Passion and Perception

Essays on Russian Culture
by Richard Stites

Edited by David Goldfrank

NAP NEW ACADEMIA PUBLISHING

Washington, DC

Printed in the United States of America

Library of Congress Control Number: 2010939058
ISBN 978-0-9828061-6-6 paperback (alk. paper)

New Academia Publishing
P.O. Box 24720, Washington, DC 20038-7420
info@newacademia.com - www.newacademia.com

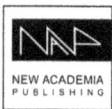

To all people everywhere
who create culture
that enriches the spirit

Contents

Acknowledgments

The late Professor Richard Stites was for thirty-three years a most valued member of the Georgetown faculty, and we could not have collected these essays and published this volume without the generous support of the university. So we graciously thank the Provost's Office, and specifically Provost James J. O'Donnell and Academic Affairs Assistant Sonia L. Jacobson; the School of Foreign Service, and specifically Dean Carol J. Lancaster, former Associate Dean Professor Peter Dunkley and former Faculty Convener Professor Charles E. King; the Graduate School, and specifically Dean Timothy A. Barbari and Associate Dean Gerald M. Mara; the History Department and specifically Professors Aviel Roshwald, Chair, Catherine Evtuhov, Amy Leonard, and Howard Spendelow, and also Administrative Assistant Djuana J. Shields; and most of all, the Center for Eurasian and East European Studies (CERES) and specifically Professor Angela Stent, Director, Associate Director Dr. Jennifer Long, Outreach Officer Sarah Dixon Klump, and Financial Officer Christina Watts.

We also must thank numerous employees of the publishing houses and other owners of copyrights to these essays for their practical assistance. Especially helpful in this respect were various academic and other staff of the Slavonic Library and Alexanteri Institute at the University of Helsinki, the Leeds University Centre for Russian, Eurasian and Central European Studies, the Russian Research Institute at Harvard University, the Harriman Institute at Columbia University, the Havighurst Center at Miami University (Ohio), the American Historical Association, and the defunct Nordic Committee for Soviet and East European Studies.

I need to single out two people, without whom this volume could not have appeared and on time for the November 18-21 2010 ASEEES (AAASS) Convention. The founder of New Academia Publishing, Professor Anna Lawton, has been a superb editor's helpmate, as well as the layout and graphic designer. And absolutely indispensible has been Stefanie Tubbs, a recent CERES M.A, who served on its staff in the summer of 2010. Enthusiastic, energetic, thorough, and responsible from start to finish, she obtained most of our permissions, located volume editors, and converted published essays into re-publishable format. She then proofread the entire manuscript, but I, as the editor of this volume, must take responsibility for any shortcomings.

David Goldfrank

Introduction

by David Goldfrank[1]

I: Richard Stites, the Man and the Scholar

I don't remember when I met Richard Stites; it seemed that, after knowing him for a while, he had always been present in my life as a historian of Russia. Any other guy with his shirt unbuttoned down to here, wearing a collection of ever-changing chains and artifacts around his neck, and constantly puffing on unfiltered Camels, would have been a fake. Richard was for real.

He knew everyone in the field and everyone knew him. He remembered your name and made you feel that you were the absolute center of attention when he talked to you–and you were. Once he came to Miami University and spoke to a class–I can't remember his topic–and got the students to look at his face and hands as he demonstrated typical Russian gestures and expressions and explained what they meant. Not for the first time, the students, and I, were spellbound.

There would be little point in gushing about Richard's knowledge of Russia, above all of popular culture. I believe he knew it better than anyone, including Russians. I recall his description of reactions from the *intelligenty* when he told them he was going off to yet another *estrada* performance: "Oh, Richard, you can't like that stuff!" But he did, and he made it come alive for the rest of us.[2]

Thus, for many of us no doubt, speaks one of his friends and editors here, Robert Thurston.

Richard Stites was born in working class Philadelphia on 2 December 1931 and grew up in a Damon-Runyanesque household, his father being a dapper, three card monte-snookering, bon-vivant bookie, and his mother nowhere in sight as of 1935. Thanks to his doting Aunt Florence, Philadelphia's Catholic schools ("four years of Latin ... with Caesar, Cicero, and Virgil"), and his own love of music and books ("historical novels, from Henryk Sienkiewycz's *Quo Vadis* to the popular ones of the day"), he obtained a first-rate education as a youth. He then attended the University of Pennsylvania, where he "was shocked to learn that historians have to go back to the sources." But learn he did, and his "senior honors thesis on Jacques-Louis David and the French Revolution" [3] foreshadowed his abiding interest in revolutionary culture. After a stint in the US Army, he matriculated at the George Washington University,[4] where he commenced his career as a professional historian and obtained his M.A. in (European) History. If his love of popular culture and lifelong fascination with World War II derived from his early life, his M.A. thesis, *Père Enfantin and the Saint-Simonians: A Study in Social Mysticism in the Romantic Period*,[5] adumbrated his other major research concerns: women's liberation, utopianianism, and Europe's sequels to the French Revolutions. His first teaching post at Lycoming College (1959-1969, with interruptions) provided that other key missing item of his future study, Russia: for his initial contract required that he also teach its history. As his later co-editor and editor Loren Graham judges:

> ... the most remarkable thing about Richard Stites is how he transformed himself during his life. Starting from a position of low knowledge of Russian history and culture, he became a master, and in a sense he became a Russian himself. No one else, in my opinion, performed this immersion as completely as Richard.[6]

Stites was also already a first-rate teacher. In the words of LTC (Ret) Gerry Lechliter, a former Lycoming student, Richard

> ... was a marvelous, stimulating lecturer who took an interest in his students. He also was a tough grader. Anyone who received an "A" worked for it. In my junior year I took his Russian History course taught early in the morning. His reputation and hour kept the class small, about eight students. In just one semester I had 83 typewritten pages of papers and had read a mountain of literature, such as Feuerbach's "Essence of Christianity." In my senior year, he was my thesis advisor and became "Richie," a friend. We

were both from Philly, and I quickly discovered he was a pool shark, among his other talents. … I learned critical thinking and expository writing in his courses because of his personal attention.[7]

Having fallen in love with Russia while at Lycoming, Stites enrolled in Harvard's history Ph.D program, where "he brought fresh air," as Peter Kenez, a former classmate and close professional colleague, remembers.[8] Another fellow student and good friend, Abbot Gleason, provided this recollection for Stites's memorial service at Georgetown on April 9, 2010:

> He had an extraordinary focus, discipline and personal ambition, totally intermingled with charm, *joie de vivre* and … generosity. His love of life was equaled only by his self-knowledge and control. He was a consummate hedonist and a great buddy. Above all, he was *svoi chelovek*. A remarkable man.[9]

Stites completed his dissertation, *The Question of the Emancipation of Women in Nineteenth Century Russia*, in 1968 on the basis of published materials located in the US Northeast.[10] He then proceeded to obtain the necessary grants to commence research in Russia, which resulted ten years later in the vast expansion of his dissertation and the publication of his first monograph, *The Women's Liberation Movement in Russia: Feminism, Nihilism, and Bolshevism, 1860-1930* (Princeton UP)—"a major event in our field," as the late Reginald Zelnik put it.[11] Helen Goscilo, another of Stites's later editors, states:

> I recall when I first encountered his superlative book on the women's movement, which impressed me not only by its excellence, but also by its meticulous scholarship and the sheer fact that a MAN had devoted so much intelligent attention to the topic.[12]

Similarly, Laurie Bernstein of Rutgers in the first of many formal tributes to him after he died:

> I still can't get over the fact that Stites covered that much ground and so early, long before most dissertation advisers were taking women's history seriously.[13]

By this time, Stites had resigned from Lycoming, done teaching stints in Denmark and at Brown and Ohio State/Lima before landing his permanent tenure home at Georgetown in 1977. As a member of that search committee, I recall the resigned attitude of his competition for the position of assistant professor, which included more than a dozen freshly minted Ph.D's who have gone on to make splendid careers in our profession. Their basic attitude was that if he wanted the job, it would be his—and right they were. Such was his reputation even before *Women's Liberation Movement in Russia* appeared. It also launched his role as model and provider and inspirer of clever chapter and sub-chapter titles, one of his signature skills. Typically, as Professor Thurston notes for *The People's War*, "… it was Richard who, during a walk around a lake outside Bochum, Germany, where we held a preparatory conference in 1993, suggested the main title of the book."[14]

While establishing himself as a mainstay of our history department at Georgetown,[15] and, during the summers, as a fixture at that "historian's paradise," the Helsinki Slavonic Library,[16] Stites threw himself madly into more sources and analysis. This resulted in his Vucinich Prize-winning *Revolutionary Dreams: Utopian Vision and Experimental Life in the Russian Revolution* (Oxford UP, 1989), which Zelnik called "the most original and least programmed book in our field."[17] Upon reading it, Nicholas Riasanovsky said to Stites: "I make you an honorary Russian."[18] Another of Stites's editors, Jeremy Smith, sums it up this way: "If Tiutchev were still around and still saying 'Russia can not be understood by intellect alone,' I would recommend him to read *Revolutionary Dreams*."[19] So it is maybe not surprising that Helen Goscilo also says about Stites, "For years I've referred to him as the Big Daddy of cultural studies within things Slavic. His range was extraordinary, his thinking imaginative, and his publications inestimably influential."[20] The three related volumes which he edited, coedited or introduced during this period: *Utopias in the Air and Ground* (Special Issue of *Russian History/Histoire Russe*, 1984), Alexander Bogdanov's *Red Star: The First Bolshevik Utopia* (Indiana UP, 1984, translation), and *Bolshevik Culture: Experiment and Order in the Russian Revolution* (Indiana UP,1985) reveal the collegaial side of Stites's work.

Now, with his "unmatched understanding of unconventional sources," to cite Zelnik once more,[21] Stites had thrust himself just as vigorously into research for his invited, third barrier-breaking monograph, *Russian Popular Culture. Entertainment and Society Since 1900* (Cambridge UP,1992).[22] This included a great deal of *sui generis* oral history research, though he never so termed all of the personal contacts he forged with members of the Soviet entertainment world. Analytically he had already boldly and perceptively gone on record juxtaposing the most basic aspect of Russian popular culture to Cold War anti-Soviet cant. Again, as LTC Lichliter (ret.) recalls concerning Stites's impact on our mid-1980's Georgetown program for the military in Upper Bavaria:

> I was at the US Army Russian Institute in Garmisch, Germany, and he showed up to give a lecture on whether Soviet society was militarized. His conclusion at the end of his presentation was, "No." A student challenged him, citing the willingness of Russians to wait in interminable lines to buy goods. Richie asked him if he'd ever been in a Russian line. "No" was the answer. Richie then said, "It's not a line, it's an amoeba," adding if patience and orderliness in lines is a criterion to judge "militarization" of a society, then one could conclude the English are militarized.[23]

In connection with the 1980s workshops on Soviet history Stites also co-edited *Russia in the Era of NEP: Explorations in Soviet Society and Culture* (Indiana UP, 1991), and two more such volumes followed upon the heels of *Soviet Popular Culture*: a co-edited collection of translations, *Mass Culture in Soviet Russia: Tales, Poems, Songs, Movies, Plays, and Folklore* (Indiana UP, 1995), and his personal brainchild, *Culture and Entertainment in Wartime Russia* (Indiana UP, 1995).

How did he do all this? James von Geldern has this recollection:

> I spent that summer in DC working in the LOC [Library of Congrss - *ed.*]. ... Needless to say, Richard and I worked the bars in the evening. For the *Mass Culture* collection, when I looked for a collaborator, Richard was, to say the least, the obvious choice. We put together a table of contents in less than a week, tracked down translations (that was in the days before the new copyright

law). Richard didn't even need to consult his notes to put together the collection; he knew it all by heart. He wrote most of the short intros to the individual pieces, and selected most of the photographs. Most important was the overall conception of the book and making representative selections that could serve as an introduction to a vast culture. We took care of that over beers.[24]

And Jeffrey Brooks, a contributor to *Culture and Entertainment* writes: "He was a no-nonsense chap on the work side, and had little patience with those who were slow to deliver on time."[25] Indeed he was impatient, for as the key figure in launching in 1993 what became the Evtuhov-Hughes-Stites-Goldfrank textbook, *A History of Russia: Peoples, Legends, Events, Forces,* as well as the *Since 1800* Evtuhov-Stites version (both Houghton-Mifflin, 2004),[26] he was also the first to complete his chapters. He then relentlessly if confidently pressed the slowest of us—the author of these words.

The genesis of the innovative *European Culture in the Great War: The Arts, Entertainment and Propaganda, 1914-1918* (Cambridge UP, 1999) is of a very different nature. Allow co-editor Aviel Roshwald to tell this story:

What I remember best is how it all started: I was teaching a course on "The First World War as Historical Watershed." Richard stopped by my office to ask me about it and requested a copy of a syllabus, which I happily handed to him. He looked through it, and said...it made him think how great it would be to co-edit a volume on the impact of the Great War on European culture. I said "sure," thinking it was just one of those friendly exchanges colleagues have about hypothetical scenarios before they go back to whatever they are actually working on. About five minutes after this exchange, Richard came knocking on my door with the scribbled draft of a brilliant prospectus. The essential issues that the volume should address were all there in germinal form—the rest, as one might say, is historiography.[27]

One of Roshwald's further comments speaks to the experience of such collaboration: "...working with Richard was a complete pleasure (not to say privilege—except that Richard never allowed you to feel that way) throughout."[28] The entire book, we might add here, exhibits a very high level of writing and analysis and covers almost all of the European combatants, except for Greeks and Turks, where no qualified authors stepped forward to contribute.

All this time Stites was energetically grinding away toward his fourth innovative monograph linking the lofty and the lowly, *Serfdom, Society, and the Arts in Imperial Russia: The Power and the Pleasure* (Yale UP, 2005). Natalia Baschmakoff, still another of his editors, gives us a nifty glimpse into his work and his ways at this time at the Helsinki "Modernization in the Russian Provinces" conference:

> Richard participated actively in the 1999 conference with a bunch of other international scholars...and graduate students from the Aleksanteri Institute ... the University of Joensuu and the University of Petrozavodsk. He was always alert, focused, interested and truly democratic–never would he have an attitude "from above" towards a junior scholar. His spontaneous interest for regions and ordinary citizens outside of the metropoles Moscow and St. Petersburg came from his interest in mass culture in general, but particularly from the magnum opus *Serfdom, Society, and the Arts*, a work-in-progress that he was writing at that period. As an author, I must say, he was a model for others: he gave his paper in good time before the deadline, without any modifications or corrections that he would send afterwards–a headache of any editor.[29]

Indeed the Finns appreciated Stites so much that they awarded him not only an honorary doctorate, but knighthood too—ceremonial sword and all!

Stites had barely submitted his initial manuscript of *Serfdom, Society, and the Arts* to the Yale press, and he was deeply at work on his fifth monograph, *The Four Horsemen: Riding to Liberty in Post-Napoleonic Europe,* a parallel and comparative history of the four related revolutionary movements personified by Rafael del Riego, Gugliemo Pepe, Alexandros Ypsilanti, and Sergei Muravev-Apostol. Yes, Stites continued to work with prodigious energy and at an amazing pace into his late seventies, to cite Baschmakoff again, "marrying events that happened at a same epoch far away from each other."[30] Yes, he did extensive original research for it in Spanish, Neapolitan, and Greek, as well as Russian archives. Yes, he integrates religion, high and popular culture, graphics, and remembrance into this

study. Yes, it does have his typical, oh-so-clever sub-chapter titles—
"In Europe's Peripheral Vision," "The Spanish Cockpit," "Charcoal
Burners," "The Friendly Society," "Catechism of Revolt," to name
a few, not to mention his concluding sequel, "The Torn Cloth of
Memory." Yes, in the opinion of more than one sophisticated reader
of his chapters, it is intellectually engaging and excitingly written.
And yes, with a total of nearly 200,000 words—ca. 70% of *Serfdom,
Society, and the Arts*—in what he reckoned as the penultimate draft
of his greatest piece of unfinished business, it will be a formidable
but manageable challenge for his literary executors to issue as he so
wished. This is not like *Serfdom, Society, and the Arts*, where he could
eliminate his planned chapter on ballet and integrate that material
within several others. *Horse*, as he liked to abbreviate the project
in his computer files, requires a separate chapter for all four of his
"men," else it will not be the book he wished so avidly and tried so
hard to see into print before "Death and Transfiguration," to quote
another of his headings, overtook him too.

True to form, as Stites awaited more feedback for *Horse* from
professional colleagues, he was already engaged, as teacher as well
as scholar, in a sixth planned innovative monograph. He planned
"to bring European fascism to the fore at its most dramatic moment: action on the Russian front" and "explore military volunteers
and Axis units from Scandinavia, the Low Countries, France, Spain,
Italy, Croatia, Hungary, Romania, and Slovakia—their motivation,
their treatment by the German ally, their behavior at the front, and
their perception by Soviet forces fighting against them."[31]

His reading and writing course on World War II film for first
year Georgetown School of Foreign Service students, which required original research at either the Library of Congress or the
Holocaust Museum, was one of his most successful ever.[32]

These few pages cannot do justice to Richard Stites, the man,
scholar, friend, colleague, and teacher, but his former Ph.D student
Hubertus Jahn, provides a fitting summary:

> "Iconoclasm" somehow comes to mind when I remember Richard
> Stites, and not just because he so incisively wrote about it in the
> Russian revolutionary context. I am thinking more about his per-
> sonality and his academic achievements generally, which were in
> many ways groundbreaking. Not that Richard was an iconoclast

in the classical religious or ideological sense. That he was most definitely not. But for me, he surely toppled a number of images and perceptions when I first met and worked with him in the mid 1980s. ... His informal demeanor, his intellectual spark and his writings immediately attracted me. We shared a deep fascination for Russian culture, high and, especially, low, a mutual interest that sustained our future academic and personal relationship. Richard was simply the ideal mentor for my Ph. D., and he was always congenial and stimulating company at Georgetown, in Russia and, crucially, in Helsinki. His originality and intellectual rigor will keep inspiring me into the future.[33]

And Robert Thurston, whose remarks commence this brief sketch, ends with the words: "If I could only sit and talk with him for an hour now..."

Don't we all feel this way?

II: The Essays

This collection of *Stitesiana* originated in his conversations with the publisher Anna Lawton, herself an active specialist in Soviet film and a Georgetown colleague, as well as old friend. His list of forty-three essays expressly excluded earlier works related to his first book, *The Women's Liberation Movement in Russia*, perhaps because they were too political and not directly connected to culture *per se*. Whether he knowingly bypassed several relevant, individual or co-authored later pieces or simply overlooked them is a mystery.[34] And whether, if such had been pointed out to him, he would have altered his original list is impossible for us to ascertain. So we have attempted to honor his wishes.

Thirty book chapters (70%), five in volumes Stites edited or co-edited and three in festschrifts, comprise the bulk of the original plan. Some of these are quite different from anything else he wrote, while others tread future or old ground for him, but usually with data, comparisons, analytical twists, or methlogical observations not found in the monographs. In just about all of his contributions to thematic collective volumes he found a way to address their main topic and at the same time speak about culture and society the way he thought best. Among the remaining thirteen essays number three scholarly journal articles, a "research note," an introduction to another's translation, a history handbook entry, an extended book review in a popular magazine, a pedagogical report for a professional organization, and five postings in study group or institute papers. Within these thirteen are located most of his analyses of specific films, commentary on current events, and recommendations for the classroom.

Few projects actually end up as envisioned. Stumbling blocks to obtaining permissions eliminated four of these essays. Even so trimmed, the volume as planned proved to be much too long, so we have cut out all of the essays, regardless of high quality and utility, which contain little or nothing not found in Stites's monographs. But we discuss all of his projected forty-three below and indicate their specific contributions and where they can be found. Researchers or aficionados, who cannot otherwise access any omitted piece, may request a copy from the author of this introduction.[35]

The celebrated medievalist Nancy F. Partner treated twelfth-century history-writing as "serious entertainment."[36] We might say the same of the impressive corpus of historical and cultural writings of the late Professor Richard Stites, both what is included here and what is not. For though readers will come to this volume with varying levels of familiarity with his work and its broad range of subject matter, and hence find some of these essays more useful than others, they will enjoy the read, as he always aimed and usually with resounding success to be, as he said, a "poet .. without the poetic license."[37]

The preliminary conversations between Stites and Lawton left for the future the ordering of these essays, so we have determined what we deem the best combination of thematic and chronological, starting with the more general, proceeding to the specific, and grouped around his second, third, and fourth monographs.

1. Russia's Cultural Coordinates

Six essays set forth Stites's approach to cultural history and cover a great deal of ground and time. They rarely introduce facts not found elsewhere in his writings, but do provide the reader a sense of his sweep and his ability to connect and integrate.

"Civilization on Trial: Noted Russian Dissident Andrei Sinyavsky Renders Judgment on the Soviet System" (1991), an extended and sympathetic if critical *The World and I* review of Andrei Sinyavsky, *Soviet Civilization: A Cultural History*[38] (1990), presents Stites's views of the dissidents of the 1960s-1970s and his overall approach to Russian culture. "Cultural History and Russian Studies" (1995), prepared for a Kennan Institute *Beyond Soviet Studies* project, is half manifesto for a combined elite and popular cultural history within its social setting and half example thereof for popular film and music, taken or adapted from two of his other works.[39] "Crowded on the Edge of Vastness: Observations on Russian Space and Place" (1999), composed for a Finnish collective volume on space in Russian culture, speaks, as Stites states, of "the juxtaposition in everyday life of an empty expanse with a cramped and crowded workspace ...[being] a strictly subjective work based on personal observations over the past thirty years."[40] The editor Jeremy Smith, sees it as "a masterpiece, although it barely began to reveal the deep interest and understanding Richard had of the place of space in Russia."[41] "Russian Symbols–Nation, People, Ideas" (2004), constituting part of a collective work on the elusive problem of malleable political semiotics, is, in the eyes of its editor, Michael Geisler, a

> … sweeping tour of Russian symbols since tsarist times ... [and]... takes the sheer wealth and diversity of Russian national symbols as a cue to remind us of the importance of considering the entire register of national symbols as a system of signification working in concert to maintain, stabilize, and reinforce the dominating constructions of collective memory.[42]

"Filling in the Cultural Landscape from Vienna to Moscow: Past and Present" (2007), based on a 2004 conference keynote address in Birmingham and placed in a Finnish festschrift, outlines nine cultural and political problems for further study. These range from the 18th through the 21st century and include two issues related to his projcted sixth monograph on Europe's Eastern Front in World War II. Finally, "Historical and Social Rhythms in Russian Culture in the 19th and 20th Centuries" (2009), written for another Finnish festschrift, attempts to show that one can distinguish for

Russia six periods over the course of 1800-1985, each of which is characterized (more or less, he concedes) by distinct output and cultural tastes, popular as well as elite.

2. Portraits of Revolution

A projected set of fourteen essays, six of which we are publishing here, is connected to *Revolutionary Dreams* (1989). Ten of these original fourteen precede the monograph in composition and hence represent stages of Stites's crafting. Revealing how he made effective use of conferences and collective volumes to present his research and writing as they developed, and thereby invite probing questions and commentary, these essays fall into two distinct categories: one, futurism and science fiction, the other, rituals and symbols.

Futurism and Science Fiction

Science fiction and other forms of futurism figured heavily in revolutionary Russian utopianism and the Revolution itself and engaged Stites's attention from the start of this project. The omitted "Utopias of Time, Space, and Life in the Russian Revolution" (1984), prepared for a Jutta Scherrer's seminar at l'École des hautes Études in January 1984, represents Stites's first published essay on Russian culture and his first stab at what would become Part III of the *Revolutionary Dreams*, "We the Community of the Future," with chapters devoted to each of these three categories.[43] The omitted "Utopias in the Air and on the Ground: Futuristic Dreams in the Russian Revolution" (1984), from a volume which he edited following a 1984 conference on utopias held in Stockholm, Turku, and a well lubricated Gulf of Bothnia ferry between these cities, boldly previews the entire monograph with his assertion that utopianism was integral to the Russian Revolution.[44]   "Fantasy and Revolution: Alexander Bogdanov and the Origins of Bolshevik Science Fiction" (1984), the introduction to the translation of *Red Star* and *Engineer Menni*, gives a fascinating literary pre-history of these works, and can also be viewed as an amplified prefiguring of the parts of *Revolutionary Dreams* devoted specifically to science fiction.[45] "Hopes and Fears of Things to Come: the Foreshadowing of

Totalitarianism in Russian Fantasy and Utopia" (1986), occasioned by a Nordic Council totalitarianism conference in Tampere, August 1984, adumbrates "Back to the Future: Nostalgic Utopia," part of his futurology and science fiction chapter. Commencing with a critique of the abuse of "totalitarianism," he describes some utopian schemes in more detail than in the book, and concludes critiquing the misrepresentation of Zamyatin's *We* as typical of a "totalitarian" Soviet science fiction, rather than as an exception.[46] "Heaven and Hell in Russian Revolutionary Science Fiction" (1987), presented to Britain's Study Group on the Russian Revolution, offers an earlier and shorter version of the book's sub-chapter similarly titled "Maps of Heaven and Hell," but with more information about some of the works considered in both, such as Yakov Okunov's *Tomorrow* (1924) and A. R. Palei's *Gulfstream* (1928).[47]

Rituals and Symbols

Symbolism, rituals, and their iconoclastic inverses likewise were prominent from the start in the Revolution and Stites's grandiose project. The omitted "Adorning the Russian Revolution: The Primary Symbols of Bolshevism, 1917-1918" (1984), also under the auspices of the British Study Group, provides an initial version of the sub-chapter "Early Signs of Bolshevism" and two Imperial Russian provincial emblems, which appear to have influenced the Hammer and Sickle design, but not included in *Revolutionary Dreams*.[48] The likewise omitted "Iconoclastic Currents in the Russian Revolution (1985)," a shorter, but more comparative draft of the chapter on that subject, arose within the nexus of American workshops on early Soviet Russia and Kennan Institute activities as part of his co-edited *Bolshevik Culture*.[49] The omitted "The Origin of Soviet Ritual Style: Symbol and Festival in the Russian Revolution" (1986), outlined at the 1985 World Congress/AAASS meeting in Washington, is a somewhat more detailed and better illustrated, earlier incarnation of parts of the first three "Festivals of the People" sub-chapters.[50] He slightly reframed it, but without illustrations, as the omitted "Festival and Revolution: the Role of Public Spectacle in Russia, 1917-1918" (1990), for a conference volume dedicated to the Revolution and Stalinism.[51]

Unfortunately we are not able to reprint here the last of Stites's relevant pre-*Revolutionary Dreams* publications, "Stalinism and the Restructuring of Revolutionary Utopianism" (1990).[52] The first half is a longer version of "Lunar Economics and Social Revolution," the initial sub-chapter of the conclusion, but without the paragraphs concerning Gastev's utopian cult of precise time and Stakhanovism.[53] One can envision the remainder, a totally different Stalinist sequel with numerous flashbacks to the utopianism of 1917-29, as an invaluable authentic, alternative conclusion to the book.

Stites continued to publish on this topic after *Revolutionary Dreams* appeared in 1989. His first of four such essays is another which we are unable to reprint, "Russian Revolutionary Culture: Its Place in the History of Cultural Revolutions" (1990), useful as a broadbrush comparison of the iconoclasm, vandalism, and new rituals and symbols of the French and Russian Revolutions.[54] As aptly put by the volume co-editor, Paul Dukes:[55]

> In his brilliant contribution, Richard Stites carried out successfully the difficult task of linking earlier chapters with one of the outstanding events of the twentieth century. ... In general, Stites avoided what he called 'sweeping comparisons of vast, complex, and very different revolutions' in his contribution to the volume, but certainly succeeded in demonstrating 'certain common features of culture building that are probably found in all great revolutions' that 'might even serve as a shorthand measure of the psychological depth of a revolution.'

"Bolshevik Ritual Building in the 1920s" (1991), in an NEP conference volume, which Stites co-edited, presents a longer and richer version of the sub-chapter "Rituals of a Counterfaith"[56] and contains, *inter alia*, data on anti-religious skits and rituals performed in schools. "The Role of Symbol and Ritual" (1997) enhances the joint Anglo-Russian-American *Critical Companion to the Russian Revolution* with several new, post-1989 sources and information on pre-Revolutionary Russian right wing rituals. Finally, "Trial as Theater in the Russian Revolution" (1998), originally from a 1991 Gauss Seminar presentation at Princeton, but using sources up to 1994 and published as "theater research," pulls together and greatly expands the scattered information in *Revolutionary Dreams* about genuine, fictive, and mock political trials. In one ironic example,

Kiev's Jewish Section of the Communist Party convicted Judaism of being reactionary and oppressive in the same courtroom where Mendel Beilis faced a ritual murder indictment in 1912.[57]

3. Culture, Popular and Otherwise

The next grouping comprises a diverse set of fourteen essays—twelve published here—related to *Russian Popular Culture*, a work which Stites conceived as a start and seed with more to follow. Only a few of these precede the book, which he completed in three years, and a goodly number amplify it to create a far richer tableau than he could squeeze into the allotted 200 pages—especially concerning science fiction, and movies, and wartime culture.

Some Miscellany

"On the Border with the Soviet Avant-garde"(1988), co-authored with Helene Jarvinen and the earliest of these, is a erudite and optimistic piece of cultural journalism, reporting on the five-day "Imatra Festival 1988" in eastern Karelia, which included all sorts of art forms, among them, a creative fusion of rock and classical musical. "Soviet Popular Culture in the Gorbachev Era" (1989), issued by Columbia's Harriman Insititute, prefigures, but with a lot of very different material, the final chapter of *Russian Popular Culture*."[58] And the omitted "The Ways of Russian Popular Music to 1953" (2004) recasts the sections of music from *Russian Popular Culture* for a collective volume on Soviet music and society with a sprinkling of fresh data, such as Dmitrii Shostakovich's early experimenting with jazz.[59]

On a different plane stands "World Outlook and Inner Fears in Soviet Science Fiction" (1990), designed for a collective work, *Science and the Soviet Social Order*, and illustrating the immense amount of research and knowledge underying *Russian Popular Culture*. Writing as a cosmopolitan literary critic attuned to social nuances, Stites gives a great sense of the sweep of this creativity and links the fruits of later Soviet sci-fi to the output of the 1920s. In the recent words of its volume editor, Loren Graham,[60]

> [it] is a superb example of Richard working at a very high level
> ... based on the mastery of an enormous literature, and then the
> tying of this literature to the history of the Soviet Union itself—
> its highs and lows, its changing fashions and obsessions, its self-
> examination.

Having prepared it before *Revolutionary Dreams* appeared,[61]
Stites provides here a seamless transition from it, as the first five
pages cover some of the same material from before 1930, while the
last twenty presage the much briefer treatments in *Soviet Popular
Culture*.[62]

Cinema

Stites's absolute immersion in Soviet film is clear in these next five
essays. "Soviet Movies for the Masses and for Historians" (1991),
written for a scholarly media publication, aims, in his own words,
"to call attention to the pedagogical utility of the mass film or the
popular movie for historians and other scholars of Russian-Soviet
culture and society."[63] This massive expansion of the discussion
of four quite different films in *Russian Popular Culture* reveals the
union of master-scholar and master-teacher in Stites and thereby
retains its value for all of us.[64] The omitted and oddly named
"Doing Film History in the Soviet Union: a Research Note" (1991),
a "research note"—brief, informative, readily availabe, and maybe
still of use to investigators—covers his favorite research haunts:
Moscow, Leningrad (so still named at the time of its writing), and
also Helsinki.[65] "Dusky Images of Imperial Russia: Prerevolutionary
Cinema" (1994), a contribution to *Russian Review* and his first
on-topic, post-*Russian Popular Culture* article, is a sweeping and
brilliant extended review of the Russo-Italo-British *Early Russian
Cinema: Films before the Revolution Now on Video*, and concludes with
recommendations for their use in the classroom. "To the Virgin
Lands: the Epic and the Idyll in the Cinematic Representation of
Khrushchev's Great Adventure" (2006), a Miami of Ohio/Havighurst
presentation and web publication, vastly expands the treatment of
one of the films covered in "Soviet Movies for the Masses and for
Historians."[66] Adding sections devoted to the "storyboard" of the

musical *Ivan Brovkin in the Virgin Lands* and to the "performance as subtext," and relating its messages to on-topic writings issued in Leonid Brezhnev's name, Stites thereby gives us his most detailed analysis of any film's utility for understanding a society at a given time. "The Pawnbroker: Holocaust, Memory, and Film" (2008), crafted for AHA's *Perspectives on History*, is a little pedagogical gem, also linking Soviet and American film production.

Wars Hot and Cold

With his longstanding interest in World War II, Stites conceived, organized, and edited *Culture and Entertaiment in Wartime Russia* (1995), a follow-up volume to the treatment of this topic in *Soviet Popular Culture*. And as he was certainly not the only person engaged in studying Russia's World War II culture, we can envision the entire package as both fruitful elaboration and original offspring of the collective endeavors that paralleled and resulted in his earlier chapter. "Frontline Entertainment" (1995), his own offering, if thematically and even somewhat textually dependent upon his earlier treatment, goes into more detail on such topics as the soldiers' favorite, Klavdia Shul'zhenko, and adult puppet shows, and raises an interesting new one, the soldiers' self-entertainment. "Heaven and Hell: Soviet Propaganda Constructs the World" (1999), designed for a general volume on Cold War propaganda, elaborates themes from both *Revolutionary Dreams* and *Russian Popular Culture*. Always insistent that culture provides a superb window into the analysis of politics, Stites combines here solid institutional analysis of Soviet propaganda organs and a survey of the satirical journal *Krokodil*, somewhat contrasted with more staid *Ogonёk* and *Znamya*.[67]

Meanwhile, Stites's habitual, intense intellectual engagement with his Georgetown colleagues produced his second collective volume on wartime culture, this time the co-edited *European Culture in the Great War: The Arts, Entertainment, and Propaganda, 1914-1918* (1999). "Days and Nights in Wartime Russia: Cultural Life 1914-1917" (1999), his own contribution, contains the relevant fruits of his research for both *Revolutionary Dreams* and *Russian Popular Culture*,[68] as well as a good deal more sleuthing among his cultural artifact-sources, such as the popular weekly *Voina*. Adding the elite to the popular, this piece is a dazzling amplification of the few pages devoted to World War I in *Russian Popular Culture*.[69]

"Soviet Russian Wartime Culture: Freedom and Control, Spontaneity and Consciousness" (2000), penned for a collective volume stemming from a 1993 conference in Bochum on Russia in World War II, perforce condenses much of what Stites had already written. The result is a very clever adaptation and variation on his earlier "Russia's Holy War" chapter, and in the eyes of the co-editor Robert Thurston,[70]

> ...of course reads beautifully. Richard drew together the themes of his title and compared them, briefly but effectively, to Russian wartime culture in World War I and to German culture in World War II. Even for those who have never before encountered this kind of material, Richard establishes not only the horror of the war but also the deep, honest, and emotional connections with Russian culture that helped make the fighting so meaningful for the people.

Continuing to move back in time from the world wars to completely fresh terrain for himself, Stites pulled off a *tour de force* regarding the culture of Russia's first twentieth century conflict, "Russian Representation of the Japanese Enemy" (2005). Comprehensive and perceptive, it is a brilliant, unique contribution to the huge, two-volume, collective work, connected to a centennial conference in Japan on the Russo-Japanese War, which we both, among others, helped to launch at an informal meeting in 2000 in Helsinki. Covering the gamut of such representations, from popular *lubki* (woodcut prints) and photos to military handbooks and symbolic poetry, and augmenting the fresh research of others with his own, he provides comparisons with other Russian wars and other countries and a gripping question for us all in this model collective volume chapter.

4. Elite and Mass Entertainment under Serfdom

Our final set of nine essays, four republished here, corresponds to *Serfdom, Society, and the Arts in Imperial Russia: The Power and the Pleasure* (2005). Four of these appeared before the monograph did, and each stands in a distinct relationship to it, illustrating again the different ways in which Stites worked with his material, presented it, and allowed it to be utilized. Our Georgetown colleague Catherine Evtuhov recalls:

> In 1993, Stites was one of the most enthusiastic participants in a Russian-American Summer Seminar – one of many exciting early post-Soviet experiments – in the city of Smolensk, entitled "A Russia That Didn't Happen?: Cultural, Social, and Political Trends in the Early Twentieth Century and their Origins." This proved to be a seminal event in the evolution of the book, which he originally intended as a monograph on Russian "high culture." Richard experienced nineteenth-century provincial culture as a revelation, diving immediately into the local archive – as well, one might add, as flirting with the kitchen ladies in the evening.[71]

"The Veselukha Tower: Social and Cultural Space in Old Smolensk" (1995), resulted from what Evtuhov called "this ten-day excursion into provincial life;" it appeared in a Finnish festschrift and enriches the monograph's overall scope with material about the representation of the various social strata in one provincial city. In her estimation, the crafting of this piece "represents a turning point for the evolution of the book by the inclusion of the provincial element." The omitted "The Domestic Muse: Music at Home in the Twilight of Serfdom" (1998), part of a collective volume linking literature, music, and society in Russia, represents an earlier, brief redaction of the monograph's similarly titled second chapter. Though only forty per cent of the book chapter in length, the essay contains useful facts not found in the latter, such as the questionable, anecdotal source for one of Stites's favorite stories: the nobleman who "required his house serfs to address him and each other in recitative."[72] "The Creative Provinces in Early Nineteenth Century Russia," (2000), prepared for an August 1999 Helsinki conference on the Russian provinces, introduces *Serfdom, Society, and the Arts* as a work in progress providing genuine local history, as it aims to recapture performers, audiences and their social settings. "The Misanthrope, the Orphan, and the Magpie: Imported Melodrama in the Twilight of Serfdom" (2002), on the other hand, appears as a greatly expanded version of the four-page sub-chapter, "Innocence and Evil in Faraway Places." Not only is this essay much richer in detail, but it presents Stites's personal appreciation of melodrama in a volume dedicated to this ever-popular, if snobbishly disdained genre.

Serfdom, Society, and the Arts itself served as a source for the five other essays originally planned in this section. The omitted "Female Serfs in the Performing World" (2007), an invited piece for the British collective volume, *Women in Russian Culture and Society, 1700-1825*, abstracts on this topic from the book, especially concerning theater and sexploitation, but explains more precisely how the celebrated serf-actress Anna Vysheslavsteva (?1817-1895) obtained her freedom.[73]

"Circles on a Square: the Heart of St. Petersburg Culture in the Early 19th Century" (2008), in an innovative, superbly illustrated collective volume on the use of visual sources for Russian history, architecturally re-visualizes for the early 21st-century reader the loci of that city's high musical and theatrical culture during a much earlier epoch within the context of both society and repertoire. In one verbal gem, Stites characterizes Mikhailovsky Square: "Unmonumental and intimate, it had no radials or small thoroughfares, but instead a small park, like a carpet that pulls a room together." [74] Without the graphics, this essay loses its punch, so we omit it.

"Cultural Capital and Cultural Heritage: St. Petersburg and the Arts of Imperial Russia" (2008) contains more fresh information and reveals the Stites some of us actually experienced as an incomparable tourist guide—but here in a preservation-oriented book, which he additionally aided by reading several other chapters.[75] Expressing a paradoxical fear that the memory as an object of study may eclipse the objects of memory themselves, he appreciates the inevitable interchange between "heritage" and "history." And as if in dialogue with his own *Serfdom, Society, and the Arts* as well as modern popular culture, he provides three brief sketches. "A Night at the Opera," rescuing Russia's most popular 19th-century opera, Aleksei Verstovsky's largely lost *Askold and Dir*; [76] a totally different "Evenings with the Orchestra;"[77] and, in "Pictures Not at an Exhibition," a review of fabulous graphic sources now in storage in the Russian Museum.[78]

"Summertime: Petersburg Suburban Entertainment in the Era of Serfdom" (2009), in a volume from a 2006 Karelian conference, which Stites could not attend but helped to plan on the Eastern Baltic dacha world, enriches his earlier presentation of popular entertainment for all classes by revisiting many of the same sources he used for *Serfdom, Society, and the Arts* and consulting a crucial new study of balls. He shows, *inter alia*, that by the 1850s, "day trippers,"[79] using the railroad to reach suburban Vauxhalls (as such places of public entertainment were termed, before *voksal* became generic for railroad station), came into their own.

"On the Dance Floor: Royal Power, Class, and Nationality in Servile Russia" (2010†), reflecting Stites's further development of some of these themes with the help of new sources, is another we are unable to reprint.[80] Prepared for a 2006 symposium in honor of Abbot Gleason and placed in a volume on the "critical subjectivity" of space,[81] this piece applies William McNeill's juxtaposition of dance and drill to the Russia of Paul I, Alexander I, and Nicholas I.[82] In the words of co-editor Mark Bassin,

> [it] offers a micro-site study of the relationship between place and power in the eighteenth and nineteenth centuries. Thanks to Peter I, Russian elites were expected to attend balls and be proficient in Western styles of dancing (sometimes to the music of serf orchestras). The ballrooms of royal palaces, merchant halls, and private estates became places to express and enact social and gender hierarchies, conduct courtships and conclude alliances, fashion personal and even national identities, and enhance status through mastery of social space."[83]

This concludes our brief survey of the forty-three essays on culture, which the late Professor Stites desired to be collected and published in a single volume. We hope that you read with pleasure as well as profit, those of interest to you, including the thirteen which we were forced to omit, and his other writings too.

And don't forget to smile, tell a joke, toast a friend, and make the most of your life, as he always did, wishing us all the very best.

Notes

1   The author of this introduction graciously thanks everyone who has contributed to it with introductory statements and, especially, the personal emails, without which it would have been impossible to do justice to our beloved late friend and colleague.

2   Personal email.

3   The citations here are from "An Interview with Richard Stites" in *Kritika* 11.1 (Winter 2010), 3 (also posted on http://hrs3.net/stites/ -- thanks to close friend and Georgetown colleague, Howard Spendelow.

4   See further, Anna Lawton, "Instead of an Obituary: Richard Stites, 1931-2010" in *Studies in Russian and Soviet Cinema* 4.2 (July, 2010): 129-34, or here, 527-33; and my 9 April 2010 Georgetown Memorial Service contribution: "The Kid from Philly," posted on http://hrs3.net/stites/.

5   Available at the George Washington University Gelman Library.

6   Personal email.

7   http://hrs3.net/stites/

8   Personal email.

9   Personal email. Curiously, their mentor at Harvard, Professor Richard Pipes, remembered Stites ten years later more as "a good guy" than as a sharp intellect: personal communication.

10   Chiefly Harvard's Widener Library, New York Public Library, and Library of Congress.

11   "Stites Festschrift: An Introduction," in *Journal of Popular Culture* 31.4 (1998), 1-5 (citation on p1). Zelnik's characterization and analysis of Stites's first three monographs and prediction for the fourth here are peerless.

12   Personal email.

13   Personal emaill post on http://hrs3.net/stites/.

14   Personal email: *A People's War: Popular Responses to World War II in the Soviet Union*, ed. Robert Thurston and Bernd Bonwetsch, (University of Illinois Press, 2000).

15   For a lovely decription of Professor Stites in his Georgetown office, see below, 527-29.

16   Stites, cited in Tapio Ollikainen, "Under the spell of the Slavonic," *Universitas Helsingiensis* (Winter, 2003), as on http://hrs3.net/stites/.

17   Zelnik, "Introduction," 2.

18   Personal communicaton from Stites.

19   Personal email: was Smith aware that a dozen years earlier, Zelnik had written in *loc. cit.*, "If ... a friendly alien being of superior intelligence ... asked me to take ... her ... to someone who would exemplify all that was best, brightest, and broadest in spirit in our little profession, I would without hesitation take her to meet Richard Stites?"

20 Personal email.
21 Zelnik, "Introduction," 3.
22 On its genesis, "An Interview," 5-6.
23 http://hrs3.net/stites/; this "amoeba" metaphor would turn up fifteen years later in Stites's "Crowded on the Edge of Vastness" article: see below, 48.
24 Personal email.
25 Personal email.
26 Really late 2003.
27 Personal email
28 Personal email.
29 Personal email.
30 Personal email.
31 "An Interview," 8.
32 *"The Pawnbroker,"* first paragraph . See below, 319.
33 Personal email.
34 Among the bypassed works are Stites's "Introduction" to *Culture and Entertainment in Wartime Russia* (Indiana UP), 1-8; his co-authored "Introduction" and "Afterward" to *European Culture in the Great War: The Arts, Entertainment, and Propaganda. 1914-1918* (Cambridge: Cambridge University Press, 1999), 1-7, 349-58; and his "Festivals of Collusion? Provincial Days in the 1930s," a "Reaction" (to a preceding article by Malte Rolf) in *Kritika. Explorations in Russian and Eurasian History* 1.3 (Summer 2000): 475-79. In this author's personal opinion, each of these would add something of value to the current volume, the last one, for example, illustrating how Stites evaluated and integrated the work of others, and, in passing, showing him as a contributor to *Kritika* at the outset of its combined revival and birth as a major journal in our field.
35 goldfrad@georgetown.edu.
36 *Serious Entertainments: The Writing of History in Twelfth-Century England* (Chicago: University of Chicago Press, 1977).
37 "Interview," 5.
38 The title is a mistranslation of *Osnovy sovetskoi tsivilizatsii.*
39 Cf. Russian Popular Culture, 76-77, 89-90, 100-1, 130-31, and below, 23-38.
40 See below, 47.
41 Personal email
42 *National Symbols, Fractured Identities: Contesting the National Narrative,* ed. Michael E. Geisler, (Hanover: University Press of New England, 2004), "Introduction," xxxiii.
43 As it turned out, Stites elaborated much of this subject matter in Part II of *Revolutionary Dreams*—"Living the Revolution," with its chapters

devoted to iconoclasm, festivals, atheism, egalitarianism, and mechanization.

44 *Utopia in Russian History, Culture, and Thought* = *Russian History/Histoire Russe* 11.2-3 (1984), 236-57.

45 See, for example, *Revolutionary Dreams*, 32-33.

46 Cf. *Revolutionary Dreams*, 188-89.

47 Cf. *Revolutionary Dreams*, 171-79.

48 *Sbornik* (Leeds), Summer 1984, 39-42, plus five plates; cf. *Revolutionary Dreams*, 83-88. The plates are viewable on http://hrs3.net/stites/ under the title: "A Provincial Origin for the Hammer and Sicle?"; and see below, 62.

49 *Bolshevik Culture: Experiment and Order in the Russian Revolution*, ed., Abbot Gleason, Peter Kenez, Richard Stites (Bloomington: Indiana University Press, 1985), 1-24.

50 *Symbols of Power: the Esthetics of Political Legitimation in the Soviet Union and Eastern Europe*, ed. Claes Arvidsson and L.E. Blomqvist (Stockholm: Almqvist and Wiksel, 1987), 23-42: cf. *Revolutionary Dreams*, 79-85, 89-92, and Figure 13.

51 *Essays on Revolutionary Culture and Stalinism: Selected Papers from the Third World Congress for Soviet and East European Studies*, ed. John W. Strong (Columbus: Slavica, 1990), 9-28.

52 In *The Culture of the Stalin Period*, ed. Hans. Günther.(New York/ London: St Martin's/Macmillain, 1990), 78-94; the sources do not go beyond 1986.

53 Cf. *Revolutionary Dreams*, 242 (very bottom)-245.

54 *Culture and Revolution*, ed. Paul Dukes and John Dunkley (London: Pinter, 1990), 132-41.

55 Personal email.

56 Cf. *Revolutionary Dreams*, 110-114; also, 122, with a bit from the chapter conclusion: The source base indicates that it was composed after *Revolutionary Dreams*, but the additional material points us to an earlier redaction of this section

57 Cf. *Revolutionary Dreams*, 107, 110, 157, 247: Perhaps it is a stretch for us to include this essay under "Rituals and Symbols," but rituals are as much "theater" as mock trials, which themselves are rife with symbolism.

58 192-94, and below, 231, 232-33.

59 *Soviet Music and Society under Lenin and Stalin: the Baton and Sickle*, ed. Neil Edmunds (London: Routledge, 2004), 23; cf. *Russian Popular Culture*, 12-16, 45-49, 74-78, 103-05, 116-21.

60 Personal email.

61 The lastest source for the essay is from 1988.

62 Cf. *Russian Popular Culture*, 153-54, 180-81.

63 See below, 273.

64 Cf., for example, *Russian Popular Culture*, 33, 91; the films are: *My Grief* (1918), *The Radiant Road* (1940), *Ivan Brovkin in the Virgin Lands* (1959), and *Déjà vu* (1989).

65 *Russian Review* 50 (1991), 481-83.

66 Cf. "Virgin Lands," paragraphs 1, 2-4, 12-13, and the nearly identical "Soviet Movies for the Masses," paragraphs 1-2, 14-16, 17-18.

67 Cf. *Revolutionary* Dreams, 171 (sub-chapter title "Maps of Heaven and Hell"); and *Russian Popular Culture*, 135 (Khrushchev on satire); and below, 351.

68 It also contains Stites's invariable textual lifting, but here with unexplained divergence: Cf. "The most famous was Leonid Pasternak's 'Aid for the Victims of War,' adapted by the Bolsheviks after the revolution for their own program" (*Russian Popular Culture*, 34), and "A 1914 poster by the established artist, Leonid Pasternak, 'Wounded Soldier,' was adapted by the Bolsheviks after the revolution for their own program" (see below, 374).

69 Cf., for example, the treatment of the film *Tears of a Ravished Poland* in *Russian Popular Culture*, 35-36, and below, 384-85.

70 Personal email.

71 Personal email.

72 *Intersections and Transpositions: Russian Music, Literature, and Society*, ed. Andrew Baruch Wachtel (Evanston: Northwestern University Press, 1998), 187-203, and esp. 199, 204, note 30; cf. *Serfdom, Society, and the Arts*, 71.

73 *Women in Russian Culture and Society, 1700-1825*, ed. Alessandra Tosi and Wendy Rosslyn (London: Palgrave Macmillan, 2007) 24-38, esp. 33-34; cf. *Serfdom, Society, and the Arts*, 249, 268, 275.

74 *Picturing Russia: Explorations in Visual Culture*, ed. Joan Neuberger and Valerie Kivelson, (New Haven: Yale University Press, 2008) 81-85, esp. 82; cf. *Serfdom, Society, and the Arts*, 14-20.

75 Personal email.

76 Cf. *Serfdom, Society, and the Arts*, 106-7, 247, 249, 251, and below, 499-502.

77 Cf. *Serfdom, Society, and the Arts*, 98-105, the section by that name, and below, 502-05.

78 Cf. *Serfdom, Society, and the Arts*, 281: Part IV Title: "Pictures at an Exhibition."

79 My own irreverent play on "day tripper" to criticize a pseudo-translator of a sacred text (since "it took me so long to find out" what he was doing), may have inspired Stites here: if so, that represents my 1% of our mutual impact in contrast to his 99% influence on me:

cf. Goldfrank, *Nil Sorsky. The Authentic Writings* (Kalamazoo: Cistercian Publications, 2008), 105, 109.

80 *Space, Place, and Power in Modern Russia. Essays in the New Spacial History.* ed, Mark Bassin, Christopher Ely, Melissia Stockdale (DeKalb: Northern Illinois University Press, 2010), 100-11.

81 Cf. *Revolutionary Dreams,* 190-204=Chapter 9: "Utopias of Space: City and Building."

82 Here also, and surely not accidently, but rather recalling his own playfulness as a father, Stites makes an oblique reference to Zorro ("On the Dance Floor," 106), the foppish hero, idolized by Richard's son Andrei at the age of five and six. One time, Richard, in his inimitable, Jimmy-Cagneyesque way, said to the lad: "Zorro is a dirty rat." "No, Papa," protested the distressed boy: "Zorro is a clean rat!"

83 *Space, Place, and Power*, 15.

I

RUSSIA'S CULTURAL COORDINATES

1

Civilization on Trial
Noted Russian dissident Andrei Sinyavsky renders judgment on the Soviet system

Stalin's daughter, Svetlana Alliluyeva, was a colleague of Sinyavsky's at a literary institute in Moscow. Years later, when he sat in jail and she was abroad, she wrote:

> Why do I see you Andrusha, my poor suffering friend, standing barefoot with buckets of cold water in your hands, your hair unkempt, and your clothes in rags?...You never did have much to say for yourself, Andrusha, and you were not the most handsome man in the world, but you had the stubborn courage to be true to yourself and honest before your conscience.[1]

The buckets of water were added by Alliluyeva, but Sinyavsky suffered enough, as much from moral anguish as from prison conditions. There is no word about convict life in this book and only a few not very kind ones about Alliluyeva. But it is drenched with sadness none the less. Its sinuous authority stems from the voice of the author, one of the towering intellectual witnesses of our time against the mindlessness of police states. His voice is deep and resonant, never strident—aching from pain but never whining. His life, his writing, his persecution, and trial under the recently vilified Brezhnev regime were the major events shaping the birth of Soviet dissidence.

Andrei Sinyavsky, now a professor of literature at the Sorbonne, is a Russian writer who came to maturity after the war. He was stunned by the arrest of his father in the last years of Stalin and shaken again by the selective revelations about the Stalinist terror made by Nikita Khrushchev in 1956. His writings, especially "On Socialist Realism" and *The Court Is in Session,* contained bitter mockery of the Soviet system and its cultural controls and thus could not be published at home. When they appeared abroad under his pen name, Abram Terts, Sinyavsky and his friend Yuly Daniel were arrested and tried a few months later, in 1966, on charges of anti-Soviet propaganda.

Political trials have often been turning points in Russian history. A century before the court condemned Sinyavsky, dozens of upper- and middle-class youth and students were rounded up by the police in the infamous Nechaev case and put on trial. Their fate catapulted hundreds more young people into the radical movement. Then the circle widened until it drew thousands into a lethal struggle against political despotism and class exploitation. That phase of the drama ended with the bloody assassination of Czar Alexander II in 1881 and the hanging of the killers. Five years after the revolution for which so many had fought and died, the victorious Bolsheviks mounted their own first major "show" trial of the weak remnant of their political foes, the Mensheviks and socialist revolutionaries. In one of the recurring ironies of history, revolutionaries were being tried by revolutionaries. In format and design, it resembled in every way the mock trials that the regime had held throughout the civil war to disgrace and demean the villains *du jour*—Woodrow Wilson, Georges Clemenceau, the leaders of the White forces, and abstract evils like illiteracy, shoddy work, religion, and child abandonment. The method was magnified by Stalin and his prosecutors into a grisly theatrical art in the famous Moscow trials of the late 1930s. But in the time of Khrushchev, who succeeded Stalin after 1953, there were no open political trials.

Great was the shock then, when, in the first years of the Brezhnev regime, the naked and ugly face of repression was unveiled again for all thinking people to see, a menacing signal that the few remaining sprouts of Khrushchev's short-lived and pallid thaw were to give way to the big freeze. The trial of two condemned writers was given limited publicity, and the masses as usual betrayed no interest whatsoever. But major figures in the intelligentsia—writers, scientists, and artists—rose up verbally in their defense. The outcry was taken up by others and grew into a continuous rumble of protest that became the dissident movement. After seven years of hard labor, Sinyavsky emigrated to Paris, where he's achieved near universal stature as a living icon of Russian literature and its moral conscience. He has not returned to live in Russia but remains in Paris, peering into the whirlpool of events and processes now unfolding in his homeland, seeking to comprehend their meaning. In doing so, he has looked back at the past, and out of his thoughts has come this appraisal of Soviet life, history, and civilization.

The English subtitle of the book is a misnomer:[2] It is in no way a "cultural history" of the Soviet Union. Strictly speaking there is no historical framework to the essay. It makes no pretense of presenting an ordered narrative or critical account of Soviet or Russian culture in our century that would include literature, theater, music, dance, cinema, and the popular arts as well as the media, the press, and something about ideology, scientific thought, and education. Its anecdotal elements are culled from all periods since 1917. And there is certainly no attempt to encompass even the main features of the Soviet cultural establishment and its creations. Literature is invoked sparingly and selectively and only to illustrate points about Russian sensibilities, revolutionary psychology, or the political system. The original Russian title, *The Bases of Soviet Civilization (Osnovy sovetskoi tsivilizatsii)*, is more accurately descriptive of what Sinyavsky does offer: a rambling and discursive monologue about politics and literature that proposes to be an interpretation of *Soviet civilization*, a term that some consider oxymoronic. Readers expecting more than this will be disappointed. But objective history and rigorous cultural analysis are not Sinyavsky's idiom. He is the quintessential Russian intellectual whose spirit comes alive in his fictional works of parody and fantasy with a moral edge. Some of this spark races through the present book.

Looking for the roots

The reader will find throughout Sinyavsky's meandering a bitter indictment of the Soviet system and of the "Bolshevik" mentality—that peculiar way of thinking and talking that combined the pseudoscientific vision of Marx's with Russian millenarian dreams. Sinyavsky, though he claims early in the book that soviet civilization is a "new" phenomenon, demonstrates vividly its deep roots in Orthodox Christian formulas and the apocalyptic expectations of the old Russian intelligentsia. Time and again he evokes the great writers of the nineteenth century for omens of things to come. In this, he follows in the tradition of the great Nikolay Berdyayev whose *Origins of Russian Communism*, printed abroad in 1937, was among the first (and remains the best) interpretation of Bolshevism as a specifically Russian outgrowth upon which the arid doctrines of Marxism were grafted. "One could devote a whole book," writes Sinyavsky, "to the borrowings or coincidences between communism and the Bible."

Communism and the revolution attempted to fulfill some of the most noble aspirations in the human soul, fundamentally to re-make the world, having repudiated everything that went before as wrong or unjust. In this sense communism enters history not only as a new sociopolitical order and economic system, but also as a new great religion denying all others.

He rightly points out the spiritual distance between Western rational atheists who merely deny God and those robust and angry Russian atheists who chose to wrestle and fight with God and who lined up sacred icons during the revolution and shot at them as if at a living enemy.

Sinyavsky disassociates himself from those in Russia and abroad who claim that "the revolution was imported and had noth-ing to do with the Russian people or Russian soil" (p. 8), a claim that often contains anti-Semitic overtones; but he also rejects the opposite view that "the October Revolution and Soviet civilization are a strictly Russian, national product" (p. 9). Throughout his dis-cussion of the early years of the revolution, Sinyavsky stresses the dogmatic, ecclesiastical side of Bolshevism, largely ignoring the emotional religiosity that seized so many believers in those years. Yet in denouncing the image-breaking compulsion that those be-lievers possessed, a compulsion to wipe out all visible reminders of the past, he gives no credit to the conservative and restraining efforts of the Bolshevik regime to preserve some of the treasures of that past.

All of this, of course, points to the undying truth that the Russian Revolution—like all major ones—was composed of two diametrically opposed forces temporarily allied against the old order: on the one hand the conscious, "modern," city-based and power-oriented "authority," *vlast'* in the Russian lexicon, embodied in Lenin; and on the other the spontaneous, antimodern, antiurban principle of anarchy and resistance embodied in the peasant partisan leader Nestor Makhno. Soviet history has been and still is, among other things, an unrelenting—now silent, now open—war between the two. Sinyavsky repudiates the premises and practices of the *vlast'* but never romanticizes the common people. To the populist images of the poet Sergei Esenin, whom he admires, he adds the lament of another great poet, Konstantin Balmont:

> You were utterly mistaken: your
> beloved people
> Are not at all the people you
> dreamed, not at all.

The old revolutionaries of the nineteenth century had placed their faith in the common people, "believing in a beautiful if somewhat misty socialism, dreaming of the advent of a new man…who would purify all of society. But when this man arrived and started shooting, the intelligentsia recoiled in horror."

Sinyavsky depicts Lenin as a cold and aloof "scholar" who injected science into the Revolution and unleashed massive cruelty for the sake of an ideology, but he does not really blame him for the larger revolution, which he attributes to World War I, the absurd and hideous fruit of the moral bankruptcy of liberal Europe, "The Bolsheviks' answer," he writes, "echoed a logical and popular demand: better a horrible end than this horror without end!" But when the horror came, in the guise of civil war, it was much worse than the bloodbath of World War I; it pitted brothers and sisters against each other, descended to savage cruelty, and implanted a Manichaean worldview among the Bolsheviks that pronounced all who did not stand with the Revolution as the embodiments of the darkest evil. It is only in the last few years that "the other side"— the defeated Whites—can be viewed by revisionist writers and filmmakers in the Soviet Union as human beings who suffered a great tragedy along with those who emerged victorious. But almost none of the present debate about these matters has a place in this book The author likens the Soviet system to a pyramid—heavy, massive, unmovable, and, he seems to suggest, unreformable.

The Stalinoid pyramid

Sinyavsky's discussion of Stalin is anecdotal and largely uninformed by any of the scholarship of the West or even of the glasnost revelations. He argues—as have many—that "Lenin's terror and centralization led perfectly naturally to Stalin," an unprovable proposition but one that is in any case far from equating the reign of Lenin with that of his successor. Indeed, Sinyavksy's entire discussion of Lenin stresses the differences in their character and style of leadership. At one point he admits that Lenin's "State of scholars" gave way to Stalin's "church-State." Sinyavsky is convincing when talking about the social bases of Stalinism and the new ruling class that emerged in the 1930s. These were common folk, workers of rural background, peasants, lower middleclass urbanites, people with "limited horizons and little education." The "primitive" ways of thinking of these simple people laid the basis of a semimagical culture in which Stalin could become a god and the stage director of a huge theatricalized polity adorned by show trials and lavish propaganda rituals, a "spectacle State" in the words of Robert Tucker, Stalin's greatest biographer. Sinyavsky speaks of "the mystery and the magic of Stalin's power," his charismatic inscrutability, his manufactured persona as the big boss, the owner, the host of all Soviet peoples in war and peace.

Sinyavsky is at his best when he writes about the Russian people as a whole and how their natural inclinations were, as he believes, degraded and distorted by the Soviet system. The theme of equality—or, more accurately, the hatred of inequality—is central to the history of the Revolution and to the current fate of the Gorbachev reforms. The strident triumphalism in the West over the imminent transformation of Soviet citizenry into their "natural" roles as acquisitive capitalists and profit seekers has recently given way to puzzlement about the resistance that the masses have displayed toward a market economy. Sinyavsky notes that the "thirst for equality has always been inherent to Russia." And again he relates this not to the imported formulas of Marxian socialism, but to Russian traditions of gross inequality that fueled maximalist aspirations to social justice. These ascended during the Revolution into huge projects for creating and maintaining equality.

Among these was the house-commune designed to release women and men from housework and provide collective living arrangements that would internalize the communist ideal through daily life. In one of his best chapters, Sinyavsky describes how this dream turned sour. House-communes — and other experiments in equality — were abandoned by the Stalinist regime and repudiated by the people. This and the housing shortage brought about the so-called communal apartment, which Sinyavsky, who lived in one for years, called a parody of the revolutionary ideal. In it residential relations turned into nasty squabbles based on family interests, small-minded efforts to control one's neighbors, and anti-intellectual hostility to those who, like Sinyavsky, stayed up late into the night reading books under communal electric lights. Here is the great irony of a revolution for ideals twisted by historical circumstances, the accelerated tempo of industrialization, political despotism, and lower-class conservatism into a mean-spirited countercommunity. The deep peasant traditions of leveling combined with the ideas of Marxism produced that marked Soviet suspicion of a neighbor's success and the impulse to "equalize" downward instead of upward. This is the rock upon which any version of capitalism may founder in the coming years — or months.

But beneath the Stalinist edifice, the Russian people — to say nothing of other Soviet national groups — have always tried to beat the system while simultaneously seeming to support it, or actually supporting it, and even fighting to the death for it as millions did in World War II. Russians are among the greatest and most skillful rule-breakers in the world. Officials, managers, workers, and consumers cannot operate under the irrational rationality of the centralized command economy. They wheel and deal and steal — from the State. The current intensity of anger and indignation about the rise in crime — gangs cheating and robbing individual citizens — was never felt by Soviets about those who looted the State, on whatever scale. Some of the great heroes of unofficial popular culture are bandits and lawbreakers, nonconformists and rebels, good-hearted swindlers, colorful entertainers famous for their alcoholic and sexual escapades. The rogue Ostap Bender from the novel *The Twelve Chairs* by Ilf and Petrov holds the crown in fiction; the late singer and actor Vladimir Vysotsky held it in real life. This is part of the recurrent dualism in Russian life: disobedience in the midst of iron conformity; universalism in tandem with xenophobia; capacious collectivism embracing narrow egoism.

We and they

Soviet Civilization is not a wholly original book. Many of its ideas, conclusions, and even concrete anecdotes can be found in previous works by Russian émigrés and even in popular journalism. Some of the patterns of Soviet life and politics are already dissolving before our eyes. In several places, Sinyavsky alludes to the current (the book was written in 1988 and updated in 1990) situation in his native country—to perestroika and glasnost—in a highly skeptical way. Events have outrun his judgments about the sincerity of reform attempts (if not about their chance for success). Serious historians will not accept many of his unqualified assertions that Stalin possessed an "oriental nature," that he was "barely educated," or that he, "as we know," had Sergey Kirov killed. But the value of this book lies not in its political punditry or historical accuracy. Students who demand immediate payoff in the coin of reliable prediction will derive little profit from it. More is the pity, because it is the wisdom contained in many of its pages that can nurture the kind of sensitivity to a nation's deep culture and mode of thinking and feeling that is so necessary to understanding something as remote and alien to our own experience.

The final pages of Sinyavsky's book are devoted to the painful and delicate Jewish question. There are no new factual revelations here. The author tells us what we know: that the latest version of Russian chauvinism has made the Jews its main target. He is clearly saddened by the news that at a public demonstration by the anti-Semitic elements of the rightwing organization Pamyat, the music of the once-sacred Soviet national anthem, "Holy War," composed in the heat of battle against Nazism in 1943, was recently sung to words that substitute "Yida" for Nazis. But Sinyavsky, a non-Jew, goes beyond pious lament to emphasize the distressing but fundamental truth that social envy and feelings of inferiority toward people who work hard, study hard, and avoid drunken escape are at the root of so much Russian enmity toward the Jews who, Sinyavsky believes, have replaced the old Russian intelligentsia that was exterminated in the turmoil of Soviet history. If "Soviet civilization" survives in a form that can accept all honest judgments, it will have to look full in the face of this hard and dreadful truth as well as many others contained in Sinyavsky's moving book.

Original publication: *The World & I* (February 1991), pp. 388-395.

Notes

1. Quoted in Abraham Rothberg, *The Heirs of Stalin* (Ithaca: Cornell University Press, 1971), 189.

2. The misleading subtitle is probably attributable to the translators or the publishers. This may be true also of the few factual errors: Zamyatin's *We* was written in 1920, not 1929 (p. 32); Ligachev's first name is Egor (sometimes rendered Yegor in English in order to capture its pronunciation) and not Boris (p. 268).

2

Cultural History and Russian Studies

The modern Middle East is not a center of great cultural achievements, nor is it likely to become one in the near future. The study of the region or its languages, therefore, does not constitute its own reward so far as modem culture is concerned.

—Morroe Berger

Cultural Imbalances

I begin with the rather negative term, "imbalances," to capture the reader's attention. Cultural studies, as I envisage it, is something that is all-embracing, studied partly for its own sake and partly for its relationship to other aspects of society. I believe that there is as yet no real cultural studies of the USSR, its antecedents and its successors. Its growth has been inhibited by two main aspects of our own culture—including our styles of scholarship: (1) the overweening investment in payoff knowledge, driven mostly by Kremlinology, about power—especially central power—and strategy, a knowledge whose main if not sole purpose is prediction; and (2) the fragmentation of disciplines that deal specifically with culture. I shall first attempt a critique of our cultural approach, then set out something of an agenda for broadening and enriching our study and teaching of Russian and related cultures.

Russian cultural studies has long been dominated, and still is, by university literature departments. In the view of many teachers of that subject in this country—not only emigrés and their students— their field of study all but ceased to exist in 1917 except for the emigration and selected "Soviet" period writers, mostly victims, martyrs, or dissidents. And for some others, literary scholarship has meant a close analysis of selected texts from the canon. For those scholars and their students, a four-way policy of exclusion has ensued: (1) the aesthetic exclusion of noncanonical works (for example, popular fiction before the Revolution) blocked out from the vision of students the vast bulk of what people actually read on the grounds that it was worthless; (2) the methodological exclusion in the once-prevailing practice of deep study of certain master texts omitted many well-known Russian writers of the nineteenth century from serious study; (3) the chronological exclusion, practiced by those who, for political and/or aesthetic considerations, did not recognize Soviet works of socialist realism as a legitimate field; (4) the linguistic exclusion, derived from the relative nondevelopment of language study of the component nationalities of the USSR (or the Russian Empire), made it seem as though Russian culture was the only culture in that empire.

The result was an extreme narrowing of the study of the written products of the Soviet people over seventy years—to say nothing of the deep past—a period that produced millions of works. Add two more circumstances to this picture. One is the fact that other fields of culture—important for their own sake as well as for their intimate and eternal interaction with print culture—have been orphaned by the hierarchical structure of knowledge that prevails in most universities, a hierarchy that places the fine arts, theater, cinema, architecture, and other things in strict subordination to literary studies. The second is the fact that the popular, "lower" or more vulgar and mass-produced and mass-oriented genres of all these arts—in other words popular culture—have until recently been almost wholly neglected or ridiculed.[1]

If I may be graphic for a moment, imagine the culture of a multinational empire as a mountain range with a dozen peaks and scores of outcroppings and foothills. Visualize then hundreds of geologists studying intensively the snowy top of one of them in the belief that they are studying the whole range. Needless to say, there are many exceptions and qualifications needed for this sweeping metaphor. But any quick scanning of American Association for the Advancement of Slavic Studies (AAASS) members, jobs, positions, departmental activities, *curricula,* conference papers, and publishing patterns will confirm its general truth.

This is not to argue that those literary specialists have wasted their time or pursued irrelevant matters. The clustering at the top is not like ten thousand angels poised on the head of a pin because our Slavic scholars have produced magnificent works of analysis and have enriched and deepened our comprehension of big cultural questions—philosophical, religious, semiotic. Nor would I deny that related cultural disciplines have been inactive. One could assemble a library of American monographs in art history, architecture, theater, music, folklore, and cinema. But the library would be small, with many of its volumes written solely within the context of their own disciplines. The narrow disciplinary approach has the advantage of placing Russian cultural production in a comparative or world context and of applying rigorously the well-established rules of analysis that each discipline has developed. But this focus sometimes means neglecting the specifically Russian or other traditions that helped to shape the various arts.

To my knowledge, there is no single modern work that treats synthetically all the arts and modes of cultural expression for any period of Russian history, and certainly none that grounds this cultural production in the historical, social, political, and intellectual context of the time.[2]

Take, for example, the reign of Alexander II (1855-81), an age of reform, of rapid intake of Western intellectual styles, and of turbulent radical activity. This was also the age of Fyodor Dostoevsky, Ivan Turgenev, Leo Tolstoy, and arguably a half-dozen other major writers and dozens of minor writers. It was the age of the insurgent group of painters called the Wanderers who defined Russian aesthetic norms for forty years. And it was the age of the Mighty Five (César Kyui, M. A. Balakirev, Aleksandr Borodin, Modest Musorgsky, and Nikolai Rimsky-Korsakov), the so-called national school of composition, as well as that of Russia's best-known composer, Piotr Illich Tchaikovsky. Add to this the various turns taken in the history of architecture, theater, and popular entertainment, and we see at once what a fabulously opulent cultural epoch it was. And beneath it all nourished a whole range of middlebrow and popular genres in literature and all the arts. Is it not remarkable that no study of the cultural interaction in this period has ever been undertaken? And yet even a cursory glance at the periodical literature and the correspondence and memoirs of the time reveals a continuous interaction and mutual enrichment of creative figures and of their relation to the historic milieu in which they lived.

The Silver Age, the World of Art, the New Religious Consciousness—have all found able chroniclers, as have the cultural currents of the avant-garde in the Soviet 1920s. But who has been bold enough to stand forth and produce works of cultural synthesis that might reveal deeper meanings of those respective eras? And what I have said here can be said for every well-established period in Russian history up to the present moment. I believe that such integrated studies would teach us much about Russian and Soviet history that has remained a mystery. And I believe that the study of all the arts would enhance the study of each; that is to say, a macrocultural panorama would lead scholars to rethink and perhaps rewrite the history of individual arts and media in a given epoch.

All this theorizing is based on a philosophy of history that ascribes to a given period of human experience within a well-defined society a certain Zeitgeist—what William Shakespeare in *Hamlet* called "the very age and body of the time." Zeitgeist does not mean that the combination of social, political, and broad cultural exploration of a given epoch will always add up to "coherence" or unity. It may, on the contrary, indicate social and cultural diversity, confusion, ambivalence, conflict, and turbulence; it may even show us that what we once considered valid segments of periodization are really false and misleading. For example, it was widely held in the 1930s that Germany, in spite of social division and political polarization, had settled into a "normal life" in the late Weimar years, 1925-29. Siegfried Kracauer, by examining only one branch of cultural production—cinema—made a convincing case in the 1940s that the psychological schisms and fissures in Weimar Germany were insurmountable. Kracauer was faulted at the time for assigning too much weight to cinematic evidence, but later historians who examined the same period with attention (however selective) to the other arts tended to confirm his argument.[3]

What have historians of Russia been doing? In recent decades, our profession has been reshaped by a flood of works on social history dealing with workers, peasants, women of various classes, merchants, teachers, physicians, bureaucrats, and others. All this work has had great value in sensitizing us to the deeper realities of Russian life. It has added a rich and heavy ballast to our knowledge about the top without displacing that top: state, dynasty, military, diplomats, aristocracy, the intelligentsia, political leaders, and so on.

But at the same time, Russian historians have always been surrounded by "culture" because so many of the notable figures in Russian history were connected with culture; because all writers of survey histories mention culture as something important; because our colleagues in Russian literature are so visible and influential in the field of Slavic studies; and because cultural themes seemed to count for a lot in the glamorous media of television and movies or publications like the *New York Review of Books*. On the other hand, a feeling of inadequacy on this issue nagged many of us. For historians, culture, when treated at all, was consigned to a chapter at the end of a textbook section or a lecture tacked on to the end of a chronological division in the course. And what kind of culture? It was usually only literature (belles lettres), and if something else got attention it was almost overwhelmingly "high culture"—the fine arts, classical music, legitimate theater, art cinema. It is fair to say that most historians of modern Russia probably engaged with culture at three points: classic nineteenth-century novels and plays (Aleksandr Pushkin to Tolstoy and Anton Chekhov); the Silver Age in literature and the arts, flowing into the revolutionary avant-garde of the 1920s; and dissident or persecuted writers of fiction in the Soviet Union.

One reason perhaps (there are others) that social historians did not do much more than this to integrate culture into our studies is that they assumed it to be yet another elite activity like diplomacy, war, government, and enterprise. And, given the traditional limited definitions of culture, that is indeed what it was. Culture was high culture and only that (and is still so treated in most accounts) and was thus an adjunct of elite life, occasionally drawing interest when it intersected with politics. I believe that the wondrous growth of social history and the recent spurt of the history of popular cultures enable us to end the artificial divisions between "history" and "culture."

The works of Jeffrey Brooks, Fred Starr, Denise Youngblood, Katerina Clark, Régine Robin, Vera Dunham, and others have given us a clearer feeling for popular tastes and values. Their work certainly reinforced my own positive feelings for popular culture and my discomfort at the huge gulf between high and popular cultures (even though these cultures are more closely related than we sometimes admit) and at the elitism that it often produces among academics. I must confess also that I had become dissatisfied with some of the "new social history," not for what it contained but for what it often left out: blood, life, élan, feelings, emotions, human expressiveness, personal relations. Some of this social history was too latent or passive, treating masses of people as statistical objects. It seems to me that the study of popular culture gives life to social history and complements it perfectly, in a way that the exclusive focus on high culture heretofore has not been able to do.

Imperial Russia and Its Cultural Universes

The rough branches of study that I have been talking about now lie before us in a square made up of four separate blocks: elite history, high culture, social history, popular culture. I believe that these may be integrated by careful and thoughtful comparison of how culture is created and consumed in society and influenced by class, gender, ethnicity, geography, and other factors. I offer some very rough notes on questions about the relation of cultures to one another, to society, and to the state—that is, to "state culture" or political culture that might be the subject of future research, graduate and undergraduate courses, and even textbook surveys. Many of these questions invite collaborative effort among people from various disciplines.

What I have in mind are studies of the relationship among various realms of culture—state culture, urban high culture, folklife, "empire" or ethnic and frontier culture, revolutionary subculture, and urban popular entertainment—in, for example, imperial Russia. This inquiry into the relationship of all the major cultural streams should attempt to relate cultural institutions and artifacts to social identities. Although some of these realms have been studied in the past, there has been no attempt to look at them as a cultural system, an interlocking edifice of ideas, values, and images in which Russian people of all classes dwelled.

Urban high culture, certainly the best known of these, particularly in its literary production, was that of Europe introduced by Peter the Great in the eighteenth century, modified and enriched by Russian elements, and institutionalized in academies, philharmonic societies, theaters, urban salons, and on gentry estates. It was limited in consumption almost exclusively to the upper and upper middle classes in town and country. High culture ought to be studied as part of social history, which is a history of taste formation, expressiveness, the dynamics of audience as a community, the role of the arts in daily intercourse, the organizational side of cultural production and its politics, the power of elitism, its relationship to European models, and its overall function in the social identity and consciousness of those who made it and consumed it.

Let us take as a specific case the visual culture of the eighteenth century, adopted by Russia from Europe. Patrons and artists of that epoch made little or no distinction between "fine arts" (painting and architecture) and the so-called minor or decorative arts. Everything was decorative, and all the arts were integrated in whole ensembles. The most elaborate and luxurious of the palaces and manor houses were designed as complex but unified works of art in which painting, sculpture, architecture, landscaping, garden planning, furniture, interior decor, and objets d'art (faience, Meissen, chinoiserie, Gobelin tapestries, porcelain, tiles, marble) were coordinated and aligned, orchestrated like the timbres, notes, and chords of a piece of symphonic music. To this one must add costume, speech patterns, and choreographed and ritualized behavior and gestures that—seen against the visual backdrop—gave art its social meaning: the theatricalization of life. Traditional art history has tended to lift certain elements—especially the oil canvas—out of this artistic ensemble and to study it as a separate subject. But such a narrow and hierarchical approach to culture pulls one branch of art out of its living context, marks it as superior to all that surround it, and then presents Russian "art" as inferior to that of the West because only one of its component genres is held up for comparison.[4]

In turning to the art of the common people, folklore or folk culture, we run into a different problem. Historians of Russian fine art have often simply ignored its role in social life, while folklorists have more often claimed that their field of study takes us inside the peasant mentality. Like Maksim Gorky, whose famous utterances in the 1930s about folk literature marked the revival of recently deceased folklorism in the Soviet Union, they believe that the history of the Russian people is encoded in their folk culture. The well-known literary historian, William Harkins, recently misread the point of Gorky's statement in the preface to a new book on the subject by Frank Miller. Taking Gorky literally, Harkins states, correctly, that the historical epics associated with folk creativity (the epics and historical tales and poems) give a distorted and factually erroneous picture of the past. But what Gorky meant, I believe, is that the entire body of folk culture—folk ditties, songs, rituals, as well as the longer folk epics—contains an accumulated record of peasant attitudes that can be decoded through careful scholarship. The fact that even before Gorky died in 1936, the Stalinist use of folklore was transformed into "fakelore"—the artificial creation of government-sponsored propaganda couched in archaic and rustic formulas—does not change the validity of Gorky's comment and does not invalidate the effort of folklorists to unravel the inner life of the village world by examining its expressive modes.[5] I would note also that in studying the depth and scope of Josef Stalin's panegyric utopia, the analysis of posters, paintings, movies, busts, and parades glorifying and deifying the leader would gain much by adding the study of Soviet fakelore. It would show that pseudoculture gains in power of persuasion when framed in "authentic" forms.[6]

But even if one is skeptical about the utility of folklore as a source of peasant thought and feeling, there are other reasons for historians to engage it. The folklife of the vast peasant population, more ancient than all the rest, flourished largely independently of high culture until "discovered" in the early to mid-nineteenth century by intellectuals, ethnographers, and revolutionaries. These outsiders reacted in various ways to incorporate it into high culture, adapt it to urban entertainment, politicize it, or suppress it. The works of Pushkin and Nikolai Gogol, of Tchaikovsky, Borodin, and Rimsky-Korsakov cannot be fully understood outside the realm of folk motifs, and for some of them, many non-Russian motifs.

Outdoor entertainment that played a great role in the public life of the urban masses and later indoor stage variations on it (*estrada*) drew freely from every level of cultural expression including that of the folk. Radical propagandists from the 1860s onward who sought the attention of workers and urbanized peasants were alive to the repertoires of folk songs and tales and tried to couch their populist, anarchist, or Marxist messages in a folkish idiom—a practice continued on through the Revolution.[7]

Finally, there were publicists of all political persuasions who looked upon folklore as the true expression of peasant life and precisely for that reason hoped to suppress it in the name of progress and European civilization. Their spiritual descendants were the antirural Bolsheviks who continued and escalated the assault on village culture in the 1920s until silenced by the prophets of Stalinist neofolklorism. Investigating the rescue operations on the remnants of folklife and folklore made by ethnologists and the assaults upon it by *Kulturträgers* and missionaries may take us beyond the brilliant work done by Richard Wortman on the psychological nexus between the populist intelligentsia and the common people and lead us further into the margins where overlapping, conflict, and social mimicry produced new forms of identity.[8]

The least studied of the rough categories I have suggested has been "empire" culture, where the Russian mainstream was reshaped by non-Russian ethnic elements, blossoming into frontier adventure, the poeticization of exotic lands, representations of empire, military iconography, the romance of the steppe, the imaging of Gypsies, cossacks, and "native peoples"—we as yet have no non-demeaning term for them—and the migration of all these elements from high to popular culture. All these topics can bring together the insights of historians, art historians, anthropologists, and literary scholars—to name just a few.[9]

Revolutionary subculture dated from the 1860s (or from the 1810s by Yury Lotman's reading of the Decembrists) and has had only fragmentary treatment by Soviet historians, who have largely idealized and heroized it but without examining its relation to the other cultures. It is interesting and revealing that nothing very much has been done about the cultural values and habits of nineteenth-century Russian revolutionaries except the obvious and endlessly repeated things about Nikolai Chernyshevsky, Nikolai Dobroly-ubov, and others on literature.[10] What I have in mind is the study of revolutionary imagery, panegyric politics, radical emotionalism (as expressed for example in song), the culture of the underlife, and emerging atheist sensibilities. (Note that I do not treat religion as a separate aspect of culture in that it takes on vastly different ritual-istic, devotional, and other forms depending on when and where it is examined.)

Urban popular entertainment became "modern" around 1900 with the import of technology (automobile, train, camera, cinema, gramophone, rotogravure presses) and soon outstripped in popu-larity almost all the rest. The new mass culture created with the help of the market and technology gave birth to new tastes, new notions of celebrity and fame, new ideas of ambition and hero worship, and a new cultural geography. One need not keep an eye constantly glued in the direction of February 1917 to appreciate how much these innovations were modifying social relations and identities.[11]

Finally—but not necessarily most importantly—we come to po-litical culture, including what Richard Wortman has called, respec-tively, "legal culture" and "the scenarios of power"—political art, court ritual, dynastic style, and the mythology of the old regime. Out of the myriad studies of the Russian bureaucracy, monarchy, local administration, judicial procedures, and the doings of the State Duma and other bodies, one always gets a sense of a peculiar Russian manner of dealing with politics and statecraft. Perhaps a "cultural" approach to politics and institutions through the study of language, rhetoric, costume, gesture, artifacts, and chancery ar-chitecture can enlighten us further about the essence of the tsarist system and how it fit or did not fit into the other cultural systems of the vast empire.

In offering the preceding topics of study, my hope—a pedagogi-cal agenda and research strategy for the profession—is that an inte-grated study of mutually interacting cultures within the nation can enrich our understanding of the whole society as well as bring once independently floating subjects into the mainstream of history.

Twentieth-Century Russia: Film and Music

In turning to the waning years of the tsarist period and the Soviet period with its aftermath, I wish to call attention to the pedagogical utility of the mass film or popular movie for historians and other scholars of Russian-Soviet culture and society. By focusing on cinema, I do not wish to abandon my belief in the importance of studying all the arts together in a given epoch (see my comments at the end of this section) but to speak concretely about movies as, arguably, the most influential of the popular arts in our century. The topic of film in the classroom is hardly new; panels have been talking for years about enriching courses through cinema and the other arts. But the practice has not yet reached many classrooms in Russian and Soviet history—to say nothing of literature or government—probably because the traditional method of using films has not proven very productive. In my observation during thirty years of teaching and talking to colleagues, that method has been usually to show the great classics of the silent screen from the 1920s and early 1930s—Sergei Eisenstein, V. I. Pudovkin, Dziga Vertov, and the others—and particularly revolutionary spectacles such as Eisenstein's *Battleship Potemkin (Brononosets Potemkin,* 1926), and films that seem to have direct political messages, such as the same director's *Alexander Nevsky* (1938), or, more recently, the jarring documentaries of the glasnost era. I hasten to add that great works of film art clearly have a place not only in the study of cinema culture but also in the history of cultural politics and aesthetic discourse. We will all continue to use them for appropriate purposes. And the value of "films of persuasion" or propaganda is self-evident.

I would argue, however, that such films are only marginally useful in understanding Russian-Soviet history and society. As recent Western scholarship has shown—and as the Soviet critics and the public have always known—the classics of Soviet cinema for the most part were not immensely "popular" either as huge box office successes or in expressing widely held values of the time."[12] This scholarship also shows that what people like in Russia is what they like almost everywhere and that what they liked in 1900 is what they still like in the 1990s—action, adventure, romance, melodrama, comedy—with of course plenty of local variation in time and place. Ideology and politics have had a much lower appeal, and artistic experiment even less—again with obvious exceptions. I might add here that the strict division between "art" or "serious" films on the one hand and entertainment movies on the other may be useful when gauging the intention of creators, but not for the final product in that both art and entertainment have produced shoddy films just as both have produced extremely good ones—quite apart from success in the market.

Extrapolating national or cultural values from popular movies is of course a problematic business filled with conceptual traps; it is not a simple operation, and we are far from a consensus about which values are actually reflected in or help shape popular culture. But the enterprise itself can reanimate some of those who are tired of the old conventions in using "film as history." Another reason for studying Soviet popular movies is that millions of Soviet people know and remember them, have felt deeply about them, and are more than willing to discuss them. This attachment rarely applies to the films of Eisenstein, Andrei Tarkovsky, Aleksandr Sokurov, and Tengiz Abuladze, which are justifiably treasured by the literati and intelligentsia—a tiny segment of the Soviet population.

Popular movies and popular culture in general can tell us more about a society in a given historical epoch than can works of high art. I hold no brief for abandoning high culture as a subject of study. On the contrary, it is essential to know it for its own sake as a precious treasury of a nation's creativity, as a counterforce and sometimes foe of the popular arts, and as their symbiotic partner. My purpose here is to suggest that popular movies can be made to speak to the student of history in the languages of their stories, acting styles, mise-en-scénes, and music in the cultural context of the era in which they were made and viewed.

Soviet popular movies are virtually unknown throughout the profession of Russian-Soviet studies. Part of the problem, of course, has been their relative unavailability compared to that of the classics for use in Western classrooms. But the birth of freedom in Russian cultural politics and the invention of the videotape and player have changed things dramatically. We are now able to introduce into our teaching the kinds of movies that have been genuinely popular for decades among Soviet people. To promote the pedagogical use and scholarly study of them, I will present a few brief remarks about the kinds of films that can be shown and the kinds of materials they contain that can be tied to historical themes—using the term "historical" in a wide sense. I will organize my remarks around four clusters of films and focus on a representative, only one of which (the second) is well-known outside the former USSR: *Be Still, My Grief* (*Molchi, grust', molchi*, 1918), *The Radiant Road* (*Svetlyi put'* [also known as *Bright Path*], 1940), *Ivan Brovkin in the Virgin Lands* (*Ivan Brovkin tselinu*, 1956), and *Déjà vu* (*Dezha vyu*, 1989). The selection is limited and arbitrary, but it does range through the century and deals with several popular genres: salon melodrama, Stalinist fairy tale, the construction epic, and the gangster comedy. Each in its own way illustrates the possibilities of reading a film for the purposes of historical understanding. I can think of no other way to make my point clear than to discuss a few of these films in detail.

The prerevolutionary decade (1908-17) was one of civil violence and peasant disorder and of increasing urban crime and social misery, but also one of material progress—city tramcars, lavish restaurants, an influx of foreign culture, and an outpouring of popular culture that captivated mass audiences and challenged the traditional rule of fine arts and high culture, By 1910 Gypsy songs, nightclubs, the cabaret, music hall reviews, and a flood of detective and adventure stories and boulevard novels of sex and ambition dominated Russian urban entertainment. The cinema, born amid the swirl of the new popular culture, was a Moloch who consumed it all: folkloric themes and narrative styles, popular music, *estrada* (the popular stage), and fiction. The omnivorous pioneers of moviemaking would devour anything that would pull a film through a camera and tell a story. When ordinary materials ran out, they hired hacks to create scripts right on the set—exactly as was done on the meadows of Astoria and the backlots of Hollywood. The greed of the studio for profit was no greater than the greed of the public for more movies.[13]

The dominant genre—half of all films made—was the salon or "bourgeois" melodrama. Neya Zorkaya has analyzed a few hundred of these using a method resembling the classic work of the folklorist V. Ya. Propp, whose "morphology of the folktale" proclaimed the structural unity of all folktale plots. Most film melodramas bear the marks of standardized production—formulaic repetition, cardboard characters, psychological shallowness, and the absence of political content. Almost all are variants on a master plot about a "slave of passion" (the title of one of them). The idyllic life of a young girl, marred only by vague malaise, is disrupted by the appearance of a seducer; her passion for him gives way to disenchantment and, at the end, tragedy ensues (suicide, ruin, murder, vengeance). Several themes are linked constantly: money, power, leisure, boredom, the need for distraction, gambling and game playing among affluent men—the main game being seduction of a young and innocent woman. The conquered prey becomes a possession, a toy to be fondled for a while and then discarded. The victims are framed in a virtuous idyll—humble or opulent: in *Be Still, My Grief,* the poor doting wife of an aging alcoholic circus acrobat; in *Children of the Age* (*Deti veka*, 1915), the young mother, happily married to a poor bank clerk; in *A Life for a Life* (*Zhizn' za zhizn'*, 1916), two happy foster sisters. The victimizers dwell in obvious settings of social decadence: expensive parties, smoking, drinking, Gypsy entertainers.

These films are filled with social and sexual tension. The contrast between innocence constructed as poor or weak and evil constructed as rich and powerful is rendered by making urbane, cruel, and impeccably dressed matinee idols break the hearts and shatter the lives of beautiful women on screen. The female superstar, Vera Kholodnaya, appeared regularly as their victim. The former dancer with the sad, gray eyes animated the celluloid world she dwelled in, a world of tainted money, opulent restaurants, champagne picnics, luxury autos careening through the night, and illicit love ending in tragedy. Of the Kholodnaya pictures, *Be Still, My Grief,* directed by Petr Chardynin, was the last of the salon psychological melodramas, a ten-year anniversary film celebrating the birth of Russian cinema and—as critics noted—a reunion of all its clichés.[14] Chardynin played Lorio, the pitiful alcoholic circus clown whose physical injury is compounded by the loss of his wife. Circus—a popular theme in movies up into the 1930s—is here a symbol of the poverty and vulnerability of entertainment figures to the allure of money and the ruthlessness of the upper classes. Kholodnaya plays Pola, the young wife who is seduced by the charms of luxurious parties and attentive men and then destroyed. The process of decay is accompanied by the then-popular title song played on violin and guitar by the begging couple (unheard by modern ears, but generally performed live in the old movie houses).

Bolshevik officials and filmmakers detested films like *Be Still, My Grief* as frothy and unserious, attuned to the decadent leisure postures of the upper class, catering to the base instincts of man, paying excessive attention to sex, violence, and crime, lacking in moral uplift and correct political content, generally uneducational, and rooted in the search for profits. Like most elites, the Bolsheviks feared that "dark forces" dormant among the lower classes could be evoked by sitting in the darkened chamber of the commercial cinema. The Bolshevik critics also hated its "theateritis": the cinematography (called "Khanzhonkovism" by later filmmakers) of long takes, intermediate shots, and a stationary camera; and the acting style called "Delsartism," a repertory of exaggerated poses and gestures coded to emotions developed on the stage by the nineteenth-century Frenchman François Delsarte and taken into popular melodrama and then films. It was against this art that many of the great film masters of the revolution rebelled. But it was precisely this sort of entertainment film that the masses rushed to see before the revolution—and after it. In late 1921 when the first private movie house under the New Economic Policy opened its doors on Tverskaya Street, it showed *Be Still, My Grief* from morning to night to full houses. With the recent showings in Europe and the United States of prerevolutionary film, we now know that some of these films were masterpieces of cinematic art.[15]

It is more than probable that widely shown films like *Be Still, My Grief* generated angry feelings toward the upper classes. Hatred and collective indignation can be engendered by the popular media; war films alone are proof of this. If hostility already festers, it can be reinforced by a cultural product that tells viewers that the makers of the movie and the public share their feelings about social morality and its outward affects—raiment, scenery, and manners. It is no wonder that slicked hair and bowler hats, prime emblems of the slimy cinematic seducers, were angrily rejected, satirized, and even assaulted under the new Soviet regime. The privileging of classical motifs in architecture and furnishing in the mise-en-scéne of the

P. I. Chardynin and Evgenii Bauer films—classical busts, statuettes, columns, cornices, Grecian urns—were meant to signify perfection, beauty, and aesthetic honesty and to provide ironic contrast to the degraded values of their owners. But to the masses they may have been simply the emblems of excessive and needless luxury of the owning classes. These images may have deepened the "vandalistic" behavior of the riotous urban lower classes in 1917-18.[16] Thus the "bourgeois" films of the prerevolutionary era, while catering to mass tastes, in a sense helped feed radicalism; and the Bolsheviks thus owed the great movie tycoons a debt of gratitude for their unintentional assistance. In any event, films like *Be Still, My Grief* can enliven and even illuminate a whole range of discussions on topics such as new versus old art, Bolshevik censorship policies, the relationship between film and audience, and the role and function of architecture and decor in the old regime.[17]

The Radiant Road (released in a cut version in the United States as *Tanya*), the product of a wholly different cultural matrix, is the pinnacle of social and political fantasy in prewar Stalinist cinema.[18] It was the last in a series of stunningly successful and long-remembered prewar musical comedies starring Lyubov Orlova, directed by her husband Grigory Alexandrov, and with music by the master mass-song composer of the era, Isaac Dunaevsky *Happy-Go-Lucky Guys* (*Veselye rebyata*, 1934), *Circus* (*Tsirk*, 1936), and *Volga, Volga* (1938). They offered a winning recipe of patriotism, cornball sentiment, spectacular cinematic effects, singable tunes, and celebration of the new Moscow. Forming the intriguing political-cultural context of these films were the easing up of the social mood in 1933-34, the sharpening of tension in 1935-36, the outward sloganizing of a "happy life," the murderous purges of 1936-38, the ascendance of the Stakhanovite mythology of production, the cultural representation of economic achievements and urban construction, and— twisting around all these—the spasmodic reordering of jazz and light music and the national campaigns to legitimize and foster a mass movement of amateur and folk culture.

In *Radiant Road*, the heroine Tanya (Orlova), a classical Cinderella with a smudged nose, rises through the textile industry to become a Stakhanovite superworker who can run hundreds of looms simultaneously and beat world records. Along the way,

Tanya learns her letters and wins the love of a clean-cut engineer—a Soviet prince charming with a pipe and a briefcase. She makes the dreamed-of pilgrimage to Moscow and is decorated by the "peasant" President Kalinin in an opulent Kremlin palace. The finale contains a splendid visual treatment of the just-completed Agricultural Exhibition in Moscow, whose Central Pavilion resembled a castle. In one of the final shots the living couple is foregrounded in front of Vera Mukhina's statue of the male industrial worker, hammer in hand, and the female agricultural worker, sickle in hand—thus proclaiming gender equality and simultaneously assuring the male engineer the dominant role in this "equal" partnership.[19] The movie asserts constantly that this plot is real life and not a fairy tale. In the finale, a chorus sings the aviation song "Ever Higher" (a colossal hit of the 1930s), which opens with the words: "We are born to make fairy tales come true." Indeed the film is roughly modeled on the rise of the then-famous female Stakhanovites, Evdokiya and Mariya Vinogradova,[20] and Orlova studied intensively on the mill floor to prepare herself for the exploits she performed on screen. Orlova plays the victorious plebeian, as she had in *Happy-Go-Lucky Guys* and in *Volga, Volga*. Social mobility through the Soviet system, a breakthrough to "consciousness" with the help of a mentor (in this case, a female schoolteacher), and triumph over a languid bureaucrat—all the ingredients of socialist realism are present. But Alexandrov and his associates rise above the usual drabness of the master plot by use of the fantastic mise-en-scéne at the conclusion, where monumental structure is framed by dream-filled billows in the sky. The uncut original (which I have not seen) has an automobile flying over the rooftops of Moscow![21] The fusion of the traditional fairy tale with metallic and mechanical furniture of modernity and with the official scenario for success accounts for the immense popular triumph of this movie—designed for and consumed by "the millions."

The Alexandrov-Orlova-Dunaevsky films can be analyzed and taught as stories of social mobility, as political mystification, as gender construction, or as musical entertainment—they were all of these. But one of the "stars" of these movies was Moscow, specifically the new Moscow construction that was represented as heroic and populist in the media. It is often argued that Stalinist architecture's celebration of state grandeur was only meant to underline the insignificance of the citizen on the street. But when a provincial woman in Moscow first gazed upon the newly finished Hotel Moskva—filmed from every angle in *Circus*—she exclaimed, "I do not know if this is a hotel or a fairy tale palace." Similarly the harbor building (or River Station) on the Moscow River, built to punctuate the completion of the Volga-Moscow canal, was meant to extend a dignified but warm welcome from the capital to newly arriving passengers from the hinterland. One of the final scenes of *Volga, Volga* shows the beautiful steamer *Josef Stalin* docked alongside this gleaming, white-columned edifice whose staircase leads up to the capital where the heroes find success and instant popularity for their amateur music.

In August 1939 the massive Agricultural Exhibition opened in Moscow and was visited by as many as twenty to thirty thousand people a day. It was a fairyland—in many ways resembling its contemporary, the New York World's Fair, in opulence and monumentality, with its domes, gothic buildings, fountains, broad walkways, a giant statue of Stalin, and the huge Mukhina ensemble.[22] These and other examples of Soviet construction and decor were deployed in the films of the 1930s not to depress and not only to impress but to enliven and animate the viewer with self-esteem and communal pride. Architecture and decor in these industrial melodramas have exactly the opposite function from what they had in the old regime melodramas: they are the status symbols of the upwardly mobile proletariat.

Ivan Brovkin in the Virgin Lands is a rustic musical that, aside from being a marvelous hour-and-a-half entertainment, summarizes and resolves several themes in the history of Soviet popular movies and marks a turning point in cultural history. It draws on two lines of scenic backdrop and social mood: the epic and the idyll. The epic of construction, a major theme in all genres of popular culture since 1917, but especially since 1928, romanticized physical labor, manual toil, and the realia of machinery against a backdrop of wilderness. During the Civil War, building something fast—such as a railroad—took on epic proportions, a fact celebrated with gorgeous cinematography in A. A. Alov and V. N. Naumov's *Pavel Korchagin* (1955), the best screen version of Aleksandr Ostrovsky's notorious novel *How the Steel Was Tempered*. In the first full sound film, Niko-lai Ekk showed another example of railroad as salvation in the *Start in Life* (*Putevka v zhizn'*, also known as *Road to Life*, 1931), about or-phan boys in the 1920s. In the 1930s Sergei Gerasimov's *Komsomolsk* (1938), offered a camera study of deforestation and town building in the Soviet Far East. In these pictures, the act of cutting down and building up is endowed with a special pathos and poetics that proved irresistible over the decades and whose cinematographic style was incorporated into the wartime epic.

The idyll came later. In the 1920s, village life was often ridi-culed in the popular arts. Folk dances, songs, and costumes were depicted as the archaic trappings of roach- and god-infested worlds of darkness—the great exception to this image of course being the work of Aleksandr Dovzhenko. But after collectivization, the new kolkhoz was romanticized as a confluence of the new and the best of the old-bicycles and hospitality, tractors and head scarves, bri-gades and peasant fertility. This theme blossomed in folk dance ensembles, paintings, operettas, novels, and films in the 1930s and 1940s and reached its apogee in Ivan Pyrev's famous *Kuban Cos-sacks* (*Kubanskie kazaki*, 1949), a cinematic kolkhoz operetta and a classic of the glossy, "conflictless" films of the late Stalin era. When tension between new and old was treated, the new was always vin-dicated—as in the most famous example, *Cavalier of the Golden Star*, a novel, an operetta, and Yuly Raizman's 1950 film starring Sergei Bondarchuk in one of his most wooden performances.

Ivan Brovkin was made in the midst of Nikita Khrushchev's Virgin Lands campaign, a drive to cultivate large tracts of land in the steppe between the Urals, the Caspian, and Siberia and in the Northern Kazakhstan. Although made only a few years after *Cava-lier*, it gave the conflict a new resolution by treating the old village and the new sovkhoz equally. The former is symbolized by rural folkways, stubborn elders, and a bride who refuses to join her man on the cultivation sites beyond Orenburg. But this standard sym-bolic characterization—almost identical to that in *Cavalier*—is de-ployed with great tact and delicacy. The old village is captured in beautifully framed color shots resembling the picture postcards of rustic life that were mass-produced before the Revolution; and it is drenched in the sounds of lovely music of the popular songwriter,

Anatoly Lepin. Out on the steppe, modernity springs forth from a semidesert under the hands and brains of the hero, his wise and kindly mentor, and a crew of young, idealistic, ethnically varied komsomols who tear open the earth and career upon it in their iron victory chariots in a civic version of savage joy. The domestic scenes of gathering, home building, and planning are done in the painterly fashion of Stalinist socialist realism.

The marriage of epic and idyll is celebrated at many levels: the wedding scene that choreographs the disorderly and energetic folk dancing along a ruler-straight street laid out on the steppe; the accordions and birch twigs on the nuptial automobile; the return of the hero to claim his bride and their journey back to the steppe on a train. The director authenticates his movie with a direct quotation from the famous potato tactics scene in *Chapaev* (1934), here having Brovkin showing his sovkhoz chairman how tractors can be deployed more effectively. Brovkin (played by Leonid Kharitonov) is a younger, more vigorous, more credible version of Bondarchuk's cavalier of the golden star, and his triumph more humane. *Ivan Brovkin* is a proclamation of moral equality and coexistence between kolkhoz life, with all the cultural baggage it retained after collectivization, and new sovkhoz life with its clean bathrooms and electric light. The film illuminates that moment in Soviet history between the relentless Stalinist exaltation of new over old that prevailed from 1928 until the mid-1950s and the exaltation of traditional village values that has been under way for thirty years and more in the words of village prose writers, filmmakers, and intellectuals of many kinds.

The reader will note that I have ignored the obvious historical aspects of this film. One is its glossy treatment of the genuine hardships and shortcomings of the Virgin Lands campaign that were generally known then and have since been well documented; even the sugary memoirs of one of its chief organizers, Leonid Brezhnev, reveal more reality than does this film.[23] The lack of amenities; the ferocious blizzards that enveloped the steppe and snuffed out the lives of the unsuspecting; the surliness of the locals; the inability of Soviet plowshares to carve open the root-entangled sward of the ancient grassland—all are missing in the film. The other historical aspect is its obvious design as a mobilizing agent to recruit needed youth—particularly women and physicians (combined in one character in the movie as in real Soviet life)—out to the Virgin Lands. In this *Brovkin* resembles the great construction epics of the 1930s, both documentary and fiction films. What could be more obvious than either of these points? Frontiering and construction invite romanticism in cinematic treatment; they make for fun, "profit," and good ideology. The American boomtown, railroad, and oil field epics of the 1930s are hardly different in this regard.

At the present juncture in film history, we are faced with flux and the unpredictable. One of the main themes of agonizing debate among Soviet filmmakers is commercialism or "Hollywoodism" and its natural offspring: romance, adventure, sex, violence, crime, and all the rest. In the midst of this debate, and a clear product of the free atmosphere of glasnost, appeared the gangster-comedy film, *Déjà vu*. A direct instance of *amerikanizm* in movies, *Déjà vu* is a hilarious Odessa Studio production set in 1925 and advertised as having "American-style action." The plot of this manic parody of the gangster film—which recalls the cinematic gifts of Billy Wilder—revolves around a Chicago Prohibition war and a Polish-American hit man sent to Odessa to wipe out an informer. The foolery explodes in the shameless quotations from old James Cagney films (very popular in Russia in the 1940s), from *The Godfather,* and from *Potemkin* (the shooting of Eisenstein's staircase scene is woven into the chase), and the reactions of foreigners to Soviet life in the 1920s, elements of which still linger to this day—particularly in tourist hotels. The large audience at the Coliseum in Leningrad (where I viewed it in early 1990) never stopped laughing and almost convulsed at the shot of a mafioso with a Civil War machine gun pointed through a loft window—a direct quotation from *Chapaev.* The lurid depiction of the Odessa criminal underworld of bootlegging, American jazz, and sex during the New Economic Policy is an affectionate reminder of another age, a sharp commentary on the kingdoms of illegality that were flourishing in the USSR in 1989 (and still are), and a sidesplitting mockery of everything Soviet and communist in the early days of the Revolution.

Déjà vu seems to herald a new era or a return to the old era of I. A. Ilf and Evgenii Petrov. If Soviet filmmakers and audiences are capable of laughing at gangsters, they are also capable of taking them seriously—which none has yet done. The makers of *Déjà vu* are, in a sense, outsiders: the director, Juliusz Michulski, is a Pole; the film was made in Odessa—that once fertile and febrile pool of Jewish comedy, musical, and cinematic talent (comedians Mikhail Zhvanetsky and Vladimir Khenkin, band leader Leonid Utesov, songwriter Oskar Feltsman, director Mark Donskoy, among others). But "outsiders" have always gotten inside the cultural center and reshaped it and themselves. Students of Russian life will certainly learn more from films openly catering to the public taste than they will from the anti-Stalinist revisionist documentaries—some of them truly masterful as art—that have come to our shores in an endless stream.

These few remarks are meant to suggest that even artless films can quicken the art of historians and enlarge their vision. Although I have formed my remarks around four titles, I do not believe that textual analysis of individual films is the only or even the most fruitful device for the cultural historian. To understand society, people, institutions, mentalities, and identities in any given epoch—and then to explain how they change in a subsequent epoch—one might take a body of films on any given theme over a long period or a more varied body within a manageable period. In doing so, one has to come armed not only with a knowledge of history and cinema but of popular culture as well—songs, stories, myths, legends, cults; performing arts such as circus, cabaret, and variety stage (*estrada*); customs, gestures, and jokes. These are the treasury of symbols and codes, the keys to the value systems of those who create and consume them. Movies and the popular culture they encapsulate may not answer questions directly, but they are sure to generate many new ones heretofore unasked. It is not too extravagant to say that all of Soviet history could be rewritten and retaught on the basis of cinema and the other arts in order to uncover national moods and feelings. Those literary and high culture scholars who have looked upon Soviet culture as a vast wasteland might even discover in it something of value; and traditional Kremlinologists might even find in the history of Soviet people something other than robotic subjects of a despotic state.

Let me now turn briefly to music, the most neglected of all arts in terms of integrating it with other matters. The neglect has sometimes been based on ignorance of or indifference to music, but more often I suspect on the belief that music is apolitical and cannot be tied to historical—social phenomena. But even if one does not share Plato's belief in the ominous influence of certain kinds of music over the emotions and minds of the Republic's citizens, one can hardly deny that music and politics intersected many times in the Soviet period of Russian history and not just in the occasional political abuse of certain classical composers (the cases of Vano Muradelli, Dmitry Shostakovich, and Sergei Prokofiev are the best known). Political leaders who claimed to represent the moral concerns and artistic tastes and interests of the masses have brought under their scrutiny music of every sort: folk, popular, jazz, prerevolutionary, foreign, classical, and rock.[24] But there is more to it than direct political meddling; entire national moods can be shaped by and reflected in music, especially popular music.

In the United States, for example, scholars and listeners both know that the whole emotional structure of popular song changed drastically and permanently around 1940-41 with the onset of the war in Europe and then in the Pacific. As proof, one may examine the music of Richard Rodgers first in partnership with Lorenz Hart in the 1930s and then with Oscar Hammerstein in the 1940s. Anyone who has even an inkling of this body of music knows at once that the change in tone was fundamental—though few people noticed it at the time. The Rodgers and Hart team in the decade of depression and recovery had produced a corpus of sophisticated, bubbly, ironic—and eminently danceable—music. It went to the head like Cole Porter's bubbles in a glass of champagne; it moved the dancing parts of the body rather than the heart. It was sassy and irreverent and belonged in spirit to the music of the preceding decade. It was not "singing" music: the lyrics of Hart were too clever and "hip" and the melody line of Rodgers relatively complex. The lyrics of his later collaborator Hammerstein, on the other hand, were eminently singable, emotional, and accessible—and Rodgers's music fit the bill perfectly.

Can a war, or a similarly potent moment in national experience, effect such a shift in popular art and in popular taste? In this question we have the key to relationship of art to life. Many scholars have tried to tie art to the other modulations of history—social change, economic development, migration, even revolution. One of the most famous of these is the study by Arnold Hauser on *The Social History of Art.*[25] But his book, though rich in detail and adventurous in conception, is ultimately reductionist since it grounds major changes in artistic sensibility in the relations of production—in other words, in narrow Marxist categories. It is not a work to be dismissed because, although Hauser's answers may not satisfy, his questions are brave and relevant. Also, it cannot be denied that social and economic change—however effected—can have a profound impact upon cultural expression. Yet it is the sudden and profound political change—revolution and war for example—that really registers a modification in popular moods, and thus in culture and art. One can hardly deny that the 1790s in France witnessed a shift in artistic styles in almost every genre and every art. At the same time one must recognize that the classical revival of the mid-eighteenth century was continued, however politicized, by the great revolutionary painters and festival managers of the French Revolution.

The Bolshevik Revolution was exceptionally self-conscious in terms of its artistic expression, and its cultural history is well known. It generated a big musical war in the 1920s and early 1930s between pure "proletarian" composers, who wanted to banish every trace of popular commercialism from song, and ordinary consumers who wanted rhythm, fun, and pathos in their songs and dances. In the 1930s, Stalin's cultural managers ended this war by an eclectic and synthetic compromise: dance and novelty tunes were permitted but not sponsored; revolutionary songs would continue to offer the pathos of struggle and sacrifice; and a new genre of "mass song" would provide the joyful element. But the joy had to be collective, optimistic, and patriotic. Hundreds of sunny upbeat marches and songs were produced by the mass composers for young communists, children, shock workers, the military, tractor drivers, and every other community that was actively helping to build socialism. "March of the Happy-Go-Lucky Guys" was written for the Komsomol in 1934; "March of the Enthusiasts" accompanied the five-year plans. The biggest nonmovie hit was Matvei Blanter's "Katyusha" (1938), destined to achieve world fame during the war. The rocket mortar invented by A. G. Kostikov and first used in the

Russo-Finnish War of 1939 was named after this song. Mass songs saturated the airwaves, film soundtracks, the stages, and the public parks; they were performed in solo, by dance bands, and by huge orchestras and choirs.

A Soviet Tin-Pan Alley composed of songwriters—mostly Jewish, many from Odessa—was assembled to produce mass songs in large numbers. Its acknowledged king was Isaac Dunaevsky, a legendary figure in the history of popular music in the USSR. Dunaevsky became the major mass song writer of the 1930s and 1940s and produced hundreds of songs until his death in 1955. He was also highly paid and honored throughout the country. A key to his success was precisely his lack of profundity or originality. His compositions, especially the film tunes, were (and still are) undeniably appealing, and they became enormous national hits in the 1930s. As mentioned above, he was the musical genius behind the great Alexandrov-Orlova musicals of that decade. *Happy-Go-Lucky Guys* launched Dunaevsky's famous "heart" into the hearts of millions, many of whom recognize it at once a half-century later. His songs from *Circus* were given massive distribution, and long before the movie reached the provinces radio listeners were singing them as if they were folk songs. The theme "Song of the Motherland" attained such stupendous popularity that it became the station signal of Radio Moscow for many years and was played on the Kremlin chimes until the 1950s. In the words of a former Soviet citizen, the music from *Circus* "helped stifle the shots that killed several generations of revolutionaries, it masked Stalin's ruthlessness and Great Russian chauvinism, and it presented to the world the benign face of an idealistic socialist state on the march."[26] At the same time it entertained millions of ordinary people.

But almost imperceptibly—first in the war years and then in the postwar era—Dunaevsky's popularity began to fade. Folk music rose into ascendance, heavily financed by the regime but also eagerly desired by the masses. On the urban scene, an idyllic, sentimental style of popular song rose as well, displacing the more urbane, town-anchored styles of the 1930s. The new force in popular music, Vasily Solovev-Sedoi, composed "Evenings Near Moscow" (known abroad as "Moscow Nights"), an elegiac celebration not of collectivized peasants, marching youth, or resolute Stakhanovites, but of innocent young lovers fondly courting in the forests outside the capital. Writers continued to compose songs of cities, but their works lacked the urban bite of earlier times, and none could compare to the popularity of Solovev-Sedoi's hit song. When its opening bars replaced those of Dunaevsky's in the Kremlin chimes, they signaled something about the burgeoning domestication and personalization of the revolution, the calming of energies, the privatization of life, and the curious shifting of gaze from the proletarian factories to the "woods outside Moscow" and to the great world of the Russian countryside beyond, a phenomenon that was matched in the emerging literary genre of "village prose."

Thus one of the effects of the great war was to make the personal a part of the national struggle, to establish a tie between historic Russia, its rural roots, and patriotism, and to legitimize private emotion. In doing so, the war fostered the sentimentalization of urban popular song and valorized country and folk music as an authentic expression of "the people" in a fashion that almost paralleled what happened in the United States at the same time. If the content and style of the American products differed clearly from the Russian (a difference arising not only from local cultural roots but also from the divergent experiences of the two nations in the war years), the shift in national mood was strikingly similar.

The National Republics and the Socialist States

What is needed for the ethnic minorities, constituent republics, and newly independent Russian states are separate, parallel studies of their cultural history to include (1) the high cultural, intellectual, religious, and spiritual traditions, including folklore and legend as well as ecclesiastical and theological history and that of popular devotion; (2) the deeply rooted and still surviving customs of everyday life and behavior, including family, gender, codes of honor, and work habits; and (3) the dominant modes of popular entertainment and use of leisure time, including socializing, reading, performance styles and attendance, radio and television, rituals and public ceremonies, styles of political discourse and interaction. These studies should be rooted in the prerevolutionary past and move through the Soviet period with an eye as to what was truly indigenous, what was imported or imposed, and what was adapted from the dominant culture (Russian) and from neighboring cultures as well. And scholars should be alert to the fact that "adapted" or syncretic forms of culture—however unauthentic they may appear—can be an important, even dominant part of people's lives.

The cultural history of Eastern Europe has been particularly disserved. Is there any work that addresses the high, folk, and urban popular cultures of the Slavic, Magyar, Romanian, Baltic, and other peoples of this region in modern times; that analyzes the role of Gypsy music, coffeehouses, operetta, folk ensembles, Jewish storytelling styles, or a dozen other elements that were a visible and audible part of the environment; or that tells us how these elements were dealt with under the communist regimes; or about Sovietization and even Russification of certain cultural practices in the region? What could enliven more the history of this culturally rich and diverse region than to go beyond (though never omit) the details of anti-Titoism, collectivization and decollectivization, reform, repression, and power struggles of the era and delve into the politics and texture of culture at every level?

Conclusions

In the Chinese idiom, I am "throwing out a brick in order to attract jade," that is, laying out some rough and crude positions in the hope that others will refine them through experience and dialogue. But here I want to stress my insistence that reform does not necessarily entail the deletion or abolition of the things we have been doing up to now. It is rather an appeal to all the disciplines to address issues that often fall between the cracks because of the traditional and legitimate interests of our own fields; to work for inclusion of cultural expression and social behavior—including politics—into a unified discourse; to add new things to those we are already engaged in; to rethink those distressing geological (and ideological) faults that divide "old-fashioned" history from the new social history, highbrow from lowbrow, literature from the "other arts." I believe that this expansion can be accomplished by turning in the following directions:

1. Increasing the number of courses on "Russian civilization" and enlarging their scope by including all the arts (high and popular) in more or less equal measure, offering a sociology of taste by showing which genres appealed to which strata of society—and why—and explaining what political significance they had in various epochs of Russian history.

2. Encouraging research at all levels on the relationship between culture and other aspects of people's lives through direction of graduate theses and dissertations and the teaching of seminars and colloquia. Publishers have a nose for new research directions and can be pushed in those directions. Scholarly conferences in general and the AAASS in particular ought to encourage this agenda in its program committees; and it certainly ought to be more responsive to those scholars who wish to use video projectors and other audiovisual devices in their presentations.

3. Emphasizing oral as well as reading fluency in Russian in history and other fields outside literature and language. I should confess a strong bias here that I have developed after sitting on several granting bodies—a bias against those economists, political scientists, and other social scientists who believe that the languages and methods of their disciplines are a kind of Esperanto that can unlock crucial knowledge about any society without knowing a word of the actual language used in that society.

4. Amplifying the study of languages of the other republics and nationalities of the area. This amplification will not happen in our universities as long as the weight of research is in countable and standardized categories such as budgets, demography, or weapons systems. Scholars of such matters can convincingly argue (and have done so successfully) that the local language is not really essential—even though, ironically, the very best of them do take language seriously. Once local cultures are seen to be important in subcutaneous understanding of a society, study of the languages will automatically follow.

5. Multiplying by many factors our use of "media" in the classroom: art, music, cinema, and television. As I indicated above, the

flowering of video culture among the general population here and in Russia, the unprecedented accessibility of musical cassettes, video, and film from Russia, and the recent interest by journals in reviewing such material in addition to traditional book reviews have enhanced our awareness of the materials at hand. Now is the time to put them to use.[27]

6. Building on present curricula and disciplines, such as literature, history, and political science, by incorporating—perhaps modestly at first—elements of cultural life and cultural history through film, slides, readings, music, videos of performance art, always in conjunction with the familiar and traditional artifacts of one's own discipline. Let me give one more concrete example: one can now expand the parameters of teaching Aleksandr Pushkin's *Queen of Spades*, a remarkable literary classic of the early nineteenth century, by following up on a close reading and textual analysis of the story with listening to Piotr llich Tchaikovsky's opera and its libretto by his brother to examine the adaptations (or distortions) of the original, taking a critical look at Alexander Benois's illustrations for the 1905 edition of that work (and many other graphic examples are available as well), and then viewing two films, Chardynin's 1910 ten-minute version (closer to the opera), and Yakov Protazanov's forty-five minute version, more faithful to Pushkin. Both the films mentioned are now available on affordable videocassettes.[28]

One could enumerate hundreds of ways to integrate cultural matters and methods into other disciplines, especially but not only history. The problem is communicating them to the profession in a systematic and organized way. Two such enterprises in recent years have been extraordinarily successful. One was the series of Summer Seminars on Contemporary Literature and Popular Culture sponsored by the SSRC and led by Nancy Condee, Vladimir Padunov, Edward Brown, and Katerina Clark. They were held at American universities and in Russian centers and included graduate students and faculty from both nations. The other, sponsored by the National Endowment for the Humanities, was a Summer Institute on Art and Artifact in Russian History, led by George Munro and Alison Hilton at the Hermitage and the Russian Museum in the summer of 1992. The students were twenty-five to thirty American professors of various disciplines, with four American professors and a staff of Russian curators, restorers, archaeologists, historians, and art historians. More of these seminars are in the making. Catherine Evtuhov and Boris Gasparov held a two-week seminar in Smolensk (1993) and Kazan (1994) for twenty American and twenty Russian participants as part of a four-year program on Russian Culture and History in various mid-sized Russian cities and towns. The virtue of such programs is that they include a dominant element of cultural study and that they are held in the country being studied. How can we generate more of them? How can we energize the profession to take culture seriously?

Culture and social science have for too long dwelt in separate houses. The task of bringing them closer together must fall to history and literature, the disciplines in Russian studies with the broadest ambit, the most imagination, the longest experience, the heaviest demographic weight in the profession—though not perhaps the equivalent power and influence. Our job will be to open our eyes and ears, as well as our minds, to the images and sounds of the past and the present and then to reach out to other fields and to each other.

Original publication: In Daniel Orlovsky, ed. *Beyond Soviet Studies.* (Wilson Center Press and Johns Hopkins University Press, 1995), pp. 306-333.

Notes

The epigraph, from Monroe Berger, is quoted in Edward Said, *Orientalism* (New York: Pantheon Books, 1978), 288.

1   For exceptions see Gerald Smith, *Songs to Seven Strings* (Bloomington: Indiana University Press, 1984); S. F. Starr, *Red and Hot: The Fate of Jazz in the Soviet Union* (New York: Oxford University Press, 1983); Jeffrey Brooks, *When Russia Learned to Read* (Princeton: Princeton University Press,198S); Richard Stites, *Russian Popular Culture: Entertainment and Society since 1900* (Cambridge: Cambridge University Press, 1992); and the works on fiction and Society by Katerina Clark, *The Soviet Novel: History as Ritual* (Chicago: University of Chicago Press, 1981); Vera

Dunham, *In Stalin's Time: Middleclass Values in Soviet Fiction* (Cambridge: Cambridge University Press, 1976); Hans Guenther, ed., *The Culture of the Stalin Period* (New York: St. Martin's Press, 1990); Régene Robin, *Socialist Realism: An Impossible Aesthetic* (Stanford: Stanford University Press, 1992); William Mills Todd, ed., *Literature and Society in Imperial Russia* (Stanford: Stanford University Press, 1978); and on cinema by Peter Kenez, *Cinema and Soviet Society, 1917-1953* (Cambridge: Cambridge University Press, 1992); Anna Lawton, *Kinoglasnost: Soviet Cinema in Our Time* (Cambridge: Cambridge University Press, 1992); Richard Taylor, *The Politics of Soviet Cinema, 1917-1929* (Cambridge: Cambridge University Press, 1979); Denise Youngblood, *Movies for the Millions: Popular Cinema and Society in the 1920s* (Cambridge: Cambridge University Press, 1992).

2   There are, of course, various works that recognize the relationships among the arts in a given time, such as Theofanis Stavrou, ed., *Art and Culture in Nineteenth-Century Russia* (Bloomington: Indiana University Press, 1983), but this is a multiauthored anthology spanning a whole century. The one single-authored example, James Billington, *The Icon and the Axe* (New York: Knopf, 1961), takes on all of Russian history and can offer no more than speculative, though stimulating, sketches from crucial periods of exceptional creativity.

3   Siegfried Kracauer, *From Caligari to Hitler: The Psychological History of the German Film* (1947; Princeton; Princeton University Press, 1974). See also Peter Gay, *Weimar Culture: The Outsider as Insider* (New York: Harper and Row, 1968); Walter Laqueur, *Weimar* (New York: Putman, 1975).

4   For alternate ways of looking at cultural production and settings, see Richard Wortman, *Scenarios of Power,* vol. 1 (Princeton: Princeton University Press, forthcoming {1995 - *ed.*}); Stephen Baehr, *The Paradise Myth in Eighteenth Century Russia* (New Haven: Yale University Press, 1991); Priscilla Roosevelt, *Life on the Russian Country Estate: A Social and Cultural History* (New Haven: Yale University Press, forthcoming {1995 - *ed.*}); and James von Geldern, *Bolshevik Festivals* (Berkeley: University of California Press, 1993).

5   For William Harkins's comments, see his preface to Frank Miller, *Folklore for Stalin: Russian Folklore and Pseudofolklore of the Stalin Era* (Armonk, N.Y.: M. E. Sharpe, 1990), ix. For an example of a historian—who has of course been challenged—using folk culture as a historical source, see Maureen Perrie, "Folklore as Evidence of Peasant Mentalité," *Russian Review* 48, no. 2 (1989): 119-43. Among the problems presented by the use of folklore are the great variations in time and place, the notorious difficulty in dating any particular version of a work, its fluid character as an oral tradition, and the ever-lurking problem of peasant irony and masking.

6   Miller, *Folklore for Stalin*; Felix Oinas, ed., *Folklore, Nationalism, and Politics* (Columbus: Siavica, 1972); Eric Hobsbawm and Terence Ranger, *The Invention of Tradition* (Cambridge: Cambridge University Press, 1983). See also the recent fascinating article by the film scholar, Mikhail Yampolsky, "The Rhetoric of Representation of Political Leaders in Soviet Culture," *Elementa* 1, no. 1 (1993): 101-13.

7   For three different perspectives on urban-rural cultural interaction, see Alison Hilton, *Russian Folk Culture* (Bloomington: Indiana University Press, forthcoming 1955); Catriona Kelly, *Petrushka* (Cambridge: Cambridge University Press, 1989); Deborah Pearl, *Tales of Revolution: Workers and Propaganda Skazi in the Late Nineteenth Century,* forthcoming (Pittsburgh, 1998 = Carl Beck Papers in Russian and East European Studies, no. 1303 - *ed.*).

8   Richard Wortman, The *Crisis of Russian Populism* (Cambridge: Cambridge University Press, 1967).

9   A beginning has been made by Michael Khodarkovsky, *When Two Worlds Met* (Ithaca: Cornell University Press, 1992), a study of the Kalmyk frontier in early modem Russia. See also Thomas Barrett, "The Remaking of the Lion of Dagestan: Shamil in Captivity," *Russian Review* 53, no. 3 July 1994): 353-66.

10 Iurii Lotman et al., *The Semiotics of Russian Cultural History* (Ithaca: Cornell University Press, 1985). A brilliant and notable exception is Irina Paperno, *Chernyshevsky and the Age of Realism: A Study in the Semiotics of Behavior* (Stanford: Stanford University Press, 1988).

11 Louise McReynolds, *The News Under Russia's Old Regime* (Princeton: Princeton University Press, 1992); Stites, *Russian Popular Culture,* chap. 1; Stephen Frank and Mark Steinberg, eds., *Cultures in Flux: Lower-class Values, Practices, and Resistance in Late Imperial Russia* (Princeton: Princeton University Press, 1994); Forthcoming is Hubertus Jahn, *Patriotic Culture in Russia during World War I* (Ithaca: Cornell University Press, 1995 - *ed.*).

12 Taylor, *The Politics of Soviet Cinema;* Youngblood, *Movies for the Millions;* Youngblood, *Soviet Cinema in the Silent Era* (Ann Arbor: UMI Research Press, 1985); Kenez, *Cinema and Soviet Society.* These books are excellent guides to popular films up to 1953. There is no comparable work as yet on the Khrushchev period. For the Brezhnev and Gorbachev eras, see Lawton, *Kinoglasnost.*

13 S. S. Ginsburg, *Kinematografiya dorevolyutsionnoi rossii* (Moscow: Iskusstvo, 1963), massive and detailed; R. Sobolev, *Lyudi i filmy russkogo do-revolyutsionnogo kino* (Moscow: Iskusstvo,1961), short and gossipy; Neya Zorkaya, *Na rubezhe stoletii: uz istokov iskusstva v Rossii 1900-1910 godov* (Moscow: Nauka, 1976), a masterly analysis of the

function of movies in popular culture; Jay Leyda, *Kino* (London: Allen and Unwin, 1960), a Western perspective by a keen critic of art film. The recent collection, *Testimoni silenzioso: Film russi 1908-1919/Silent Witnesses: Russian Films, 1908-1919,* ed. Yury Tsivian et al. (Pordenone, Italy: Biblioteca dell' Imagine, 1989) is a gold mine of catalog data and commentary (in English and Italian) on the old silents (the Indiana University Press edition is identical to this one except that the title is reversed). About thirty of the films discussed in this book are now available on ten videocassettes (see n. 28).

14 Tsivian, ed., *Silent Witnesses,* 478-84.

15 The screenings that I know about took place beginning in 1989 in Pordenone, Italy, and in Munich, Paris, London, Los Angeles, and Washington, D.C., where, at the Library of Congress, about seventy were presented in the winter of 1992.

16 See Richard Stites, "Iconoclastic Currents in the Russian Revolution," in *Bolshevik Culture,* ed. Abbott Gleason et al. (Bloomington: Indiana University Press, 1985), 1-24.

17 For purposes of illustration, I have given only one example from the wealth of ideas on social relations, identities, mentalities, and ethnographic realia (including costume, gestures, interior decor, leisure habits) that can be detected from the vivid imagery of this body of films—even granting that seventy is a small sample of the two to three hundred surviving films and the approximately two thousand films made in the tsarist period, including those from private studios in 1918-19.

18 For the background, see Richard Taylor, "Boris Shumyatsky and the Soviet Cinema in the 1930s: Ideology as Mass Entertainment," *Historical Journal of Film, Radio, and Television* 6, no. 1 (1986): 48-64.

19 In Soviet iconology, the woman had come to be identified with the countryside and thus with a relatively nurturing role in society, in spite of her prominence in the urban work force, and the man with the city, the factory, the machine—and thus power. See Gail Warshofsky Lapidus, *Women and Soviet Society* (Berkeley: University of California Press, 1978); Richard Stites, *The Women's Liberation Movement in Russia* (Princeton: Princeton University Press, 1978).

20 Lewis Siegelbaum, *Stakhanovism and the Politics of Productivity in the USSR, 1935-1941* (Cambridge: Cambridge University Press, 1988), 76, 80, 173, and passim for the realities behind the Stakhanovite mythology.

21 A detailed analysis of this film by the late Maria Enzensberger will appear in Richard Taylor and Derek Spring, eds., *Stalinism and Soviet Cinema* (London, New York: Routledge, 1993 - *ed.*). One ought to put this fairy tale motif in the context of world cinema of the 1930s: the

Universum-Film-Aktiengesellschaft (UFA) musicals of the Nazi period, the Hungarian drawing room comedies, the "White Telephone" films of fascist Italy which drew on the former, the adventure fantasies and colonial epics of Alexander Korda in England, and Hollywood, which of course possessed its share of Central European dream makers and fantasists: Ernst Lubitsch, Billy Wilder, Ferenc Molnár, Michael Curtiz (Kertesz Mihaly, earlier an agitprop film director for Béla Kun's Soviet regime), and the lesser-known storytellers, Melchior Lengyel and Lajos Biro.

22 Milka Bliznakov, "Architecture as Decorative Art" (unpublished manuscript); Vladimir Papernyi, *Kultura "dva"* (Ann Arbor: Ardis, 1985). A Western visitor to Moscow in 1936, Kurt London, after lamenting the vulgar array of porticoes, parapets, cornices, and friezes of Hotel Moskva (then used for delegations of workers and peasants), cites this explanation of its decor from a Soviet citizen: "These people, who very often only live in poor huts, are to see that the greatest luxury is thought fit for their reception. They are to return home with the feeling that they are citizens of a great and wealthy country. That increases their self-respect and strengthens their allegiance to a regime which affords them such princely hospitality." *Seven Soviet Arts* (London, 1937), 259-61.

23 L. I. Brezhnev, *Trilogy: Little Land, Rebirth, the Virgin Lands* (1978; Moscow: Progress Publishers, 1980), 231-398.

24 See Starr, *Red and Hot*; Stites, *Russian Popular Culture.*

25 Arnold Hauser, *The Social History of Art,* 2 vols. (New York: Knopf, 1951).

26 Mark Kuchment in *Soviet Observer* (January 26, 1989), 4.

27 *American Historical Review, Russian Review, Soviet Union,* and *Slavic Review* have introduced film and video reviews.

28 *Early Russian Cinema: Films before the Revolution Now on Video.* Ten VHS videos; 28 films. Milestone Film & Video, 175 West 96th Street, New York, N.Y. 10025; telephone (212) 865-7449. Price: $29.95 each, $250.00 for the set of ten. My review of the set appeared in *Russian Review* 53, no. 2 (1994): 285-95 (see below, here, 289-306).

3

Crowded on the Edge of Vastness
Observations on Russian Space and Place

Through the vastness of the land ran a chain of hills and beneath them lay a long valley and through the valley flowed a deep and wide river and on the banks of the river was a cabin and in the window of the cabin sat a maiden weaving.

This is a paraphrase of the conventional opening of many Russian fairy tales. At the core of my inquiry lies the duality in Russian feelings—almost never articulated—about space, a seamless conjunction of acrophilia and claustrophilia. I employ these terms by reversing those used in Elena Hellberg's reference to Peter the Great's agoraphobia and claustrophobia—but the duality is the same.[1] Put briefly, the focus is on one of the many complexities of Russian space—in metaphor and in life—the juxtaposition in everyday life of an empty expanse with a cramped and crowded work space—shops, libraries, archives, ticket offices, hotels, and other public institutions. My essay is a strictly subjective work based on personal observations over the past thirty years rather than a rigorous scholarly treatise based on a large database.

Let me offer a few concrete examples before attempting to explore deeper meanings. At the St. Petersburg Railway Station in Moscow, an enormous building two blocks long, the front doors facing the square are locked. One must walk around the station along the sides up to the train tracks and then back the entire length of the station hall to a ticket office, wait in line, and then go back to the train—six blocks instead of two blocks. The St. Petersburg Moscow Railway Station has an enormous empty hall with no benches, surrounded by tiny booths enclosed in glass with a little closed window to speak through as you bend over. The waiting room is up two floors and four staircases. If you wish to sit while waiting for your train, you must take your luggage up there to the benches. Then of course there is the railway carriage in which you must walk to the far end to get on and then walk back to your seat. The St. Petersburg Central Ticket Office on Griboedov Canal has the familiar layout: a cavernous hall ringed by tiny booths and offices fronted by glass from which are cut minuscule windowettes through which you can talk to the clerk—if you bend—who sits in her cramped space. Not a single place to sit. From the minuscule service openings stretch queues that are amoeba-shaped, never straight, showing an aversion to geometric order.

Take another kind of site: the famous research center, Pushkin House in St. Petersburg. It has big, randomly used, offices and a lot of lobby; both the Manuscript Reading Room and Library are small, the former with eleven reading tables tightly squeezed together. In Moscow, the Glinka Museum and Library has three floors with huge empty spaces in the middle, surrounded by small offices. In its library, the area is so cramped that one cannot use the card catalogue without carrying the trays to the table—of which there are a few, with chairs crammed together. Most other libraries possess enormous proportions but have tiny reading rooms with chairs jammed together and card catalogues closely aligned. Everywhere the story is the same: empty unused expanses and tiny cramped places for the workers as well as the customers, readers, clients. Why this astonishingly unbalanced use of space?

Inner Spaces

Within these tiny work-sites, three principles seem to dominate: impregnability, irregularity, and domesticity. The first—the bastion mentality—begins at the door, narrow single entrances usually at the wrong end of a building—that is, away from the normal route of approach. These doors seem to say 'Do not come in. Why are you here? Do not disturb. Come back tomorrow.' Very often they do speak with signs: Out to Lunch, Cleaning Day, Inventory Day, or simply Closed—with no explanation. The doormen at empty cavernous restaurants in Soviet times turned away hopeful diners with the words 'no room.' It still happens. All these signs and habits of the workplace reflect the peculiar and specific indifference to, sometimes even an aversion to providing comfort or convenience to the public. Handiness for the multitudes is an unspoken taboo of urban Russian life. But the very space that is fortress-like to the everyday visitor can become porous when even the flimsiest of personal relations are established. A guest can be taken into places where other employees are never permitted, can be seated in the middle of an office at someone's desk in order to work. A tiny place is cleared amid papers and books. This small intimate inner work space is collective, everybody's, nobody's. The accompaniment to this is the lack of dedication, commitment, responsibility to a task that requires long-term attention and concentration—things that are associated in Western societies with one's own desk, computer, telephone, workbooks, records and all the rest. The very social topography of an office is created by the casual—or better to say 'distanced' or 'estranged' attitude to work itself. And yet the interchangeability of stations is often accompanied by a ferocious sense of narrow specialization and absence of lateral communication. No one knows and no one wants to know anything outside the immediate range of duties. No one has the right to perform another's task: 'she's not here today; I can't help; not my job; she took the keys with her on vacation; come back in a week.'

Irregularity is a relative concept and perhaps involves a culturally biased aesthetic judgment. But here I am concerned with function: desks jammed together can impede pedestrian motion, chairs unmatched to desk size cause discomfort and fatigue, long distances between stations that require regular mutual traffic might (and do) require workers to walk through several rooms a hundred times a day to take or deliver material to another party— even though there is no particular reason for this distance. Sections, departments, work stations, and desks grow up accidentally, spontaneously, ad hoc, and at random—pretty much in the way that the ancient *prikazy* of Muscovy did—without prior planning. In a society famously based on central economic planning, one will find the most unplanned work space. Once it is there, it is there. Any suggestion to rearrange furniture or personal space in a more rational way is viewed with utmost suspicion. 'This is how we do it,' 'I don't know why: or 'it is not important' are the usual replies to questions or suggestions. Tradition can thus be instantaneous.

By domesticity, I mean the workplace as home, club, and surrogate family. There is a gender element here. Most offices are staffed by women. They bring domestic and neighborhood values into the workplace, making it a home away from home. In between service to the firm or its customers (readers, clients, guests, citizens making inquiries), the day is filled with talk—to each other or on the telephone. The talk is personal, family-oriented, quotidian matters that take priority over all other matters, including and especially the business in which they are employed. Lunch is a sacred time when—besides ingesting some food—the business of life can be continued. The emotional sustenance that women and some men obtain from their Home-at-Work and their fellow employees cannot be underestimated. And the notion of transforming the workplace into a relatively cold, impersonal, site of efficient labor would require an entire cultural and psychic restructuring—a wrenching process.

As at home, audible conversations and telephone talk take place in spaces that are normally held quiet in other societies (reading rooms, for example). The boundaries within the work space are fluid. Ancient routines and procedures consume needless hours of useless work and tons of paper. Restaurants, libraries, museums, academies function as independent republics in their daily procedures. Customers are unwelcome interlopers. A common though unspoken attitude: this is our collective, this is how we do it, we are not interested in efficient service to clients or to saving them or us time. The sense of time and space is of course inseparably linked to efficiency and productivity.

Outer Spaces

My discussion of the inner spaces of Russian urban work culture in some ways explains the non-use of available empty rooms. It seems clear that employees, if offered the option of spreading out and moving into the large halls available, would decline, preferring to remain in the intimacy of their 'family offices' or workplace clubs. Spreading out would mean individuation of work stations and distance from their colleagues. Part of the reason for such abundant empty space in Russian edifices is of course the Russian and Soviet architectural traditions of grandiosity and monumentality. Big is good, big is strong.[2] To those workers who inhabit booths and counters, the surrounding cavernous lobbies, halls, reception rooms, galleries and the like are alien spaces, full of strangers who are there to disrupt their own private time by asking questions, ordering tickets or books or buying things.

What about front doors, grand entrances, and frontal outdoor space—so often encountered in, for example, museums and other public places? Elena Hellberg-Hirn has again highlighted a key feature of Russian spatial culture in her observations about narrow back door and side door entrances though which thousands of people are ushered.[3] Why not pass them through the front? The facades of Imperial Russian buildings contained the ceremonial or parade entrance reserved strictly for the owner's family and guests or for high officials in a government house. All others had to come through different apertures—usually at the rear. (Cf. the trades-men's and servant's entrances in the West.) But after the Russian Revolution, the masses, especially the honored proletariat, were not tradesmen or servants but the alleged rulers of the state. And yet, the parade entrance mentality was retained; you just could not allow ordinary people in through those grand entrances. Then who would be allowed? No one, because to invite the rulers and other privileged Soviet elements would be to admit the real but inad-missible fact of privilege and inequality on a visible public scale. The same explanation probably applies to the open areas in front of some public buildings. These were organic parts of the ceremonial entry way, not to be violated by crowds. Only in the theaters, for practical reasons of ticket collecting and directing people to their seats, did the grand entrances remain open.

One of the interesting features of Russian spatial culture is the way it contradicts a fundamental self-image of the national charac-ter: *gostepriimstvo*—hospitality and welcoming generosity. But this trait—certainly rooted in social reality—had its obverse side in Rus-sian traditional practices. Stranded travelers, Holy People, friends and relatives, and the nearby *barin* were indeed given lavish wel-come. But the bread and salt were not extended to any passerby; old

Russian villages were plagued by bandits, horse thieves, escaped convicts (in the nineteenth century when it was still fairly easy to escape), unwanted beggars, or even foreign troops. The personnel in government chanceries and waiting rooms were notorious for their hostility and contempt toward petitioners. Soviet xenophobia and paranoia amplified this trait. The present-day Russian edifice continues to exude hostility and wariness to visitors. If you wander into space where you have no business, may God protect you from the verbal abuse of a *vakhter* or *babushka* at the checkpoint. One of the greatest failures of the Soviet regime was its unwillingness or inability to induce mutual respect and *dobrota* among its people. A side result of this is the near absence of politeness and good manners among strangers in public places.

But there are still other dimensions to the spatial world. If the home is private and the workplace semiprivate, how can we characterize the surrounding urban space? In Soviet times and partly still today, this area fell into two categories which I shall call public and common—both in a sense belonging to nobody or to everybody. Public space is sacral, municipal, honorific, civic. Its squares and parks, lobbies and reception areas are maintained by the state and selectively open to the citizens. Common space is no-man's land: staircases and landings, courtyards, back-alleys, station halls, most rest rooms. Timo Pirainen has noted the visible difference between the use of this space in Western Europe and in Russia. In the latter one is struck by the stark contrast between the relative neatness and order and even comfort inside the private apartment and the utter neglect—dirt, decay—of the common areas adjacent to it.[4]

In Western European cities, this contrast is much smaller and in some places non-existent. Orderly residences are often surrounded by neat and well-kept environs; public and private space seem to flow into each other. To some observers, this is a mark of civic consciousness and even civil society. The neatness of European streets and homes has always been one of the first things Russian travelers westward have noted—from border crossings into eastern Prussia in the eighteenth century to shopping trips in Helsinki in our time. The irony of these cultural crossings resides in the fact that so many intellectuals among those Russian visitors, from the playwright Denis Von Vizen onward, have found in European spatial culture a clear sign of crabbed natures, cramped souls, and petty bourgeois sensibilities—all in contrast to the vaunted Russian need for grand spaces, the open road, and a sense of freedom.[5]

Meaning

Western office workplaces tend to be spread out, with easy lateral communication. Service areas are usually bright, welcoming, and open. Think of the physical properties of customer-clerk encounters in travel agencies, banks, libraries, and post offices: an open counter, sometimes a seat for the client, and rarely a window. The human topography is different as well. Professionalism means leaving intimacy, family, personal concerns at the door (in theory, and mostly in practice as well). One has one's own desk, personal space, responsibility, and some work privacy—allowing one to measure one's own work and achievement—and allow others to measure it as well. Interchangeable desks are uncommon as is the practice of handing over an employer's desk to a visitor or outsider. This capitalist rational environment has been the target of cultural attack and satire almost from the very beginning, its most resonant artifact being the cinema—*Modern Times* in the 1930s, *The Apartment* in the 1960s, *Brazil* in the 1980s—each probably more influential than the various anti-capitalist science fiction dystopias of our century. But one thing is clear, the capitalist workplace has separated to a significant degree the job from the home and family. How to construct the moral balance sheet between depersonalization and productivity is a matter for some serious consideration by social scientists.

The Russian work culture that I have impressionistically—but I believe accurately—described throws some light on the fate of the petty-bourgeoisie, a topic now being explored in a very learned treatment by Timo Vihavainen. He demonstrates again and again that the concept itself was so fluid as to serve any kind of ideological justification for social policy. Only one constant remained: an eternal aversion to petty bourgeois values, however defined at the moment. In this respect Soviet ideologists differed from the old Russian intelligentsia who zeroed in on petty bourgeois mind (*meshchanstvo*) as philistine and vulgar.[6] If the family-as-community-and-work-unit, as formulated by Proudhon, is a fairly accurate summary of the petty bourgeois outlook, then the Soviets, willy-nilly, helped or allowed it to lodge itself at the very base of its system. Not only did the Soviet family retain its own world at home as the unit of primary loyalty (even when surrounded by neighbors in a communal apartment), but it brought its ethos into the workplace as well. And in this sense, the millions of offices and stalls and counters across the land constituted a Proudhonian substructure upon which reposed a Marxist centralized planned society. This is one of the greatest ironies in the richly ironic tapestry of Russian history.

But in Russia's case, the roots of the alleged petty-bourgeois family and its work habits is the peasant village with its own notions of space, time, motion, and order. I have dealt with these in a chapter called 'Man the Machine' of a previous book.[7] There I try to describe those mentalities and practices as they contrast to the work-pace of modern industrial societies. The resulting gulf between these habits and the needs of an aspiring Soviet industrial culture of efficiency and productivity produced two startling phenomena. In the 1920s, desperate Soviet enthusiasts of time and motion—the disciples of Henry Ford and Frederick Taylor—conceived sweeping utopian devices designed to end the space-time culture of peasants and turn them into mechanized, clock-driven workers: the Scientific Organization of Labor and the League of Time. In the 1930s, under Stalin, a more manipulative and selective apparatus was put in place: shock work and the Stakhanovite movement.[8] None of these practices went deep into Soviet work styles and ethos. The regime in fact shielded the entire economy from structures of incentives and penalties that would gradually have created a modem work culture—including punctuality, alertness, lateral communication, and the rational organization of space.

And at what price? Spatial irrationality is closely linked to other aspects of the culture of work and service. All of the Russian practices mentioned above sharply diminish the level of efficiency at work. The total effect is multiplied by the impact that each act or practice has upon everyone else. In the course of a day, one potentially productive worker at any task will lose about a third or even half a day's work due to the cumulative power of other citizens' work habits. Here I offer a fictional but plausible scenario.

10:00-5:00, a good enough workday in winter time. Citizen X plans to spend two hours in the library, have a business lunch with Y at 12:00, go for rail tickets at 1:00, meet another colleague, Z, at 2:00 for a half hour, and then ride for half an hour to the university for teaching and consulting from 3:00 to 5:00. Call it a day and go home at five.

The reality we all know. The reading room, without prior announcement (nobody's business but theirs), has been taken over for a special staff meeting—even though there are seven other equally large rooms available for it. So X crosses town to another library and thus has only about 45 minutes of actual work that morning. Back to the meeting point for lunch. Y arrives forty minutes late because his plumber did not show up on time to do essential repairs. All nearby eating places are either 'full' (though nearly empty) or have long lines, so they go to a fast-food place and make it a short and not very productive stand-up business lunch. Then X gets to the railway ticket office at 2:00 instead of 1:00 and finds it closed for lunch until 3:00. Since the ticket is essential, he waits. The ticket seller returns from lunch at 3:15, but her computer is down and the repairman has not yet come to fix it. After waiting in line at another window, X has his ticket by 4:00. He has of course missed his 2:00 o'clock appointment with Z thus throwing off Z's schedule as well. He calls the university, but no one answers the phone because the receptionist has left early for the day to do the shopping and no one else in the office cares to answer it (not their job). X rushes to his class and finds that all the students have left because he is more than one hour late.

The total professional productive work time for X on that day: 45 minutes and about 15 minutes of business talk with Y. But note that Y and Z will face similar if not worse inefficiencies during the day as will practically every resident of a major Russian city. And if X, Y, and Z are relatively efficient people who want to do productive work, think of all those who are indifferent or even hostile to their jobs. This is all too obvious and familiar to those who have lived in Russia, even for a short time. What is striking and revealing is that no Russian I have ever met (inside the country) would venture to make an analysis of the real causes of an unproductive day, or week, or year. In the old Soviet days, the typical reaction of a critic—a dissident or someone indifferent to the Soviet system—would be: "it's the fault of our system," meaning socialism. In recent times, the comment is: "we are in a difficult time of transition." A more honest and cogent reply that I have often heard—though no more trenchant analytically—is: "it's Russia."

Though I have broadened the focus from spatial matters to the more general features of the Russian work style, space remains a key ingredient. After all, unless one has an aesthetic agenda, space—empty or full—is interesting only as it relates to the people in it or kept out of it. It seems to me that the working place defines the workers and vice versa. In gender terms, as long as offices remain a *posidelka* for women and a village *mir* for men, productivity is not likely to increase or the work culture change. Men are more mobile through the day and certainly possess more power and get bigger wages; but it is doubtful if their collective efforts are more productive than those of women. They simply do different things in their nonwork-related segments of the working day. When and if the work environment changes in a drastic way, it will bring forth a serious mental trauma and a chorus of lamentation which will, I believe, make the better-known pain of economic destitution seem mild by comparison.

To those who may have *Schadenfreude* at the prospect of such irrational people suffering for their sins, I address a few words. I cannot really apologize for the rather harsh assessment I have made of work styles and use of space in the service sector. I do not believe that hiding unpleasant truths is doing anyone a favor. On the other hand I write out of affection for those who staff those, to us, outrageously inefficient workplaces. Although still plagued by a passive attitude to the job, Russians are not by nature lazy or inefficient people. Given sufficient incentive and a supportive environment, they can perform miracles of productivity. And those grim faces that we so often encounter at service points belong to the same people who—on acquaintance—can prove to be marvelous hosts and true friends. I believe that Russians will be a lot more content in the long run in terms of comfort, convenience, and rewarding work when the old ways are abandoned and new ones adopted.

But as a historian, I am more interested in the roots of the Russian-Soviet use of working space than in speculation about

the future (which interests me as a citizen). This volume addresses questions about Siberia, the broad Russian land, the symbol of
boundless freedom, *volya;* and Siberia as the historic land of prisoners, of unfreedom; the broad Slavic soul and the narrow confines of
daily existence; the crowded peasant *izba* and the spacious Russian
steppe. After a half-dozen years of perestroika and almost a decade
of political freedom and the market, I for one am persuaded that
not all of the peculiarities of Russian spatial and world culture are
attributable solely to Soviet socialism. Perhaps historians and literary scholars will someday uncover the deeper layers.

Original publication: In Jeremy Smith, ed. *Beyond the Limits: The Concept of
Space in Russian History and Culture.* Helsinki: SHS, 1999, pp. 259-269.

Notes

1 My references to Elena Hellberg-Hirn, Timo Pirainen, and Timo Vihavainen are to their remarks at The Winter Seminars in Advanced
   Russian HIstory at the Renvall Institute, 1998.
2 See Vladimir Papernyi, *Kul'tura dva* (Chicago, 1985) and other historians of Soviet architectural style.
3 See her contribution to this volume ("Ambivalent Space: Expressions of
   Russian Identity," in Smith - *ed.*), 49-69.
4 Ekaterina Gerasimova "Sovetskaya kommunalnaya kvartira: istoriko-
   sotsiologicheskii ocherk." Paper. Renvall Institute, Helsinki, 1998. Here
   she describes the eternally unsuccessful efforts of laws and committees
   to have the inhabitants care for common space; Pirainen's remarks at
   the Winter Seminars — see note 1.
5 An Englishman in the 1830s observed that Russian towns were, per
   capita, three times the size of English ones: Robert Bremner, *Excursions
   in the Interior of Russia,* 2v. (London, 1840), 2: l64. Vast unused space for
   town planning seems natural in such an immense country as Russia;
   but that use of space did not transfer to intimate settings.
6 Svetlana Boym, *Commonplaces: Mythologies of Everyday Life in Russia*
   (Cambridge, Mass., 1994).
7 Richard Stites, *Revolutionary Dreams* (New York, 1989); see also Nicholas Vakat, *The Taproot of Soviet Society* (New York, 1962).
8 Lewis Siegelbaum, *Stakhanovism and the Politics of Productivity in the
   USSR, 1935-1941* (New York, 1988).

4

Russian Symbols: Nation, People, Ideas

One can waste a lot of time, space, and verbiage on definitions particularly of such a loaded word as "symbol" and its derivatives. It has become so overused that frequently writers (myself included) have had to fall back on alternatives such as "emblem" or "metaphor." Those words are not interchangeable, but recourse to them shows how engrossed are interpreters of our era (or working in our era) with the need to summarize and to substitute signs for sentences or even words. I will also employ the word "image," which, in the words of Julia Kristeva, is a "bearer of hypnotic emotion."[1] The element of emotion in her phrase needs no further comment, but her "hypnosis" is suggestive of the deep impact of some images and their ability to induce something like robotic or involuntary behavior. To Kristeva's stress on the cerebral and the unconscious, I would add the physical force of imagery—often indicated by the term "visceral" when speaking of spontaneous or elemental responses. And, as anyone who has ever been truly angry or afraid knows, certain signs can be just as stomach churning as a word. Signs having the widest national resonance in the nineteenth-century Russian Empire were the tsarist emblems; the Orthodox religious symbols; and the various devices connected with Slavic legends as embedded in folklore, Panslavism, middlebrow print culture, and—at the turn of the century—modernist art.[2]

The history of the tsarist double-headed eagle has been traced many times from its origin in Byzantium, where it reflected the division of the late Roman Empire into its Western and Eastern components with capitals in Rome and Byzantium (Constantinople) respectively. When the latter fell to the Ottoman Turks in 1453, some

Russians claimed a kind of *translatio imperii* from one Orthodox Christian realm (Byzantium) to another (Muscovite Russia). The eagle, along with court rituals, some terminology (Caesar = Tsezar = Tsar), and more than a few legends, entered the Muscovite cultural universe in the fifteenth century. Since then, its treatment in monarchical-imperial heraldry grew from relatively simple representation to extremely elaborate mountings, surrounded by orb and scepter and by various subordinate shields with their own armorial bearings. Like royal motifs elsewhere, the eagle flew out of the throne rooms and palaces onto public buildings, fence posts, jewelry, bookplates, and hundreds of other surfaces and housings. The Romanov eagle (often so-called although it was adopted long before that dynasty arrived in 1613) was deployed in all sorts of ways to denote hegemony as well as protection and patronization over Russian institutions under imperial sway. In the official seal of the Academy of Art, for example, the outstretched eagle's wings are paralleled by sunrays announcing enlightenment, and both of its heads are on guard against the foe (ignorance? philistinism?). The eagle perches astride the triple motif of the Academy of Fine Arts: the capital of a doric column, a bust, and a palette.[3] This was one of hundreds of examples of the graphic intertwining of imperial power with all branches of public life. The mass production of signs by the Ministry of Court and the mint was well under way in prints, books, medals, and icons.[4] The sheer number of imperial eagles explains why it took years to erase them or tear them down after the 1917 Revolution.

If the tsarist coat of arms and its assertive bird could serve as a marker of dynastic majesty and imperial unity, it could also cause offense. The rampant wings of the eagle and its terrifyingly open beak were used again and again by hostile foreigners as additional proof of potential Russian aggression. Cartoonists had a field day with it all over Europe. Perhaps the most palpable example of this ploy is a famous painting, *The Attack* (1899) by Edvard Isto, now located in the National Museum of Finland in Helsinki. This huge and dramatic canvas shows a chaste young woman garbed in white holding a book titled *Lex*. The maiden is Finland, and she and her laws are being menaced by a ferocious and gigantic eagle hovering in the forbidding sky and tearing out the pages of the book.

Drawing on well-established European representations of nations as women—Marianne, Germania, Britannia—the picture was as effective a bit of political art as was the contemporary nationalist tone poem *Finlandia* by Jean Sibelius.

It may stretch things a bit to gather in non-graphic arts that were put into service of the monarchy and call them symbols. But one of the weaknesses in studying graphic materials out of context is that the people affected by them were conditioned by other artifacts—songs, anthems, stories, and even "moving" clusters and vehicles of symbols such as parades, receptions, and all kinds of ritual gatherings. The last of course were regular features of life in the capitals and often in the provinces as well when royalty came to call. As to the more crystallized works of culture, it is important to underscore that the reign of Nicholas I was one of the pinnacles of national and imperial consciousness, particularly in the 1830s, when the doctrine of official nationality was enshrined in the slogan "autocracy, Orthodoxy, and Nationalism." It was coined by Minister of Education Sergei Uvarov in 1834 and has been the subject of many fine scholarly investigations.[5] The reign of Nicholas I was the supreme moment of autocratic power in Russian history and, if that power might have been hollow, its representation was vigorous indeed.

Of the three major cultural artifacts that clustered around the dynasty, the first was the new national anthem. Many composers, including Mikhail Glinka, tried their hand. But it was the version of the courtier and amateur composer General Alexei Lvov that prevailed: "God Save the Tsar" (1833). By his own admission, Lvov tried to combine in that anthem the spirit of church, people, and army. Thenceforth it was played continuously all over Russia at every conceivable occasion, often repeated in times of great enthusiasm or national trauma.[6] A year later came the most popular monarchist historical drama of the age: Nestor Kukolnik's *The Hand of God Has Saved the Fatherland*, a historical play about the Time of Troubles (1605-13), which premiered in January 1834 at the Alexandrinsky Theater. This hazy spectacle is a colossal bore to read, and yet it made a vivid impression on audiences—merchants as well as aristocracy—and became an immediate favorite of the tsar.[7] Indeed, so closely was it associated with the dynasty that in

1866, in the aftermath of the failed assassination attempt against Nicholas's son, Tsar Alexander II, the play was revived in order to arouse patriotic emotion.[8] To complete the representation of the national-dynastic nexus, Mikhail Glinka's still famous *Ivan Susanin* or *Life for the Tsar* debuted in 1836, another tale of 1613. In this one, a common peasant sacrifices his life to save the first of the Romanov dynasty. All these productions reinforced one another and formed a symbolic system that was far more important and understandable than simply a collection of static images.

Although towns were replete with imperial eagles, especially on their central squares where government buildings were clustered, the locals had some leeway in constructing their own heraldic symbols. These usually contained beasts indigenous to Russia and prominent in folklore and folk art: bears, foxes, fish. Sometimes a hammer was displayed on a town's shield to indicate craft and industry, and sometimes sickles to suggest proximity to the soil. Both of these were probably partial inspirations for the later Soviet hammer and sickle motif (see below). Here and there the blade of a "saracen" (read Mongol or Polovetsian—i.e., medieval invaders from "the East") was set against the straight sword of "the West." The city of Yaroslav had a bear holding a halberd. Moscow invoked St. George. The assembly of provincial coats of arms onto the imperial shield was common and was to be adopted in the USSR for the fifteen republics.[9] Similar to the towns, military units combined elements of religion and dynastic fervor as in a 1900 standard of a dragoon regiment: a gonfalon emblazoned with the words "God is With Us," a memorable phrase from Tsar Nicholas I's response to the revolutions of 1848. An infantry regiment of the same era featured Veronica's veil with the face of Jesus and captioned in Old Slavonic print style.[10]

The Orthodox icon, of Byzantine origin, has been the subject of many a commentary by art historians and is far older than the symbols of autocracy. The social history of religion also reveals that icons were probably the most ubiquitous of Russian symbols. Not only did all churches contain them, but virtually every Orthodox peasant cabin had its icon corner as did many an urban residence. The practice was later cleverly adapted by the Bolsheviks as "Red Corners"—usually a little picture of Lenin. The icon and the gonfalon (a perpendicular banner with a religious picture on it) were mobile artifacts as well. Thousands of pilgrimages in the prerevolutionary decades featured crowds carrying them in long marches to some holy shrine as well as around the church at Easter and for sacramental occasions. The great realist painter Ilya Repin incurred criticism in his famous canvas *Religious Procession in Kursk Province* (1880-83) because an icon was being borne in the picture by an obvious drunk. Gonfalons were easily adapted to battlefield use in Russia's many wars; and in the traumatic Civil War of 1918-21 between Reds and Whites, the gonfalons of the White Army (along with their Christian chaplains) made a neat contrast to the red banners of the Red Bolshevik forces.

Folk symbolism played many roles in Russian life. The horse, chicken, and hybrid *sirin* (bird-woman), in addition to populating folktales and songs and their use as ornament for peasant cabins, were drafted into the fine arts. Alexei Venetsianov's *Spring* (1820s) employed a peasant woman walking between two horses for his plowing scene in an otherwise conventional canvas. Later in the century, such motifs were taken up wholesale in the Abramtsevo art colony, *The World of Art* journal and its exhibits, and the Ballets Russes of Diaghilev—to mention only a few. To a huge quarter of the creative intelligentsia, being Russian around 1900 was precisely identified with being able to adapt, deploy, and appreciate these marvelous vestiges of village life that allegedly encapsulated the true Russian soul.[11]

The question of peasant national identity or consciousness cannot be easily resolved, but it seems clear that long after the emancipation of the serfs in 1861 peasant identity—if symbolized at all—revolved around Orthodoxy and "peasantness." Peasants actually called themselves and each other *pravoslavnye* (Orthodox people) or *krestyane* (peasant folks or Christian folks), and thus the Byzantine crosses and icons as well as the images from folklore played a far greater role in national "identity" than the dynastic devices. This does not mean that Russian peasants ignored or demeaned the tsar. In fact they were attuned to what is called "peasant monarchy" or sometimes "naïve monarchy"—the notion that a benevolent and distant tsar was deprived of the knowledge of rural injustice and persecution by wicked landowners or bureaucrats. This belief, or sometimes only its utterance, had fueled several major peasant up-risings in early modern times up to the 1770s. At many points in Russian history, peasants had "found" or used a fictitious or forged "Golden Charter," allegedly signed by the tsar and granting free-dom to the peasant serfs. By the turn of the century, peasant mobil-ity, wide-scale travel, and ingress into the cities and factories had—through reading, conversations, and observation—broadened horizons and developed among a wide sector of the lower classes a kind of national consciousness as Russians, not only in the ethnic sense but in the sense of subjects in the Russian Empire.

Another subsystem of signs that burst forth on several occa-sions was Panslav iconography. Russian Panslavism was a loose but widespread political ideology of the nineteenth and early twentieth century that preached the natural solidarity of the Slavic peoples (usually omitting Poland because of a mutually hostile his-tory) under the leadership of tsarist Russia and in opposition to alleged common foes: the Ottoman Turks always, the Germans and Austrians sometimes. Panslavism's greatest moment came in the mid-1870s before and during the Russo-Turkish War of 1877-78. All levels of graphic art were put to work in order to illustrate the main facets of that struggle as seen by the Panslavs: the enormous cruelty of the Turks toward Serbs and Bulgarians who were fighting for their freedom; the blood nexus between Slavic Russians and their little Balkan brothers; and the mystique of the Orthodox Church, which bound those peoples to Russia and which sacralized the struggle against the Ottoman Empire.

Petr Ilych Chaikovsky's *Marche slave*, the best known of these productions, added Romanov support by quoting "God Save the Tsar" in the finale of this musical composition. Wartime demoni-zation, of course, was nothing new in Russian culture: cartoons, popular art, and various satirical pictures had been flowing our through the eighteenth and early nineteenth centuries, its high point occurring during the 1812 French invasion of Russia. But the Panslav episode contained something very modern, and very self-conscious.

Just as anthropologists worth their salt would never leave an island armed only with a record of totemic signs, but would make notes on costume and custom as well, we should take note of the

social symbolism embedded in the clothing styles of old Russia—
one more system to be utterly rejected (for a while) in Soviet times.
Walking around Moscow in 1830, an observer would know who
was (male) gentry and who was not simply by observing facial hair.
Gentry had shaven faces, and almost all others had beards (except
in the army). Peasants, merchants, priests, and many townsmen
retained the biblical chin to distinguish them from the "Roman"
and pagan classes created by Peter the Great in the eighteenth century. Similarly, the dress was divided along European/Russian lines
(except for non-Russian ethnic groups). Attempts to cross the line
evoked tension (the merchant dressing as a lord) or scorn (Konstantin Aksakov, the Slavophile, assuming beard and faux-peasant costume). The beard became well-nigh universal after 1860 or so (once
again in line with European stylistic shifts), but the dividing line
through class apparel remained pretty thick up to 1917. Needless to
say, other daily life appurtenances (housing, possessions, furniture)
and activities (dance, gestures, manners) projected a "sign" valori-
zation as well.

Against all the above ranged the "nihilists" of the 1860s and
their radical cousins right up into the 1920s. For them the trick was
to reject everything about the old regime and the older generation,
and especially its visual culture—the first order in the "presentation of self." Bad-mouthing Pushkin and Raphael and exalting Mo-
leschott, Darwin, or Marx formed the intellectual style; bad hair
and drab clothing the outward affect. Women excelled in this because there was more to challenge: beautiful tresses, narrow waists,
large busts, cosmetics, and other cogs in the beauty machine. As
a statement of her rejection of the "bourgeois" (actually "aristocratic") world, the nihilist woman cut her hair, dressed plainly, and
scorned physical attractiveness.[12]

It goes without saying that those who went on to become
warriors against autocracy and religion came to hate the symbolic
worlds of those institutions. In order to create for themselves an
identity as a "nation within a nation," they also developed a symbol
set of their own. Among the most affecting of these was the Sign
of the Convict: paintings, underground journals, book covers, and
illustrations released oceans of sympathy by showing the long lines
to Siberia, the ace of diamonds sewn on the backs of the condemned,

the grated window of a prison cell, whips, manacles, and the gibbet. Dungeon-like fortress cells drew on the imagery of early-nineteenth-century romantic prisoners, real or fictitious—Silvio Pellico, Byronic heroes, Beethoven's *Fidelio*, the Decembrists[13]—and of the unfortunate Populists or Marxists rotting away in jail or exile. The revolutionary generation of 1905 was celebrated in a fin-de-siècle mode: the bloody monster posters and the decadent style of gothic and grotesque that was also used in socially critical high culture, pulp fiction, and movies.

During World War I, the greatness of Russia and the rightness of its cause was embodied in mass-produced portraits of the tsar and his symbols: flag, double-headed eagle, anthem. The name of the capital since the time of Peter the Great, St. Petersburg, was changed to Petrograd to give it a Slavic ring; de-Germanization took a much more menacing turn when Russian-Germans (and even people with "foreign-sounding names") were beaten up and their shops looted. There were no major war heroes among the commanders, and so history had to be enlisted: the 1812 invasion and Tolstoy's *War and Peace* were often and inappropriately invoked. The regime tried to co-opt Marshal Kutuzov's victory over Napoleon in 1812 by calling the current struggle "The Second Fatherland War" in a 1914 *Hymnbook of the Triple Entente*, adorned with draped Allied flags.[14] Heroic leaders of the past—Alexander Nevsky, Dmitry Donskoi, Minin and Pozharsky, Suvorov, and Kutuzov—stood in for the missing ones in this war. For combat heroes, readers and viewers had only a few air aces and the colorful young Cossack Kuzma Kryuchkov, who allegedly impaled eleven Germans on his lance and whose image was reproduced hundreds of times in books, posters, and even postcards. But in this war, Russia was culturally and symbolically weak, compared with the Soviet effort in World War II.[15] The state played a minor role in propaganda. After the first flush of patriotism in 1914, the symbolic and cultural contribution to the war effort declined visibly, marking as it did the diminution of a war spirit among large segments of the population. Signifiers can remain effective long after the signified has lost its charisma. But for how long?

The Revolution of 1917 set off all kinds of symbolic contests. Some "modern" slogans, symbols, and rites were organized by various groups associated with the February Revolution and the Provisional Government: a funeral of those killed in the February uprising, decked out as deliverance and martyrology; hagiographical appearances of Old Revolutionaries and political prisoners of the tsarist period; and various freedom parades. Some support groups of the Provisional Government ventured into more synthetic symbology. For example, the volunteer Shock Battalions, including women's units, were formed to support the war effort (still raging as the eastern wing of the Great War). They bore aloft dark banners adorned with the rather crude but legible device "Freedom or Death!"[16] The government itself, however, remained rather unimaginative: it adapted "La Marseillaise" (read: Revolution of 1789 plus an Allied anthem) and retained a tamed version of the Romanov eagle.

When Lenin came to power, the brooms began to sweep the symbolic arena more vigorously. A contest was mounted among artists for a new state symbol, and among the many entries (which included castles and cornucopias, crosses, axes, zigzags, and triangles) the winner was a device featuring a hammer, a sickle, and a sword—representing the three social categories that allegedly made the Bolshevik Revolution: industrial worker, peasant, and soldier. Lenin for several weeks fought the prize committee to remove the sword as a belligerent signifier. He won out, and the hammer and sickle were then placed alongside a star upon a banner of solid red, the color that had long evoked radicalism and the working class in the nineteenth century. The red star, possibly suggested by a 1908 Bolshevik utopian novel, Alexander Bogdanov's *Red Star*, became an emblem of the new Red Army and later adorned the towers of the Kremlin. As a token of solidarity with revolutionary workers of the world, a European socialist hymn, "The Internationale," was adopted without any debate as the new party anthem (there was no national anthem until wartime).

The very name of the country now ruled by Lenin was changed twice before the dissolution of 1991: in 1918 it was declared the RSFSR, Russian Federated Soviet Socialist Republic—a recognition both of multinational form and political-economic content. With the reincorporation by 1922 of non-Russian border areas that had broken away during the Civil War, the new designation adopted was USSR—Union of Soviet Socialist Republics, an amalgam that was represented millions of times—in books, pictures, subway station friezes—by the Soviet coat of arms that included the local seals of each of the (eventually) fifteen republics. Along with the Soviet nomenclature of the state and of political bodies all levels came a strong drive, especially in the 1930s, to create a transcendent "Soviet" identity, although—ironically—the government insisted on an ethnic identification in every person's passport.

One of the great symbolic (and real) shifts occurred a few months after the Bolsheviks came to power. In March 1918 they moved the capital from Petrograd to Moscow, for strategic reasons having to do with centrality and its distance from the German army. This move also afforded the fledgling regime a wonderful opportunity to deepen its "Russian" trappings. Even as the Bolsheviks were launching or supporting numerous modernizing and utopian renovations in life, they were able to draw upon the rich symbolism of the ancient city that had been the capital of the first large, centralized Russian state from the fifteenth century to 1713, with its Kremlin, twisting streets, heartland location, and various associations with Muscovy's original princes and tsars. The creation of St. Petersburg early in the eighteenth century by Tsar Peter the Great had produced a cultural shock to many Russians due to its distance from Old Moscow, its European architecture, and its symbolic significance as a "Window to the West." A key element in the revival of Russian nationalism in the nineteenth century was the Moscow mystique in the ideology of the backward-looking Slavophiles—all Muscovites—and in the styles and vocabularies of the art world, particularly its nostalgic and folkish dimensions. Although the Bolsheviks shared few of these romantic-archaic visions of the city, they nonetheless inherited the sense of tradition that the old city emitted.

The new Soviet government had many missions to perform on the symbolic front: demonize its enemies, glorify itself, neutralize its former colleagues, and modernize the masses. The first—demonization—was (as it usually is) the easiest. The Bolsheviks possessed clear advantages here. They drew upon the labors of some very talented pro-Bolshevik artists who dredged up and modified entire historical layers of graphic and other art that exalted the poor and the weak over the rich and the strong: European Jacobin and labor discourse, Russian popular prints and folktales, and radical posters of 1905. The images became so set in the early years that they could be recycled for every new struggle; thus the fat capitalist, monarch, and priest of Civil War-era imagery later worked well under Stalin in the new apparel of economic saboteur, fascist invader, or NATO warmonger. Though early Bolshevik political art has been rightly admired for its skill and imagination, it was not really that original: the corpulent factory owners of Eisenstein's 1920s films hardly differ from those of D. W. Griffith in his 1916 *Intolerance.* All the same, the Revolution allowed the Bolshevik artists to reach with both hands back into the deep past for heroes and demons. With one hand they unearthed the dragon slain by the converted Roman soldier who had become St. George and had been enshrined in Byzantine and thus Russian Orthodox Christianity as the ultimate warrior. With the other they reached into classical antiquity for the Hydra slain by Hercules. All four figures fit nicely into revolutionary iconography, which was supremely political and combative — as were the inspirations. Hercules was morphed into the muscular Red Army fighter-proletarian opposed to the "hundred-headed" foe, that is to the fifteen intervening powers of the Civil War who sided with the Whites; and St. George could be made to look pretty good in a red shirt. As often happens in propaganda (religious or political), the loathsome, scaly, slimy monsters were probably more effective than the cardboard heroes.

Self-glorification of Soviet power and socialism was simply the other face of the coin. Cultural artifacts inscribed the Bolshevik claims to social justice, equality, and a coming prosperity, among many other virtues.[17] Cartoon and poster depicted square-jawed Red Army men bayoneting the enemy-reified images of capitalism, religion, and militarism. Handsome peasants turned the rural world upside down by ousting the superfluous landowners. Pictures of the Soviet leaders were arrayed on collages with Lenin at the sacred center, very much as in the Orthodox iconostasis or altar screen on which the church displayed its hierarchy of saints surrounding the Holy Savior. Lenin's death and transfiguration created an entire industry of myth and symbol.[18]

Neutralizing former colleagues was a bit trickier. Soviet leaders were ambivalent about the "precursors" of Bolshevism: the Populists, Anarchists, and Mensheviks. Those who cried out against Soviet autocracy were shot, imprisoned, or sent into emigration. Yet the regime continued to tolerate the more complacent surviving "ancients," the veteran members of the nineteenth-century People's Will and Land and Freedom; and it even enthroned a few as icons of the holy struggle against tsarism as gathered into the Society of Former Prisoners and Political Exiles.[19] Although symbolic and rhetorical wars erupted about their role in the prehistory of 1917 and even about the appropriateness of logos showing prison bars on the society's journal, the authorities in the 1920s were still ready to smile tolerantly on the nostalgic work of these aged warriors. Under Stalin, all smiles ceased. The society with all its redolent symbolism was brutally dismantled and some of its members were liquidated. Stalin would not suffer any kind of alternate current of history to challenge the one he created in the 1930s.

Officially, modernization to the Bolsheviks meant making the population abandon religion for science, rural values for urban ones, sexism for equal rights for women, sloth for time-motion efficiency, ethnic hostility for "Soviet" national identity. And in truth, the early Bolsheviks worked for these goals with great vigor and even sincerity, however much their progress was partially reversed under Stalin in the 1930s. The history of one symbolic treatment, that of women, can best illuminate the problem. The earliest depictions of men and women together seemed egalitarian. Boris Kustodiev—a major figure of pre- and post-revolutionary art—executed a folkish diptych with a male on the left with hammer and a female on the right with sickle, denoting a bigenderal struggle for revolutionary values. But the culturally suggestive implements undercut the egalitarian symmetry of gender construction. The industrial hammer was an emblem of city, machine, and power, while the sickle was one of rural life, superstition, and—by extension—female backwardness. The image was at least balanced in the 1920s by a wide band of representation of women in "advanced" and "progressive" roles. But, again, under Stalin, women's images—paralleling the laws passed and the policies put in place—were permanently demoted to second place in virtually every kind of cultural statement, the most famous of these being Vera Mukhina's statue of the male industrial worker with hammer and the female collective farmer with sickle standing slightly behind him.[20]

Many a book has been written about the kinds of symbols that inhabited the arts of socialist realism from the 1930s onward: tractors, factory smokestacks, airplanes, and all sorts of humanoid embodiments of the Stalinist virtues.[21] Some of these softened or faded in the quieter years after Stalin's death, though never fully disappearing. During World War II, however, glimmered the beginnings of the regreening of Russia. Folk ensembles, blending traditional dance and music styles with Soviet values and kitsch, had been created by the state in the mid-1930s and they blossomed luxuriantly during and after the war. The birch tree had far more emotional resonance on the wartime screen than any shot of a factory. In fact official priorities now encouraged rural landscape painting, much neglected in previous years. Even the new 1943 anthem reflected an amplification of national values. In order to downplay world revolution and allay the fears of his allies (Britain and the United States), Stalin abolished the Communist International (Comintern, 1919-43) and simultaneously substituted a new, rather boastful and chauvinist "State Hymn" (music by Alexander Alexandrov, words by Sergei Mikhailkov) for "The Internationale" with its obvious message of world revolution. Great Russian chauvinism prepared the way for the long good-bye to the sinewy symbolic forms of early utopian Bolshevism and helped sustain the school of Village Prose that so dominated fiction for three decades before the collapse of the USSR.

With the demise of the Soviet Union in 1991, the new symbols pushed out of the ground by the force of glasnost and perestroika of the previous five years created a landscape of multicolored vegetation. Old growths, savagely cut down by the Revolution or subtly camouflaged in late Soviet times—village ways, church architecture, Rus antiquities—sprung up again. But they were crowded by transplants from other climes—the "West." If a symbol is a visual statement of identity (among other things), then procapitalist T-shirts, BMWs, Rolex watches, and a hundred other visible and audible artifacts were truly symbols of a "rejoining" to the outer world. But it was no longer the world of railroad carriages, silent movies, decadent journals, or jazz, but of a vastly transformed global culture. How were Russians to define themselves as a nation symbolically in the swirl of this cultural deluge?

Inventing a new state symbol of the nation—flag and coat of arms—could hardly be up to that immense and perhaps hopeless task. Still, Russians could be made, at least on ceremonial occasions, to perceive that the rulers of the state possessed and endorsed some vision of national identity. This could be no more than a fragment of a vision if only because the multiplication of competing "hypnotic" signs had intervened on a vast scale in the twentieth century for this now literate population—a fact hardly unique to Russia. But what kind of fragment would Russians get? The decision was largely that of one man: Boris Yeltsin. In 1991 a new state flag of the Russian Federation was announced. It turned out to be the old one—that of the Romanovs: three bands of red, white, and blue. Thus it was in no way a parallel to the Bolshevik adoption of a completely new flag of red; but, though a reversion, it was also a clear reversal—a very loud rejection of seventy years of symbolism in which that red cloth had allegedly unified a great people and also mesmerized radicals on five continents. Next came the coat of arms. Here there were parallels to the commissions and debates under the Provisional Government in 1917 and then under Soviet power in 1918. In the 1990s, when the Russian Federation's Ministry of Culture and the Archives Administration were preparing the new coat of arms, controversy erupted at once over the proposal to reinstate the famous double-headed eagle. The alternative suggestions are revealing of the mix of sentiments among the sign-making politicians and scholars. In addition to the old eagle, among the entries as central motif on the shield were a bear, a crane, and a horseman.

The bear of course had for centuries inhabited popular cartoons, folktales, bear ceremonies, folk-fair shows, and the circus. Among the most popular silent films of the 1920s had been the gothic tale *The Bear's Wedding*, with a script by Commissar of Enlightenment Anatoly Lunacharsky. To Western observers—even at the most primitive level—however, the bear meant "the big bear" that hugged its neighbors to death.[22] The Spanish diplomat and writer Salvador de Madariaga in the 1920s told a fable at a disarmament conference in Geneva about how each species at an analogous conference of forest animals called for the abolition of certain "weapons" of their foes: beaks, claws, teeth, long legs, and so on. But the bear proposed total disarmament in the woods so that all could live peacefully in his comradely embrace. This sign was clearly unbearable for an armorial bearing, though we have no data on the nature of the objections by Yeltsin's committee.

Crane and horseman could offer no encoded threat to the world, for they were hardly known outside Russia to be Russian symbols. The horseman appears everywhere—one of a pair flanking a peasant woman in folk ornament, in the omnipresent St.-George-and-the-dragon depictions, and in famous and popular paintings of the nineteenth-century "Wanderers" school of realist art. The crane is more obscure. According to certain legends, Russian warriors who perished on the battlefield were transformed into cranes who would fly for all eternity—this giving rise to a song and a drama on that theme and to the title of the renowned 1957 film *The Cranes Are Flying*. In 1992, probably in the face of discord in the first committee over these issues, a new committee took up the work. R. G. Pikhoya of the Russian Archives Administration and the artist E. I. Ukhnalev were put in charge. In 1993 the new emblem was ready: a red shield on which is emblazoned a golden double-headed eagle, with three crowns, an orb, and a scepter; in the insets were placed shields of St. George and the dragon.[23]

But there is an inside story, which was told to a group of American professors at the Hermitage in 1992 in the midst of the symbolic debates. G. V. Vilinbakhov, an official of the Hermitage and in effect the heraldmaster of the Russian state, had just traveled to Moscow to present Yeltsin with two possible variants of the Ukhnalev eagle: one with wings modestly folded (as in that of the Provisional Government of 1917) and the other with flaring wings. Yeltsin chose the latter, thus opting for the image that had been so offensive to many people under the older of the old regimes.[24] In addition, in order to "de-unionize" the new country and stress its Russianness, it was named the Russian Federation—minus the terms "soviet" and "socialist" from the old USSR designation. The Stalinist anthem of 1943, full of references to "the Soviet Union," was replaced by one of the great choral numbers from Glinka's *Life for the Tsar.* Thus Russia's first widely recognized composer, who had lost out in his own time (see above), for a while had his name on Russia's most important piece of symbolic music. When Yeltsin's successor, Vladimir Putin, came to power, however, he decided to return to a modified version of the old Soviet anthem, posing the rhetorical question: "Is it true there is nothing to remember in the Soviet period of our country's existence except for Stalin's camps and repressions?"[25] Citing other accomplishments from the Soviet era, such as the victory in World War II and Yuri Gagarin's first spaceflight, Putin argued that the Soviet anthem enjoyed broad popular support as a symbol of Russia's military strength and international status. The old Soviet anthem[26] is still sung by the Communist Party at its gatherings. Alarmists in Russia, probably overreacting, interpreted Putin's action as a sign of a return to other aspects of the Soviet system. But Putin wants to keep the tricolor double-headed eagle for the national flag and emblem, and use the red banner only for the army.

Full circle? Not even a small stretch of the circumference. Symbols do not work as they once did, for reasons partly explained above. Leftist symbols with universal pretensions have been weakened in our century precisely by their global reach and are now seen as comic outside and tired inside the few communist countries that remain. Rightist symbols, precisely because they were anti-transcendental, had to be rooted in real or fake national soil: yokes and arrows, twisted or fiery crosses, fasces, iron wolves, steel helmets, medieval falcons. And then of course European fascists and their admirers in Ireland, China, and the United States also relied on shirts—whether black, brown, silver, blue, or green (never socialist red or royalist white). In the terror-stricken thirties and forties, how brilliantly they stood out in the sea of men's dull fashions; and in our time how quickly they would be lost in the peacockery of our sartorial landscape. In this sense the age of movement symbolism is on the wane—at least for a time.

At this moment in history, Russian nationhood, scantily clad in the eagle and the tricolor, must move beyond symbolic assertiveness in order to say what it is. Bur first, it has to determine what it is.

Original publication: In Michael Geisler, ed. *National Symbols, Fractured Identities: Contesting the National Narrative*. Hanover: University Press of New England, 2004, pp. 101-117.

Notes

1   Julia Kristeva, Lecture at Georgetown University, October 1999.
2   Elena Hellberg-Hirn, *Soil and Soul: The Symbolic World of Russianness* (Aldershot, UK, 1998).
3   *Imperatorskaya Sanktpeterburgskaya Akademiya Khudozhestv: Kratkii istoricheskii ocherk* (SPB, 1914), title page.
4   See Richard Wortman, *Scenarios of Power: Myth and Ceremony in Russian Monarchy*, vol. I. (Princeton, N.J. 1995).
5   Ibid.
6   Richard Stites, "The Domestic Muse: Music at Home in the Twilight of Serfdom," in Andrew Wachtel, ed., *Intersections and Transpositions: Russian Music, Literature, and Society*, 187-205. (Evanston, Ill., 1998).
7   Laurence Senelick, ed., *National Theater in Northern and Eastern Europe, 1746-1900* (New York, 1991), 359.
8   Boris Varneke, *History of the Russian Theater* (1939), tr. B. Brasol (New York, 1951), 242.
9   See *Gerby gorodov Rossii* (Moscow, 1998).
10 N. A. Soboleva and V. A. Artamonov, *Simvol Rossii* (Moscow, 1993), 128-29.
11 Alison Hilton, *Russian Folk Art* (Bloomington, Ind., 1995).
12 Richard Stites, *The Women's Liberation Movement in Russia: Feminism, Nihilism, and Bolshevism, 1860-1930* (Princeton, N.J., 1978), 99-114.
13 Decembrists were radical officers who launched a failed uprising in St. Petersburg on December 14, 1925.
14 Soboleva and Artamonov, *Simvol Rossii*, 177.
15 For World War I: Hubertus Jahn, *Patriotic Culture in Russia during World War I* (Ithaca, N.Y., 1995), and Aviel Roshwald and Richard Stites, eds., *European Culture in the Great War: The Arts, Entertainment, and Propaganda* (Cambridge, 1999); for World War II: Stites, ed., *Culture and Entertainment in Wartime Russia* (Bloomington, Ind., 1995).
16 Soboleva, and Artamov, *Simvol Rossii*, 141. The best work on this period is Orlando Figes and Boris Kolonitsky, *Interpreting The Russian Revolution: the Language and Symbols of 1917* (New Haven, Conn., 1999).
17 Richard Stites, *Revolutionary Dreams: Utopian Vision and Experimental Life in the Russian Revolution* (New York, 1989).
18 Nina Tumarkin, *Lenin Lives: The Cult of Lenin in Soviet Russia* (New York, 1994); Claes Arvidsson and Lars Erik Blomqvist, eds., *Symbols of Power* (Stockholm, 1987).

19 Sandra Pujals, "When Giants Walked the Earth" (Georgetown University dissertation, 1999).

20 Victoria Bonnell, *Iconography of Power: Soviet Political Posters under Lenin and Stalin* (Berkeley, 1997).

21 Hans Günther, ed., *The Culture of the Stalin Period* (London, 1990).

22 David Goldfrank, *The Origin of the Crimean War* (London, 1994), front cover cartoon.

23 G. V. Vilinbakhov, *Gosudarstvennyi gerb Rossii, 500 let* (St. Petersburg, 1997).

24 Vilinbakhov showed us both these images in his talk at the Hermitage.

25 David Hoffman, "Putin Seeks Restoration of Soviet Symbols," *Washington Post*, 5 December 2000, A40.

26 The former anthem was composed during the war by general Alexander Alexandrov, director of the Red Army ensemble, with words by Sergei Mikhalkov, a well-known conservative and father of the film directors Nikita Mikhalkov and Andron Konchalovsky.

5

Filling in the Cultural Landscape from Vienna to Moscow
Past and Present

I might well have titled this informal piece "Some things that a historian of Russia would like to know about Eastern Europe." Being no specialist on the region, I apologize in advance to those who have already written about these subjects or who are aware of such writings in generally accessible languages. Amid the flood of so many wonderful monographs that enlighten us on the details, it would be a boon to professional and layman alike to have more synoptic and interpretive works that link together some comparable matters in East European history—and that history to Russian studies as well. In particular, it would be enlightening to the Western academic community, students, and general public for scholars of the Other Half of Europe to retrieve the colorful panoramas of the social and cultural life of people whose past has so often been seen as the dark side of a Dark Continent. In this short sketch, I want to lay out a few topics that might help fill the gaps in our knowledge and to relate issues that have seldom been taken together. I offer a personal wish-list about some issues that have long piqued my interest and in some cases have been prompted by my own researches in Russian history.

The Creative Serf

I will begin with the golden age of the Central and East European nobility in the eighteenth and early nineteenth centuries when the Polish szlachta, Hungarian magnates, and Croatian landowners held serfs; and when, until the revolution of 1848, Phanariotes and Romanian Boiares held slaves in the Ottoman Provinces of

Wallachia and Moldavia. In the study of rural Eastern Europe, we have many works in English on comparative land tenure, village life, juridical bonds, crop yields, peasant parties, and noble classes. Among the many, I mention the books by Jerome Blum, Ivo Banac, and Arno Mayer.[1] Missing from the picture are serf actors, musicians, and painters. This is one of the subjects of my most recent book which deals with serfdom and the Russian cultural scene up to 1861.[2] It has been constantly noted in music history and biography, though with little comment about the context, that Joseph Haydn was a kind of musical house servant of the Esterhazy princes. How many Haydns and lesser Haydns, free and unfree, served in the great manor houses of Eastern Europe? What kind of music did they make? And, most interesting of all, how did they live, as artists and as men and women? Were they in effect cultural slaves, as they often were in Russia, subject to the whims—sexual, occupational, or punitive—of the master? Were unfree painters cut off at the peak of their genius to be sent to the pantry or the field? Did those living in serfdom or other variants of indenture or dependence perform operas and plays—again as in Russia—in estate theaters where they assumed the roles of kings or princesses? And with what psychological effects? A comparative study by one or more scholars might uncover a whole world of creative servants or serfs who enlivened the cultural life of a private sphere among the privileged, and who perhaps both suffered and flourished in their own personal lives.

Tales from Beyond the Vienna Woods

Music is among the most neglected of the arts as far as historians are concerned. When you get it at all in a general treatment, you do not get much. For example, in a 411-page general historical survey of late nineteenth century Europe, Norman Stone devoted a few pages to music — all by canonical composers. The longest passage, an interesting treatment of one of Gustav Mahler's symphonies, offered a learned comment on his use of modulation.[3] And that was about all. Professional musicologists have certainly scoured the musical past, but they tend to speak in technical language and to focus, quite naturally, on the masterpieces in the canon (or on "authentic" folk forms). The experience of music in the life of the great majority of urbanites high and low in social status gets little attention. Let's take the old Habsburg Monarchy whose capital was long acknowledged to be the musical capital of Europe. As I glanced through some standard histories of that empire, I found the usual focus on the great composers from the first and second Vienna schools and a few others. But this great empire also gave us not only the very well-known Bohemians Dvorak and Smetana, the waltz family of the Strausses, and the Hungarian operetta masters Lehar and Kalman; but also the lesser-known but at the time eminent Carl Goldmark of Hungary, Emil Reznicek of Vienna, and the still popular Franz von Suppe, born in Split (Spalato), who composed a *Missa dalmatica* as a youth. The music of these and a half-dozen other Habsburg composers filled the radio concert airwaves in the twentieth century, as did that of the Romanian Emil Ivanovici whose "Danube Waves" became popular as "The Anniversary Waltz." At least as well-known at the time of course were the ubiquitous Gypsy ensembles and folk song and dance troupes and their amateur counterparts in the villages.

Could not this vast musical mosaic and its social framework — publishers, recordings, orchestras, performers, schools, virtuoso systems (such as that surrounding Fritz Kreisler) — be connected to the mainstream history of a multicultural state, to its social and ethnic components, and even to politics? Quite aside from the absolutely essential role played by musical ensembles in the great symbolic jubilee of the Habsburgs in and that of the Kingdom of Hungary — Millennium in 1896, small forms, domestic music-making, concerts, and operas served as a crucial part of the texture of everyday life.[4] And is it possible to doubt that the extraordinarily large participation of Jewish musicians throughout the empire had no social and cultural repercussions?

Casablanca Man

During the short-lived Hungarian Soviet Republic of 1919, a young filmmaker working for Bela Kun's Communist regime made an eight-minute silent film called *My Brother Has Returned*, which I have viewed twice in the Helsinki Film Archives. It dealt with a fictional Hungarian soldier, briefly shown, who, while a World War

I POW in Russia, had become a Bolshevik—a character and a scenario that fit not only Bela Kun, but also Josip Broz Tito and many another future Communist luminary. On arrival in Hungary, the returning Bolshevik in the movie waves a proletarian banner. Actual newsreel footage of a May Day parade is shown, and then the movie ends. The director of this film, Kertesz Mihaly, soon left Hungary to escape the anti-communist and anti-Semitic butchery that came in with the White counter-revolutionaries led by Admiral Miklos Horthy. From Vienna and Berlin, Kertesz eventually made his way to Hollywood where he became successful as Michael Curtiz who gave us, among many other famous films, the 1942 Warner Brothers' *Casablanca*. Two questions have nagged me for many years: why did so many Hungarians become successful in the British and American film industry?; and what other kinds of cultural artifacts were promoted by that desperate 1919 revolutionary government which dispatched trains to the countryside filled with toothbrushes, combs, and gallows as well as propaganda?[5]

In regard to Eastern Europe as a creative pool, there is a very rich study entitled *An Empire of their Own: How the Jews Invented Hollywood* by Neal Gabler[6] that tells part of a big story: the fate of a handful of immigrants from Eastern Europe and the Russian Empire who reached American shores: Louis B. Mayer from a Russian shtetl who headed MGM; the Polish-born Samuel Goldwyn and the Warner Brothers who headed their own studios; the Hungarians William Fox (Vilmos Fuchs) of 20th Century Fox and Adolf Zukor of Paramount, to name only the top rank. To these we can add innumerable others who flourished in England or America: the Korda brothers and Emmerich Pressburg of Hungary, Billy Wilder from Galicia, and dozens of screenwriters and directors. We may also add the film composers Dmitry Tiomkin, Franz Waxman, Max Steiner, and Miklos Rosza to the roster. These men virtually created the big Hollywood film score style in the 1930s and 1940s. When Tiomkin won an Academy Award for the musical score of *High Noon*, he unashamedly thanked his "collaborators" down through the years: nineteenth- and early twentieth-century Russian and East Central European composers.

I said that Neal Gabler's book gave us part of the story: the fate of talented East European Jews who became producers in the Hollywood studio system. The book omitted non-producers and non-Jews. Most important, Gabler offered little on the role of the cultures and everyday life of the East European place of origin in the Hollywood men's later tastes and values. Of coffee-shop wits and cabaret culture we know a good deal, thanks to the works of Harold Segel and Laurence Senelick.[7] But what was on offer in the fin-de-siècle metropolises of Mitteleuropa, the Christian villages, or the Jewish shtetls that fed into the special styles of humor, farce, shtick, baroque adventure, or sentimental melodrama. To take Hungary again, the names of Mor Jokai, Baroness Orczy, Lajos Biro, and Melchior Lengyel are not present in the Western-language histories I have read. Like cowboy writer Karl May in Germany, the prolific Jokai was the most widely read author of his time in his native land; Lengyel and Biro became prolific script writers for Ernst Lubitsch and Billy Wilder.

A Black International?

This is a dark and rather delicate subject, yet one that I think invites synthetic treatment: the role of clergy in the right-wing politics of Central and Eastern Europe before and during World War II. I am not speaking of the Vatican or of a macro-history of the Christian churches for which studies abound. I have in mind something like six characters in search of an anthology or a synthetic treatment. The names are well known: Father Ignaz Seipel, Chancellor of Austria in the 1920s, supporter of the Heimwehr and of clerical corporate fascism; the radical Slovak nationalist Father Andrej Hlinka of the Hlinka Guard in Czechoslovakia; Monsignor Jozef Tiso, wartime dictator of Slovakia and ally of Hitler; the activist Orthodox priests in the Romanian fascist Iron Guard; the infamous Catholic clergy who worked in the death camps of the fascist Ustashe in Croatia. All have been studied separately, but to my knowledge, there is no book that links and analyzes and compares their programs, ideologies, and—when relevant—style of governance. This story is part of an old and painful war and is full of moral and methodological traps, not least of which is the mendacious literature produced in postwar Communist regimes that endeavored to smear all churches with the brush of fascism and collaboration. A serious overarching look at fascism and the cross might help set the record straight.

Underground

I have read somewhere that in the Nazi ruled Gouvernement-General of Poland during World War II, playing in public or broadcasting the music of Frederic Chopin was prohibited. Chopin's music of course first got politicized in Paris in the 1830s by the composer himself who tried to enlist support for the cause of his countrymen. He, Adam Mickiewicz, and other émigrés were creating the image of Poland as a crucified nation. Chopin's music was invoked in a major way by the pianist Ignazy Paderewski who eventually became the resurrected Poland's first Prime Minister, in 1918. During World War II, was it only Hollywood composers who used the Revolutionary Etude and the Polonaise in A Flat major as the sound track for Polish patriotism and resistance? Or was it happening on the ground? A Hungarian folk song (used by either Kodaly or Bartok, I cannot recall which) was similarly prohibited when that country fell under Nazi occupation. I wonder what we might learn about the depth and contours of Nazi occupied Europe by examining the conquerors' mode of selecting censorship targets, the level of enforcement, and resistance to it. (Think of some of the scenes in the recent film *The Pianist*.) Did Serbs interned in Ustashe camps sing Partisan or Chetnik songs; did Orthodox priests intone the litany?

While on the subject of violent occupations, how did the Soviet authorities treat the local cultural activities of Poles, Belarusians, Ukrainians, and Jews during their two-year occupation of that borderland during the Nazi-Soviet Pact of 1939-1941 (aside from looting pianos and accordions)? And, on a related matter, how interesting would it be to compare prisoner self-entertainment and entertainment of their captors in the POW and death camps of Axis and Soviet Europe? There will surely be those in our profession who would consider such a scholarly pursuit to be an exercise in criminally trivializing the experience of those victims.[8] This view in fact has been voiced in other contexts by some Western scholars who believe that the study of social history or cultural history (by historians as opposed to specialists in cultural disciplines) of the Soviet Union, especially in the Stalin period, is tantamount to an apologia for the system or at least to deflecting attention from the totalitarian nature of the regime and its monstrous atrocities. Needless to say, I do not hold to this view.

Memory and History

Much has been written in recent years about the relation of memory to history—usually other people's memory. But historians have a memory problem also. Historians, myself included, sometimes forget that history did not end in the year we started teaching. When I began in 1959, the year 1953 seemed to be pretty much the end of the grand narrative of Soviet and East European history. The rest was current events or grist for the mill of political science. For some reason, historians like myself tend to shy away from the immediate past. If we lived through it and remember it, somehow it does not seem like "history." This, I confess, is a weakness. Only recently has even the distant Khrushchev period taken on the dimensions of a full-blown historical epoch.[9] The Brezhnev and the Gorbachev eras are close on its heels. Political scientists in Europe and America have done yeoman work in trying to synthesize the recent past—I think especially of Stephen White's useful series of volumes on the Gorbachev years and after and the works of Robert Service and Richard Sakwa.

How might historians of Eastern Europe shine new light on the Communist period of this region—1945-1989? We have many books on cinema, literature, and art. So again I hark back to music, the neglected muse. A recent Georgetown doctoral dissertation explored the politics of conflicting musical cultures in divided postwar Berlin, where extra-musical factors often drove the concert repertoires, professional associations, program notes, and many other things.[10] This was a cultural microcosm of the early Cold War in which musical establishments East and West were creating their identities in the face of the Other, with Soviet and Allied authorities playing a crucial role. Certainly a similar approach could be applied to that other eminently musical capital, Vienna, where it was said—four elephants sat in a rowboat: the British, French, Russians, and Americans.

A promising area of comparative exploration with even greater scope—"fakelore"—occurred to me when I examined the Stalinist politicization of folk culture in the 1930s. We all remember how, in later decades, the world was charmed by such traveling dance troupes as the Igor Moiseev Ensemble. "Such vigorous and talented people! Such a deep culture!" were the frequent reactions of foreign audiences, and not only from Lefties. And who could deny this to the Moiseev dancers? The subliminal message might have suggested: happy Soviet peasants. This was certainly part of the original intention of the Stalinist cultural managers of the 1930s. But this game goes way back, how far I am not sure. I mentioned earlier the jubilees of the Habsburg Monarchy and of the Kingdom of Hungary. On both of these occasions, peasant folk dancing in traditional costume held a prominent place in the festivities. Think only of the economic and social conditions of nearly barbarized peasants of Ruthenia, way off in the corner of the empire and contrast it to the images projected of healthy, well-fed rural dancers in the public celebrations. Things did not change all that much in the interwar period of East-Central European independence when the only agrarian party regime in history to that point was brutally overthrown and its leaders tortured and murdered (Stambolisky in Bulgaria); when peasant parties were routinely marginalized; when land reform failed in most of those countries; and where peasants were co-opted into genuinely fascist parties, such as the Iron Guard in Romania. In the 1930s, royal and other dictatorships regularly deployed cultural images of peasant well-being by means of folk dance and folk song festivals—as did their Communist successors after World War II. What riches of cultural politics might be excavated in a comparative survey of this phenomenon all over Eastern Europe and Russia in the nineteenth and twentieth centuries.

Where Have All the Trabis Gone?

Which brings us to Soviet culture and its imitators in Eastern Europe. The pulling down of Lenin and Stalin statues from Tallinn to Sofia and the joyful celebrations that accompanied those acts make it perfectly easy to understand why a comparative study of Stalinist culture in Eastern Europe has not galvanized scholars of late. Some of that stuff was genuinely repulsive and some was harmless kitsch. But might we not ask what meanings it had in the various satellites? The recent German film *Goodbye Lenin!* raises some intriguing ideas. Wolfgang Becker's ironic valentine to Eastern European communism suggests immense possibilities for exploring a certain perspective on the Ost (the East) a perspective that the Germans now call Ostalgie—a qualified nostalgia for aspects of a lost world. In Russian it has led to all kinds of Retro-Stalinism, Sotsart, and so on. If some hip Germans are restoring Trabi cars, are the Czechs doing so with Tatras, and the Serbs with Yugos? Is this harmless trivia, or can it cause us to think comparatively about Fiats and Porsches—the folks who gave us fascist bombers and Nazi tanks fifty years ago? Chic Germans are also throwing vintage costume parties where the guests dress up in Young Communist uniforms and red scarves. One can hardly imagine Nazi costume parties in Germany at any point from 1945 until this day—except for underground skinheads whose apparel would have a wholly different purpose. (Interestingly enough, in Hungary, the Hammer and Sickle emblem and other Communist symbols are forbidden by law.) For young Germans, are the Commie costumes and other markers of the past, when edited against shopping malls and Coca-Cola trucks, just good-humored pranks, signs of deeper malaise with consumerism, or something altogether different? And let us try to imagine, if we can, how such cultural recapturing might compare with, for example, Stefan Zweig's utterly different masterpiece of Habsburg memory.[11]

Inclusiveness

In discussing a recent book on globalization and Russian youth culture, a reviewer advised the contributors to reach beyond tastes in pop music, movies, and fashion in examining the mental life styles of youngsters and young adults; and to seek out their interest in higher learning and classical culture, among other things.[12] The review reflects a problem that vexes many of us who write about culture: namely that you cannot please everybody. The reviewer spends much time talking about a book that the authors (including Hilary Pilkington, one of Britain's most prolific scholars) should have written. Over the past three decades or so, social historians at least implicitly scolded those purely political historians who studied only the elites. Cultural historians taxed social historians for ignoring the expressive life of the cohorts and classes they examined. And some of us who dealt in popular culture gently jibed the profession for treating culture, when they did treat it at all, strictly in terms of the canon, and usually only literature. Now the tables might be turning again, and rightly so. We can only do so much, and there is no sense in faulting anyone for not doing it all. Yet, when exploring the life of any given social group, we ought to canvass all sides of its cultural profile. Concretely, one could ask in a comparative way across the region from Vienna and Berlin to Moscow and Vladivostok what mixtures of tastes and habits inform any particular cohort: to what extent they consume products of the Old Regime (the Communist period), of the Old Old Regime (the tsarist period or the interwar East European independence period), and of the domestic and global culture and/ or folkways of the present. Needless to say, such studies can go beyond a survey of crystallized culture (songs, movies, products) and—as most such scholars now do—pick up on folkways and everyday habits.

The Sexy Comrade and the Clash of Cultures

Let's conclude with a journey into love—east-west love and capitalist-communist love. For a long time, the Bolsheviks frowned upon and even forbade intermarriage between Soviet citizens and those from the decadent West (i.e., practically everywhere else). In the 1920s, when sex was still a hot topic of debate in Russia, one stern Bolshevik physician went even further. A marriage between a Menshevik and a Bolshevik, he said, was equivalent to the mating of an orangutan and a crocodile (though he did not indicate which was which).[13] To Western film-makers, the idea of cross-ideological romance was too good to bypass: the result was the classic comedy film, *Ninotchka* (1939), directed by Ernst Lubitsch and with a screenplay co-scripted by Billy Wilder—both children of Mitteleuropa. In this film, the female commissar, though seduced by a Westerner and by the West itself, was at least allowed to retain some of her positive socialist values. Not so during the Cold War when strong American heroes liberated a girl enslaved by communism, as in *Never Let Me Go* (1953), with Clark Gable—a crude reworking of the Byronic harem rescue tale. In real life, intermarriage got rolling in the 1950s and 1960s, largely as a result of scholarly exchanges. We all know the tensions that these unions sometimes produced. In recent years, the press has been exploring German East-West intermarriage. In one, between a "Wessie" (West German) man and an "Ossie" woman, the persisting differences in cultural values were overcome, in the man's case, by the strong attraction to his wife, driven by what the reporter called "socialist exoticism," a kind of "orientalism in one country" (the subtitle of a recent book about the two Italys).

Who knows? Studying these peculiar corners of culture and society might prepare scholars and practitioners elsewhere about what is to come—for example when, after, and if certain communist regimes collapse or are drastically transformed, North Koreans marry South Koreans, Mainland Chinese marry Taiwanese, and Island Cubans marry Miami Cubans. Long live the clash of cultures!

Original publication: *Varietas et Concordia: Essays in Honour of Professor Pekka Pesonen On the Occasion of His 60th Birthday.* Eds. Ben Hellman, Tomi Huttunen, Gennady Obatnin. Helsinki: Slavia Helsingiensa, 2007, pp. 161-171.

Notes

1 J. Blum, *The End of the Old Order in Rural Europe.* Princeton: Princeton University Press 1978; I. Banac and P. Bushkovitch (eds.), *The Nobility in Russia and Eastern Europe.* New Haven: Yale University Press 1983; A. Mayer, *The Persistence of the Old Regime: Europe to the Great War.* New York: Pantheon 1981.
2 R. Stites, *Serfdom, Society, and the Arts in Imperial Russia.* New Haven: Yale University Press 2005.

3   N. Stone, *Europe Transformed, 1878-1919*. Cambridge, Mass.: Harvard University Press 1984, 400-402.

4   P. Lendvai, *The Hungarians: A Thousand Years of Victory in Defeat*. Princeton: Princeton University Press 2003, 310-328.

5   T. Hajdu, *The Hungarian Soviet Republic*. Budapest: Akadémiai Kiadó, 1979, 73-79; A. Kaas & F. de Lazarovics, *Bolshevism in Hungary: The Bela Kun Period*. London: G. Richards, 1931, 160-69; J. Cunningham, *Hungarian Cinema: From Coffee House to Multiplex*. London: Wallflower, 2004; J.C. Robertson, *Casablanca Man: The Cinema of Michael Curtiz*. London: Routledge, 1993.

6   N. Gabler, *An Empire of their Own: How the Jews Invented Hollywood*. New York: Doubleday 1988.

7   H. Segel (ed.), *The Vienna Colke House Wits, 1890-1930*. West Lafayette, Indiana: Purdue University Press 1993; H. Segel, *Turn-of-the-century Cabaret: Paris, Barcelona, Berlin, Munich, Vienna, Cracow, Moscow, St. Petersburg, Zurich*. New York: Columbia University Press 1987; L. Senelick (ed.), *Cabaret Performance, Volume I: Europe, 1890-1920*. New York: PAJ 1987.

8   As it happens, a recent (2006) scholarly article has appeared on German POWs in Russia in *The American Historical Review*, the premier historical journal of the United States.

9   W. Taubman, *Khrushchev: The Man and his Era*. New York: Norton 2003.

10 E. Janik, "Music in Cold War Berlin: German Tradition and Allied Occupation." Georgetown University PhD Dissertation, 2001.

11 S. Zweig, *The World of Yesterday*. Lincoln: University of Nebraska Press 1964 [1943].

12 H. Pilkington et al. (eds.), *Looking West: Cultural Globalization and Russian Youth Culture*. University Park: Pennsylvania State University Press 2002; reviews in *Slavic Review*, 63/1 (Spring 2004), 206-207.

13 R. Stites, *The Women's Liberation Movement in Russia*. Princeton: Princeton University Press 1978, 381.

6

Historical and Social Rhythms in Russian Culture in the 19ᵗʰ and 20ᵗʰ Centuries

One of the most useful instruments of historical prose, periodization, allows some measure of interpretive clarity, yet often underplays the insistent force of continuity and overlap. In laying out a series of arbitrary eras of modern Russian cultural development, I have, within a short space, tried to achieve the former and avoid the latter. My approach—a study of the arts in a social and political context—hopefully affords the possibility of some success in this endeavor. As one period succeeds another, I indicate the presence and function of those persistent themes and practices that continue to roll along beneath a surface of an expressive culture that was much more visible and worthy of attention by the cultural leaders of the time, and that eventually became canonized. What follows then is a series of interpretive sketches of three discrete eras of the nineteenth century and three of the twentieth that reconstruct what cultural life meant to society at the time as well as what has come down to us through the filters of aesthetically elite perspectives. To do this is to retrieve from the dustbin now-forgotten artifacts and whatever they contained that caught the imagination and approval of those who saw or heard them—minor or even "bad" works of famous creators and now obscure works of others not so famous. Thus a truly historical examination of culture demands a survey of taste as well as of the immortal and eternal works that have survived the test of time. For modern Russia the keys to such an approach—digging for the ephemeral—are found in "society"—those who saw, read, or heard works of art and culture in each successive period; in the power of the state; and in national identity.

In the Twilight of Serfdom, 1801-1861

The teleological term "twilight" reflects what we know but not what contemporaries knew. Many deplored serfdom, some fought verbally against it, and Tsar Nicholas at least foresaw its eventual abolition. But few if any in the years between 1801 and the post-Crimean era lived with the expectancy that it would soon disappear. That bonded labor defined Russian society in manifold ways can be no news to Russian historians. That it also undergirded and even shaped much of its culture directly and indirectly is perhaps not so well known. To speak of only the most obvious effect, it gave hundreds of amateur poets, dramatists, composers, musical performers, painters, and other art figures among the nobility the leisure and the means to create. The literary character, Matvei Kirsanov from Turgenev's *Fathers and Sons*, represented hundreds if not thousands of real-life counterparts who pursued music as a domestic hobby and recreation.

What noble landowners and serf-owners produced by proxy, in the form of serf creative labor, loomed even larger. Lords of rural manor houses and urban mansions, beginning in the mid-eighteenth century, harnessed whatever talent they could find on their estates and trained them in the arts. Serf choruses regaled noble families and their dinner guests at table.

The eccentric Count Skavronsky required all his servants to address him only in the form of operatic recitative rather than in speech. Individual musicians exhibited their skills for the master and his neighbors. Whole orchestras were composed exclusively of serf musicians. Some of these, when intermixed with noble amateurs, took on great symphonic works of the time, including a cycle of Beethoven concerts performed on an estate deep in the provinces during the 1820s. More commonly, serf orchestras supplemented the serf theaters that sprang up in the late eighteenth century and continued to function in some places right up to emancipation. On the boards, serf men and women acted out the roles of Carthaginian queens or Celtic warriors in opera and drama, or of villains and victims in adapted European melodramas. The permanent theaters erected by such magnates as the Yusupovs and the Sheremetevs ranked with those in the capital in elegance and construction and in the production values of décor and costumes. On occasion, land-owners purchased individual serf artists and performers and even entire orchestras or theatrical troupes. Thousands of serf painters, sculptors, and skilled decorators served their masters on the estates. To have one's own serf portraitist in residence was an emblem of chic. Until 1817 and occasionally afterwards, wealthy lords sent their serfs to the St. Petersburg Academy of Arts for training and then brought them back into servitude.

The question of how far serf artists could go in self-expression and mobility became a major moral issue among those liberal nobles committed to human justice and free development. Violinists, singers, or painters trained to the highest degree of artistry, sometimes even abroad, could not only be forced to spend their lives isolated in the service of a rural estate, but—at the master's whim—could have their lives reversed and ruined by being reassigned to the field or the pantry. Scandals and exposures of abuse arose periodically and fed many a work of fiction dealing with the tragic fate of the unfree artists. Aside from Alexander Herzen's story "The Thieving Magpie," most of these works are long forgotten. Painful incidents of wasted talent led a circle of humanitarian aristocrats to form a society in the 1820s dedicated to buying freedom for talented serf artists and financially supporting them. Prominent artists of the Academy, such as Karl Bryullov and Alexei Venetsianov, helped to wrest the vital document of manumission from a stubborn serf-owner for the talented artist Taras Shevchenko, later famed as the great Ukrainian writer and national hero. Women suffered double jeopardy in the world of serf performance: the truly gifted ones as artists enchained to a particular household; all of them as potential targets of sexual abuse. Certain serf theaters became notorious as nothing more than facades for a serf harem. The luckiest serf performers, aside from those few who were set free, gained permission to act in the network of provincial theater troupes that emerged early in the century and were run as businesses by private entrepreneurs. By 1861 a hundred or more stages were staffed partly by serfs on a system of non-estate labor which freed them to move around, earn money, and pay the requisite fee (*obrok*) to the master. By the time of the emancipation, the vast bulk of theatrical life in Russia was to be found on the provincial circuit.

Western scholars have sometimes divided in their judgment as they weighed the immense cultural production of serfs, sometimes at a high level, against the suffering of unfree painters, musicians, and actors. Soviet historians of the arts deftly faced the issue with a simultaneous (if often muted and generic) condemnation of servitude with a proud exaltation of the art produced. Since the collapse of the USSR, Russian scholarship has tended to stress the latter over to the former.

The Russian state had relatively little control over or interest in the vast world of the provincial stage or of culture produced on manorial estates. Its principal art-producing and art-training institutions were the state-owned Imperial Theater system, the Academy of Arts, and the Capella or Court Choir. The Imperial Theaters—three houses in St. Petersburg and two in Moscow—held a monopoly over the theatrical life of the two capitals until the 1880s. The Academy, founded by Catherine II and still standing proudly on the banks of the Neva, modeled itself on the French academy in organization, terminology, and curriculum and ran an outpost in Rome for advanced students. The Capella, sited right off the Moika River near the Winter Palace, specialized in sacred choral music. All of these cultural institutions drew upon the lower classes for students and staff but in varying degrees. The Capella, where composer Mikhail Glinka once worked, drew a large contingent of its boy singers from Ukraine, usually purchased serfs. Students at the Theater School came from the lower ranks of society, including serfs, orphans, children of soldiers, and townspeople. The serfs within these groups were set free upon entering state training programs. The Academy was more complicated. It drew from the nobility as well as from the social strata of the other schools, but serf pupils remained unfree unless emancipated by their owners. In 1817 they were officially excluded. Choirboys were shunted into free but servile occupations when their voices changed. Graduating artists could achieve, fame, fortune, and even social standing, depending on talent. Actors could achieve even greater fame, but not fortune since they were low paid by the state. They also remained, as elsewhere in Europe, shadowed by social and moral taboos, with no chance of social prominence.

Serious instrumental, symphonic concert music—the least

studied of all the arts in Russia—lacked any kind of state school or institutional roof until 1862, with the founding of the St. Petersburg Conservatory. Concert societies abounded, some of them with nominal court sponsorship or nomenclature. But most classical music activity in this era remained a private affair of amateurs and schools. Promising composers like Glinka and Anton Rubinstein went abroad for advanced training. Noble dilettantes hired foreign tutors for themselves or for their serfs. Thus, while "good" European music was being heard all over the empire in homes and in halls where foreign virtuosos, including Franz Liszt and Hector Berlioz, performed, no professional training center existed in Russia for would-be professional composers and musicians. One result was the long lasting dominance of German symphonic players.

The national and aesthetic content of the art produced in Russia during this period is a subject so vast, that only a few sketchy remarks may be offered here. Literature is treated elsewhere in the volume. Two waves of national expression overtook Russia. During the Napoleonic Wars, dramatists turned their plays into thinly veiled patriotic diatribes or even outright chauvinistic ballet scenes of drama or music. Graphic artists took on the French enemy with scorching satire, though academic canvases continued to ply the compulsory mythological, historical, and biblical themes. Nobles rushed to learn their "native" tongue and to do folk dances as Gallophobia reached its zenith. But this quickly attenuated after the 1812-1814 wars. Under Nicholas I, when no national threat loomed up, the impulse came from above in the doctrine of Official Nationalism; and from within in the historical dramas of Nestor Kukolnik and Nikolai Polevoi and Glinka's opera, *A Life for the Tsar* (1836)-many of them set during the Time of Troubles in the seventeenth century when Russia was threatened by Polish invasion.

Painters, weary of the stringent rules of the Academy—though without breaking from it—turned to Russian genre subjects: interiors, villages, taverns, street scenes of the big city. In the 1840s and especially the 1850s, "realism" came into vogue and was yoked to Russianness of content and style. The merchant plays of Alexander Ostrovsky and the peasant plays of Alexei Pisemsky marked a culmination in the search for what was considered authentic national expression in theater. Beneath all of these forms of cultural production—high, middle, and sometimes, low— the folk culture of the Russian peasantry—crafts, songs, dances, tales—continued along in its timeless fashion, quite distinct from the forms of art practiced in the capitals and provincial towns and estates. Only later did this rich body of popular expression get co-opted and adapted on a major scale by a new generation of artists, choreographers, and composers.

The Flowering of the Arts, 1861-1900

Needless to say, this period far outshines the previous one in terms of the lasting fame of its cultural creations. Not only did Tolstoy and Dostoevsky enter the mainstream of European culture, but so did Tchaikovsky and a few other composers. The break should not be exaggerated. Creators during the reigns of Alexander II and III (1855-1894) built upon the accumulated experiences from the age of serfdom—including the widespread practice of amateurism in music and performance. More important, certain myths need to be explored and in some cases exploded in order to understand the full richness and complexity of the cultural landscape.

One of these myths concerns the alleged long lasting and un-bridgeable schism between the authentic Russian national music of the Mighty Five and the "imported," Western styles of Tchaikovsky and other luminaries of the conservatory system. The story in out-line is well known. Anton Rubinstein, a professional piano virtu-oso and composer, got the ear of influential courtiers in the 1850s and convinced them to back a conservatory which opened in St. Petersburg in 1862, followed soon by one in Moscow. On the heels of this, the circle of Mily Balakirev started the Free Music School as a counter-conservatory where advanced technique and musicology were underplayed and Russianness promoted—in contrast to the Germanic faculty and styles of the conservatories. The Balakirev group eventually crystallized under the nickname, *kuchka* (fist or handful)—or Mighty Five: Balakirev, Modest Musorgsky, Alexan-der Borodin, Nikolai Rimsky-Korsakov, and Cesar Cui.

In theory more than in practice the Five stressed their sponta-neous self-taught character, a holdover of the amateurism of the past. Indeed, all but Balakirev long held positions wholly outside music—Musorgsky and Cui as army officers, Rimsky-Korsakov as a naval officer, and Borodin as a chemistry professor. The initial rivalry between the Five and the Conservatory was marked by some ugly outpourings among some of the Balakirev followers of chauvinism and even anti-Semitism aimed at Rubinstein. The obsessive focus on the schism obscures several things. Tchaikovsky won the friendship of some of these men, including Rimsky-Korsakov who actually became a conservatory professor. Interaction among the two groups was common; both groups of composers employed native motifs as well as Western orchestration in their works, though certainly Musorgsky in particular moved much further away from accepted musical forms in his masterpieces-the operas *Boris Godunov* and *Khovanshchina.* But Cui, the most vociferous of the Five in his "nationalism," also wrote the most eclectic music. Indeed the cross-fertilization engendered much of the genius in both schools and raised Russian art music to a level comparable to the best in Europe in the late nineteenth century.

Beyond the two capitals and often impervious to the rivalries there, musical life unfolded and spread to the provinces at a rapid rate in the late nineteenth century. The growth of local conservatories and concert societies, the freeing of the serfs, and the outreach of the railway network all contributed to the rise in musical activity and public consciousness. The St. Petersburg Conservatory set dozens of virtuosos on their way to world renown. The city of Odessa became a virtual fountain of brilliant Russian Jewish violinists. Keyboard and orchestral virtuosity was not far behind as the world was soon to learn.

Another schism—the Wanderers vs. the Academy painters—has also suffered distortions. In 1863, fourteen Academy artists, led by Ivan Kramskoi, declined the academy's degree and set out on their own. The issue was the assignment for final examination of a mythological theme. In the conventional account, the dissenters formed the school of Traveling Exhibits (thus the misnomer Wanderers or *Peredvizhniki*), spread art throughout provincial Russia, and introduced Russian national themes and social criticism in their realist canvases from the 1860s onward. In fact few of the Fourteen became members of the Wanderers, a group formed seven years after the mutiny. Though often compared to the radical Populists (*Narodniki*) who in the 1870s "went out to the people" to stir up revolution, the painters did not settle among the rural masses but rather took their shows to various provincial towns—certainly a factor in the emergence of art consciousness and an art market. But their break with the Academy has been overblown. Just as some Mighty Five composers made peace with the conservatories, so some Wanderers returned to their alma mater to teach. The Academy and the Wanderers often exhibited together in St. Petersburg and in the provinces as well. And the vaunted theme of social protest among the latter soon gave way to more neutral landscape art, historical canvases, and various kinds of national thematics. For all of their innovations, the early Wanderers owed much of their technique if not their subject matter to the school that had trained them. In terms of world reputation, however, the painters gained much less in their own time than did the composers of the Russian national school.

The key figure in the transformation of Russian theater, Alexander Ostrovsky, virtually ruled the stage in the 1860s and 1870s and for a long time after his death as well. He launched his dramatic career with a series of plays about merchant life in Moscow and the provinces, culminating in *The Storm* (1860). Well-known is the stir among the radical intelligentsia, represented by Nikolai Dobrolyubov who interpreted his plays as a social critique of mean-spirited merchants. But Ostrovsky's advent also launched a brief though little known, schism between those actors of the Imperial Theater who took to his down-to-earth realistic characters, with their often crude language and gestures, and the more staid performers who resented the smell of caftans and greased boots. Ostrovsky widened his dramaturgy, turned the footlights on a whole spectrum of social classes and everyday life, and became the most performed of all Russian playwrights in his native land. Largely due to his efforts, the tsarist regime ended the theater monopoly in the two capitals in the 1880s. The cultural specificity of his work, a delight to Russian audiences, has never had success on foreign shores. Late nineteenth-century musical theater, however, was to have spectacular renown around the world. The operas of Musorgsky, Tchaikovsky, and Rimsky-Korsakov have been captivating foreign audiences for a century. Russian classical ballet, thanks to the choreographical genius of Marius Petipa and the music of Tchaikovsky and others, has had even greater success.

Two elements of society outside the ring of elevated artistic creators contributed to the efflorescence of high Russian culture in this era. Russian merchants, much maligned by the intelligentsia in their time, began roughly at mid-century patronizing Russian contemporary art, particularly painting. Among many, Pavel Tretyakov stands out as one of the seminal figures in sustaining the work of late nineteenth century Russian painters, particularly those of the Wanderers school. Merchants also avidly supported theater, both in its traditional habitat (especially the Moscow Maly Theater) and in their own lavish homes where opera and other arts were performed and supported. Even classical music won the material favor of wealthy merchants and businessmen, particularly Mitrofan Belyaev. Soviet historians, for obvious reasons, underplayed or explained away the impressive role of Russian merchants in the art world. In recent years, Russian and western investigators have produced numerous volumes on the life of the merchantry, its role in society, and its patronage of the arts, thus addressing a long neglected aspect of the social history of art.

The peasant played a very different role in Russian high art, chiefly as the object of yet another "discovery" of Russian rural national life. Beginning in this period and quickening after 1900, composers and painters sought out the eternal values of their culture in village life. Patronizing distortions, clichés, and romanticization aside, the artists who drew on folk themes to inspire their muses contributed enormously to the images that elites—both Russian and foreign—came to have of Russian national life.

An Age of Silver and Electricity

The upsurge of urbanization, acceleration of industry, and new technology such as the movie camera, rotogravure, electricity, trains, and cars added to the cumulative complexity of Russian society, and of its cultural output. The explosion of the mass circulation press, loosening of the censorship after 1905, and magnified contacts with Western Europe and other parts of the globe added their force to the widening awareness of the world among creators and consumers. Something like an art market throbbed in Moscow and St. Petersburg, floated by new money. The Wanderers and the Academy continued their own traditions—both realistic and eclectic—but new styles and foreign products began to crowd them. The *World of Art*, a journal and a movement launched by Sergei Diaghilev and his colleagues brought fresh new painting and illustration styles into vogue. The Russian *moderne*, paralleling the European Art nouveau, Sezession, and den Stil, dipped deeply into Russian folk, religious, and medieval themes as well as oriental and decadent art. Symbolist poetry inspired striking, dream-like and allusive canvases, posters, and magazine covers. The rash of periodicals that erupted during the Revolution of 1905 utilized neo-Gothic approaches in order to terrify viewers and comment on the bloody repressions of the tsarist regime. The enormous upsurge of sexual topics in all the arts led illustrators to depict Russia as innocent but voluptuous nude young women being devoured by dragon-like creatures representing the authorities. In the half decade or so before the Great War, numerous new schools of avant-garde painting, some suggested by Russian poetry, jostled one another for attention: Neo-Primitivism, Rayonism, Cubo-Futurism, Constructivism. The riot of brash and creative innovation of this era would continue on into the post-Revolutionary age for some time—in particular those aspects of Futurism and Constructivism that deified speed, machinery, and modern urban life.

Architecture, which had suffered somewhat from uninspired eclecticism and Victorian clutter after the glorious age of the Empire style, c. 1800-1850, experienced a powerful pseudo-traditional revival matched by modernist sensibilities in the works of Fedor Shekhtel and other masters whose railroad stations and mansions of the affluent stand as monuments to lavish imagination, attentive scholarship, and sound engineering principles.

Under the acknowledged leadership and tuition of Nikolai Rimsky-Korsakov at the St. Petersburg Conservatory, the established forms of Tchaikovsky and the Five continued to dominate classical music, privileging national themes done up in a brilliant orchestral palette and fashioned into operas and tone poems based on Russian folklore. Sergei Rachmaninov and Alexander Glazunov appeared as faithful guardians and developers of these traditions, the latter in symphonic and choral works, the former in many genres. The odd man out in this period, Alexander Scriabin, in what was labeled a mystical impressionistic manner, broke with the conventions and produced exotic music that even to this day defies categorization. In the meantime, the flood of virtuosos and conductors took Russian music all over the country and abroad. One of the cultural tragedies of this era, the escalation of anti-Semitism and pogroms, led many of these figures who were of Jewish background to emigrate, thus enriching the world with their spectacular talents. War and revolution would hurl other more prominent figures out of their land of birth: conductor Sergei Koussevitsky and violinist Nathan Milstein, to mention only two, and a number of popular song writers and film composers.

On the musical stage, it can justly be said that Russia produced a dance art that conquered the world. Diaghilev—an impresario with refined taste rather than an artist himself—brought together one of the most sparkling collections of talents in the history of that art: designers Leon Bakst and Alexandre Benois; the composer Stravinsky; the choreographer Michel Fokine; and the dancers Anna Pavlova, Tamara Karsavina, and Vaclav Nijinsky—among many others. They took Paris by storm with *Petrushka*, *The Firebird*, and *The Rites of Spring.* In the last, the unheard-of tonalities and rhythms of Stravinsky's music and the deliberately "barbaric" movements of the dancers did indeed unleash a storm of both praise and abuse at its scandalous premier in Paris in 1913—a landmark in the history of modern performance that has made an indelible mark on world culture.

So too did the advent of the Moscow Art Theater founded by Konstantin Stanislavsky and Vladimir Nemirovich-Danchenko in 1897. The two most famous dramatists whose works they staged, Anton Chekhov and Maxim Gorky, pulled in audiences on five continents. Although Gorky's depiction of "the lower depths" and his premonitions of class struggle were of their own time, they were later exalted in Soviet culture and thus migrated to the stages of other communist-dominated countries. With no need of state sponsorship, Chekhov's *Uncle Vanya*, *Cherry Orchard*, and *Three Sisters* still live on due to the universal appeal of ordinary upper and middle class people adrift in a world they do not understand. But

Stanislavsky's greatest impact on theater was in the realm of acting. In his repertory company, there were "no small roles, only small actors." He erected an invisible "fourth wall" and fitted his stage with authentic furnishing in order to approach the fullness of illusion. He devised a "system" of acting that required psychological depth and plausible gestures in order to fight the still clinging habit or declamation and playing to the audience. His ideas came to be immensely influential, particularly in the United States where Lee Strassberg adapted some of the master's techniques into his own "method acting" in New York, a style that still prevails on American movie screens. In the prerevolutionary era, the daring avant-garde director Vsevolod Meyerhold challenged Stanislavsky's stage realism with his contrasting "modernist" theories of audience participation, stylized movements, and extravagant material in a "theater as theater" without illusions.

Popular culture, a problematic term, came into play on a large scale as a basically urban phenomenon appealing to mass tastes, from the middle to the lower classes. Gypsy music, tango dancing, and "cruel songs" met the needs of those who would never see a concert or opera. Pulp fiction of adventure, comedy, and melodrama created a mass readership in Russia for the first time, thus providing some clues about popular values and tastes. Those themes were taken up by the new medium of cinema in the period from 1908 (the year of the first Russian feature film) to 1917. Recently, scholars in Russia, Britain, Italy, and America have also revived and restored a number of film masterpieces, revealing the long unknown genius of cinematic directors of the period. The term *estrada* embraced circus, nightclub, cabaret, and other popular stages. All these forms, taken together made up the vast bulk of the culture consumed in the pre-revolutionary years, far exceeding in audience the elite forms of high culture for which the world now remembers that era. An even tinier cultural output, radical subculture, appealed to revolutionaries and their working-class clients and consisted of protest songs and placards held aloft during strikes and demonstrations. This largely underground corner of culture had very little impact on the population at the time as did the ephemeral patriotic propaganda broadsheets, cartoons, and stories of the Russo-Japanese War.

For a long time, historians tended to focus on the dark side of prewar culture—the Symbolist poets' apocalyptic visions of total destruction, novels of eroticism and suicide, and decadent themes in graphic art. By examining the broad cultural landscape, high and popular, recent scholarship has painted a more complex picture, one of many cultures and taste communities, numerous genres free of cosmic pessimism, and narrative plots about normal life, exploration, comic situations, and even self-revelation. While the study of culture alone can offer no absolute key to the "social health" of a nation in any given era, a broad based approach to it can at least challenge the one-sided impression, drawn exclusively from fin-de-siècle thematics, of a civilization doomed to destruction.

The Ill-Tempered Revolution

The provocative ruptures of Silver Age culture seem tame compared to those instituted by the Bolsheviks who came to power in Russia in 1917. Though the record was jagged and uneven, certain forms of expression were attacked all through the first revolutionary decade, particularly after the Civil War (1918-21). During the years of NEP or New Economic Policy (1921-29), when the authorities had the time and energy to launch their assaults, critics assailed artistic production that seemed to them "un-socialist" because it was associated with Old Regime Russia, bourgeois Europe and America, or the "backward" Russian peasantry. Self-styled "proletarian" groups in literature, music, architecture, and other arts led the attack, though they were not uniformly backed by the political leaders. Musical life provided the most vivid battleground in the cultural wars. Roughly five kinds of music found themselves under the gun: traditional classical music for its links to the despised Russian and European past; modernist music (atonalists, for example) for its inaccessibility; urban song for its alleged petty-bourgeois lapses in taste; folk music for its identification with the" idiocy of the countryside"; and religious music for its obvious polarity with an atheist regime. Siding with the proletarian position, a group known as the Engineerists fostered machine music played on factory equipment. It enjoyed little success due to the reaction of workers who had no interest in hearing concerts made from the sounds of their workplace. The Russian Association of Proletarian Musicians fought these forms vigorously in favor of their own brand of proper musical expression—the proletarian choir singing revolutionary songs. Even so, the conservatories continued training and performance in the classical styles; restaurant bands blared away with jazzy dance tunes and sobbing gypsy songs; and a few Russian modernists composed variants on serial or atonal music.

The music wars were paralleled in the other arts, and the result—as in music—was an uneasy, if brilliant, mosaic of all kinds of experimental and traditional forms. Revolutionary mystery plays, working class Blue Blouse and TRAM productions, Meyerhold's biomechanical displays, and Stanislavsky's theater all fed into the theatrical scene of the 1920s. Detective and science fiction tales often found more readers than novels about the revolution. Great cinematic geniuses such as Sergei Eisenstein emerged with films of revolutionary spectacle, marked by innovative editing and casting, while masses of urbanites preferred imported movies such as *The Thief of Baghdad* or *Robin Hood*. The world of graphic art became inhabited by the most advanced ideas in representation. And both architecture and poetry succumbed to the craze for ultramodern Futurism. Since Bolshevism promoted a Marxist ideology of industry, urbanism, and machines, even the most daring of the experimental arts seemed to fit that mindset—however alien they might seem to ordinary people. With the coming of the Cultural Revolution of 1928-31, the proletarian activists attempted to shut down all styles of art and culture not congenial to their single-minded and maximalist view of society and culture; and their temporary successes threw a blanket of conformity and fear over almost all cultural production.

From the ascension of Stalin onward, official Soviet writers about the 1920s tended to dismiss the more adventurous cultural outpourings as hopelessly utopian and even harmful to the working class. Indeed many practitioners of the Soviet avant-garde of the NEP period were repudiated and even exterminated in the 1930s. By contrast, Western students of literature, cinema, poetry, theater, and the fine arts saw that earlier revolutionary period as an age of giants, the last great display of Russian creative genius—equivalent in its way to the Weimar period in German history. Political historians in the West have divided in a different way. Those associated with the totalitarian school saw the 1920s as nothing more than a prelude to Stalinism. A good deal of its cultural achievements, they correctly maintain, lauded the values of communism. Those that did not were constantly harassed or were able to flourish because the government was too busy with other pressing matters. This kind of teleological argument—with always one eye gazing toward the coming Gulag system—is fueled by a top-down view of history, emphasizing power rather the creators themselves who are seen as either irrelevant or doomed. The problem with such arguments is that they tend to dismiss or demean one of the most protean moments, with all its flaws, in Russian cultural history.

Invented and Revived Traditions: The Stalin Era

For various reasons—some unconnected with culture per se—Stalin and his confederates in turn shut down the Cultural Revolution in the early 1930s, calling it nihilistic and "petty-bourgeois." New cultural chiefs introduced two principles to replace it: Socialist Realism and mass culture. The first originally concerned itself with literature. A congress of writers, including Gorky who had returned from emigration, declared after much debate that Soviet literature must have the double aim of describing reality and projecting the world to come. The main formulae of Socialist Realism were partly derived from Gorky's pre-revolutionary works, such as *Mother* (1906), and some Soviet novels of the 1920s. Banished wholly from this new corpus were excessive introspection, decadence, pessimism, overt sexuality, racism, religious themes, and most speculation about the distant future (as in the science fiction of the 1920s). Required were positive heroes of either sex who surmounted obstacles along their way to building socialism, in a plot that ended on an upbeat. This "masterplot" often included an older and more seasoned mentor who cooled the excessive hot blood of youth and showed them the proper way to proceed. The same approach informed many dramas and films of the 1930s, as well as paintings that contained narrative elements. Optimism and the triumph of light over darkness became de rigueur. Avant-garde daring and complexity (usually decried as "formalism") was jettisoned in favor of mass accessibility.

But the canons of Socialist Realism did not account for all of the culture of the Stalinist era. Certain traditions held firm all through the turbulent 1920s and even the Cultural Revolution. Others slipped back in. Classical symphonic music of the past, the ballets of Marius Petipa and Tchaikovsky, and the operas from the Russian and European repertoire were exalted by the Soviet regime. It paid outstanding artists well and even titled them and it subsidized their institutional homes: the Leningrad Philharmonia, the Moscow State Orchestra, the Kirov and Bolshoi Theaters. Othello, Medea, and Don Carlos trod the stages of dramatic theaters. Stanislavsky and his method reigned supreme at the Moscow Art Theater. Various operetta, children's, and estrada theaters catered to a broad public with a minimum of political message. Through the new medium of radio, all these offerings were broadcast throughout the population of the 11 republics of that decade. To the extent that these forms were part of what has been called "the Great Retreat" they by no means represented a social-political reaction or revival of Old Regime values. Rather they represented what is long familiar to historians as social mimicry and cross over. "Bourgeois" values can often be found where there is no bourgeoisie in the usual sense. Like gentrification, it represented social striving though the medium of taste or distinction. The Soviet leaders had been lower or lower middle class revolutionaries and journalists with little in the way of refined upbringing. Once in power, they donned the attributes of a ruling elite and cloaked the alleged socialist content of the system with mixed signs of humble origins (clothing and language) and high style (opera attendance). For Stalin himself, this also meant the escalation of the personality cult of the leader inaugurated in 1929 to massive proportions from the 1930s onward.

"Mass culture"—particularly in film and song—compressed and popularized these themes by means of widespread distribution in simpler languages. Celebration of socialist construction, enthusiastic youth, explorers, and aviators shaped many of the mass songs and movies of the era. Even the very popular and often zany musical comedies of Grigory Alexandrov—such as *Happy-Go-Lucky Guys* (a jazz musical), *Circus*, and *Volga, Volga*—with their superstars and singable tunes, smuggled in sermons promoting Soviet values of loyalty, hard work, and upward mobility. By the mid-1930s however, jazz music was associated with decadence and either out-lawed or sweetened and sanitized beyond recognition. As a whole, the Stalinist cultural genres worked together, mutually reinforcing the ideology and accepted mores of the regime. Since virtually all means of public cultural expression were tightly controlled, and even subject to creative command, no alternatives were available to the population and no flood of imported arts threatened to erode the system.

Until the appearance of a masterful history by S. Frederick Starr of Soviet jazz in the 1980s, popular and mass culture of the Stalin era went almost completely unnoticed by historians. That book loosed a flood of works on the topic among Western historians. Beginning with the new openness inaugurated by Mikhail Gorbachev in the late 1980s, Russians who lived through the cultural life of the Stalin era voiced conflicting opinions about it. Critics, stressing that mass culture covered up the horrors of the period, deemed it no more than false propaganda supporting an evil system. Defenders recalled the joy that songs and movies brought to the masses in troublous times. As memories faded and debates lost their ideological edge after the collapse of the Soviet Union, Stalinist mass culture was transformed into a kind of retroactive system of campy and kitschy artifacts and marketed for nostalgia value.

A certain degree of erosion did set in, however, during the Great Patriotic War of 1941-45, though even here it occurred in the context of top-down policies. Knowing full well that emotion trumped abstraction in a deep crisis such as war, the leaders partly underplayed Marxist rhetoric (without ever abandoning Communist ideology) in favor of compromises with religion, exaltation of historical figures, old-fashioned patriotism, and friendship with the Allies. Stalin abolished the League of the Godless, founded in the 1920s, and made a deal with the Orthodox Church. Religious persecution virtually ceased and some churches were reopened. In return, the Metropolitan of Moscow praised Stalin as the leader of the nation's cultural forces and urged parishioners to lend full support to the regime and the war effort. The ease-up on Russia's ancient faith fit perfectly with a reemphasis on traditional Russian, as opposed to Soviet, patriotism. Stalin's speech of November 7, 1941, invoked military and cultural giants of the past. The regime issued a mammoth print run of Lev Tolstoy's novel of the 1812 invasion of Russia by Napoleon, *War and Peace,* and the stirring strains of Tchaikovsky's symphonies were heard all over the land. Urban-production themes gave way to rural ones. Poetry, films, and songs drew on the rich imagery of Russian landscape, small town, home and family life. The personal and emotional held sway over the bombastic styles of the 1930s. The most harrowing and affecting war films personalized the struggle by framing it around the lives and tragedies of female martyrs and partisan leaders.

Official views of foreign powers underwent two jarring shifts. Through most of the 1920s and 1930s, an era that Kremlin leaders perceived as one of "capitalist encirclement," they saw Nazi, fascist, authoritarian, and democratic governments as no more than variants of each other. By the mid-1930s, Nazi Germany took its place as the preeminent menace, reflected in the 1938 Eisenstein film *Alexander Nevsky.* During the Nazi-Soviet Pact, 1939-41, anti-German propaganda was replaced by verbal assaults on Britain and France (until the latter fell to Hitler's armies in 1940). Artifacts such as the Eisenstein film were shelved. With the invasion of the USSR by the Third Reich, all this was reversed. Britain and, in December 1941, the United States were heralded as virtuous allies in the anti-fascist war for human justice. As a gesture of solidarity, Stalin in 1943 abolished the long dormant Comintern or Third International. The U.S. Lend Lease program hurled tons of trucks, vehicle parts, and canned food into the Soviet Union. Along with it came recordings of American jazz bands. Red Army and other jazz ensembles, now officially permitted, quickly emerged and gained enormous popularity among troops and civilians alike. Although the regime magnified official values once again after the Soviet victory at Kursk in 1943, the partial wartime "thaw" or softening of cultural rigidity continued to the end of the hostilities in 1945.

The postwar era, also Stalin's twilight years (1945-53), brought a renewed crackdown on Soviet culture. The leadership, speaking in the voice of high-ranking Party chief Andrei Zhdanov, lashed out at the creative community. Zhdanov attacked Anna Akhmatova for poetry published during the wartime relaxation of the rules; and Mikhail Zoshchenko for satirical sketches held to be anti-Soviet. At a congress of composers, Zhdanov took Shostakovich and Prokofiev to task for their abandonment of "correct" values in musical composition: flowing melody, national themes, a humane optimism, and accessibility. Some film makers sinned, it was claimed, by downplaying the role of the Communist Party in movies about the war. Jazz—once again officially linked to American decadence—came to an end. The campaign against cosmopolitanism took an even uglier turn when the wrath of the regime fell upon the Jewish intelligentsia. The arrests and executions and the closing of the few surviving Yiddish cultural institutions were politically motivated but had the effect of throwing a dank pall on an already constricted arena of creation and performance. Although this is the least studied period in Soviet cultural history, it seems certain that it was the most dismal and unoriginal; and that the crackdowns in all walks of life so dampened creative life that, right after Stalin's death, voices were raised in favor of more freedom.

Spring Thaws and Wintry Frosts: 1953-85

Soviet public culture after the death of Stalin evolved in fits and starts, though always within the general parameters established in the 1930s. In fiction, Stalinesque war novels and triumphalist celebrations lasted and even swelled through the Khrushchev and Brezhnev periods. Socialist realist production novels continued to appear as well. Yet in every branch of the arts, new sensibilities found their way into the open, fueled by postwar social and intellectual undercurrents. The frightful loss of males in the war, the resultant phenomenon of the "lonely women," the sheer exhaustion of the population, and the sharply diminished power of the urban-progressive myth of socialist construction all contributed in various ways to the new cultural thematics. The Khrushchev family reforms of the 1950s that eased up on divorce and abortion legislation of the 1930s, reflected the regime's—and the public's—recognition of the importance of private life and the private sphere. A series of what came to be called "women's films" took on deep and urgent questions about family life and women's daily burdens and emotional stresses. Filmmaker Kira Muratova was especially known for pursuing this examination in a series of sensitive films. The workplace came into view as something much more complicated and human than what was portrayed in the formulas of obstructionist bureaucrat-heroic struggler for the just way-wise mentor. The Thaw of the 1950s allowed novelists such as Ilya Ehrenburg and Vladimir Dudintsev to explore this life with greater honesty. Even World War II, one of the regimes sacred myths, received more complex treatment by filmmakers of the 1950s.

Two large audiences displayed a thirst for something more in culture than official slogans and prim performance. One was mature educated readers, urban and rural, who began to devour an emerging genre of fiction later known as "village prose." Novels and stories by writers such as Fedor Belov and Valentin Rasputin described in bleak terms a decaying countryside, scarred by environmental ruin and inhabited by hopeless characters—especially old women—lacking a future. By extension, much of village prose, by identifying rural life with the real Russia, was implicitly announcing the decline of the nation itself. Invoking old values of community, simplicity, and even religion, the authors of this genre were not so subtly repudiating the picture of a "radiant future" under Communism promised to the Russian and Soviet people since the first days of the Bolshevik Revolution. Partly because of its use of aesopian language, partly because it took no overt political position, and partly because Soviet leaders shared the sense of nostalgia emanating from village prose, its authors were not persecuted as dissidents.

On the urban front, quite another sense of dissatisfaction surfaced during the years of Khrushchev and Brezhnev: the need for self-expression and cultural products that titillated, aroused, amused, and entertained in a way that Soviet culture did not. Young folks, called style-hunters, chased after Western clothing, jazz (partly rehabilitated in the 1950s), and later rock. Bold creative spirits wanted to write controversial stories, artists to paint abstract pictures, poets to write non-canonical verses, actors to put on absurdist and outrageous plays. Novelists wrote for the drawer, knowing that their controversial works would never see light. The Khrushchev regime's rejection of Boris Pasternak's *Doctor Zhivago* and its allowance of Alexander Solzhenitsyn's *One Day in the Life of Ivan Denisovich* clearly framed the limits of dissent. Avant-garde art shows were berated by Khrushchev and physically wrecked by bulldozers under Brezhnev. Plays, pop concerts, dance hall events, and even school musicals were routinely closed down by snooping police or Young Communist patrols. One of the cultural tangents where state met youth was science fiction, a massively popular genre in the late twentieth century. SF in turn helped fuel young male enthusiasm for the regime's vaunted Scientific Technical Revolution and its space program. All these cultural contestations, combined with the import of Western rock and jeans, did not bring down the Soviet regime, as some observers have claimed. But they did set the stage for a large-scale public critique and repudiation of Soviet culture once the lid flew off. That happened after Mikhail Gorbachev came to power in 1985.

Two underground forms of cultural life have yet to be integrated into the history of the public culture in this thirty-year period: dissidence and prison camp life. Each has spawned numerous very valuable studies, but, since each also formed a counterculture in opposition to the official culture, links between the two spheres have yet to be explored in a systematic fashion. And, although many important works on various aspects of this Soviet Old Regime, 1953-1985, have enriched our picture of it, scholars have yet to produce a synoptic and interpretive overview.

Global and Local

Glasnost or openness, Gorbachev's first and most visible and audible change in Soviet life, was literally heard round the world. It upended the cinema industry, freed the press, allowed long forbidden Russian and foreign literary works to fill the bookstalls, sanctioned huge and sometimes rowdy rock concerts, and permitted virtually every kind of artistic expression short of pornography (and sometimes even that) and outright racism (though that popped up as well). The year 1989 seemed to mark the pinnacle of the most exciting period in modern Russian cultural ferment. The excitement lay not so much in the quality of the output but rather in the conflict among a whole array of artistic goods on offer. Never before or since had Russians seen so much open, public, and legally sanctioned combat in the arts. Except for a few cranky voices, the Silver Age had produced little friction between high and popular culture, between Russian and foreign, or among various realms of art—folk, high popular—though within each branch of the arts debates had raged. In the headiness of the revolutionary decade, c. 1917-29, each brand of radicalism frowned at its rivals, and they all deplored "bourgeois" culture. But few voices defending those being attacked could be heard. Apostles of "decadence" were gone or silenced. With glasnost, things were different. All sides were given voice, and the cacophony possessed a healthy intonation of totally free debate.

Since the fall of Soviet power in 1991 and the founding of the Russian Republic, cultural issues, with some exceptions, have not raised the ire of critics the way they had a few years earlier. Russia, with all its faults and distortions, enjoys a normal cultural climate with its expected feuds and egos, its snooty elitists and its envelope pushers. Only the future will tell us if the lean towards more control and authoritarianism in the government treatment of the media will descend into cultural obscurantism and reaction.

Original publication: In Elina Kahla, ed. *The Unlimited Gaze: Essays in Honour of Professor Natalia Baschmakoff*. Helsinki: Kikimora Publications, 2009, pp. 2-29.

II

PORTRAITS OF REVOLUTION

Futurology and Science Fiction

Rituals and Symbols

Futurology and Science Fiction

7

Fantasy and Revolution
Alexander Bogdanov and the Origins of Bolshevik Science Fiction

"Blood is being shed [down there] for the sake of a better future," says the Martian to the hero of *Red Star* as they are ascending to Mars. "But in order to wage the struggle we must *know* that future." The blood he speaks of was the blood of workers shot down in the streets of St. Petersburg, of revolutionaries put against the wall of prison courtyards, of insurgent sailors and soldiers, of Jewish victims of pogroms in the Russian Revolution of 1905. And by "that better future" he means not the immediate outcome of the revolution but the radiant future of socialism that will dawn on earth after the revolution has triumphed everywhere. In order to inspect the coming socialist order, the hero—a Bolshevik activist named Leonid—has accepted the invitation of a Martian visitor to fly with him and his crew to Mars.

In this manner Alexander Bogdanov, a major prophet of the Bolshevik movement and one of its most versatile writers and thinkers, begins his utopian science fiction novel *Red Star*, first published in 1908. The red star is Mars; but it is also the dream set to paper of the kind of society that could emerge on Earth after the dual victory of the scientific-technical revolution and the social revolution. Bogdanov, a professional revolutionary, was one of those people, peculiar to revolutionary societies of our century, who moved easily back and forth between the barricade and the study table, the prison cell and the laboratory. He was a physician and a man of science; and he was the first in Russian fiction to combine a technical utopia, grounded in the latest scientific theories of the time, with the ideas of revolutionary Marxism. This was the central theme of both *Red Star* and his other novel, *Engineer Menni*.

★

Bogdanov's revolutionary Martian fantasy grew out of his personal experiences as a Marxist during the Revolution of 1905, the popularity of science fiction in Russia around the turn of the century, and his still developing theory of tectology, the science of systems thinking and organization. Bogdanov was born in Tula in 1873 to an educated family, studied science and psychology in Moscow and Kharkov, and received a medical degree in 1899. By that time he had also become a Populist and then a Marxist. On the surface, Bogdanov's path from medicine to revolution appears typical of radical Russians of that age in that so many of them—Mark Natanson, Fëdor Dan, Vera Figner, among others—had begun their love affair with "the people" by learning how to cure their physical illnesses. Unlike most of them, Bogdanov did not abandon science for revolution: rather, he deepened and extended his study of physiology, technology, and natural science and combined them with his own version of Marxian sociology. An early member of the Marxist Russian Social Democratic Party—the matrix of Bolshevism and Menshevism—Bogdanov worked as an underground agent, fomenting agitation and disseminating propaganda among workers, students, and educated society in Moscow as well as in provincial towns far distant from the two capitals. In terms of on-the-spot experience, he was one of the best informed of the Social Democrat leaders about actual life and labor conditions in Russian cities. As a physician he was also keenly aware of the social misery of poor people in the burgeoning factory centers of industrializing Russia. His repugnance for the contemporary city reveals itself in his loving description of the utopian factory settlements of *Red Star* and the dreadful working conditions in *Engineer Menni*. Numerous arrests and terms in exile punctuated his revolutionary career, and these experiences—often called the university education of radicals—threw him into contact with like-minded young thinkers and rebels such as Anatol Lunacharsky, future Bolshevik Commissar of Education and Culture, Fëdor Bazarov, a well-known economist, and I. I. Skvortsov-Stepanov, publicist, economist, and writer on atheism.

When the newly formed Russian Marxist party split into Bolsheviks and Mensheviks in 1903, Bogdanov—like the hero of *Red*

Star—chose the more impetuous and revolutionary current of Bolshevism headed by Lenin. Bogdanov was among the original Bolsheviks (not yet a separate party), one of those "twenty-two," with Lenin as the central figure, who fashioned in Switzerland early in 1904 a group dedicated to disciplined revolutionary action. In the stormy years of war and revolution from 1904 to 1907, Lenin and Bogdanov were close associates, with Lenin mostly in emigration and Bogdanov inside Russia organizing and directing the underground network of party cells and organizations. In 1905 the social unrest that had been brewing since the 1890s exploded in a revolution that swept over the vast expanse of the Russian land. In an unprecedented display of revolutionary energy, workers, peasants, soldiers, sailors, intellectuals, teachers, students, schoolchildren, priests, actresses, musicians, and people of every rank of society revolted; they demonstrated, shouted down their former masters, fought, struck, boycotted, burned out manor houses, and in every imaginable way disrupted society. In the midst of this ferment, Tsar Nicholas II issued a constitution and created a parliament. Then the authorities struck out with vengeful fury to punish the insurgents and restore order to the beleaguered empire. Martial law, drumhead trials and shootings, brutal punitive expeditions, and murderous repression of urban uprisings crushed the radical wing of the revolution and drowned it in blood.

Bogdanov, like thousands of other revolutionaries, was seized with the spirit of insurgence, heroism, and hope. He saw what superior military technology could do against insufficiently armed and organized revolutionary forces. And yet the revolutionary élan generated by the recent events was so highly developed that even in the summer of 1907, when the tide was visibly and rapidly ebbing, Bogdanov was still hoping for a resumption of action that would turn the tide again. This led him to a tactical quarrel with Lenin, who was convinced that the revolution was over. And it led Bogdanov to write *Red Star*—a novel of revolutionary optimism set in a far-distant utopia.

The spectacle of fire and devastation in the 1905 revolution formed the backdrop for Bogdanov's story. The revolution is the scene of the opening and the closing chapters, and it also underlies the fantasy world of Mars. The voyage itself and the accompanying technological explanations, though striking in predictive detail, were not wholly original. "Mars, gleaming red and hateful," had been the object of fascination to astronomers since antiquity. But the man most responsible for generating public speculation about life on Mars for almost a century was Giovanni Schiaparelli, whose observations in the late 1870s and early 1880s from a Milan observatory led him to use the word *canali* to indicate the straight lines he detected on the surface of the planet. The word, normally meaning channels or natural waterways, was quickly mistranslated as "canals," suggesting massive engineering projects, a huge labor force, and advanced minds (it had recently taken ten years to dig a hundred miles of the Suez Canal). The specter of human life on Mars was fleshed out by the American astronomer Percival Lowell, who claimed to have identified four hundred canals by 1900. His *Mars and Its Canals* (1906), with its depiction of a complex network of man-made waterways, great engineers, and a struggle against a dying environment, may have been a direct inspiration for Bogdanov.

The first novel to capitalize on Schiaparelli's "canals" was Percy Gregg's *Across the Zodiac*, which appeared in London in 1880, complete with "apergy"—an antigravity substance—huge canals, an engineer hero, advanced humans, and orange vegetation with red foliage, all discovered by human astronauts. More ambitious and plausible was Kurd Lasswitz's *Auf zwei Planeten* (1897), which brought large-eyed Martians to Earth. In an elaborate plot, Martians and Earthmen, Martian militarists and pacifists, are locked in friction. The issues are finally resolved in favor of democracy and peace. (A generation of German scientists was raised on this novel, although it was banned by the Nazis in the 1930s for its exaltation of internationalism and antimilitarism.) In 1897-98 also appeared the much more famous *War of the Worlds* by H. G. Wells, a writer who enjoyed enormous popularity in Russia at the time. Bogdanov in 1908 may have drawn from all of these, updating them with the latest speculation in science and technology, including the writings of the Russian rocketry pioneer Konstantin Tsiolkovsky. What Bogdanov added was a communist utopia on Mars.

But there was also a rich native tradition of utopian science fiction to draw from. From about 1890 to the eve of the Revolution of 1917, at least twenty Russian tales of utopian societies, fantastic voyages, and interstellar space travel appeared. Some of these were blatant copies of the numerous Western science fiction novels that were widely circulated and serialized in translation in the same period. Others drew on native Russian utopian dreams of the nineteenth century, such as Vladimir Odoevsky's *The Year 4338* (1840), Nicholas Chernyshevsky's *What is to Be Done?* (1863), and Vladimir Taneev's *The Communist State of the Future* (1879). Still others were antisocialist tracts written in the form of "warnings" of the danger of utopian collectivism, materialism, and a dehumanizing high technology—predecessors of the famous anticommunist dystopias of the mid-twentieth century: Eugene Zamyatin's *We* (1920), Aldous Huxley's *Brave New World* (1931), and George Orwell's *1984* (1948). In addition to these, scientific and popular science journals of the period were full of stories and speculations about rocketry, space travel, alien life, and new forms of energy and fuel. There is hardly anything in the technology of Leonid's voyage to Mars that did not appear either in scientific writings or in the science fiction of the period before 1907.

The industrialization of Russia in the 1890s and the accompanying growth of technology, transport, and urbanization opened up broad vistas for utopian speculation. A whole series of European and American utopias appeared in Russian translation between 1890 and 1905: the works of August Bebel, Friedrich Engels, Karl Kautsky, Atlanticus, and Lili Braun, with their exaltation of electricity, communal apartment living, and the technologizing of everyday life, captured the imagination of Russian socialists who were looking for the ultimate purpose of revolution to inspire themselves and their followers—a dream of a golden future where men and women could work, study, and love in total freedom, harmony, and community, liberated from the backwardness, poverty, and greed which had always tormented humanity. In this sense utopia was seen by Bogdanov (through the eyes of his hero) as a weapon in the arsenal of revolution: a snapshot of man's future that would dazzle the eye of the worker and inspire him more deeply than could the arid words of party programs.

Studies of reading habits in tsarist Russia have shown that the urban lower classes were far more interested in adventure tales than in polemical propaganda. Bogdanov, who had close connections with workers, knew this. And socialist writers had no monopoly on futuristic fantasy. In 1895 the engineer V. N. Chikolev wrote an "electric tale" of a coming world transformed by technology, particularly electricity, that could provide everything human life needed, including musical concerts. L. B. Afanasev's *Journey to Mars* (l901), on the other hand, was a warning against industrialization per se, whether capitalist or socialist. Using Martian society as a vehicle, the author related how the appearance of cities, roads, and factories turned the simple, primitive, trusting, rural Martians (read the peasants of Russia) into greedy, competitive, cannibalistic brutes and egoists—into what Afanasev called "the nervous society." More devastating yet was N. Fëdorov's *An Evening in the Year 2217* (1906), with numbered citizens, monstrous conformity, abolition of marriage and family, sex by appointment, and a lifeless socialist urban milieu of glass and stone—a virtual prototype for Zamyatin's *We.*

Bogdanov, in constructing his utopia on Mars, was not indifferent to the dangers of collectivism and high technology projected by some of the anti-utopian fantasies of the late tsarist epoch. He may well have had some of the dark warnings in mind as he set out to describe, through Leonid's narrative, the "self-adjusting" and socially just world on Mars. Indeed, he was acutely aware of the dreadful consequences of a premature revolution in a backward society. But a deep-seated belief in the rational power of "systems" prevented him from descending into the depths of social pessimism or cosmic fear—a feeling that enveloped many thinkers after the failure of the 1905 revolution.

Bogdanov's systems thinking, still developing when he wrote *Red Star*, eventually blossomed into a full-scale theory which he called "tectology." The term, borrowed from Ernst Haeckel, denoted a study of the regulatory processes and the organization of all systems, a "general natural science." As a physician and a political ideologist, Bogdanov was struck by the systemic analogies between living organisms and societies, between scientific and social organizations and processes. His main goal was to suggest a super-science of organization that would permit regulative mechanisms to preserve stability and prevent cataclysmic change in any of life's major processes—including the production and distribution of goods. As a Marxist he believed this to be possible only under a system of collective labor and collectivized means of production; but he also believed that Marx had to be updated by means of contemporary scientific and organizational discoveries. The complex theory of organization that he devised and revised in the 1910s, tectology, has often been cited as an early version of cybernetics or systems thinking. Thus one of the functions of *Red Star*, with its highly elaborate Martian system of feedback, information control and retrieval, statistics, protocomputers, regulation, and "moving equilibrium," was to lay out the author's first thoughts on the theory that has won him so much attention in recent years, both in the Soviet Union and in the world at large.

Bogdanov combined his Marxist convictions, his revolutionary experiences of 1905, and his facility for technological projection in his fantasy of life on Mars in the early twentieth century. Failed revolutions and even enforced isolation, as in a counterrevolutionary prison cell, have often produced free flights of fantasy. Nicholas Chernyshevsky wrote the famous utopian "Dream of Vera Pavlovna" in *What is to Be Done?* while languishing in the Peter Paul Fortress. The terrorist Nicholas Kibalchich designed a flying machine in 1881 while awaiting his execution (a crater on the Moon now bears his name). Nicholas Morozov, a long-time inhabitant of the Schlüsselburg Fortress prison, wrote in 1910 a lighthearted account of a voyage to the moon describing the joy of flight experienced by himself and his fellow astronauts—all former political convicts. The revolutionary euphoria that had seized so many thinkers and writers in the years 1905-07 and had produced so many apocalyptic visions and assorted dreams of an imminent New Jerusalem also permeated the spirit of Bogdanov and endowed his social vision with a sense of immediacy and hope. A rank-and-file Bolshevik of the period recalled that he and his comrades read Bogdanov's novel with enormous enthusiasm and saw it as a sign of renewed and triumphant revolutionary upheaval. What they overlooked at the time, as he later admitted, was the novel's principal theme: the organization of society in the socialist future. Yet the high drama of the work lies precisely in the wonderfully contrived juxtaposition of a unified, harmonious, serene, and rational life on Mars with the chaotic, barbarous, and self-destructive struggles of the peoples and social classes of the twentieth-century.

★

The vegetation on Bogdanov's Mars (as on Wells's) is red, and the hero calls it socialist vegetation. This is one of the few playful devices in the novel. For the most part *Red Star* is a straightforward science fiction utopia. Leonid, the protagonist, is a Bolshevik at the time of the 1905 Revolution caught up in political work and a dying romance. A mysterious comrade from the south of Russia revels himself as a Martian, explains his mission on Earth, and invites Leonid to Mars. The episodes of the Revolution and the voyages are the frame of the story; at its center is the description of Martian society. The irony, an almost invariable feature of science fiction utopias, is particularly sharp in the contrast between a Russia devoured by "problems" and a Mars where such problems have long since vanished.

In Russia, for example, three major problems that beset society and state were the peasant question, the national question, and the labor question. But on Mars there were no peasants. Farming had been industrialized, and rustic life—which Marx had called idiotic—no longer existed. Nor were there any nationalities. Mars, with a population smaller than Earth's, had an ethnically homogeneous race with a single language (another utopian dream, by the way, made popular in Russia at that time by the Esperantists). Workers or laborers existed, of course: but since everyone was a worker who produced according to capacity and consumed according to desire, there was no "labor question" as such. Bogdanov also addressed on Mars the vexing question of the opposition and contradiction between city and countryside—a big problem of Russian social history up the Stalinist times. Unlike More, Campanella, and Morelli, Bogdanov does not aspire to destroy the countryside. Unlike Rousseau, Ruskin, and Morris, he does not aspire to destroy the city. He creates a whole new kind of arrangement that is neither country no city, though retaining elements of both.

On Bogdanov's Mars there is no state and no politics, although there are clothes made of synthetic material, three-dimensional movies, and a death ray. People are quartered in various kinds of urban and semiurban planned settlements, such as the Great City of Machines or the Children's Colony. Voluntary labor alternates with leisure and culture, and the drama of life is provided by the never-ending struggle with the natural environment—not with other people. The climax of the story occurs when someone tries to alter this Martian scenario.

The systemization of the productive process is the main focus of the hero's interest. Factories are operated by electrical power and fully automated. "Moving equilibrium" is maintained by data retrieval machinery in all enterprises. Data on stockpiles and inventories, production rates, and labor needs according to specialty are channeled into a Central Institute of Statistics, which collates and computes the information and sends it where it is needed. Since consumption is unlimited, all work is voluntary and unpaid. Short workdays and the rotation of jobs reduce the menace of alienation and psychic enslavement to the machine. Bogdanov, though he certainly revered machines, feared and hated the system of capitalist production that made human beings appendages to machinery. He thus not only fought against the so-called Taylor System of industrial labor but also against the Bolshevik "Taylorists"—particularly Alexei Gastev, the greatest proponent of man-the-machine mentality. Planning, productivity, labor discipline, and recruitment—all problems of developed industry outlined in the novel—became issues of heated debate among Soviet planners of the 1920s and 1930s. No wonder that Bogdanov's novel was sometimes invoked at the dawn of the First Five-Year Plan by economic chieftains and planners.

Equality and collectivism are the social values held in highest esteem by Martians. Even on the voyage out, the captain's role as commander is deemphasized and he is ranked along with the rest of the crew as a specialist. Rules and regulations are minimal and are based upon science, not on philosophical or religious moral values. Coercive, authoritarian, categorical "norms" were as repugnant to the author as they had been to Nietzsche, whom Bogdanov had once admired. Equality expressed itself on Mars in many ways: the absence of gender in names, unisex clothing, and the businesslike intercourse among people, free of superfluous greetings and empty politeness—reminiscent of the Russian nihilists of the 1860s. There are people of superior talent on Mars, but they are afforded no special prizes or recognition in life or after death. The monuments on Mars are erected to commemorate historic events, as products of collectives wills, and not to heroes. After the Russian Revolution of 1917, a kindred surge toward anonymity, egalitarianism, collective creativity, and iconoclasm burst forth for some time before it was repudiated by the authorities, who soon began to set up live heroes, stone statues, and cultic idols of the Revolution. Bogdanov's ultimate gesture of fraternal solidarity on Mars was the "comradely exchange of life" in which mutual blood transfusions were employed to prolong life.

Bogdanov clung to his vision of collective creativity after the Revolution of 1917. In a reply to Gastev written in 1919, he said that in proletarian cooperation, comradely recognition of competence would replace authority and force in the workplace and that leadership roles would be rotated according to the task and the talent:

> The proletarian collective is distinguished and defined by a special organizational bond, known as *comradely cooperation.* This is a kind of cooperation in which the roles of organizing and fulfilling are not divided but are combined among the general mass of workers, so that there is no authority by force or unreasoning subordination but a common will which decides, and a participation of each in the fulfillment of the common task.[1]

From his central premises about collectivism, anti-individualism, and a wide arena for personal choice, Bogdanov's depiction of other features of Martian life flow neatly and consistently. The scenes in the Children's Colony, where upbringing is collective, in the hospital, where suicide rooms are available, and in the Museum of Art, where the themes of facing death and the dignity of labor are celebrated—all these are extensions of Bogdanov's social philosophy. They also reflect debates then current among the intelligentsia about childrearing, family, and education, about suicide, which ran rampant after the collapse of the revolution of 1905, and about the meaning and function of art.

But the recurrent discussion of sex and love requires more than a passing comment. Debate on the "sexual question" reached a crescendo in Russia at the very moment when *Red Star* was published. Love, marriage, divorce, birth control, abortion, prostitution, and sexuality were hotly discussed in the media, especially in the years between Leo Tolstoy's *Kreutzer Sonata* (1889) and Michael Artsybashev's *Sanin* (1908). Outraged society took issue particularly with sexual "decadence" as illustrated in *Sanin*; and the many nuances between "comradely union," free love, and promiscuity were canvassed endlessly in the press and in popular brochures. The accompanying wave of suicides in 1907 and 1908 led cultural critics of the time to link sensualism and suicide as forms of self-destruction and escapism born of the recently failed revolution and the upsurge of repression. Among socialists in Russia the debate on sex was especially painful and ambivalent because socialism generally inscribed high moral behavior as well as personal liberation on its banner. In 1908 a socialist woman physician, A. P. Omelchenko, linked *Red Star* and *Sanin* in a book attacking free love and upholding the family.

How did Bogdanov treat the sexual issue under communism? Leonid in fact does resemble Sanin, the vulgar amoralist of Artsybashev's creation. Both are in love with life and sneer at the notion of moral duty. But there the similarity ends. Sanin is a wild libertine and seducer who scorns all values and all causes. Leonid, on the other hand, finds personal expression in the proletarian cause and, though he believes that polygamy is more life-enriching than monogamy, he does not practice it until he arrives on Mars. There his shallow Nietzscheanism undergoes a series of shocks. Leonid's advanced and conventionally radical ideas on sex seem old-fashioned indeed on a planet where the "liaison," "affair," "romance," and "marriage" have the same meaning. Bogdanov, like his contemporary and fellow Marxist Alexandra Kollontai—who shared many of Bogdanov's ideas on collectivism and antiauthoritarianism—was groping experimentally toward a reasonable and yet warmhearted solution to the question that has plagued so many dreamers and social reformers throughout the ages: how to reconcile personal freedom with the need for long-time loyalties, commitments, and emotional stability. Dr. Omelchenko, gently chiding her fellow socialist, Bogdanov, proclaimed that the family, not free love, would be the social base of the new socialist order because it did not violate the spirit of collective life and labor but rather enhanced it. Not surprisingly, a recent Soviet edition of Bogdanov's novel saw fit to omit Leonid's ruminations on marriage and sex.

After the survey of society mandatory in almost all utopias, Leonid is permitted to enter into an emerging drama, one that threatens to pit planet against planet, man against man. Bogdanov extricates his hero and returns him to the explosive urban battle-fields and barricades of Moscow as the Revolution of 1905 nears its climax.

★

The circumstances under which *Engineer Menni* was written in 1912 were very different from those of 1907. Bogdanov's dream of an imminent upsurge of the proletarian offensive in Russia was ill-founded. By 1908 the reaction was in full swing and tsarist authori-ties were in full command of the situation. Many members of the intelligentsia and of educated society at large fell into a mood of postrevolutionary despondency and withdrawal. Mysticism, the occult, and even what was then considered pornography came into vogue. Social daydreamers now sought salvation in personal lib-eration and predictions of a revolution of the spirit. Some former revolutionary thinkers turned to religion—and even to conserva-tism and nationalism. Those who clung to revolutionary political tactics and programs were either banished to the fringes of the Russian state or forced into emigration. Bogdanov was among the latter. The expatriate world of Russian revolutionaries—Geneva, London, Paris, Stuttgart, Capri—was a world of disappointed men and women who lashed one another with bitter recriminations and ideological squabbles. One of these differences of opinion was the break between Bogdanov and Lenin.

At the end of *Red Star*, Bogdanov makes fleeting reference to the Old Man of the Mountain, an invaluable, hardheaded, but somewhat conservative and inflexible revolutionary leader. Bogdanov was clearly referring to his comrade Lenin. The two men fell out over philosophical and tactical questions. The philosophical controversy had begun to emerge years earlier when Bogdanov embraced the epistemological theories of Ernest Mach, the Austrian scientist who denied the existence of a material world independent of the observer.

To Mach the world was only organized perception and nothing more. Bogdanov's acceptance of "empiriomonism," as this latest version of a very ancient idea was called, evoked an assault from George Plekhanov, the father of Russian Marxism, who wounded Bogdanov to the quick by addressing him in print as "Gospodin" (mister) instead of as "comrade." Lenin kept his own hostility to Machism muted for some time, until, in 1908, he could no longer contain it and wrote the famous massive polemic *Materialism and Empiriocriticism.* This was after the appearance of *Red Star.* Lenin mentioned the novel only once, briefly and obliquely, in an ironic comment about Lowell's *Mars and Its Canals.*

The philosophical duel merged with the political fight, of more recent duration. This latter was based upon Bogdanov's insistence on the possibility of mounting a new armed uprising in 1907 and 1908. Because of this he diverted party funds into revolutionary partisan operations and vigorously opposed Bolshevik participation in the new parliament. The break which ensued was, in the last analysis, caused by a fundamental difference between an increasingly rigid and ideologically authoritarian Lenin and a Bogdanov whose encyclopedic knowledge of the sciences and whose personal proclivities toward revolutionary action could not be reconciled to the views of a self-appointed and self-righteous leader. Bogdanov recalled years later in his autobiography that the barracks and prisonlike atmosphere of his school had taught him as a schoolboy "to fear and to hate those who coerce and to flaunt authority."

Bogdanov spent the years 1908-1914 in Western Europe. He and his associates retreated to Italy, to the island of Capri, where Gorky had been living since 1906, and founded a party school for workers. Bogdanov, Lunacharsky, Gorky, Bazarov, and Skvortsov-Stepanov, now estranged from Lenin's party, taught there, as did non-Bolsheviks Trotsky, Pokrovsky, and Menzhinsky. All of these men would hold important posts in Soviet life after the revolution, at least for a while. Bogdanov continued to develop his system of tectology; Gorky and Lunacharsky engaged in what was called "god-building"—the attempt to forge a religion out of socialism. And all of them tried to create the basis for a new proletarian culture. By the time of the composition of *Engineer Menni* in 1912, most Bogdanov's friends had drifted back into the Bolshevik party. Bogdanov aban-

doned active political work in 1911 and devoted his time exclusively to the organizational science and proletarian culture. *Menni* was
one of the fruits of this decision.

Engineer Menni combines the then-current speculation about
the natural history of Mars with a plausible story of canal construction and class struggle. It is a historical novel about economic development, political change, and revolutionary labor movements
on Mars in the seventeenth century—anticipating the events of
Bogdanov's time by three hundred years. The structure of the history is straightforward Marxism, schematic in places but cleverly
contrived. By placing the class struggle in "nowhere" (utopia),
Bogdanov universalizes the Marxist scheme of history, suggesting
that something like it would happen "everywhere." To dramatize
the process, Bogdanov provides fictitious characters who represent
various aspirations of struggling forces in the painful process of
Martian modernization. These are not brilliant portraits, but they
are far from being simple pasteboard figures speaking political
platitudes. Menni, the chief protagonist, is a sympathetic person,
upright and decent, but one who happens to be on the wrong side
of the barricades in the fight between progress and conservatism.
In his rigid logic and rugged individualism, he resembles in many
ways the Nietzschean and Darwinian characters in some of Ayn
Rand's novels (her formative years were spent in revolutionary Russia). Bogdanov's technological premise was taken from Schiaparelli
and Lowell. The latter's theory of man-made canals for irrigation
was long opposed even in his time and was definitely disproved in
the 1960s and 1970s by the Mariner and Viking missions. Mars and
Marx,[2] the red planet and the red philosopher, are thus combined
to provide the historical explanation of the communist society described in *Red Star.*

Engineer Menni is a novel about socialists and labor leaders,
capitalist villains and blind aristocrats—but it is especially a novel
about engineers, a profession that has played an enormously important role in Russian and Soviet development in the last ninety
years and is only recently being studied by serious scholars. Despite Bogdanov's desire to play down the hero and the individual
of great talent, technological heroes dominate this book: Menni, the
engineer of genius, master of planning and efficiency, and his son

Netti, who, like Bogdanov himself, devotes his later life to an encyclopedic study of work and an all-embracing science of organization. It was precisely this celebration of technocratic power, of the
technical intelligentsia, and of self-correcting systems and moving
equilibria based on science, and the corresponding downplaying of
proletarian energy, party authority, and class struggle, that caused
orthodox Bolsheviks to look askance at the author—a man who
lived before his time.

In the scene depicting a workers' meeting, Bogdanov discloses
some of the elements of his theory of "proletarian culture." Like
the Bolsheviks with whom he had just parted company, Bogdanov
(through the voice of Netti) teaches a doctrine of sacrifice of the few
in the present time for the welfare of the many not yet born; unlike
them, he also insists upon fairness in all human relations, including
the treatment of enemies. Bogdanov believed in the inherent egalitarianism of all workers (who address each other as "brothers"),
but also was painfully aware that the intelligentsia and the more
politically and socially aware workers, while able to represent the
aspirations of an entire class as a species, rise above the proletariat and become detached from them. The problem of the elite who
know and the masses who are constrained to *believe* is poignantly
illustrated in the moving lament of the bewildered worker at the
meeting.

Bogdanov's answer—again voiced by Netti—is the creation of
a unified science of organization that will link all the sciences, currently fragmented, to the processes of labor and life. And in the debate between Menni and Netti, father and son, the author presents
his own sociology of ideas and feelings and an original gloss on the
Marxian philosophy of history.

★

How were these novels received in Russia? The moderate Populist
journal *Russian Wealth* dismissed *Red Star* as trendy, derivative, and
unmoving. Neither wing of Russian Social Democracy reviewed
it. On the other hand, a Bolshevik reviewer of 1918 recalled, as
we have seen, how inspiring the novel was to rank-and-file party
workers even after the revolution had subsided. After the Bolshevik Revolution of 1917, *Red Star* became very popular and was reprinted at least five times inside the Soviet Union, including once

as a supplement to a very widely read popular science magazine, *Around the* World. "The first utopia embellished with proletarian pathos," as one critic has called it, was well received in Party circles after the Revolution. A writer in *Messenger of Life,* a journal for proletarian culture, announced that Bogdanov's utopian vision contained scientific laws and features of life already discernible in the revolutionary Russia of 1918.

The most incisive review of *Red Star* was written by Lunacharsky just as it came out. He praised the poetry and prophecy of innovation and the scientific insight of Bogdanov's futurology, defending the author from literary purists who might object to his pedestrian style. Bogdanov's art was in his contrasting of the "crystal atmosphere of rationality that reigns on Mars," its lack of drama, color, and passion, with the stormy scenes of Earth's contemporary life. Lunacharsky saw the brutally analytical speech of Sterni, the would-be destroyer of Earthlings, as the high point of the novel

Bogdanov's predictions of 1908, put into the mouth of Sterni, are eloquent indeed. Like the American socialist Jack London, whose *Iron Heel* was written in the same year, Bogdanov warns of the coming time when capitalists and ruling classes would use the latest technology to persecute and provoke the proletariat into a premature uprising which the provocateurs would then crush. On the militaristic *revanchisme* of the day Sterni says:

> Patriotic fervor intensifies and becomes extremely acute after military defeats, especially when the victors seize a part of the loser's territory. The patriotism of the vanquished then takes the form of an intense and prolonged hatred of the victors, and revenge becomes the ideal of not just the worst groups—the upper or ruling classes—but of the entire people, including the best elements, the toiling masses.

Bogdanov also perceived the growth of what Lenin would call "social patriotism" in 1914, the desire of European Marxist Social Democrats, in defiance of their allegiance to internationalism, to fight off and defeat the national enemy. Socialists, says Sterni, in reference to a Terrestrial-Martian war, "would start a bitter and ruthless war against us [Martian liberators], because they would never be able to reconcile themselves to the killing of millions of their own kind to whom they are bound by a multitude of often very intimate ties." The most striking of all these passages, one that must have jolted both Lunacharsky and Bogdanov in later years, referred to the possibility of a revolution and the establishment of a few islands of socialism surrounded by a hostile capitalist sea. These would be beleaguered by the capitalist states. "It is difficult to foresee the outcome of these conflicts," says Sterni, "but even in those instances where socialism prevails and triumphs, its character will be perverted deeply and for a long time to come by years of encirclement, unavoidable terror and militarism, and the barbarian patriotism that is their inevitable consequence. This socialism will be a far cry from our own."

Engineer Menni attracted less attention than had *Red Star*, coming as it did in 1913, when hopes for revolution were not high. The Populist journal *Testaments* was very negative and considered it dry, schematic, and contrived. Lenin wrote to Gorky in 1913: "Just read his *Engineer Menni.* Another case of Machism and idealism, but obscured so that neither the workers nor the silly editors at *Pravda* understood it." The Bolshevik reviewer of 1918 referred to above recalled that the mood of skepticism and pessimism was so deep among his people when *Menni* came out that they could not apprehend its extravagant picture of the socialist victory on Mars. But he also suggested that Menni's dream of bringing proletarian culture to the masses was now within reach of the new regime. In later years both *Red Star* and *Menni* were criticized for placing too much emphasis upon the "progressive" technocracy—that is, the engineers—and not enough upon the creative role of the proletariat. Yet contemporary Soviet critics recognize Bogdanov as the authentic founder of Soviet science fiction. He was, in the words of one historian of the genre, the "first writer of Russian science fiction to combine a well written technological utopia with scientific Marxist views on communism and the idea of social revolution."[3]

Bogdanov's works pointed the way to an enormous blossoming of revolutionary science fiction in the 1920s, a period that saw the publication of about two hundred works of this kind, most of them dealing with the two main themes of Bogdanov's work: capitalist hells, militarism, frightful weapons, greed, and exploitation leading to catastrophe; and communist heavens adorned with life-easing technology and complete social justice. Eugene Zamyatin's *We* (1920), called by Ursula LeGuin the greatest of all science fiction novels, was, in its pervasive imitative irony, an emphatic repudiation of Bogdanov's utopia—its technology and its rationalism, as well as its version of socialism. Yakov Okunev, a popular Soviet science fiction writer of the 1920s, borrowed *Red Star*'s computerized society for his *The Coming World* (1923). Alexis Tolstoy's once famous *Aelita* (made into a classic silent film) again featured two planets, Earth and Mars, and two revolutions, though with a political premise about Mars opposite to that of Bogdanov's. One writer, Innokenty Zhukov, even incorporated Bogdanov's title into his fantastic tale: *Voyage of the Red Star Detachment to the Land of Marvels* (1924). The "land of marvels" is Earth in the year 1957, after a communist revolution has transformed it into a unified planet resembling that of Bogdanov's Mars. Examples of Bogdanov's influence on the golden age of Soviet science fiction are legion, Soviet critics proclaim it, in spite of residual hostility to Bogdanov as a thinker. It is no exaggeration to say, as the foremost Western authority on Soviet science fiction, Darko Suvin, has said, that Bogdanov was the progenitor of this genre in Soviet literature.

By the time he finished *Engineer Menni* in 1913, Bogdanov had abandoned the active political struggle and was devoting himself to research and theorizing on a wide range of subjects, scientific, philosophical, and cultural. During World War I—whose horrors he had foreseen—he returned to Russia and served as a military physician at the front. After the Bolsheviks came to power he threw himself into the Proletkult, the proletarian culture movement that he had helped to found before the Revolution, and established thousands of cells and studios all over Soviet Russia and issued a huge number of publications with enormous circulations.

Bogdanov did not rejoin the Communist (formerly Bolshevik) Party but held several high posts in academic and economic institutions. After 1921, with the dismantling of the independent Proletkult movement at the behest of Lenin, Bogdanov devoted himself fully to scientific work and experimentation. In 1926 he founded the Institute for Blood Transfusion as a way to realize his dream, first described in *Red Star*, of performing the "comradely exchange of life." He gave his own life in this cause, so characteristic of the utopian experiments generated by the Revolution: in 1928, while carrying out a transfusion on himself, he died.

Bogdanov's works circulated in hundreds of thousands of copies in the 1920s, including several editions of *Red Star* and *Engineer Menni* in huge printings. Though he ceased to wield political or philosophical influence, Bogdanov nonetheless remained a major figure in the intellectual landscape of the early Soviet years. Nicholas Bukharin, still a prominent communist political leader and a disciple of Bogdanov, wrote his obituary in *Pravda*, stressing Bogdanov's personal courage and revolutionary boldness in giving his life "as a victim" and praising his intellectual breadth and influence. Bukharin called *Red Star* "one of the best socialist 'utopias.'" When the novels were reissued after the author's death, discussion of them came into vogue once again as the Soviet Union entered that fatal and frenetic period of its history known as the Pyatiletka (Five-Year Plan), the Great Break, or the Revolution from Above. During the debates and reports at the outset of the Five-Year Plan, G. M. Krzhizhanovsky, an engineer and one of the architects of the plan, made oblique reference to Bogdanov's great canal projects on Mars. In 1929, the famous city planner L. M. Sabsovich likened the plan to "the great projects" of *Red Star*. Indeed the atmosphere had become filled with revolutionary utopianism once again, with its frantic energy and wild dreams of the refashioning of cities of Earth, and of mankind. But this last burst of utopia soon gave way to a massive despotism undreamed of even in the most extravagant fantasies of Alexander Bogdanov.

Original publication: Alexander Bogdanov, *Red Star: The First Bolshevik Utopia*. Bloomington: Indiana University Press, 1984, pp. 1-16.

Notes

1   Quoted in Kendall Bailes, "Alexei Gastev and the Soviet Controversy over Taylorism, 1918-24," *Soviet Studies*, 29/3 (July 1977), 380.
2   Xarma, the Martian socialist philosopher in the story.
3   A. F. Britikov, *Russkii Sovetskii nauchno-fanticheskii roman* (Leningrad: Nauka, 1970), 55.

8

Hopes and Fears of Things to Come
The Foreshadowing of Totalitarianism in Russian Fantasy and Utopia

For most students, almost the only reference point for the relationship between Russian science fiction and totalitarianism in the Soviet Union is the well-known dystopian novel of Eugene Zamyatin, *We* (1920), widely translated and published outside the USSR and enjoying a vigorous popularity in this year of Orwellian retrospective. Orwell knew the Zamyatin novel and was obviously influenced by it although his own book, *1984*, reversed some of Zamyatin's central visions. In the 1950s, when both novels enjoyed wide circulation in English and when the notion of totalitarianism was being fleshed out by Arendt, Friedrich, Brzezinski, and others, the Zamyatin-Orwell scenarios—loosely and wrongly fused—became in fact the vehicle for popular mass perceptions of this apparently new and frightening phenomenon.[1] But Zamyatin's *We* sprang out of a rich and teeming literary and psychological context: a whole world of science fiction, social dreams, utopian visions and projects that excited the imaginations of Russians from about 1900 to 1930. I would like to describe that world and to analyze the hopeful visions of utopia, the fearful specters of dystopia, the reality of Soviet Russia in the light of these hopes and fears, and the relevance of all of this to totalitarianism.

But first I feel obliged to describe my own views of the concept "totalitarianism." The word itself originated (as *totalitarismo*) in the rather heavy handed rhetoric of Italian fascist apologetics in the 19205 and 1930s—after Mussolini had come to power. Since Mussolini had admired Lenin's methods and had been a militant Marxist before the Great War, since Georges Sorel had admired them both, and since both Italy and the USSR were ruled by a single party, some linkages were already apparent. This linkage was amplified in the minds of some people after 1933 by the fact that Hitler's party was a National Socialist Workers' party and by other allegedly Marxoid (the word is Adam Ulam's[2]) elements in Nazi and fascist movements and regimes. The idea was muted during the grand alliance of 1941-5 but revived again in full force with the advent of the Cold War and the Red Scare in the United States. A whole community of reputable scholars now began to elaborate a novel theory of totalitarianism that tended to weld together the twin evils of fascism and communism. The moral similarity between the two was quaintly underlined by Senator Joseph McCarthy's use of the term "brutalitarian" to describe Communist regimes. My comments have to do with its use and its misuse.

The concept was certainly useful in demonstrating in great detail the similarities between certain aspects of the political culture of, say, Stalinism and Hitlerism: the police state, the absence of legal restraint and civil liberties, the single party, the attempts at regimentation and mobilization, the dynamics of economic planning, the leader cult, and so on. And in this it performed a necessary service in exposing the foolishness and naivety of those who saw fascism and communism as antipodes: the former as a boundless evil, a tool of high capital, a reversion to barbarism and the latter as progressive, democratic, and humane. On the other hand, the theory often obscured as much as it revealed, particularly on two matters: the genuine difference between Nazi Germany and Stalinist Russia, and the profound divergence between the totalistic Communist party rhetoric and the everyday life, culture, and reality in Soviet Russia in the 1930s and 1940s. It failed to show that "civil society" in the sense understood in the West, though clearly abridged in both societies, continued to exist in Nazi Germany in the form of private fortunes, property and dwellings, independent farming, churches, and popular culture in the old manner—all this in spite of twelve years of "total" power in the hands of the Führer and his party. In Soviet Russia after 1928, most of this was harshly dismantled and eliminated. There was also an enormous difference in the perception and roles of women in these two societies. Furthermore, in spite of the drastic elimination of civil society in Soviet Russia, everyday life never reflected the visions of the planners and leaders, of the totalitarian modellers, or of the utopian fantasists I am about to describe.

The Urban-Socialist Utopia

Although Russian utopian dreaming and action had deep roots in history and had given birth to a small but interesting corpus of literature,[3] "social fantasy" or utopian science fiction as a distinct genre with a continuous history only got underway with the beginnings of industrialization in Russia at the turn of the twentieth century—just at the moment when Marxism also first became an intellectual force in Russia. The impetus for utopianizing—as for Marxism—was the sudden growth and the public perception of industrial cities, technology, and a proletariat.

Like the models for economic growth, much of the management and capital, and the technology of Russia's surge to industrialization, the first utopian speculations in this era of industry and technology were imported: Edward Bellamy's *Looking Backward* (1889), Lili Braun's *Female Labor* (1892), Atlanticu's (Karl Ballod) *A Glimpse into the Future State* (1898), August Bebel's *The Society of the Future* (1905), and a few "futuristic pictures" by Karl Kautsky.[4] Except for Bellamy, the authors were German and (except for Ballod) members of the Marxist Social Democratic Party. All of them envisioned a distinctly urbanized, industrialized, and technologized world of collective labor and life. Interestingly enough the most harshly anticapitalist, the most militarized and regimented, and the most concretely egalitarian of these utopias—Bellamy's—was also the most popular in prerevolutionary Russia.[5]

But the most important and directly influential Russian utopia was the two-novel epic of a communist society on Mars by Alexander Bogdanov, *Red Star* (1908) and *Engineer Menni* (1913).[6] Bogdanov was a leading Bolshevik, a scientist and a doctor, and a coleader with Lenin of the party in the early years, but he broke with Lenin at the time he wrote his first novel—which is heavily suffused with anti-authoritarianism and anti-elitism. On communist Mars, the "red star," peasant, labor, and ethnic questions which so plagued Russia in 1908 were eliminated by the mechanization of agriculture, the construction of ultra-modern cities, the free choice of labor according to the classic canons of Marx, and the merging of the population into a single unit speaking one language. Factories were electrically operated and fully automated, and the "moving equilibrium" of supply, labor assignment, and production needs were minutely calibrated by data retrieval machinery, cybernetics, and protocomputers. Equality and collective work, comradeship, and the full emancipation of women were the binding social values of Martian life. Rules were based on "science" and not religion or philosophy. Rank and deference did not exist, nor did coercive and authoritarian norms. People wore unisex clothing and had gender-less names and treated each other in a comradely and business-like fashion—without the polite adornment of manners. Superior talent was its own reward. And there were no monuments to the heroes and heroines of the past—to the people described in Bog-danov's second novel, *Engineer Menni,* wherein the foundations of communism were laid on Mars, along with its canals, in the seventeenth century. Art was used to celebrate the collective efforts of the masses, past and present. Bogdanov's ultimate form of fraternal solidarity on Mars was the "comradely exchange of life"—the use of mutual blood transfusions to prolong life.

The *Red Star* cycle was the prototype of a whole genre of revo-lutionary science fiction in Soviet Russia in the 1920s, when over 200 science fiction works appeared. Bogdanov's vivid contrast be-tween capitalist-militarist Earth and communist-harmonious Mars provided the writers of the 1920s with innumerable opportunities to project current Soviet reality (at that moment a one-party state in the midst of a backward economy and a relatively pluralist soci-ety and culture) far into the future when a world revolution would have erupted, communism would have emerged triumphant across the globe, and peace and happiness would have dawned for the hu-man race.[7] Typical of this scenario was Yakov Okunev's *The Coming World* which depicted the entire land surface of the earth linked together in a single global megalopolis, and "all-world city" of the year 2123. People worked 2-3 hours a day, the bulk of production being carried out by machines and organs of administration and accounting (Lenin's compulsive daydream in *State and Revolution*) which had replaced force and wealth and politics. Machines con-troled the machines. At the center (not pinnacle) was an elected council of computer statisticians without power other than to check and control output. The hairless citizens looked alike; gone were crime, prostitution, exploitation, and famine as well as specialization of labor (no professors, no scholars), private property, home-owning, and shame. Everyone worked. "You will want to work" says the smiling guide, Stern, to his newly awakened guests from the year 1923. There were no classes—only a single communist family united to fight nature, not each other. Freedom was the only law. Its meaning? Quite clear: "All citizens of the World City live as they want—but they all want what everybody wants."[8]

The source of all disharmony and agony in the corning ages, according to Soviet science fiction of the 1920s, was capitalism. The villains were usually either power- and profit-hungry American racist usually either tycoons (partly lifted from Jack London's *Iron Heel* (1908) as in V. Orlovsky's *Horror Machine* (1925), or Germanic "mad scientist" types, descended from Frankenstein and made into a universal cliché by Hollywood at about the same time) as in Alexander Beylaev's *The Lords of the World* (1929). And in this also, Soviet science fiction was taking up Bogdanov's theme of a feudal-capitalist earth as a ball of fissionable human hate and greed ready to destroy everything on its surface in the name of patriotism, honor, and colonies.[9]

Science fiction did not float in the margins of the Revolution: its major themes were accompanied by movements that worked to introduce them into life. The extravagant urban visions of science fiction were shared by a remarkable school of architects and town planners in the late 1920s and the early 1930s who dreamed up mammoth schemes of urban conglomeration and deurbanization.[10] Technological daydreaming and speculation thrived also; Tsiolkovsky's rocket experiments, Rynin's designs for the conquest of space, Lenin's scheme for civilization through electrification, and a whole circle of scientists, religious adepts (followers of Nikolai Fedorov) and even bureaucrats who believed in the prolongation of human life and the resurrection of the dead.[11] Universal labor liability was of course part of the Marxist program: Trotsky tried to militarize labor during the civil war, and his successor Frunze dreamt of a permanent militarization of society.[12]

A "cultured" attitude toward work was approached from two

directions: the Komsomol morality movement to replace religious values with modern (therefore work-oriented) ones, and Gastev's Central Institute of Labor and Kerzhentsev's League of Time—both designed to transform the bumbling peasant into a machine-like smooth-functioning productive unit. The ultimate goal of "communalism"—consuming and dwelling together in a comradely collective—was tried out in at least three different arenas: the house-commune designed by revolutionary architects, the rural communes where food and tasks were shared, and the pure student commune of the city where *everything*—including friendship, space, and underclothing—were shared.[13]

In all, or almost all, of the utopian science fiction works from Bogdanov onward—the issue of women's role in society was addressed in a very emphatic and forthright manner. Women were depicted as equals in the same way that the Zhenotdel—the Women's Section of the Communist Party (1919-1930)—was working to make them in real life. In fiction this was often underlined by physical and sartorial similarity of the two sexes. Futuristic women were also emancipated from housework which was now the function of communal institutions, with the assistance of household technology. And women were sexually free: nowhere in Soviet life or in fiction was there ever any talk of regimented sex or prohibition of sex—except in the usual juridical categories. The women's liberation movement in the Russian Revolution, and its reflection in science fiction, contained no hint of either the sex-by-ticket system of Zamyatin's *We*, the sex-as-opiate solution of Huxley's *Brave New World*, or the Anti-Sex League of Orwell's *1984*.[14]

Pervading the entire tableau of the future world was practical egalitarianism in everyday life—not the cut-out symmetry of a Babeuf in which all humans were thought to be equal in capacity, but where hierarchy, the inequality of wages, and the psychosocial structure of deference had been eliminated. And this also was in the spirit, if rarely in the practice, of revolutionary egalitarians of the early Soviet years, manifested as levelling of wages in some instances, humble dress for high officials, iconoclastic and nihilistic assaults on old culture, anti-intellectualism, and housing arrangements.[15]

The Counter-Utopia and the Dystopia

The world of fantasy, like the world of myth and legend, reveals and evokes deeper layers, archaic dreams, and longings that may better describe *feelings* about the future than the more conventional acts of political adherence. Russian science fiction on the eve of war and revolution was a dialogue of fantasy and a duel of dreams: bright and hopeful utopias of progress, with strong urban, technical, and socialist elements generated counter-utopias of alternate scenarios and dystopias of fear and warning. The fictive discourse was a prelude, remarkable in its predictive detail, to the better known literary wars of utopias and counter-utopias in the Revolution itself. The authors of these pre-revolutionary works were of three kinds: well-known literary names (Bryusov, Kuprin) whose ambivalence and talent give their books literary distinction; political journalists and publicists of the right; and popular writers who are otherwise almost unknown.[16]

The non-socialist variety of futuristic speculation first took the form of "wartopia" or geopolitical romance such as A. Belomor's *The Fateful War of 18??* (1889) and I. I. Romanov's *Sketches* (1891), featuring a coming war, assorted Austrian, Jewish, or papal villains, and the preservation of Holy Russia at the end. A. Krasnitsky's *Behind the Raised Curtain: A Fantastic Tale of Future Things* (1900) was the most interesting of these. The "future things" were submarines, a European holocaust and war, a colonial rebellion, a foiled attempt to create a Jewish empire in Central Europe, and the emergence of a regenerated Russia—religious, patriotic, monarchic, with its capital renamed Petrograd and ruled by a Russian God of Truth (*Pravda*), Goodness, and Love, and heading an All-Slavic political union. A more concretely conservative counter-utopia was N. I. Shelonsky's *In the World of the Future* (1892), an attack on Bellamy and on socialism, but not on technology as such. Television (*telefot*), tunnels, antigravity machines, and all manner of supertechnology existed. But cities have been eliminated and people have returned to the land, living in individual dwellings, widely scattered and separate from each other in self-sufficient families. Religious, bearded elders presided over this privatized exurbia of the 30th century.[17] These counter-utopias were all vivid reflections of a malaise that was creeping over the Russian sensibility in the 1890s, a fear of ethnic minorities, of centrifugal national movements, of turbulent proletarians and cerebral radicals, and of menacing European powers—all threatening to subvert or destroy what one historian has called the "reactionary utopia"[18] of traditional Russia, the Russia of Church, tsar, and perceived pastoral harmony.

But counter-utopia was, in a way, simply the antimodern mirror image of the urban-socialist utopia and as such neither very convincing nor arresting. The dystopia on the other hand, with its biting irony and its extravagant projections of then current trends, possessed greater literary value and intellectual force. The first of them, like the first utopia of this period, was a foreign import, Paolo Mantegazza's *The Year 3000*, published in Russian translation in 1898.[19] Its distant Land of Equality in the Indian Ocean, with cities such as Andropol and Tyranopol, is characterized by universal symmetry, identical clothes, looks, and homes, mandatory simultaneous dining, state-organized marriage sanctified by a "sanitary tribunal," numbered citizens, and a rigid scheduling of sexual intercourse. Mantegazza, a physician and a specialist on sexology, may have been the first to introduce the ubiquitous theme of sexual control into modern antisocialist dystopian literature. Its format was apparently borrowed for the virtually unknown *Everything in the Year 2217* (1906) by N. Fedorov. In it, Citizeness No. 437-2221 resides in a socialist city—St. Petersburg—of stone, steel, and glass with networks of balloon buses and moving sidewalks. All citizens are compensated according to need and there is no cold, hunger, or disease. But all are expected to exchange sex freely with anyone who desires them by registration and appointment. Children are anonymous and are raised by the state. The heroine and her male friend are alienated: they long for individual love and a family and are willing to exchange the abundance of heat, light, food, and schooling for the risky conditions of bygone peasants whom they read about in the "old books"—a life of deprivation and recurring misery, but with the opportunity to choose their own style of living. Fedorov's book was the closest thing to a Russian anticipation of Zamyatin's *We* (and Orwell's *1984*) before the Revolution.[20]

The real master of the dystopian genre was Valery Bryusov who began his dark search of the future with *Earth* (1904) set in the

"City of the Future Times," an underground labyrinth of geometric rooms, passages, and machines, unexposed to natural light and air. *The Republic of the Southern Cross* (1904-5) has its capital, Starry City, at the bottom of the globe, its center set squarely on the South Pole beneath a dome of glass with all streets radiating out from it. In this metropolis of 50 million people and of identical houses and artificial heat and light, all needs are cared for by the state, though only skilled metal workers have full rights. But behind the welfare facade, "the directors" enforce a hideous regimentation and conformity of life, as well as a rigid police control—though it is never quite clear whether it is technology, socialism, or capitalism that is the target of Bryusov's satire. *The Last Martyrs* (1906) describes a future revolution during which the iconoclastic and barbarian revolutionaries liquidate the last martyrs of the old intelligentsia and their religious cults, their elitist culture, and their sexual decadence.[21]

The counter-utopia and the dystopia did not give up the ghost after the Bolshevik Revolution: on the contrary, although their numbers dwindled sharply due to censorship, those that appeared were even sharper in their focus and more articulate in their political scenarios. Of the former genre, two deserve comment: Alexander Chayanov's *Journey of my Brother Alexei to the Peasant Utopia* (1920) and Peter Krasnov's *Beyond the Thistle* (1922). Chayanov was an economist with populist leanings whose utopia—set in the year 1984—was the result of a victorious rising of peasants and SRs against the Bolsheviks in the 1930s. It is a rural democratic republic in which the major cities have been destroyed or drastically reduced in size, and where technology is used largely to assist agriculture and defend the land (the latter type including a rain machine used against German invaders in 1984). Traditional peasant customs and costumes complete this fictional version of the nineteenth-century populist vision. Krasnov's novel was a pure dream of monarchist restoration: after a half century of Bolshevik misrule, famine, and isolation, the last Romanov heir to the throne marches triumphantly on a white horse from the Himalayas to Moscow and creates a dreamland of Orthodoxy, nationalism, and autocracy, with youth militarized in patriotic bands (Krasnov was living in Weimar, Germany when he wrote the novel) and a selective use of technology (high speed flying trains for long distance and horses and sleighs for short-term transport.). Both these authors were destroyed by the Stalin regime.[22]

Zamyatin was luckier and managed to emigrate. His novel *We*, a monument of twentieth century political fiction, was not just a clever projection by a foreboding genius. It was an answer: to Bogdanov's sanitized world on Mars, to the cult of the machine and Soviet Taylorism in its earliest phase, to the super-rationalists who envisioned the phasing out of independent thought and communication and of a machine-administered world, and to the architects and poets who proclaimed the City as the model for the coming world.[23]

In this strange, fear-laden corpus of prediction, several themes recur again and again. One is the hatred of industrialization-modernization-technology-urbanization that were alleged to produce neurosis, an erosion of healthy traditions, values, and community, and the destruction of man's most precious possession: nature. So potent is this theme in some of the works that their anticapitalism is at least as strong as their anticommunism. A second theme is the discomfort at the prospect of an all-embracing welfare system that would alleviate the eternal evils of man's existence— ignorance, poverty, disease, war—but would leave him enmeshed in soul-killing boredom. And the most menacing of all is the theme of regimentation, conformity, and the control of personal—particularly sexual—life. Zamyatin's book combines them all in a picture of absolute entropy—a world without passion, feeling, or fantasy, a world in which the Well-doer and the Guardians perform fantasectomy upon their people in order to excise the harmful mechanisms of love, rebellion, and imagination.

... and Soviet Reality

Let us set these major dystopian themes from Russian science fiction and utopia against the reality of Soviet Russia. Leaving aside the semantic and theoretical debates about the much abused word "modernization" there is no doubt that both in the East and in the West its components—industrialization, technologizing, and urbanization—are blazened across the coat of arms of the twentieth century. The Bolsheviks proclaimed it before, during, and after the

Revolution and ever since: their vision is no idyll but a buzzing machine of global proportions. Starting especially with the five year plan of 1928, the conscious push to mechanical modernity has brought its share of neurosis connected with speedy transformation, mobilization, migration, adjustment to the town, building and rebuilding, cultural adaptation, and sheer physical labor calibrated to the rhythm of the machine. It has also threatened to destroy the beauties and treasures of the natural environment, with plans of linear cities to interlace the vast green of Siberia. And, since science and a reverence for material technique are so intimately linked to all this, modernization has also reinforced the atheist and the anti-rural and anti-traditional elements in Russian society. Nothing like the geometric perfection of Fedorov, Zamyatin, or Bryusov is on the horizon—though the path toward it is certainly littered with psychic and aesthetic victims. But in all of this, the difference between the communist and the capitalist visions and procedures has been mostly a matter of tempo. Comparison between Zamyatin's *We* and Frederik Pohl and C. M. Kornbluth's *Space Merchants* is a vivid illustration of this point.

The matter of welfare, peace, harmony, and order being the engine of massive boredom and suicidal malaise is an extremely intriguing one. In Russia, the first important example of it was the dialogue between Chernyshevsky, author of the utopian *What is to be done?* (1863) and Dostoevsky's impassioned and continuous assault on crystal palace and anthill serenity. It has been a major theme in twentieth century science fiction as well as a prominent motif in conservative criticism of the so-called welfare state in any guise. One need only recall President Eisenhower's sweeping comment about Sweden, socialism, and suicide to get a flavor of the "pop" version of the facile formula. But, like much else in science fiction projections, the fear of "total welfarism" is not measurably applicable to Soviet life—in Stalin's time or now. In many sectors of life the USSR is in the early or middle stages of modernization and society is plagued with alcoholism, inefficiency, overwork for some, underemployment for others, chronic shortages, sexism and the whole range of what in nineteenth-century Europe were called social maladies. The extraordinarily uneven development of Soviet society has created a sociotechnical mosaic, with quasi-primitive "collective farming," a black market, and a creaking trade network coexisting with a crack military and scientific research establishment. Boredom is not a quantifiable commodity: but the kind of boredom that exists in the Soviet Union does not spring from over-coddling of the population.

George Orwell's totalitarian villain of *1984*, O'Brien, voicing his love of repression for its own sake, offered the metaphor of "a boot stamping on a human face—forever." Repression and permanent terror were seen in the classic formulations of the 1950s as endemic to totalitarianism. In prerevolutionary dystopias, physical violence and state repression played a very small role; the emphasis was on boredom and regimentation. It was the prophetic genius Zamyatin who foresaw that the conventional violence of 1920, arising from revolution and class war, and the extravagant dreams of mind-control held by a few, could combine into the terror-machine of mass arrests, executions, and the Gulag. The very peculiar feature of the Stalinist terror, the show trial, ironically enough, had never been foreshadowed in fiction. It seems to have emerged out of deep Russian traditions of public mockery and shame, the inquisition, and revolutionary experiment with ritual, carnival, and outdoor spectacle—in which enemies, "wreckers," and poor workers were publicly flayed in effigy.

Regimentation and conformity, however, were at the very center of the fearful visions of dystopia. The source of this fear is not hard to discern: it was the utopians themselves. Even among those utopian writers who did not conjure up the vision and who loathed it, their constant and almost universal invocation of equality as a central principle for future societies, their worship of technology and the Cartesian images that seemed to accompany it, and their usually unsatisfying and unconvincing picture of innocent state power (or its absence) provided sufficient material for those whose confidence in benign human nature was low to begin with. Regimentation is a relative thing of course. It is true that Soviet society has never come close to the universal regimentation and conformity envisioned by Zamyatin and wished for by eccentric writers such as Nikolai Punin and Eugene Poletaev who demanded that the Revolution produce a Germanic, racist military-productive machine,[24] and by more practical military men such as Mikhail Frunze who wanted the "militarization" of society. On the other hand the power to invoke a near total mobilization (as was tried in 1941-5), the permanent machinery of mobilization (the mass organizations), the large-scale (but not total) control of the economy, and the enforcement of a high level of conformity in culture clearly distinguish Soviet political life from what we in the West call civil society and "freedom," however much we internal critics may lament the scope of that freedom.

In the early years of the Revolution, Alexei Gastev, an industrial poet and a prophet of Taylorism in the work force, desired to mechanize and robotize human labor, to annihilate fantasy, and to eliminate passion and feeling from the human psyche—indeed to reduce all discourse and communication to a mathematically coded language.[25] His dream was Zamyatin's nightmare. It was precisely these dangers—images of which had flickered constantly through the pages of prerevolutionary dystopian science fiction—that Zamyatin saw as entropy, the emerging menace to mankind, newer, more subtle "and more invidious than even the mechanics of despotism and repression. Hannah Arendt's *The Origins of Totalitarianism* appeared in 1951, *We* was republished in 1952, and the Brzezinski-Friedrich symposium came out in 1956. To a world numbed by the horrors of World War II and revelations about the Soviet purges and camps, it was not difficult to imagine and believe the popularized and filtered versions of these books which painted Soviet life as a black prison house whose inhabitants marched around like robots locked in fear.

No one who has ever lived in or visited the Soviet Union with eyes and ears open could be persuaded that the Russians have been transformed into robotized people devoid of fantasy or human emotions. Their pattern of gestures, motions, and work rhythms could accurately be described by that colorful Russian term "lyrical disorder" but not by Taylorized motions. Gastev in fact was purged in the 1930s and his Scientific Organization of Labor (*Nauchnaya Organizatsiya Truda*) movement has remained a parody of his dream, contemptuously dismissed by Soviet workers nowadays as *Nenuzhnaya Organizatsiya Tuneyadstva*—an Unnecessary Organization of Parasites.

Conclusion

The two points I am trying to make in this essay are very simple. The first is that Zamyatin in 1920 seems to have embraced *all* the fears from prerevolutionary dystopia about the coming nightmare as well as his own dismay at some very extravagant though never realized fantasies at large when he wrote the book. *We* gained currency in the West precisely at the point when the theory of totalitarianism was being mapped out. Since no Bolshevik utopian science fiction, with its hopeful visions and humane arguments, was ever translated, *We* was taken as the statement of the Russian literary imagination (it was, I hasten to add, by far the best in terms of literary quality) about the Soviet "utopia" in practice. *We/1984* was the combined popular image of the Nightmare State for a whole generation for college and high school students who knew little or nothing of the nuance and analyses of Brzezinski, Friedrich, and the others.

The second point, derived from common sense and observation, is that while Soviet Russia has since the death of Stalin painfully but clearly moved away from whatever degree it approached the totalitarian model, and has become a certain version of the authoritarian regime—or in Robert Tucker's arresting image—"the ruins of the fantasy state,"[26] popular and even official imagery of the Soviet Union in the West has retained much of the flavor of dystopian and totalitarian images of the early 1950s, Jeane Kirkpatrick's "long, dark night" being among the most recent and prominent of these images.[27] This is not to argue that Stalinist Russia was somehow "better" than Orwell's Oceana or Zamyatin's One State—in some ways it was more hideous. Nor do I wish to deny the lingering elements of Stalin's nightmare in present Soviet reality. I merely wish to point out that since the essence of scholarship and understanding is differentiation and discrimination, one ought to distinguish between what dystopians fear and what utopians hope for, between "the dream of a perfect order" and the stages along the road to that order, and between elegant and unifying theories and human realities.

Original publication: *Nordic Journal of Soviet and East European Studies* vol. 3, no. 1 (1986), pp. 1-20.

Notes

1 See Luther P. Carpenter, "1984 on Staten Island" in Irving Howe, ed., *1984 Revisited: Totalitarianism in Our Century*, New York: Harper, 1983, 72-85 for some scanty evidence on American reading habits in the 1950s.

2 Adam Ulam, *The Unfinished Revolution*, New York: Random House, 1960.

3 For an introduction to it, see the collection *Utopia in Russian History, Thought, and Culture*, a special issue of *Russian History*, Winter, 1984, eds. Lars Kleberg and Richard Stites; for a sampling of texts, *Pre-Revolutionary Science Fiction: an Anthology*, ed. Leland Fetzer, Ann Arbor: Ardis, 1982.

4 Bellamy, *Budushchii vek* and *Cherez sto let*, both St. Petersburg, 1891, were the first two of several translations of *Looking Backward*; Braun, *Frauenarbeit und Hauswirtschaft*, Berlin, 1891, appeared in Russian as *Zhenskiy trud*, 1892; Ballod's *Ein Blick in den Zukunftstaat*, Stuttgart, 1898, as *Gosudarstvo budushchego*, 1906 with a preface by Kautsky; the last section of Bebel's *Die Frau und der Sozialismus*, Zurich, 1879, dealing with the future, was translated and republished many times: see *Budushchee-obshchestvo*, Moscow: Kolokol, 1905; for a sampling of Rautsky's speculations in Russian translation, see *Sotsialnaya reforma na drugoi den posle sotsialnoy revolyutsii*, Rostov-na-Donu, 1905. Discussions of some of these, from different perspectives, may be found in Stites, *The Women's Liberation Movement in Russia*, Princeton: Princeton University Press, 1978 and Daniel Tarschys, *Beyond the State*, Stockholm: Läromedelsförlaget, 1971.

5 Alexander Nikoljukin, "A Little-Known Story: Bellamy in Russia," in Sylvia Bowman, ed., *Edward Bellamy Abroad*, New York: Twayne, 1962.

6 For texts of the novels and commentary: Alexander Bogdanov, *Red Star: The First Bolshevik Utopia*, ed. Loren Graham and Richard Stites, Bloomington: Indiana University Press, 1984.

7 For an introduction to it, see: A. F. Britikov, *Russkiy Sovetskiy nauchno-fantasticheskiy roman*, Leningrad: Nauka, 1970, 56-102; and Darko Suvin, "The Utopian Tradition of Russian Science Fiction," *Modern Language Review*, 66, 1971, 139-59.

8 Ya. Okunev, *Grysadushchiy mir: utopicheskiy roman, 1923-2123*, Petrograd: Priboi, 1923.

9 V. Orlovskii, *Mashina uzhasa*, Leningrad: Priboi, 1925; A. Belyaev, *Vlastiteli mira*, Leningrad: Krasnaya Gazeta, 1929. For the roots of this theme, see: Jack London, *Zheleznaya pyata*, Moscow: Obshchaya Biblioteka, 1918.

10 For the best introduction to this subject, see S.F. Starr, *Melnikov: Solo Architect in a Mass Society*, Princeton: Princeton University Press, 1978.

11 Konstantin Tsiolkovsky, *Science Fiction*, Adam Starchild (ed.), Seattle: University Press of the Pacific, 1979; N. A. Rynin, *Mezhplanetnye soobshcheniya*, Leningrad: 1928; Michael Hagemeister, "Valerian Nikolaevic Murav'ev (1883-1931) und das 'Prometheische Denken' der frühen Sowjetzeit" in Muravev, *Ovladeniye vremenem*, Moscow, 1924; Munich: Sagner, 1983, reprint.

12 Trotsky's disastrous experiment is well-known; it sprang out of wartime conditions. For M. V. Frunze's "voennizatsiya obshchestva" see his *Izbrannye proizvedeniya*, Moscow, 1934, 192-201.

13 These experiments are reviewed in Richard Stites, *Revolutionary Dreams: Utopian Vision and Experimental Life*, forthcoming (New York: Oxford University Press, 1989 - *ed.*).

14 There was, to be sure, a movement called "revolutionary sublimation" launched by Dr. Aron Zalkind, a Bolshevik physician, whose very puritanical "twelve commandments of a communist" in the 1920s had some vogue among Komsomol enthusiasts—but it never took hold of the Party as such, not to mention the Soviet population. For discussion and documentation, see Stites, *Women's Liberation Movement*, ch. 11.

15 I have treated this phenomenon at some length in my essay "Iconoclastic Currents in the Russian Revolution," in Abbott Gleason *et al.*, eds., *Bolshevik Culture*, Bloomington: Indiana University Press, 1985, 1-24.

16 Some of these are anthologized in Fetzer, *Pre-Revolutionary Russian Science Fiction*.

17 Belomor, *Rokovaya voina 18??* *Goda*, SPB: Golike, 1889; Romanov, *Ocherki*, SPB, 1891; Krasnitsky, *Za pripodnyatoyu zavesoi: fantasticheskaya povest o delakh budushchago (XX vek)*, SPB: Trei, 1900; Shelonsky, *V mire budushchego: fantasticheskii roman*, Moscow: Sytin, 1892.

18 Heinz-Dietrich Löwe, *Antisemitismus und raktionäre Utopie*, Hamburg: Hoffmann und Kampe, 1978.

19 Paolo Mantegazza, *L'anno 3000*, translated as *Budushcheye chelovechestvo (3000 god)*, SPB: Pavlenkov, 1898.

20 Nikolai Fedorov (probably a pseudonym), *Vecher v 2217 godu*, SPB: Gerold, 1906.

21 Bryusov, *Zemnaya os*, 2 ed., Moscow: Skorpion, 1910, contains all the stories.

22 I. Kremnev (pseud. of A. V. Chayanov), *Puteshestviye moyego brata*

Alekseya v stranu krestyanskoy utopii, Moscow, 1920 and trans. in R. E. F. Smith, ed., *The Russian Peasant, 1920 and 1984*, London: Cass, 1977; P. N. Krasnov, *Za chertopolokhom*, Berlin: Dyakov, 1922.

23 Zamyatin, *We*, 1920; New York: Dutton, 1952.

24 E. Poletaev and N. Punin, *Protiv tsivilizatsii*, 1916; Petrograd, 1918.

25 "Man the Machine," a chapter in my *Revolutionary Dreams*, is devoted to the Gastev phenomenon. A brief study of his literary work is Kurt Johansson, *Aleksej Gastev*, Stockholm: Almqvist & Wiksell, 1983.

26 Tucker, "Does Big Brother Really Exist?" in Howe, ed., *1984 Revisited*, p. 102.

27 Jeane J. Kirkpatrick, *Dictatorship and Double Standards*, New York: American Enterprise Institute, 1982.

9

Heaven and Hell in Russian Revolutionary Science Fiction

If the Golden Age of American Science Fiction is said to have begun in the mid-1920s with Hugo Gernsback, I think we may be entitled to talk of "the red age"—Soviet science fiction (SF) of the revolutionary period, 1917-1930. Three major forces propelled this genre into popular prominence: prerevolutionary SF traditions; science-worship in the 1920s; and revolutionary utopianism. As to the first: most of the themes in prerevolutionary SF and utopianizing—dating from the 18th century—flowed into the first Bolshevik SF utopia: Alexander Bogdanov's *Red Star* (1908) and its sequel *Engineer Menni* (1913). The latter is a historical fantasy about canal-building and class struggle on Mars in the seventeenth century; the former, set in the Russian Revolution of 1905, tells of the odyssey of a Bolshevik to Mars—the red star—now transformed into a communist utopia. The familiar elements in these novels were space flight, interplanetary rivalry, the ironic contrast of two worlds, the exposition of an idealized order to the visitor from Earth, and projected technology. The new elements were the concrete use of the ultimate Marxist vision of a society where everyone works according to ability and consumes according to need (the first such application of Marx to fiction), and the self-regulating, computerized economy—a feature of Bogdanov's developing theory of Tectology.

The feverish preoccupation with the future of technology and the use of science for social salvation is a feature of twentieth century revolutions in backward societies: a compensatory wish-dream in which a Promethean faith in human reason and scientific genius is seen as the instrument of transforming poor, weak, unorganized, and semiliterate countries into clean, strong, modern, and efficient ones. Among the many schools of futurology in the 1920s were: Bogdanov's Tectology or the fusion of all sciences into a universal organizational science; Alexei Gastev's N.O.T.—the Scientific Organization of Labor through the quasi-robotization of the Russian worker; Platon Kerzhentsev's related League of Time for the scientific elimination of inefficiency in time, space, motion, and order in everyday life; Konstantin Tsiolkovsky's rocket research and N. A. Hyoin's Society for Interplanetary Communication; and Bio-Cosmism which taught eternal life, the revival of the dead, conquest of the universe, and the inalienable right to room in space.

By "revolutionary utopianism" I mean the numerous enthusiastic movements that sprang up spontaneously in the Revolution with purpose of remaking human life, the environment, and the personality form the bottom up—and as soon as possible. Among the most important movements were: iconoclasm, the thorough destruction of old culture and its values; carnivalism, the destruction of the old order with the help of laughter and celebration; militant atheism, the elimination of God and the creation of a new morality for the proletariat; egalitarianism, the equalization of income, personal appearance, and living conditions, and the elimination of deference and hierarchy of all kinds; urbanism, the planning of new giant cities; and communalism, experiments of living, eating, and spending one's leisure time in orderly communes.

Two of the major themes of an older Russian science fiction literature were "capitalist hell" and "communist heaven." The former theme draws its inspiration from Jack London's *Iron Heel* (1908), which was translated into Russian before the Revolution and made into a film in 1919. It transformed Marxist teachings about capitalism into vivid and comprehensible prophecies about its evil powers. One of the earliest representatives of the first theme was Aleksei Tolstoi's famous *Aelita* (1923, which was also filmed), in which the plot of Bogdanov's harmonious, communist Mars fighting against the vicious capitalist world was inverted: the heroes of the Russian Revolution did not go to Mars in order to learn, but in order to free the inhabitants of the "fifth Technocracy," a fascist slave state, led by coldly calculating engineers. In his later work, *Engineer Garin's Death Ray* (1924), a man aspires to become a fascist-type dictator by means of a super weapon. Fascism (which came to power in Italy in

1922) raised its ugly head again in Marietta Shaginian's (pseudonym Jim Dollar) *Mess Mend: or A Yankee in Petrograd* (1923), in which the world is described as having been divided into a peace-loving, technologically advanced socialist bloc and a capitalist-imperialist bloc in which coolies and workers are exploited and poverty prevails. Yakov Okunev's *Tomorrow* (1924) reverses the gloomy conclusions of London's *Iron Heel*. The Wheat King and other millionaires who support the racist and chauvinism Western government incite workers into strikes in order to get rid of them and establish a militarist-capitalist-clerical order. But they are defeated after the communist takeover of the Atlantic fleet. The army of German workers attacks Paris and the army of the Soviet Union liberates India; then a worldwide federation of Soviet states is established with London as its capital.

A.R. Palei's *Gulfstream* (1928) is both more ambitious and more subtle than Okunev's book. His "capitalist hell" is the United States where very advanced specialization, humdrum routing, regulated family life, compulsory TV, and the gradual loss of the faculty of speech are balanced by modern machines, short working days, high salaries, safe working conditions and welfare. It is, in other words, a Zamyatin-like nightmare in the world of capital. The Republic of Soviets of the Old World (The Soviet Union, China, and Japan)—where children have such names as Rem, Roza, and Electra—sends its techno-knights to fight against enemies with the help of orange beams in order to help workers to liberate themselves. A similar theme, in which American workers are described as robot-like monsters (like the oxen and the primitives which Taylor regarded as ideal for his own Taylor system), is present in Alexander Beliaev's book, *Struggle in Space*, which is about an aerial war between the United States and the Soviet Union (for which reason the U.S. Air Force financed its translation into English).

There were many SF novels in the 1920s like the ones described here. Let me make a few generalizations about them. First, the genre resembles those "war utopias" published in Europe prior to 1914 and in the 1920s and 1930s. But the depictions of "capitalist hell" and war derive their origins in part from pre-revolutionary Russian novels in which fear of neighbors (especially of Austria), ethnic minorities (Jews in particular), and destructive technologies were expressed. In spite of all of the Marxist rhetoric and hopes of future harmony and decency, a kind of paranoid nationalism and xenophobia, that became so familiar in the era of Cold War, were already present in these works.

Another feature common in early Soviet science fiction literature was its attention to one of the major evils in "capitalist hell," the Taylor system, an intensive labor and management efficiency system created by Frederick Winslow Taylor from Philadelphia. The system was regarded as exploitative and dehumanizing by many workers and labor leaders at the beginning of this century. The attitude of Bolsheviks to "Taylorism" was ambivalent in the 1920s; Lenin supported it, Alexei Gastev made it into a religion, other Bolsheviks opposed it. This contradiction appeared in the science fiction literature as well. In the communist positive utopia, rationalism, symmetry and mathematical precision were seen as liberating values. In the capitalist negative dystopia, the dark side of mechanical work and senseless robotization was emphasized. It is ironic that the latter treatment of mechanization formed the central theme in Zamiatin's nightmarish single state in the dystopia *We*.

"Communist heavens"—sometimes incorporated as happy endings in the novels depicting capitalist hell—formed alternatives to the misery and horror of private enterprise, racism, and militarism. "How could anyone make a socialist revolution in a country like this without dreamers?" Lenin asked at the beginning of the revolution. This remark was quoted in the preface to Vivian Itin's *Land of Gonguri* (1922), which was the first post-revolutionary mechanism (i.e., mechanized utopia - *ed.*). Itin (1894-1945), a former student of law, had fought during the revolution in Siberia, pronounced death sentences in the local courts of justice, and closed down churches. His hero, a sixteen-year-old Bolshevik, who is awaiting execution by Kolchak's troops in Siberian, is dreaming of Gonguri, a "more perfect world" where streets wander through a continuous garden with squares of mirrored glass and palaces of gold and topaz; where every building is a city with tens of thousands of residents; where construction of new cities is performed as a festival at incredible speed; where monuments are raised to events and not to individuals (a notion taken right out of *Red Star*); and whose citizens live without government, crime, war, or violence and who partake of a substance that endows them with love and the ability to fly. The customary contrast is presented by scenes of horror and devastation on war-torn Earth. Gonguri is an atypical utopia of the period: though resembling Bogdanov's Mars, it is a utopia *ex machina* in both senses of the word, full of machines and created out of interplanetary travel rather than out of revolution. Its "communism of the heart" puts it closer to the exoticism of Rider Haggard's *She* and James Hilton's *Lost Horizon* than to the visions of Marx. The pathos of the hero's execution was matched in real life by the fact that peasants bought the novel and used it for cigarette paper and that the author was purged by Stalin in 1936.

In contrast, Yakov Okunev's *Coming World* (1923) is the quintessential piece for the genre. The author was a prolific journalist and a seasoned atheist debater. His vision of the year 2123 is of an "all-world city" connected by tunnels and bridges so that one can literally walk around the world through city streets. Identical dwelling houses support on their rooftops all public buildings. There are no states, nations, or frontiers. Cable TV and electronic grids unite the planet in a single communications system. The economy is run by computers and machines, overseen by a rotating committee of technocrats, elected not to rule but to check, account, and control—as in Bogdanov and as in Lenin's famous dream of future statelessness and the "administration of things" in his 1917 work, *State and Revolution.* People are hairless, shameless, and egalitarian. Everyone works. "You will want to work," explains a guide to the visitors from the year 1923. Gone are war, prostitution, exploitation, famine, private property, and coercion. Here to stay are harmony, order, and comradeship. There is but one law: freedom. This is defined as follows: "All citizens of World City live as they please—but everybody wants what everybody else wants."

A dozen variants on this scenario sprang into print in the 1920s, each with its own piquant predictive details. V. D. Nikolskii's *In a Thousand Years* (1927), for example, added synthetic food, the restoration of human organs, and prolonged life of the species; and Innokenty Zhukov's frolicking *Voyage of the "Red Star" Pioneer Detachment to the Land of Marvels* (1924), set in 1957, had the usual harmonious, communal, technologized, peace-loving globe, but also a children's movement, Esperanto, moving sidewalks in garden cities, flying homes, and women liberated and elevated to high positions.

The last communist SF utopia before the anti-utopian curse of Stalin descended was Yan Larri' s *The Land of the Happy* (1931), an exceptionally vivid and detailed description of the U.S.S.R. in the 1980s, with the usual supercities, garden rings around the towns, Zamiatin-like technology, skyscrapers, and personal flight. Equality is underlined by the universal use of the familiar *ty* (thou) and identical costumes. But those costumes (unlike Zamyatin's "unifs") are worn only during the five hours a day of compulsory or socially necessary labor; after that people wear what they choose. And they have real names (Neon, Maiya, Nefelin, Shtorm) and not numbers as in *We*. The unusual feature of Larri's book is the stress on youth culture, leisure, communal meals, and vacation life in such resort hotels as Sun Valley, Happy Fisherman, Calabria, Gay Pilot, Evening Stars, and Future. The book rings with laughter, debate, and fantasy within the fantasy world. One character suggests reducing all library books in the world (including the works of Comrade Stalin!) to shorthand for the sake of space. *Land of the Happy*, from internal evidence as well as specific remarks in the preface, was clearly an answer to Zamiatin's *We*. The debate over space colonization recalls the latter; but the use of super-technology is benign and there is a Soviet of a Hundred instead of the dread Well-Doer of Zamiatin. In responding to Zamiatin, Larri may have gone too far in depicting a happy, egalitarian, and consumer-oriented future, and his insult to Stalin could not have gone unnoticed. He wrote no more utopias; nor did anyone else for the remainder of the Stalin regime. Larri himself was purged in 1941.

There is a great deal to be analyzed in Soviet utopian fiction of the revolutionary period, but I will make only two main points, both in relation to Zamiatin's *We*, a novel too well-known for me to recapitulate its story and its message. First it is important to remember that Zamiatin did not write *We* before all these books appeared. His dystopian impulses arose even earlier: at the specter of modern Western industrialization and mechanization which he saw at first-hand while living in England; during the Revolution when he witnessed extreme forms of techno-fantasy and the robotization of workers in the visions of Alexei Gastev and others; and, without doubt, in reaction to Bogdanov's *Red Star.* But it is certainly true that some of the elements of entropy which he feared remained prominent in the science fiction of the 1920s: super-technology, visual and social uniformity, glass and steel urban worlds, big weapons and space exploration plans, and a pervasive rationalism in life.

On the other hand, revolutionary SF can also be read as an answer to Zamiatin, some of the authors having read *We* even though it was never published in the U.S.S.R. Even those who did not know it continued Bogdanov's fundamental argument that man could live in a totally communist, industrialized, and "self-regulated" society in a state of genuine humanitarian equality, freedom, harmony, and peace, without dictators, cults of personality, regimentation, and repression. This warm-blooded and sincere dream, whatever we in the late twentieth century may think of it, was at the very centre of the revolutionary age of Soviet science fiction.

It was not, of course, the only kind of hope and vision that arose from the Revolution. Accompanying the Red Utopia of Bolshevism-urbanist and forward looking as the Green Utopia, only faintly suggested in "the land beyond the green wall" of Zamiatin's *We.* In SF it appeared at least twice: in Alexander Chaianov's *Journey of My Brother Alexei to the Peasant Utopia* (1920) and in Peter Krasnov's *Beyond the Thistle* (1922). The first, written, by a populist-minded economist, envisioned an overthrow of Bolshevik power in the 1930s, and a self-sufficient deurbanized peasant society of the year 1984. It was legally published in the Soviet Russia but its author was purged in the early 1930s. The second, by a defeated White Cossack general, was published in Germany in 1921. Its dream was of a restored Russian, Orthodox, conservative, Romanov monarchy built on the ruins of Bolshevik mismanagement and famine (the famine of 1921 was actually raging when Krasnov wrote the book). Both of them employed advanced technology selectively for defense, long-distance travel, and the enrichment of agriculture—but displayed a hatred of large cities and super modernization for its own sake. These were not adventitious fantasies floating in the void. They appeared in the context of the "green movement" of independent peasants and partisans in the Civil War, of rural and pastoral utopianizing in *belles lettres* (Sergei Esenin), and in the nostalgia of many Russians—at home and abroad—for a lost world of perceived rustic harmony and order.

Utopian SF came to an end in 1931 and disappeared until after the death of Stalin. SF in the 1930s and during the World War II presented near rather than far projection, emphasized realizable technological growth rather than techno-fantasies, and put stress on "capitalist hells," espionage, and war. The anti-Bolshevik utopographers were of course wholly suppressed: Zamiatin forced into emigration in 1931; Chaianov purged at about the same time; Krasnov arrested by Soviet forces at the end of the war and hanged in Moscow. But pro-Bolsheviks felt the wrath of Stalin as well: at least two, Itin and Larri, are known to have been arrested. The genre was itself repudiated. The Great Leader, his economic managers, and his literary magnates had no interest in abstract fantasy—they wanted to promote practical results in present day economic growth and technical applications. Stalin himself, who spoke of the joy of Soviet life in 1936, clearly had no affection for pictures of happiness in a future dictatorless, "self-regulating" society and in images of mass consumerism. Most important of all, we know from his general policies, he detested the social values that lay at the very foundation of these utopias: freedom, individual consumption, communalism, brotherhood, internationalism, warm-blooded spontaneity, statelessness, absolute equality, and anti-authoritarianism. So the revolutionary red age of Soviet SF ended, even though the production of SF continued throughout the Stalin period. But the real science fiction was to be found in Soviet political reality itself, in what Robert C. Tucker calls The Fantasy State. At the centre of that fantasy was the Beloved Comrade Stalin—all alone.

Original publication: Study Group on the Russian Revolution. *Sbornik* (now known as *Revolutionary Russia*) 13, 1987, pp. 60-64. Leeds, England.

Selected Bibliography

Beliaev, A. *Vlastiteli Mira*. Leningrad, 1929.

Bogdanov, A. *Red Star: the First Bolshevik Utopia*. Bloomington, 1984.

Chaianov, A. (pseud. I. Kremnev) "Journey of My Brother Alexei to the Peasant Utopia" in R.E.F. Smith, ed., *Russian Peasant*. London, 1976.

Iivonen, J. "Utopiat vernäjänkeilisessa kirjallisuudessa 1780-luvulta 1920-luvulle," *Portti*, 4 (1983).

Itin, V. *Strana Gonguri.* Kansk, 1922.

Krasnov, P.N. *Za chertompolokhom.* Berlin, 1922.

Larri, Y. *Strana schastlivykh.* Leningrad, 1931.

Nikolskii, V. *Cherez 1000 let.* Leningrad, 1928.

Okunev, Y. *Griadushchii Mir.* Petrograd, 1923.

Okunev, Y. *Zastrashnii den'.* Moscow, 1924.

Palei, A. *Golfshtrem.* Moscow, 1928.

Shaginian, M. (pseud. Jim Dollar) *Mess Mend: ili Yanki v Petrograde.* Moscow, 1924.

Stites, R. "Stalin: Utopian or Anti-Utopian?" in J. Held, ed., *The Cult of Power.* New York, 1982.

Stites, R. "Utopias in the Air and on the Ground" in L. Kleberg and R. Stites, eds., *Utopia in Russian History, Culture, and Thought* (the Stockholm-Turku Utopia Conference), special number of the journal *Russian History* (December, 1984).

Stites, R. "Utopias of Time, Space, and Life," *Revue des études slaves* (Summer, 1984).

Susiluoto, I. "Tieteiskir jallisuudan suuri Scina ja utopia Punatähti," *Aikakone*, I/4 (Fall, 1982).

Suvin, D. "The Utopian Tradition of Russian Science Fiction," *Modern Language Review*, 66 (1971).

Tolstoy, A. *Aelita.* Moscow, 1923.

Zamiatin, E. *We.* New York, 1952.

Zhukov, I. *Puteshestvie zvena "Krasnoi Zvezdy" v stranu chudes.* Kharkov, 1924.

Rituals and Symbols

10

Bolshevik Ritual Building in the 1920s

Ritualism—the use of created forms of symbolic behavior for devotional and celebratory moments in life—found its way into many corners of the Russian Revolution. The emergence of a search for new ritual as part of a Bolshevik religion reveals much about the transition from the revolutionary utopianism of the Civil War period to the revolutionary experimentalism of the 1920s. Many Bolsheviks were seized by the vision of War Communism as a permanent order and an ideal structure. When this vision receded in the early 1920s, some revolutionaries turned to another form of utopia building—experimental life from the bottom up. The years of NEP were an ideal setting for social and cultural experimentation. On the one hand, the partial restoration of capitalism engendered fierce hostility among committed communists, particularly veterans, workers, and radical intellectuals. Some of these tried to fight, repudiate, or even forget the realities of NEP by creating experimental enclaves of equality, community, and innovative culture or by drastically reordering old institutions. On the other hand, the very atmosphere of peace and normality, of relative tolerance and pluralism, created a sympathetic environment for leisurely culture building on a trial-and-error basis.[1]

The ritual race for Russian souls was one of these experiments. Its roots can be found in the intellectual current within early Bolshevism known as god building, launched after the Revolution of 1905 by the writer Maxim Gorky and the future commissar of enlightenment Anatolii Lunacharskii. It was based on a desire to infuse socialism with a religious element. Although Lenin, the leader of the Bolshevik Party, fought it angrily, god building recurred in many guises in the first decade after the revolution of 1917: in the arts, in the debates over communist morality, in the cult of Lenin, in revolutionary festival. Lunacharskii bowed to Lenin's ban on god building as a movement but never abandoned its religious kernel. He envisioned socialism as immediate community and faith triumphant, its basic human attributes as love and solidarity, and its historical agent as the proletariat. This was expressed in his own writings and speeches, in the kind of art he favored, and in the content of the early festivals that he promoted—particularly the massive theatrical spectacles in Petrograd in 1919-20 that were enveloped in myth, martyrdom, sacrality, and holy joy. But the broad religiosity of the early outdoor festivals (*prazdniki*) diminished in the 1920s, giving way to a heavy politicization and instrumentalism.[2]

Bolshevik observers of culture in the early 1920s were alive to the ritual and theatrical elements unfolding in all kinds of arenas. There was often a kind of reductionalism in the rhapsodic appeals of some to turn all of life into theater and all of theater into church. But it became increasingly clear that revolutionary forms and symbols, modes of expression and gathering—the festivals of revolution—did not in and of themselves provide the basic elements of a new religion: community rites of celebration, dedication, or mourning that evoked emotional forces transcending political and civic needs. But what kind of rites were needed? How could they be constructed? Of what use would they be? On these matters considerable acrimony was called forth.

Part of the problem resided in the nature of the ritual that would be replaced. The peasant way of life (*byt*) was determined by a system of values, customs, and folkways, varying from one community to another according to local history and the organization of economic life. Inseparable from *byt* was *obriad* (literally rite or ritual), a system of symbols and symbolic behavior rooted in tradition, displayed or performed in connection with the seasonal and life cycles. The imagery and lexicon of traditional Russian ritual were drawn almost exclusively from the Orthodox church calendar, though often heavily infused with pre-Christian pagan elements. These rituals possessed theatrical and aesthetic values for people who had almost no contact with the art and theater of high culture. More important, they possessed practical and instrumental significance, in that peasants believed very concretely in their established function. Legitimacy and salvation were vested in the proper ceremony of naming children, entering wedlock, and laying souls to rest. For the community as a whole, periodic rituals provided a rich and colorful social life, punctuated by convivial feasts and often ending in the fleeting moment of release—freedom from backbreaking toil, drunkenness, brawling, and sexual misbehavior. Rituals embedded family history and life-cycle events in the memory of the entire village, thus affirming the importance of each person in it. Some of these practices—though diluted through adaptation—migrated to the urban milieu.[3]

Judging from the literature advocating and accompanying the new ritual, the advocates had two kinds of things in mind. On the political and practical side, they opposed the old ways in order to fight religion with their own "visible Church," introduce a tone of rationality into lower-class leisure, struggle against drinking and fighting, promote labor stability, teach loyalty to the regime, and in a general way impose an urban order upon a rural mass seen as backward. On the idealistic side, they proposed to emotionalize the revolution, promote a spiritual image of Bolshevism, and—it seems likely—provide some symbols of class consciousness for the working class at a time when such consciousness appeared to be ebbing.[4]

Recognition of the problem began during the Civil War but found a focus only after the debacle of the Young Communist (Komsomol) Christmas Carnival of 1922. Suggested by an enthusiastic promoter of atheism, the economist I. I. Skvortsov-Stepanov—who was also an ardent opponent of god building—this episode was one of the landmarks of the antireligious campaign of early Bolshevism. All over Soviet Russia, Young Communist agitators staged mocking parades parodying religious belief, the clergy, the saints, and even the gods of Christianity, Judaism, and Islam. The public reaction was so negative that the practice was discontinued and leaders began searching for a more subtle way to replace religion. One of these was ritualism. The main spokesmen for it were Mikhail Kalinin, "peasant" president of the republic; P. M. Kerzhentsev, a Proletkult theater specialist; Leon Trotsky; Emelian Iaroslavskii, founder of the Godless League; and the urbane and literary physician V. V. Veresaev. Kalinin quoted peasants who were asking him for surrogate rituals. Trotsky observed that workers were already creating their own ritual forms. Kerzhentsev viewed civic ritual as part of the theatricalization of life. Iaroslavskii stressed the need to move beyond the mocking carnival. Veresaev, the most thoughtful of them all, mapped out the relationship of ritual to the rich and healthy world of emotions. They all argued that since religion was being discouraged and taken away from the people, something had to be given back to them. To do so, they further argued, was not a capitulation to religion but an appropriate mode of peaceful competition with it—one that would give rise to a new communist spirit.[5]

After a good deal of conference talk and journalistic ventilation, the party in October 1923 issued a circular recommending communist public festivals and private rituals. Of the first, Iaroslavskii was the main interpreter. He promoted "revolutionary countercelebrations," sober and joyous—processions with revolutionary songs and music, lectures and reports, and reasonable games—all timed for the cycles of the seasons to compete with church holidays. These festivals, supplementing the already established holidays of the revolutionary calendar, were to eschew mockery and insult but were to offer fun as well as enlightenment, perhaps embellished by a voluntary act of labor in order to woo youth away from the prayers and drunkenness of the old holy days. After the misconceived Komsomol Christmas, a Komsomol Easter had been organized in 1923—not a one-day act of carnival but a kind of unholy week of antireligious consciousness, raising speeches replacing the mockery. Published guides on Communist Easters described reports, charades, songs, poems, tales, stories, legends, quotations from atheist "masters," and skits such as "The Political Trial of the Bible," "The Komsomol Petrushka," and a "Trial of God."

A foreign visitor who witnessed the Leningrad counter-Easter of 1924 tells of Pioneers singing "materialist" songs, displaying slogans such as "The Smoke of the Factory Is Better Than the Smoke of Incense," and performing an atheist play to an audience of a thousand. Eventually a whole new counterfestival calendar emerged made up of "parallel" days, opposing Electric Day to Elijah Day, Forest Day to Trinity Sunday, Harvest Day to the Feast of the Intercession, and the Day of Industry to the Feast of Transfiguration.

The problem was that if the performances were salted with antireligious skits, they descended back to carnival; if they were not, they were dull.[6]

The result was a shift in the realm of invented traditions from public display to the more intimate spheres of community and family. In the local community the focus for new ritual was the club, envisioned by some as a surrogate church or civic temple. An early apologist for the Palace of Workers, repudiating the old tsarist People's House (*Narodnyi Dom*) as an arena for "bread and games" to lull the masses, and scorning the bourgeois clubs as shelters for the card games and banquets of the affluent, described the workers' palace as "a cultural building for a new, healthy life of the proletariat."[7] The problem was to transform the workers' club of the revolutionary period (which had been, like those of 1789 and 1871 in France, psychological staging areas of revolutionary political action) into something solemn, joyous, and celebrative of the new order, without descending to banality.

A barrier to the fulfillment of this ideal was the dichotomy between the designers and the users of the club—a dichotomy that has often beset religious congregations in modern times. The exterior forms and the interior space of the clubs were in many ways congenial to the utopian speculations that accompanied the revolution. Architectural experimentation, fueled by self-consciously radical impulses, coincided with the turn toward indoor ritual and a search for the forms of community. The earliest clubs were opened in the premises of confiscated mansions or public edifices. But almost at once there appeared grandiose plans for huge central palaces of labor, followed by projects for local clubs in neighborhoods and enterprises. They varied little in interior content: library, dining room, large auditorium for solemn occasions, music room, theater, and recreational facilities. Variations of the name "workers' club" (*rabochii klub*) abounded: Workers' Palace, House of Lenin, Proletarian House, House of Workers, Palace of Culture (and of Rest), and so on. The earliest projects bordered on fantasy, with grandiose structures resembling medieval cathedrals, the Hotel de Ville in Paris, railway stations, and chateaux. In the mid-1920s, especially with the work of the brilliant architect Konstantin Mel'nikov, clubs become more functional and more like the places where their users worked. These buildings provided—on paper—a broad range of collective activities, public services, and a grand setting, often with imaginative use of partitions for self-changing space.[8]

A sense of what went on inside may be gained from the report, based on "long observations" of a workers' club written by a ritual advisor and specialist in the 1920s. The closest thing to a quasi-religious ritual was the frequent meeting to honor special people or events. According to his observations, the decor was uniformly artless, routinized, and often inappropriate: red table cover, a bust or portrait of a leader, slogans on the walls, and a dais; and on particularly "festive" occasions, the bric-a-brac of a bygone age—crepe paper, paper lanterns, a fir tree. Music was provided by a brass ensemble which offered "flourishes" to punctuate the proceedings and endless renderings of the "Internationale."

Meetings were usually poorly timed, too long, and stilted—consisting of repetitive speeches, the awarding of prizes, the marches of the honored up to the dais. The formalism and the passivity of the spectators led the observer to assess the whole routine as "boring, dreary, and tiresome." His offhand remarks about the eternal awkwardness of ushers who carried banners up to the front reveal in a flash how the easy grace of the outdoor festival with its stately reverence and its familiar catalogue of movements and gestures became cramped inside the artificial premises of the new "workers' church." In the schools, communist ritual took the form of antireligious propaganda: a skit about Science Triumphant, a mock church service, a choral singing of "the antireligious Internationale," a verse about "The Priest and the Devil," and a collective declamation called "Storming the Trust of Heaven."[9]

At the level of family life-cycle ritual, the Bolsheviks made an effort to drape the three main junctures of human life—birth, marriage, and death—in revolutionary clothing. Octobering (*Oktiabrina*), the dedication of newborns (called Starring [*Zvezdina*] in some places), was the most celebrated of these. It began haltingly and sporadically in the Civil War but began to spread in the early 1920s. Trotsky, hearing of a mock ceremony of "inspection" of a newborn child of workers by their factory comrades, saw it as a spontaneous expression of a new workers' ritual culture. No survey of Octoberings was ever published, but it seems to have taken hold in factory towns in the early 1920s. One of the first recorded in detail (November 22, 1923) took place in Kharkov, where a baby daughter was Octobered and presented with a gift—a portrait of the infant Lenin. The parents delivered a verbal promise to raise the child in the spirit of communism, the "Internationale" was sung, and choruses performed folk songs. The reporter claims a wide influence thereafter in the vicinity of Kharkov.[10]

At an Octobering in a Moscow club, a detachment of Pioneers with flag and drum chanted "We are the Young Guard of Workers and Peasants" as they escorted a mother to the dais. "The child belongs to me," she declaimed, "only physically. For spiritual upbringing I present it to society." The Pioneers then folded the baby in a red banner and vowed to enroll her in their unit. Since the Soviet law of 1917 permitted all citizens to change their names at age eighteen, some adults began to follow suit. A group of women workers, hoping to promote Octobering, had themselves renamed at a club ceremony as the "Vanguard of the New Life" amid some muffled guffaws from the menfolk. After a few months, they reclaimed their old names, except for one, Avdotiia, who had taken the name Revolution (*Revoliutsiia*) and was ever after known as Auntie Revo (*Tëtya Reva*).[11]

The new names given to Octobered babies offer a code to the values officially revered in the early years. The French Revolution had invoked the shades of classical figures (Brutus, Hannibal, Gracchus); and European Social Democrats had tried to popularize socialist names (Lassallo, Marxina, and Primo Maggio in Italy; Bebelina in Germany). The few dozen Russian "revolutionary" names that I have uncovered from the period divide in the following way:

Revolutionary Heroes and Heroines

Spartak, Marks, Engelina, Libknekht, Liuksemburg, Roza, Razin, Mara, Robesper, Danton, Bebel', Vladlen, Vladlenina, Ninel, Il'ich, Il'ina (all variants of Lenin); Bukharina, Stalina, Budena.

Revolutionary Concepts

Pravda, Revmir (revolution and peace), Konstitutsiia, Revdit (child of the revolution), Dotnara (daughter of the toiling people), Era, Karm (Red Army), Barrikada, Giotin (Guillotine), Bastil', Tribuna, Revoliutsiia, Krasnyi (Red), Kommuna, Parizhkommuna (Paris Commune), Proletarii, Buntar' (rebel), Fevral', Mai, Oktiabrina, Serpina (from sickle), Molot (hammer), Smychka (alliance of workers and peasants), Volia (will or freedom), Svoboda (freedom), Dinamit, Ateist, Avangarda, Iskra (spark), Marseleza (Marseillaise).

Industrial, Scientific, and Technical Imagery

Tekstil, Industriia, Traktorina, Dinamo, Donbass, Truda, Smena (shift), Radium, Genii (genius), Ideia, Elektrifikatsiia.

Culture, Myth, Nature, Place Names

Traviata, Aida, Les (forest), Luch (light), Poema, Okean, Orel (eagle), Solntse (sun), Zvezda (star), Razsvet (dawn), Atlantida, Brungilda, Minevra [sic], Monblan (Mont Blanc), Kazbek, Singapur.

There were the usual cases of error, resulting from misunderstanding of words. In 1919, peasants in a commune named their daughter "Markiza" (Marquise), thinking it irreligious and somehow vaguely foreign. Other names chosen included Commentary, Embryo, and Vinaigrette.[12]

It is hard to assess the semiotic significance of this because we do not know how many people were given which of these names. But in musing about what kind of people endowed and bore them (mostly workers), one feels an element of magic. Names in fact are magical in many so-called primitive and not-so-primitive cultures. This particular invented ritual was an expression of the wish to create a new reality by means of imagery, to populate the world with humans called Spark, Joy, Will, Electric, Rebel, and Barricade, and to fashion living monuments to the recent and distant heroic past (Vladlen, Spartacus). But it was also an almost mystical quest for another world by giving image to what is perhaps the most intimate possession of any human being. In their variety, color, and rich associative capacities, the revolutionary names of the 1920s represented a sensibility exactly opposite to that of those people who aspired to a collective identity for the masses. And it was also a national and generational revolt against the Greco-Russian Orthodox culture of the past with its ancient and limited repertoire of Aleksandrs, Andreis, Sofiias, Petrs, and Tatianas, though some tried to do this by choosing pre-Christian Slavic names, such as Mstislav or Sviatopolk, that had fallen into disuse in modern times.[13]

From the perspective of the ritual designers, Octobering possessed many distinct virtues. By allowing the couple to choose the baby's name, it rejected the custom of many villages for the male head of the household to make that choice. By providing the parents with a suggested list of "revolutionary" names, it reduced the number of people bearing names of saints (among whom had been very few workers, peasants, intellectuals, or radicals), and also eliminated another excuse for holiday observance: the traditional name day of the saint. By holding the naming in a club or factory or village reading room and allowing the local Bolshevik or manager to officiate with the aid of a Pioneer detachment, it excluded the clergy. By skipping the watery immersion in a damp church building and substituting a red banner for the white baby shawl, it promoted both good health and Bolshevik symbolism. And by treating the mother as an equal and prominent celebrant, it visibly repudiated the church's practice of banning women from the church until forty days after childbirth.[14]

Getting married at a Red Wedding—instead of at the dry civil registry office or in the church—had a dual significance. Its form showed a desire for the solemnity, decor, and ritual that were wholly absent at marriage registry offices. Its content treated the wife and the husband as legally, politically, and symbolically equal. During the French Revolution, the policeman Joseph Fouché had wanted Temples of Love built to stage all weddings. Such edifices did not bloom in the Russian Revolution, and the civil office remained a cramped, crowded bureau where couples got married in twenty minutes without so much as a rose or a ring. Some people obviously wanted more, as did the prophets of the new ritualism.[15]

Red Weddings appeared at about the same time as the Octobering ceremonies. Critics such as Veresaev thought them banal. He described one, of December 1924, in a club of leatherworkers: a red covered table, a portrait of Lenin, the vows of bride and groom to each other and to communism, reports and speeches, a wedding gift for the new couple—works by Lenin and Zinoviev—and the mandatory "Internationale." Village Red Weddings added the traditional custom of *chastushka* (the declamation of witty folk sayings) and *khorovod* (round dance and song). Among the peasants, attempts were made to insert industrial imagery into the feast by employing the new Ford tractor, adorned with red flags, as a wedding carriage. But the custom did not catch on in the countryside— peasants wanted something longer, more solemn and elaborate, followed by a day or two of carousing. In 1925, according to one estimate, 75 percent of peasant weddings were still held in church. Even in the industrial towns, there is no sign that the Red Wedding became a universal or even mass phenomenon. [16]

Here, too, the Red Wedding had some advantages over the Orthodox wedding. It was shorter, requiring far less expenditure of energy, and it advanced and signaled the doctrine of the equality of the sexes, an official position of the regime. This had appeal to some urban elements. But for the peasants, it apparently had little. Furthermore, the Red Wedding, even at its most elaborate, lacked the stunning beauty and magnificence of the Orthodox nuptial service—the song, the incense, the costumes, the rings signifying an unbroken life together. Furthermore, the church wedding was preceded by extremely stylized and theatrical preliminary rituals of courtship, matchmaking, serenading, wailing, improvised jokes, and carefully choreographed movements; and it was crowned by a joyous feast of dancing, eating, and drinking. The lamentation on the coming loss of freedom for the bride and the graphic display of the bloodstained sheet from the wedding couch as proof of virginity may have seemed to Bolsheviks debasing to women, but these customs were part of an ancient tradition and thus were revered by most peasants. In fact, the village wedding was the central event in the life of every person, and, for women especially, its signs and gestures were interlocked with the whole culture of folk tales, folk songs, epics, laments, sayings, and customs. Desacralizing the wedding was an assault on rural culture as a whole. [17]

The revolutionary funeral—it is significant that no neologism was applied to it and it was officially called "civic burial"—was the most problematic of the invented rituals and the most resistant to innovation. At the root of the problem was its origin as a martyr's funeral. Drawing on nineteenth-century precedents, the genre had emerged in 1905 with the funeral of Nikolai Bauman and found artistic stylization in the painting *Red Funeral* by Isaak Brodskii (1906). This style was adopted and amplified in the first great Bolshevik interment, that of Moisei Uritskii, held in September 1918. With its guard of honor, the lying in state in luxurious surroundings, the huge cortege with ornate red catafalque, the carriage escort and lone caparisoned horse, rows of bedecked armored cars, and over-flying aircraft, it far surpassed the obsequies of former martyrs of the revolutionary movement. The city boss Grigorii Zinoviev displayed the full power of Petrograd's ceremonial magnificence and mobilized an entire city for the most elaborate funeral seen there since the interment of Aleksandr III in 1894—and even more dazzling in that the public was in full presence for the entire day, with dispersed units touching almost every neighborhood in the huge city. It became a model for hero funerals in the Civil War and prefigured most of the elements in the Lenin funeral of 1924, an event of stupendous importance. For the next two years, revolutionary burials became a regular feature in the street life of Russia.[18]

But not all people who die are revolutionary martyrs or heroes. The Orthodox church panikhida, a work of extraordinary textual richness and beauty, continued to attract masses of people, and not only in the countryside. Even at radical Kronstadt in the early days of the revolution, fallen sailors were given an Orthodox requiem on Anchor Square followed by a general singing of the "Workers' Marseillaise." As tension between church and state mounted, people began searching for alternative and politically acceptable ways to bury their dead. A peasant in 1919 asked Kalinin what kind of service the regime had in mind and if it was really necessary for him to bury his son—who was no revolutionary—to the strains of "You Fell Victim." New forms began to appear ad hoc, uneasy blends of old pious forms and modern political speeches. Veresaev described them in the mid-1920s as arid: a sterile chamber for the wake, mourners with nothing to do, and the customary eulogy for the departed—all of it leaving a void instead of an affirmation of life for the survivors. For poor workers, the rites were empty and cold. Veresaev proposed a wholly new ceremony with original music (instead of the eternal Chopin or the revolutionary funeral marches): sounds of sorrow to evoke genuine emotion followed by triumphant cadences to celebrate continuing life, a choreographed tableau of white-robed young women (recalling the maiden mourners of Orthodox funeral rites), and the mourners' participation in a great catharsis—in other words, an unabashed public display of emotion in the company of loved ones. But even Veresaev conceded that a "symphony of scarlet and black banners and a forest of marvelous palms" was suitable for a great national leader—such as Lenin.[19]

Some hoped to achieve the democratization of death by the use of crematoria. The first European crematorium had been built in Milan in 1876, and many major cities of Europe had them; but none had been allowed in Russia because of the power of the Orthodox church. As early as 1919 architects began designing ceremonial crematoria, bearing such names as "To the Heavens" and "Phoenix" and taking the shape of basilicas, towers, castles, and churches. But in some of these, the lying-in-state halls came in different sizes, indicating hierarchy even in death. This was simply a reflection of the heroic burial culture that was well underway and of the fact that when "important" funerals took place, factories were sometimes closed. Yet the crematorium seemed to promise a mode of neat standardization. Trotsky urged speedy cremations and simple ceremony with red flags, the funeral march, processions, eulogy, and a rifle salute.

The architect Mel'nikov devised a "crematorium-columbarium" for ordinary people where the "family ritual would be revolutionized in a stroke, transcendent beliefs broken down, and the cause of sound health advanced." The first Soviet crematorium was opened in 1927 in the nonfunctioning Donskoi Monastery in Moscow which possessed cellars deep enough for the construction of incinerators and machinery. It contained a Farewell Hall of 150 seats. By the end of 1928 over 4,000 bodies had been cremated there, most of them by "administrative" process (that is, cadavers assigned to it by various institutions, presumably hospitals and morgues). Among the first "volunteers" who requested cremation in their testament were Skvortsov-Stepanov and Aleksandr Bogdanov, who was working to extend human life through blood transfusion.[20]

The fiery machines of the crematoria were the perfect emblem for the Bolshevik way of death: clean, rational, and economical. But this particular fire did not spark the emotions of the majority of Russians who continued to look to the life-giving earth for their place of final rest. The sculptor Sergei Konenkov dreamed of a new kind of cemetery for the future:[21]

The very concept of a "cemetery" will change. They will be parks of good memories. In them, the grateful descendants will "recall" those who did not spare themselves in the name of the common good. Young life will seethe around magnificent works of sculpture and under the canopies of beauteous trees. These parks will become places of leisure and the pride of every Soviet city.

Except for the seething youth, such places have in fact sprouted up in Soviet Russia: the Mars Field in Leningrad, the Revolutionary Necropolis on Red Square, the various military-revolutionary sections of the Novodevichi in Moscow and the Aleksandr Nevskii Lavra and Volkov Cemetery in Leningrad, and the huge memorial grounds containing those fallen in World War II. They are places of immeasurable sadness as well as of national pride and love of homeland—but in this they hardly differ from the overgrown Orthodox churchyards that continue to cover the Russian land.

Revolutionary funerals became the norm for party leaders and other prominent figures in Soviet life. They were also observed by ordinary people, provided—as often happened by way of compromise—that a priest could intone the last rites before the civil ceremony or that a church service was allowed to follow it. Again, Bolsheviks could claim a rational advance over traditional funerals where women and family members questioned the deceased in lamentations about why he had abandoned them by dying, and where women regularly received less ritualistic attention in their burial services. But the civil burials also displayed inequality of a different sort expressed in size of musical accompaniment (often a guitar for a humble person and bands of varying sizes for the elite), length and complexity of ceremony, and symbolic importance of the interment site.[22]

The communist ritual movement of the 1920s did not become a mass phenomenon as it would in the 1960s.[23] Only limited sectors of the urban population, mostly workers and intellectuals, took to it; and the government made no serious effort to sustain it. Peasant dislike or indifference, too, is easily understood: rural people of the older generation missed the little glasses of vodka and appetizers, the cry of "it's bitter," the priest, and the dancing at weddings; the plates of food for the dead; the mysteries, beauties, joys, and ebullience of country-style ritual. One reporter described a "new" wedding in a small town where the guests were expected to partake of cakes and tea and listen to political messages! But there was hostility to ritualism among communists as well. Some Young Communist League members seemed to distrust acts of piety and "beauty" no matter how Bolshevized. A 1930 encyclopedia entry on rituals asserted that "with the development of culture, rituals lose their significance." In the same year we hear of Young Militant Godless children playing "antireligious" military games in which a correct answer about God or atheism enabled the answering team to capture an enemy soldier or fortress, a clear reversion to the tough mode of war on God. Militant and military now converged.

Soviet institutions abandoned the rituals of the 1920s thereafter and succumbed to dry bureaucratic forms. Club meetings of the 1930s adorned their trees with red stars and bayonets and listened to such soul-searing lectures as "The Class Essence of Christmas."[24] Vitalii Zhemchuzhnyi, a filmmaker and writer for the avant-garde *Novyi Lef,* put his finger on the malaise in a critique of ritual building in 1927. "The spreading or propagation of some sort of novel, invented ritual," he wrote, "is an absurd utopia." Archaic ritual, he conceded, symbolized reactionary values. But artificial ritual was worse, since it preserved old elements but had no link to popular psychology. Only an "organic" system of ritual, built over time, could replace the ritual of tradition. He was right and wrong. Invented political and social rituals in nineteenth-century Europe had shown themselves fully capable of taking root if given time to grow. At a more visceral level lurked the deophobia of some communists. Emelian Iaroslavskii, in a striking anecdote, told of a comrade who, in order to avoid the odious prospect of a Red funeral which he considered immoral and barbarous, had endowed his body to a soap factory. This was the fear of a "communist *dvoverie*"—the simultaneous existence of two religions (both retrograde): Christianity and the ritualized communism of a new priesthood, holy day, God (Marx), scripture (his works), angels (the Red Army), and hell (for class enemies). Bolshevism, in this phobic vision, was becoming a religion in reverse. The distaste for it was Lenin's hatred of god building taken to its logical conclusion.[25]

The collapse of Soviet ritualism was of course part of the larger failure of the Bolsheviks to create a new religion around their ideals, myths, and values. For a while, the cult of Lenin seemed to offer a suitable substitute for traditional religions. But, as Nina Tumarkin has shown, the power of that cult began to fade in time and was in the late 1930s weakened by a cult of Stalin. The intensification of the war against God during the First Five-Year Plan also spelled the end of Bolshevik ritual building. Christmas trees were banned in 1929, and Santa Claus was unmasked as an ally of the priest and the kulak; churches were closed, and the antireligious carnival was once again unleashed. A parallel termination of the interesting discourse on communist morality which had occupied many writers in the late 1920s undercut all the other elements of god building in that period. In a larger sense Bolshevism—as the journalist Maurice Hindus observed at the time—while possessing some outward attributes of a religious faith, was actually a nonfaith because it was not forgiving, possessed no deity, exalted science and technology, and offered a "revolutionary" ethics instead of a universal and humane one. Berdiaev noted Bolshevism's lack of inward drama and depth, its weakness in religious psychology, and its pedantry. Years later—and from an entirely different perspective—Mao Zedong voiced his view very succinctly and honestly: "Marxism-Leninism has no beauty nor has it any mystical value. It is only extremely useful."[26]

The relevance of this rather minor exploration of cultural forms of the Russian Revolution ought to be obvious. First of all, if the quest for ritual is seen in combination with other experimental or innovative practices of the period, it should lay low the myth that the 1920s were a "nonutopian" time—a period of hard-headed common sense flanked by the two great utopian and experimental eras of War Communism and the Cultural Revolution of 1928-31. If anything, the NEP period was even more experimental because various groups had the freedom, leisure, and security to test out new human relationships. They were also highly motivated to do so precisely in order to keep the flame of revolutionary myth alive in the drafty and dank landscape of semicapitalism and "bourgeois remnants" of the 1920s. Ritual building was part of a counterculture that sought to affirm October in the face of hard economic realities, harsh physical conditions, and the compromise with the old world (as many perceived the NEP to be). The debate in the Young Communist League over morality and "how to be a good communist" was a perfect reflection of this. Ritualism was its reified counterpart—the visual, kinetic, and symbolic edifice that every value system needs in order to take root or survive. Enthusiasts of a new Bolshevik ritual clearly wanted to enrich and vary life under Soviet socialism and not reduce it or render it less meaningful by submitting it to political or economic machinery. Finally, it goes without saying that the limited success of community and family rituals in the towns was not matched by any success at all in the countryside-a statement that can be made for a whole range of innovative experimentation during the 1920s. This was further proof that urbanites and peasants continued to dwell in two different worlds.

Original publication: In Sheila Fitzpatrick, Alexander Rabinowitch, and Richard Stites, eds. *Russia in the Era of NEP: Explorations in Soviet Society and Culture*. Bloomington, Indianapolis: Indiana University Press, 1991, pp. 295-309.

Notes

1   This is one of the arguments of my book *Revolutionary Dreams: Utopian Vision and Experimental Life in the Russian Revolution* (New York, 1989).
2   For a brief and competent summary of Lunacharskii's religious sensibility, see Jutta Scherrer, "L'intelligentsia russe: sa quête de la 'vérité' religieuse du socialisme," *Le temps de la réflexion*, II (1981), pp. 113-52. For a reading of the revolutionary festivals, see James Von Geldern, *Festivals of Revolution* (forthcoming = *Bolshevik Festivals, 1917-1920*, Berkeley, 1993 - *ed.*), and Stites, "The Origins of Soviet Ritual Style: Symbol and Festival in the Russian Revolution," in Claes Arvidsson

and Lars Erik Blomqvist, eds., *Symbols of Power: The Esthetics of Political Legitimation in the Soviet Union and Eastern Europe* (Stockholm, 1987), pp. 23-42.

3   V. Ia. Propp, *Russkie agrarnye prazdniki* (Leningrad, 1963); Y. M. Sokolov, *Russian Folklore*, trans. C. R. Smith (Detroit, 1971); Mary Matossian, "The Peasant Way of Life," in W. Vucinich, ed., *The Peasant in Nineteenth-century Russia* (Stanford, 1968), pp. 1-40; and K. V. Chistov and T. A. Bernshtam, eds., *Russkii narodnyi svadebnyi obriad* (Leningrad, 1978).

4   See Diane Koenker's essay, above, for the diminution of class consciousness among workers in the 1920s (= "Class Consciousness in Socialist Society: Workers in the Printing Trades during NEP," in *Russia in the Era of NEP*, pp.34-57 - ed.).

5   M. K. [M. I. Kalinin], "Novyi byt," *Krasnyi pakhar*, I (1919), pp. 13-15; *Deietali Oktiabria o religii i tserkvi* (Moscow, 1968), pp. 6-7; V. [P. M.] Kerzhentsev, "Teatr kak vneshkol'noe obrazovanie," *Vneshkol'noe obrazovanie*, 2-3 (Feb.-Mar. 1919), pp. 23-28; L. D. Trotsky, *Problems of Everyday Life* (1923; New York, 1973); Iaroslavskii, *Protiv religii i tserkvi*, 3 vols. (Moscow, 1932-5), vol. III, pp. 220-24; V. V. Veresaev, *Ob obriadakh starykh i novykh* (Moscow, 1926), pp. 5-8; C. Binns, "The Changing Face of Soviet Power: Revolution and Accommodation in the Development of the Soviet Ceremonial System," *Man*, 14 (Dec. 1979), pp. 594-95.

6   Binns, p. 595; Yaroslavskii, *Religiia i R.K.P.* (Moscow, 1925), p. 47; Iaroslavskii, *Protiv religii*, vol. III, pp. 61-63; *Komsomol'skaia Paskha* (Moscow, 1924); Ia. Rezvushkin, *Sud na bogom* (Moscow, 1924); P. Sheffer, *Seven Years in Soviet Russia* (London, 1932), pp. 34-39; F. Kovalev, *Kalendar' religioznykh prazdnikov* (Kharkov, 1930).

7   V. E. Khazanova, ed., *Iz istorii Sovetskoi arkhitektury*, 2 vols. (Moscow, 1963-70), vol. I, pp. 134-35.

8   Ibid., vol. I, pp. 134-43, 150-55, and vol. II, p. 7 (illust.); Kathleen Berton, *Moscow: An Architectural History* (London, 1977), pp. 211-12; Vittorio de Feo, *URSS: architettura, 1917-1936* (Rome, 1963), p. 112; S. F. Starr, *Konstantin Melnikov: Solo Architect in a Mass Society* (Princeton, 1978), pp. 128-47.

9   M. Danilevskii, *Prazdniki obshchestvennogo byta* (Moscow, 1927), pp. 3-13; F. F. Korolev et al., *Ocherki po isloni Sovetskoi shkoly i pedagogiki, 1921-1931* (Moscow, 1961), p. 294.

10 Trotsky, *Problems*, pp. 45-47; Ivan Sukhopliuev, *Oktiabriny* (Kharkov, 1925); A. M. Selishchev, *Iazyk revoliutsionnoi epokhi* (Moscow, 1928), pp. 179-80; and Jenifer McDowell, "Soviet Civil Ceremonies," *Journal for the Scientific Study of Religion* (1974), pp. 267-68, for examples of obscure places where these rituals were performed.

11 Veresaev, *Ob obriadakh*, pp. 22-26; Danilevskii, *Prazdniki,* p. 4.

12 M. Kol'tsov, *Izbrannye proizvedeniia*, 3 vols. (Moscow, 1957), vol. I, p. 574; R. Fueloep-Miller, *The Mind and Face of Bolshevism* (New York, 1965), pp. 193-94; Sukhopliuev, *Oktiabriny*, pp. 20-30; M. K., "Novyi byt"; and personal information from bearers of revolutionary names. For comparisons, see H. de Man, *Psychology of Socialism* (London, 1928), pp. 156-64, and E. M. Thompson, *The Making of the English Working Class* (New York, 1963), p. 407. Science fiction utopias of the period abound in names of this sort.

13 For invented ritual, see Eric Hobsbawm and Terence Ranger, eds., *The Invention of Tradition* (Cambridge, England, 1983). Diane Koenker's small sample of six renamed babies (her essay, above {*op. cit.*, p. 49 - *ed.*}) presents an interesting case for analysis: two Vladimirs, two Rosas, one Margarita, and one October. Vladimir is the ultimate Russian Orthodox saint's name, but it was also widely adopted at that moment, in many variants (see my list), because it was Lenin's first name. Rosa or Rose (*Roza* in Russian), though not common (except among Jews), was not unusual, yet it was a popular revolutionary name also because of its association with the Polish-German revolutionary martyr Rosa Luxemburg. Margarita, more popular in some non-Russian areas of the Soviet Union, may have been the only conventional name in this sample.

14 Natalie Moyle, "Death in Life: The Role of Women in Russian Ritual," unpublished ms.; Janna Gross, "Krasnyi Obriad," unpublished ms. I thank the authors for access to their work.

15 For the civil (ZAGS) wedding, see Stites, *The Women's Liberation Movement in Russia* (Princeton, 1978), pp. 363-64. Fouché, cited in Ernest Henderson, *Symbol and Satire in the French Revolution* (New York, 1912), p. 409.

16 Veresaev, *Ob obriadakh*; Vadim Bayan [V. I. Sidorov], *Kumachevye gulianki: khorovodnye igry* (Moscow, 1927), pp. 16-25; G. B. Zhirnova, "Nekotorye problemy i itogi izucheniia svadebnogo rituala v russkom gorode serediny XIX-nachala XX v.," in Chistov and Bernshtam, *Russkii narodnyi svadebnyi obriad*, pp. 32-47; M. Hindus, *Red Bread* (Bloomington, 1988), p. 197; Trotsky, *Problems*, p. 46; R. Pethybridge, *Social Prelude to Stalinism* (London, 1974), p. 55 (wedding figures). See also Helmut Altrichter's essay, above (= "Insoluble Conflicts: Village Life between Revolution and Collectivization," *Russia in the Era of NEP*, pp. 192-209 - *ed.*).

17 Moyle, "Death in Life"; Zhirnova, "Nekotorye problemy."

18 On the Bauman funeral, see Abraham Ascher, *The Russian Revolution of 1905: Russia in Disarray* (Stanford, 1989), vol. I, pp. 262-64; *Vestnik*

Oblastnogo Komissariata Vnutrennikh Del, 2 (Sept. 1918), pp. 64-71 (Uritsky's funeral, illust.). See also *Plamia*, 67 (Oct. 19, 1919), pp. 1-2, for the funeral of General A. P. Nikolaev, who was hanged by the Whites. The motifs of his and Uritskii's funerals are similar to those of a funeral of the 1860s depicted in *Sergei Vasilevich Gerasimov* (Moscow, 1951), p. 11. On Lenin's funeral, see Nina Tumarkin, *Lenin Lives!* (Cambridge, Mass., 1983).

19 P. Avrich, *Kronstadt* (Princeton, 1970), p. 173; M. K. "Novyi byt"; Fueloep Miller, *Mind*, p. 196; Veresaev, *Ob obriakakh*, p. 9.

20 Khazanova, *Iz istorii,* vol. I, pp. 214-15; Trotsky, *Problems*, p. 46; Starr, *Melnikov*, p. 35; Gvido Bartel, "Istoriia i statistika Moskovskogo Krematoriia," *Zdravookhranenie* (1929), pp. 106-108; Alexander Bogdanov, *Red Star: The Fint Bolshevik Utopia*, ed. L. Graham and R. Stites, trans. C. Rougle (Bloomington, 1984).

21 Quoted in Vasily Komar and Alexander Melamid, "In Search of Religion," *Artforum*, vol. 18, no. 9 (May 1980), no pagination.

22 Moyle, "Death in Life"; Gross, "Krasnyi Obriad"; and Daniel Kaiser, "Death and Dying in Early Modern Russia" (Kennan Institute Occasional Paper, 1986).

23 For the revival of communist ritualism after Stalin's death, see Christel Lane, *Rites of Rulers* (Cambridge, England, 1981). Arguments at the time of the revival (in the early 1960s) parallel those of the 1920s about the need for emotion and beauty in ritual events: I. Kryvelev, "Vazhnaia storona byta," *Kommunist*, 8 (May 1961), pp. 65-72; D. Sidorov, "Vazhnaia forma ateisticheskogo vospitaniia," *Partiinaia zhizn'*, 6 (Mar. 1963), pp. 49-51; and O. Poleshko-Polesskii, "Khoroshie traditsii," ibid., pp. 52-54.

24 McDowell, "Soviet Civil," pp. 267-68 (qu. p. 267); *Tseli i zadachi Soiuza Bezbozhnikov* (Ulianovsk, 1928), pp. 41-42; N. Amosov, *Na detskom antireligioznom fronte* (Moscow, 1930), pp. 47-48; Merle Fainsod, *Smolensk under Soviet Rule* (New York, 1963), p. 440.

25 Vitalii Zhemchuzhnyi, "Protiv obriadov," *Novyi Lef* (Jan. 1927), pp. 43-47; Iaroslavskii, *Protiv religii*, vol. III, p. 223. For Europe, see Hobsbawm and Ranger, *Invention.*

26 Hindus, *Great Offensive* (New York, 1933), pp. 182-89; idem., *Humanity Uprooted* (New York, 1930), p. 41; Nicholas Berdyaev, *The Origin of Russian Communism* (London, 1937), pp. 158-78. Mao is quoted in W. Rosenberg and M. Young, *Transforming Russia and China* (Oxford, 1982), p. 182.

11

The Role of Ritual and Symbols

Before the Revolution

Major human shake-ups—wars, revolutions, religious revivals, social movements and cultural awakenings—have generally produced symbols: visual, auditory and even tactile texts designed to arouse collective emotions. Signs invested with meaning—easily legible like the Christian cross, or encoded like the graffiti of modern urban youth—form a paralanguage. When embedded in a public ceremony such as a festival, parade or spectacle, the symbols are combined with gestures and words to flesh out the social drama. It is rarely difficult to trace the origins of particular elements of the spectacle back to pagan, classical, folk or various local traditions. The revolutionary rituals of modern times were of course "invented traditions" built in turn on earlier traditions that were also invented. But the historical genealogy of signs and choreographed movements (mass song, marches) alone cannot tell us much about the meanings intended and received at the moment of invention, presentation or performance. Ritual "texts" must be analyzed within the larger political frame.

Like all revolutions, the Russian revolution of 1917, and its continuation during the civil war of 1917-21, drew its symbolic language largely from inherited forms which were adapted to the purpose at hand. The deepest layer of derivation was pre-Christian Russian cyclical and seasonal ceremonies and their rituals which included magic incantation, cathartic destruction of devils, and wild release in song, dance and feasting. All these passed into Russian Orthodox Christianity, which crystallized into outdoor processions and indoor sacramental solemnities combining hierarchical order, sacred images, music, stationary worship and luxurious displays of vestments and ornament. The ecclesiastical affects of this tradition were partly retained by the Provisional Government in 1917 and wholly abandoned by the Bolshevik regime that succeeded it. On city streets or at fairs, the most widespread popular form of gathering for performance was the folk festival or funfair, with its dazzling array of foods, games, amusements and carnival shows—a perfect vehicle for later revolutionary holiday celebrations.

The Petersburg or imperial era of Russian history (1703-1917) was marked by the prominence of imported European ritual forms that transformed a crucial portion of interior and exterior space: parade, court ceremony and ball. The military review, established in the eighteenth century, was neither religious nor popular in any sense: it was a sign of state power, not so much of combat preparedness but of order commanded from the top. From about the mid-eighteenth to the mid-nineteenth century, the parade dominated the appearance of almost every Russian town. The highly elaborate uniforms were meant to flaunt power and dazzle viewers; the visible ranking and command structure to reinforce hierarchy and obedience; the geometrical and mechanical forms to impose an urban diurnal clock. One could measure time of day more accurately by the changing of a guard detail than by the ringing of church bells. Revolutionaries could dispense with the court ceremony, coronation festivity and gentry ball, but not with the parade, since soldiers played such a great role in the presentation of the revolution on the streets of Petrograd. It was relatively easy to "proletarianize" military parades even before the Bolsheviks took power because army uniforms had gradually been simplified in the later nineteenth century and fancily attired officers were no longer in evidence. Breaches of the new parade "etiquette" in 1917—the funeral of Cossacks killed in the July street fighting and General Lavr Kornilov's public appearances—were seen as jarring throwbacks to prerevolutionary ritual forms and interpreted by hostile observers as counterrevolutionary.

A later development in public ceremonial life of the tsarist era was the patriotic pageant. Begun by Panslav enthusiasts in the 1860s and 1870s, it was meant to celebrate "popular" wars—particularly the Russo-Turkish War of 1877 and World War I. The Panslav affairs were marked by large public indoor benefit meetings, featuring speeches, songs and musical performances; religious services in solidarity with the South Slavs; and the creation of heraldic banners that were sent to the front. In World War I, patriots revived the genre. M. I. Dolina, a dedicated monarchist and reactionary propagandist, gave hundreds of patriotic benefit concerts that offered folk songs, balalaika bands, martial wind ensembles, regimental choirs, songs set to the words of the famous Bessarabian anti-semite publicist Pavel Krushevan, texts provided by the Russian right, and readings of official edicts. An interesting, though not original, device used by Dolina was the patriotic *tableau vivant*—actors dressed as Suvorov, Kutuzov, and other national-military heroes, frozen alongside common people for the visual contemplation of the audiences. The juxtaposition of genres and the staged mixture of social orders were designed to promote a picture of all-Russian solidarity and loyalty.

The most immediately relevant form of pre-revolutionary ritual—that of the radical sub-culture—was of course wholly illegal in tsarist times. It developed underground, in secret meetings in the woods or in protest demonstrations—the word *demonstratsiia* becoming a synonym for parade or march in the revolution and in Soviet times. Beginning in the 1890s, meetings were held to celebrate the newly proclaimed international holiday, May 1; speeches were framed by a singing of the *Internationale,* the hymn of the Second or Socialist International, founded in 1889. Protest marches and funerals of fallen comrades became more common during the revolution of 1905. Red banners, songs—including revolutionary funeral dirges—were the bare accompaniment of these moving texts but the visual austerity was more than compensated for by the emotional texture and quasi-religious aura.

The February Revolution

The first days following the fall of the monarchy in March 1917 were marked more by spontaneity than by ritual—which implies rules, textual continuity and repetition. Parallel actions in many cities were too close in time for this to have been social mimicry. They included large crowds of all classes assembling in the main squares or boulevards or in front of public buildings where new authorities had set up shop—self-appointed municipal leaders or soviets. The crowds cheered "free Russia" in a spirit of generalized joy and social solidarity; and they honored recently freed political prisoners or veteran radicals. In Petrograd, the celebratory pattern culminated in the first public collective gesture: the burial of those killed in the February overthrow. In almost every one of its components, the interment spoke of social harmony and peace. Planning was jointly done by a largely middle-upper-class Provisional Government and the Petrograd Soviet — also middle-class in leadership, but with a lower-class base; the crowds were socially heterogeneous; and the theme was harmony at the dawn of a new era. Marching columns, their assembly at the Field of Mars—the burial ground-banners and slogans, red-draped buildings, severe dress, and revolutionary funeral hymns were the chief ingredients. Hardly noted in eyewitness accounts was the absence of church participation—a thoroughly novel development in public solemnities.

The next major city-wide celebration displayed a different visual and kinetic face. This was the burial of the seven Cossacks killed defending the Provisional Government during the July Days. It combined the church procession and military review of bygone days: the traditional pomp of the armed forces and a requiem mass at St Isaac's Cathedral, one of the holiest shrines of the capital whose history was closely connected with the monarchy. This funeral was literally a sign of the times, a semiotic counterrevolution reflecting perfectly the aspirations of the more conservative elements in the Provisional Government and those further to their right. Between the burials of the first and second sets of martyrs, public rituals and performances still spoke of relative social and national solidarity—political evenings and "revolutionary concerts" featuring *tableaux vivants* and the presentation of old radical veterans in the majestic setting of the imperial theatres. But the political division of the city and the country as a whole had grown tremendously. The differences between the Provisional Government and the Petrograd Soviet over war, army life, social reforms and revolutionary change were matched in the very style of proceedings of the two bodies housed in the same building, the Tauride Palace.

One could hardly imagine two assemblies more different in appearance and manners. The buttoned-down lawyers, professors and industrialists of the Provisional Government in one wing of the Palace tried to conduct business in an orderly legalistic manner adhering to the old rules of the Duma. In the Petrograd Soviet in the other wing, mass participation was taken literally, as several thousand roughly-dressed factory hands, recruits and frontline veterans shouted out of turn and voiced their emotions in speeches flowery and crude. The apparent chaos of the Soviet meetings—resembling those of a village *mir*—was misleading: positions were advanced, votes were held, measures were taken. Bespectacled socialist intellectuals stumbled over sleeping sergeants with rifles in hand and were choked by the smell of *makhorka*, the cheap tobacco of the common folk. Some were repelled; but most of them were thrilled to be rubbing shoulders with "the people." The extraordinary juxtaposition of these two bodies and their outward appearance and gestural language were as much a key to the deep gulf dividing Russian society as were their political agendas. Their symbolic and political worlds continued to diverge up to the Bolshevik takeover in October 1917.

Soviet Symbols

The Provisional Government had taken as its seal and currency motif a modified double-headed eagle of the Romanovs, visually domesticated with folded wings, and minus the accoutrements of autocracy—orb and scepter. The French Republic's *Marseillaise* with Russian lyrics had served as an unofficial anthem. When the Bolsheviks took power, their new Soviet regime donned a different symbolic attire to create an identity around its social base and its aspiration to create a new world. This was accomplished by replacing the old seal, flag and anthem. The national seal caused the most excitement and controversy. Lenin and Anatoly Lunacharsky, the Commissar of Enlightenment, held a competition among artists whose entries provided a dazzling and even amusing array of motifs including futuristic squares and wedges. The one chosen as most likely for adoption contained three implements meant to symbolize the classes who made the revolution or for whom it was made: the sickle for the peasantry, the industrial hammer for the proletariat, and a short sword for the army. Lenin objected strenuously to the sword's militaristic associations. This was winter-spring 1918 in the midst of peace negotiations with the Germans at Brest-Litovsk. Lenin, bending over backwards to present Soviet Russia as a nation of peace, argued against it in committee for weeks until the offensive weapon was removed.

The remaining hammer and sickle (both frequently used in old provincial heraldry) was framed by a reassuring wreath adorned with classical elements, including the Roman fasces—a bundle of rods wrapped around an axe. The fasces was later removed, possibly in response to its adoption by the fascist regime in Italy. The first official appearance of the new Soviet emblem was on the cover of the first constitution of the RSFSR in summer 1918. The hammer and sickle was then planted on the corner of the new red flag. The name 'hammer and sickle' was widely used thereafter for factories, communes, schools, and other institutions.

The arrangement of the hammer and the sickle (in Russian the word order is always "sickle-and-hammer"—*serp i molot*) on flag and seal makes no statement about a superordinate-subordinate relationship between the two signs and what they stand for. But when poster artists began incorporating them into their art, they almost invariably depicted a man holding the hammer and a woman with the sickle. In later readings, this meant associating man with industry, machine, city, power and the future; women with agriculture, rural backwardness, nurture and fertility. Here, where art history and political history—so often segregated from each other—intersect, it is important to distinguish between intention, function and reception. We can rarely know the intentions of artists at the time of creation and there is no way of discovering what symbol makers and poster artists "meant" when they gendered the pictures mentioned above. It is reasonable to suppose that they simply copied forms from the life they knew—particularly in the recent war years when men in factories and women in the fields were very much a national norm. Similarly there are no clues about what viewers thought or felt when they looked at visual gendering. Therefore, in interrogating the "function" of this kind of motif, historians have no evidence that it was intended to identify women with agriculture and men with industry as an ideological position or cultural statement. The real function of the material, then, is not so much as a "sign" of the regime's thinking, but rather as a signal for historians to start looking for real evidence of the gendering of town and country, a search that might not have occurred to them without close examination of the iconography of the time. To do more than this is to engage in ahistorical theorizing.

Reconstructing a new public face for the revolution also required renaming and replacing public signs of the old regime. During World War I, students had gone around the capital replacing German with Russian names on street signs. The city itself was renamed from St Petersburg to Petrograd. For self-protection during a rage of anti-'German' pogroms in Moscow, Russians of German, Latvian, Jewish or Scandinavian descent rushed to adopt Slavic-sounding patriotic names like Romanov or Serbsky (Serbian). Hammer became Molotov, Berg became Gorskii, Taube became Golubev, Schwartz became Chernov, Schmidt become Kuznetsov, and Eiche became Dubnov. In 1918, Bolshevik renaming of streets and squares began and later spread to the renaming of cities—Petrograd into Leningrad after Lenin's death in 1924 being one of the first. Tsarist emblems and monuments were torn down. Lunacharsky ensured that some of the more artistic statues remained untouched, but most monuments to tsars and tsarist heroes were pulled down in ceremonial acts. To replace them, Lenin presented a plan of "monumental propaganda"—public unveiling of hero figures.

These visual ornaments received great fanfare in the early years of revolution. The objects of statuary art chosen by political leaders were of cultural and radical figures of European and Russian history. The cultural set was presumably meant to tie the revolution to canonized tradition, and the political set to establish a revolutionary genealogy from Spartacus through the French revolution, the utopian socialists, the European Marxists and—paralleling it—the Russian radical tradition from Radishchev and the Decembrists to 1917. Lenin, believing in the inborn passivity of a mass audience, ordered that the unveiling of the statues be accompanied by lectures indicating the precise significance of the monuments. The figures were unveiled during special holidays at key points in the city, with talks by such important political orators as G. E. Zinoviev and A. V. Lunacharsky. Thus the faces of great socialists, writers and former state criminals now replaced the massive equestrian replicas of monarchical Russia.

Soviet Festivals

The great festivals and holiday celebrations swirling around the unveiled statuary were not as spontaneous as those of the February revolution; and they soon hardened into highly organized and ritualized performances. From 1918 to the end of the civil war, Petrograd, Moscow, and other towns within the Bolshevik-controlled heartland came alive on May Day, Revolution Day (November 7) or for special congresses, with colorful floats, parades, wall decorations, fireworks and lights, and a variety of outdoor theatricals. Some of the most talented artists of the day splashed their glowing paints over public places to create a carnival appearance. These earliest celebrations tried to blend tradition with modernity. In a created festive atmosphere, the barkers, puppeteers, marchers, and speech-makers mocked the enemies of the revolution and burned straw figures of White and Interventionist leaders. Big outdoor theatricals deployed thousands of performers and technicians in the staging of battles, *tableaux vivants*, mystery plays and historical revolutionary epics. By the end of the civil war, the Soviet festival style was largely in place, surrounded by stylized slogans and symbols that had emerged from the revolutionary years.

Original publication: In Edward Acton, Vladimir Iu. Cherniaev, and William Rosenberg, eds. *Critical Companion to the Russian Revolution 1914-21.* Bloomington and Indianapolis: Indiana University Press, 1997, pp. 565-571.

Further reading

von Geldern J., *Bolshevik Festivals, 1917-1920* (Berkeley: University of California Press, 1993).

German M., *Art of the October Revolution* (New York: Avrora, 1980).

Kenez P., *The Birth of the Propaganda State: Soviet Methods of Mass Mobilization, 1917-1929* (Cambridge: Cambridge University Press, 1985).

Lane C, *Rites of Rulers* (Cambridge: Cambridge University Press, 1981).

Mally L., *Culture of the Future: The Proletkult Movement in Revolutionary Russia* (Berkeley: University of California Press, 1990).

Mazaev A. I., *Prazdnik kak sotsialno-khudozhestvennoe iavlenie* (Moscow: Nauka, 1978).

Stites R., "Adorning the Russian Revolution: The Primary Symbols of Bolshevism, 1917-1918," *Sbornik* (Leeds, England) 10 (Summer 1984).

Stites R., *Revolutionary Dreams: Utopian Vision and Experimental Life in the Russian Revolution* (New York: Oxford University Press, 1989). See pp. 270-3 for sources and literature in Russian.

Tumarkin N., *Lenin Lives!* (Cambridge, MA: Harvard University Press, 1983).

Verner A., "What's in a Name? Of Dog-Killers, Jews, and Rasputin," *Slavic Review* 53, 4 (Winter, 1994), pp. 1046-70.

Wortman R., *Scenarios of Power* (Princeton: Princeton University Press, 1994).

12

Trial as Theatre in the Russian Revolution

In an extraordinary passage of *The Mind and Face of Bolshevism,* the Hungarian journalist and philosopher, René Fueloep-Miller, made this observation in the 1920s on the innate theatricality of the Russian people:

> If a Russian recounts an incident in company, in his political club, or even in the street, he does not for long confine himself to verbal description. Suddenly, he sends a gesture into space, like an arrow from a bow, at the same time giving a cue to another in the circle, who immediately becomes an actor in the drama. Though at first the whole thing looks like a very excited discussion, soon many emphatic gestures and words creep in and an increasing number of bystanders begin to take part in the scene. Suddenly the recital takes living form: chairs and tables are shifted with a few touches, and soon stand in a particular relation to each other and to the events being enacted. Men and things are now subject to new and different laws. Those taking no part look on in astonishment and soon become an audience, just as the story, which was at first merely related, becomes reality and attains complete actuality in the people acting and the improvised scenery…This lasts as long as the anecdote enacted, then the company at once returns to ordinary life…and the members of the circle sit smoking and talking again in their former quiet tones as if nothing had happened.[1]

This description is based on the experience of a very observant man. From it, he concludes that the Russian, by nature and in utter distinction from the European, seizes "every opportunity of passing from the real to the theatrical." Further he states that there is a sort of primitive religious consecration about everything theatrical in Russia, and it would almost seem as if they still felt all artistic creation as a sacred process, and the actor as a social hierophant.[2]

On first hearing such words, a normally skeptical scholar will likely consign them to the realm of ethnic fantasy, that arrogant tendency to leap from the minute example to the sweeping generalization. But to anyone familiar with the Russian scene or long acquainted with Russian people, they cause a thrill of recognition. One sees in the mind's eye at once the playlets and mini-melodramas enacted daily in the streets and trams and buildings of St. Petersburg and Moscow: the eloquent narrator who sculpts the air as he relates a story, the excited women who argue over an episode of street life, the dramatic debates in bars and restaurants—where talk is much freer than in offices or schoolrooms. We may leave aside the author's argument for the uniqueness of Russian theatricality (which cannot be sustained). But his main point is that Russians are theatrical both as players and as public. Fueloep-Miller also argues in the chapter "Theatricalized Life" that the Bolsheviks exploited this passion for performance art in everyday life in their propaganda campaigns of the revolutionary epoch. That application is the focus of my argument—in particular the theatricalization of court trial.

But did the passion actually exist among the masses? And if so, how and what did the Bolsheviks know about it? The evidence for the first comes from the realm of pre-revolutionary theatre. At an 1844 performance of Victor Ducange's *Theresa, the Orphan of Geneva* in the provincial town of Astrakhan, a spectator, having witnessed a murder on stage and hearing the villain deny his guilt, cried out from the audience: "You lie, you son of a dog, you bandit. You killed [her]. Look at these good folks [in the theatre]; they are witnesses. Am I right, friends?" This episode was fairly typical of audience behavior in the theatre—not only in Russia. Later in the century, "popular (*narodny*) theatre"—an elite attempt to bring culture to the masses along with moral uplift—offered classic stage works by Alexander Ostrovsky, Nikolai Gogol, Anton Chekhov, and others to workers and peasants. Here spectators tended to reify all abstract ideas, to identify with characters, to feel themselves part of the action, to applaud and celebrate the righteous life, to endorse harsh retribution against the sinful, to see theatre as a moral instrument, to kibitz and shout at performers, and to be puzzled by social types alien to them—such as lawyers.[3]

The courtroom drama itself had roots in folk culture. Among the Cossacks, *The Trial of Ataman Burya* was a well-established folk drama which survived until World War I. Ataman, or chieftain, Burya—a figure from the folklore surrounding the sixteenth-century Cossack Ermak—meted out justice to the traditional enemies of the lower classes: landowners, merchants, and innkeepers. The performance was partly improvised and partly based on oral traditions and set speeches as well as audience participation. The interesting thing about the last is that audience members accused the defendants who, in turn, tended to incriminate themselves in the course of their testimony.[4] Both the Cossack setting and the intricate forms of accusation would have reflections in revolutionary trials—mock and otherwise.

Political theatre took on massive dimensions during the Revolution. All the theatres were opened up to the masses and whole blocks of tickets were often assigned to factory workers. Revolutionary dramatists sought popular audiences for radical spectacles, pageants, and carnivalesque holiday shows. The huge Proletcult movement staged thousands of pieces for soldiers, workers, and peasants. The organizers of Bolshevik agitation and propaganda were quick to spy the possibilities of staging propaganda which, like mass singing and graphic art, was especially suitable for a still largely illiterate population. Agit-trains and boats carried mobile players to the front lines of the civil war and to the remote villages where they performed agitplays or showed agit-films—vehicles with a single, sharp message acted out before the eyes of the local population. In fact, there was a widespread movement during the early years of the revolution to theatricalize almost every aspect of the new life.[5]

How the courtroom trial made its way into this genre of entertainment and enlightenment is not yet clear. It might have been the result of Bolshevik experience with early revolutionary tribunals. During the visionary and maximalist period of "War

Communism," written law and legal professionalism were scorned in favor of "revolutionary consciousness" or the alleged spontaneous preference of the masses for instinctive justice over ponderous judicial procedures.[6] In practice, this often meant untrammeled abuse of power and even judicial murder. In the first great Bolshevik political trial, that of Sofya Panina—ironically an eminent figure in the popular theatre movement—the prosecution bowed to the concept of revolutionary jurisprudence by asking for public denunciations from the floor! But the audience, comprising mostly workers who supported Panina, did not rise to the call.[7]

The trial-as-theatre or political mock trial that appeared in the early years of the revolution was a fusion of popular theatre and the revolutionary tribunal. It was called "agit-trial" (*agitsud*) and had a distinctly didactic purpose: to convince the auditors of the guilt of the accused (whether person, thing or concept) by means of vivid acting and realistic staging. In the earliest cases, actual judges were often used to add authenticity to the show. The topics of the trials fall into the categories of health, work, habits, morality, religion, history, and culture.

In the realm of public health and disease prevention, the Bolsheviks were determined to reverse the largely passive government policies of the past and activate an entire nation in the struggle. Massive campaigns and posters were employed to teach people signs of disease and good sanitary habits. The Moscow Theatre of Health Education and the Drama Circle in the Ministry of Health put on plays exposing the dangers of patronizing prostitutes. The "Trial of Zaborovna" (from the word "indecent") featured an actress playing a prostitute who had infected a soldier. The play was preceded by weeks of sensational advanced publicity which implied that it was an actual case. Judges, prosecutors, defense attorneys, and witnesses were assembled at the trial site and the audience was empanelled as the jury. The German observer Fanina Halle tells us that such proceedings were frequently staged by the Central Council for Combating Prostitution (founded 1922) in conjunction with anti-prostitution "weeks" and half-weeks throughout the country.[8]

A major issue of social and medical health in the 1920s was child abandonment. The scenario of a mock trial published in 1924 by the Maternity and Infancy Protection network dwelt upon the social intricacies of this question. In it a twenty-year old mother leaves her month-old son at a health centre and fails to return. The baby is already ill and in need of breast feeding. But in the course of the trial, the audience learns that the delinquent mother is an ex-peasant from an indigent family recently employed in a factory and then laid off. She has been taken in and betrayed by a skilled worker who evicts her from his room after she becomes pregnant. She has also received bad advice and ill treatment from socially shady characters. After detailed testimony from experts and witnesses, the accused is found guilty on all counts of neglect but—in view of her "proletarian" background, her poverty, and the harsh conditions of her life—she is merely required to resume the care of her child; and the father is ordered by the court to pay her one half his monthly wage for support. The case was conducted in a wholly realistic fashion, complete with authentic settings, court language, and procedures of the time. The creators of the drama urged its performance in all factories, clubs, and village centers, hoping that at least one or two prospective mothers would learn the proper social lessons from it.[9] In both these instances—and the frequent trial of drunks—a high degree of realism was created. But pure fantasy and parable were also employed as in the trial of a louse who was found guilty of spreading typhus.[10]

The Soviet concern about the nation's work habits, including punctuality, neatness, good order, overall efficiency, was—and remains in the new Russia—a major one. The worker-poet Alexei Gastev in his Central Institute of Labor endeavored to teach workers a robotic culture of the machine; and Platon Kerzhentsev—a theatre critic among other things—created in his short-lived League of Time (1923-5) an efficiency army to monitor every walk of life for violations of the rational use of space, time, and motion. Among the many methods used to promote efficiency in the population was the trial of offenders against it. In factories, malfunctioning machines were put on trial, with witnesses and physical evidence designed to acquit the machine itself of guilt in order to prove the "guilt" of clumsy workers who mistreated the machinery. In the villages, cows were exonerated in show trials in order to reveal the real source of low milk yields: the unscientific peasant.[11]

In a 1924 mock trial, a Komsomol (Young Communist) girl

was indicted for marrying a NEP-man (businessman of the New Economic Policy era) in church. Crossing class lines in marriage was denounced as a political "sin" by some upholders of the new morality, one of whom declared the marriage of a Bolshevik and a Menshevik to be equivalent to mating an orangutan with an alligator.[12] A NEP-man was considered worse than a Menshevik; he was a capitalist shark feeding legally off the proletariat. An ideal communist woman could have no truck with that sort of person. To marry in church was an even more grievous sin, since communists were supposed to be atheists. 350 workers attended this "trial" which lasted four hours. They thought they were attending an actual court proceeding and they hailed the verdict rendered by the court: expulsion from the Komsomol. Then the actors went home and the trial was revealed to have been staged.[13]

Religion was assaulted frontally, especially after 1925 with the formation of the League of Militant Atheists who flooded the country with printed matter, films, lectures, and radio shows about the perils of superstition and religious belief, God in general and the special gods of Christians, Jews, and Muslims were mercilessly mocked by Komsomols and other militant youth groups. Gods, saints, priests, and faiths were assaulted in almost every cultural arena of the time. During an unholy week in 1923, put on as a counter to the Easter season, enthusiasts mounted a play called *The Political Trial of the Bible.*[14]

On Rosh Hashanah, 1921, the Jewish Section (*Evsektsiya*) of the Kiev party organization put the Jewish religion on trial. The Evsektsiya was set up to encourage and control Yiddish cultural outlets, oppose Judaism, and win over the Jewish working class to communism. For added spectacle, it was held in the very courtroom where Mendel Beilis, the celebrated victim of a ritual murder frame-up, had been tried in 1913 by tsarist authorities. Witnesses were called to corroborate the indictment: a well dressed Jewish lady who sent her child to Heder (Jewish school) in order to display her high social position; a Rabbi who testified that he taught religion in order to keep the masses ignorant and a corpulent member of the bourgeoisie, among others. Any spectator who dared to protest was arrested on the spot. Although the public was apparently unconvinced, the "court" brought in a death sentence for the Jewish faith.[15]

History, especially recent events inspired many court shows. Petrograd workers indicted and tried the long deceased Father Gapon—notorious for his role in Bloody Sunday—on the anniversary of that 1905 massacre. Admiral Kolchak, generals Wrangel and Yudenich, and other White commanders took their turn in the dock as did the Entente interventionist powers and the German Freikorps and the police murderers of the revolutionaries, Rosa Luxembourg and Karl Liebknecht. The most elaborate of these was *The Trial of Wrangel*, put on in the autumn of 1919 in the Kuban district of the Northern Caucasus. The playwright Vsevolod Vishnevsky has left a vivid description of the setting. Hoping to win over the local Cossack population, the Bolsheviks endeavored to present a clear-cut portrait of their current foe, the White commander Baron von Wrangel who was generally known for his savage treatment of prisoners. An estimated audience of 10,000 Red Army soldiers, peasants, Cossacks, and their wives and children made their way in peasant carts and carriages from miles around to the outdoor spectacle. The sight of the multitude of peasant women frightened the only professional actor in the company. Since he was playing the role of Wrangel, he feared he would be lynched by the angry mob.[16]

The outdoor courtroom drama began with the reading of the charges. The court entered and the entire assembly rose to its feet. Then "Baron Wrangel" was questioned and cross-examined by angry and emotional interrogators, largely improvising from a few sketchy notes. "Tell me, did you hang people in Tsaritsyn and at such and such a factory on the Volga also?" asked the prosecutor. "Yes," replied Wrangel. On and on went the accusations: rape, murder, mass execution of workers and peasants, treacherous dealing with foreign capitalists, selling out Russia to the imperialists. Witnesses appeared from every front and from behind the White lines, confirming the atrocities and the treason of Wrangel and his forces. "A wealthy merchant tells of the charms Wrangel holds for the bourgeoisie...Each witness represents a type, a particular social class, and gives a lively picture of recent events." All the while, the crowd erupted in vivid participation and shouts. At the end of the trial, the prosecutor turned to the audience, as the accused trembled in his box, and asked them: "Citizens, what is to be done with the condemned?" "Cut him to bits, shoot him," is the answer.

He was then led away in chains. In this trial, also, the actor doing Wrangel enmeshed himself in a web of contradictions. Since the huge audience was largely Cossack, one may speculate as to how much the organizers of this play consciously adapted the style of *Ataman Burya.*[17]

Cultural backwardness was assaulted in various types of agit-trials. One was a "prosecution of the enemies of books." After White troops burned books and gutted libraries during General Yudenich's drive to Petrograd in 1919, the charred remains were displayed in a coffin for several days and then buried with full military pomp. After the "funeral," enemies of the book—including speculators—were tried. Agit-trials were not limited to Moscow and Petrograd. Workers' clubs in Ekaterinburg in the Urals organized a trial of the "White Poles" and tax-resisting kulaks. Those in Tambov province brought to justice and jailed "illiteracy." Sometimes the scripts were provided by Russian literary material. Chekhov's story "The Evil Thinker" (*Zloumyshlenik*) inspired a Trial of Popular Ignorance for six performances in Vyatka; in May 1921 alone it was seen by 1500 people. Servants of capital were tried there on the basis of Alexander Kuprin's famous story, "Moloch." In several provinces, old fashioned marriage and family life, as described by the nineteenth-century playwright Ostrovsky, were arraigned. Chekhov and Ostrovsky, incidentally, were precisely the ones most used by the pre-revolutionary intelligentsia in the popular theatre for the masses.[18]

Organizers of agit-trial argued over how much they should be scripted and how much improvised. Given the frequency of their performance and discussion about them in the 1920s, there can be little doubt that the people who staged real political trials of opposition parties in the twenties, of the alleged saboteurs at the turn of the decade, and of the "enemies of the people" during the great purge of the 1930s availed themselves of the techniques used in the trial-dramas. The Moscow Trial of the oppositional Socialist Revolutionary party in 1922 was the first major one. It was designed to crush the last remaining party in Russia still in opposition, the party that had arguably been the most popular in Russia in 1917. The Bolsheviks were explicit in announcing this as a show trial, an educational vehicle. It was preceded by meetings and demonstrations of workers denouncing the accused; and by street carnival and puppet shows ridiculing the Socialist-Revolutionary leaders. When a designated defender of the Socialist-Revolutionaries, Theodor Liebknecht, brother of the German communist martyr, arrived in Moscow, he was greeted with the slogan, "Cain, Cain, where is your brother Karl?" In the middle of the trial, a workers' demonstration was permitted into the courtroom to harangue the accused for several hours. The Soviet documentarist, Dziga Vertov (D. A. Kaufman) shot a newsreel film of it which was exhibited in theatres even before the proceedings were over.[19] Party leader Grigory Zinoviev, soon to be a victim of one himself, called this show trial" a great step forward in the cause of the political instruction of the very broadest masses in town and country."[20]

The Shakhty Trial of fifty-three Russian and foreign engineers and managers accused of sabotage and treason was held in the Nobles' House in Moscow from 18 May to 4 July 1928. Here the prosecutor of the Socialist-Revolutionaries, Nikolai Krylenko, joined with the future prosecutor in the purge trials, Andrei Vyshinsky. Krylenko, perhaps in an effort to invoke a civil war memory, dressed in riding breeches, and puttees, his shaved head glistening under the Klieg lights that were set up for filming the trial. In addition to almost one hundred reporters—Soviet and foreign—more than 100,000 spectators including school children, workers, and peasants, viewed a portion of the one-and-a-half month long trial by means of a frequent change of shifts. No material evidence was presented by the prosecution—only the confessions of the accused and testimony by some hostile witnesses. Many of the charges were, even then, seen to be invented; cruelty to civil war prisoners was even lodged against some of the accused—a possible tie-in to the mock trials of Wrangel and others. The American correspondent Eugene Lyons, at that moment still sympathetic to the Soviet regime, called the treason charge "a figment of Soviet stagecraft." The pattern of confessions retracted publicly and then repeated after an absence from the courtroom strongly suggested coercion and fraudulent evidence. Five of the condemned were executed.[21]

The other trials of this period followed roughly the same pattern. They all included elaborate advertisement and preparation, mobilization of indignant masses demanding the maximum penalty, partial scripting, rehearsal and collusion of the accused, prepared witnesses, partial intervention of the audience, exaggerated and false charges, and—apparently—mass belief in the justice of the proceedings. In the matter of the charges against accused people (as opposed to concepts or problems), the great purge trials of the 1930s were far more fantastic. The real trial was staged as a play and the organizers doubtless hoped that the audience at large—the nation—would concur with the harshest sentences if they could be convinced of the guilt of the accused. Popular audiences before the revolution, it will be recalled, were insistent that the outcome of a drama include righteous and stem retribution for moral laxity. Peasants, however, played resistance politics with the state in many spheres. During a brief interval of experimental democracy and multi-candidate elections, some peasants nominated priests; anti-Stalinist underground folklore circulated freely; and some peasants even ventured to pray for the souls of the departed Zinoviev and others tried in Moscow and killed in the purges. In late 1937, rural district show trials were held in which the collective farmers were able to testify against officials in the dock who had recently plagued them. Their focus was purely local, but the mode of denunciation resonated with that of theatrical trials.[22]

There is no direct evidence that the political show trials were inspired in their methods by the theatricalized trials of the revolution and 1920s. But theatre and politics were so closely intermixed in this period that proof of a direct association is hardly necessary. Playacting was used to agitate, inform, convert, and mobilize; to vitalize and concretize political and cultural messages to the masses in a country whose uneducated populace had difficulty with the new political lexicon when seen in printed form (a Red Army veteran in 1922 was unable to understand the words "USSR," "Soviet," and "socialism").[23]

The political trial had for the Bolsheviks several functions: to expose, punish, and frighten the enemy; to educate the masses about vigilance and righteousness; and to legitimize their own judicial procedures with a semblance of popular endorsement and participation. The Bolsheviks could not bring themselves to hold real trials outdoors in full view as in the mock trials; nor did they stage outdoor executions as a consciousness raising device. But they clearly believed in the educational value of show trials. Lenin, shortly before the opening of the Socialist-Revolutionary trial of 1922, angrily demanded from the Commissariat of Justice "model trials" (*obraztsovye protsessy*) and severe measures including the firing squad for speculators and oppositionists.[24]

The theatrical trial of the Russian revolution lies along a continuum. At one end is pure trial, marked by the judicial procedure of its own time and place. At the other end is pure theatre—a staged fiction designed for dramatic entertainment. Between them lies the trial *in absentia*, with real people and juridical issues; the moot court, whose purpose is to teach trial procedure and justice; and the Kangaroo court, whose judicial outcome is predetermined. The theatrical trial or judicial drama was a mock trial that helped give shape to the real political trial. It was one of numerous methods—often called simply propaganda—used by the regime to create "truth." The word for truth in Russian, *pravda*, also means justice. To the peasant mind, these were all but inseparable. Just as Charles Maurras once claimed that French national honor was higher than justice because without the former there could be no justice, so many Russian peasants—and their city cousins—believed that truth had to be just and vice versa. Since many of them seemed also to believe that dramatized action was "true," theatre and theatricalized politics was an eminently suitable means of social communication. In this context, the Bolsheviks must be credited with great imagination and a deep understanding of the mentalities of the uneducated population. And they must also bear the guilt of incorporating an originally liberating artifice of the revolution into a hideous murder machine.[25]

Original publication: *Theatre Research International*, 23(1): spring 1998, pp. 7-13.

Notes

1   René Fueloep-Miller, *The Mind and Face of Bolshevism* (1926; 2nd edition, New York, 1965), p. 135. This article was originally presented to the Gauss Seminars at Princeton University in 1991.

2   Jeffrey Brooks, *When Russia Learned to Read* (Princeton: Princeton University Press, 1984); Richard Stites, *Russian Popular Culture: Entertain-*

ment and Society Since 1900 (Cambridge: Cambridge University Press, 1992), chapter 1.

3   I. I. Lavrov, *Stsena i zhizn v provintsii i v stolitse* (Moscow, 1889), p. 50; Gary Thurston, "Theatre and Acculturation in Russia from Peasant Emancipation to the First World War," *Journal of Popular Culture*, 18. 2 (1984), pp. 3-16; "The Impact of Russian Popular Theatre, 1886-1915," *Journal of Modern History*, 55/2 (June, 1983), pp. 236-67.

4   James Von Geldern, *Bolshevik Festivals, 1917-1920* (Berkeley: University of California Press, 1993), p. 109.

5   Peter Kenez, *The Birth of the Propaganda State* (Cambridge: Cambridge University Press, 1985); Richard Stites, *Revolutionary Dreams: Utopian Vision and Experimental Life in the Russian Revolution* (Oxford & New York: Oxford University Press, 1989); Lynn Mally, *The Culture of the Future* (Berkeley: University of California Press, 1990); Richard Taylor, "Agitation, Propaganda, and the Cinema: the Search for New Solutions," in *Art, Society, Revolution: Russia, 1917-1921,* ed. N. Å. Nilsson (Stockholm: Almqvist & Wiksell, 1979), pp. 237-63.

6   On traditional peasant justice, see Stephen Frank, "Popular Justice, Community, and Culture among the Russian Peasantry, 1870-1900," *Russian Review*, 46/3 (1987), pp. 239-65.

7   William Rosenberg, *Liberals in the Russian Revolution* (Princeton: Princeton University Press, 1974), pp. 278-82. Panina was accused of pilfering funds from the People's House that she managed.

8   Fueloep-Miller, *Mind and Face,* pp. 139-40; Ella Winter, *Red Virtue* (New York: Harcourt, Brace, 1933). p. 189; Fannina Halle, *Women in Soviet Russia* (London & New York: Routledge, 1933), pp. 227-31.

9   *Sud nad materyu podkinuvshei svoego rebenka...Instsenirovka* (Moscow, 1924).

10 N. A. Gorchakov, *Istoriya sovetskogo teatra* (New York: Chekhov, 1956), p. 88.

11 Stites, *Revolutionary Dreams*, p. 157.

12 Stites, *The Women's Liberation Movement: Feminism, Nihilism, and Bolshevism, 1860-1930* (Princeton: Princeton University Press, 1978), p. 381 (cf., above, 86 and 88, note 13 - *ed.*).

13 *Moskovskii pechatnik,* 21 (April, 1924), p. 19, cited in Diane Koenker, "Class Consciousness in a Socialist Society: Workers in the Printing Trades During NEP," in Sheila Fitzpatrick, et al., eds., *Russia in the Era of NEP: Explorations in Soviet Society and Culture* (Bloomington: Indiana University Press, 1991), p. 41.

14 Stites, *Revolutionary Dreams*, pp. 108-110. See also Arto Luukkanen, *The Party of Unbelief: the Religious Policy of the Bolshevik Party, 1917-1929* (Helsinki: Studia Historica, 1994).

15 Zvi Gitelman, *Jewish Nationality and Soviet Policy* (Princeton: Princeton University Press, 1972). For a sane treatment of the Bellis case itself, see Hans Rogger, *Jewish Policies and Right-Wing Politics in Imperial Russia* (London: Macmillan, 1985), pp. 40-55.

16 A Soviet movie actor of the 1930s exhibited a similar reluctance to portray the villain, in this case in a Stalinized film version of the Kirov murder: *Great Citizen*. Moira Ratchford, *Stalinist Myth and the Popular Movies of the 1930s* (MA Thesis, Georgetown University, 1989).

17 Vishnevskii, "Dvadtsatiletie sovetskoi dramaturgii," in *Sovetski dramaturgi o svoëm tvorchestve* (Moscow, 1967), pp. 149-S0. Von Geldern, *Bolshevik Festivals*, p. 110; Fueloep-Miller, *Mind and Face*, p. 140.

18 Fueloep-Miller, *Mind and Face*, 140-1 and *passim*.

19 *Cinema in Revolution*, edited by L. and J. Schnitzer and Marc Martin (London: Seeker and Warburg, 1973), p. 78. Vertov had also filmed the trial of the Civil War hero and frame-up victim, Filip Mironov. Vertov's brother, Boris Kaufman, achieved cinematic glory in quite a different trial milieu as the cameraman for Sidney Lumet's Hollywood film, *Twelve Angry Men*.

20 Marc Jansen, *A Show Trial under Lenin: the Trial of the Socialist Revolutionaries, Moscow, 1922* (The Hague & Boston: M. Nijhoff & Hingham, MA, 1982), p. vii, and *passim*.

21 Kendall Bailes, *Technology and Society under Lenin and Stalin* (Princeton, Princeton University Press, 1978), 69-94; Eugene Lyons, *Assignment in Utopia* (New York: Harcourt, Brace, 1937), pp. 114-133.

22 See Sheila Fitzpatrick, *Stalin's Peasants: Resistance and Survival in the Russian Village after Collectivization* (Oxford & New York: Oxford University Press, 1994), chapters 9, 11.

23 Jeffrey Brooks, "Public and Popular Values in the Soviet Press, 1921-1928," *Slavic Review*, 48/1 (Spring, 1989), pp. 16-35.

24 V. I. Lenin, *Polnoe sobranie sochinenii*, 5th edition, XLIV (Moscow, 1970), p. 400.

25 It is not certain when the practice of agit-trial died away, but it was still being used during World War II: see "Teatr kak sredstvo sanitamoi agitatsii," *Sovetskoe zdravokhranenie*, 1-2 (1943). My thanks to Bart Goldyn of Georgetown University for finding this article.

III

CULTURE, POPULAR AND OTHERWISE

Some Miscellany

Cinema

Wars Hot and Cold

Some Miscellany

13

On the Border with the Soviet Avant-Garde

Helene Jarvinen, Richard Stites

"Imatra Festival 1988" celebrated young Soviet art of the 1920s and the 1980s during five days in late June in Imatra, Finland, a few miles from the Soviet frontier. It was the first live demonstration of Soviet avant-garde of its kind held outside the USSR. About three dozen Soviet artists, musicians, poets, actors, and filmmakers— mostly in their twenties and thirties—were brought in by various Finnish culture and friendship societies to exhibit some of the latest cultural fruits of *glasnost* and *perestroika*.

Imatra is set in the forest and lake district of Old Karelia, now the easternmost region of Finland, and is adorned by the magnificent Lake Saimaa, the Vuoksi River, the Imatra Falls, and the stunning monument of turn-of-the-century Jugendstil architecture, Usko Nystrom's Imatra State Hotel, a favorite playground of the nobility in the days when Finland was a Grand Duchy of the Russian Empire. The 1988 festival events were held in the bright and spacious Imatra Cultural Center—alive with blonde wood, glass and native stone—the State Hotel, and local restaurants. There were a few minor blemishes: rock critic Artemy Troitsky, who was to have lectured about Soviet music of the 1920s and 1980s, went to the United States instead; and there were mix-ups in scheduling and transportation. On the other hand, the smallish audiences mixed easily with the artists and there was time to talk to them informally between shows and after hours.

The art was on permanent display throughout the festival. Upstairs hung a large show of Alexander Rodchenko with pieces rarely seen in the West, on loan from the Tampere (Finland) Rodchenko Society and from Soviet collections. Downstairs was offered a whole array of Moscow and Leningrad painters: Vladimir Sulyagin, Evgeny Dybsky, Sergei Volkov, Nikola Ovchinnikov, Sven Gundlakh, and others. The symbolism ran from a collage about AIDS (a recurring theme in Soviet cultural discourse) to a U.S. flag with Orthodox crosses for stars on the canton. Sulyagin (b. 1942), one of the few artists there over forty, combines Constructivism (his bow to the 1920s) and Russian Christianity in portraits of Dostoevsky, Mandelshtam, Bakhtin, Jesus, and the four evangelists. Dybsky (b. 1955) is a self-styled meta-realist landscape painter who attempts to combine human conflict and harmony in his canvases. During intermissions, artists talked about their works to assembled listeners.

The three main musical events were by Kamil Chalyaev, Sergei Kurekhin, and the AVIA rock band. Chalyaev (b. 1962) illustrates the extreme mobility in career and fluidity in style of modern serious Soviet musicians. Trained as a conductor at the Moscow Conservatory, he has worked in jazz combos, in rock groups (including the now famous Bravo), with Komsomol—Young Communists—ensembles, and as a conductor of a church choir. He has also performed in drama (a recent play called *AIDS in Time of Plague*), in underground musical events, and in concert with his own "Sinfonia." He is inspired, he says, by Tschaikovsky, Stravinsky, and Joy Division. On stage in the vast Carelian Hall, he deployed a whole army of gadgets, scrap metal, chimes, mobiles, and musical instruments, including his main vehicle, the double bass. Chanting as he knocked and struck, Chalyaev produced a sonority which recalled the "noise orchestras" and factory performances of the 1920s.

Sergei Kurekhin (often rendered Kuryokhin in the West) is a world-class musician. Born in 1954, he began playing rock before studying classical forms, and his range of activity and style is enormous—rock leader (of Pop Mekhanika), piano soloist, conductor, composer, and musical impresario. In the stark and intimate frame of Kalevala Hall, he exploded in a virtuoso performance at the grand piano equipped with an electronic keyboard and cassette plug-in: blues, boogy-woogie, fifties rock 'n roll, folk, classical waltzes from one end of the nineteenth century and ragtime and tango from the other end, alternating complicated counterpoint of the baroque with big hard rock sounds and the occasional musical joke—all in a single number. In the middle of it, he fell off the piano bench and climbed underneath the huge instrument to explore the acoustical dimensions of its wood and its pedals.

From time to time he would joined by Sergei Letov-Kropotkin — in a Bolivian robe, bare feet, and beads — who blew into an astounding bumber of wind instruments including flutes, pipes from South America and Vietnam, a bass clarinet, a soprano saxophone, and a wildly improvising tenor sax.

Kurekhin says that "jazz is dead," but he himself is alive to practically every other form of musical expression, including serial composition, aleatory and improvisational performance, and the sounds created by electronics and computer, as well as traditional instruments. Although no slavish imitator of the 1920s experimental music, he is a confessed admirer of the early Shostakovich and of the "machine music" composer, Alexander Mosolov, long forgotten, now revived, and once world famous for his 1928 composition *The Factory* (*Zavod*). Kurekhin is clearly a major force in contemporary Soviet music, both popular and "serious."

The AVIA rock concert was the zenith of the festival and the best-attended event. VIA in Soviet parlance means "vocal and instrumental ensemble," but to the cutting edge of the rock world, it also denotes pallid, bland, and "safe" music. AVIA was conceived as an "anti-VIA" phenomenon. Nikolai Gusev, its personable founder, described to us the constant turnover in groups such as his, not composed of eight players and nine "fizkultura" performers. They filled the Carelian Hall with incredible sounds and sights. A bewigged band member, dressed in the garb of a 1920s poet, declaimed verses from a tribune in the manner of Mayakovsky, commenting on socialist realism, skateboards (now a big street "trend" in Russia), and *perestroika*. Against a background of Futurist slogans and Constructivist sets, the band, including brass and three saxes, played Russian rock in sharp rhythms and almost stratified sonorities, with sudden turns into folksong, marches, 1930s mass song, and an unexpected jocular allusion to "Home on the Range." The climax of this spectacular and ironic display of musical-political erudition was a chorus line of eight female fizkulturists, in stark black ties and shirts with white shirts, who emulated the precision movements of a machine in a deliberate reference to Meyerhold's "biomechanics" style of theater from the 1920s and the monumental Stalinist gymnastic shows of the five-year plan period—but then in an incredibly swift and controlled transition broke into the Twist, which the band joined as the music from the age of Chubby Checkers soared to a maximum volume.

We have rarely seen such an electric performance anywhere. The audience seemed struck into silence for a few seconds after the last note thundered—and then erupted into massive applause, shouts, and whistles.

Two documentary film people showed their wares during one of the daytime sessions: Olga Sviblova and Tatyana Yurina. Sviblova, a trained psychologist, wrote the script for *The Black Square*, which deals deals with the fate of avant-garde art in the Soviet Union by means of stills of the big experimental art figures of the 1920s, especially Malevich, footage of NEP Moscow, Stalinist socialist realism, a marvelous sequence showing Khrushchev as "art critic" in the 1960s, and interviews with well-known contemporary artists—including Ilya Kabakov, Erik Bulatov, and Grisha Bruskin on matters of creativity, freedom, isolation, and fear. Her *Krivoarbatsky 12* is a restrained but affectionate tribute to the great experimental architect of the 1920s, Konstantin Melnikov, a figure now well known to students of the Soviet Union from S. Frederick Starr's book about him. Melnikov's architectural vision is stressed—the Paris pavilion, the workers' clubs, the outlandish designs that never got off the board, and his bizarre circular house at Number 12, Krivoarbatsky Lane, lovingly caught by the camera. Yurina's works are in a slightly different key: her tribute to the beauties of the Russian language and her lament about its politicization and debasement reflect a current of cultural nostalgia whose principal voice nowadays is Dmitry Likhachev. And her witty *All Sold Out in the Theater of the Absurd* is an anthology of footage about human folly since the invention of the movie camera, ranging from English royalty and Stalinolotry to death camps, bombs, and a lesbian wedding. Her next project, she tells us, is a documentary about the Miss Moscow beauty contest.

The feature film of the festival—alas, the only one—was Oleg Teptsov's *Mister Designer* (*Gospodin Oformitel*) from Lenfilm, with a score by Kurekhin. It is being promoted as "the first Soviet horror film," which is reasonable if one discounts Kozintsev and Trauberg's

The Greatcoat from the 1920s. But the film's real roots are in the guignole productions of the prerevolutionary Russian studios, which churned out vampires, satans, black masses, and all manner of decadent "horror." Set in the years 1907-1914, *Mister Designer*'s baroque plot revolves around an artist and interior decorator who purchases a woman's cadaver from the morgue in St. Petersburg to use as a model. Predictably, she comes back to life to haunt and torment the designer. The theme of picture, artist, and model locked in fateful conflict was a common theme in symbolist movies of the 1910s. The cinematography is impressive, if not exactly daring: unusual angle shots, colored filters for different moods, and the beautifully handled motif of the Four Horsemen—this time in an open touring car in relentless pursuit through a black rainy night. But the real star of this film is the artwork of *fin-de-siècle* ambience, *art noveau* interiors, sprawling Jugenstil homes of the affluent, and Oscar Wilde costumes. There is more than enough art, cinematic and otherwise, to please the intelligentsia, and enough erotic suggestiveness and shock to pull in general audiences as well.

The most provocative event at Imatra, *Birthday*, began out on the lawn that stretches between the amphitheater and the Vuoksi River when a totally bald young woman displayed her naked skull through a circular hole in a huge black plastic cloak and the crawled, in agonizing slowness, across the grass to the theater door. The audience then piled into the tiny Imatra Hall to watch a performance (not a play) by a Leningrad experimental folkloric ensemble called, simply, Tree. They began with some ironic fairbooth buffoonery, set to the piano music of Scott Joplin, which contained a touch of menace—tossing iron pipes dangerously near the spectators. Then under dim light on the black plastic floorcover, they reenacted the birth of life on earth, twisting in agonized gyrations their almost wholly nude bodies, discovering self, "others," love, pain, and even war. An hour or so of these symbolic acrobatics was followed by a kind of finale—a rather frightening explosion of hysterical laughter, aggression, and the bursting of water bags all over the theater. Although visually exciting as a mimetic display of unfolding ambivalence and human contradiction in the rawest kind of setting, the performance probably fell short of its intention to shock because of its excessive length—and perhaps also the acute discomfort of the space in which it was held.

The setting of the last event we attended was althogether different: a restaurant in the center of Imatra where all were free to dine and drink during the performance. It was fundamentally an evening of Konstantin Kedrov—multimedia show of poems, slides, music, and dance. The music was provided by the Soviet composer, Nina Artistova, and was accompanied by a standard modern male-female dance number. The slides—all Soviet moderns—were chosen by the poet who declaimed in a soft-resonant voice, conveying—as he wished—a sense of pure sound and pure rhythm floating freely in space. The entire production was dubbed *The Unleashed Square*.

In conversations at the table afterwards, Kedrov spoke about his art in a way that seemed to embody the whole spirit of the Imatra Festival—and partly at least of Soviet avant-garde art in general. Through admiring of Bely, Tyutchev, and especially Khlebnikov (and much less of Pushkin, Lermontov, and Mayakovsky), Kedrov stressed originality—his own and that of the artists assembled, not beholden to the revered giants of the past.

The ring of *glasnost* was clearly audible in the festivities at Imatra this summer, but it was not blaring, defiant, or self-consciously ideological. The mechanics of the invitation process was such that the usual establishment was bypassed. The artists clearly did what they wanted to do here, and these were things unthinkable in the days before Gorbachev. The trumpeting of the 1920s theme is certainly tied in to other currents in Soviet intellectual and political life that harken back with longing to the years of Lenin and the NEP. But for the new avant-garde it is also just a way of having fun, of leaping over two intervening generations and linking up with the last genuinely vibrant period of Russian high culture, of playing with forms that were once considered dangerous, nihilistic, or destructive. The great musical jokes and parodies and the historical allusions make wonderful entertainment for a knowledgeable audience and for the performers themselves—as they freely admitted. Yet all the signs at Imatra '88 point to a new road for the avant-garde, indeed many roads, that will lead in directions undreamed of by anybody at this moment of joyous and serious ferment in Soviet culture.

Original publication: *The Soviet Observer*, vol. 1, no. 13, 29/9/1988.

14

Soviet Popular Culture in the Gorbachev Era

What does popular culture reveal about a society? It charts the different ways that people enjoy themselves in their free time in space of their own choosing—home, at friends', on the street, or in places of public relaxation. Its genres and media can uncover deeper values, the "solutions" in life about order, romance, family, deviance, friendship, and work. The reordering of popular culture now occurring in the USSR opens up this assortment of problems and solutions to full scrutiny and free discourse, with sometimes surprising revelations. Recent movements and shifts in reading habits, show attendance, film and television viewing, musical tastes, and non-structured leisure indicate a rapid growth of amateur culture —performance art, music, graphics, and hobbies. These changes also reflect a decentralization of cultural life through the spread of electronic media, especially video players, and an emerging recognition by the authorities of the legitimacy of spontaneously generated culture from below. And they demonstrate an accompanying "system" of alliances, friendships, networks, partnerships, patronage relations, and celebrity interlock that links "stars" of popular culture with the Other arts and with influential leaders of Soviet society, journalism, and politics.

Strong currents of iconoclasm, demythologizing, and open irreverence in all genres of popular culture are demonstrated by nude pictures and obscene lyrics in public places and heretofore unseen levels of shock and violence in movies and TV. This has evoked a complicated but very visible and audible countercurrent of resentment, envy, and hostility. The present cultural duel recapitulates many themes of the critique leveled by a moralizing intelligentsia in the 1900s and in the 1920s against popular forms of entertainment, such as boulevard literature, risqué variety shows, jazz, and "trashy" movies. It is also the culmination of recent decades of infighting in repertory committees, censors' offices, ideological headquarters, and all arenas of entertainment. At the core of the present struggle is the Gorbachev challenge to the spirit of the Brezhnev era, whose culture was recently called one of "vulgar optimism [which] covered everything with a vigorous phrase and a glistening smile."[1]

Traditional studies of Soviet culture have overwhelmingly focused on high culture, especially literature. Popular culture may reveal more about society because it is an interlocking system, a vast code of meanings and symbols that migrate from one genre to another and that function in a special way for the majority of Soviet Russian citizens. The best way to get to the values that popular culture bears, represents, and promotes or rejects is to survey it as whole. It is also necessary to approach this subject with an open mind, to discard the notions that only politically dissident culture in Soviet society is legitimate or authentic or popular, that cultural rebels are *ipso facto* politically motivated, and that official, traditional, and old-fashioned tastes are imposed from above and have no following among the people.

The Most Reading Nation on Earth?

Soviet commentators have long claimed that their people are the world's most voracious readers (*samyi chitaiushchii narod'*). Now Soviet critics are questioning this with anguished lamentations about the alleged decline of reading habits. This complaint, which has risen in cycles since the late nineteenth century, says that the masses are turning from reading to other forms of relaxation, or that they are reading the wrong things. A typical recent article, by the critic Maria Chegodaeva, juxtaposes "real" art (which is cathartic, cleansing, deeply stirring, and able to evoke tears or laughter) with what the author calls "comforting art" (popular culture and reading matter which are light, easy to consume, and unburdened with big ideas). She likens comforting art to its social setting—the cozy individual apartment which is rapidly replacing the old communal flat and the "homey life" that is as psychologically and culturally "indoors" as it is physically, a life removed from the storms and passions of reality. The author seems to shudder as she cites a recent example—a cartoon history of Russia. Literary critic Nikolai Miroshnichenko wrings his hands over a poll that reports that only 45 percent of adult males read books regularly, a figure that would seem impressively high in many other societies but which reflects a decline in the USSR. Alluding to the present passion for television and popular music among the young, he concludes wistfully that the USSR has become "the most dancing nation." He and many other observers are upset by amateurism and vulgarity in writing and by the fact that the "lesser" genres of books, such as crime and historical novels and science fiction, are crowding out serious literature in readers' preference.[2]

In terms of book sales and magazine publication, the two most popular writers in recent years are Valentin Pikul and Iulian Se-menov. Pikul draws on the Russians' fascination with the upper-class lifestyles of the tsarist past, an area neglected by Soviet historians.[3]

Semenov's bestselling thrillers, such as *TASS is Authorized to Announce*[4] and *Seventeen Moments of Spring*, have been made into enormously popular television series. Western readers of Frederick Forsythe, Tom Clancy, and Robert Ludlum may find it hard to understand Semenov's appeal. It stems from his ability to draw on an internal code of Soviet reading habits, memories, and sensibilities, very cleverly combining the familiar (references to Hemingway and the Spanish Civil War, feminized villains, and learned cops) with titillating elements of the new (exotica, atrocities, light sex, more open social criticism, and knowing allusions to the inner circles of film and entertainment celebrities). Semenov also presents the realia of KGB investigative procedures and technologies, which he knows intimately, and, like Pikul, writes about the history that Soviet historians have neglected—in this case Nazi Germany.

Science fiction has been an extremely popular genre since its vigorous revival in the late 1950s, following an entire generation of neglect and unofficial banning under Stalin. As with detective fiction, it reflects readers' tastes and curiosity and lifts them out of the everyday world into another time and space. It also provides adventure, suspense, and puzzling situations, and takes standard jabs at capitalism. But unlike the detective genre, science fiction creates scenarios that may seem anti-Western in form but which can be interpreted as critiques of Soviet society and policy. The built-in obsession with the frontiers of science and with rapid technological advances appeals mightily to its main audience: young urban males, especially those with aspirations for a scientific or technical career. In the 1980s, Soviet science fiction seems to be moving in a trendy, Western-style direction. In the early 1980s appeared the "Aelita" annual award for excellence in science fiction (inspired by Alexei Tolstoy's 1923 novel and analogous to the American "Hugo"). In 1988, a major author, Dmitry Bilenkin, called for Soviet science fiction fan clubs and magazines in emulation of those in advanced, scientifically literate countries. Well-known Science fiction writers have come out openly for *glasnost'* and *perestroika*. This summer, one of the most famous of them, Eremei Parnov, lashed out against the "medieval era" of Stalinism, and a subcommittee of the Writers' Union dealing with adventure and entertainment fiction resolved to turn their art to the struggle against "reaction"—in other words against the foes of Gorbachev.[5]

In addition to science fiction, detective novels, and historical pot-boilers, a proliferation of subgenres is now evident. There is no Soviet "horror" novel as yet, but translations of Stephen King are very popular. And recent critical reactions to Iurii Nikitin's East-West love and sex novel, *Hologram*—with its scenes of resort romance, real flesh in hotel bedrooms, a starry-eyed young American woman visiting the Don, foreign bars, drunken tourists, and a total absence of ideas—indicate that writers have crossed a great divide that might revive old Russian traditions of boulevard novels and perhaps even move on to gothics, candlelight romances, doctor-nurse tales, and other pulp styles that are so massively popular in North America and Western Europe.[6]

Show: Beyond the Bolshoi and the Taganka

When Western travelers think of Soviet theater, names like Kirov, Bolshoi, Taganka, Liubimov, Shatrov, and Tovstonogov come to mind. Yet many millions of Soviet citizens have never been to these places or seen works written or directed by these men. For most

Soviets, the stage means local theaters, amateur companies, touring ensembles, the circus, or variety shows of all kinds—known in Russian as *estrada*. Amateur theater has been expanding for years and the atmosphere of *glasnost'* has pushed the movement to full speed. Thousands of self-financed companies—private in almost every way—are springing up all over the USSR. In Moscow, for example, Blackboard, Nikita Gates, Chekhov Street, and Moscow Experimental have joined a syndicate called "Echo," which has a two-year plan to operate on a collective contract based on economic accountability (*khozrazchet*). The variety of formats, styles, and arrangements with authorities is infinite. The sort of avant-garde performances that the American theater specialist Alma Law witnessed some years ago—plays put on in suburban train cars and in private flats—are now out in the open. A recent performance of Tree, a Leningrad experimental group, would have been unthinkable before the onset of the Gorbachev era: near nudity, audience shock, dark references to the Red Army, and so on. It is doubtful that such avant-garde theater will become popular. But those "studio" theater groups who embrace topical themes (rather than the eternal or existential) seem to have a better chance of garnering large audiences. Such themes have included break-dance, disco, and commentary on the Afghanistan war.[7]

Even the hallowed circus ring is not immune to the winds of change that are blowing over the cultural landscape. Recent press accounts have told of circus tyrants dethroned, of rude treatment of artists by bosses, of improper safety devices and resultant injuries and deaths, and of extreme inequalities of pay. But since *perestroika* also means responsiveness to audiences, and since Soviet audiences love the circus just the way it is—an estimated 100 million Soviets attend each year—it seems unlikely that structural changes will lead to changes in style or artistry.[8]

Russian *estrada* (the word is derived through French from the Spanish word for low stage) includes the entire world of show—variety, cabaret, nightclub, vaudeville, operetta, and popular music concerts—and can be either live or on television. Live *estrada* is next in popularity to television and movies. It involves hundreds of thousands of concerts put on for tens of millions of people each year, placing its attendance figures far ahead of drama, opera, and ballet. A multi-genre show, *estrada* combines music and comic satire.

Soviet standup comedy is virtually unknown outside the country and may sound like an oxymoron. In fact, it is one of the great glories of popular culture in that country. Its roots are in fairground barkers who regaled, amused, and insulted onlookers from a wooden box in bygone days, in variety and cabaret shows at the turn of the century, in the towns of the Jewish pale, and in the revolutionary satire of the 1920s.[9] The father of modern Soviet stage comedy was the late Arkady Raikin. Raikin possessed the gift of the ghetto—that peculiarly Jewish approach to humor that combines searing satire with gentle sympathy for our flawed humanity. He walked the edge of official censure for four decades, delivered sharp social commentary, and survived the Stalin and Zhdanov cultural pogroms. His routines, which were lengthy, complex, even learned, were topical and more theatrical than those of American comics, with their chains of one-liners, and certainly less salty than either European cabaret or American nightclub comedy. He used structure and narrative with a stunning cumulative effect and embellished it with a repertory of gestures and voice registers that kept Soviet audiences roaring with laughter.[10]

There are dozens of *estrada* comedians, including Raikin's son Konstantin, a brilliant comic narrator. Another, Mark Olshevsky, speaks of the improvisational quality of comic routines and the importance of a direct, almost physical, rapport with the audience.[11] The Soviet comedian must not only amuse and entertain, but also display empathy and an understanding of everyday problems: work, in-laws, dating, corruption, bureaucracy, and especially neighbors (who in the Soviet context are often across the wall, not the hall). Satirical comedy is partly created by its audience and its environment. The laughter connecting the standup comics to their listeners about the shortcomings of Soviet life may be more socially significant than the muted exclamations and breathless silences of the Taganka theater that Western visitors have so often noted.

Estrada comedy is changing in two ways. A movement is on to organize all its artists into a union parallel to that of writers, composers, and filmmakers. Of greater cultural importance is the growing perception among professionals that it is becoming more difficult to produce irony and satire through Aesopian language because the new openness in public discourse cuts at the heart of oblique social satire. This means that comedy may have to become bolder, more vulgar and direct. What this will do to the popularity of *estrada* comedy, which is still immense, is impossible to say.[12]

The Silver Screen

When the superb metaphorical anti-Stalin film *Repentance* appeared in Moscow, Western press reports spoke of massive attendance nightly at Moscow cinemas. But my straw poll of non-intelligentsia workers and employees in Soviet towns in the summer of 1987 indicated overwhelmingly that almost none had seen the film or planned to (and that the one who had did not understand it). Western film scholars have shown that Soviet audiences in the 1920s did not rush to see the masterpieces of Eisenstein and Pudovkin that all intellectual filmgoers adore. The masses went to see Mary Pickford and Douglas Fairbanks; foreign films about cowboys, Tarzan, criminals, and the thief of Baghdad; and Soviet productions that dealt with Western-style adventure, vampire bears, or low comedy.[13] Soviet movie audiences today, like those the world over, have not changed much since the birth of cinema. They still prefer films of action, adventure, and pure entertainment over allegorical, symbolic, experimental, or philosophical films.

The 1986 revolt of Elem Klimov and other directors against the cinematic old guard has been much noted of late. It has affected the release of many previously shelved and censored films and it seems to promise both greater artistic freedom and more attention to the market. This can be achieved, as it was in the 1920s, by financing artistically worthy but poorly attended films with the receipts from popular ones. Critics recognize that audiences do not flock to see Gleb Panfilov's *Theme* (about the personal crises of a writer and a would-be Jewish émigré) or Alexei German's *My Friend Ivan Lapshin* (a grim portrait of provincial life in the early 1930s). Detective movies, film critic R. Sobolev observes, are "the locomotive of the box office." But, he concludes, since most Soviet crime movies are trashy, the industry should allow more well-made foreign films of that genre to be imported. He suggests the James Bond movies, which at least possess irony and wit. Audience survey research reveals that three quarters of the movie-going public are young people who want action, compelling themes, and exciting plots.[14]

Movie theater audiences are diminishing in the face of the competition provided by upgraded television shows and televised films and by the rapid growth of video players, both legal and underground. *Rambo*, *The Last Tango in Paris*, and *One Flew Over the Cuckoo's Nest* are among the favorites of video audiences. *Tootsie* was a smash hit in Soviet movie houses. Filmmakers will have to satisfy the obvious taste among youth for adventure, violence, eroticism, and shocking cinematic treatments of madness. The "first Soviet horror film" (so advertised) was *Mister Designer* (1988), an entertaining piece of gothic art, but far too tame to slake the thirst for shock that seems to be growing.[15]

The industry is responding in a variety of ways. One is the widely touted but still rather formless scheme for "new model films" by independent or semi-independent studios. Another is Forum, a cinema cooperative created in the summer of 1988 by Rudolf Fruntov to produce and distribute films. (The film industry was to have moved to self-financing as of January 1, 1989.) The director Mikhail Belikov, who visited the United States last year, has revived a grandiose version of a scheme hatched in the 1930s for a "Soviet Hollywood" in the Crimea (its creator, Boris Shumiatsky, was executed in the purges). Belikov's is called Kinograd or Cinema City, blending elements of Rome, Hollywood, and Disneyland. It calls for a planned city to be located in the Carpathian Mountains as a filmmaking center for the Soviet bloc; a tourist resort with hotels, a zoo, and a huge amusement park; a technical research center including a library, museum, and costume warehouse; and a colony of mockup historical cities to serve the needs of the studios. Kinograd is to be financed through revenues from tourism. A scheme of "Hollywoodization" such as this—however it might turn out—could not have been aired publicly before the advent of glasnost'.[16]

Moviemakers are also tapping into two current trends in Soviet life: the drastic revision of history and the explosion of rock music. For the former, the documentary is in the lead with major productions such as *More Light* and *Risk-2*, which partially restore the historical truth about the Russian Revolution, early Bolshevism, and

Stalinism. A half-dozen shorter documentaries shown this summer at a festival in Finland deal with the rehabilitation of artists, architects, and writers silenced or destroyed in the 1930s, or harassed and persecuted in the 1960s and 1970s. The most effective and disturbing documentary on the rock generation is the Latvian film *Is It Easy to be Young?* (1987) by Juris Podnieks. Some specialists believe that the documentary will soon occupy a major place in Soviet cinematography.[17]

Feature films pay less attention to history and more to current problems of alienated urban youth, sexual tension, and hooliganism. Rock film scores and rock musicians appear in these more frequently. In *The Burglar* and *Courier* (both 1987), it is a backdrop. But in *Assa* (1988), rock culture is the symbol of a coming era just as a mafia-like boss is emblematic of the corrupt age about to fade away. *Little Vera* (1988) is the most wrenching of these films to date. An unvarnished close-up of working-class life in a provincial city with scenes of dancehalls and disorderly youth, it shows moments of sexual intimacy between a boy and a girl unprecedented on the Soviet screen.

The Blue Screen

Even more important than film is television. "Television has become the pre-eminent medium of mass communication in the Soviet Union," writes Ellen Mickiewicz. "It is the medium that has created the first mass public in Soviet history."[18] This striking statement is buttressed in her recent book by hard data and compelling arguments. She shows that television is accessible to 93 percent of the population, that 150 million people watch TV news daily (80 percent of all adults), and that some 63 percent of workers and intelligentsia (which included the white collar class as a whole) claim this medium as the chief source of both information and moral values. News and stories dealing with the United States exceed in popularity those about the socialist bloc or the Third World. On recent shows, the chief U.S. correspondent presented meticulous demonstrations of American voting machines and of fast-food retailing procedures. In programming, the entertainment sector—already huge—is getting larger, though still proportionately smaller than on U.S. television.

The massive expansion of television popularity has evoked criticism. The Soviet intelligentsia, to a greater extent than the American educated elite, is still somewhat alienated from the general offerings on television. The eminent scholar and standard-bearer of culturally conservative values, Dmitry Likhachev, sees television as a "great force" but one that is littered with bad programs—a wholly familiar complaint in "media" societies. Irina Tolmakova, a high official in the children's book industry, calls it simply "a terrorist and aggressor who tries to oust literature."[19]

The line between popular and educational TV is blurred in the Soviet Union: news is viewed by tens of millions and "pop" shows sometimes contain motifs of uplift or politics. But the extremes of each are quite visible. Purely educational programs do not possess mass appeal. As elsewhere, Soviet viewers like to watch adventure films, popular music shows, comedy reviews, and games and youth shows. The game show *Ready, Girls?* (*Nu-ka, devushki?*) combines friendly competition in silly tasks, celebrity figures, and a jocular atmosphere. Audiences love it. Sketches of daily life and takeoffs on lazy clerks and officious bureaucrats give the public at home what Soviet viewers have long sought for in live *estrada.* Audience preference for light entertainment is not new, and the political excitement of *glasnost'* does not seem to have diminished it.

However, new things are going on. The old morning exercise program has become an aerobics show of chic females gyrating to rock music in the background. Rock is used to open news and commentary shows and something like music video can be seen on Soviet television. Most dramatic and most representative of the Gorbachev era is the dynamic interview and call-in show on topical issues. Mickiewicz calls one of these, *The Twelfth Floor*, "the most interesting program on Soviet television" and "probably the most popular."[20] In it, the visual medium clearly out-dramatizes the press in treating rock culture, drug abuse, prostitution, Afghan veterans, youth disaffection, violence, and corruption with unprecedented candor and energy. On this and similar shows in recent months could be seen young Soviet neo-Nazis expounding racist opinions, body builders explaining why they beat up punks, and rockers telling why they do not belong to ordinary society. They pick up the public anger and the sharp clashes of opinion among their interviewees and respond to it with sympathy and a desire to defuse tensions and solve problems.

Television is *the* mass medium today in the Soviet Union, and *glasnost'* is its guiding principle. Real news, politics, social candor, and popular entertainment of a new order are its content. The study of television reveals two important developments that are crucial to the understanding of its relationship to other realms of popular culture. First it has already caused a reduction in the public's consumption of reading matter, theater, shows of all kinds, concerts, and cinema-viewed movies. All of these have registered fall-offs. Mickiewicz claims that all other previous uses of leisure time, including visits to friends, have decreased. Second, the new principle of news in the Gorbachev era is *operativnost'* (timeliness), an effort to authenticate and enliven the new openness by giving viewers what they want to know immediately and by concretizing the world and its unfolding events. This seems to be a direct response to Mikhail Gorbachev's remarks at the XXVII Party Congress on the dullness of the media and the need to infuse them with life and respond to actual audience preferences.

Television news and entertainment mutually frame and define one another. Frankness and timeliness in news coverage and analysis is paralleled by the sharpening of the themes of popular culture as a whole. Live popular genres are not disappearing, but much of their production is being transferred to television. The paradoxical result is that while some standardization is required in order to present most genres to the mass public on the blue screen, timeliness and openness in their performance make the innovations in popular culture accessible to almost everybody in the Soviet Union simultaneously. These include historical revisionism, strident social commentary, iconoclastic styles of dress and speech, and audacious criticism of authority.

Leisure Culture

Scholars sometimes exaggerate the importance of high culture over low, of one genre over others, of all cultural production over unstructured leisure activity. One of the most perceptive observers of Soviet life, John Bushnell,[21] has shown that leisure culture has been surprisingly autonomous and stable in this century. Its main ingredients have been visiting (or entertaining) friends and going out (*progulki*). The latter term can mean street promenade, but more often denotes simply being with companions outside the home, workplace, or school. People can be at cafes, bars, restaurants, or "hangouts" such as street corners, parks, and hotel entrances. There they talk, tell jokes, flirt, neck, play cards, dance, or generally have fun. Urban Russians visit or hang out not because of poor housing or because of the shortage of alternative cultural opportunities. Rather they do so by choice, something that some Kremlinologists believe the Soviet people have never possessed.

The restaurant is the major locus of urban leisure in Soviet towns, especially for those eighteen or over. Bars, clubs, and cafes are small and few in number, though new ones are springing up all the time. Even restaurants are hard to get into because service people and managers dislike crowds and the prospect of overwork, and because their food supplies are sometimes depleted by the employees themselves. But the attractions of restaurants are manifold: the bright, noisy hall (often called a "stable" by their denizens), the conviviality of the table, a talkfest, appetizers and vodka (after 2:00 P.M.), live music, and—because Russians have retained the European custom of combining dancing with dining—a room full of dancing partners. Soviet dance floors revel in energy, eclecticism, and in the generational mix that has all but disappeared in societies where popular culture is strictly stratified by age or style and where dancing has been largely separated from dining. Soft rock bands are displacing the old pop and swing combos but the range is still very wide—from the upscale kitsch *estrada* of Moscow's Starry Skies Restaurant to the blaring saxes and brass of the Metropol in Leningrad.

People in the USSR do all kinds of things in their spare time from familiar hobbies such as sports (a vast activity deserving of a special study), chess, book hunting and icon-collecting to the lesser known ones of pet care, motorcycle hockey, and collecting pins, records, and Beatles' memorabilia. In big towns the *fartsovshchiki* or dealers seem to derive psychic joy from the time and energy they spend on buying and selling on the black market. Less shady, but still shadowy, is the tremendous activity involved in organizing underground shows, concerts, and garage rock, assembling high-tech paraphernalia (speakers, video players), and participating in a *tusovka* or happening. Fashion, makeup, hairstyle, and perfume have occupied urban women at least since the 1930s, a part of the *embourgeoisement* that overtook Soviet society from that time. In the era of Gorbachev, this has been given a sharp boost by the emerging image of Raisa Gorbacheva, by the ascendance of fashion designer Slava Zaitsev into global prominence, and by the staging of the first Miss Moscow contest (soon to be the subject of a scathing Soviet documentary).[22]

For urban Soviet youth, many of the above activities interlace with their persistent habit of hanging out together in groups or gangs that share the same taste—groups of constantly changing shape and composition. In the past few years, a new street culture has arisen that is popular in two senses: it is the chosen leisure form of those in it and, because of its expressive nature, it is an object of entertainment for the general public. On Moscow's Arbat Street and at the Bitsevsky and Izmailovo parks, one sees not only daring new outdoor art shows, but a whole marketplace of cultural forms—break-dance (which flourished from about 1984 to 1986), rock bands, singers, poets, youngsters in bizarre costumes, trinket sellers. It is the same array of elements which twenty years ago linked the hippie hangouts of a score of American and European cities into a single culture.[23]

Rock and Roll is Here to Stay

The driving force behind much of the urban youth culture of large Soviet cities is rock music. The Soviet establishment has long tried to exert some control over the production of popular music by promoting "mass songs" of patriotism, revolutionary optimism and sentiment, and by allowing the resurrection of old forms such as Gypsy, urban, and folk music, as well as pop styles from Europe. The old forms and the foreign imports are still immensely popular, at least among people over thirty. For decades, the contending alternative to these was jazz, whose struggle for official acceptance lasted until the sixties. No sooner was it accepted that the popularity of jazz declined, partly under the impact of emerging rock music.

Like jazz, rock had to fight the same battle for two decades. By the late Brezhnev years it was almost fully accepted and had become the most popular type of music among young Soviets.[24]

There was a time when scholars who looked at popular music at all saw it only in jazz or in the great guitar poets or bards, Bulat Okudzhava, Aleksandr Galich, and Vladimir Vysotskii. This tradition is by no means dead (though two of the above singers are) and a new star has arisen to carry it on: Aleksandr Rozenbaum. Furthermore, the cult of Vysotskii (who died in 1980) is still very much alive and broader in social scope than the cult of rock. Nevertheless, rock is in the ascendant. The much-revered Boris Grebenshchikov of Aquarium has become almost a cult figure for Soviet urban youth. There is a very strongly perceived spiritual element in Grebenshchikov and Vysotskii before him that distinguishes them sharply from their Western counterparts, though this is not the only reason for their popularity.

Under Gorbachev, formerly proscribed rock bands were recognized and now all styles of rock are blossoming—hard, soft, punk, art, folk, fusion, retro, and heavy metal. Some estimate the number of registered rock groups at 250,000. While the music of Soviet rock closely resembles that of the West right down to instrumentation and electronic gear, Russian players have ceased singing it to English words and are developing a Russian lyrical style. Professional rockers belong to one of about 200 concert agencies and they perform in clubs, restaurants, concert halls, radio shows, television programs, recording studios, and films. They are paid according to the assessments of official agencies on the basis of appeal, skill, training, and content of lyrics. Amateurs get no state bookings or pay but are free to drift from gig to gig, to shape their own programs, and to make informal wage deals. Beyond the pros and paid amateurs are the genuine amateurs, a whole world of garage bands, barracks groups, and workplace ensembles who play for themselves and friends. Rock clubs and laboratories offer a further variant in employment and performance opportunity. The net result is that a great deal of rock performance is unmonitored.

Soviet rock, like jazz before it, has many well-placed friends and allies. The popularity of such groups as AVIA, Black Coffee, Aquarium, Time Machine, Stas Namin, Bravo, Pop Mekhanika,

Kino, Arsenal, and Avtograf has brought them celebrity and contacts with other figures in the art and entertainment worlds. A well-known composer of Soviet pop (singable and danceable, but neither jazz nor rock), Raimond Pauls, promotes an open market place for all kinds of music. Alla Pugacheva, the superstar of Soviet pop, has actively supported rock musicians. Andrei Voznesenskii, viewed by many as the leading Soviet poet, is an enthusiastic promoter of Grebenshchikov, whose group was once outlawed. Rock operas, such as *Juno and Avos* (1981), with lyrics by Voznesenskii, have endowed rock with respectability for some people, as have decorous rock concerts, festivals, and interviews on television. Rock has invaded film, both documentary and feature. Critic Oleg Panov calls rock music the folklore of the Scientific Technical Revolution and urges the public to take it seriously, admit its vast popularity, and criticize it intelligently.[25]

But rock has also made enemies because of its style and its social overflow. The loudness and the harsh vocal phrasing assault the ears of older people, including those in power, who for decades have tuned in to smoother pop music, imported or Soviet. Rock lyrics such as "get out of control" or "my father is a fascist" are offensive to devotees of Leninism and to those who recall the war against "fascism" in 1941. A rock lament on the lack of places for couples to make love ends like this:

> *In summer we can go together to the woods*
> *But it takes an hour to get there*
> *And if the local yobs [fuckers] get you*
> *You risk being beaten into a pile of shit.*

Or the boast of a corrupt bureaucrat:

> *I am a man of the people*
> *The people chose me*
> *And raised me over the years.*
> *That's how it is, boom, boom, fuck you;*
> *That's how it is.*

Song titles such as "Atheist Twist" or names of groups such as Pig or Mister Twister (from the name of a universally known children's verse) can be offensive to an older generation. Drugs, alcoholism, corruption, and urban nihilism—the stuff of everyday *glasnost'*—are ideal materials for the sharpened tongues of rock singers. Rock players have fainted into the audience and shepherded livestock onto the stage. On the visual front, hairstyles and costumes range from the hippie look of the 1960s to mocking replicas of Russian civil war uniforms.

If, as *estrada* comics claim, verbal satire is now losing its punch, rockers are filling the void with satire of sound, sight, and gesture. Like the popular music of other eras and places, rock has produced a subculture that is carried onto the streets: a lexicon, facial expressions, gestures, clothes—a code and ethos shared by its members and serving to define its identity. Heavy metal fans call themselves *metallisty*, a term associated by older people with the steelworkers of the October Revolution. As a recent study of the inner life of the Leningrad rock counterculture shows, the Soviet rock generation, like the Russian nihilists of the 1860s or like the American hippies of the 1960s, have raised a personal and cultural revolt and not one that is engaged in political dissidence.[26]

Of all the manifestations of popular culture in the Gorbachev era, rock is seen as the most negative by its enemies. Some of these are musical competitors. Pop composers are distressed by rock singers who write their own songs—and collect their own royalties. Traditional crooners, such as Iosif Kobzon and Muslim Magomaev, are not only losing ground to rock singers but are sometimes even mocked by them. Jazz and big band figures, who fought for years in order to gain recognition, state publicly that rock is not music at all. A poignant and typical example is Konstantin Orbelian. This smoothly attired leader of the Armenian State Estrada Orchestra, with its big band sound, is a child of the Stalinist purges who fought against all odds to make it to the top of popular music only to find that nowadays his kind of music is ignored by "nearsighted managers" and television producers. Zhanna Bichevskaia, a very popular folk-revival singer, complains that children now "listen to non-descript music."[27]

Of greater social and political import is the opposition to rock, or certain forms of it, by cultural conservatives who cover a wide range of the political spectrum. Elements of the press have called rock "musical alcoholism" and a "creature of the C.I.A." In 1987 a Red Army officer identified heavy metal with Zionism and the once powerful writer Sergei Mikhalkov linked rock bands to AIDS, prostitution, drugs, crime, and finally treason. The rightwing group *Pamiat'* puts the matter simply: "Rock groups are satanism." Yegor Ligachev, the recently downgraded Politburo "conservative," opposes the "spread of primitive music" and urges a return to folk and classical music. A group of influential ruralist writers claim that rock is "mentally and morally damaging." Aleksandr Iakovlev, a main force in the Gorbachev reform movement, on viewing American rock on television, said "such things we shall never accept." Dmitry Likhachev sees popular music of the present moment as all "wild rhythms and stupid words."[28]

Is this merely a verbal war or does the anti-rock current possess a social base? Informal youth groups and gangs have been around for a long time but have become more diverse and more publicized in the last few years. They include Afghanistan war veterans (*afgantsy*), vigilantes who visit mob justice on speculators and grafters, bikers, sports fan gangs (*fanaty*), body-building cultists, neo-Nazis (*fashisty*), and a whole array of street gangs distinct from and usually hostile to punks, hippies, and rockers. Juvenile violence and vandalism among working-class and vocational school youth in provincial industrial towns and ports and in the proletarian suburbs of big cities has been much in the news lately. Some of it is fueled by resentment of the privileged youth of Moscow and Leningrad (called *goldeny* by one television interviewee). The best known of these gangs is the Lyubery, named from the Moscow district of Lyubertsy. Bodybuilding—very popular now on Soviet media—is their main hobby, and they have adopted special clothing, names, rituals, and a way of walking. Moved by a kind of angry redneck patriotism, the Lyubery identify rock music, its cultural style, and its devotees with the West, and ultimately with disloyalty. They have travelled to downtown Moscow to beat up rockers and hippies, cut their hair, and smash their artifacts. Victims and foes of the Lyubery perceive a natural (and perhaps active) alliance between the culturally conservative intelligentsia and the street gangs.[29]

Gorbachev, Glasnost', and Popular Culture

Mikhail Gorbachev has sent two strong signals about how *glasnost'* relates to popular culture: his comment on the need for more responsive media and his 1987 remark at a Central Committee meeting about the need for greater trust in young people. Media echoes have tied this to the upsurge of rock culture: newspapers encourage giving the music a hearing, and television interviewers let the rockers speak for themselves. There is at least a tentative alliance among reform leaders, media managers, a segment of the intelligentsia, and the huge rock community. At the same time, the authorities, the Komsomol, and entertainment industry leaders are trying to tame and co-opt rock music culture, to deflect it from nihilistic directions without eliminating its vigor—a difficult task. The operating principle seems to be that it is politically safer to allow openness in popular culture than not to. Such a policy risks offending the cultural conservatives, but that is the nature of politics.

Many of the changes in popular culture noted here had beginnings in the pre-Gorbachev era. But a new function in the present era is to disseminate in popular and digestible forms the muckraking and revisionism of journalism. In the past, fun and social criticism (tightly constrained) were further apart. Now the two are often combined and they illustrate for the masses both past realities and present problems. This disturbs some as much as it delights others. But much of eccentric popular culture can be defused and legitimized by its very appearance on television in a respectable setting. The whole process is replete with backlash, gaps, and contradictions. It is harder to remain patient in time of ferment than in time of stagnation.

The potential results (the realities are as yet unmeasured) of the thaw in popular entertainment are twofold. First, it can give those who favor reform a greater sense of participation in national renewal by seeing problems dramatized or fictionalized in song, story, television drama, or comedy routine. The audience thrill of identification supplements what people get from news and political language. Secondly, the diverse content of the emerging popular culture reinforces pluralism—existing or in embryo. Religious freedom, greater privacy, personal security and autonomy, preservation of past culture, and conservation of nature are not only promised in speeches, but celebrated in the popular arts. All of this raises hope for the emergence of greater civic consciousness among the Soviet people, a prerequisite for any passage to the long awaited civil society.

Original publication: In *The Harriman Institute Forum*, I: 3, March 1989, pp. 1-8.

Notes

1   Evgenii Sidorov quoted in Anthony Olcott, "Glasnost' and Soviet Culture," M. Friedberg and H. Isham, eds., *Soviet Society Under Gorbachev* (New York, 1987), 118.

2   *Sovetskaia kul'tura* (hereafter as *SK*), July 30, 1988, 4; Olcott, "Glasnost'," 107.

3   Klaus Mehnert, *The Russians and their Favorite Books* (Stanford, 1983) 32, 50-1, 85, 155-60. Pikul's popularity has not diminished since this book appeared. On historians and Pikul, see Mark von Hagen's discussion in *The Harriman Institute Forum*, I: 11 (November 1988).

4   Now available in paperback translation (New York, 1988). Analysis of his works in Walter Laqueur, "Julian Semyonov and the Soviet Political Novel," *Society*, XXIII/5 (July-Aug. 1986), 72-80.

5   Richard Stites, "Vision and Value: World Outlook and Inner Fears in Soviet Science Fiction," the next essay in this volume. (The citation in the original is misleading - *ed.*).

6   Olcott, "Glasnost," 109. See Anatolii Rybakov's indignant review of *Gologramma* in *Literaturnaia gazeta* (hereafter as *LG*) Sept. 7, 1986, 3.

7   *Soviet Life* (Sept. 1986), 52-3; *Current Digest of the Soviet Press*, 39: 11 (1987), 17; *Ogonek*, 2 (Jan. 1987), 32-3; *Soviet Observer* (hereafter as *SO*) (Sept. 29, 1988), 1, 5.

8   *SK* (Nov. 13, 1986), 5.

9   E. M. Kuznetsov, *Iz proshlogo russkoi estrady* (Moscow, 1958); S. S. Klitin, *Estrada* (Leningrad, 1987).

10 E. D. Uvarova, *Arkadii Raikin* (Moscow, 1986); Iu. Dmitriev, *Estrada i tsirk* (Moscow, 1977), 102-6; *Teatr Arkadiya Isaakovicha Raikina* (Videotape, 1987).

11 *SK* (Jan. 20, 1987), 5.

12 *Ibid.* (Dec. 18, 1986), 5; *LG* (March 11, 1987), 8.

13 Richard Taylor, *The Politics of Soviet Cinema* (Cambridge, Eng., 1979); Denise Youngblood, *Soviet Cinema in the Silent Era* (Ann Arbor, 1985).

14 *LG* (March 11, 1987), 8. The best introduction to recent Soviet film history is Anna Lawton, "Toward a New Openness in Soviet Cinema," in Daniel Goulding, ed., *Post New Wave Cinema in the Soviet Union and Eastern Europe* (Bloomington, 1988), 1-50.

15 *SK* (Nov. 25, 1986), 4; *People* (Apr. 6, 1987), 18-19, 28; *SO* (Sept. 29,1988), 5.

16 *SK* (July 30, 1988), 7-8; Taylor, "Boris Shumyatsky and the Soviet Cinema in the 1930s," *Historical Journal of Film, Radio, and Television,* VI: I (1986), 43-64.

17 Lawton, "Rewriting History: a New Trend in Documentary Film," *SO* (Sept. 29, 1988), 6.

18 Ellen Mickiewicz, *Split Signals: Television and Politics in the Soviet Union* (New York, 1988), 204.

19 *Ogonek* (Aug. 1985), 22. See also *SK* (July 18, 1988), 8. Kristian Gerner, "Soviet Television Viewing in Sweden" (ms.).

20 Mickiewicz, *Split Signals*, 177-8; Jonathan Sanders, "A Very Mass Media: Soviet Television," *Television Quarterly*, xxii:3 (1986), 7-27; Nick Hayes, "Glasnost and the Politics of Soviet Media" (ms.).

21 "Urban Leisure Culture in Post-Stalin Russia" in T. Thompson and R. Sheldon, eds., *Soviet Society and Culture: Essays in Honor of Vera S. Dunham* (Boulder, 1988), 58-86.

22 *Washington Post* (hereafter as *WP*), Sept 8, 1988, C8 (motorcycle hockey) and Apr. 6,1988, C1, C5 (Miss Moscow). On fashion, see *People* (Apr. 6, 1987), 31, 133-5; *SK* (Nov. 29, 1986), 8; and *Ogonek*, 10 (March 1987), 7.

23 *Ogonek*, 12 (March, 1987), 18-21; Nancy Condee and Vladimir Padunov, "The Frontiers of Soviet Culture: Reaching its Limits?", *The Harriman Institute Forum*, I:5 (May, 1988), 2.

24 S. F. Starr, *Red and Hot: the Fate of Jazz in the Soviet Union* (New York, 1983); Artemy Troitsky, *Back in the USSR: the True Story of Rock in Russia* (London, 1987). See also Paul Godfrey, "The Leningrad Rock Community," in J. Riordan, ed., *Soviet Youth Problems* (Bloomington, 1989).

25 *SK* (Nov. 16, 1986), 3-4 and (Jan. 10, 1987), 4; *Ogonek*, 11 (March, 1987).

26 Troitsky, *Back in the USSR, passim.* Godfrey, "Leningrad Rock Community" (lyrics).

27 Troitsky, *Back*, 99; *Pevtsy sovetskoi estrady* (Moscow, 1985); *SK* (July 20, 1988), 5; *Ogonek*, 49 (Dec. 1986), 17.

28 Troitsky, *Back in the USSR*, 125, I31; Pedro Ramel and Sergei Zamascikov, "The Soviet Rock Scene," *Kennan Institute for Advanced Russian Studies Occasional Paper*, No. 223, 10-11; *WP* (Feb. 18, 1988); (Nov. 27, 1987); (Apr. 20, 1988); *Ogonek*, 31 (Aug. 1985).

29 Bushnell, "Moscow Graffiti" (ms.); Riordan, "Teenage Gangs, 'Afgantsy', and Neofascists," in *Soviet Youth Problems*; *LG* (March 4, 1987), 1.

15

World Outlook and Inner Fears in Soviet Science Fiction

Much of the commentary on contemporary Soviet science fiction suffers from an insufficiency of historical understanding. Unlike similar genres in Western nations, Russian science fiction, known by the somewhat more lyrical name of *nauchnaia fantastika*—science fantasy—was born into a setting of backwardness in material life, small but flourishing islands of high culture and academic eminence, and a visionary and largely radical intelligentsia who dreamed of remaking Russia into a land of social justice and technical competence. In 1890, about the time that a continuous tradition of science fiction arose there, Russia was very far from either goal. With the onset of industrialization, the older dreamy and millenarian traditions of social fantasy gave way to a "harder" genre of scientific speculation. After a decade or so of technological speculation about such things as the wonders of electric power and modern weapons, Russian Marxism was linked with this technical genre in Aleksandr Bogdanov's *Red Star* (1908), a communist utopia set on the planet Mars. Out of it—as out of Gogol's "Overcoat"—flowed the main strands of revolutionary science fiction for the next two decades. Bogdanov's red and rosy vision was matched and challenged by a series of antisocialist works offering either the frightful specter of a totalitarian future or a counterutopia of antimodern, pastoral escape.[1]

This dialogical pattern was repeated in the revolutionary decade 1920-1930 under Soviet power in an environment of Party dictatorship, a mixed economy, and relative pluralism in society, artistic experimentation, and utopian experiment. The revolutionary storm that blew over Russia and shook away portions of the old order also irrigated the intellectual landscape of early Soviet life, from which sprouted a lush crop of futurology. Physicists, geologists, astronomers, and biologists vied with journalists and literary figures to speculate in the press about the coming character of a world made perfect under communism. Scientists of the New World spoke of prolonging human life, while mystical philosophers with roots in the Old World insisted on the possibility—indeed the moral need for—abolishing death altogether and revivifying all of deceased humanity. Bolshevik worship of the machine, cults of Ford and Taylor, and a frenetic technolatry suffused the arts, the theater, and the military, and shaped all kinds of revolutionary discourse. The tractor became an emblem of modernizing the countryside and fighting religion. Aviation—as a physical binding force in the vast spaces of the USSR and as another symbol of modernity—became a public hobby. Scientists and laymen alike, driven by an intense interest in outer space, saw distant stars as more fortresses for bolshevism to storm along the way to cosmic liberation.[2]

Soviet science fiction in this era, though drawing much from Bogdanov and other prerevolutionary writers, was ruled by the atmosphere of optimistic and limitless change—a collective eulogy to Prometheus and Marx. The revolutionary age, 1917-1930, witnessed a mounting wave of utopian vision and experiment: culture building, egalitarianism, collective creativity, moral brotherhood, sexual revolution, and urbanization inspired thousands of intellectuals, students, and workers to point demonstratively to the glimmering daybreak of their tomorrow. The grim, prosaic realities of daily existence for most Soviet citizens of the period endowed this vision with exceptional pathos. On a time scale, utopianism could be divided into present, near future, and distant times to come. In the first category were the social experimenters of the time, in particular the hundreds of city people and country folk of the communal movement—like-minded comrades of both sexes who lived together, pooled their meager earnings, divided the labor, shared all goods, and tried to cement friendship in a familylike setting. In the near-future category were architects, city planners, economists, and sociologists, who drew blueprints for new schemes of structures, space, and population density—deurbanizing dispersal across the land, conglomerations of towering house communes, fantastic cities and anticities to replace the decaying metropolises of Old Russia. And in the category of further speculation, the science fiction writers took on the depiction of an entirely new world to come.[3]

On peering into the future worlds of the most popular and characteristic of the science fiction works of this period, we see in a flash both the tremendous euphoria that the Revolution had breathed into popular writers (most of them non-Party fellow travelers sympathetic to communism) and the endless horizons it opened to them through the device of blending Marxism with "Marsism." The plots and situations were trivial and remarkably similar. One can speak confidently of an almost common scenario of a world environment, an eco-technical system of governance, and human relations. The dominant motif is the world city, or world-as-a-city: an urbanized planet shaped by technology, with mountains moved and seas rearranged, with megacities and a citified globe. In one example the planet is so completely urbanized that one can travel from Australia to Central Russia by walking or riding along city streets. London and Paris are conjoined; Moscograd is an urban blanket of concrete, steel, and glass. Highways repose upon pillars which themselves house thousands of dwellers. Tracks encircle the earth like musculature; an endless parade of aerostats, ethoronephs, airbuses, and skycars transport citizens to the far ends of the world. Nature (if it is permitted at all) is a vestigial adornment of the urbs or a setting for children's colonies.[4]

Government and economy as such do not exist in the communist future world. Production, processing, and extraction are performed by machines and their tasks coordinated by other machines. Computers calculate all production and distribution of the world's resources in proto-cybernetic systems akin to that on Bogdanov's Mars. In one novel mechanically harvested and packed foods are pulled through underground vacuum tubes from agrocenters and delivered to urban dwellers. No one need work very much, yet everyone does. As the quintessential utopian host puts it in *The Coming World* (1923), "You will want to work."[5] Labor is pleasant and rotational. All the contradictions lamented by Marx are gone: the manual-mental, the male-female, the city-country, and the private-public. Who rules? Either no one at all or a faceless set of rotated leaders or elders. In the first case a kind of "machine politics" in the literal sense manages the only struggle left to humanity, that between man and nature—in other words, production, feeding, and supply. The noneconomic sector is conflict-free. In some cases a Council of a Hundred or some such shadowy body—never elucidated—makes general policy and oversees the big machines. Both politics and economics have disappeared. The usual array of fancy technology is on full display (processed food, personal flight, and so on), with special emphasis on transport, aviation, space flight, and—bowing to Lenin's compulsive dream—total electrification. The world sparkles with light and enlightenment.

Peopling this wondrous universe are the expected paragons of communist virtue. They do not compete, hoard, covet, engage in social climbing, steal, rape, kill, sell their bodies or souls, or make war. The familiar static harmony of most classical utopias ensures serenity and peace. Vernean pairs of protagonists are often employed to examine and narrate the new ways: an arid professor for the technology and a down-to-earth younger companion to inspect life and love. Equality is palpable here: unisex clothing and haircuts, androgynous shapes, absence of deference and differential reward, egoless friendships, comradely cooperation—all of these drawn not only from the utopian corpus and various stages of socialist ideology, but also from schemes and practices in the everyday Russia of the 1920s. No politics, no conflict, no struggle for existence, no apparent anxieties. What, then, is the meaning of life? The authors give no direct answer, but they seem to share two assumptions. The first is that the absence of violence and struggle is happiness enough. One might pause a moment to recall what most of these writers had recently witnessed in their country in the years 1914 to 1922 and the conditions of their present life. The second—a standard reply—is that there is drama in the continuous struggle against nature or the exploration of space in order to see (or liberate) other worlds. But the authors limit their explication of utopian happiness to stock descriptions of rituals and spectacles of the most banal order: the disturbingly familiar radiant faces, the collective song, and the joyful reverence toward one's own world, one's own existence.[6]

The pendant to utopian communist heaven in this literature is the capitalist hell. The road to utopia is hardly ever analyzed, but in most cases it arises in the aftermath of an apocalyptic war between the forces of emergent socialism (often specified as an "Eastern" federation) and the resistant evil empires of the capitalist West— Germany, England, or the United States. These are dictatorships, fascoid despotisms, industrial hells, slave states, plutocracies, or feudal and militaristic fossils. As in Jack London's *Iron Heel* (1907), the inspirer of them all, the workers are brutalized or drugged with mass culture and religion, their leaders provoked into vain uprisings and then massacred. A whole genre of "war scare" fantasy grew up, rooted in the era of fear that preceded the First World War. Atomic explosions, skies blackened by bombers, death rays, mad scientists, and supervillains who would rather blow up the world than hand over their property menace the peace of Russia and her allies. Extraordinary scenes of battle, star wars launched from satellites, underwater armadas, proletarian mutinies, and armies of liberation mark the pages of Soviet fantasy. The most popular of them, Aleksandr Beliaev's *Struggle in the Atmosphere*, depicts a war with America so grim and comprehensive that the U.S. Air Force had it translated and published in the 1960s. In the end, the capitalists are beaten and their subjugated peoples led into the light of humanitarian justice.[7]

The "dialogue of dreams" that began before the Revolution could not be conducted openly, and so the ratio of hope and fear was reversed in the 1920s. Pessimistic novels and alternate routes to happiness were rare and often masked. The most influential of these was Eugene Zamiatin's *We*, a political dystopia about a nightmare collectivist state so famous that it scarcely needs discussion. Until 1989 it had never been published in the Soviet Union.[8] Two observations need to be made about it. First, it was not an answer to Soviet science fiction, because it preceded all the works I have just described; indeed, some of those novels may have been hopeful answers to Zamiatin. But *We* was an answer to something: partly to the Bolshevik visions of modernization, machine worship, and authoritarianism, and partly to the general wave of scientific technicism that Zamiatin (an engineer who had lived in England) saw as the principal menace of the twentieth century. *We* was a classic warning and a supreme work of art. At a lower level of expression were three counterutopias that offered a pastoral vision of the future. Apollon Karelin's *Russia in 1930* (1920) was an anarchist projection of a stateless world fictionalized and set a decade ahead. Aleksandr Chaianov's *Journey* (1920) was a peasant utopia of the year 1984 which combined social justice, private farm property, technology, and deurbanization. Finally, the nostalgic *Beyond the Thistle*, written by the Cossack general Peter Krasnov, in Berlin in 1921, chronicles the return of the Romanov dynasty to Russia in the mid-twentieth century to preside over a resuscitated Muscovite, Slavophile, and faintly fascist religious state.[9]

The dialogue of dreams ended in 1931—as did most other kinds of dialogue. The anticommunist utopians and dystopians had been almost voiceless anyway. But the officially tolerated and encouraged genre of communist science fiction utopia was also silenced. The last of the genre, Ian Larri's *Land of the Happy* (1931), had satirized Stalin and Kaganovich (Larri and some other science fiction writers were actually purged).[10] But the reasons went much deeper than this. Mere fellow travelers were held in suspicion under the new censorious literary culture of socialist realism. Strict controls were imposed on all writers—especially popular ones. The private press and journals that had printed much of the early science fiction were now nationalized. After Larri—and until a few years after Stalin's death—Soviet science fiction avoided the proscribed topics of far projection, utopia, and pictures of social justice and stateless equality, and dealt instead almost exclusively in near futures, new weapons, production norms, espionage, and wrecking. The Stalinist "single state" (the name of Zamiatin's antiutopia) could not tolerate blueprints of a bright future that was easily contrasted with some of the harsh realities of the 1930s, or even detailed treatments of capitalist abuse of workers. It was now forbidden to glorify equality and scorn deference, hierarchy, and authoritarian ruling styles. The whole corpus of science fiction fell into the dreary doldrums of conformity and instrumentalism for a quarter century.

Revival

After Stalin's death in 1953, some of the more notorious terror captains were shot; millions were eventually released from camps;

and, in the years 1956-1962, a very large and visible anti-Stalinist campaign was conducted. This partially cleared the literary air of the fear that had hung over it for thirty years. Also, a number of novel developments in Soviet scientific-technological achievement and awareness came to maturity in the mid-1950s: the launching of *Sputnik* in 1957, the revival of public discussion of systems thinking,[11] and the reinstatement of freer modes of scientific discourse in general. In the midst of this euphoric time, Ivan Efremov, a paleontologist, published *The Mists of Andromeda* (1957), called by Darko Suvin "the first utopia in world literature which successfully shows new characters creating and being created by a new society, that is the personal working out of a collective utopia." Efremov depicts a refined race of the distant future, a unified planet with a single language, possessing neutral names (as opposed to the "revolutionary" names often used in the 1920s such as Youth, Revo, Spark, Joy, Will), and eager to explore outer space. Its many innovative elements include a knock at Stalin through the character of Bet Lon (probably referring to the Russian word *beton*: concrete, or hard), and the prominence of women characters as equals to men. It was the first communist utopia in thirty years. Although opposed by some in the Stalinist literary establishment, it was a huge success, enjoying twenty-four editions and translation into twenty-three languages before the author's death in 1972.[12]

Andromeda opened the floodgates for a deluge of new Soviet science fiction, called by an American critic the "second great age" in the history of this genre, and by a Soviet writer "our own 'Campbellian Golden Age,'" thus comparing it to American science fiction of the 1930s and 1940s. Closet science fiction writers, popularizers and writers of other fiction, and—most important—dozens of professional scientists, researchers, and engineers "crossed over" into a now legitimized field of speculation. Efremov replaced Bogdanov as the new Gogol, laying out for an entire generation previously taboo themes and endless possibilities for refinement and development of his ideas and suggestions. Efremov himself remained the leading figure until his death. Science fiction volumes now began to appear in circulations of one hundred thousand copies and were sold out instantly—a pattern that would continue with periodic crackdowns and falloffs—until the 1980s.

The first such crackdown, came in the late 1960s—after the fall of Khrushchev and the inauguration of the stricter Brezhnev regime—in connection with the works of the Strugatskii brothers (whom I discuss in more detail later in this chapter).[13]

By the mid-1970s Efremov was gone, and the atmosphere of political control had led to a shift into more personal and apolitical themes and a vague sense of malaise among writers. The genre not only survived, however, but increased in output and variety. By the early 1980s a kind of tacit compromise had been reached between the purveyors of fantasy and the censors, represented in the works of Kirill Bulychev: science fiction would not be subjected to the rules of "social command" (purely pro-Soviet works of realism and optimism); and the writers would refrain from wandering into the territory of alternative political utopian vision. And so it largely stood until the era of glasnost.[14]

Who are the writers? Who are the readers? An estimate from the mid-1970s suggests that about six hundred writers have produced works of science fiction—fifty or so as full-time science fiction authors.[15] A dozen or more of these have achieved high visibility in the West in translation: the Strugatskii brothers, Dmitrii Bilenkin, Bulychev, Mikhail Emtsev and Eremei Parnov, Vladimir Savchenko, Anatolii Dneprov, Il'ia Varshavskii, Olga Larionova, Gennadii Gor, E. Voiskunskii and Isai Lukodianov, Vladimir Gakov, and several others. Notable is the dominance of male writers (no one of the stature of Ursula LeGuin has emerged among females) and the frequency of writing partnerships. A few of these authors were born before the Revolution of 1917 (Gor, Varshavskii, Efremov), a few more in the Civil War period and the 1920s (Dneprov and Voiskunskii, for example). All these men were deeply involved in the Second World War. The rest were mostly children of the 1930s who came to maturity and received their education after the war. A rather large percentage did not begin writing science fiction until the Efremov thaw of the late 1950s. In contrast to American and many other communities of science fiction writers, the great majority of the Soviet writers have a serious scientific background: geology, paleontology, chemistry, physics, mathematics, astronomy, ethnography, oceanography. And most of the others are also "scientists" in the European sense—that is, scholars of the humanities or social sciences, including a Japanologist (Arkady Strugatskii) and a specialist on Burmese history (Bulygin).

It is harder to speak with assurance about the readers' market for science fiction, but it is certainly possible to make some broad statements. Most fiction of this sort reaches the public through anthologies such as *Fantastika* (published on an irregular schedule since 1962), books and journals published by Detlit (children's literature), Znanie (Knowledge), and Molodaia Gvardiia (Young Guard, the Komsomol outlet). In the 1960s the circulation for the average book was about 100,000, in the 1970s 200,000 to 300,000. As of the 1970s almost two-fifths of the roughly 2,500 to 3,000 titles of Soviet science fiction published since 1917 had appeared since 1957. In addition, between 1917 and 1970 some 1,500 foreign works had been printed in various Soviet languages, most of them since 1957. Among the most popular authors are Isaac Asimov, Ray Bradbury, Kurt Vonnegut, Robert Heinlein, and the classics of Wells and Verne. Censors attached to every publishing house, at least until recently, scrutinized Soviet science fiction works to prevent the leakage of specific technical and scientific details, discoveries, and secrets. This was done because of the heavy crossover from active scientific work to fiction. Most readers, apparently, are young, male, urban skilled workers, members of the technical intelligentsia—scientists and engineers. Half are of the age group fifteen to twenty-five—pupils and students. This pattern and the estimated number of readers (2 to 3 percent of the population) is similar to that in the United States, except that there are rather more older readers in the USSR. Inquiries into the motivation for reading such works have yielded the following: curiosity about the future, interest in science and technology, and moral content. The genre is known to be a magnet for drawing the young into scientific careers.[16]

Contemporary Science Fiction

Before examining some of the major themes of Soviet science fiction, I want to examine how it compares with popular science futurology. These have a common purpose: to make science accessible, a particularly acute problem in less highly developed countries. It seems clear that science fiction does a much better job.

In two examples of scientific futurology, one from 1957 and the other from 1976, what we see is mostly descriptive technologizing. The book *Russian Science in the Twenty-first Century* contains portraits of future foods, cities, transport, amenities, resources, industrialized agriculture, electric power, and oceanic exploitation. Even in the chapters about the "good life" of the coming age—on schools, homes, town life—there is not a single speculation about the nature of man, his reshaping, his relationship to the environment, or the special nature of socialism or communism in that environment. L. E. Etingen's *Mankind in the Future: Its Appearance, Structure, and Form* gives a timetable of changes in the human organism from 1967 to 2030, by which time humanity is seen to be experiencing organ transplants on a regular basis, along with implantation of artificial organs and electronic mechanisms, personality and intelligence modifications through medicine, biomechanical stimulation of the growth of organs, a symbiosis of man and machine, direct communication between persons and between persons and computers, chemical control of aging, and the prolonging of life.[17]

In these and similar studies the technical is divorced from life— emotions, relationships, family, taste, political problems of power, individuality, cooperation, love, and all the rest. These questions are, of course, taken up separately in works on sociology and Communist party program commentary, but rarely are the two fitted together. Soviet science fiction attempts to do this in a variety of ways. All the problems just enumerated have been treated in science fiction in the last twenty-five years, but they are usually accompanied by an examination of their effects on people and their society, by ironic twists, unexpected outcomes, anxiety, failure, reversals, or details about the role of technology in everyday life. With few exceptions, the problems are treated individually, in stories. The deficiency in Soviet science fiction futurology is the working of all these themes together into a grand mosaic, a master blueprint of what science and society will look like and how they will interact in a better world.

Nevertheless, the genre is rich in insights into Soviet mentalities. One Soviet critic sees science fiction as a bridge between different cultures (she seems to be including communist and capitalist as well as national cultures), and between scientists and the masses within society.[18] Science fiction writers pose necessary questions: How are we changing? What will come of it? How does technological "improvement" impinge on society, on men and women, on the biological structure of the species? What is the role of science in a world full of mutual hostilities and marked by the ambivalence of most people toward science? Science fiction themes in the USSR—and I deal here only with the Russian-language corpus, and not with that of other nationalities—include very broad-based and variegated alternative worlds and cultures, space travel, extrapolation into the unknown, technological fantasy, and ecological awareness, and they are usually sensitive as well to problems of social welfare and security, aesthetics, and the meaning of happiness. These themes reflect a whole range of opinions about Soviet mores and values, about the capitalist West, about the past, and about the future. In comparing this body of work to the science fiction of the revolutionary period, we see that modern works are much more scientifically literate than the older ones. It is also apparent that the genre has gone beyond the bounds of socialist realism and possesses a sharp critical edge. Some of it is good literature. Knowledgeable people claim that it is also equal in merit to Western science fiction.

I have arbitrarily organized my discussion around the following themes: the "problem" of science; the use of technology; Soviet values; anticapitalism; social criticism; and antimodernism. The last flows naturally into the realm of dystopia and into the puzzling works of the Strugatskiis.

To the layman in the modern world, the problem of science is the contradictions it creates: the growing rift between "two cultures"; the explosion of unabsorbable knowledge; the creative urge to invent and develop a thing to its outer limits, including "things" that can destroy the entire planet through a trivial accident. In this matter, Soviet science fiction offers nothing particularly new, although the expression of anxiety may have a peculiarly Russian or Soviet character. The Dr. Frankenstein with a test tube, the mad scientist, the doomsday weapon, and the death ray were common elements of 1920s science fiction, and always attributed to evil capitalists. Contemporary science fiction has come a long way; it recognizes the danger to be universal and not class bound. Vladimir

Savchenko's hero in *Self-Discovery* (1967) muses over the familiar repertoire: poison gas in the First World War, the death camps of Nazi Germany and their technology of extermination, Hiroshima, and the present balance of terror. No direct allusion to a possible Soviet-made disaster is apparent; but, as in most discussions of this question, it can be inferred.[19] Dmitrii Bilenkin, in "The Ban," has the world's most respected scientific figure falsify his evidence and suppress a discovery in order to save mankind from its evil potential. Sudden global holocaust is not the only perceived danger. Bilenkin specializes in warnings. In one of his stories prospective parents are required to pass a battery of examinations in moral values to determine their fitness for reproduction. In another space explorers unwittingly blind an entire planet with their search beams. In still another a painter has found the last piece of undeveloped nature and settles down to capture it on canvas when a "servorobot" appears from nowhere to prepare his food and a storm of green rain descends to kill the mosquitoes that are annoying him.[20]

Some writers believe that the way out of this threat of mindless and untrammeled scientific growth is to create more smart people—"smart" being identified with wise and humane in almost all positive Soviet characters. Professor Tsesevich in Pavel Amnuel's "Today, Tomorrow, and Always" wishes to multiply the number of geniuses and abolish "mental inequality." Savchenko in *Self-Discovery* has the hero manufacture new people one by one by means of a computer. Echoing some motifs of the "nihilist" science-worshiper Dmitrii Pisarev, uttered a century earlier, he laments the inertia and egoism of the masses and sets out to make new people brimming with energy and brains. The production of such people would fill the gap in competence and integrity—so obviously lacking in the negative characters around him—give science a broader social base, link the elite more closely with the untutored, and finally better control the increasingly uncontrollable aspects of science and technology. Savchenko rounds out his decision by facing the moral dilemmas inherent in it: the denial to man-made people of childhood and family; the danger of the "processing" of created humans as voters, prostitutes, soldiers, or commercial commodities.[21]

The scientists in the Soviet science fiction of our time are a varied and complicated lot—not always the strong and virtuous Bolshevik heroes of the early days who did no wrong and made no mistakes. They are fallible, weak, puzzled, energetic, brave, devious, ambitious, even lazy. The heroes are better than the average, to be sure: they try. And the reality of their condition is far more convincing than the equivalent in older works of socialist realism. One gets the feeling in almost all of this fiction that the general public, while perhaps ignorant about science, holds science and its practitioners in high regard. The scenes of scientific conferences are held in resplendent palaces of learning and other dignified settings. Within the scientific community fossilized types abound, sometimes bearing indicative names of the sort used by Griboedov in the nineteenth century. A perfect example is Professor Mesozoiskii in one of Savchenko's tales, whose prehistoric views match his name. Heroes and heroines battle against "mesozoic" attitudes all the time.[22]

Internationalism and cosmopolitanism in science, in the most literal sense, is a major background motif in the years since Stalin's death—and quite unthinkable, of course, during his regime. Soviet scientists in fiction, whether in future or present scenarios, are constantly flying off to foreign capitals for conferences and consultations. Limitless travel, a world community of science, permanent mutual communications—sometimes instantaneous—learned friendships and collaboration, central information depositories, a sense of international equality and a single spirit of open inquiry are almost mandatory in the longer novels that deal with global crises. Internationalism in science fiction contains an element of pathos, given the actual restrictions on scientific cooperation in some quarters, but it clearly reflects the broad opinion of Soviet scientists themselves and forms a permanent buffer to the occasional anticapitalist stories and themes. Historical references in the works celebrate intellectual community in the same way: the names of Norbert Wiener, Einstein, Bohr, and many others are constantly invoked and properly credited with the scrupulousness of a scholar with a footnote. Nothing could be further from Zhdanov's intellectual pogrom of the late 1940s, when Russians were flaunting their "own" science and crediting themselves with every sort of discovery and invention.[23]

The treatment of new technologies is not really separable from scientific progress as such, but it operates fictionally on a more concrete level and therefore deserves an analysis of its own. Soviet science fiction is modernist and Promethean as a rule. Some authors are still playing the Stalinist-period game of merely projecting replicas of what the government is doing now—as in a short piece by Mikhail Greshnev, "Sagan-Dalin" (1984), which features the dream of two scientists of a future city, another BAM (Baikal-Amur Mainline), another giant power station, another vision of a streamlined, populated, industrial Siberia, a dream originally sketched in a striking prose poem, "Express" (1916), by the proletarian poet and apostle of Taylorism Alexei Gastev.[24]

Then there is the usual assortment of plausible toys for the future: airbus, videophone, robot, time machine—all of them familiar to readers of nineteenth-century fantasy, even in Russia. Far more interesting, though of course also not novel, is the notion of computerizing all of life and work. Savchenko gives us a computer factory the size of a television set which receives orders for computer systems, calculates the requirements, plots the correct circuitry, and prints out a thin plate in twenty seconds to be mailed to a client (factory, hospital, traffic control headquarters) and plugged in. In another story he suggests the application of cybernetics to personal affairs and daily life, to manage independently all kinetic and organizational tasks and allow the unburdened human brain to deal with creativity, love, friendship, pleasure, and other presumably nonorganizable matters.[25]

Dmitrii Bilenkin and Vladlen Bakhnov take up where Savchenko leaves off: scientizing emotions, dreams, and psyche. In "What Never Was," Bilenkin's main character falls into a voluptuous reverie on love, nature, and serenity so real that he thinks he is living it. But the dream has been manufactured and fed to him by a "biowave" method used to prevent depressives from committing suicide. In "Personality Probe" Bilenkin uses collective cognition to allow students in an experiment to think together without voicing their thoughts aloud, with periodic and automatic feedback through phonoclips of solutions arrived at. The wittiest of these devices are in Bakhnov's "Cheap Sale": a "mood battery" to regulate the emotions and store up joy for later use in moments of adversity; reified emotions that can be "put on" and taken off; a love potion to inspire creativity (not procreation); and "fond memories" for the enjoyment of selective nostalgia.[26]

The most imaginative invention I have seen in this literature is Savchenko's "computer womb" for the generation of new and brainy scientists. In *Self-Discovery*, which draws on the myth of the homunculus and cybernetic research, the hero, Valentin Krivoshein, builds three new people by combining his own organism and thoughts with a computer. Biology, systemology, bionics, electronics, and chemistry are enlisted in an elaborate system for feeding impulses into the machine, which then follows the metabolic control patterns of Krivoshein through his brain waves and creates not a clone but a replica with desired variants of size, personality, looks, and brainpower. A remarkable episode in this story, written twenty years before Chernobyl, is the vivid description of an atomic reactor explosion, the burning of graphite rods, the deliberate self-radiation of Krivoshein, and his self-cure through immediate protection of bone marrow and marathon showers.[27]

The darker side of technology does not escape the scrutiny of modern science fiction writers. Bilenkin offers novelty with a twist: the "time bank," in which one can save up useless time (time spent standing in line, for example) and later retrieve it for serious purposes. It is the Taylorist equivalent of the "mood battery." Taylorism in everyday life and the battle against wasted time (and motion) had a lively history in the 1920s when the NOT (Nauchnaia Organizatsiia Truda, or Scientific Organization of Labor) movement tried to mechanize and robotize the rustic Soviet labor recruit, and when the League of Time tried to schedule the lives of all people by the clock and by a rigid division of the day into useful time morsels. In Bilenkin's story it all falls apart, just as it did in real life fifty years ago. Soviet censorship and control are mildly ridiculed (or so it seems) by Il'ia Varshavskii's "phenotype" and Bakhnov's "Ahmeter." The first is a sensor beam which locates students on any part of a huge campus to summon them in for a talk. The second is a machine that measures the exclamations of art appreciators in order to determine the authenticity and artistic worth of a painting—an unequivocal sermon against gauging the value of art, as in the traditional Soviet way, by the number of people who can understand it.[28]

One more illustration is perhaps worth a note: Viktor Pronin's story "The Power of the Word," which deals with ESP and telekinetic energy, the former having a long history in Russian science fiction although banned under Stalin as a subject of speculation. This tale shows how a "simple" cleaning woman can move objects with the power of her mind. The implication is made clear: in addition to the social application of this power that can lighten the burdens of everyday life, its military application would make it so dangerous that it would soon render nuclear weapons obsolete.[29]

In the realm of Soviet values and their relationship to realities, ethnicity and gender are dealt with in Soviet science fiction in the same way they are dealt with in general fiction (as far as I can judge from wide but spotty reading in the latter). Ethnicity is treated according to the official position, whereas gender is treated in accord with reality. The topic of ethnicity in literature is always a delicate matter, particularly in cultures where a myth of complete equality and harmony is officially held. In stories with a Soviet setting, the main characters are almost invariably Russian. But characters with Georgian, Armenian, Ukrainian, Tatar, or Central Asian names are common and are often situated in high places in the academic, scientific, or administrative community. Aside from passing references to swarthy skin, black eyes, or "unpronounceable" names, no issue is made of their national origins. They form in a sense the minority backdrop for the action. Crews of spaceships in futurist stories are multinational. Only a few identifiably Jewish characters appear: one, Erik Erdman of Odessa, is a prominent coprotagonist of *World Soul* (one of whose coauthors is Jewish). I have found no anti-Semitism, no tension over ethnic interaction, no false exaltation of Jews. One may read this collective text (together with all other official statements on Soviet nationality policy) either as a hypocritical device masking the actual ethnic problems of the USSR or as a commendable way to foster tolerance of non-Russians who conform to the general values of Soviet society.[30]

The general treatment of gender—specifically of women—in a genre that is male dominated is closer to the realities of Soviet society. That reality includes a relatively high level of opportunity in science, technology, and professional life (compared to other societies and to Russia's past), overbalanced by vertical and horizontal segregation in the workplace, lower wages and prestige, relative powerlessness in all walks of life, and the burden of the "double

shift"—full-time work as well as the responsibility for home management, domestic work, and child care. Some writers, such as
Efremov and Sergei Snegov, have tried to upgrade women into
major figures in their fiction. Others, especially the Strugatskiis,
have opened themselves to charges of overt sexual chauvinism,
particularly in *The Snail on the Slope*, in which females play negative
roles and the female gender even symbolizes a kind of evil force.
In the mainstream of Soviet works the treatment of women characters is more realistic. They are always a minority on expeditions
or scientific teams, are intelligent and well educated but distinctly
overshadowed by the men, are often subordinate to theoretical
equals, are nurturing and inspiring rather than dynamic and active. Whether scientifically competent or not, the women seem to
be more materialistic, more down to earth, more skeptical of free
flights of imagination—more "womanly" in the stereotypes that
have dominated Soviet imagery since the 1930s. Soviet science fiction is clearly a genre written by men and for men. It differs from
its Western counterpart in the absence of overtly sexual scenes and
the coarser kind of male attitudes toward women.[31]

Although, in a general sense, women seem less enamored of
technology in the stories I have read, there is nothing like a "feminist" science fiction or specifically feminist utopia. American feminist utopias of the 1970s tackled the matter of technology head on,
displaying hostility to violence and ecological destruction and repudiating the vision of technology as synonymous with human
progress. In these works women are aligned with nature, and the
male use of technology to make war against nature is equated with
male dominance over females. The fact that this perspective has not
emerged among Soviet science fiction writers, male or female, says
something about the level of a feminist consciousness in the Soviet
Union.[32]

Attitudes toward the state and authority do not emerge very
sharply, except in the bolder dystopic works, which I discuss later
in this chapter. Most science fiction is very vague on the ideal state,
or nonstate, of the future. Like the novels of the 1920s, recent ones
allude to shadowy councils and galactic committees of wise people, usually men, with an occasional essay into machine-run politics and fuzzy references to consensus or computer calculation. It

is on this issue apparently that the limits of political alternatives bump up against censorship and self-censorship. Fundamental questions of individual freedom and social or intellectual rebellion are hardly addressed. The most interesting characters are usually those who fight against bureaucratic forces, mindless conformity, and careerism—but they do so in the name of values that are fully accepted in official Soviet life, and in this respect are almost identical with themes in general literature since the 1950s. The texture of everyday life is decidedly urban. There are few peasants or collective farms. Soviet town life is familiarly depicted—restaurants, tram rides to the institute and university, lecture halls, laboratories, academic councils and dissertation defenses, *komandirovkas* (official trips), "ordinary" sexism, but not yet much on street violence, alcoholism, drugs and *fartsovchiks* (dealers), blue jeans, and rock bands.[33]

Anti-Western polemics in the 1920s helped to focus anxieties about the world without producing ambivalence in the reader. The format was strictly we-they/good-evil. This element is rare in modern Soviet science fiction, as compared to the earlier period, and especially the Stalinist years, when it was reduced to the crudest forms, very much resembling the treatment of Germans and Japanese in American popular culture in the prewar and wartime years. Matters are more complicated nowadays. One finds various kinds of jibes against the West in recent stories. For example, when unexpected disaster ensues after two Soviet scientists develop a "world soul," the American press accuses the Soviet government of spreading an epidemic. In the same story the Soviet hero is disgusted with a social system (capitalism) in an unspecified South American country because it produces prostitution. Spartak Akhmetov in "Shock" (1984) is still deploying the old clichés of soulless decadence in a modern Western city—a bleak cityscape, faceless people, leaden skies, derelicts lying on the streets ignored by the heartless crowd, suicides, and a culture of neurotic haste—fairly reminiscent of one of the earliest Russian fictional assaults on European industrial society, "A Journey to Mars" (1901). In Liudmila Sveshnikova's "How to Outwit Pain" (1984) a lonely American widow who has lost her husband and son in some distant imperialist war retreats into reveries and loses touch with the world. Aleksandr Potupa's

"Effect of a Lucky Man" (1984) tries to show the extreme mutual distrust that pervades mendacious Western society. These are all rather formulaic and pallid critiques, without depth; most of them could be interpreted as Aesopian critiques of the Soviet scene, which possesses its own quotient of mistrust, indifference to suffering, prostitution, and a distant war in which the Joe Sr. and the Joe Jr. of Sveshnikova's story could easily be replaced by the fathers and sons who died in Afghanistan.[34]

Somewhat sharper in their bite are the scenarios in *World Soul* whose main premise is the obliteration of private thought and secrecy. Aside from the many other complications this creates, it forces capitalist businessmen in the West to disclose their profits and shady practices and to tell the truth about their products—thus eliminating advertisement and forcing firms into bankruptcy. Amnuel's recent "Innocent" traces the career of a Harvard-educated scientist who is so intent on pursuing his experiments to the very end—even though he knows that they will endanger the species, the environment, and the entire planet—in the interest of "truth" and to satisfy his intellectual ego that he brings the world to the brink of disaster and is arrested and charged with irresponsible crimes toward humanity. And a 1985 fantasy describes in great detail how American corporations and government agencies develop new modes of electronic surveillance, including bee-shaped sensors that fly among the citizens, pick up their conversations, and try to apprehend the mood of the people.[35]

When we attempt to isolate and categorize varieties of social criticism in modern Soviet science fiction, we face two problems. The first is epistemological and has to do with determining the line between anticapitalist and antisocialist critiques, the latter easily produced through Aesopian modes of expression. Further, one must search for the equally elusive boundary between legitimate social criticism and political dissidence. The moral dilemma for the Western student is the danger of attributing dissidence to works in which it was never intended.

Most of the critical material in these stories refers to Stalinism—either its fearful past or its lingering presence in Soviet life. Straightforward references to the purges can sometimes be found in the biographies and memories of heroes, as with Savchenko's character who muses over his father, a Red Cossack in the Civil War, who was arrested in 1937. No more than those last three words is offered; and for all Soviet readers, no more is needed. With Il'ia Varshavskii and others, we are left to wonder whether or not the dreadful gulag-like camps, the slave labor, and the brutal guards (such as the "stupids" in Bulychev's "Half a Life") are only Kaf-kaesque fantasy and spaceship conventions or allusions to the real thing, which flourished in Stalin's Russia longer than it did in Hit-ler's Germany.[36]

Contemporary careerism and opportunism, especially in high places, offers the most fertile field for alerting readers about the remnants of the mentality of Stalin's ruling class. The extraordinari-ly entertaining story "Success Algorithm" by Savchenko creates a computerized program for success in life by feeding in the clichés of amoral upward mobility: "You scratch my back and I'll scratch yours"; "An eye for an eye, a tooth for a tooth"; "Don't rock the boat"; "Dog eat dog"; and "Every man for himself." The completed program even teaches the user the facial language of hierarchy and deference.[37] An unforgettably obnoxious figure in *Self-Discovery* is a perfect illustration: Harry Haritonovich is a fluffy, vain, false, well-turned-out toady, bootlicker, backbiter, and conformist who man-ages to push through a wholly worthless dissertation because the board is too lethargic and routinized to stop a man with connec-tions. An angry outburst from one of the positive characters sums up the author's view: "And *don't* we [in the Soviet Union] have peo-ple who are ready to use everything from the ideas of communism to false radio reports, from their work situation to quotes from the classics [of Marxism] in order to become wealthy and have a good position and then to get more and more for themselves, at no mat-ter what cost?"[38]

But beyond the banalities of ordinary careerism lies what we might call "reptilian careerism," familiar to all who have studied the history of Soviet science and the arts. It has to do with advanc-ing or holding one's privileged position through character assas-sination of prominent but vulnerable people. A masterful rendition of this is Bilenkin's "Personality Probe," in which a famous nine-teenth-century writer, editor, and publicist (who also wrote science fiction, by the way), Faddei Bulgarin, is brought back to life by a classroom of computer students. Bulgarin, the king of the "reptile" press in the reign of Tsar Nicholas I (1825-1855), made a specialty of slandering his rivals and spreading poisonous gossip about them in high places. His most famous victim was the poet Aleksandr Pushkin. The twentieth-century students reconstruct Bulgarin in a "phantomatic" holograph resembling ectoplasm or a three-dimensional apparition and then subject him to a withering interrogation about the immortality of his career—a perfect vehicle for exposing to the knowledgeable reader the shameful, not-so-distant history of many Soviet intellectuals.[39]

Another target is the "masses," sometimes disguised in other national identities, sometimes not. Many stories contain contemptuous allusions to consumerism, materialism, philistinism, mindlessness, conformism, and the herdlike shape of the unspecified mass—an inert mediocrity. This has been a favorite target of abuse in the West from Nietzsche and Ortega through H. L. Mencken to Ayn Rand, often a rather easy target for cheap shots. Soviet writers must be circumspect; they can hardly be permitted to attack "the working class" as such, for it is still the mythical hegemon of Soviet culture. But they do it nonetheless, lamenting the palpable power of mob inertia against the creative or innovative spirit of scientists and the gap between elitist science and mass ignorance. In the many instances of bribery through gadgets, the facile purveying of alcohol to oil the way, and corruption at various levels, one can even see glimmers of the massive "second economy" that is visible almost everywhere in Soviet urban life (and even in some rural areas) but could not until recently be openly discussed as a pervasive phenomenon.[40]

Conservatism and resistance to healthy change appear everywhere. Often they are embodied in the stuffy blimps who inhabit research centers, institutes, and academies—such as Professor Voltamperov in *Self-Discovery*. A different twist is provided in Amnuel's "Higher than the Clouds, Higher than the Mountains, Higher than the Sky" (1984). The protagonist, Log (from the Greek *logos*, for "word" or "reason"), lives in a village somewhere in time and space but wishes to travel widely and discover other worlds (perhaps also a mild reference to the travel restrictions to the West placed on Soviet citizens). The village elder tells him: "A sensible man will not travel from one settlement to another when life is difficult and the same everywhere. Doesn't the law teach us this?" But Log persists in wanting to know what is out there, higher than clouds, mountains, and sky. Imprisoned by the community, he escapes to pursue the "beautiful sickness of mind" — the urge to know and to master.[41]

Social control and overpowering mediocrity flow into the prominent theme of antimodernism, familiar to readers of Soviet literature in the last two decades as expressed in village prose, or the exaltation of traditional Russian rural, national, and even religious values. Science fiction writers are more oblique than the *derevenshchiki* and focus on the harmfulness of useless machinery and excessive technology. In Iurii Medvedev's "Love for Paganini," a zealous scientist on Mars decides to transform nature beyond recognition in his society. Mars is already a highly technical utopia, and the inhabitants resent his compulsion to change the climate on Neptune, move mountains and seas, and invent an antimelancholy device, an atomizer of moonlight, and an audible replicator of ocean waves. In the end, the Martians send him to earth and allow themselves to keep in touch with the beauties of the past—revering Paganini as well as Euripides.[42]

Aleksandr Petrin, in "Vasil Fomich and the EVM," unveils a mild but firm variety of Luddism in the modern workplace. The EVM, or Electronic Calculator, is introduced into an office and greeted with skepticism by the bookkeeper Vasil Fomich (a very archaic name). He believes that personal labor and human psychology (and, presumably, the abacus) are better able than an insentient machine to do his job and meet the plan. He wins this duel: the employees produce their quota, the plan is met, the bonuses are meted out, the machine is expelled, and Vasil Fomich is the hero. It is tempting to read in this the coming wave of resistance by the Soviet office force (overwhelmingly female at the lower ranks) to personal computers and other forms of machinery. But Luddism, fictional or real, has never long delayed the march of technology in modem societies. Liudmila Ovsiannikova's "Machine of Happiness" is another expression of the malaise over the rapid development of a machine culture. She may be voicing the Soviet woman's perspective (not, however, a Western feminist one) when she identifies machines of happiness with appliances to ease the weight of everyday life and questions the utility of machines that carry cosmonauts to the moon. Is this the voice also of grass-roots men and women who long for consumer goods and who wonder at the awesome expenditures for space programs?[43]

Unlike utopia, dystopia has not been subjected to endless searches for typology. I do not wish to violate this tradition, but I do suggest here at least a basic dividing line between the dystopias of entropy and those of energy. The former is the more familiar and finds its classic expression in the One State of *We*, a frozen world of symmetrical regularities, uniform appearance and motion, cyclic existence, and mathematized ritual. Ideally, nothing happens in the United States; it is locked in entropy. The second type releases an evil force, a wave of destructive energy. Around the time of the Revolution of 1905, Valerii Briusov—a well-known poet of the day— had written several stories of both genres. In "Earth" the planetary city-state lies underground and the hero fights to let in the air—and then dies. In "Republic of the Southern Cross," an Antarctic megalopolis of high technology and surface welfarism explodes with a strange disease that reverses the behavior of all the inhabitants and wreaks disaster on society.[44]

In modern Soviet science fiction we have Varshavskii's miniature tale "The Violet." In it the earth has become a ball of continental cities from pole to equator, two miles deep into the earth and thirty miles above; no nature, no soil, no verdure exists. A small child, taken to the bowels of the earth in order to visit a "field" in the museum of antiquities, weeps for the death of a flower. In *World Soul* a polymer growth from a fragment of seaweed blossoms turns into a biotosis, or "world soul," a universal telepathic computer that links all minds together, generates empathy, and opens communications. Its coinventor argues that the biotosis simplifies and automates the world, makes government truly democratic, abolishes deception, and eliminates violence (since each person suffers when any individual does). "Life is simpler and happier," he says; "the scope of [people's] feeling has grown from the single 'I' to the 4 billion 'we.'" Critics in the novel point out that the biotosis causes transformations, accidents, tragedies, pseudo resurrections, insane visions, and death; and that even if its chaotic energy is corrected, it will mark the end of human will and the ascendance of a "supercybernetic" collectivist machine that will destroy individuality.[45]

The path of the Strugatskii brothers—the Soviet science fiction writers best known to Western readers—has been called by one critic "paradise lost," or a journey from utopia to dystopia, by another as an agonizing struggle between their utopian visions and the dystopian forces around them. Whatever the case, it is apparent that their vision has developed, opened out, and become desimplified. An example from each of the two basic periods of their production can serve as illustrations. Their first major science fiction work, following directly in the tradition of *Andromeda*, was *Homecoming* (1962), a utopia of the twenty-second century, inhabited by physically and spiritually superior people and run by a world council. Russia has become the first communist society and the nucleus of planetary perfection. There is a moving flashback to the siege of Leningrad (1941-1944) and then a pause at a statue of Lenin: "Lenin stretched out his hand over this city, over this world. Because this is his world; he envisioned it this way—radiant and lovely—two hundred years ago." The Strugatskiis have retrieved all the romanticism of the 1920s, all the Promethean force of the *chelovek vsemogushchii* (omnipotent man), the serenity and humaneness of the revolutionary vision.[46]

Ten years later, in *The Ugly Swans* (1972), we have a dictatorship deploying its security forces, the Legion of Freedom, or "woodpeckers," against the "slimies"—outcasts and rebels whose status is openly compared to that of Negroes and Jews—who crave books and ideas, maintain a high moral standard, and vacillate between utopian and dystopian visions (a fairly close description of the Soviet underground intellectual community, including but not coterminous with the dissidents). Between these two novels the Strugatskiis obviously underwent an intellectual and emotional change, in addition to a broadening of their perspectives through exposure to the writings of Kafka and the Polish science fiction writer Stanislaw Lem. Their stories became more problematical, more complex, more cryptic—perhaps a way of warding off the measures taken against their work by censors in the late 1960s and 1970s, but more important, a sign that Soviet Science fiction has passed far beyond the rosy simplicities of the revolutionary age. The work of the Strugatskiis is a major fictional corpus; it deserves (and has received) lengthy analysis in its own right. It is still impossible to gauge how representative it is of Soviet science fiction as a whole or how reflective of the values of science fiction audiences.[47]

In Retrospect

It would not be a gross oversimplification to say that Soviet science fiction has seen three main ages: the Age of Bogdanov (1908-1931); the Age of Stalin, who created much fantasy but wrote no science fiction (1931-1956); and the Age of Efremov (1957 to about 1970). The first age was dominated by sweeping optimistic utopianism in the midst of a deplorably backward society; the second by tight control of fantasy and imagination and a sharp narrowing of thematics; the last by a renewed flash of utopian hope fueled by a de-Stalinizing thaw and by a maturing culture of scientific and technical achievement. What has occurred in about the last two decades is not so easy to characterize because our perspective is too short. This recent period resembles very much the world around us—full of patternless confusion, fluidity, blends of bright hope and dark fear, new dialogues of dream and nightmare.

Thus the history of science fiction in the Soviet Union seems to show a natural fit between certain periods of the genre as a whole and the historical backdrop against which it appears. Some might see this simply as a result of "command literature," a reflection of new styles and programs of Party leaders. But it is surely more than that. Although it is impossible to track the history of social values directly by reading science fiction, it does give a feel for some of the most significant attitudes that writers—and thus many of their readers—hold about the outer world, technology, progress, scientific morality, professionalism, and a dozen other elements of the collective, educated Soviet mentality.

What is the promise of the new period that is opening up before our eyes, this age of glasnost and perestroika? It is, of course, very difficult to speculate about an era that is in such rapid flux. But some straws are in the wind. First, there are some indications that readership of science fiction may be growing. No data are available, but cultural critics have been bewailing the decline in "serious" reading among the citizenry and a rise in "low" reading tastes — that is, for the detective story and science fiction. This is a perennial complaint, to be sure, but one that gathers force almost daily.[48] With the extraordinary lessening of censorship, science fiction may join the enormous trend in popular culture toward exploring hitherto unmentionable dimensions of life — including sex, social abuses on the grandest scale, and democratic criticism of the regime itself. And it may lead to the more experimental modes of literary expression that are emerging rapidly in the arts, especially in film. Thus far, however, I have seen no clear-cut examples of open eroticism or of avant-garde aesthetic forms in the genre of science fiction. Yet neither is there any sign of the racism that has crept into the writings of some belletristic writers — particularly Viktor Astaf'ev.

Similarly, it is hard to discern any major shift in the political thrust of Soviet science fiction, but there are signs that some of the most influential writers are squarely in the camp of Gorbachev-style reform. In March 1987 the Council on Adventure, Entertainment, and Science Fiction of the powerful Union of Writers convened for the purpose of discussing the role of this genre of writing in combating reactionary propaganda — one of the code words for antiperestroika thinking. Among its members were Eremei Parnov, A. Kazantsev, the Strugatskiis, Dmitrii Bilenkin, G. Gurevich, Olga Larionova, E. Voiskunskii, and V. Revich — in other words, the crowned heads of Soviet science fiction of the last two decades.[49]

Old books have a way of inspiring new ones, especially old forbidden books of explosive content that have been long suppressed. Masses of Soviet citizens have at long last had the opportunity of reading Evgenii Zamiatin's classic dystopian science fiction thriller *We*, written in 1920 but not published in the Soviet Union until 1989. In his introduction to the first Soviet edition, the critic V. Lakshin pulls no punches, relating the novel not only to its revolutionary context — particularly War Communism and the visions of Gastev, Bogdanov, and Taylorism — but also to the barbarities and hypocrisies of high Stalinism. The literary echoes to this book — and there are many — may have the effect of drawing science fiction into further political speculation and fantasy. In any case, it is hard to imagine Soviet science fiction remaining untouched by this cultural bombshell from out of the past (particularly with the publication in Russian of Aldous Huxley's *Brave New World* and George Orwell's *1984*).[50]

Taking Huxley for inspiration in his article of July 1988, "O, Brave New World," Eremei Parnov, a dean of science fiction letters, cast a passionate glance at the Stalinist past, which he described as a lapse into medievalism, the recurrence of darkness that seems to happen every century. Parnov's target is not only the cruel repressions and stupendous errors of Stalin but the legacy of twisted truth, the cult of Big Brother (his words), and the lies that are the main foe of human reason, sanity, and global survival. Prejudice, racism, and noxious mythologies were the fruits of that ugly time; and at the intellectual core of the Stalinist deformation, says Parnov, was the death of science—all science—and the bigoted exclusion of new fields such as cybernetics. Parnov's cry of collective conscience is striking not only because of his acknowledged stature in the community of science fiction, but also because it appeared prominently in the mass publication *Soviet Culture*.[51]

Equally moving was the last essay of Dmitrii Bilenkin, who died soon after its publication. It was his farewell address to the readers of the *Science Fantasy Annual*. Bilenkin wished to broaden the range of science fiction, to widen its content, and, by implication, raise it to the same level as "literature"; to spread its appeal, as happens in advanced industrial societies that are leaders in science and technology, by the spontaneous formation of nationwide science fiction fan clubs. In the coded idiom of perestroika, Bilenkin told his readers that in a rapidly changing world, the people must prepare themselves spiritually and intellectually for adaptation to the unheard-of novelty of the coming age. The failure to make such a mental adjustment, he warned, leads to psychological disorientation, a flight from reality, spiritual paralysis, and a "hatred of progress."[52]

Thus some major figures in this exciting genre are plainly on the side of reform, of change, of a betterment of Soviet society, and closer links with those nations in which science is free and dynamic. None of this tells us, however, what the coming fate of Soviet science fiction will be. Its traditional role, in times of relative freedom, has been to popularize technology and science, to indulge in healthy fantasy, to promote civic virtues, to tell a good story, and—at times—to offer oblique social and even political criticism. Works performing the last-named function may now be drowned in the flood of what Andrei Bitov has called "half-food" or docunovels[53]— that is, books by village prose writers who want to protect ancient Russian rural values as well as natural resources and historical-political exposés such as *Children of Arbat* by Anatolii Rybakov. To put it more bluntly, social criticism is now so prominent in the daily press that fiction writers may lose interest.

But the current growth of belletristic fantasy in Russia can also compete with science fiction since major Soviet writers, like those of the "magic realism" school in Latin America, are treating large philosophical themes in a setting of lyrical fantasy. In other words, lines are blurring between mainstream and genre science fiction writing. The likely outcome is that new writers of science fiction will turn more to highly scientific and technical subjects and exploit the leading edge of world scientific experiment, research, and speculation.[54] Whatever happens, it is certain that Soviet readers—and perhaps outsiders too—can look forward to many surprises, twists, and rich insights into how the scientific community and science itself are going to function in the heady years ahead. It is highly doubtful that even a reactionary antiperestroika turn could stop the flood that is now released.

Original publication: In Loren Graham, ed. *Science and the Soviet Social Order*. Cambridge, Mass.: Harvard University Press, 1990, pp. 299-324.

Notes

1   For background, see Richard Stites, "Hopes and Fears of Things to Come: The Foreshadowing of Totalitarianism in Russian Fantasy and Utopia," *Nordic Journal of Soviet and East European Studies* 3, no. 1 (1986), 1-20 (and above, 135-51 - *ed.*); Richard Stites, "Utopias in the Air and on the Ground: Futuristic Dreaming in the Russian Revolution," *Russian History* 11, nos. 2-3 (Summer-Fall 1984), 236-257; and Alexander Bogdanov, *Red Star: The First Bolshevik Utopia*, ed. Loren Graham and Richard Stites (Bloomington: Indiana University Press, 1984).

Concerning the material in this chapter, I wish to thank Tanya

Stites for research assistance, Jarri Koponen of Helsinki for use of his science fiction collection, and Mark Adams and Alexander Batchan for commentary.

2   This experimental atmosphere is the subject of my book *Revolutionary Dreams: Utopian Vision and Experimental Life in the Russian Revolution* (New York: Oxford University Press, 1989).

3   For the relationship among these visions, see Richard Stites, "Utopias of Time, Space, and Life in the Russian Revolution," *Revue des études slaves* 56, no. 1 (1984), 141-154.

4   For an introduction to the genre, see A. F. Britikov, *Russkii-sovetskii nauchno-fantasticheskii roman* (Moscow: Nauka, 1979); Darko Suvin, "The Utopian Tradition of Russian Science Fiction," *Modern Language Review* 66 (1979), 139-159; and Leonid Geller, *Vselennaia za predelom dogmy* (London: Overseas Publications, 1985). My thanks to Mark Adams for this book.

5   Ya. Okunev, *Griadushchii mir: Utopicheskii roman* (Petrograd: Priboi, 1923), p.44.

6   See, for example, V. Itin, *Strana gonguri* (Kansk: Gos. izd., 1922); and V. D. Nikolsky, *Cherez tysiachu let: Nauchno-fantasticheskii roman* (Leningrad: Soikin, 1927).

7   See A. R. Palei, *Golfstrem* (Moscow: Ogonek, 1928); and A. R. Belyaev, *Bor'ba v efire* (Moscow: Molodaia gvardiia, 1928).

8   Evgenii Zamiatin, *My: Roman, povesti, rasskazy* (Moscow: Sovremennik, 1989).

9   Zamiatin, *My* (1920; reprinted, New York: Interlanguage Literary Associates, 1967); A. Karelin, *Rossiia v 1930 godu* (Moscow: Vserossisakaia Federatsiia Anarkhistov, 1920); and P. N. Krasnov, *Za chertopolokhom: Fantasticheskii roman* (Berlin: Diakov, 1922).

10   Ian Larri, *Strana schastlivykh* (Leningrad: Leningradskoe oblastnoe izd., 1931).

11   See Ilmari Susiluoto, *The Origins and Development of Systems Thinking in the Soviet Union* (Helsinki: Suomalainen Tiedeakatemia, 1982).

12   Darko Suvin, *Metamorphoses of Science Fiction* (New Haven: Yale University Press, 1979), p. 269; Ivan Efremov, *Tumannost' Andromedy*, trans. G. Hanna as *Andromeda: A Space-Age Tale* (Moscow: Progress. 1980). Also see G. V. Grebens, *Ivan Efremov's Theory of Soviet Science Fiction* (New York: Vantage. 1978); and Ben Hellman, "Paradise Lost The Literary Development of Arkadii and Boris Strugatskii," *Russian History* 11. nos. 2-3 (Summer-Fall 1984), 313.

13   Suvin, "Utopian Tradition," p. 153; Vladimir Gakov, ed., *World Spring*, trans. R. de Garis (New York: Collier, 1981), p. ix; and Patrick McGuire, *Red Stars: Political Aspects of Science Fiction* (Ann Arbor: UMI Research Press, 1977), pp. xiv, 18-23.

14 McGuire, *Red Stars*, p. 23.

15 Ibid., pp. 93-94.

16 Ibid., pp. 85-92. 95-99; Peter Nicholls et al.. eds., *Encyclopedia of Science Fiction* (London: Granada, 1979), p. 212; Ariadne Gromova, "At the Frontiers of the Present Age," in C. G. Bearne, ed., *Vortex: New Soviet Science Fiction* (London: Pan, 1970), pp. 9-26. *Fantastika* is an annual of about 350 pages, printing twenty to twenty-five stories and articles.

17 S. Gorschev [Gorshchev] and M. Vassilev [Vasilev], eds., *Russian Science in the Twenty-first Century* (New York: McGraw, 1959); and L. E. Etingen, *Chelovek budushchego: Oblik, struktura, forma* (Moscow: Sovetskaia Rossiia, 1976).

18 Gromova, "At the Frontiers."

19 Vladimir Savchenko, *Otkrytie sebia: Roman* (Moscow: Molodaia gvardiia, 1967), trans. A. Bouis as *Self-Discovery* (New York: Collier, 1979). It is worth noting that the Soviet film *Letter from a Dead Man* has as its premise a Soviet-caused accidental nuclear holocaust.

20 "The Ban," in Dmitrii Bilenkin, *The Uncertainty Principle*, trans. A. Bouis (New York: Collier, 1978), pp. 46-54; "Final Exam," ibid., pp. 23-28; "Strangers' Eyes," ibid., pp. 63-73; and "The Painter," ibid., pp. 132-137.

21 Pavel Amnuel, "Segodnia, zavtra, i vsegda," in his *Segodnia, zavtra, i vsegda: Sbornik nauchno-fantasticheskikh rasskazov* (Moscow: Znanie, 1984), pp. 4-63 (esp. p. 23); and Savchenko, *Self-Discovery*, pp. 36, 119-120.

22 Vladimir Savchenko, "Success Algorithm," in H. S. Jacobson, trans., *New Soviet Science Fiction* (hereafter cited as *NSSF*) (New York: Collier; 1979), pp. 140-191. Also see Anatolii Dneprov, "Formula for Immortality," ibid., pp. 113-140, a blast against "apolitical" scientists whose research is used for destructive purposes.

23 For one example of internationalism in science, see M. Emstev and E. Parnov, "The Pale Neptune Equation," in *NSSF*, pp. 192-231.

24 Mikhail Greshnev, "Sagan-Dalin," in Spartak Akhmetov, ed., *Fantastika 84: Sbornik nauchno-fantasticheskikh povestei, rasskazov, i ocherkov* (Moscow: Molodaia gvardiia, 1984), pp. 6-18. For Gastev's utopia, see Charles Rougle, "'Express': The Future According to Gastev," *Russian History* 11, nos. 2-3 (Summer-Fall 1984), 258-268.

25 For a sampling of science fiction gadgetry, see M. Emstev and E. Parnov, *World Soul*, trans. A. Bouis (New York: Collier, 1978); and the discussion of robots by E. Voiskunskii, in "'Stremitsia k chelovechnosti,'" his introduction to *NF: Sbornik nauchnoi fantastiki*, 23 (Moscow: Znanie, 1980), pp. 3-6. For those examples cited, see Savchenko, *Self-Discovery*, p. 211; and "Success Algorithm." Those who know Soviet

urban life from the inside (or who have read the works of Iuri Tri-
fonov) will appreciate the pathos of such inventions.

26 "What Never Was," in Bilenkin, *Uncertainty Principle*, pp. 55-62; Bilenkin, "Personality Probe," in *NSSF*, pp. 54-74; and Vladlen Bakhnov,
"Cheap Sale," ibid., pp. 97-104.

27 Savchenko, *Self-Discovery*, pp. 168-169, 178-183, passim.

28 "Time Bank," in Bilenkin, *Uncertainty Principle*, pp. 159-163. For the
historical antecedents in Soviet Taylorism, see "Man the Machine," in
Stites, *Revolutionary Dreams*; Il'ia Varshavsky, "The Duel," in *NSSF*, pp.
9-14; and Vladlen Bakhnov, "Beware of the Ahs!" ibid., pp. 105-114.

29 Viktor Pronin, "Sila slova," in Ivan Chemykh, ed., *Fantastika 85* (Moscow: Molodaia gvardiia, 1985), pp. 57-67.

30 Emstev and Parnov, *World Soul*, passim.

31 For a sober analysis of women's status in the Soviet Union, see Gail
Lapidus, *Women in Soviet Society* (Berkeley: University of California
Press, 1978); and Barbara Holland, ed., *Soviet Sisterhood* (Blooming-
ton: Indiana University Press, 1985). For women in science fiction, see
McGuire, *Red Stars*, pp. 46-47; and the manuscript by Diana Greene,
"Male and Female in *The Snail on the Slope* by the Strugatskys," cited
with the author's permission. Some examples are Amnuel, "Segod-
nia" (Irina), and "Zveno i tsepy" (Alena), in *Segodnya*, pp. 125-155; and
Svetlana Yagunova, "Bereginia" (Lyudmila), in Akhmetov, *Fantastika
84*, 124-149.

32 Patrocinio Schweichart, "What If...Science and Technology in Feminist Utopias," in Joan Rothschild, ed., *Machina ex dea: Feminist Perspectives on Technology* (New York: Pergamon, 1983), pp. 198-224.

33 See McGuire's discussion of the state in *Red Stars*, pp. 36-49. The issue of
free speech is taken up in Iuri Moiseev, "Pravo na giperbolu," in Akhmetov, *Fantastika 84*, pp. 63-68; that of interference in the domestic affairs
of another society by Stanislav Gagarin, "Agasfer iz Sozvezdiia Lebedia,"
ibid., pp. 91-105, as well as in many of the Strugatskiis' novels.

34 Emstev and Parnov, *World Soul*, p. 96; Spartak Akhmetov, "Shok," in
Akhmetov, *Fantastika 84*, pp. 105-118; Liudmila Sveshnikov,. "Kak per-
ekhitrit' bol'," ibid., pp. 182-190; and Aleksandr Potupa, "Effekt Laki-
mena." ibid., pp. 190-197. The Mars tale is L. B. Afanas'ev, "Puteshestvie na Mars," *Niva* (January and March 1901).

35 Emstev and Parnov, *World Soul*, p. 76; Pavel Amnuel, "Nevinoven," in
Segodnya, pp. 155-162. Iurii Moiseev, "Angel-eko," in Chernykh, *Fantastika 85*, pp. 81-90.

36 Bulychev's *glupye* are translated "gloopies" in "Half a Life"; *Half a Life
and Other Stories*, trans. H. S. Jacobson (New York: Macmillan, 1977),
pp. 1-49. Il'ia Varshavsky, "Escape," in *NSSF*, pp. 28-41.

37 Savchenko, "Success Algorithm."

38 Savchenko, *Self-Discovery*, p. 121.

39 Bilenkin, "Personality Probe."

40 For one example, see Emstev and Parnov, *World Soul*, passim.

41 Pavel Amnuel, "Vyshe tuch, vyshe gor, vyshe neba," in *Segodnya*, pp. 162-191; see esp. pp. 169, 190.

42 For perspectives on village prose, see G. Hosking, *Beyond Socialist Realism* (London: Granada, 1980); and Katerina Clark's contribution to this volume (Chapter 9, "The Changing Image of Science and Technology in Soviet Literature," *Science and the Soviet Social Order*, 259-98 - ed.). Iurii Medvedev, "Liubov' k Paganini," in Akhmetov, *Fantastika 84*, pp. 18-32.

43 Aleksandr Petrin, "Vasil Fomich i EVM," in Akhmetov, *Fantastika 84*, pp. 174-176; Liudmila Ovsiannikova, "Mashina schastya, " ibid., pp. 62-63; and a brief discussion of the issue in Dmitrii Bilenkin, "Proverka fantastikoi," in *NF sbornik nauchnoi fantastiki*, 22 (Moscow: Znanie, 1980), pp. 3-6.

44 Valerii Briusov, *Zemnaia os'*, 2nd ed. (Moscow: Skorpion, 1910), contains these and other stories. They have been widely translated. For a good translation of one story set in the context of other Russian science fiction works, see Leland Fetzer, ed., *Pre-Revolutionary Russian Science Fiction: An Anthology* (Ann Arbor: Ardis, 1982), pp. 229-243.

45 Il'ia Varshavsky, "The Violet," in *NSSF*, pp. 1-8; and Emstev and Parnov, *World Soul*, p. 124 and passim.

46 Hellman, "Paradise Lost," pp. 314-315; and Darko Suvin, "Criticism of the Strugatskii Brothers' Work," *Canadian-American Slavic Studies* I, no. 2 (Summer 1972), 286-307.

47 A. and B. Strugatskii, *Gadkie lebedi: Povest'* (Frankfurt: Posey, 1972). For varying perspectives on the Strugatskiis, see the works of Britikov and Geller, already cited, and T. Chernysheva, "Utopiia i ee evoliutsiia v XX v.: Na primere tvorchesta A. i B. Strugatskikh," *Canadian-American Slavic Studies* 18, nos. 1-2 (Spring-Summer 1984), 76-84.

48 Anthony Alcott, "Glasnost and Soviet Culture," in M. Friedberg et al., eds., *Soviet Society under Gorbachev* (Armonk, N. Y.: M. E. Sharpe, 1987), pp. 101- 130.

49 *NF sbornik nauchnoi fantastiki*, 32 (Moscow: Znanie, 1988), p. 204.

50 V. Lakshin, "Antiutopiia Evgeniia Zamiatina," *Znamia* 4 (April 1988), 126-130.

51 Eremei Parnov, "O divnyi novyi mif," *Sovetskaia kul'tura*, 26 July 1988, 6.

52 D. Bilenkin, "Realizm fantastiki," in *NF*, 32 (1988), 184-203.

53 *Washington Post*, 8 September 1988, C8.

54 Unless the impact of *We* is too irresistible.

Cinema

16

Soviet Movies for the Masses
and for Historians

The purpose of this paper is to call attention to the pedagogical utility of the mass film or popular movie for historians and other scholars of Russian-Soviet culture and society.[1] The topic of films in the classroom is hardly new; panels have been talking for years about enriching courses through cinema and the other arts. But the practice has not yet reached many classrooms in Russian and Soviet history—to say nothing of literature or government. I believe this is because the traditional method of using films has not proved very productive. In my observation during 30 years of teaching and talking to colleagues, that method has been either to show the great classics of the silent screen from the 1920s and early 1930s—Eisenstein, Pudovkin, Vertov, and the others—and particularly "revolutionary spectacles" (to use a term of Peter Kenez) such as Sergei Eisenstein's *The Battleship Potemkin* (*Bronenosets Potemkin*, 1926); or to show films which seem to have direct political messages—such as the same director's *Alexander Nevsky* (1938) or, more recently, the revisionist film of Tengiz Abuladze, *Repentance* (*Pokayanie*, 1986). I hasten to add that great works of film art clearly have a place not only in the study of cinema culture but also in the history of cultural politics and aesthetic discourse. We will all continue to use them for appropriate purposes, and the value of "films of persuasion" or propaganda is self-evident.

I would argue, however, that such films are only marginally useful in understanding Russian Soviet history and society. As recent Western scholarship has shown—and as the Soviet critics and the public have always known—the classics of Soviet cinema for the most part were not immensely "popular" either as huge box-office successes or in expressing widely held values of the time.[2] This scholarship also shows that what people liked in Russia is what they like almost everywhere and what they liked in 1900 is what they still like in the 1990s: action, adventure, romance, melodrama, comedy—with of course plenty of local variation in time and place. Ideology and politics have had a much lower appeal and artistic experiment even less—again with obvious exceptions. Extrapolating national or cultural values from popular movies is of course a problematic business filled with conceptual traps; it is not a simple operation and we are far from a consensus about which values are actually reflected in or help shape popular culture. But the enterprise itself is full of intellectual tingle that can reanimate some of those who are tired of the old conventions in using "film as history." Another reason for studying Soviet popular movies is that these are the ones that millions of Soviet citizens know and remember, have felt deeply about, and are more than willing to discuss. This rarely applies to the films of Eisenstein, Tarkovsky, Sokurov and Abuladze, which are (justifiably) treasured by the literati and intelligentsia—a tiny segment of the Soviet population.

My view is that popular movies and popular culture in general can tell us more about a society in a given historical epoch than works of high art. I hold no brief for abandoning high culture as a subject of study. On the contrary, it is essential to know it for its own sake as a precious treasury of a nation's creativity, as a counter-force and sometimes foe of the popular arts, and as their symbiotic partner. My purpose here is to illustrate how popular movies can be made to speak to the student of history in the languages of their stories, acting styles, mise-en-scène, and music in the cultural context of the era in which they were made and viewed.

Soviet popular movies are virtually unknown throughout the profession of Russian Soviet studies. Part of the problem, of course, has been their relative unavailability compared to that of the classics for use in Western classrooms. But with the double revolution of glasnost in Soviet cultural politics and the invention of the videotape and player, this has changed dramatically. We are now ready—or are on the verge of being ready—to introduce into our teaching the kinds of movies that have been genuinely popular for decades among Soviet people. In order to promote this, I wish to present a few brief remarks about the kinds of films that can be shown and what kinds of materials they contain that can be tied to historical themes—using the term "historical" in a wide sense. I will organize my remarks around four clusters of films and focus on a representative, only one of which (the second) is well-known outside the USSR: *Be Still, My Grief* (*Molchi, grust', molchi*, 1918), *The Radiant Road* (*Svetlyi put'*, 1940), *Ivan Brovkin in the Virgin Lands* (*Ivan Brovkin na tselinu*, 1959), and *Déjà vu* (1989). The selection is limited and arbitrary but it does range through the century and deals with several popular genres: salon melodrama, Stalinist fairy tale, the construction epic, and the gangster comedy. Each in its own way illustrates the possibilities of reading a film for the purposes of historical understanding.

The decade of pre-Revolutionary Russian cinema (1908-1919)[3] was one of civil violence and peasant disorder and of increasing urban crime and social misery but also one of material progress—city tramcars, lavish restaurants, an influx of foreign culture, and an outpouring of popular culture that captivated mass audiences and challenged the traditional rule of fine arts and high culture. Gypsy songs, nightclubs, the cabaret, music hall reviews, and a flood of detective and adventure stories and boulevard novels of sex and ambition dominated Russian urban entertainment by 1910. The cinema, born amid the swirl of the new popular culture, was a Moloch who consumed it all: folkloric themes and narrative styles, popular music, estrada, and fiction. The omnivorous pioneers of movie making would devour anything that would pull a film through a camera and tell a story. When ordinary materials ran out, they hired hacks to create scripts right on the set—exactly as was done on the meadows of Astoria and the backlots of Hollywood. The greed of the studio for profit was no greater than the greed of the public for more movies.[4]

The dominant genre—half of all films made—was the salon or "bourgeois" melodrama. Neya Zorkaya has analyzed a few hundred of these using a method resembling the classic work of the folkorist V. Ya. Propp whose "morphology of the folktale" proclaimed the structural unity of all folktale plots. Silent film melodramas bear the marks of standardized production—formulaic repetition, cardboard characters, psychological shallowness, and the absence of political content. Almost all are variants on a masterplot about a "slave of passion" (the title of one of them): the idyllic life of a young girl, marred only by vague malaise, is disrupted by the appearance of a seducer; her passion for him gives way to disenchantment and, at the end, tragedy (suicide, ruin, murder, vengeance). Several themes are linked constantly: money, power, leisure, boredom, the need for distraction, gambling and game playing among affluent men, the main game being seduction of a young and innocent woman. The conquered prey becomes a possession, a toy to be fondled for a while and then discarded. The victims are framed in a virtuous idyll—humble or opulent: in *Be Still, My Grief* the doting wife of an aging alcoholic circus acrobat; in *The Children of the Age* (*Deti veka*, 1915) the young mother, happily married to a poor bank clerk; in *A Life for a Life* (*Zhizn' za zhizn*, 1916) two happy foster sisters. The victimizers dwell in obvious settings of social decadence: expensive parties, smoking, drinking, gypsy entertainers.

These films are filled with social and sexual tension. The contrast between innocence, which is poor or weak, and evil, which is rich and powerful, is rendered by making urbane, cruel, and impeccably dressed matinee idols break the hearts and shatter the lives of beautiful women on screen. The female superstar, Vera Kholodnaya, was their regular victim. The former dancer with the sad grey eyes animated the celluloid world she dwelled in, a world of tainted money, opulent restaurants, champagne picnics, luxury autos careening through the night, and illicit love ending in tragedy. Of the five Kholodnaya pictures I have seen,[5] *Be Still, My Grief* was the last of the salon psychological melodramas, a ten-year anniversary film celebrating the birth of Russian cinema and—as critics noted—a reunion of all its clichés.[6] Chardynin played Lorio the pitiful circus clown, whose physical injury is compounded by the loss of his wife. Circus—a popular theme in movies up into the 1930s—is here a symbol of the poverty and vulnerability of entertainment figures to the allure of money and to the ruthlessness of the upper classes. Kholodnaya plays Pola, the young wife who is seduced by the charms of luxurious parties and attentive men and then destroyed. The process of decay is accompanied by the then popular title song played on violin and guitar by the begging couple (unheard by modern ears, but generally performed live in the old movie houses).

Bolshevik officials and film-makers detested films like this as frothy and unserious, attuned to the decadent leisure postures of the upper class, catering to the base instincts of man, paying excessive attention to sex, violence, and crime, lacking in moral uplift and correct political content, generally uneducational, and rooted in the search for profits. Like most elites, the Bolsheviks feared that "dark forces" dormant among the lower classes could be evoked by sitting in the dark chamber of the commercial cinema. The Bolshevik critics also hated its "theateritis": the cinematography (called "Khanzhonkovism" by later filmmakers) of long takes, intermediate shots, and a stationary camera using an imagined theater audience as its point-of-view, and the acting style called "Delsartism," a repertory of exaggerated poses and gestures coded to emotions, developed on the stage by the nineteenth-century Frenchman François Delsarte, and taken into popular melodrama and then films. It was against this art that the great film masters of the Revolution rebelled. But it was precisely this sort of entertainment film that the masses rushed to see before the Revolution (and after it: in late 1921 when the first private movie house under NEP opened its doors on Tverskaya Street, it showed *Be Still, My Grief* from morning to night to full houses).

It is more than probable that widely shown films like *Be Still, My Grief* generated angry feelings toward the upper classes. Hatred and collective indignation can be engendered by the popular media—war films alone are proof of this. If hostility already festers, it can be reinforced by a cultural product that tells viewers that the makers of the movie and the public share their feelings about social morality and its outward affects—raiment, scenery, and manners. It is no wonder that slicked hair and bowler hats, prime emblems of the slimy cinematic seducers, were angrily rejected, satirized, and even assaulted under the new Soviet regime. The privileging of classical motifs in architecture and furnishing in the mise-en-scène of the Chardynin and Bauer films—classical busts, statuettes, columns, cornices, Grecian urns—were meant to signify perfection, beauty, and aesthetic honesty and provide ironic contrast to the degraded values of their owners. But to the masses, they must have been simply the emblems of the excessive and needless luxury of the owning classes. This may have deepened the "vandalistic" behavior of the riotous urban lower classes in 1917-1918.[7] Thus the "bourgeois" films of the pre-Revolutionary era—while catering to mass tastes—in a sense helped feed radicalism, and the Bolsheviks thus owed the great movie tycoons a debt of gratitude for their unintentional assistance. In any event, films like *Be Still, My Grief* can enliven and even illuminate a whole range of topics such as new versus old art, Bolshevik censorship policies, and the relationship between film and audience.

The Radiant Road (1940; released in a cut version in the U.S. as *Tanya*), the product of a wholly different cultural matrix, is the pinnacle of social and political fantasy in prewar Stalinist cinema.[8] It was the last in a series of stunningly successful and long-remembered prewar musical comedies starring Lyubov Orlova, directed by her husband Grigori Alexandrov, and with music by the master mass-song composer of the era, Isaak Dunayevsky: *The Happy Guys* (*Veselye rebyata*, 1934), *The Circus* (*Tsirk*, 1936) and *Volga, Volga* (1938). They offered a winning recipe of patriotism, cornball sentiment, spectacular cinematic effects, singable tunes, and celebration of the new Moscow. In the background and forming an intriguing political-cultural context stood the easing up of the social mood in 1933-1934, the sharpening of tension in 1935-1936, the outward sloganizing of a "happy life," the murderous purges of 1936-1938, the majestic ascendance of the Stakhanovite mythology of production, the cultural representation of economic achievements and urban construction, and—twisting around all these—the spasmodic reordering of jazz and light music and the national campaigns to legitimize and foster a mass movement of amateur and folk culture.

In *The Radiant Road*, the heroine Tanya (Orlova), a classical Cinderella with a smudged nose, rises through the textile industry to become a Stakhanovite superworker who can run hundreds of looms simultaneously and beat world records. Along the way, Tanya learns her letters and wins the love of a clean-cut engineer—a Soviet Prince Charming with a pipe and a briefcase. She makes the dreamed-of pilgrimage to Moscow, and is decorated by the "peasant" President Kalinin in the opulent Kremlin Palace. The finale contains a splendid visual treatment of the just completed Agricultural Exhibit in Moscow, whose Central Pavilion resembled a palace. In one of the final shots the living couple is foregrounded in front of Vera Mukhina's statue of the male industrial worker, hammer in hand, and the female agricultural worker, sickle in hand—thus proclaiming gender equality and simultaneously assuring the male engineer the dominant role in this "equal" partnership.[9]

The movie asserts constantly that this is real life and not a fairy tale. In the finale, a chorus sings the aviation song "Ever Higher" (a colossal hit of the 1930s, although written in 1920), which opens with the words: "We are born to make fairy tales come true." Indeed the film is roughly modeled on the rise of the then famous female Stakhanovites, Yevdokiya and Mariya Vinogradova[10] (Orlova studied intensively on the mill floor to prepare herself for the exploits she performed on screen). Orlova plays the victorious plebeian, as she had in *The Happy Guys* and in *Volga, Volga*. Social mobility through the Soviet system, a breakthrough to "consciousness" with the help of a mentor (in this case, a female schoolteacher), and triumph over a languid bureaucrat—all the ingredients of socialist realism are present. But Alexandrov and his associates rise above the usual drabness of the master plot by use of the fantastic mise-en-scène at the conclusion where the monumental structure is framed by dream-filled billows in the sky. The uncut original (which I have not seen) has an automobile flying over the rooftops of Moscow![11] The fusion of the traditional fairy tale with metallic and mechanical furniture of modernity and with the official scenario for success accounts for the immense popular triumph of this movie—designed for and consumed by "the millions."

The Alexandrov-Orlova-Dunayevsky films can be analyzed as stories of social mobility, as political mystification, as gender construction, or as musical entertainment—they were all of these. But one of the "stars" of these movies was Moscow, specifically the new Moscow construction that was represented as heroic and populist in the media. It is often argued that Stanlinist architecture's celebration of state grandeur was only meant to underline the insignificance of the citizen on the street. But when a provincial woman in Moscow first gazed upon the newly finished Hotel Moskva—filmed from every angle in *The Circus*—she exclaimed: "I do not know if this is a hotel or a fairy tale palace." Similarly the harbor building (or River Station) on the Moscow River, built to punctuate the completion of the Volga-Moscow canal, was meant to extend a dignified but warm welcome from the capital to newly arriving passengers from the hinterland. One of the final scenes of *Volga, Volga* shows the beautiful steamer "Joseph Stalin" docked alongside this gleaming white columned edifice whose staircase leads up to the capital where the heroes find success and instant popularity for their amateur music. In August 1939 the massive Agricultural Exhibition opened in Moscow and was visited by as a many as 20-30,000 people a day. It was a fairyland—in many ways resembling its contemporary, the New York World's Fair, in opulence and monumentality—domes, gothic buildings, fountains, broad walkways, a giant statue of Stalin, and the huge Mukhina ensemble.[12] These and other examples of Soviet construction and decor were deployed in the films of the 1930s not to depress and not only to impress, but to enliven and animate the viewer with self-esteem and communal pride.

Ivan Brovkin in the Virgin Lands is a rustic musical that, aside from being a marvelous hour-and-a-half entertainment, summarizes and resolves several themes in the history of Soviet popular movies and marks a turning point in cultural history. It draws on two lines of scenic backdrop and social mood: the epic and the idyll. The epic of construction, a major theme in all genres of popular culture since 1917—but especially since 1928—romanticized physical labor, manual toil, and the realia of machinery against a backdrop of wilderness. During the Civil War, building something fast—such as a railroad—took on epic proportions, a fact celebrated with gorgeous cinematography in Alov and Naumov's *Pavel Korchagin* (1955), the best screen version of Ostrovsky's notorious novel *How the Steel Was Tempered*. In the first full sound film, Nikolai Ekk showed another example of railroad as salvation in *The Start in Life* (*Putevka v zhizn'*, also known as *The Path to Life*, 1931), about orphan boys in the 1920s. In the 1930s Gerasimov's *Komsomolsk* (1938), offered a camera study of deforestation and town-building in the Soviet Far East. In these pictures, the act of cutting down and building up is endowed with a special pathos and poetics that proved irresistible over the decades and whose cinematographic style was incorporated into the wartime epic.

The idyll came later. In the 1920s, village life was often ridiculed in the popular arts. Folk dances, songs, and costumes were depicted as the archaic trappings of roach- and god-infested worlds of darkness—the great exception to this of course is the work of Dovzhenko. But after collectivization, the new kolkhoz was romanticized as a confluence of the new and the best of the old—bicycles and hospitality, tractors and headscarves, brigades and peasant fertility. This thematic blossomed in folk dance ensembles, paintings, operettas, novels, and films in the 1930s and 1940s, and reached its apogee in Ivan Pyriev's famous *Kuban Cossacks* (*Kubanskie kazaki*, 1949), a cinematic kolkhoz operetta and a classic of the glossy, "conflictless" films of the late Stalin era. When tension between new and old was treated, the new was always vindicated—as in the most famous example, *The Cavalier of the Golden Star* (*Kavaler Zolotoi zvezdy*), a novel, an operetta, and Yuli Raizman's 1950 film starring Sergei Bondarchuk in one of his most wooden performances.

Ivan Brovkin, was made in the midst of Khrushchev's Virgin Lands campaign—a drive to cultivate large tracts of land in North Kazakhstan in the steppes between the Urals, the Caspian, and Siberia. Although made only a few years after *Cavalier*, it gave the conflict a new resolution by treating the old village and the new sovkhoz equally. The former is symbolized by rural folk ways, stubborn elders, and a bride who refuses to join her man on the cultivation sites beyond Orenburg. But this standard symbolic characterization—almost identical to that in *Cavalier*—is deployed with great tact and delicacy. The old village is captured in beautifully framed color shots resembling the picture postcards of rustic life that were mass-produced before the Revolution, and it is drenched in the sounds of lovely music of the popular songwriter, Anatoli Lepin. Out on the steppe, modernity springs forth from a semi-desert under the hands and brains of the hero, his wise and kindly mentor, and a crew of young, idealistic, ethnically varied Komsomols who tear open the earth and careen upon it in their iron victory chariots in a civic version of savage joy. The domestic scenes of gathering, homebuilding, and planning are done in the painterly fashion of Stalinist socialist realism.

The marriage of epic and idyll is celebrated at many levels: the wedding scene which choreographs the disorderly and energetic folk dancing along a ruler-straight street laid out on the steppe; the accordions and birch twigs on the nuptial automobile; the return of the hero to claim his bride and their journey back to the steppe on a train. The director authenticates his movie with a direct quotation from the famous potato tactics scene in *Chapayev* (1934), here having Brovkin showing his sovkhoz chairman how tractors can be deployed more effectively. Brovkin (played by Leonid Kharitonov) is a younger, more vigorous, more credible version of Bondarchuk's cavalier of the gold star, and his triumph more humane. *Ivan Brovkin* is a proclamation of moral equality and coexistence between kolkhoz life, with all the cultural baggage it retained after collectivization, and new sovkhoz life with its clean bathrooms and electric lights. The film illuminates that moment in Soviet history between the relentless Stalinist exaltation of new over old which prevailed from 1928 until the mid-fifties and the exaltation of traditional village values which has been underway for 30 years and more in the works of village prose writers, filmmakers, and intellectuals of many kinds.

The reader will note that I have ignored the obvious historical aspects of this film. One is its glossy treatment of the genuine hardships and shortcomings of the Virgin Lands campaign that were generally known then and have since been well-documented; even the sugary memoirs of one of its chief organizers, Leonid Brezhnev, reveal more reality than does this film.[13] The lack of amenities, the ferocious blizzards that enveloped the steppe and snuffed out the lives of the unsuspecting; the surliness of the locals; the inability of Soviet ploughshares to carve open the root-entangled sward of the ancient grassland—all this is missing in the film. The other is its obvious design as a mobilizing agent to recruit needed youth—particularly women and especially physicians (combined in one character in the movie as in real Soviet life)—out to the Virgin Lands. In this, *Brovkin* resembles the great construction epics of the 1930s, both documentary and fiction films. What could be more obvious than either of these points? Frontiering and construction invite romanticism in cinematic treatment: it makes for fun, "profit," and good ideology. The American boomtown, railroad, and oilfield epics of the 1930s are hardly different in this regard.

At the present juncture in film history, we are faced with flux and the unpredictable. One of the main themes of agonizing debate among Soviet filmmakers is commercialism or "Hollywoodism" and its natural offspring: romance, adventure, sex, violence, crime, and all the rest. In the midst of this debate, and a clear product of the free atmosphere of glasnost, has appeared the gangster-comedy film, *Déjà vu* (*Dezha vyu*, 1989). A direct instance of *amerikanizm* in movies, *Déjà vu* is a hilarious Odessa Studio production set in 1925 and advertised as having "American style action." The plot of this manic parody of the gangster film—which recalls the cinematic gifts of Billy Wilder—revolves around a Chicago prohibition war and a Polish-American hitman sent to Odessa to wipe out an informer. The foolery explodes in the shameless quotations from old James Cagney films (very popular in Russia in the 1940s), from *The Godfather*, and from *Potemkin* (the shooting of Eisenstein's staircase scene is woven into the chase); and the reactions of foreigners to Soviet life in the twenties—elements of which still linger to this day, particularly in tourist hotels. The large audience at the Coliseum in Leningrad (where I viewed it in early 1990) never stopped laughing and almost convulsed at the shot of a mafioso with a Civil War machine-gun pointed through a loft window—a quotation straight from *Chapayev*. The lurid depiction of the Odessa criminal underworld of bootlegging, American jazz, and sex during NEP is an affectionate reminder of another age, a sharp commentary on the kingdoms of illegality that now flourish in the USSR, and a side-splitting mockery of everything Soviet and communist in the early days of the Revolution.

Survey research reveals that three quarters of the movie-going public are young people who want action, compelling (*ostrosyuzhet-nye*) themes, and exciting plots. Detective movies, writes the well-known film historian, Romil Sobolev, are "the locomotive of the box office," and since, he claims, most Soviet crime movies are trashy, the industry should import more well-made foreign ones such as the James Bond cycle which at least possess irony and wit.[14] Police, detective, and crime films have always had a following but their social significance has been low. Recent crime plots have at least incorporated current black market themes, some violence and sex, and rock music. But Soviet directors have not been successful either in conveying the real horror of organized crime (as done for example in Robert Evans' *Cotton Club* or Sergio Leone's *Once Upon a Time in America*) or in parodying it (as in Billy Wilder's masterpiece *Some*

Like it Hot). Two "straight" crime pictures I saw last winter failed utterly to do either. *The Perfect Crime* (*Ideal'noe prestuplenie*, 1989) is a model of how not to make a picture. Its wholly stylized setting is a cross between Estonia and Mars; the rest is cheap sex, amateur violence,[15] and poor acting. *Crime Quartet* (*Kriminal'nyi kvartet*, 1989), based on the case of MIF (myth) or Mikhail Iosifovich Feldman's crime ring in Omsk, is about four cops on the trail of racketeers who kidnap the son of one of them. The elements in it of suspense, camaraderie, and violence seem artificial and alien either to Soviet or Western cinematic traditions.

Déjà vu, however, seems to herald a new era—or a return to the old era of Ilf and Petrov. If Soviet filmmakers and audiences are capable of laughing at gangsters, they are also capable of taking them seriously—which none has yet done. The makers of *Déjà vu* are, in a sense, outsiders: the director Juliusz Michulski, is a Pole; the film was made in Odessa—that once fertile and febrile pool of Jewish comedic, musical, and cinematic talent (comedians Mikhail Zhvanetsky and Vladimir Khenkin, bandleader Leonid Utesov, songwriter Oskar Feltsman, director Mark Donskoy, among others). But "outsiders" have always gotten inside the cultural center and reshaped it and themselves. The end of poor imitations of Hollywood popular products is in sight. Any nation that can produce and successfully market a film like *Déjà vu* (which the critics, of course, hate) can do the same for every genre. The "Russianization" of rock music over the past decade is an obvious precedent for this. What is happening to popular movies at present is that all talents are being let loose and all themes launched uncensored. Cross-fertilization, the market place, and art will do the rest. If this happens, we may be able to enjoy Soviet movies as well as sitting through them in order to tease out their social or historical significance. Students of Soviet every-day life will certainly learn more about it from films openly catering to the public taste than they will from the anti-Stalinist revisionist documentaries—some of them truly masterful as art—that are coming to our shores in an endless stream.

These few remarks are meant to suggest to colleagues that even artless films can quicken the art of historians and enlarge their vision. Although I have formed my remarks around four titles, I do not believe that textual analysis of individual films is the most fruitful device for the historian. What does the historian want? To understand society, people, institutions, mentalities, and identities in any given epoch—and then to explain how they change in a subsequent epoch. It is therefore wiser to take a body of films on any given theme over a long period or a more varied body within a manageable period. In doing so, one has to come armed not only with a knowledge of history and cinema but of popular culture as well—songs, stories, myths, legends, cults; performing arts such as circus, cabaret, and variety stage (estrada); customs, gestures, and jokes. These are the treasury of symbols and codes, the keys to the value systems of those who create and consume them. It is not too extravagant to say that all of Soviet history could and should be rewritten and retaught on the basis of cinema and the other arts in order to uncover national moods and feelings. Those literary and high culture scholars who have looked upon Soviet culture as a vast wasteland might even discover in it something of value, and Kremlinologists might even find in the history of Soviet people something other than robotic subjects of a despotic state.

Original publication: *Historical Journal of Film, Radio, and Television* 11.3 (Oct. 1991).

Notes

1   I wish to thank the All-Union Scientific Research Institute for the History of Cinema (VNIIK) and Gosfilmofond in Moscow and IREX for arranging film viewings for me in the winter of 1989-90.

2   Richard Taylor, *The Politics of the Soviet Cinema, 1917-1929* (Cambridge, England, 1979); Denise J. Youngblood, *Movies for the Masses: Popular Cinema and Soviet Society in the 1920s* (Cambridge, England, 1992); idem, *Soviet Cinema in the Silent Era, 1918-1935* (Ann Arbor MI, 1985; reprint Austin TX, 1991); Peter Kenez, *Cinema and Soviet Society from the Revolution to the Death of Stalin* (London, New York, I.B. Tauris, 2001). These books are excellent guides to popular films up to 1953, as is Anna Lawton, "Towards a new openness in Soviet Cinema," in: D. J. Goulding (Ed.), *Post New Wave Cinema in the Soviet Union and Eastern Europe* (Bloomington, IN, 1989), pp. 1-50, for the Brezhnev and Gorbachev eras (expanded and published as, *Kinoglasnost': Soviet*

Cinema in Our Time (Cambridge: Cambridge University Press, 1992 - ed.); there is no comparable work as yet in English on the Khrushchev period (such a book appeared more recently, Josephine Woll, *Real Images: Soviet Cinema and the 'Thaw'* (London: I, B. Tauris, 2000 - ed.). For parallel discussion of other popular arts, see: S. F. Starr, *Red and Hot: the Fate of Jazz in the Soviet Union* (New York, 1983); Jeffrey Brooks, *When Russia Learned to Read* (Princeton, NJ, 1985); Richard Stites, "Soviet Popular Culture in the Gorbachev Era," Harriman Institute Forum (March, 1989); and the works on Socialist Realist fiction by Vera Dunham, Katerina Clark, and Regine Robin.

3   Including films made by private studios in 1917-1919, which continued the traditions of the previous era.

4   S. Ginzburg, *Kinematografiya dorevolyutsionnoi Rossii* (*The Cinema of Pre-Revolutionary Russia*) (Moscow, 1963), massive and detailed; R. Sobolev, *Lyudi i fil'my russkogo dorevolyutsionnogo kino* (*The People and Films of Pre-Revolutionary Russian Cinema*) (Moscow, 1961), short and gossipy; N. Zorkaya, *Na rubezhe stoletii: U istokov massovogo iskusstva v Rossii 1900-1910 godov* [Between Two Centuries: The Sources of Mass Art in Russia 1900-1910] (Moscow, 1976), a masterly analysis of the function of movies in popular culture; J. Leyda, *Kino. A History of the Russian and Soviet Film* (London, 1960), a Western perspective by a keen critic of art film.

5   The others are: *The Children of the Age* (*Deti veka*, 1915), *Mirages* (*Mirazhi*, 1916), *A Life for a Life* (*Zhizn' za zhizn*, 1916), and *The Last Tango* (*Poslednee tango*, 1918).

6   Yu. Tsivian et al. (Eds) *Silent Witnesses: Russian Films 1908-1919* (London & Pordenone, Italy, 1989), pp. 478-84.

7   See Richard Stites, "Iconoclastic Currents in the Russian Revolution," in: Abbott Gleason et al. (Eds) *Bolshevik Culture* (Bloomington, IN, 1985).

8   For the background, see: Richard Taylor (1986) "Boris Shumyatsky and the Soviet Cinema in the 1930s: ideology as mass entertainment," *Historical Journal of Film, Radio and Television*, 6(1), pp. 48-64.

9   In Soviet iconology, the woman had come to be identified with the countryside and thus with a relatively nurturing role in society (in spite of her prominence in the urban work force); the man with the city, the factory, the machine—and thus power. See: Gail Lapidus, *Women and Soviet Society* (Berkeley, CA, 1978), and Richard Stites, *The Women's Liberation Movement in Russia* (Princeton, NJ, 1978).

10   Lewis Siegelbaum, *Stakhanovism and the Politics of Productivity in the USSR, 1935-1941* (Cambridge, England, 1988), pp. 76, 80, 273; and see passim for the realities behind the Stakhanovite mythology.

11 See the detailed analysis by Maria Enzensberger of this film also known as *The Radiant Path*, in: Richard Taylor and D.W. Spring (Eds) *Stalinism and Soviet Cinema* (New York, Routledge, 1993).

12 M. Bliznakov, *Architecture as Decorative Art* (unpublished manuscript); V. Paperny, *Kul'tura "dva"* [The "Second" Culture] (Ann Arbor MI, 1985). A Western visitor to Moscow in 1936, Kurt London, after lamenting the vulgar array of porticoes, parapets, cornices and friezes of the Hotel Moskva (then used for delegations of workers and peasants), cites this explanation of its decor from a Soviet citizen: "These people, who very often only live in poor huts, are to see that the greatest luxury is thought fit for their reception. They are to return home with the feeling that they are citizens of a great and wealthy country. That increases their self-respect and strengthens their allegiance to a regime which affords them such princely hospitality." *Seven Soviet Arts* (London, 1937), pp. 259-61.

13 L. I. Brezhnev, *Trilogy: Little Land, Rebirth, the Virgin Lands* (Moscow, 1980), pp. 231-398.

14 R. Sobolev, "Grustnye priklyucheniya prikyuchencheskogo fil'ma" ("The Sad Adventures of an Adventure Film"), *Literaturnaya gazeta* (Literary Gazette), 11 March 1987, p. 8. Sharply conflicting opinions on "popularity" and "commercialism" in cinema were voiced openly at the November 1989 Soviet-American Film Conference in Moscow.

15 It is a curious fact that Russian-Soviet cultural products rarely replicate the realities of torture, murder, sadism and violence, and not because these things do not exist there. A recent crime film showed a gangster pressing a red-hot flatiron into the belly of his victim, and a cartoon in *Krokodil* (*Crocodile*) has the female viewer apply this scene to current shortages as she says to her husband: "Let's join the racketeers; they have irons!"

17

Dusky Images of Imperial Russia
Prerevolutionary Cinema

Prerevolutionary movies are *terra incognita* throughout the profession of Russian-Soviet studies in this country because they have been almost completely unavailable for use in Western classrooms or even for viewing by scholars and teachers. To my knowledge, until this year only one fiction film of that era, roughly 1908 to the end of commercial production in 1919, was available for purchase or rent: Iakov Protazano's masterful *Father Sergius* (*Otets Sergii*), made in 1917 in private studios and released in 1918. One may add to this a few tantalizing seconds of footage from the documentary, *Birth of Soviet Cinema.* But thanks in part to the collapse of the Soviet system of highly guarded film monopoly and of official values that despised the films made in tsarist times, and in part to the spread of video culture, this situation has changed dramatically. We are now able to introduce into our teaching (and research) the kinds of movies that masses of people watched in the last decade or so of the Russian Empire. Credit for this goes to Iurii Tsivian and other Russian film scholars and archivists who in 1989 brought the first major showing of prerevolutionary cinema to a marathon festival in Pordenone, Italy. With their Italian and British colleagues they produced a magnificent annotated catalogue, *Silent Witnesses*, as a guide to the surviving films of the epoch.[1] Since Pordenone, the exhibit has traveled around Europe and the United States.[2]

To judge how representative the collection under review is, we must recall that in the tsarist period approximately sixteen hundred films were known to have been made in private studios, Russian- and foreign-owned. Most have been lost. Of the surviving few hundred, seventy or eighty have been included in the traveling exhibit.

Of these, twenty-eight are contained in this collection: one newsreel, one documentary, and twenty-six fiction films of folklore, comedy, historical drama, literary adaptation, and melodrama. Prospective viewers will want to explore the historical-cinematographic contexts of the era, which are easily gotten in a number of studies.[3] For readers who may contemplate acquiring the collection, I will say something about each of these films, though more about some than others, reflecting the interests of a social and cultural historian more than those of a cineaste. At the end I will offer some general remarks about the collection as a whole. However, specialists concerned primarily with aesthetic values will be pleased at the selection made by Ian Christie of the British Film Institute, an eminent scholar and critic. A historian might make other choices, but the selection is a fine one, offering great variety and high quality, both in a visual and a literary sense. It is certainly representative of the genres shown in the larger traveling exhibit.

The categories used by the organizers and packagers of the films are inevitably artificial—combining in each cassette (volume) three or four films by particular directors or on loose themes: *Beginnings, Folklore and Legend, Starewicz's Fantasies, Provincial Variations, Chardynin's Pushkin, Class Distinctions, Evgenii Bauer, Iakov Protazanov, High Society,* and *The End of an Era.* The first five volumes run from forty to sixty minutes each; the others about ninety minutes. Each cassette or volume contains from two to four films. The shortest, the footage on the actress Vera Kholodnaia's funeral, lasts only a few minutes; the longer ones an hour or more. This makes the collection wonderfully adaptable to classes of almost any kind, especially since the visual quality of most of the films is extraordinarily fine and the subject matter engrossing—as cultural documentation, as entertainment and as cinematic art. A word about titles and sound. All the films are of course silent, many of them untitled. This plus the fragmentary status of a few sometimes makes continuity a problem but also a puzzle and a challenge for those who are willing to learn the art of watching silents and decoding gestures. Where intertitles exist, they are shown in the Russian original and in the generally accurate translations of Julian Graffy.[4] The tinkling piano accompaniment of Neil Brand reminds us that silent films were almost never shown without musical background. His tunes are eminently suitable for the moods of the films, with even an occasional "ethnic" allusion in the music.

It seems to me useful to discuss the films using categories (however arbitrary) relevant to scholars of various disciplines interested in the era: newsreel and documentary, current events, history, popular ethnography, literary inspiration, comedy, and melodrama. The only newsreel, *The Funeral of Vera Kholodnaia*, is a two-minute segment showing the priests, family and vast crowds who in 1919 followed the film actress's bier in Odessa, to which she had repaired after the Revolution and where studio life continued until the Whites were defeated. This brief newsreel is an interesting reminder of the power that Kholodnaia, the "queen of the linen screen," wielded on audiences in her brief but brilliant career. It probably served as the inspiration for the scene of moviegoers' adulation for a female star in Nikita Mikhalkov's *Slave of Love* (1975), the most famous modern evocation of movie life in the last days of the studios. *A Fish Factory in Astrakhan* (1908), one of a series called "Picturesque Russia," is an early travelogue common in the first years of Russian cinema. (The first non-newsreel film shot on Russian soil was a similar piece on the Don Cossacks). The camera lingers on the docks along the Volga deltas, the boats, fisherman, stevedores, cleaners, scalers, salters—women and Bashkirs prominent among them—at work in providing the fish delicacies that we will see being devoured with champagne and vodka in films about the haute monde.

The three fictionalized treatments of newsworthy events deal with the prewar years, World War I and the February Revolution. An early "docudrama;" *Departure* [or *Flight*] *of a Great Old Man* (Protazanov, 1912, 38 minutes, titled) mixed real footage with acting, featured the turbulent last days of Lev Tolstoi, and cast his wife in such a bad light that she successfully petitioned to have it banned in Russia. The main theme is how she and Vladimir Chertkov, the "chief Tolstoian," tried to shield him from the realities of everyday life, including their mistreatment of his peasant neighbors. Visually impressive is the footage of the convent where Tolstoi's sister lived and the great railway yards at Astapovo where Tolstoi left the train for the last time. These events and movements, by the way, were all headlined in the daily press, to whose readers Tolstoi was a celebrity and a literary icon.[5] Most important is the startling depiction of Tolstoi and his ideas on religion, the common people and the simple life. Starewicz's wartime *Lily of Belgium, or the Suffering and Rebirth of Belgium* (1915, 13 minutes, titled) combines stop-frame animation with live characters in a lyrical but clearly propagandistic emotional allegory in which Belgium, the tender lily, is destroyed by marauding Germans, who are portrayed as beetles with cannons and war vehicles and who are finally bested by a folk-dancing and concertina-playing Russian pine cone. The film was commissioned by the Skobelev Committee, the chief organizing body of Russian World War I propaganda.

Evgenii Bauer's *The Revolutionary* (1917, 31 minutes, titled) was made right after the February Revolution of 1917. Its scenarist and principal, the Georgian Ivan Perestiani, was a great screen actor of the period and went on in the Soviet years to direct one of the most popular adventure films of the 1920s and after: *Little Red Imps*. In *The Revolutionary* he plays a radical of indeterminate political persuasion who, in a scene reminiscent of a Repin painting, is arrested by the gendarmes (the first truly negative depiction of the Okhrana in Russian cinema history) and bids goodbye to his young son. In Siberian exile, he languishes amid the other convicts. Upon his release as an old man he is, like many real counterparts of the time, feted as a "martyr of freedom" by the crowds and immediately takes up the patriotic line of the Provisional Government to "finish the war to victory." His errant son, a Marxist, is quickly converted to the war party and they both enlist.

Strictly speaking, no genuine historical drama appears in this collection, although that was a popular genre, particularly the military spectacles on 1812 (at least three of them), the Crimean War (*Sevastopol*) and so on. But two films reviewed here deal with actual historical figures. One is of great magnitude, the other trivial, but both were the subject of enduring legend. The first was *Stenka Razin* (Romashov, 1908, titled), the first Russian-made fiction film. It is only eight minutes long, crudely acted by wildly gesticulating theater actors and extras who posture with swords and wine bottles. Its sole focus is on the jealousy of the seventeenth-century bandit rebel, Stepan Razin, who throws his captive Persian princess, suspected of infidelity, into the waves of the Volga (actually an inlet near St. Petersburg). It is a pity that the accompanist did not play the famous theme song about Stenka Razin that was used in the original showings, a minor flaw that can easily be rectified in the classroom by substituting a tape of "Iz-za ostrova na strezhen."

Princess Tarakanova (Hansen, 1910, 15 minutes, titled) is a better film, though hardly more realistic. The sets, costumes and camera work are very impressive, with some effective deep-focus shots. Modern viewers will certainly enjoy seeing how filmmakers in 1910 visualized the court of Catherine with its Orlovs, Tolstois and Golitsyns. The operatic acting is pure "delsartism," a code of gestures, staggers and lurches created in French theater to signify specific emotions through visual means. "Tarakanova" (a name she never used) was an obscure pretender to the Russian throne whose tragedy was fictionalized in the enormously popular 1883 story by G. P. Danilevskii.[6] In 1775 she was kidnapped in Italy and brought to Russia where Catherine the Great had her thrown into the ravelins of the Peter and Paul Fortress, where she perished of disease (or in the mythical account was drowned by the waters of the Neva, which flooded her cell). The movie actually provides both endings, the latter derived from the K. D. Flavitskii painting of the 1860s, reproductions of which were a commonplace in prerevolutionary homes. The dungeon sequence must have evoked great interest from an audience who had never before seen the inside of one: no scenes of the incarceration of political prisoners were permitted until the February Revolution, though scenes of jailed criminals were, as for instance in the series *Light-fingered Sonka.*

Several of the films in the series can be considered "ethnographic," using the term loosely to indicate attempts to capture, however modestly and clumsily, some of the visible attributes of non-Russians, of Russian peasants and their folkways, and of people of bygone ages. A three-minute film, *Drama in a Gypsy Camp near Moscow* (Siversen, 1910, untitled), the first made by the Khanzhonkov studio, is very disappointing in this regard. Filmed in a park in Kuntsevo (now inside Moscow), it offers no more than a fleeting glimpse of a *tabor* (encampment) and a cast of real Gypsies. In the fragment offered, the viewer will see only the opening and the finale, with no explanation of a plot, designed to reinforce all the clichés about that eternally maligned people: the gambling away of a fiancée in a card game, her murder at the hands of the loser, and his own sui-cide. *Wedding Day* (Slavinskii, 1912, 15 minutes, untitled) is among the least interesting of a film series on Jewish life produced by Jews in Poland, in the Pale and in Moscow. Like the others, it shows that middle-class Jews copied the furnishings, pictures and interiors of Russian and Polish homes. But of *shtetl* life it offers only the briefest glimpse: a dying wife and an outdoor wedding under the *hupah*. A much better choice would have been *Leon Drey* (1915), the story of a heartless Jewish gigolo who is also staunchly devoted to his family. Like other Jewish films made before the Revolution, *Leon Drey* goes beyond pieties as well as bigotry to display the universal flaws of people as well as their virtues.[7]

More interesting are the ethnographic details and the histori-cal and socio-geographic visions of the filmmakers of the time. In *A 16th-Century Russian Wedding* (1909, 10 minutes), the director Goncharov interweaves folkloric realia, copied from the historical paintings of Konstantin Makovskii, with a faux-melodrama ending in a comic surprise. In the original, two young people from boyar families fall in love and then discover that their marriage to each other has been arranged. They feign sorrow and disappointment until finally left alone in the bridal chamber, where they smile and happily embrace. Unfortunately, this cut omits a few of the crucial frames where the ruse is revealed. Movies like this, including the excellent *Boyar Orsha* (1910; not in this collection), attempted to re-capture the life of Old Muscovy—a nostalgic trend of the time that reached all the way to the court of Nicholas II. The various gyra-tions of parents, matchmakers, bridal pair and guests add kinetic archaeology to the iconographic archaeology of the static pictures made by nineteenth-century artists, creating filtered images based on antiquarian research.

Merchant Bashkirov's Daughter (Larin, 1913, 34 minutes), is, though untitled, a model of clarity and continuity as well as a shocking drama based on a real event in eighteenth-century Nizh-nii Novgorod.[8] Set in the 1910s in Iaroslavl Province, the film tells of a wealthy hereditary Russian merchant (a portrait of his ances-tor hangs on the wall) who plans to wed his daughter to another elderly merchant. But, as in so many *domostroi* dramas, the young woman loves a younger man, a shop clerk for her father. It would be unkind to reveal the thread of the story, which includes an accidental death, coerced sex and a truly grisly denouement. In contrast to films like *Tarakanova*, it is remarkably realistic, offering details of everyday life: the carriage and the costume of the merchant, with blouse under a frock coat and bobbed hair; the deference of the wife who serves while men eat, drink, bow, face the icon, and cross themselves; and the ritual toasts made in the home contrasted with the brutishness of drinking in the tavern. The most poignant scene in this harrowing film, used as the logo of this collection, is of the doomed couple kissing in silhouette beneath and arch, through which one sees the church in Iaroslavl across the Volga River.

The "literary" films demonstrate that canonized Russian writers were being mediated to the masses on the screen as well as in the print media and the schools. In the case of Aleksandr Pushkin, adaptation for cinema was an important episode in the lengthy process of literary cult-building that culminated during the Stalin period in the 1937 celebrations of the centenary of his death. Vasilii Goncharov's *Rusalka* (1910, 9 minutes, titled) was among the earliest film adaptations of Pushkin, and one of the best, though rather far from the original, which features the tempting of a pious monk. The film tells the story of a prince who abandons a miller's daughter to marry an upper-class woman. The forlorn girl throws herself into the Dnieper River and lives there amid the water sprites. The prince returns to the riverbank to find that the miller has gone mad; he himself is lured down into the depths of the river. The final underwater scene of water sprites dancing around the corpse of the prince is both chilling and ethereal.

Brigand Brothers, another Pushkin adaptation by Goncharov (1911, 22 minutes, titled), traces in flashback the life of two orphan brothers who eventually become bandits. The flashback is narrated by one brother who is now leader of a pack of Volga brigands. (The other brother has been killed.) Like some of the bandits in the stories analyzed by Jeffrey Brooks, the narrator remains unrepentant but sentimental and self-pitying, remorseful about this brother's death but exultant in the memory of robbing and feasting.[9] *Little House in Kolomna* (Chardynin, 1913, 20 minutes, titled), the most delightful comedy in the collection, shows off a bit of Pushkin's prose wit, the charms of the naughty and flirtatious Parasha (played by

Sofiia Goslavskaia), and the great versatility of Ivan Mozzhukhin, the most famous actor of prerevolutionary cinema. Apparently no people or era is immune to the comic device of a cross-dressing man; witness Mozzhukhin hilariously doubling as an imperial hussar officer and a chambermaid. The lively conversations between the two females offer a fine visual lesson on how Russians actually move their hands and faces when they speak.

Two versions of *The Queen of Spades,* one by Chardynin (1910, 10 minutes, titled) and the other by Protazanov (1916), are justly contrasted in the liner notes, but one should not ignore the former even if it is clearly the inferior of the two. Like the original Pushkin story, Chardynin's is driven by the thematic of the "romantic agony" of the early nineteenth century and is done with macabre apparitions and a generally theatrical atmosphere. Its stilted posturing, balletic ballroom dancing, clutched foreheads and other formulaic signs rigidly copy Delsarte's stylized vocabulary of gestures. The actor playing German (or Hermann) is too tall, bulky and clumsy—without a hint of the "fatal" temperament Pushkin ascribes to him. The sets are crudely sketched and Liza descends into a cardboard Winter Canal (following the Tchaikovsky opera rather than the Pushkin story). But the compositions are busy and well assembled, the apparitions of the countess and the cards on the wall are well executed, the timing is neat, and the whole production is short and tight. Protazanov's *Queen of Spades* (45 minutes, titled) is now recognized as a masterpiece of silent cinema. It is a blend of three times and three cultures—the age of Catherine the Great in the flashbacks, the age of Pushkin in the main action, the age of World War I and modern art in the execution. The first two are evoked brilliantly in the costumes and sets. Mozzhukhin playing Hermann takes us to the world of his contemporaries in his movements, his makeup, and his madness: the cabaret singer Aleksandr Vertinskii and his powdered face, the blood-sucking spiders and serpents of symbolist and decadent imagery, the use of Benois illustrations in the sets, and the victimized women and neurotic gambling males of film melodramas. Protazanov's super cinematic treatment of the old countess's reveries of youth culminates when her would-be lover appears at the door in her dream as she awakes and sees the frightening Hermann framed in the same door. The crisis of Hermann's obsession is exquisitely suspenseful—even to those who know the dénouement—as Hermann plays out the secret of the Three, the Seven and the Ace of Spades. The director's use of deep interiors, double rooms and arches, waist-high shots, shadows and lighting effects, and slow fades between narrator and narrated combine to make this a film that can be seen again and again for its technical virtuosity. One may also commend Neil Brand for his skillful and restrained use of the *Dies Irae* in the crucial scenes.

Folklore, legend and rustic humor figure in Nikolai Gogol's *Christmas Eve*, a part of his 1831 collection of stories, *Evenings on a Farm near Dikanka.* Wladislaw Starewicz, the pioneer of stop-frame photography and animation, made an extremely lively 1913 adaptation of it (42 minutes, titled) with Ivan Mozzhukhin as the devil and other competent performers as Oksana, Vakula the Smith, Chub, and Prince Potemkin. Its eighteenth-century characters engage in dancing, sledding, flying, moon theft, sexual intrigues, courtship, broad comedy antics, and camera tricks—including a scene with flying *galushki* (unfilled *pelmeni).* One of its episodes, in which male visitors are put in a bag as soon as a new one comes to Solokha's door, recalls the folk tale about the libidinous priests who are trapped in a bag. Readers who are tempted to share Vladimir Nabokov's verdict on these Gogol stories as unfunny would do well to view this film as they read the original.[10] Starewicz's *The Dragonfly and the Ant* (1913, 8 minutes, untitled), an early animated film, is Ivan Krylov's fable about the industrious ant and the lazy dragonfly and the moral drawn from it. A Chekhov story becomes *Romance with a Double Bass* at the hands of Danish-born director, Kaj (Kai in Russian) Hansen, an entertaining 1911 film (8 minutes, untitled) about carefree life at the dacha and male and female swimmers whose clothes are stolen.

There are two comedies, other than those of belletristic provenance. *The l002nd Ruse* (Bauer, 1915, 14 minutes, untitled) takes its title from Vladimir Azov's stage comedy, *The 1001st Ruse*, itself a reference to *A Thousand and One Nights.* The film is a delightful and totally sexist romp about wifely "feminine wiles," which the husband tries to interdict by reading a book of "Oriental Wisdom." It handles infidelity in the light manner of French cinematic farce and allows the woman to cuckold her husband—all to an arrangement of Camille Saint-Saëns's *Danse macabre* on the piano. In the other "bourgeois" comedy, *Antosha Ruined by a Corset* (Puchalski, 1916, 25 minutes, titled), the husband is the unfaithful partner undone—after a long chain of visual gags—by the forgotten corset of a visiting lady friend. It was one of twenty-four comedy films in the "Antosha" series (1915-18) by Anton Fertner, a Czech-born actor. The restaurant scene, with Brand's Slavic-Gypsy-Jewish musical backup, is particularly evocative of the affluent lifestyle. Given the massive bloodletting going on at the war front as these two movies were being screened, it is tempting to speculate about audience reaction—but we have no way of knowing.

The "bourgeois" melodrama, with its clear formulaic repetitions, was the most important genre of film from about 1911-12 onward in that more of them were made than any other single genre. In many of them, a masterplot prevailed: the idyllic life of a young girl, marred only by vague malaise, is disrupted by the appearance of a seducer; her passion for him gives way to disenchantment and, at the end, tragedy (suicide, ruin, murder, vengeance). Several themes are routinely linked: money, power, leisure, boredom, the need for distraction, gambling and game-playing among affluent men (cards and the races). The main game is seduction of a young and innocent woman. The conquered prey becomes a possession, a toy to be fondled for a while and then discarded. The victims are framed in a virtuous idyll—humble or opulent. The victimizers dwell in settings of obvious social decadence. The films are filled with social and sexual tension. The contrast between innocence (which is poor or weak) and evil (which is rich and powerful) is rendered by making urbane, cruel and impeccably dressed matinee idols break the hearts and shatter the lives of beautiful women on screen. The female superstar, Vera Kholodnaia, was their regular victim. Kholodnaia, a former dancer with sad grey eyes, animated the celluloid world she inhabited, a world of tainted money, opulent restaurants, champagne picnics, luxury autos careening through the night, and illicit love ending in tragedy.

The collection happily includes some good examples of the masterplot as well as a few variants. *The Peasant's Lot* (Goncharov, 1912, 35 minutes, untitled) is a grim if familiar depiction of the precarious condition of the rural scene where a fiancée's life is ruined by a fire that burns down her home. Harsh economic realities are enmeshed with marital plans when the dowry deal can no longer be met by a family who has lost everything. The rejected bride goes to the city to work as a servant in a wealthy home in order to earn back her dowry. She is, as any adult audience would have expected by 1912, seduced by the master and turned out of the house. Tolstoi's *Resurrection*, the police blotter and the medical inspector's records offered evidence enough of this common occurrence. Though the scenes of harvest and cabin-raising are beautifully shot, they do not obscure the unbending economic realities of village life. Yet it is the town that is the young peasant woman's undoing, the town whose cold, mechanical character is captured brilliantly as she stands in the middle of a busy street criss-crossed by menacing tram cars, and whose cruelty is deployed by merciless upper-class men who prey upon helpless servants.

As the next five films indicate, Evgenii Bauer is the dominant director in this collection. In *Child of the Big City* (1914, 34 minutes, titled) he reverses the usual process of ruination: the rich young man named Victor becomes the victim of a poor orphan girl and seamstress, Mariia. There is a grainy, melancholy shot of her before she meets her rescuer: she sits at the window of her gloomy flat unable to participate in the bright outside world. (This shot is famous in the iconography of movie stills and adorns the cover of the book, *Silent Witnesses*.) After Victor takes her from the dank world of basement laundries and sweatshops and spends all his money on luxury, the reversal takes place: he, broke and disillusioned with the high life, longs to move into a "modest" flat with his love; she suggests in a letter (composed as she cynically smokes a cigarette) that he find a "modest" girlfriend. Mariia's arrival at the top and her simultaneous corruption is established in a shot of her reclining on a chaise longue, à la Madame Recamier in Jacques-Louis David's famous canvas; a Grecian statue hovers over her head—a typical Bauer touch. Her moral degradation is completed when she steps over the body of Victor, who has taken his own life on her doorstep, and calls to her entourage: "To Maxime's or we'll be late!"

Silent Witnesses (1914, 50 minutes, titled) is one of the finest of the Bauer melodramas. The story is simplicity—and familiarity— itself: an effete snob, cad and useless Oblomov type tampers with the affections of a servant girl who is the granddaughter of the doorman at the residence of an upper-class family. He is in love with Hélène, a slinking and perfidious young society woman, but seduces the maid nonetheless. The scene in which the maid has to remove Hélène's boots is psychologically harrowing, as is the heart-rending moment of the grandfather's anger and disappointment at the "sin" of the jilted girl—another victim of heartless city folks. Bauer is completely in control as he renders cinematically the utter coldness of the affluent crowd and the world of fabulous interiors, restaurants and auto cars in which they move. *Daydreams* (1915, 35 minutes, titled) was based on an 1898 Belgian symbolist novel of Georges Rodenbach. The protagonist, crazed by his wife's death, cuts off one of her braids and sets out to find a close substitute for her. At a performance in a small opera theater of Giacomo Meyerbeer's *Robert le diable*, with its ghoulish scenes of open coffins and the rising corpses of dishonored nuns performing an eerie seduction dance, the deranged widower falls in love with one of the singers who resembles his late wife. His obsession with the dead wife alienates the manipulative opera singer and he finally strangles her with the braid of hair. *Daydreams* is one of the best of the many films of that age inspired by mystical, decadent and even necrophilic themes.

My personal favorite of the Bauer films in this collection is *Life for a Life* (1916, 48 minutes, titled), based on a novel by Georges Ohnet. Its importance as the archetypical Russian cinema melodrama is enhanced by the quality of the cast: Olga Rakhmanova as the mother, a key figure who cherishes her two daughters and finally kills the prince-villain and fakes his suicide; Liliia Koreneva as Musiia, the less attractive natural daughter who loves and marries the prince; Vera Kholodnaia as Nata, the adopted daughter who loves the prince but weds an adoring businessman (movingly played by Ivan Perestiani), betrays him, and suffers from her sin; Vitold Polonskii, a perennial matinee idol and screen rogue of the time, as Prince Bartinskii, who marries Musiia for her money, sleeps with Nata, squanders money at the races, forge his friend's signature, faces arrest, refuses to confess, and is killed by his mother-in-law. The finale offers the representative "Russian ending" for melodrama—almost always a panorama of disaster and wrecked lives.

Equally prominent in the film is the national style of interior decor that Bauer employed with great effect movies. The underlying theme of the film—and of many others—is the folkloric (not Marxist) belief that "money is the root of all evil."

For Happiness (not *For Luck* as on the cassette; Bauer, 1917, 32 minutes, titled) is a supremely upper-class story of a wealthy widow, her daughter and a lawyer caught in a love triangle. The mother (played gracefully by Koreneva), by overindulging her daughter "for happiness," insures the unhappiness of all three. The architecture and interior sets in Moscow and the Crimea are truly voluptuous, and the outdoor scenes are rich in bright sunshine and stark shadows. The scenic element clearly outweighs the dynamics of a weak plot. One is again tempted to speculate about audience reaction. Watching affluent people suffer perhaps diluted the element of envy and hostility that lower-class viewers might have had toward their "betters," as it apparently did for those millions of Russians who viewed *The Rich Also Cry* series on television in recent years.

Behind the Screen is the last entry in the last cassette, entitled "The End of an Era." It is a thirteen-minute fragment (one reel of an eight-reel 1917 film) starring Mozzhukhin and his wife Nataliia Lisenko as themselves. Its alternate title, *A Life Destroyed by Fate,* hints at a plot that is unknown to us. *Behind the Screen* is a fitting finale to the collection. Its theme—lives destroyed by fate—is a central one of the Russian movie melodrama. It also depicts the departure of two actors from the world of filmmaking and shows the interior of a Moscow studio. Particularly touching and symbolic of the coming end of an era is the scene of Mozzhukhin leafing through old stills of himself in his most famous movies—including several from the present collection.

What can Russianists do with these films? This magnificent collection offers endless possibilities to teachers and scholars of Russian history, literature, theater, folklore, popular culture, art, architecture, society, and even politics. One may focus on the aesthetics of cinema through the oeuvre of the main directors—Chardynin, Starewicz, Bauer and Protazanov.[11] In the realm of acting styles, Mozzhukhin's wide range is demonstrated in many performances, but one will discover multiple performances and diverse roles by other actors and actresses as well. Unfortunately, the art of Vera Kholodnaia, with her trademark panting breath, mobile mouth, doleful eyes, and graceful movements, is poorly represented. One hopes that Milestone will, in its next issue, include the moving *Be Still, My Grief*, one of her finest performances, or even her final film, *The Last Tango*.

Students of turn-of-the-century art styles, especially architecture and interior design, will find a treasure house in these films, particularly those of Evgenii Bauer. He attended a school of architecture and sculpture and studied with the famous architect, Fedor Shekhtel, and so imbibed and helped transfer to the screen notions of abundant space as a marker of luxury. The new architecture was indeed cinematic and the Bauer corpus is a documentary record of Russian styles.[12] His use of stereoscopic space and moving camera creates striking cinematic effects. The privileging of classical motifs in architecture and furnishing in the mise-en-scène of his films signify perfection, beauty and aesthetic honesty and provide ironic contrast to the degraded values of their owners.

For literature courses, let me give a concrete example of what can be done to expand the parameters of teaching Aleksander Pushkin's *Queen of Spades*, that remarkable literary classic of the early nineteenth century. After a close reading and textual analysis of the story one can watch and listen to Tchaikovsky's operatic version and/or read his brother's libretto in order to examine the adaptations (or distortions) of the original. Alexandre Benois's illustrations for the 1905 edition of that work are available (as are many other graphic examples). Then one can view the two films, Chardynin's version, closer to the opera, and Protazanov's version, more faithful to Pushkin. The possibilities of such a discussion can easily be imagined.

What do the films tell us about Russian society and life in the twilight years of the empire? One needs to be modest and cautious about deriving social meaning from the art of a given era, particularly given the very limited source base that this collection constitutes. Yet the sampling, small as it is, is fairly representative of the films made, and the cinema had surpassed all other forms of mass entertainment by the time of World War I. The films say something about the values of those who produced them and, indirectly, something about those who watched them. But since there is no single set of values in any production of culture or consumption, the challenge is to try to estimate what people of various classes, ages, genders and so on might have perceived on the screen and how they might have reacted to it. In the last analysis, cinema offers no clear set of answers, but it certainly suggests new questions about crime and social misery and about material progress and consumer culture at various levels, about the roles and identities of porters, doormen, man-servants, housemaids, cooks and chauffeurs, as well as merchant families, idle princes, businessmen, gamblers, actors, and rakes—and it does so in a vivid and immediate form that supplements traditional written sources.

There are a hundred ways to extract meanings from and enrich teaching with *Early Russian Cinema*; any enthusiast of Russian society and culture will see them at once. I wish to add a few words of advice, based upon my own use of films in academic courses. Students of the present generation need to be prepared for "Russian" tempos, which were deliberately slow. Since there was no talking, audiences needed to read intertitles and absorb them, to follow the continuity of the filmmakers, and—most important of all in the melodramas—to "co-think" with the protagonists as they reacted to the unfolding plot. This dynamic of screen time and reaction to events strikes modern viewers as ponderous, but it was "meditative" and reflective. Students who have seen no Russian film styles other than the rapid editing of Eisenstein and who have grown up with the fast cutting of MTV need to view the films of another age through the eyes of the people of that age. In terms of content and thematics, students raised on expectations of neat and happy resolutions will also have to come to grips with the prolonged suffering and the often rather sudden "Russian endings" (meaning unhappy ones) that almost universally marked the melodrama.

Watching the occasional untitled film or the ones with missing reels presents no major problem, though some close attention to movement and gesture is required. The titles that have been restored, with great labor, are very legible. The cassette boxes contain only sketchy data about each film, so the viewer would be well advised to have the book *Silent Witnesses* at hand; perhaps Indiana University Press will soon put this expensive book into an

English-only paperback edition. *Early Russian Cinema* now takes its place beside two other masterful collections of recent years, *The Glasnost Film Festival* (twenty-four documentaries of the 1980s) and *Red Silents* (ten classics mostly from the 1920s). If it is a success, perhaps we can hope that many more films of this and other periods of Russian cinema history are made available in such an attractive and practical format.

I wish to thank my friends and colleagues Catherine Evtuhov, Boris Gasparov, and especially Josephine Woll for expert advice and assistance on this article.

Original publication: *Russian Review* 53.2, April 1994, pp. 285-295.

Notes

1   Yury Tsivian et al., *Testimoni silenziosi: film russi 1908-1919/ Silent Witnesses: Russian Films 1908-1919* (Pordenone, 1989), a gold mine of catalogue data and commentary (in English and Italian). The Indiana University Press edition (1990) is identical to this one except that the title is reversed. Foreign showings and production began in 1896; the commentary in this volume dates from when native Russian production began in 1908.

2   My viewing of some eighty to ninety prerevolutionary films took place in Moscow (1989), London (1990), and at the "Russian Silent Film, 1908-1919" showing put on over the course of three months at the Mary Pickford Theater in the Library of Congress in 1992. I wish to thank the All-Union Scholarly Research Institute of Cinematography and Gosfilmofond in Moscow and IREX for arranging archival film viewings for me in 1989-90; Richard Taylor and Ian Christie for inviting me to the conference on Soviet cinema in London in 1990; and Patrick Loughney of the Motion Picture Division of the Library of Congress for many kindnesses.

3   In addition to *Silent Witnesses* one may consult S. Ginsburg, *Kinematografiia dorevoliutsionnoi Rossii* (Moscow, 1963); R. Sobolev, *Liudi i filmy russkogo dorevoliutsionnogo kino* (Moscow, 1961); Peter Kenez, *Cinema and Soviet Society, 1917-1953* (Cambridge, 1992), chap. 1; Iurii Tsivian, *Istoricheskaia retseptsiia kino. Kinematograf v Rossii, 1896-1930* (Riga, 1991); and Jay Leyda, *Kino: A History of the Russian and Soviet Film*, 3d ed. (Princeton, 1983). For parallel discussion of the other popular arts see Neia Zorkaia, *Na rubezhe stoletii. U istokov iskusstva v Rossii 1900-*

1910 godov (Moscow, 1976); S. F. Starr, *Red and Hot: The Fate of Jazz in the Soviet Union* (New York, 1983), chap. 1; Jeffrey Brooks, *When Russia Learned to Read* (Princeton, 1985); and Richard Stites, *Russian Popular Culture: Entertainment and Society since 1900* (Cambridge, 1992), chap. 1.

4   Errors are few and inconsequential: the misspelling of the name of Admiral Greig (a historical personage) in *Princess Tarakanova* and of Viarskaia, a character in *Daydreams*; in *Rusalka*, the prince asks the sprites, "Where have you come from?" not, "Where are you?" In the Siberian burial scene of *The Revolutionary*, the word "Farewell" becomes "Forward." But Graffy also fixes misspellings in the titles ("Nity" for "Naty" in *Life for Life*). Some of the restored Russian titles seem not quite accurate.

5   Louise McReynolds, *The News under Russia's Old Regime: The Development of a Mass-Circulation Press* (Princeton, 1991), 226. In this film and in *The Revolutionary*, the accompanist plays the opening theme from Tchaikovsky's *Queen of Spades* but does not do so in the two films on that subject. I thank Boris Gasparov for identifying the music.

6   G. P. Danilevskii, *Beglye v Novorossii*; *Volia*; *Kniazhna Tarakanova* (Moscow, 1983), with an essay and notes by Emiliia Vilenskaia. I thank Catherine Evtuhov for this reference.

7   In an interesting article on Yiddish films in the Bolshevik period, J. Hoberman does not mention this background. See "A Face to the *Shtetl*: Soviet Yiddish Cinema, 1924-36," in *Inside the Film Factory: New Approaches to Russian and Soviet Cinema*, ed. Richard Taylor and Ian Christie (London, 1991), 124-50. A few comments on the prerevolutionary Jewish films can be gleaned from the sections of *Silent Witnesses* on *Leon Drey* (pp. 268-70) and *The Sorrows of Sara* ([1913], p. 176), both of which I have seen, and on *L'Haim* ([1911], pp. 102-4) and *Vera Chibiriak or the Truth about the Beilis Case* ([1917], p. 384), which I have not seen.

8   This event occurred sometime before 1767 and became the subject of a play by P. I. Felonov, *Bez viny vinovataia*, first staged in Kazan in 1875. See *Pervyi shag: provintsial'nyi literaturnyi sbornik, 1876* (Kazan, 1876). Catherine Evtuhov found this collection in the Nizhnii Novgorod archives.

9   Brooks, *When Russia Learned to Read*, 166-213.

10   *Nikolai Gogol* (1944; reprint ed. New York, 1959), 30-32.

11   For interesting material on Protazanov in the Soviet period, and thus for continuities between the two eras, see Denise Youngblood, *Movies for the Masses: Popular Cinema and Soviet Society in the 1920s* (Cambridge, 1992), chap. 6; and idem, "Return of the Native: Protazanov and Soviet Cinema," in Taylor and Christie, *Inside the Film Factory*, 103-23.

12   See William Brumfield, *The Origins of Modernism in Russian Architecture* (Berkeley, 1991), for the best introduction to this magnificent cultural development.

18

To the Virgin Lands
The Epic and the Idyll in the Cinematic Representation of Khrushchev's Great Adventure

This essay is meant to call attention to the role of performance art as a code and subtext in mass films or popular movies.[1] Teachers and researchers in history and other scholars of Russian-Soviet culture and society increasingly make use of such films. Cinema reviews feature in journals such as *American Historical Review, Russian Review,* and *Slavic Review.* Literary scholars tend to look at intertextuality, among other things; film studies people often focus on the formal attributes of film. Film-as-history in the classroom caught on in our profession a long time ago and professors routinely use it to enrich their courses with visual material. But traditional ways of screening mostly offer the masterpieces of cinematic art or the obvious "films of persuasion." Sergei Eisenstein's *The Battleship Potemkin* (*Brononosets Potemkin,* 1926) serves both purposes on a grand scale. I have found that these great works have limits in getting inside the mentalities of the people who saw them at the time of release—and later. The classics often failed to appeal to mass audiences in the way that popular movies did—musicals and movies of romance, comedy, and action-adventure. My purpose here is to illustrate through a single example how popular movies can be made to speak to the student of history in the languages of their stories, acting styles, mise-en-scène, music, and particularly performance art in the cultural context of the era in which they were made and viewed.

The film under discussion, *Ivan Brovkin in the Virgin Lands,*[2] a rustic musical of 1958, appeared at a major turning point in Soviet cultural history where history failed to turn. It draws on two lines of narrative, scenic backdrop and social mood: the epic and the idyll. The epic of construction, a major theme in all genres of

popular culture from 1928 to the 1950s—romanticized physical labor, manual toil, and the realia of machinery against a backdrop
of wilderness. During the Russian Civil War (1918-1921), building
something fast—such as a railroad—took on epic proportions, a
fact celebrated with gorgeous cinematography in Alexander Alov
and Vladimir Naumov's *Pavel Korchagin* (1955), the best screen version of Ostrovsky's notorious socialist realist novel *How the Steel
was Tempered* (1932-1934). In the first full sound film, *Start in Life*—
also known as *Road to Life* (*Putevka v zhizn*, 1931)—director Nikolai Ekk utilized the railroad as salvation in a story about orphan
boys in the 1920s. Sergei Gerasimov's *Komsomolsk* (1938) offered a
camera study of deforestation and town-building in the Soviet Far
East. In these pictures, the act of cutting down and building up was
endowed with a special pathos and poetics that proved irresistible
over the decades and whose cinematographic style was incorporated into wartime epics.

The Soviet idyll emerged in the 1930s alongside the epic. In the
1920s, village life had often been ridiculed in the popular arts. Folk
dances, songs, and costumes were depicted as the archaic trappings
of roach- and god-infested worlds of darkness. The great exception
to this of course is the work of Oleksandr Dovzhenko. But after
Soviet collectivization in the early 1930s, the new *kolkhoz* (collective
farm) was romanticized as a confluence of the new and the best
of the old—bicycles and hospitality, tractors and head scarves, brigades and peasant fertility. This thematic blossomed in folk dance
ensembles, paintings, operettas, novels, and films in the 1930s and
1940s, and reached its apogee in Ivan Pyrev's famous *Kuban Cossacks*
(*Kubanskie kazaki*, 1949), a cinematic kolkhoz operetta and a classic
of the glossy, "conflictless" films of the late Stalin era. In contrast
to the epic, which is driven by the motif of dynamic change, this
film represented the ultimate static utopia where nothing changes
except the decimal point in production figures. When tension between new and old was treated, the new was always vindicated—as
in the most famous example, *Cavalier of the Golden Star*, a novel, an
operetta, and Yuly Raizman's 1950 film starring Sergei Bondarchuk.

Ivan Brovkin was shot in the midst of Nikita Khrushchev's Virgin
Lands campaign—a drive to cultivate large tracts of land in the
steppes between the Urals, the Caspian, and Siberia and in Northern

Kazakhstan. Although released only a few years after *Cavalier*, it gave the conflict a new resolution by treating the old village and the new *sovkhoz* almost equally. The former is symbolized by rural folkways, stubborn elders, and a bride who refuses to join her man on the cultivation sites beyond Orenburg. But this standard characterization—almost identical to that in *Cavalier*—is deployed with great tact and delicacy. Its traditional trappings are contrasted and intercut with the epic plot of the new Virgin Lands campaign. Out on the steppe, modernity springs forth from a semi-desert under the hands and brains of the hero, his wise and kindly mentor, and a crew of young, idealistic, ethnically varied Komsomols (Young Communists) who tear open the earth and careen upon it in their iron victory chariots in a civic version of savage joy. The domestic scenes of gathering, homebuilding, and planning are done in the painterly fashion of Stalinist socialist realism.

Storyboard

Ivan Brovkin in the Virgin Lands revolves around a demobilized peacetime soldier's decision in the 1950 to leave his *kolkhoz* in order to go as a volunteer tractor driver to the Virgin Lands and help turn the barren grass land of the region into an enormous grain basket. The film opens to the ring of an army bugle and a military march. An artillery unit, after strenuous gymnastic exercises, is being mustered out, thus establishing a familiar theme: the link between military ardor and socialist construction campaigns. Whereas the tank drivers in the 1940 film *Tractor Drivers* had gone off to a Moscow factory, a Georgian vineyard, and a Ukrainian collective farm upon terminating their service, Brovkin chooses to continue that service in what Leonid Brezhnev, comparing World War II to the Virgin Lands, called a "great battle won by the Party and the people."[3] When Brovkin goes home to say farewell to his kolkhoz, he encounters the dual conflict in the story: his fiancée Lyubasha (played by D. Smirnova) dissolves in tears at his decision and declines to accompany him as his bride; her father, the kolkhoz chairman, is angered at the imminent loss of his best worker. Once ensconced at one of the Virgin Lands units, the Komsomol Sovkhoz (Young Communist State Farm), Brovkin fits in easily, but his work ethic is eroded by the absence of his sweetheart. The Sovkhoz director finally persuades him of the value of the new Soviet project and sends him back to fetch his beloved. They both return as the film ends.

Embedded in the story are the contrasting but complementary images of new and old, town (out on the steppe) and village (kolkhoz), epic and idyll. The old is destined to lose in the struggle, in line with Khrushchev's continual efforts to hasten the advent of communism by consolidating kolkhozes into large amalgams and fostering more sovkhozes. But the victory is softened with nostalgia and romance for the loser. Brovkin's home farm, the kolkhoz he deserts, has an "old time" look, with many of the visual and auditory qualities of the pre-Soviet Russian village which is captured in beautifully framed black-and-white shots resembling the prints and picture postcards of rustic life that were mass-produced before the revolution.[4] No church bells ring out. But the houses are fronted by white picket fences; the kolkhoz chairman wears the belted peasant shirt and bloused boots; and women, as they serve the men at table, are garbed in traditional-looking dresses, though in fact they are Soviet made cotton prints. Lyubasha wears braids and her lovelorn lamentation is set in a birch grove. On the village street at eventide, young women of the kolkhoz sing stylized folk songs as the men stroll by with accordions as in the old peasant promenade. Brovkin tries to console and win over his girlfriend by serenading her with song and accordion, while Lyubasha, the chaste village maiden, reluctantly stays inside by the window and weeps. It is a Mickey Rooney-Judy Garland moment set in a folkloric rural Russia.

The epic face of the film begins to unfold on that great emblem of modernity, the train, which rolls in a straight line out toward the Orenburg steppe. The ur-Russianness of the story is slightly diluted when a non-Russian Soviet Asian Virgin Lander, Abaev (played by T. Zhailibekov), becomes Brovkin's new sidekick, a slightly clownish figure who acts in the manner of the old Soviet (and Hollywood) "quaint ethnic types." He is in fact a holdover from the first Brovkin film (*The Soldier Ivan Brovkin*, 1955); and his name, as Michael Rouland suggests, "signals a link to the popular turn-of-the-century Kazak poet and 'friend of the Russians,' Abai Kunanbaev."[5] Socialist Realism kicks in hard when Brovkin meets the director of the sovkhoz—also an ex-artilleryman—who becomes his mentor in work and in love. In short, he helps his love-sick and malingering brigadier to snap out of his melancholy yearning for the faraway Lyubasha by summoning up, with the aid of flash forward footage, energetic pictures of hard work and rewarding production figures. One is again reminded of Brezhnev, who recalled how he helped and hovered over underlings of less developed consciousness. Once back in gear, Brovkin again evokes the theme of production-as-tactics by acting out the famous potato scene from the film *Chapaev* (1934), known to every Soviet moviegoer. The potatoes are now stand-ins for tractors instead of Civil War partisan formations.[6]

To unleash an epic, one must have formidable obstacles to overcome. The camera provides convincing visual evidence, via capacious long shots of the immensity of the steppe, the challenge of the untilled soil, and perilous climatic changes. Brezhnev recalled with fondness "the tractor columns battling their way across the roadless blizzard-swept expanses."[7] He speaks of "the primeval nature of the steppe" and other hardships.[8] Both in the flash forward dream scenes and in real-time sequences, the film fills the vast landscape with "grunting, snorting trucks" and the relentlessly rolling tractors that slice the resistant soil, cultivate it, and harvest its mountains of grain.[9] Paralleling the carving up of the land, the director captures the rapid collective construction of housing and public buildings for the sovkhoz population: individual cottages, even for singles, and service edifices—including the official wedding office. The forbidding distance from the Russian heartland is conquered by technology: an airplane arrives with new volunteers and Brovkin's visiting mother.

Performance as Subtext

What makes production epic films like this so memorable, of course, is not the banal love plot and labor scenario, but the music and the performance. Imagine the plots of *State Fair* and *Oklahoma* without the music and lyrics of Rodgers and Hammerstein. But categorizing this film according to familiar Western genres does not work very well. Unlike musicals in rustic settings such the above-mentioned American musicals, *Brovkin* does not stop the action for set pieces; rather it integrates song and dance into the story at every stage, reinforcing comedic, emotional, and celebratory effects. Only the off-screen orchestral scoring of the field production and other scenes departs from the otherwise realistic narrative. It thus retains a strong rhetorical character, which allows the "messages" to be folded in without excessive intrusion. Furthermore, both familiar tunes and the newly composed but clichéd score connect easily for viewers who have heard it or something like it on the radio and on recordings for years and thus allows them to identify with the people who sing it or work to its strains. And *Brovkin* rises above the simplistic cinematic epics of the Stalin years in the way it fleshes out and complicates the tension between two visions. A good dramatic opera alternates musical and performance styles between opposing worlds—for example the scenes of amorous encounter and those of a menacing dungeon. In this film the chiaroscuro arises from the clever juxtaposition of idyll and epic and its brilliant illustration in performance art.

The film skillfully sets up the coming contrast of nature and modernity by drenching the kolkhoz scenes with the sad-and-sweet melodies redolent of old-time village life. Composed Russian "folk" songs of course date back to the late eighteenth century; in the Soviet era they undergirded a virtual cultural industry, along with the invented folk ensemble. The traditional songs and those provided by the popular songwriter, Anatoly Lepin, reek of folk or fake-folk stylization. One in particular owes much in structure and rhythm to Vasily Soloviev-Sedoi and Mikhail Matusovsky's canonical paean to innocent love, "Evenings Outside Moscow" (known in the West as "Midnight in Moscow," 1955), written shortly before the *Brovkin* film was released.

The wedding at the Virgin Lands sovkhoz makes some concessions to tradition: garlanded vehicles, flowing scarves, folk dance, and *chastushka*. But the men in attendance are wearing newly made European-style suits and ties. In the kolkhoz scenes, the singing and dancing, independent of all fieldwork, are performed only on the village streets. Out on the steppe, by contrast, the music is synchronized with labor and production and the score tracks the path of the agrarian vehicles as the tractor drivers and harvesters sing their hearts out. The singing becomes an instrument of agrarian bounty and these scenes seem to be reversing a popular saying, as cited by Brezhnev: "Only let there be grain and the songs will come of themselves."[10] An indoor dance is interrupted by a radio "performance" announcing super-worker competition winners, and the director's monologue on his farm's production achievements is applauded as in a play. If the kolkhoz songs recall a deeper past, the Virgin Lands singers draw on Komsomol and quasi-patriotic marches with the upbeat rhythms and four-square optimism of the great Stalin-era composer, Isaac Dunaevsky. The sovkhoz director and Brovkin's mentor converts him back into a Soviet-style taste for work not only with words and images of production victories, but by singing to him in—of course—a lovely bass voice, in the manner of the father in *La Traviata*. Joyful declamation has displaced the bittersweet longing of the "folk" idiom. In the final scene, the sadness of departing from the village has been overcome. The espoused couple stands on the train's back platform and look happily into the looming distance as they speed along the track across the steppe. For them, *toska* for a fading world has given way to nostalgia for the future. "The virgin lander," wrote Brezhnev years later, "is a historic figure and represents a heroic age."[11]

Conclusion

The marriage of epic and idyll is celebrated at many levels: the wedding scene that choreographs the disorderly and energetic folk dancing along a ruler-straight street laid out on the steppe; the accordions and birch twigs on the nuptial automobile; the return of the hero to claim his bride and their journey back to the steppe on a train. Brovkin (played by Leonid Kharitonov) is a younger, more vigorous, more credible version of Bondarchuk's cavalier of the gold star, and his triumph more humane. *Ivan Brovkin* proclaims a kind of moral and cultural equality and coexistence between kolkhoz life, with all the cultural baggage it retained after collectivization, and the new sovkhoz life with its clean bathrooms and electric lights. At the same time, it tilts the equation in favor of a new way of life, the product of youthful "storming" and wise planning of Kremlin elders. It voices a fond farewell to the old farm and announces the headlong rush to agrarian utopia. The film illuminates that moment in Soviet history between the relentless Stalinist exaltation of new over old that prevailed from 1928 until the mid-fifties and the exaltation of traditional village values which was now beginning in the works of village prose writers, filmmakers, and intellectuals of many kinds.[12] As for real entertainment on the ground in the Virgin Lands, Brezhnev mentions, almost in passing, that Lyubov Orlova and several other popular screen stars came there to put on shows in the manner of the troop entertainment brigades of World War II. But he was apparently more interested in the airplane hopping from site to site than in their performances.

The reader will note that the film ignores certain obvious historical aspects of its subject matter. In the spring and summer of 1954, some 300,000 Komsomols and other volunteers entrained eastward. The plan was to cultivate some 13 million hectares of soil. Within a few years, the campaign became an "agricultural and ecological disaster."[13] Film and press treatments largely glossed over the genuine hardships and shortcomings of the first phases of the Virgin Lands campaign that were generally known even at the time and have since been well-documented. Even the sugary memoirs of one of its chief organizers, Leonid Brezhnev, reveal more of the reality on the ground than does this film. The lack of amenities, the ferocious blizzards that enveloped the steppe and snuffed out the lives of the unsuspecting, the surliness of the locals, the inability of Soviet ploughshares to carve open the root—entangled sward of the ancient grassland—all this is missing in the film. Distortion comes also in the monochromatic treatment of the festive culture of the Virgin Lands. "Alongside the officially sponsored spirit, there arose an undercurrent of pure individualism celebrated in such songs as 'We Drink to the Malcontents, the Different Ones,' expressing what was probably the deepest layer of values among the young who were mostly apolitical—certainly not dissident but bored with the magniloquent words and gestures of the parent state"[14]— precisely the ones that dominate the film. Lev Kopelev recalled that, like other youth working far from home, "'virgin-landers'... put distance between themselves and the ruling, 'industrially' standardizing civilization, the gloomy clichés of propaganda, and all kinds of cultural work done according to plan." No trace of this phenomenon appears in *Brovkin*, which played only to the positive.

This can hardly surprise. Frontier life and construction invite romanticism in cinematic treatment: it makes for fun, audience appeal, and good ideology. The American boomtown, railroad, and oilfield epics of the 1930s are hardly different in this regard.

But very much present is the movie's obvious design as a mobilizing agent to recruit needed youth. The studio that produced it, the Gorky Central Studio of Children's and Youth Films in Moscow, specialized in combining targeting young people with a blend of moralist and socialist values. Women and especially physicians (combined in one character in the movie as in real Soviet life) were also objects of recruitment for the Virgin Lands campaign. In this *Brovkin* resembles the great construction epics of the 1930s, both documentary and fiction films. However, in the end, and in reality, women were the ones who sustained the home and the public services more than becoming heroines of the mechanical revolution in the fields. In Soviet iconology, the woman had long come to be identified with the countryside and thus with a relatively nurturing role in society (in spite of her prominence in the urban work force); the man with the city, the factory, the machine—and thus power.[15]

How well the propaganda of this film and in other media actually worked in creating genuine enthusiasm for the project is hard to know.[16] The numbers—even though gained by a combination of pressure for conformity and the still buzzing atmosphere of last years of the thaw–are impressive enough. Yet it seems that the most important element in this movie turns out to be–in the light of what came after—the ultimate failure of the epic. I refer not to the concrete failures of the Virgin Lands in agricultural output, but of the much deeper failure in subsequent decades of the entire epic project in Soviet life. Brezhnev's Baikal Amur Magistral program of the 1970s resembled the previous construction dramas superficially, but the old spirit of enthusiasm and the romance of construction, eventually soured and yielded a great breakup or divorce between rural and urban values and social life, as depicted so brilliantly and poignantly by the village prose authors. And so it is that the aesthetically inferior but popular film can sometimes unwittingly catch moments in a historical watershed.

Original publication: www.units.muohio.edu/havighurstcenter/publica-
tions/documents/Stites06.pdf as "[Draft 2] Virgin Lands. The Movie,"
new title supplied by Richard Stites himself to Anna Lawton; re-format-
ting and footnote completion by Stefanie Tubbs and the editor.

Notes

1   Richard Taylor, *The Politics of Soviet Cinema 1917-1929* (Cambridge,
    1979); Denise Youngblood, *Movies for the Masses: Popular Cinema and
    Soviet Society in the 1920s* (Cambridge: Cambridge University Press,
    1992). Peter Kenez, *Cinema and Soviet Society, 1917-1953* (Cambridge:
    Cambridge University Press, 1992); Josephine Woll, *Real Images: Soviet
    Cinema and the Thaw* (London: I. B. Tauris, 2000); Anna Lawton, *Kino-
    glasnost: Soviet Cinema in Our Time* (Cambridge: Cambridge University
    Press, 1992). For parallel discussion of the other popular arts, see Rich-
    ard Stites, *Russian Popular Culture* (Cambridge: Cambridge University
    Press, 1992).
2   *Ivan Brovkin na tseline* (Gorky Studio, 1958), directed by Ivan Luki-
    inskii. Filmed on location at the Komsomol Sovkhoz in Orenburg
    Oblast.
3   L. I. Brezhnev, *Trilogy: Little Land, Rebirth, the Virgin Lands* (1978; Mos-
    cow: International Publishers, 1980) 231-398 (p. 244). Brezhnev, a Par-
    ty official overseeing the program at that time, repeats the World War
    II and the Virgin Lands campaign throughout his memoir (pp. 249,
    253, 297-98, 310, 329).
4   *Pozdravitel'naya otkrytka v Rossii (konets XIX veka–nachalo XX veka)*, ed.
    Yuri Kombolin (St. Petersburg: Trade House Konstantin, 1994).
5   Personal communication from Michael Rouland, a close student of
    Central Asian history and culture.
6   Brezhnev, *Trilogy*, 236, 247, passim. See Katerina Clark, *The Soviet Nov-
    el: History as Ritual* (Chicago: University of Chicago Press, 1985), for
    the mentor figure in Soviet fiction.
7   Brezhnev, *Trilogy*, 321.
8   Ibid, 250, 266-67, 353, 380.
9   Ibid, 324.
10 Ibid, 233.
11 Ibid, 301.
12 Ibid, 374-75. For the wartime brigades, see Stites, "Frontline Enter-
    tainment" in *Culture and Entertainment in Wartime Russia*, ed. R. Stites
    (Bloomington: Indian University Press, 1995) 126-40 (or below here,
    329-348). Al. Romanov, *Lyubov Orlova v iskusstve i v zhizni* (Moscow:
    Iskusstvo, 1987) makes no mention of this episode.

13 William Taubman, *Khrushchev: the Man and his Era* (New York: Norton, 2003), 263.

14 Stites, *Russian Popular Culture*, 144-45 and 222 n. 28. Kopelev quoted in Gerald Stanton Smith, *Songs to Seven Strings: Russian Guitar Poetry and Soviet "Mass Song"* (Bloomington: Indiana University Press, 1984) 42.

15 See Gail Lapidus, *Women and Soviet Society* (Berkeley: University of California Press, 1978) and Stites, *The Women's Liberation Movement in Russia* (Princeton: Princeton University Press, 1978); Victoria Bonnell, *Iconography of Power: Soviet Political Posters under Lenin and Stalin* (Berkeley: University of California Press, 1997).

16 Woll, *Real Images*, the best book on 1950s cinema in English, discusses *The Soldier Ivan Brovkin* (pp. 14-16), but not its sequel. She quotes (p. 149) a puzzling 1962 attack on quite another film, but endorsing *Ivan Brovkin*: "Everyone knows that when *Ivan Brovkin* came out, 25,000 tractor and combine drivers set out for the Virgin Lands territories. That's what the Party wants." Woll indexes the quote under *The Soldier Ivan Brovkin*, though the reference seems to be for the sequel.

19

The Pawnbroker
Holocaust, Memory, and Film

I have been using films in courses for a number of years—on Russian popular culture; the United States and the USSR in the 20th century; and, most recently, Europe in World War II: History and Film, designed as a pro-seminar for first-year students in the School of Foreign Service at Georgetown University. Except for a few clips, I use full-length films, mostly fiction features ranging from black-and-white ones of the 1930s to more recent releases from Germany, Russia, and the United States. Only with the complete film can the student get a real sense of the story, the characters, and the historical content. I have a block of two two-hour classes in a media room. I usually give a lecture on a Tuesday and we watch the film on Thursday. For longer films, I shorten the Tuesday lecture and start the film showing which is completed on Thursday—with some time set aside for discussion. This is supplemented with short papers integrating lectures, films, and readings. The final research paper requires work at the Library of Congress and/or the U.S. Holocaust Memorial Museum and Research Center. Judging from feedback, this has been the most successful course of my 48-year teaching career.

Although the course ranges far and wide over various campaigns and home fronts, the Holocaust plays a key role, from the first weeks (a clip from *Der ewige Jude*, followed by *The Wannsee Conference* and *Schindler's List*) to the last film, *Judgment at Nuremburg*. Needless to say, other films, such as *The Pianist*, would make a good fit. Since my course is not on the Holocaust *per se*, it does not address the experience of survival after the war, and for that reason I want to talk about a film that is in my view the most moving depiction of that experience, superior even to another fine treatment of the theme, *Sophie's Choice*.

I have chosen the American film, Sidney Lumet's *The Pawn-broker* (1964). Why? Because until the release of Steven Spielberg's *Schindler's List* in 1993, which now tops my list, I considered Lumet's the finest American fiction feature movie ever made about the Holocaust and, as I hope to demonstrate, belongs in any course on the Holocaust where film is used. The story centers around Sol Nazerman, a New York pawnbroker and Holocaust survivor. His searing experience in Europe and the loss of his wife and children have left him bereft of human sympathy—an embittered, heartless shell of a man. In and out of his shop come down-and-out ghosts of Harlem's underlife—an abandoned pregnant girl, drug addicts, Caribbean hooligans, déclassé white folks on the skids, a pitiful self-educated black man. Nazerman treats them all with icy indifference and wards off the sympathetic attentions of his Puerto Rican shop assistant and a well-meaning social worker. Tragedy again assaults him at the end as new evil forces beyond his control—personified by a pimp played by the magnificent Brock Peters, fresh from *To Kill a Mockingbird*—conspire to bring violence into his life and transform him into a full human being once again.

Pawnbroker—a New York film, a memory film, and a Holocaust film—lights up the screen on many levels: acting, direction, sets, music (by Quincy Jones), and especially cinematography.[1] As to the last, Lumet had previously teamed up with cameraman Boris Kaufman in *Twelve Angry Men* (1957). Kaufman was one of three talented brothers who made silent movies in the Soviet Union during the 1920s. One brother, Mikhail, played the title role in the Moscow documentary *Man with a Movie Camera* (1929); the director of that film was the third brother who adopted the name Dziga Vertov. While Vertov went on to became one of the world's leading experimental documentary filmmakers and theoreticians, Boris Kaufman emigrated to the United States. He did not carry with him the fast-cutting montage of that early Soviet era. Instead he worked in a gritty realistic mode. Two moments in *Pawnbroker*, among many, stand out for sheer visual evocation: the low-angle camera shot of the lawnmower brought in to be pawned by petty crooks and the gloomy panorama of dawn over Manhattan—

a scene whose desperation is matched visually only by the alcoholic's tortured trek through the city in Billy Wilder's *The Lost Weekend* (1945).

Rod Steiger, already eminent for his role in *On the Waterfront* (1954), here renders his finest performance, reaching a dramaturgical and psychological climax in a monologue where, in "teaching" his young ambitious helper about money, he launches into an impassioned capsule history of his people. "You begin with several thousand years during which you have nothing except a great, bearded legend," doomed to a peripatetic mercantile existence. In this shocking sequence, Nazerman opens his bitter sermon in a professorial tone, rises in frenzy, and ends with a guttural screaming of the epithets applied to the Jew down through the ages—"a sheeny, a mockie, and a kike." The scene can be disturbing, even offensive, to Jew and Gentile alike—and yet it is essential in etching Nazerman's pain and isolation in the form of historical consciousness.[2]

The actual scenes of the Holocaust—restrained and stylized— all appear in flashback. This is where the emotional power of the film is at its strongest. The memory of a single survivor, stripped of piety and self-pity, has turned him into a twisted though less lethal and totally non-ideological version of his cruel persecutors. He is immune to the suffering around him. As he begins to realize the delusions under which he is living, the anguish deepens—cleverly enhanced by the oft-used device of flashing light from his eyeglasses and at the tragic end by a wordless scream of pain that artists and filmmakers have been employing since the time of Goya.

The film has nothing to say about Hitler or the Nazis as political phenomena. It tracks the impact of horror on a Jewish survivor in America 15 to 20 years after the event. By the mid-1950s, as two eminent historians have argued, most American Jews—having lost no immediate family in that European tragedy—were thriving, and public expressions of anti-Semitism were taboo.[3] Holocaust memory, though never dead, had been driven deep into the consciousness, and writing creatively about it remained an agonizing task.[4] Putting it on screen still posed a challenge to a Hollywood whose largely Jewish magnates had almost always shied away from Jewish themes in their movies.[5]

In those years, the writer Edward Louis Wallant had been

sitting in a relative's pawnshop observing its ways. And while studying at the Pratt Institute in New York, he met a survivor of the death camps.[6] His 1961 novel, *The Pawnbroker*, became the basis for Lumet's film. Reviewing it in the *New Republic*, film critic Stanley Kauffman wondered why, since so many other Jews had "adjusted" to something like a normal life, a Sol Nazerman was created to represent the experience.[7] No one can answer this question.

The literature on Holocaust survivors is immense and can easily be marshaled as the historical context of this film, if only to show the wide variety of responses to their tortured past. The film appeared in 1964, barely 20 years after the liberation of the death camps in Europe and at a moment in American history when moviegoers were being fed largely by big budget technicolor productions. A fruitful assignment might be student interviews of survivors who saw the film at the time of its release. Another would be to contrast it with the stories told in William B. Helmreich's *Against All Odds: Holocaust Survivors and the Successful Lives They Made in America.*[8] The kind of closure embodied in *The Pawnbroker* complicates the story of Holocaust memory. When set against, say, the documentary epilogue of *Schindler's List*, the range of discussion will unroll in and of itself about how history, fiction, and film shape each other in the popular mind. What could all this mean to 18- to 22-year-old moviegoing students who are trying to come to grips with a distant past?[9]

For a course in Jewish history, the monologue on the Diaspora alone would provide ample provocation for discussion. And for the really adventurous among those who teach courses on New York City or on film noir, the colorful cast of multiethnic characters, and Harlem itself as contrasted to the blandness of the Long Island suburb where Nazerman lives, and the very darkness of the story, the photography, and the setting all offer a chance to depress, elevate, enlighten students, and perhaps even transform the way they, as historians, will henceforth look at movies—in or out of the classroom.

Original publication: American Historical Society *Perspectives on History* 46.1, January 2008, pp. 30-31.

Notes

1   Sidney Lumet, *Making Movies* (New York: Vintage, 1996).

2   The script version is even harsher than the novel's original: Edward Louis Wallant, *The Pawnbroker* (New York: Macfadden, 1962), 43.

3   Maurice Isserman and Michael Kazin, *America Divided: The Civil War of the 1960s* (New York: Oxford University Press, 2000), 252-53.

4   Irving Howe, *World of Our Fathers* (New York: Schocken, 1976), 626-27.

5   Neal Gabler, *An Empire of their Own: How the Jews Invented Hollywood* (New York: Pantheon, Doubleday, 1988). For German "silence" on the Holocaust in the same period, see David Cook, *A History of Narrative Film*, 2d ed. (New York: Norton, 1990), 853-54.

6   David Galloway, *Edward Louis Wallant* (Boston: Twayne, 1979), 156.

7   Stanley Kauffman, *A World on Film* (New York: Dell, 1966), 132.

8   William B. Helmreich, *Against All Odds: Holocaust Survivors and the Successful Lives They Made in America* (New Brunswick: Transaction Publishers, 1996).

9   The very useful *Teaching about the Holocaust: A Resource Book for Educators* (Washington: The United States Holocaust Memorial Museum, 2001) lists histories, memoirs, novels, and films, but makes no mention of *The Pawnbroker*.

Wars Hot and Cold

20

Frontline Entertainment

The frontline concert brigade (*kontsertnaia frontovaia brigada*) was a particular kind of performance vehicle that fit perfectly into the wartime design for reaching the troops with art that was entertaining, uplifting, morale-building, and of course politically correct. In it one finds a mix of virtually all the performing arts as well as a close interlock with nonperforming arts (cartooning, fiction). Neither its content nor its form was novel. The mixture of genres on stage goes back to European and prerevolutionary Russian traditions of variety show and cultural evening (called in Russian *vecher* or *kontsert*) that were preserved in Soviet performance art. Revolutionary spectacles, *estrada* (popular stage) concerts, workers' club entertainments, and even Kremlin command performances—all featured a blend of "high" and "middlebrow" numbers, verbal texts, music, and dance. The men and women who staffed the brigades in World War II came from theater, concert hall, ballet, opera, the world of popular music (stage, recording, and radio), folk ensembles, circus, puppetry, standup comedy, literature, and the movies. The cultural offering was correspondingly eclectic: at one end the light genres; at the other, the classics. Like Soviet radio, the brigades offered a mix; and to add to that mix, troops frequently performed for the performers: singing their own songs or "delivering" shells and bombs, autographed by entertainers, to the enemy after the concert.[1]

In form, the wartime brigades were a revival of the mobile agitation units sent to the front on trucks, trains, and riverboats during the Russian Civil War. In the 1920s, mobile culture was practiced with great vigor by youth, women's, and godless organizations, though entertainment was often subservient to numbingly dull political messages. During the stormy years of collectivization and cultural revolution, more organized cultural "crusades" were unleashed on the countryside. Once artists came under full centralized control in the early 1930s, they were expected not only to avoid certain themes and cleave to certain aesthetic rules (those of "socialist realism"), but also to carry out tasks assigned to them by the state, to mount concerts in factories and military units across the country, and to forge formal links (called *sheftsvo*) with the armed forces, enterprises, and institutions. Theaters and orchestras toured the peacetime barracks, camps, and naval bases; and when sporadic fighting broke out in the Soviet Far East with Japan in the late 1930s, companies were sent there as well. This activity was upgraded for the wars in Eastern Poland, Bukovina, and Finland in 1939-40 and greatly amplified after the German invasion of 1941.[2]

The production of popular culture during the war was a result of both voluntarism and mobilization, but the latter occurred to a degree undreamed of in other belligerent states, even Nazi Germany. This was especially true of live performance. The main organs of control and deployment were the Committee on the Arts, the Central Committee of RABIS (the Union of Art Workers—a startling formulation in itself). These committees, composed of thoroughly politicized art bureaucrats, received orders from military authorities and other organs and carried them out with great vigor. That mobilization of the arts began on the very first day of the war, June 22, 1941, is not such a remarkable thing given the long experience alluded to (see Kenez, this volume, for cinema mobilization). On day two of the invasion, RABIS sent out a circular to embarkation points, recruiting offices, and railroad stations informing troops that "wherever units of the army or navy can be found, art workers will be sharing their lives. Now as never before, art will be a mighty and warlike means of victory of communism over fascism."[3]

The organizational, numerical, and geographical scope of this operation was enormous by the standards of the time. To the front lines, the rear areas, and the towns were dispatched local branches of theaters, whole theater companies, and mixed brigades. RABIS was assisted by the Moscow TsDRI (Central House of the Arts), the Chief Political Administration of the Army, and other groups.

Artists and performers of every kind could be seen lining up at TsDRI, waiting for assignments: the soprano A. V. Nezhdanova, the composer Dmitrii Kabalevskii, the architects A. V. Shchusev and Lev Rudnev, the painter Pavel Konchalovskii, and the pianist, Vladimir Sofronitskii. A typical order mandated on July 16, 1942, that the students in the fourth year at the State Institute of Theatrical Arts, Russia's main drama school, were to evacuate along with the Moscow Arts Theater to Saratov, there to form frontline theatrical brigades. A few scattered figures will give a sense of the tempo and density of activity. By October 1941, the government had sent out forty-two *estrada* brigades; by May 1942, sixty-one. At the local level, in Moscow Oblast during the first week (June 22-July 2), 450 concerts involving 700 artists were performed; and by early September, 3,000 concerts and fifty spectacles were mounted in the city of Moscow alone. As the Germans were approaching Leningrad, the authorities sent out Agit-Trucks with speakers and performers, including the noted film actor Nikolai Cherkasov, star of the 1938 anti-German film, *Aleksandr Nevskii.* In Rostov Oblast, thirty-six brigades with 992 artists gave over five hundred concerts. Odessa during the first ten days presented 250 concerts; Ordzhonikidze, 140; Irkutsk, 184.[4]

Various flat and probably inflated claims have been made about the total picture. About 3,800 theater-concert and circus brigades were formed and deployed in the first year of the war, 700 from Moscow, 500 from Leningrad, and the rest from elsewhere. One participant claims that some 45,000 artists serving in 3,720 brigades performed over 400,000 concerts at the front. A similar claim puts it at 42,000 artists in around half a million performances. Another, more modest estimate, talks of more than 100,000 performances given at the front in the war years. Six hundred stage artists were decorated. Real totals may never be known, since many performances were unnoted or uncounted. Because of the huge numbers of troops and their vast dispersion, the brigades could never have saturated the armed forces. What impresses is the variety of places visited and the sheer mobility of civilian entertainment brigades in a war and a country noted for transport hunger. Although older and infirm artists and those needed to perform for the bigwigs stayed at home, a large number of the prewar stars of stage and screen appeared in front of the soldiers and sailors. How many troops were reached? If official figures were exaggerated, they may have been balanced by the fact that concerts were given in shifts—to dragged-out troops just relieved, pilots back from raids, ships pulling in to ports—thus extending the outreach that was recorded.[5]

The brigades made their way to every front on warplanes, boats, trains, and wagons, by cutter through mined waters, along a front bombed and shelled, across mine fields, arriving at trenches, bathhouses, and foxholes. Sometimes they got lost or were stopped by sentries and sent back. Impromptu forest theaters with stage and dressing rooms were organized; more often the "theater" was a glade, an open field, a truck bed, the deck of a warship, a hangar (see illustration below). The comedienne M. Mironova, dressed in a light blue ball gown and silver slippers, regaled her audience from a float in the middle of a swamp. Standup comedian Vladimir Khenkin did his routines right on an airfield: the concert would stop, pilots would mount up, fly off and drop bombs, and then return to yell for a continuation of the show. Conversely, German air raids or offensives often provided "intermissions"—lasting as long as three hours. Actors sometimes had to help build defenses. In battle, some were caught in the fire, killed, or wounded. One touring company captured by the Germans was thrown alive into a well. Artists traveled light, usually without sets or costumes, though the troops preferred realistic re-creations of the original sets, theater, and costumes. Memoirs of performers cite audience size ranging from three to 1,000.[6]

Concert during a lull in fighting. *Illiustrirovannaia istoriia SSSR* (Moscow: Mysl', 1974), 375.

Performances were held on all points of the compass: Vladivostok, a monastery in the Carpathian Mountains, Murmansk, Northern Norway, the polar seas, the Black and Baltic Seas—and hundreds of points between. Asians from warm climes wrapped in fur hats and quilted jackets found themselves in snowy north Russia in the fall of 1942 when the First Tadzhik Frontline Brigade put on national songs, dances, and comedy. Ethnic variety prevailed in the brigades: Jews, Poles, Asians, Caucasians, even recently vanquished Baits. Between jaunts to the front, artists raised morale in the rear-area cities. In Moscow, the popular big-band leader, Leonid Utesov, on learning about the invasion, quickly abandoned a concert of music adapted from Ivan Dzerzhinskii's 1935 opera *Quiet Don* to a program of patriotic songs. Satirist Nikolai Smirnov-Sokolovskii quickly invented the monologue, "Hitler will be Beaten." Actors' groups known as "Living Newspaper" offered poster-like crudity to induce high emotional responses. In beleaguered cities like Odessa, the *politotdel* (political arm) of the Communist Party ordered the formation of a brigade which gave five or six concerts every day during the seventy-three agonizing days of the siege. These concerts offered local patriotic and Jewish motifs in their songs and comedy acts: as the siege ended the entertainers boarded one of the last evacuation ships to the Northern Caucasus, where they continued to entertain. Leningrad witnessed 25,000 performances during the three-year blockade. When the only remaining theater in the city, the Musical Comedy, opened, it was filled every night in spite of cold, hunger, shells, and sale of tickets for bread rations (400 grams per ticket).[7]

What kind of cultural offerings did the brigades bring with them? Music, readings, poems, dance, one-act plays, scenes, lectures, circus acts, comedy routines. The very first artists to hit the frontline circuit represented in miniature the shape of the coming enterprise: literary readers Sergei Balashov and N. Efros; comedians Mikhail Garkavi, Vladimir Khenkin, Lev Mirov, E. Darskii, V. A. Dykhovichyi, M. Raskatov; singers Lidiia Ruslanova and Klavdiia Shul'zhenko; dance team Anna Redel and Mikhail Khrustalëv. To urban Russians (or those ruralists who possessed a radio), these were household names from the world of contemporary entertainment.

Soviet performers thus brought not only cherished songs, poems, and plays—but also the pleasure of live celebrities who needed no more introduction to the Russian combatant than did the names of their American counterparts to GIs: Eddie Cantor, Al Jolson, Bing Crosby, Judy Garland, Jack Benny, or Bob Hope. Differences in style were significant, to be sure: there were no poetry readers or folk ensembles in the American armed forces entertainment network.

Poetry and prose readings had long been part of the Russian scene in public events. Russians adore the music of their language and the expressiveness of verse and rhyme; they listen with rapture to public readings live or on the radio. In choosing material to be uttered to the troops, it became apparent at once that the defiant and declamatory hoorah-patriotic themes of the immediate prewar period and the early months of the war struck a dissonant chord. Readers and reciters—mostly actors from stage and radio—had to find the right voice and tone in order to avoid the ring of falsity. They culled the classics with great care. Pushkin's epic poem, "Battle of Poltava," could easily be applied to the hope for another decisive victory over a foreign invader.[8] The verse of the revolutionary poet Vladimir Maiakovskii inspired Sergei Balashov, a theater actor and dramatic reader for the stage and radio. He gave live one-man readings of Russian, Soviet, and foreign prose and poetry replete with gestures, costumes, and music. In the war, he declaimed Maiakovskii's verses on a submarine and among tankers and—a habit of many—wrote some verses on a torpedo to be "delivered" to a German ship hull. From Mikhail Lermontov, Lev Tolstoy, and Maxim Gorky, actors drew well-quoted passages memorized by Soviet schoolchildren as well as fresh works by the Soviet writers Mikhail Sholokhov, Konstantin Simonov, Aleksei Surkov, and Aleksandr Tvardovskii. Foreign classics were sometimes used to unmask the difference between "good Germans" and Nazis. Heinrich Heine's satire helped to explain German barbarism. (The use of a Heine monument in the Soviet occupation zone of Germany for this contrast can also be found in the famous postwar film, *Meeting on the Elbe*.) Nonfiction readings of essays, newspaper articles, and pamphlets were occasionally offered as a way of giving voice to journalism.[9]

The whole idea of comedy on the Soviet warfront may come as

a surprise to Westerners who have been led (by misunderstanding and distortion emanating from both sides) to see Russians as fundamentally humorless, and to those who see nothing funny about war. The latter assumption also disturbed some Soviet critics in the early months of the war, until it was shown that soldiers—even those who lay dying in hospital—wanted to laugh at the old familiar foibles of everyday life as well as at the German enemy. Stage comedy, though constricted by political censorship, had never disappeared from public life in the USSR, and a whole generation of radio and stage personages were at hand to generate cathartic laughter. Humor of another time and place may not travel well over the decades, but a stretch of the cultural imagination may help explain why soldiers guffawed to this rich and cruel ditty recited by comedians at the front after the German defeat at Stalingrad:

> Frau Greta hasn't slept for days.
> Her Fritz does not respond
> To all those letters she has sent
> To the back of the beyond.
> "Mein Gott, what's happened to my Fritz
> Who's fighting on the Volga,
> And battling near some Stalingrad,"
> Thinks poor, distraught Frau Greta.
> It's time to realize, dear Frau,
> Your letters will not reach him now.
> Fritz is gone and simply is:
> "No Longer at This Address."[10]

On the same theme, Stalingrad, a comedian acted out a famous wartime poster showing Hitler in a wedding dress, weeping because he lost his "ring", i.e., the twenty-two German divisions encircling Stalingrad. Stand-up performers from the capitals like Arkadii Raikin, later to be the king of the Soviet comedy stage, maintained a certain level—hilarious but correct—of urban amusement. Others, like Iurii Timoshenko and Efim Berëzin had worked together before the war and, when drafted, began to do shows based on their invented characters, Galkin the Cook and Mochalkin the Bath Attendant. Their skits, dialogue, ditties, dances, and routines were drawn from life on the company street, dugout, and front line. It was loose, unstructured, improvised, and coarse, resembling village fun-making, wedding parties, toasts, and jokes as well as prerevolutionary folk fair entertainment. Timoshenko used an exaggerated Ukrainian accent and vocabulary to project a bumpkin image—in a way that was, at the time in many places, nonoffensive. The down-to-earth quality of this entertainment was also found in the numerous adaptations of Tvardovskii's picaresque farce, *Vasilii Tërkin,* one of the most popular wartime writings, but probably known better to the troops in its acted versions than in the original written one.[11]

The warring nations of 1939-45 showed an extraordinary tendency to exalt and revere classical music and, through media promotion, turn it into something like a popular art (see Robinson, this volume). The occupied nations treasured their own musical heritage, particularly the romantic productions of the previous century. The music of Dvořák, Chopin, Rachmaninov, and Grieg on American radio and in movies was associated with the heroic struggles of beleaguered peoples. In war-racked Russia the most mournful strains of Chopin, Beethoven, and Chaikovskii filled the concert halls and airwaves. Liudmila Shaposhnikova, a drama student touring the front, thought that many of the troops were unprepared for classical music, and indeed had never heard any. But in fact, they received it well, although some of the pious accounts of audience reception—like accounts of the masses in 1917-18 hearing their first concerts—ought to be taken with caution. Most of the classical offerings were art songs, arias, or solo instrumental selections—usually squeezed in beside popular entertainment. For obvious logistical reasons, no one had to sit through Beethoven's *Eroica Symphony* or Wagner's *Ring.* For example, after a violinist at the front played Chaikovskii's "Sentimental Waltz" accompanied by a guitarist, the latter then played the famous popular wartime song, "Dark Is the Night," from the movie *Two Warriors.* The dancer Tamara Tkachenko—later famous as a folk choreographer—recalls giving fifty-one performances in seventeen days in the region of the old Napoleonic invasion route. Her company included *estrada* and radio stars and the extremely popular folk singer Lidiia Ruslanova.[12]

What about martial music at the front? This was, perhaps not surprisingly, less popular than it had been in the period of military buildup and war scares of the late 1930s. Songs about the armed forces (such as the famous "Katiusha") were important as self-entertainment when sung by the troops; and "patriotic songs" about love of the land had wide appeal. Big bands—jazz or pop orchestras—used them regularly in frontline concerts. But those about combat—fighting, action, violence—were avoided by the brigade performers. Viktor Belyi and Iakov Frenkel (a proletarian composer and a mass-song lyric writer) wrote "Song of Five Heroes," about "five sons of the Motherland" who are killed in a tank battle. But combatants did not care to hear this kind of song when being entertained, though they did sing them themselves (see Rothstein, this volume). Military bands were of course ubiquitous, as in all armies, and the big ones went on tour. The giant Red Army ensemble split itself into four detachments and went off to different sectors. Half of their 1,500 concerts were given at the front. But their repertoire was as much "folkish" as it was martial.[13]

The explosion of officially promoted and spontaneously organized folk performance art in the Patriotic War is one of the most visible signs—of which this volume speaks so many times—of the deepening nationalism, traditional nostalgia, and collective emotionalism of those who fought and suffered in it. It is also a prime example of how the goals of the regime and popular feelings could be temporarily fused in cultural forms. The folk revival had begun in the mid-1930s as part of Stalin's cultural legitimation program, and the folk ensemble with peasant costumes and balalaikas became a familiar part of the cultural landscape. In wartime, these ensembles were sent to the front; and by 1944 the folk revival had erupted into a major cultural wave of festivals in Moscow, recently liberated Leningrad, Rostov, Gorky, Sverdlov, and Saratov; at the last concert nine hundred singers from thirteen choirs joined forces. The most popular folksinger of the era, Lidiia Ruslanova, was among the most wanted entertainers in the frontline brigades. Military units with no access to the mobile brigades put on their own amateur folk productions. However it may have been exploited for political purposes in other times, the groundswell of folk music reflected the depth of national feelings ignited by the struggle for existence.[14]

The bandleader Leonid Utësov once claimed that song had more instant emotional power than mere verse, in that the music added feelings to the words. There can be no question that song, especially what is loosely known as popular song, held the greatest emotional sway for the audiences of the entertainment brigades. The range of requests by the troops was very wide, but tilted toward love songs, nostalgic romances, and the light and frothy melodies of prewar days, including those from musical comedy films sung by Liubov' Orlova and written by Russia's foremost popular songwriter, Isaac Dunaevskii. Frontline fighters did intone solemn hymns such as the emotionpacked "Sacred War," but preferred hearing other things from the brigade entertainers. Pop and jazz reigned supreme.[15]

Among the songbirds who delivered what was desired at the front, by far the most famous—then and in memory—was Klavdiia Ivanovna Shul'zhenko. Caught in Erivan when war broke out, she and her colleagues in the Jazz Ensemble of Vladimir Koralli entrained to Leningrad and volunteered to tour the front. They went straight from the train station to headquarters and were enrolled in the army—Shul'zhenko holding the rank and uniform of a private. She recalled her first sortie to the front on a bus through the city drenched in autumn rain, past deserted buildings with windows like blinded eyes, empty trams arrested on their tracks like frozen cattle, monster-like flak balloons rising from frozen bridges and canals. Sharing the hunger, fatigue, and fear of the massing troops, she and her comrades gave concerts in the morning for departing units, in the afternoon for the wounded, and in the evening to those in the rear—all accompanied by crashing shells and bombs. Shul'zhenko gave five hundred performances in one year alone. Like other artists, she worried about the appropriateness of her "light" prewar fare—love songs, tangos, and foxtrots—given the somberness of front life. And like those others, she was persuaded by the warriors themselves who begged her to sing "the old songs" of love. A pilot, on seeing Shul'zhenko in uniform, asked her to put on a peacetime dress "so that things will be as in the prewar days."

So Shul'zhenko—or Klava, as the troops called her—sang her 1930s hits about old love letters, about "fiery Chelitas and ornery Lolitas," about sadness and lost affection. These were sentimental, eminently personal and intimate romances that had once been assaulted by sturdy "proletarians" as counter-revolutionary. Like her counterparts Vera Lynn of England, Zara Leander (a Swede by birth) of Germany, and Edith Piaf of France, Shul'zhenko's appeal was in her style: the gestures, the clarion voice, and the unabashed but skillfully deployed emotionalism made her a national icon. Lt. General of the Air Force Vasilii Golubev said later, in the pious rhetoric of postwar recollection, that her songs were as necessary as bombs and shells in the war. Women and men combatants alike saluted her, wrote to her, shared meals with her. Soon she became the most celebrated entertainer in the country. An airman about to bailout of his crippled plane heard her voice on the radio and flew in on "one wing." Her biggest hit was "Little Blue Kerchief," which became her theme song. In February 1942 she sang it in the film, *Concert for the Front Lines* (*Kontsert-frontu*), a morale-builder starring among others the actor Igor Il'inskii, Raikin, Utësov, Ruslanova, and the clown Karandash. As a film it was a show about show people, roughly equivalent to Hollywood's *Stage Door Canteen* and to the German UFA Studio's *Wunschkonzert.* Shul'zhenko was named Meritorious Artist of the RSFSR in September 1945.[16]

The success of big-band jazz was the result of three things: the genuine popularity it had achieved during those years in the 1920s and 1930s when it was not being persecuted; the concessions to popular taste that differentiated the years 1941-45 from those before and after; and the American alliance. Without discounting the power of emotional memory, one reason that millions looked back (and some still do) with nostalgia to the war years was the looser cultural milieu of the time. Soviet jazz of the 1930s, like that in Nazi Germany, had been curtailed and smoothed out in the manner of American "high-society" bands who promoted the sweet over the hot. The big bands of Boris Renskii, Iakov Skomorovskii, Aleksandr Tsfasman, Utësov, and others played American tunes such as "All of Me" and "Sunny Side of the Street." There was so much demand for jazz music by the troops that railwaymen, aviators, cooks, and the NKVD formed their own outfits. A group of students at the Leningrad Conservatory formed the Sympho-Jazz Ensemble and toured the front. When the American film *Sun Valley Serenade* appeared on Soviet screens in 1944, the popularity of Glenn Miller's style rose to new heights.[17] The best wartime jazz leader was "Eddie"

(Adolph, but called Adi or Edi) Rosner, a Berlin-born son of a Polish-Jewish émigré. Rosner fled into Soviet territory at the beginning of the war and ended up in Moscow, from where he toured the front with his band. An admirer of the American trumpeter and band leader, Harry James, Rosner banished the balalaika and concertina from his orchestra and played straight American jazz.[18]

If Rosner was the most "authentic" jazz-band-leader, Leonid Utësov (Vaisbein, or Weissbein, 1895-1982) was certainly the most eclectic and popular. Born in Odessa, he had made a career in pre-revolutionary Jewish vaudeville and became a jazz pioneer in the 1920s and then the star of a zany but spectacularly successful musical-comedy film of the 1930s. When war began, he mobilized his band and, with Moscow as his base, ventured to the Urals, Siberia, the Soviet Far East, the front near Kalinin (Tver), and to the Volkhov front, with his daughter Edit as vocalist. His touring cycle, totaling more than two hundred concerts, resembled those of the Agit-Trains of the Civil War period. His band appeared in Leningrad and in his home town, Odessa, after these cities were freed from German occupation and blockade.

Utësov's shows were pure *estrada*: a synthesis of big-band music, pop and patriotic songs, comedy, and dance. His slapstick humor, which owed much to the Marx brothers and Ted Lewis, but had been curbed in the late 1930s, was now permitted full scope. Utësov had an ear for the currently popular. He staged the immortal "Wait for Me" with a reply sung by a female voice "I'll Wait for You;" and when his band played "Dark Is the Night" at a Moscow theater, the audience stood up to sing along. A careful impresario, he could bow to official solemnity by composing the "Knight's Fantasy" (Bogatyrskaia Fantasiia), blending themes from the Battle of Poltava and victory over Napoleon in 1812, and by playing Dunaevskii's anthem-like "Song of Motherland," Shostakovich's Leningrad Symphony, and the exalted "Sacred War." But he could also combine a tribute to Russia's allies with the desires of his audience in songs like "It's a Long Way to Tipperary" and "Bombardiers" (sung in English and Russian by Edit Utësova), a straight adaptation of the American hit, "Comin' in on a Wing and a Prayer." Even anti-Nazi novelty tunes about Baron Zilch and Fieldmarshal Filthy were reminiscent of Spike Jones's once-famous "Right in der

Führer's Face." During the siege of Odessa, Utësov sang "Mickey (Mishka) of Odessa" over the airwaves:

> You're Mickey of Odessa and you know what that means.
> That terror, fear, and sadness are absent from your soul.
> You're a seaman, Mickey, and sailors never cry.
> And never lose their courage or lose heart.

Utësov's great success lay in merging sweet-jazz elements with the wartime mood and employing the kind of topical pathos that the American Al Jolson did at about the same time by adding a generous portion of "heart" to every song he sang.[19]

The theater world did not remain stationary. The All-Russian Theater Society called for a "defensive anti-fascist repertoire of modest format performances." In practice this meant Russian and European classics and Soviet prewar and wartime pieces. Mounted on stage also were special pastiches of Lenin's life and wisdom from plays and from movies such as *Man with a Gun*, a Civil War political melodrama of the 1930s. Some entire theater companies toured the front and the rear; others sent part of their staff as itinerant acting brigades to perform selected scenes—often flanked by musical and comedy shows. The Red Army Theater in Moscow vacated its mammoth star-shaped edifice, was evacuated to Sverdlovsk, and from there radiated teams to front or rear. The Malyi Theater actress, forty-one-year-old Elena Gogoleva, along with Igor Il'inskii and others, was dispatched to the west and south of Moscow to put on scenes from Aleksandr Ostrovskii, Shakespeare, Gorky, and others for about three weeks in the winter of 1942, doing forty shows at fifteen different points along the front. Bomber pilots in their audience thanked the brigade as they set out to give their own "concert" to the Germans. On the eve of its departure for the front in August 1942, a brigade from the world-famous Moscow Art Theater debated the relevance in wartime of a classical repertoire but were soon convinced by the soldiers' enthusiastic reception of Pushkin's *Stone Guest*, Dostoevskii's *Brothers Karamazov* (a dramatic reading), Chekhov's *Three Sisters*, and Satan's monologue from Gorky's *Lower Depths*.[20]

Light entertainment on stage receded in the rear area for a

while due to the harsh psychology of the moment and the need for blackouts. But it too was soon enlisted for the war. Circus and *estrada*, with their traditions of mobility and variety, were perfectly suited to frontline entertainment. In Moscow, a theater of light satire, Little Hawk (named after the Soviet pursuit plane), was launched by veteran actor David Gutman, who persuaded the authorities that a "fighting theater" was needed. Staffed by well-known writers, comedians, and musical figures, it offered barbed verses, sketches, and one-acters relevant to the war. Axis politicians were presented as losers: Vichy French leader Pierre Laval fell off a high wire; Romanian dictator Marshal Antonescu sang off key; strongman Mussolini could not lift his weights; and the boxer Hitler was knocked out. Front-theater troupes freely adopted these themes. In the circus, the great clowns Karandash, Vitalii Lazarenko, and the Durov brothers had only to re-costume their old political targets Kerenskii, Lord Curzon, and Makhno into Nazi villains. Karandash introduced a dog dressed as Goebbels to bark out a report to the Führer. The Durovs put on The Three Gs: Gitler (Hitler), Gimmler (Himmler), and Goebbels, all played by dogs. These characterizations, along with the perpetually freezing and miserable "Winter Fritz," were inspired by political cartoons and posters.[21]

Puppet theater, an art designed primarily for children in most Western countries, was a popular adult entertainment in Russia — before the war, and before the revolution. The Obraztsov Central Puppet Theater was divided into two teams at the start of war; one in Moscow, the other in Vladivostok, where it entertained sailors of the Pacific Fleet. The Far Eastern company returned to Moscow for a few days and then were off on a five-river journey which took the evacuated theater (hit by a bomb) to Ufa and then to Novorossiisk, which became its home. The puppeteers put on more than four hundred shows in towns and villages, army camps and hospitals, frontline dugouts and partisan forest encampments. Among their acts were a mini-operetta, "On the Rooftops of Berlin," with cats as the main characters and "Meeting of Dogs," with Hitler as a shepherd dog and Admiral Horthy, the political chief of Hungary, as a black mongrel who bites Antonescu.[22]

Operetta was another great night-out favorite of the Soviet urban population and had been since the turn of the century. By nature frothy and apolitical, it had suffered bumps in the early cultural revolutions but was legitimized by the mid-1930s. Grigorii Iaron, a longtime performer in the Moscow Operetta Theater, described the dilemmas of his art in time of war. On July 22, 1941, the company was giving a summer performance of the Viennese operetta *Silva* in the Mirror Theater of the Hermitage Garden in Moscow. In mid-performance, Iaron yelled "air raid" and although the audience wanted the show to continue, it was stopped. In October the theater was evacuated along with many others to the Volga. On returning to the capital the company resumed its work in early 1942 with *Wedding at Malinovka*, a 1937 farce about the Bolshevik struggle against the Ukrainian anarchist Nestor Makhno. Iaron claims that the audience felt a rare moment of identification with the present when the singing hero, surrounded by choristers from the Red Army Choir, promised revenge on the German occupiers of 1918.

War was no easier to blend into operetta than had been revolution. A few dealt directly with a wartime theme: *A Tale of the Forest*, about partisans; *The Ocean Covered Vast Expanses*, about sailors; and *Girl from Barcelona*, a fantastic concoction about a communist refugee to Russia from the Spanish Civil War menaced in 1941 by her ex-fiancé, who serves with the invading Spanish fascist Light Blue Division. An attempt to adapt the nineteenth-century nationalist popular fiction of Mikhail Zagoskin was not a success. Laughter, melody, and — yes — froth is what the public still wanted. *Silva* remained the undying favorite. *Maritza* by the same composer (Imre Kalmán) had not been done since 1915; when revived, it had to be purged of such lines as "I will dream about her belly button and her short transparent skirt."[23]

A word about self-entertainment at the front: this was encouraged by some commanders as a morale builder when there were no brigades and in the long hours and days between combat engagements. A talented performer would take the initiative or be ordered by an officer to organize shows from among the troops. Song and dance, accompanied by assorted instruments —guitar or accordion—were the staples. Since women served within or alongside many units in this war, sometimes the genders were mixed on stage doing dance styles of the time and of past time: hopak, waltz in a tap-dance manner, or the long-forgotten "Crimean Tatar Girl." Witnesses also describe spontaneous readings out loud from Ehrenburg, Simonov, Surkov, Tvardovskii, and Gorky or couplets, jokes, rhymes, sayings, and anti-fascist ditties. Iurii Nikulin, later a famous clown and then director of the Moscow Circus, got his first performance experience in the front lines as an amateur in the ranks.[24]

Did the Soviet experience with frontline entertainment differ in any substantial way from that of other belligerents? The only country to match it in scale was the United States, through the agency of the United Service Organizations (USO). Formed in 1941, it coordinated the voluntary efforts of Christian, Jewish, youth, and other private welfare agencies to provide various social and spiritual services to the armed forces. Its most visible function was troop entertainment provided by volunteers from radio, movies, the night club circuit, and even the legitimate stage. Like Soviet brigade members, American performers put on shows of mixed genres; unlike them, they offered very little in the way of classical selections and very much in the way of leggy females. USO troupes had to travel immense distances — Africa, Europe, the Pacific — to reach the fighting forces and, like the Soviet show-people, sometimes endured the danger of enemy fire. In both cases, they represented expressive links to the home front, supplemented by radio (see Von Geldern, this volume) and an occasional film. Verbal and photographic evidence of Soviet soldiers laughing at comedians recalls footage of the reaction of GIs in the Pacific to Bob Hope; and there is no reason to doubt that the catharsis of real laughter was authentic for both armies in the lull between battles.

We know very little about tensions between civilians and the military, audience and actors, officers and men, women and men, or ethnic groups. The brigades drew from all major nationalities; a fairly large percentage of the entertainers were Jewish, reflecting their prewar prominence in the arts and particularly in popular and mass culture.[25] Was there a hierarchy that determined who got to be entertained, such as officers, certain units, branches, proximity to front? Did privilege and power determine which performers served in brigades, as opposed to those who remained in the rear or those who got drafted and lost their lives as soldiers? (The circus aerialist, Ivan Shepetkov, was one of the twenty-eight Pan-filovites who perished before Moscow in 1941.)[26] Recollections of both performers and veterans about the relations between brigades and troops are bathed in mutual affection. Their descriptions of heroic men and women combatants are couched in folkloric and pious terms. Almost all the brigade entertainers recall the days of war with solemn joy. According to some, they were well fed and clothed, certainly better than most soldiers and most civilians too. One natural offshoot of the prewar *sheftsvo* relationship between the military and the entertainment world was fraternization and even intermarriage of elite officers and celebrities.[27]

On the content of entertainment and its impact on the troops we can speak with some certainty. Some of it was orchestrated from the center. Political officers, on orders from above, could manufacture spontaneities; and the programs, routes, and repertoires were closely screened, if not planned, much more than in other wartime societies, where censorship was more defensive and passive than active. This does not mean that there was no heart, no emotion, no room for ad-libbing in the relations between performer, genre, and audience. Soldiers were not averse to contemporary war themes, even though some performers wanted to delete the death of Arkadii in Simonov's play, A *Lad from Our Town*; evidence of repertoires shows that home-related themes were the most wanted and the most offered. In the case of jazz, it is clear that soldiers' own desires were considered. The troops wanted laughter, satire, and fun, song and dance; and they were happy to take small doses of high culture along with it. They were no more interested in seeing enacted battle scenes after a day of fighting (even if such scenes could be done believably) than had been workers in hearing industrial machinery concerts mounted during the Civil War.[28]

Wartime entertainment spread and deepened culture among the population. The evacuation of orchestras and theaters and the concerts and performances in out-of-the-way places was the cultural counterpart of the relocation of industry, which brought new kinds of markets and employment opportunities to far-flung regions. Even allowing for exaggeration and patriotic posturing and the nostalgia of the aged, one is struck by the glow of memory among the entertainers—for each other, for the men and women at arms, and for the general population in a bonding that few nations experienced in that war. This memory partly accounts for the vast and enduring popularity of those who performed at the front. About long-term influence upon the arts themselves one can speculate that performance styles changed and actors' understanding of life deepened. Many interrupted studies to go to the front, a move that delayed but did not hurt careers. The most historically interesting facet of wartime entertainment was that it expressed something like real values of millions of people on certain matters: not purges or executions or party politics; but on homeland and friendship, love and loyalty, gender roles and recent traditions. It showed a public resurgence of the "personal life, intimate feelings, deep emotional authenticity, and even quasi-religiosity" of which I spoke in chapter 1. The most terrible of all wars, for all its frantic cruelty and devastation, had revealed a closer glimpse of the heart and soul of a nation than had been seen for some time.

Original publication: *Culture and Entertainment in Wartime Russia*, Richard Stites, ed. Bloomington and Indianapolis: Indiana University Press, 1995, pp. 126-140.

In this essay, Stites refers to five other contributions to *Culture and Entertainment in Wartime Russia*:
p. 328: Peter Kenez, "Black and White: The War on Film," 157-175.
p. 334: Harlow Robinson, "Composing for Victory: Classical Music," 62-76.
p. 335: Robert A. Rothstein, "Homeland, Home Town, and Battlefield: The Popular Song," 77-94.
p. 342: James von Geldern, "Radio Moscow: The Voice from the Center," 44-61.
p. 344: Richard Stites, "Introduction: Russia's Holy War" (Chapter 1), 1-8.

Notes

1   For tsarist and revolutionary roots of military entertainment forms, see E. M. Kuznetsov, *Iz proshlogo russkoi estrady* (Moscow, 1958); Richard Stites, *Russian Popular Culture: Entertainment and Society since 1900* (Cambridge, Eng., 1992), chap. 1; Hubertus Jahn, *Patriotic Culture in Russia during World War I* (Ph.D. diss., Georgetown University, 1989); James Von Geldern, *Bolshevik Festivals, 1917-1920* (Berkeley, 1993);

Peter Kenez, *The Birth of the Propaganda State* (Cambridge, Eng., 1985); *Russkaia sovetskaia estrada*, ed. E. Uvarova, 3 vols. (Moscow, 1976), 1 (1917-30), 2 (1930-45), to be cited as RSE.

2   *Ocherki istorii russkogo sovetskogo dramaticheskogo teatra*, 3 vols. (Moscow, 1954-61; to be cited as OIRSDT); 2, 528-31.

3   O. A. Kuznetsova, "Estrada v period velikoi otechestvennoi voiny," RSE, 2, 371-97 (372).

4   *Iskusstvo v boevom stroiu: vospominaniia, dnevniki, ocherki* (Moscow, 1985), to be cited as IBS, pp. 15-26, 98; OIRSDT, 2, 529.

5   Kuznetsova; Irina Vasilinina, *Klavdiia Shul'zhenko* (Moscow, 1979), p. 60; on transport problems, see Holland Hunter, "Successful Spatial Management," in Susan Linz, ed., *The Impact of World War II on the Soviet Union* (Totowa, NJ, 1985), pp. 47-58.

6   Kuznetsova; IBS, pp. 23-24, 72; OIRSDT, 2, 533-34.

7   ISS, pp. 47-56, 72; Leonid Utësov, *S pesnei po zhizni* (Moscow, 1961), p. 176; Kuznetsova, p. 6 and passim. I. Zim, "Raskinulos more shiroko," *Sovetskaia kul'tura* (April 13, 1965): 1. Living Newspaper was a proletarian drama form that had risen in the 1920s.

8   At Poltava in 1709, Peter the Great inflicted a major defeat upon the Swedish invading forces.

9   IBS, pp. 8, 24; Kuznetsova; Sergei Balashov, "Slushaite, tovarishchi potomki," *Iskusstvo estrady: sbornik* (Moscow, 1964) pp. 13-78; OIRSDT, 2, 533.

10 G. Terikov, *Kuplet na estrade* (Moscow, 1987), p. 125; Lev Mirov and Evsei Darskii performed their entire routine before a burned and bandaged soldier in hospital: *Mastera estrady* (Moscow, 1964), p. 108.

11 For the constant interchange between poster art and theater, see N. I. Smirnova, *Sovetskii teatr kukol, 1918-1932* (Moscow, 1963), pp. 322-41; IB5, pp. 108-11; Iurii Dmitriev, "Dvadtsat' s gakom," *Teatr* 5 (1965): 105-109. For the comic roots: A. F. Nekrylova, *Russkie narodnye gorodskie prazdniki, uveseleniia i zrelishcha: konets XVIII-nachalo XX veka* (Leningrad, 1988) and Kuznetsov, *Iz proshlogo*. On *Tërkin*, see: *Sovetskie pisateli na frontakh Velikoi Otechestvennoi voiny*, vol. 78 of 2 parts *Literaturnoe nasledstvo*, (Moscow: Nauka, 1966), 1, 563-601.

12 IBS, pp. 20, 26-29, 249. On *Two Warriors* and its hit song, see Rothstein (this volume) and Stites, *Russian Popular Culture*, pp. 113-14.

13 *Pesni Velikoi Otechestvennoi voiny* (Moscow, 1945), a songbook published by the defense ministry, p. 14, for "Song of Five Heroes." General treatments: Rothstein (this volume - see Rothstein, here, before Note 1 - *ed*.); Suzanne Ament, "Soviet Songs of World War II" (ms.): Arnol'd Sokhor, *"Katyusha" M. I. Blantera* (Moscow, 1960).

14 Frank Miller, *Folklore for Stalin: Russian Folklore and Pseudo-folklore of*

the Stalin Era (Armonk, N.J., 1990); Stites, *Russian Popular Culture*, pp. 78-79, 108-109. On Ruslanova: S. Frederick Starr, *Red and Hot: the Fate of Jazz in the Soviet Union* (New York, 1983), p. 186; Leningrad Radio documentary on her life, January 19, 1990: *Muzykal'naia zhlzn'* (May 1975): 18-19; and *Poët Lidiia Ruslanova*, record sleeve notes.

15 Rothstein (this volume); Ament, "Soviet Songs of World War II"; Al. Romanov, *Liubov' Orlova v iskusstve i v zhizni* (Moscow, 1987), p. 192: P. F. Lebedev, *Pesni rozhdënnye v ogne* (Volgograd, 1983), p. 6; L. Dani-levich, *Muzyka na frontakh Velikoi Otechestvennoi voiny* (Moscow, 1948), p.22.

16 V. V. Dementev, *Pesni i sud'by soldatskie* (Tashkent, 1982); Vasilinina, *Klavdiia Shul'zhenko*, pp. 60-79.

17 As they occupied cities of Eastern Europe, Soviet authorities found and confiscated many movies — local and foreign, mostly German and American. "Chattanooga Choo-Choo" from *Sun Valley Serenade* be-came a virtual anthem for jazz fans. These were called "trophy films" and became very popular in postwar Russia: Starr, *Red and Hot*, pp. 193, 237-38; Stites, *Russian Popular Culture*, pp. 125-26; Kenez, *Cinema and Soviet Society, 1917-1953* (Cambridge, Eng., 1992), pp. 213-14. For jazz in Nazi Germany, see Michael Kater, *Different Drummers: Jazz in the Culture of Nazi Germany* (New York, 1992) and Detlev Peukert, *In-side Nazi Germany* (New Haven, 1987).

18 Starr, *Red and Hot*, pp. 183-94; IBS, p. 330.

19 Stites, *Russian Popular Culture*, pp. 103-110; Utësov, *S pesnei*, pp. 173-38; Dmitriev, *Leonid Utësov*; Starr, *Red and Hot*, pp. 183-94; *Leonid Utësov: Recordings of the Forties and Fifties*; *Leonid Utësov: zapisi 40-kh-50kh godov*.

20 OIRSDT, 2, 528-43; IBS. pp. 7-26, 59-66, and passim.

21 M. Krimker, "Pervyi frontovoi: k 25-letiiu moskovskoi bitvy," *Sovets-kaia estrada i tsirk*, 12 (Dec. 1966), 3; Kuznetsova; S. M. Makarov, *Sovets-kaia klounada* (Moscow, 1986), pp. 93-119.

22 Sergei Obraztsov, *My Profession* (Moscow, 1981); IBS, pp. 89-97. Hun-garian and Romanian troops participated in the invasion of Russia and still nurtured mutual hostility over Transylvania.

23 Grigorii Iaron, *O liubimom zhanre* (Moscow, 1960), pp. 193-206.

24 IBS, pp. 213-20, 271-84.

25 Jack Miller, *Jews in Soviet Culture* (New Brunswick, N.J., 1984), pp. 65-106.

26 OIRSDT, 2, 542-48; *Tsirk: malenkaia entsiklopediia* (Moscow, 1979), p. 373.

27 IBS, pp. 22, 25. On the military-theater linkup, see Stites, *Russian Popu-lar Culture*, pp. 69-70.

28 OIRSDT, 2, 535-39. For those concerts, Stites, *Revolutionary Dreams: Utopian Vision and Experimental Life in the Russian Revolution* (New York, 1989), p. 136.

21

Heaven and Hell
Soviet Propaganda Constructs the World

Three late Stalinist movies came out as the 1950s opened: *Composer Glinka,* on the depth and glory of Russian high culture; *Kuban Cossacks*, on the wealth and joy of Soviet life; and *Meeting on the Elbe,* on the menacing power of the main foe of the Soviet people: the United States. Together, they contained the basic conceptions of Soviet Cold War propaganda in the 1950s. The themes of heaven and hell—simplistically wrought in the films—were developed through the 1950s, reflecting new Soviet achievements (especially in space), new foreign interests (as in the Third World) and new menaces—real and perceived—from the West.

The Media

The weakness of tsarist propaganda in the First World War had reflected a basic distrust of popular sentiment for any cause. The private sphere of patriotic culture suffered from the disconnect between high and popular culture, one exalting the power of mind, the other of the body. These failures were largely overcome in the Bolshevik propaganda of the early years which contained two novel features: great experimental and artistic exuberance; and the welding of popular and high culture forms that exalted both the physical bravery and the spiritual (i.e., revolutionary) energy of the Russian people. In the Stalinist 1930s, artistic innovation was abandoned and the system of 'socialist realism' that replaced it was far more stodgy. But it did have some success in closing the mind-body gap: in literature by the thematic use of robust and muscular proletarians guided spiritually by intellectual mentors;

and by related devices in the other arts. Equally important, the good-vs.-evil, heaven-vs.-hell imagery of the revolutionary era was deepened and broadened in Soviet propaganda.[1] Soviet experience in the Patriotic War of 1941-5 swelled the Manichaean element to frightful, though understandable, proportions. The German invasion, the occupation and the atrocities could not be forgotten (though parallel Soviet ones were) and the 'cult of the Second World War' remained a subtext for the emerging propaganda of the Cold War that began in the late 1940s and reached its most ferocious point in the last years of Stalin. The memory of the terrible days of the war held such sway in Soviet minds about defence—physical and psychological—that the visual and verbal lexicon of that war's propaganda culture was almost wholly adopted for the Cold War. After Stalin's death in 1953, the deep forms of Soviet propaganda resisted change even when the content was modified in the detente of the later 1950s.[2]

Soviet Cold War propaganda was rooted in primal notions of heaven (the Soviet Union) and hell (the capitalist world, and especially its superpower leader). Its rhetoric was thus soaked in self-praise and wicked abuse. Some of the themes, of course, were mirror-imaged in Western propaganda. But the Soviet product was distinguished by its relative uniformity, a product of the near total government control over both media and message. In the outer ring of the control system lay the ideological matrix: Marxism-Leninism, *partiinost* (Party loyalty and esprit), nationalism and the enshrined memories of the Revolution and especially the Second World War. The regime reinforced these values through a carefully controlled educational system, real and latent sanctions, self-censorship and mass culture.

A tight web of organizations radiated from the centre. The Central Committee of the Communist Party had its Department of Agitation and Propaganda (Agitprop), an organ of ministerial status—indeed its chief in 1949, the hardliner Dmitry Shepilov, later became editor of *Pravda*, the Party newspaper, and then Foreign Minister in 1956-7. In 1957, Agitprop controlled thousands of schools and hundreds of thousands of employees, each provided with a fat book called *Guide for the Propagandist*. All major and some minor speeches of the Soviet leaders were fed into the media. Separate sections of Agitprop reached deeply into publishing, the press, radio, the schools; into mass organizations such as trade unions, women's and youth groups; and into the unions of artists, theatre workers, cinematographers and writers.[3]

On the foreign front, Agitprop held sway over the Youth Festivals that, starting in the late 1940s, were held in Prague, Vienna and other cities with the purpose of mingling the assembled Communist youth of the Soviet bloc with sympathetic counterparts from around the world. Agitprop had its hand in the Cominform, a lame successor of the defunct Comintern, TASS, the Soviet news agency, and the World Peace Council which was vigorous in Stalin's famous 'peace offensive'. Beyond these, Moscow had strong ties with the various labour internationals, the International Union of Students and the Women's Federation of Democratic Youth—each with its own organization, conference schedule and press.

The Soviet state, separate from but wholly entangled with and subordinate to the Communist Party, had its own organs of cultural propagation, many of them parallel to the Party's. Under the Ministry of Culture fell most of the formal cultural life of the country. For about a decade after the Second World War, the USSR was almost completely isolated from regular intercourse with the West. This began to change in 1955 under Minister of Culture Nikolai Mikhailov who opened up cultural exchanges. Such ministerial initiatives were of course unthinkable without the permission of the highest leaders, and those leaders were embarked upon a New Course in foreign policy and cultural thaw.[4]

In the face of this elaborate machinery, many in the West complained of the advantage held by the USSR in the great struggle for hearts and minds. Though the complaint had some virtue, the USSR by no means held all the cards. It is an often overlooked fact that in 1957 only some 5000 Soviet citizens were working abroad and thus in place to rub shoulders, shake hands and talk directly with the rest of the world. In contrast, about 580,000 Americans were employed abroad, to say nothing of the tens of thousands of European and American tourists who roamed the globe each year. The fact remains that the Soviet Union, by its own choice, was lacking in direct contact with the world. Nor can the rush of tourists to the Russian lands in the 1950s (about 10-15 000 American tourists and many from other Western countries visited the USSR in 1957) offer good evidence of propaganda advantage. Who influenced whom? Tourists were largely either impressed by the remnants of high culture or appalled by the food or the inefficiency—with many nuances in between.[5]

Inside the USSR, there was of course no private press and so the state could speak to the masses, if not in a solo voice, then through a very small choir. All papers were in a sense house organs. In the 1950s, *Pravda* printed 5 million copies daily. Some 2500 magazines in 56 languages were published at the rate of about 42 million copies a year. Book publishing was also a state monopoly. Russians called themselves 'the most reading people in the world' and not everything they read was propaganda. For foreign consumption, a state firm called International Books produced about 100 million copies of 900 titles a year. In 1956, 147 shortwave stations beamed 2000 hours of news to the world in a week. At home, some 9000 radio sets and 28 million wired speakers received radio broadcasts in 1960. The wired speakers offered one or two programmes to virtually every urban home. TV was still relatively inconsequential since only about 3 million sets were made.[6]

After the low point of contact with the West between 1945 and 1953, a gradual change began with the launching of cultural diplomacy which a major scholar of the subject defined as 'the manipulation of cultural materials and personnel for propaganda purposes'. The Ministry of Culture's opening of cultural and educational exchanges in the mid 1950s was built on the work of an earlier organization, VOKS or All-Union Society for Cultural Relations with Foreign Countries dating from 1925. The new organ was called the Union of Soviet Societies for Friendship and Cultural Relations with Foreign Countries. At its centre, the Moscow House of Culture hosted foreign visitors. Twenty such organizations existed in the USSR during the 1950s and many others in the Republics—each one with a direct tie to a particular country and headed by a prominent Soviet cultural or academic figure.

The French cultural exchange was one of the first of the bilateral programmes, beginning in 1954-5; other European states followed suit. By 1959 an exchange programme with the United States was operating. Out of the agreements came the machinery for the exchange of artists and entertainers on the one hand, and on the other educational exchange ranging from undergraduate students to young faculty. Goskontsert—the State Concert Agency—handled the first; various academic agencies the second. Such agreements were bound to break the ice at a personal level, but they did not stop the flow of propaganda (from either side) and were always subject to the needs or whims of foreign policy.[7]

What was the content of the Soviet culture and propaganda that was transmitted through these mechanisms to its own citizens and to folks all over the world? The Cold War propaganda content of culture was relatively low and certainly got much lower after the death of Stalin: spy novels, banal anti-warmonger verses, occasional jabs at Western culture in performance entertainment and graphic art – especially the cartoon. A recent Russian article recalling how the 'image of the enemy' was forged in those years offers only a few novels about the persecution of blacks in the United States.[8]

Here I will explore the zone that seemed to carry the most Cold War messages to a large number of readers: *Ogonëk* (Little Flame) and *Krokodil* (Crocodile), two of the most important mass circulation illustrated serials of social satire and Cold War propaganda. *Ogonëk* was a slick weekly of about thirty pages, lavishly illustrated with photographs and reproductions of paintings and other graphic material interspersed with short feature articles—history, culture and fiction. As an uplift publication, its level of critique and abuse of foreigners was low and it specialized in the 'home' side of propaganda: the riches of Russia's cultural heritage, Soviet achievements in science and industry and miscellaneous human interest stories about popular heroes: cosmonauts, scientists, superworkers and the like.

Krokodil, on the other hand, was a fairly crude tabloid devoting about two-thirds of its pages to permitted 'social criticism'. Khrushchev had strong thoughts about this: 'Satire is like the surgeon's scalpel: you find harmful growths inside a human body and like a good surgeon you remove them right away. But to know how to wield the weapon of satire skilfully the way a surgeon uses his knife, to remove the deadly growth without harming the organism—that requires mastery.'[9] This 1963 admonition describes neatly the frame in which satirists could work in the 1950s: they could strike out at social abuses but not at the system. Not only was political repression unmentionable but so were common social practices such as wife-beating and sexual harassment in the workplace. Only occasionally—especially around International Women's Day—would mistreatment of the female sex, usually in economic or education rights, be mentioned.

A key to changes in *Krokodil* over the decade is to compare the cover of the first issue of 1953, months before Stalin died, with that of the last issue of 1959, three years after Khrushchev's de-Stalinization speech. The first contains a beautiful watercolour of the Volga-Moscow Canal, with Soviet youth waving and heading for a great white ship in the lock. Both motifs had been featured in the notorious Stalinist film *Volga, Volga!* (1938) which exalted the marvels of river transport and masked the terrible death toll from forced prison labour that had built the canal. The illustration was a rather tired celebration of Stalin's technical achievements of the 1930s. On the cover of the New Year's Eve edition of 1959 we have Soviet rockets pointed toward the moon, Venus and Neptune. Stalin's handiwork has been down played and Khrushchev's technical achievements in space put on display. The arc of this process can be traced in this and all other periodicals in the years between 1953 and 1959.[10]

Cold War propaganda in *Krokodil* in the early 1950s was a continuation of the late 1940s; the softening came and went strictly in line with current foreign policy, swinging from harsh condemnation to mild détente but never warming up. Other periodicals matched the pattern. In the 1950s, almost all the major themes were on display. In 1959, the last year of the decade, Khrushchev's visit to the US toned down the Cold War rhetoric and imagery; but this was only a phase in the continuing modulation of détente and refroidissement leading right up to the Gorbachev period. The cruder level of *Krokodil* perhaps reflected a belief that lower taste culture was more amenable to propaganda. For contrast, I examined a few issues of the more elitist *Znamya* (Banner), the organ of the Union of Soviet Writers. It contained much less Cold War material: some occasional satire and cartoons—usually rather dull visually.

The cartoon was the main and probably most noticed vehicle of the two-sided Cold War narrative: the peaceful development of a historically great and progressive people on the road to socialism and prosperity; the aggressive interference of the United States and its allies in Europe. The artwork is fun, and some of the artists, particularly Kukryniksy—an anagram for three cartoonists—were very skillful. But most of them were also painfully repetitious. The quality the cartoons in *Krokodil* lay roughly between that of an American comic book of the period and a fairly good aquarelle. *Ogonëk's* were better, but less charged with Cold War messages. Villains were depicted as angular monsters, with elbows jutting out in menacing positions, a sinister style developed in early Soviet iconography, for example B. V. Ioganson's famous 'Interrogation of Communists' (1933). The fat capitalists of the 1950s were modelled on those of the revolutionary era. But they were now overshadowed by militarists. Some of the more paranoid cartoons had their parallel in the West, as for example V. Svetalin's 'Black Spider Web' spun around the globe by the CIA.[11]

The Message

I have selected a few thematic categories that best recapture the spirit of the time: the virtuous USSR; revanchism in Western Europe; the United States as the main enemy; and the Third World.

The overall picture of Soviet life in the time of the Cold War was a cross between an idyll and an epic. The idyll was provided by pastoral scenes, warm home life, peaceful citizens going about their business in an aura of optimism. Folded into this was the epic of high energy achievements in technology along the road to progress. Cultural workers were constantly urged to promote a feeling of optimism, the so-called *lakirovka*—glossing over reality with a smile. Songs of chaste love filled the airwaves. A key element in the idyllic image was growing prosperity. Matching the optimistic films of the late Stalin period were the sweetened pictures in the mass press of domestic life and the urban round. A truly laughable example imagined the evolution of the female shopper who in 1947 carried an *avoska* (the net bag you have with you in case some products appear); as the years go by her bag gets bigger and her wearing apparel more chic until by 1952, she is hauling two pieces resembling luggage stuffed with consumer goods. The imagery continued through the 1950s, and though the gap closed somewhat, the image was always several steps ahead of reality.[12]

Technological achievement had always been part of Soviet self-projection, especially since the launch of the First Five-Year Plan in 1928. Factory and farm outputs covered the pages of mass journals as did production figures blasting out of the radio receivers. Khrushchev's agricultural reforms were especially vaunted. But the emphasis changed after *Sputnik* in 1957, a major propaganda boon as well as a genuine fruit of Soviet science. The space theme was surrounded by pious biographies of cosmonauts, dozens of new science fiction space adventures, and an anti-religious campaign that tried to use planetary exploration as a weapon against traditional belief in heaven's power. A concise summary of the decade's themes was on display in the very fetching cover of *Krokodil's* first issue for 1959 with its spirited steed made of corn (maize), the crop that Khrushchev hoped would solve the agricultural problems of the USSR. On page 2, a red train is speeding on its way to Communism, and on page 4 another Soviet rocket is on its way to the celestial heavens.[13]

Russian high culture was constantly presented as ballast to the ship of contemporary life. After the assault on it in the 1920s, the Stalin regime had legitimized the arts of the tsarist period. Films and books in the late 1940s exalted nineteenth-century Russian scientists, inventors and art figures. Tolstoy and Tchaikovsky were displayed as cultural icons. An illustrated spread on the great novelist and the world famous composer in *Ogonëk* in 1953 explained that the Russian Revolution had made their works accessible to the masses. Frederick Barghoorn may have exaggerated somewhat when he argued that the Soviet love of classical music was presented by propaganda as a token of advanced civilization and as the sign of a peace-loving nation. But it was true that many in the West were properly impressed by the widespread attention given to high culture in Soviet life.[14]

The tableau of a peace-loving population anchored in a great culture and building a new society—not a wholly distorted one—had to be speckled with permitted criticism in the form of satire. In practice this meant mild exposés of un-Soviet behaviour in cartoons and reports on abuses: red tape, bad workmanship, mismanagement, alcoholism, corruption, insensitivity of bosses, excessive divorce and non-payment of alimony, and even boring lectures!—

the venial sins of Soviet socialist life that were contrasted to the mortal sins of the capitalist world. Soviet satire took up the fight. Good satire has to be open, free and biting. The Soviet brand was limited and rather flat. But the overwhelming presence of the genre certainly reveals the concerns of the regime as well as its incapacity to deal with the roots of social issues. Corruption, for example, was presented as a minor if recurring flaw when in fact it was a component part of that system. The same was true of family abuses. A cartoon showed a man dreaming about the Soviet motto 'Strengthen the Family' as he gazes at photos of his five ex-wives and several children and wonders 'which one [shall I strengthen]?' Alcoholism was often attributed to religious superstition as in a cartoon showing a priest using large vodka tumblers as bells.[15]

The glorification of the Soviet armed forces, a quite understandable phenomenon for that time, was seen abroad as evidence of aggressive intentions. Western threat-inflators, especially those in the Pentagon, were able to fatten their war budgets by showing clips of military hardware on Red Square in May Day parades. Such displays had a multiple purpose: to intimidate enemies; to honour the armed services on which the regime depended; and to strike a spark of patriotic enthusiasm among the population. The coverage in the popular magazines affirmed that the Soviet people were fully prepared to fend off any kind of aggression against their way of life. Thus the themes of the tranquil everyday, progress and armed might were knit together in a communication system that was always at the ready to modulate its messages in response to any foreign policy switches.

In contrast with the blandness of domestic messages, those pointed at the outer world were sharper, infused with emotion, panic, even hatred. The new postwar enemy in the West was demonized as the next round of invaders or war-makers just as the recent enemy had been demonized. Though often conflated with American aggression, the European foe was given special themes: revanchism, neo-Nazism, and Europe as puppet of the United States.

The Soviet regime mounted peace offensives and simultaneously depicted the West as enemies of peace. Western scholars often claimed that the Russians did not really want peace, or that their leaders did not—though some of these scholars conceded that the USSR wanted to avoid war in order to build up material successes, an argument with little logic. But the Soviets did distort when they accused their enemies of wanting a new war against the Soviet Union. This line was softened but not abandoned in 1956 when at the Twentieth Party Congress peaceful coexistence became official doctrine. The peace offensives in and of themselves lacked much magnetism. It is really easier to fight against bad things than for good things. The 'anti-peace camp' evoked the most forceful and malicious coverage in the Soviet mass press. An early example was the full-page cartoon of peace demonstrators marching past a building in which the usual wicked band—policeman, hangman, Nazi, Klansman, Japanese warlord and banker with a fat cigar— were hatching their nefarious anti-peace plots.[16]

For the NATO countries, 'neo-Nazism' and revanchism were folded into the older caricature of Europe as the realm of bankers and capitalists. Sabre-rattling rather than labour exploitation was now the principal vice of the ruling class. It proved easy to recostume the warmongers of Bonn, London and Paris as Nazis virtually identical to the bony, rat-like figures of wartime propaganda. A 1953 article in *Ogonëk,* to take a typical example, exposed the shady political past of corrupt right-wingers in West Germany. A 1957 cartoon has an inkwell composed of the heads of Hitler and Goebbels into which a neo-fascist journalist dips his pen adorned with a dollar sign. His task: slandering the USSR. A banal 1959 verse by Samuil Marshak, a talented children's writer, accompanied a cartoon by the famed Kukryniksy about NATO generals goose-stepping with missiles on their highkick shoe soles. In 'Short Memory' (1959), a fat soldier with an A-bomb goose-steps over Hitler's grave. Both Hitler's skeleton and the modern soldier hold in their hands plans for world domination. Germans were not the only 'murderers at large'; General Franco appeared regularly, and a particularly chilling coloured cartoon presented a French court releasing wartime collaborators and appointing them judges.[17]

A major Cold War theme was the constant effort of the United States to rearm, control and direct Europe's energies and forces against the Soviet orbit. This was linked with American support of revanchist neo-Nazis serving in Bonn. Divide and conquer motifs also came into play when Britons were warned about US intentions. A 1958 cartoon revealed that the 'American Gift to the British Lion' was a top hat with a target painted on it. A subtype was designed to generate enmity between allies. In a colour cartoon, German militarists resembling pirates, with daggers in their teeth, climb a ladder made of cannons in order to break into the chamber of a young French girl wearing a Liberty Cap—the latter being a rather lame attempt to remind the French of their revolutionary tradition. A scathing version of the wedge involved American tourists standing across the Grand Canal from St Mark's Cathedral in Venice wondering why the natives complained of their lot with such a marvellous view; in the shadow lurks an impoverished Venetian family living in a slum.[18]

Most of the puppetry material was extremely dull, but the peak was probably reached in an astounding orgy of graphic hatred by Yury Ganf, a regular cartoonist for *Krokodil*. It is the ultimate panorama of evil embracing all the themes of US dominance, puppetry and Nazi revival in one large picture showing every corner of Europe deluged with war fever and militaristic frenzy. The problem was overkill and a level of abstraction that suggested a political line of Agitprop rather than concrete information. Some nuances emerged about unfair trade practices, arms shipments, and currency manipulation—but these too come across as dull and flat. The doctrine articulated by Goebbels and Hitler about the effectiveness of repetition was adopted by the Soviets to an excruciating degree.[19]

In the Soviet media, the United States was the easiest target, the embodiment of pure evil long before Ronald Reagan applied the term to the USSR. America was seen as the chief supporter of imperialism, capitalist exploitation and bourgeois culture in the world. Charges against 'puppetization' of Europe had produced an unremitting series of cartoons and reports in *Krokodil* illustrating how Americans took away cheap housing, mistreated the locals, abused women and stole art treasures in Britain, France, Germany and Italy. Oddly enough, the specifics of aggressive American foreign policy did not loom large in iconography. The evil was usually more abstract. Korea, for example, got relatively little notice in the mass journals after the truce. But a particularly nasty and well-executed cartoon showed a Clarke Gable look-alike as an American pilot being told that North Korea had just opened an Academy of Sciences. As his plane is being loaded with bombs, he lights a cigarette and answers: 'I wonder how to get into it.'[20]

Soviet writers always spoke of the 'camp of peace' in reference to their supporters in the peace campaigns. A clever cartoon in *Krokodil* has the FBI ordering the police to 'put all those in the camp of peace into this [concentration] camp.' When raw hostility was revived after the warm interlude of 1958-9, Khrushchev gave a speech to shock workers telling them that the pilot of the famous U-2 flight, Gary Francis Powers, was in jail; he then invited Soviet citizens to visit the wreck of his plane on display in Gorky Park of Rest and Culture.[21]

Propagandists found no difficulty combining the theme of American aggression with neglect of the common people. Big Pentagon budgets meant low social services. One cartoon showed a restaurant where 'only one party' was served—the generals being fed with gold—while the hungry patrons of education, the arts, and health care were ignored. A Soviet visitor to New York contrasted the lifestyle of the rich and powerful—Mrs. Vanderbilt, her wardrobe, mansion and luxurious parties—with the desperate existence of the homeless in Central Park. Union persecution and unemployment, a major trope of the 1930s, appeared from time to time. A miners' strike in 1950 in New Mexico and a US film about it, *Salt of the Earth* (1953), was reviewed in *Krokodil*. True democracy was always contrasted to that of the Yankees. A prominent Stalinist ideologue, David Zaslavskii, wrote a double-edged piece on 'The Constitution Under Lock and Key'. It worked the theme around a report on the deposit of the Declaration of Independence and the Constitution in a bomb-safe location. Democracy, like the newly guarded documents, was indeed locked away from the masses by a nuclear obsessed regime.[22]

Race was the key question in American society in the 1950s, though it was not then recognized as such. Soviet writers and artists ventilated this issue from a rather crude ideological perspective. They were not wrong about the depth of racism but their treatment was one-dimensional. An objective approach would have required an acute knowledge of American society—North and South—and an accompanying recognition of racism in the USSR, a recognition that could not be tolerated. To be fair, the Soviet coverage of American racism was not so much mendacious as uninformed. Ironically, its projection of United States race relations was weaker than the reality. The few novels about racism did not plumb the depths of the 'Negro question'. Persecution of black schoolchildren, the blight of poverty and the different styles of small town and big city racism were there. But Soviet works idealized and patronized black people by placing figures from the intelligentsia as their saviours. One fictional hero was clearly modelled on the American Communist singer, Paul Robeson, a man of great heart and ambition but who knew little more about the life of his people than did the Soviet writers. A Russian sailor's memoirs contained a scene in Seattle where an armed mob chases a poor black worker in order to beat him, kill him and—in the words of a female pursuer—poke out his eyes. The vignette is reminiscent of Eisenstein's film *October* (1925) featuring umbrella-wielding bourgeois women aiming at the eyes of a Bolshevik street fighter; and of the 1936 film *Circus* with its Kansas lynch mob on the loose. The formulaic treatment is not very convincing.[23]

Occasionally a clever note was struck. In 1957, Radio Moscow effectively contrasted Soviet space exploits and American racism by announcing that a Soviet satellite would pass over the American town of Little Rock, Arkansas, a place recently shaken by a major civil rights struggle. A *Krokodil* cartoon scored some points in another juxtaposition: at a peace-related track event, an American bystander—unmistakable in his Hawaiian shirt—looks on and dreams of lynching a participating black athlete.[24] But irony must have hung heavy in the air when, a decade later, African students rioted on Red Square against the racist treatment they were suffering in Moscow.

On the culture front, a regular feature of *Krokodil* was a collage of illustrated book covers of American pulp fiction—including Mickey Spillane and his hero, Mike Hammer (an avid anti-Communist)—as examples of the US export of filthy hate literature for profit. Sergei Konenkov, a famous sculptor who had once rubbed shoulders with the avant garde, reviewed the American art scene and observed that it was ugly and lacking in 'national form', a bow to the 1948 Party line of Andrei Zhdanov who had demanded that art always reflect deep national roots. The recurring campaigns against jazz, abstract art and Western commercial culture were designed to uphold the regime's own taste in culture that was historical and traditional.[25]

Bolshevik graphic art about colonialism in the early years had been extremely vivid, springing as it did from great hopes about the collapse of the British Empire, a Russian victory in the Great Game and the unleashing of the fury of the masses of Asian and African toilers and coolies. Part of the drama arose from the theatricality of the otherwise rather unsuccessful Baku Congress of Toilers of the East in 1920. The famous (and falsified) 1920s painting depicting British officers witnessing the execution of the Twenty-Six Commissars of Baku was an added inspiration as was a similar scene in the Pudovkin film, *Storm over Asia*. The political art of the 1950s had lost much of this vitality. The 'Third World' card in Soviet foreign policy did got get played until Khrushchev came to power, and it developed rather slowly. But where there was policy—even in embryo—there was political caricature.

A striking 1953 *Krokodil* cartoon showed a dozen officials and wounded officers running up to a Colonial Minister with reports of insurrection in Kenya, Rhodesia, Malaya and other hot spots in the British orbit. Another took up Indochina: a very fat French officer blocked on one side by the Vietnamese People's Army and on the other by an American arms mission. The best for this period dealt with as yet uncharted terrain: Latin America. In Guatemala, the Arbenz government was nationalizing some of the land of the United Fruit Company, an icon of Yankee imperialism. In the picture, a scowling United Fruit executive with palm beach suit, panama hat and swagger stick is embarking from the shores on a steamer as the Guatemalan peasants and workers exhort him to go home.[26]

Khrushchev escalated the Third World target on his visit to the UN in New York in 1960: after some critical remarks on Soviet policy by the British representative, Khrushchev said: 'If the colonialists now rail at me, I am proud of the fact; it means that I am loyally serving the peoples who are fighting for their freedom.' It must be said, in regard to another realm of propaganda work, that

Soviets posted abroad, few though they were, did rather better in learning languages, showing sensitivity to native cultures and promoting cultural exchanges with the Third World—especially with nonaligned states such as India. The mass journals were full of reportage about the Committee for the Solidarity with the Nations of Africa and Asia.[27]

Détente

It is still mildly shocking after paging through years of invective, to come to a *Krokodil* cartoon of female dancers from the Berezka Dance Ensemble weaving their (folk)way across Manhattan's Broadway outside the famed Metropole. This was a good-natured congratulations to the dancers on winning the hearts of American audiences—which they did. The cultural exchanges were paying off in mutual goodwill. For a long time, Bolshoi ballerina Maya Plisetskaya was not permitted to travel abroad for fear of a propaganda defeat by defection. Khrushchev recalls that, on hearing of it, he finally allowed her to go on tour. Her foreign appearances and those of others scored high in creating an aura of Soviet stability and high culture. Even the Red Army Chorus captivated the public in Paris, Brussels, London and Prague—as revealed in the sugary pictures of *Krokodil*. In return the American Ice Follies in Moscow were portrayed as melting the ice statues labelled 'Cold War'. The most famous icebreaker was the young Texas pianist Van Cliburn, who won the Tchaikovsky competition in Moscow in 1958. Rave reviews appeared in the staid journal, *Soviet Music*, which had always kept its distance from politics and whose foreign coverage had naturally focused on Europe. Van Cliburn was the hero of the hour to millions of Soviet citizens—with the blessing of the regime.[28]

All this did not signal the end of the Cold War; negative propaganda articles and cartoons continued to appear—sometimes in juxtaposition—among the encomiums to Western artists. But the air had cleared up for a while. Khrushchev himself acted as a sort of cultural exchange figure during his 1959 visit to the United States, allowing the American people for the first time to see a Soviet supreme leader up close. *Krokodil* made much of this in a September issue. On the cover, an American newsboy shouts the 'Good News!'

that Khrushchev is in New York, Russians are on the moon and the Cold Warriors are in shock. *Ogonëk* printed a wonderful black-and-white photo of two wise heads—both very bald—of Eisenhower and Khrushchev under the headline 'America Applauds its Exalted Guest.' As part of his charm offensive in Hollywood, Khrushchev addressed the head of 20th Century Fox, Spiros Skouras, as 'Dear brother Greek' in reference to the shared Byzantine Orthodox heritage of the Russians and the Greeks.[29]

The Union of Writers checked in with a glowing account of the trip in *Znamya* adorned with the leaders 'We can breathe more freely now' and 'America is closer.' Though only temporary, the aura of detente brought the decade to a close. The New Year's edition of *Krokodil* offered a very friendly picture of a young Russian and an American greeting the New Year with a bottle of champagne in an ice-bucket with the caption: 'Let us have only this ice between us.' And on the back cover, as if to balance and affirm the thought on page 2, was pictured a failed banquet of warmongers.[30]

The Meaning

In Soviet life, there was usually a wide gap between organization, efficiency and effectiveness. On paper, the industrial establishment looked marvellous, but its output was meagre. The propaganda establishment was well-organized and its personnel fairly efficient. But how effective was the product? Surprisingly, the Harvard specialists who interviewed Soviet émigrés in the 1950s found that many of the regime's values had sunk in pretty well, even in that sample of people who were by definition hostile to the Soviet government.[31] By the late 1960s, there was a good deal of scepticism. However, some beliefs and attitudes that matched those of the mass press could still be encountered, though voiced more politely.

My estimation is that in the 1950s, the home-front material was pretty well accepted. Based on decades of socialization and loyalty training and delivered in an aura of peace following a frightening wartime experience, domestic-oriented propaganda was reassuring, though probably more to the majority of small-town and rural people than to urban intellectuals. Enemy imagery was, I believe, less effective due partly to its exaggeration and monotony. Ordinary Soviet citizens—like those elsewhere—paid less heed to international affairs and high politics than to their own daily lives. In the big cities there surely reigned a continuum of hostile rejection, plain disbelief, curiosity, ambivalence, friendly but cautious interest and acceptance of the propaganda about the outer world.

One certainty is the change in Western intellectuals' response to Soviet propaganda. Quite aside from the new political environment on all sides, Soviet propaganda of the 1920s warmed the hearts and ignited the brains of many Western intellectuals in the Comintern and salons and circles from Berlin to New York and in between. Part of the attraction was the political excitement of the young revolution, but part of it also was its cultural packaging adorned with the art of the avant garde. The Soviet Cold War propaganda of the 1950s was emphatically lacking in both these elements.

Original publication: In Gary Rawnsley, ed. *Cold War Propaganda in the 1950s*. London: Macmillan, 1999, pp. 85-103.

Notes

1   For the First World War, see Richard Stites, 'Days and Nights in Wartime Russia', in Aviel Roshwald and Richard Stites (eds), *European Culture in the Great War: The Arts, Entertainment, and Propaganda, 1914-1918* (Cambridge, New York: Cambridge University Press, 1999) pp. 8-31 (and here, below, 367-399).
2   Nina Tumarkin, *The Living and the Dead: the Rise and Fall of the Cult of World War II in Russia* (New York: Basic Books, 1994); Richard Stites (ed.), *Culture and Entertainment in Wartime Russia* (Bloomington: Indiana University Press, 1995).
3   Derek Scott, *Russian Political Institutions* (New York: Allen & Unwin, 1961) p. 188; John Garrard, *Inside the Writers' Union* (New York: Free Press, 1990).
4   The classic works: Frederick Barghoorn, *Soviet Foreign Propaganda* (Princeton, NJ: Princeton University Press, 1962), and *The Soviet Cultural Offensive* (Princeton, NJ: Greenwood, 1960); *The Soviet Image of the United States* (New York: Associate Faculty Press, 1950).
5   Barghoorn, *Soviet Cultural Offensive*, p. 7 for figures.
6   H. McCloskey and J. Turner, *The Soviet Dictatorship* (New York:

McGraw-Hill, 1960) p. 586; Kurt London, *The Making of Foreign Policy, East and West* (Philadelphia: Lippincott, 1965), p. 301.

7   London, *The Making of Foreign Policy, East and West,* pp. 7-8.

8   Stites, *Russian Popular Culture: Entertainment and Society Since 1900* (Cambridge: Cambridge University Press. 1992). Chapters 4-5; S. N. Burin, 'Kak sozdalsya 'obraz vraga'', *Amerikanskii ezhegodnik* (1994) pp. 36-52.

9   Quoted in Stites, *Russian Popular Culture,* p. 135.

10 *Krokodil,* 1 (10 January 1953); and 30 (30 December 1959).

11 *Ogonëk,* 43 (October 1953), 14-15.

12 *Krokodil,* 12 (30 April 1953), 8-9.

13 *Krokodil,* 1 (10 January 1959).

14 *Ogonëk,* 44 (October 1953), 9; Barghoorn, *Soviet Cultural Offensive,* p. 1.

15 *Krokodil,* 1 (10 January 1953), 5; 9 (10 January 1959), 15. See also Edward Crankshaw, *Khrushchev's Russia* (Harmondsworth: Penguin, 1959), p. 73.

16 *Ogonëk,* 1 (1951), 38.

17 D. Melnikov and L. Chemaya, 'Bonnskie revanshisty·. *Ogonek.* 38 (September 1953). 14; Kukryniksy, *Po vragam mira!* (Moscow, 1982), pp. 34-5; *Krokodil,* 13 (10 May 1959), 11; 3 (30 January 1953), 11.

18 Kukryniksy, *Po vragam mira!,* p. 52; *Krokodil.* 13 (10 May 1953), 16; and 17 (20 June 1953), 16.

19 *Krokodil,* 7 (10 March 1953), 14; and 31 (30 October 1953), 8-9.

20 Barghoorn, *Soviet Cultural Offensive,* p.19; *Krokodil,* 1 (10 January, 1953), 12; and 1 (20 January 1953), 12. Propaganda on Korea in the fighting phases was very heavy but I have not treated this topic. A 1951 example compares General Douglas MacArthur, commander-in-chief of the UN forces in Korea at the time, to Hitler: *Ogonëk,* 2 (January 1951), 21-2.

21 *Krokodil,* 4 (10 February 1953), 9.

22 *Krokodil,* 4 (10 February 1953), 8; G. Ramadin, 'Nyu-Iorkskie kontrasty', *Ogonëk.* 4 (January 1951), 19; *Ogonëk,* 35 (September 1953), 22-3; 'Konstitutsiya pod zamkom', *Krokodil,* 1 (10 January 1953), 10.

23 Burin, 'Kak sozdalsya'; Vasily Kucheryavenko, *Na amerikanskom beregu* (Moscow, 1951).

24 John Gunther, *Inside Russia Today* (London: H. Hamilton, 1957), p. 79; *Krokodil,* 22 (18 April 1953), 10.

25 V. Chichkov, 'Don-Kikhot amerikanskii', *Krokodil,* 22 (18 August, 1953).13; Konenkov, 'Yarmarka iskusstv', *Znamya,* 2 (1953), 126-31. See also *Ogonek,* 5 (January 1951), 31.

26 *Krokodil,* 10 (10 April 1953), 10; 22 (18 August 1953), 13; and 29 (October 1953), 8.

27 *Khrushchev in New York* (New York. 1960), p. 209; *Ogonëk,* 36 (September 1959), 5.

28 *Krokodil*, 1 (10 January 1959), 9; 10 (10 April 1950), 10; 5 (20 February 1959), 16. See also *Khrushchev Remembers* (London: Deutsch, 1970), p. 575 and *Sovetskaya muzyka*, 6 (June 1958).

29 *Krokodil* (20 September 1959); *Ogonëk*, 39 (September 1959), 1-4.

30 *Znamya*, 11 (November 1959), 156-73; *Krokodil*, 36 (10 December 1959), p. 2 and back cover.

31 Raymond Bauer et al., *How the Soviet System Works* (Cambridge, Mass.: Harvard University Press, 1956).

22

Days and Nights in Wartime Russia
Cultural Life, 1914-1917

> Like a prisoner hurled into a deep, empty well, I cannot say
> where I am or what awaits me. Only one thing has been
> given me to know; in the fierce and relentless struggle with
> the devil—the principle of material force—victory will be
> mine. And then matter and spirit will join in harmonious
> splendor, and the kingdom of universal will be ushered in.
> —Anton Chekhov, *The Seagull*, 1896

The wartime culture of Russia has until recently been little studied[1]
for several reasons: the Soviet historiographical enmity towards
most of those engaged in it; the near exclusion from literary and
art history of things that smell of propaganda or popular culture;
and—most important—the absence of a real historical memory of
that war in Russia, a memory that was buried beneath the remembrance of the revolutions of 1917 and the civil war that followed.
A moment's reflection will remind us that this is one of the many
historical phenomena that have divided Russia from the West psychologically in our century.

The Cultural Landscape

The political frame surrounding cultural life in wartime Russia was
composed of three blockades: the physical one, political censorship, and the "mental blockade" of boycottism. The first, erected by
distances, battlefields, danger zones, and naval forces in the Baltic
Sea cut Russia off from most of Europe. The regular flow of cultural

products and people virtually ceased. (One interesting side effect of the blockade was that Finnish subjects of the tsar were deprived of European films and began watching Russian ones.) Russian artists and writers were stranded in the West or arrested in the Central Powers countries and often unable to return home. Visiting theater troupes and orchestras were mostly immobilized. Censorship kept bad news to a minimum and stifled antiwar or other protest voices. Frontline correspondents were carefully monitored and the radical subculture of the previous decade was silenced. All of this reinforced the mental blockades erected against the culture of the enemy, past—with some nuances—and present. The renaming of Petrograd and of city streets and the anti-German riots reflected and fueled hatred or fear of enemy influence. Even music by German composers long dead—Mozart, Beethoven—was prohibited in certain concert halls. It became illegal for the German language to be spoken in public places. Dachshund dogs were sometimes killed on the streets.

What were the cultural responses to the war? A few preliminary observations can be stated at once. First, the state played a very small role in culture: its "Skobelev Committee"—named after a chauvinistic nineteenth-century Russian general—had been formed by Skobelev's sister during the Russo-Japanese war. During the Great War, it produced some films, concerts, and unimaginative graphics but remained relatively inactive, in striking contrast to the mammoth efforts made by some of the other belligerent states. The Russian monarchy was uncomfortable with mobilizing mass opinion and sentiment: it had been wary of an upsurge of Panslavism in the 1870s during the Balkan struggle; and its brief experiment with state-directed unions ("police socialism") had backfired in 1905. Unlike the other major belligerent states, the tsarist regime distrusted elements in society that could have worked with it for a major propaganda effort.

A second observation is that Russian high culture writers and artists had difficulty responding directly to the war because of reservations about the programmatic or "occasional" use of art and, for some, because of ambivalence about the war itself. The intellectual idiom of nuances, interior rumination, and transcendent vision fit poorly with such a direct and brutal experience as war. Many who began as fiery patriots became lukewarm after 1915. Conversely, the purveyors of popular culture proved better able and willing to deploy their traditions and forms of expression into propaganda. The gap between high and popular culture was far from complete. High-toned Symbolist poets did write for the popular press and talented artists did make war posters. Yet, the elevated elite could not match the forcefulness and the in-your-face simplicities and distortions of pulp fiction, stage routines, and cinema.

Poetry and Fiction

Many literary figures were gripped by agony, ambivalence, or silence: in December 1914, the Symbolist poet Zinaida Gippius wrote that "it is a sin to write poems now" and spoke of the "wisdom of silence." When writers did produce war-related poetry or fiction, it was usually marred by chauvinism or by lack of conviction. A pro-war posture was held by most of the great writers, but it was expressed in essays, journalism, and philosophizing about Neo-Slavophilism, Panslavism, and apocalypse. Writers, artists, and scholars signed a manifesto "to the Fatherland and to the Civilized World," announcing a struggle with the "Germanic yoke" for the freedom of mankind. Maxim Gorky was a signatory. Writers, according to one of them, were enraged at the Germans. From left to right, with a few exceptions, intellectuals initially lined up behind the government. Critics then and now view most wartime literature as banal and monotonous. The darling of prewar salon poetry, Igor Severyanin (1887-1941), allowed himself to end a piece with the words: "Blessed be the people! Blessed be the war!" The marriage of literary creativity with power diminished the value of the former; and the excessive repetition of slogans was almost equivalent to "literary silence." The defeats of 1915 took a severe toll on the optimistic patriotism of the first months. Some writers withdrew "to Parnassus," as a Soviet critic later complained, but others began to evince cautious opposition to the Russian army's wartime treatment of the civilian population—particularly the Poles and the Jews (Segel and Roshwald, this volume). Leonid Andreev, Fedor Sologub, and Gorky used the journal *Shield* for this purpose. Eventually Gorky rallied some writers around opposition to the war itself. Although *Shield* did not improve the literary quality of their output, it did display honorable opposition to anti-Semitism. Sologub in particular described the "fatherland" as a home for all its people, including the Jews.[2]

The most prominent pre-war literary school had been the Symbolists. Their wartime poetry was declamatory and vaguely patriotic in an abstract spiritual sense—but a bit closer to real things and people than their historiosophical speculations. The division over the war itself opened slowly. Andrei Bely, Aleksandr Blok, and Valery Bryusov at varying tempos turned against it; the others either supported it with verbal vigor or remained ambivalent. The most divided was Gippius who privately opposed and publicly— though cautiously—supported it. Vyacheslav Ivanov, Konstantin Balmont, and Fedor Sologub firmly supported the war. Dmitry Merezhkovsky, like his wife Gippius, wavered. Fittingly, the Symbolist poets preferred allegory, allusion, and mystical speculation; and their works in every genre—fiction or not—were enveloped in quasi-religious metaphor. In this respect they resembled others of the religious intelligentsia (often called Godseekeers) and occult writers (see below, pp. 388-390).

A few Symbolists wrote in the popular press but their pre-war stance of aloofness from social turmoil for the most part kept them from any kind of direct engagement with the war. Only Bryusov visited places near the front as a journalist, but he never saw fighting and returned to private life after nine months. Blok, escaping the draft through connections, got assigned engineering duty behind the lines in the Pinsk marshes for a short time. The others spent the war in the two capitals and in summer resorts and dachas, thus matching the intellectual remoteness from the real war with physical separation. Symbolists explored the "landscape of the soul" rather than the rational and material world or the fields of battle. Their view of reality is foreshadowed in the Chekhov quotation at the head of this chapter.[3] Avant-garde literary movements proliferated in the 1910s, often descending to mutual antagonism: Acmeism, Imagism, Futurism, Cubo-Futurism and many others produced a brilliant stream of literary art, often in collaboration with the plastic arts. The very nature of their enterprise—abstraction, transrational language, cosmic speculation, *épatage*—flourished well outside the cultural conversation about the war.

Popular fiction functioned in a different way. By this term I mean what critics called vulgar: stories—serialized or issued in cheap paper editions—with simple plots, strong narratives, clear-cut heroes and villains. This fiction said nothing profound or intelligent about the 1914 war or about war itself. Its backtext was newspaper stories and chauvinist journalism rather than religious or philosophical discourse. The racist portraiture of the enemy in cheap fiction hardly differed from that of the intellectual writers—except that its form was physiological and folkloric. It contained no inner exploration and no political agenda except demonization and heroization. Well-trained in etching good and evil and generating suspense, pulp and middlebrow writers easily adapted to patriotic themes during World War I. But the war theme did not predominate. In the first ten months, the genre of popular fiction that led all others in book purchases in the capital was the middlebrow "woman's novel" of sex, love, and career written by Anastasiya Verbitskaya, Olga Bebutova, Evdokiya Nagrodskaya, and Lidiya Charskaya. These writers had long provided a mass readership with scenes of illicit sexual liaisons backstage, on trains, at spas, and in "exotic places"; and this element fitted easily into war tales, just as pre-war spy and war-scare scenarios were easily converted into wartime fiction.[4]

Stage

A similar dichotomy prevailed between "legitimate theater" and the popular stage. Few plays on wartime themes were mounted in the great theaters, considered by many as temples of art. Aside from Andreev (see below, p. 379) and a few Symbolists whose works were mostly unstaged, playwrights steered clear of the topic and the repertoires remained classical European and Russian. Konstantin Stanislavsky deepened his work on the "method" in his by-then conventional Moscow Art Theater (MAT). Some claim that MAT was infused with a Tolstoyan pacifism. But this was hardly more than a rarefied and gentle humanitarianism as shown in its production of Dickens' *Cricket on the Hearth*, a protest against war. Aleksandr Tairov's experimental Chamber Theater (founded in 1914) "recoiled from contemporaneity," whether in peace or war. Its doctrine of cerebral and archaic staginess discounted audience and outside world. Said a critic in 1916: "a melancholy and depressed mood pervaded Moscow. But art was being created on Tairov's stage which knew no Moscow, of the past or of the present—did not know or wish to know." Vsevolod Meyerhold moved along two tracks: the mainstream stage with big classics new and old; and his studio where he explored *commedia*, Kabuki, and Spanish baroque—all of them oblivious to the war.[5]

The more commercial theaters staged a few anti-Kaiser potboilers. The best-attended Russian stage was the circus, which supplemented its regular fare with marvelous balletic reenactments of battles, glorifying the Russian forces and maligning Germans, Austrians, and Turks. Appealing more to upper and middle classes were patriotic evening concerts of readings mixed with choirs and folk ensembles that exalted throne and nation. Inspired—and often sponsored by—pre-war rightwing patriotic groups, these events constituted the closest thing in performance art to an official dynastic reading of the war.[6]

Art

Most of the modernist and avant-garde schools of visual art – Cubism, Futurism, Rayonnism, Suprematism – turned to inner visions or to universal ideals, but not to the war. Among the notable exceptions were Vladimir Mayakovsky, Kasimir Malevich, and David Burlyuk who created hundreds of cartoon-like works in 1914, though their patriotic phase was short lived. Only a few artists fought in the war, Pavel Filonov and Georgy Yakulov among them. Mayakovsky went to the front as a war artist. Mikhail Larionov served only a few weeks and was wounded; though inspired by popular soldiers' art before the war, he did not address it during the Great War. Most artists remained in the cities. Marc Chagall, Ivan Puni, Natan Altman, Ed Lissitzky, and Vasily Kandinsky returned from abroad. During the war years, Russian easel painting became more abstract. Cubo-Futurism reached its peak and Suprematism and Constructivism were born, though the world learned of these last only in the 1920s when an international art network was reestablished. Like the European Dadaists, the Russian avant-garde dwelt in a mood of political uselessness. Its competing schools

Kasimir Malevich, *Private of the First Division,* 1914.
Oil on canvas, 53.7x44.8 cm. Reproduced by permission of the Museum of Modern Art, New York.

busied themselves with reinventing art: Futurism, the vision of the outer machine; Constructivism, that of the inner machine; and Suprematism, Malevich's reductionist vision of the world. Publicly, modern artists were virtually impervious to the direct experience of the war.[7]

Germany's Kaiser Wilhelm II choking on the Belgian bone. Pem, untitled. *Sovremennaia russkaia i inostrannaia karikatura i voina,* no. 18, 9x14 cm. Reproduced by permission of the Slavonic Library, University of Helsinki.

Popular graphics—postcards, cartoons, posters—offered narrative propaganda art that resembled pulp fiction and the plebeian stage but with terser messages and more biting wit about the Kaiser and company, Russian heroes, and historical ghosts done up in raw colors and dramatic diagonals with texts resembling those of the folk broadside (*lubok*—a captioned picture). Some of the best cartoons were done by Alexander Lebedev for the covers of the popular weekly, *The War.* Philanthropic societies flooded Russia with patriotic graphics—many of them executed by disciples of the realist Itinerant Movement—which promoted war bonds, hatred of a barbarous foe, and sympathy for the suffering victims at home, on the front, and in allied countries. A 1914 poster by the established artist, Leonid Pasternak, "Wounded Soldier" was adapted by the Bolsheviks after the revolution for their own program. Millions of pictures were produced in a wide variety of styles, often blurring the line between "art" and popular graphics. Artists employed antique Slavonic lettering, Christian motifs, and *lubok* styles on war posters depicting German and Turkish atrocities and Russian war heroes.[8]

Music

Orchestra musicians were not exempt from service as such. At first many avoided the army, and those who went were only nominally soldiers. But in 1916 the draft caught up and one can only wonder if their wartime experience resembled that of Fritz Kreisler who said that in war, "centuries drop from one, and one becomes a primeval man, nearing the cave-dweller in an incredibly short time."[9] The draft, the railroad jam, high prices, and the takeover of some halls for hospitals cut down on symphonic music concerts. All but two big ensembles in Moscow collapsed when war descended: the Imperial Russian Musical society and the private orchestra of Sergei Koussevitzki (Kusevitsky). The latter's bimonthly shuttle between the capitals was reduced due to transport problems. Ironically, audiences expanded. The thirst for Russian and the allied countries' serious music was great in these years (as it would be in 1941). The solemnity and emotionalism of Russian music in particular no doubt played a psychological role—as it often did in times of stress. An ugly debate sprang from the press about performing "alien" music. Koussevitzki received threats for playing older German works in public. His main repertoire was Russian and French. Almost all his concerts were for the benefit of soldiers, their wives, the Union of Cities and—in one case—Jewish relief (Koussevitzki was Jewish). By 1916, the draft had eroded his ensemble and his concertizing declined.[10]

Like many other artists, the major serious composers and performers largely missed the war altogether by staying abroad if caught there or avoiding the draft if at home. In a wider sense, their art—whether traditional or modernist—could not fit a patriotic mold. Their letters are filled with musical and professional concerns, and the war hardly figures at all, though a few did give concerts for war benefits. Igor Stravinsky, stranded in Europe, recalled: "My profound emotions on reading the news of the war, which roused patriotic feelings and a sense of sadness at being so distant from my country, found some alleviation in the delight with which I steeped myself in Russian folk poems." Alexander Scriabin continued working out his modernist or Silver Age mystical themes, religious visions, and experimental sonorities. He saw the war as "spiritual renewal for people ... even though it destroys them mate-rially." His main preoccupation in the last months before his death in 1915 was planning a monumental performance of his music in India.[11]

Sergei Rachmaninov toured Russian cities with Koussevitzki to raise money for the war effort. Although he produced *All Night Vigil* (The Vespers), *Vocalise,* and some songs, Rachmaninov's depression about the war induced a creative gap for a few years. Sergei Prokofiev wrote some of his greatest early works during the war. Aloof from patriotic rhetoric, he ignited a few minor musical scandals with his Second Piano Concerto and *The Scythian Suite.* One critic vacuously linked the turbulence of his modem music in 1915 to the "ferment" of a world at war. Prokofiev composed, played, and conducted at elite musical sites and theaters and toured the provinces. A lesser known but important composer, Nikolai Myaskovsky (b. 1881) was directly affected by the struggle: serving at the front as an officer, he wrote home in disgust that "everyone is fed up with the war"; although he was productive before and after the war, he wrote no music during it.[12]

In the world of musical theater, the fabled Ballets Russes was scattered and nearly dissolved by the war. Artists assembled and reassembled at the urging of impresario Sergei Diaghileff (Dyagilev) and some members spent a good part of the war across the Atlantic. Though many male dancers were called up, the dancer Sergei Grigoriev missed the draft due to health reasons and joined Diaghileff: he recalls the voyage from the United States back to Europe in a ship bearing "ammunition, horses, " and the Russian Ballet." Nijinsky lived under house arrest in Budapest for a while. Those released tended to rendezvous in Europe—not at home because it was simply too hard to get there. In Russia, state theater "budgets were cut. The choreographer Mikhail Fokin put on *Stenka Razin,* dealing with a seventeenth-century peasant rebel, set to Borodin's *Prince Igor* music; *Eros,* set to Chaikovsky's *Serenade for Strings*; and Mikhail Glinka's *Jota Arogonese* (from the 1840s) at the Marynsky Theater (later Kirov). Amidst this show of tradition, Fokin did salute the allies in a number called "Dances of the Nations." The nearest that the famed dancer, Tamara Karsavina, got to war was to observe bayonet drill in Theater Square outside the

Marynsky. Escape and diversion were the driving force of wartime ballet stage; and its mission, wrote Karsavina, was to "protect the eternal treasure" of classical art.[13]

Opera was no more affected by war than ballet. Indeed the only sign of war in all theaters was the repeated playing of the Russian and allied national anthems to ardent crowds who applauded and bowed to the ambassadors' boxes. The greatest singer of the age, Fedor Chalyapin (Shalyapin), financed two military hospitals and sometimes sang to the patients. His visit to bombed-out Warsaw and briefly to an empty battlefield produced a photo opportunity and some lachrymose moments in his memoirs. The lofty social circle of Paléologue was probably representative of the capital's elite; their salons featured the nineteenth-century art songs of The Mighty Five composers and other Russians.[14]

In less exalted spheres, music played the war. Anthems and band music—a prominent outdoor genre since the time of Nicholas I—were in full evidence at public performances. Concerts by the Andreev Balalaika Ensemble, founded a few decades earlier, and the recently formed Pyatnitsky Folk Ensemble enlisted stylized "folkish" art in the patriotic cause. But once again, "neutral" genres won out: tango, folksongs, urban romances, Gypsy tunes, and early imported American Ragtime continued to dominate the sheet music and phonograph market and the restaurant and cabaret scenes. I have seen no soldiers' songs that actually emerged from the ranks (see below for songbooks, p. 393); reports and iconography tell us that the men sang at the front as they had in previous wars and brought their accordions with them.[15]

Cinema

The film industry came to Russia in 1896 and the first Russian-made feature was shot in 1908. The movies' familiar blurring of popular and high culture makes cinema art difficult to pigeonhole. The vast bulk of production in the war consisted of popular entertainment films of various genres—historical-literary epics, comedy, and crime—unrelated to the war. Among the light films that Emperor Nicholas II viewed at the headquarters of the High Command was *Secrets of New York*, a detective serial from Pathé.

The biggest entertainment medium of the time, cinema paid scant attention to the war after 1914-1915. Directors of genius—Evgeny Bauer and Yakov Protazanov—lent their talents to popular genres, particularly sexual melodrama, highlighting class and gender cruelty in which a poor female is victimized by an affluent man. Did this generate anger toward the upper classes? Popular media, regardless of the producers' intentions, may have created as much class hatred as anti-foreign feelings. It is still unclear how much wartime resentment at dodgers and dandies fed into the violence of the 1917 revolutions.

Among the war-related films with higher pretensions, three different versions of Lev Tolstoy's *War and Peace* were shot, celebrating the 1812 victory over Napoleon and thus suggesting a successful outcome of the present war. The most original state-sponsored work was the stop-motion film entitled *Lily of Belgium* (see below, p. 383). Popular war films were mostly skilful adaptations of crime or detective stories, with the villains now dressed up as spies, traitors, or brutal German officers. The Skobelev Committee, with only four cameramen at the front, monopolized newsreels and took very little footage.[16] Unlike that of other belligerents, Russian cinema had virtually no impact as foreign propaganda.

The Major Themes

Disentangling themes from cultural products is an artificial act since most of them were jumbled together. But it may help to examine the treatment of the more prominent topics: enemies, victims and allies, the "Russian soul," and the meaning of war.

The Enemy

Ridicule was poured on all Germans, but two "types" invited special abuse: the corseted, monocled, spike-helmeted Prussians: and the Bavarians arrayed in fat beer bellies, sausages, clay pipes, and Lederhosen. Kaiser Wilhelm remained the primary object of scorn and hate. A *lubok* called *Carnival Sideshow: Satan Wilhelm and the German War* contained a malicious rhymed satire attacking all ethnic Germans and a crude cartoon of the Kaiser with insane eyes and twisted moustaches. Whipping up hatred for the enemy, especially the Germans, proved surprisingly easy, since anti-German feelings (often submerged in a generalized resentment of the West) were latent among many Russians—common folks as well as intellectuals. Anti-Germanism focused on national stereotypes and militarism. Cartoons on Belgium showed Prussians with spiked helmets and sabres impaling babies. A full-color poster called *German Barbarism* made its point by showing a Zeppelin airship dropping bombs on a defenseless city—as happened in Poland and Belgium early in the war.[17]

The exalted literary figures had their own version of German barbarism. In instances too numerous to reference, they turned geography and history around and equated the Germans with the Mongols and other "eastern hordes" (Conclusion, this volume). One of the most popular writers of the pre-war period—with a readership much larger than those of Andreev, Gorky, or Blok—was Lidiya Charskaya, who exploited the war in a collection of stories called *Fear Not Your Own Troops*, melodramatic tales with cardboard characters and relatively implausible coincidences. Most of them begin with gentle pre-war idylls which are then shattered in 1914. In one story, a flirtatious young Russian maiden at a Bohemian watering spa (in Austria-Hungary) in the summer of 1914 falls in love with a German who, after the war breaks out, shoots her father and has her stripped at a railroad station. Other tales described the wounds of war, and women burying their dismembered men. There are no real battle scenes, no psychology, and no national insight. But these easily read tales of misadventure at the hands of a devilish people were what sold in the book stalls.[18]

Germans inside Russia were especially hated. Students painted over German street signs; a crowd sacked the German embassy and smashed statues; a reader complained of gothic type in a newspaper. Russians of German, Latvian, Jewish, or Scandinavian descent rushed to adopt Slavic-sounding patriotic names like Romanov or Serbsky (Serbian). Names were changed from Hammer to Molotov, Berg to Gorsky, Taube to Golubev, Schwartz to Chernov, Schmidt to Kuznetsov, and Eiche to Dubnov. The reason was survival: not only were "Germans" being fired without proper vetting of their identity; they were also being beaten up and even killed. When the police rounded up "aliens" in 1915, they took in more non-Germans (including British and French citizens) than Germans! The culture reflected this with a vengeance: stories, plays, and films warned the public against the enemy within. Zinaida Gippius's story "The German," dealt with a little Latvian boy who, because of his foreign name, is taunted by schoolmates who call him "the German." When he discovers his true ethnic identity, the child is happy to learn from his mother that as a Latvian he is also "Russian." Newspapers accused Baltic Germans *en masse* of disloyalty—the evidence in one paper being that Count Zeppelin, German designer of the formidable airship, was married to a Baltic German woman.[19]

The detective thriller was easily adapted to spy stories combining adventure with patriotism. In a Charskaya story, a vindictive German Russian national has his unfaithful wife raped and her Russian lover shot. The film *Amid the Thunder of Cannon* treated the war as a backdrop to an interethnic triangle in which Fritz Müller, the son of a German factory owner in Russia, lusts after the young Vera (Faith) who is loyal to the Russian Sorokin. In wartime Müller and Sorokin are drafted into the Russian army and Vera becomes a nurse. Müller not only shows his true colors by deserting to the Germans, but he tries to rape Vera and kill his rival Sorokin. Villainy is punished and the heroes are rescued by a squadron of Cossacks in the last scene.[20]

The Symbolist Fëdor Sologub—the fiercest of the anti-Russo-Germans—wrote a play, *Edge of the Sword*, which is as racist as anything in popular fiction. In one way it resembles the central premise of the famous Nazi anti-Semitic film, *The Eternal Jew* (1940) because it proposes an essentialist view of the Russo-German residing permanently behind the mask of assimilation. The main character—a Russian German—seems both Russian and civilized in every way; he courts a good Russian girl but turns out to be a traitor and a murderer. The wise Russian characters who see through him are a clairvoyant sister of the girl and some holy pilgrims. The same writer's play *Seeing Off* (1914) displays deep resentment of Baltic Germans and lays on a "natural" brotherhood of Estonians and Russians against the old common foe. This and other works also assaulted home-grown Russian Germanophiles as somehow ethnically blind. These works, brilliantly analyzed in Hellman's work, display the intimate relationship between the late-blooming mysticism of the Silver Age and modern national hatred bred from essentialist philosophical positions.[21]

Austria was seen as a foe of a different order, weaker than Germany, led by a senile old man (Emperor Franz Joseph), filled with ethnic groups who surrendered in droves to the Russians, and the owner of an important Russian war aim—Galicia, populated by Poles, Ukrainians, and Jews, and seen by Russians as theirs by right of ancient Kievan cartography. In the title story of Charskaya's *Fear Not Your Own Troops*, Galician Polish noble girls are frightened by the specter of approaching troops whom they take to be ferocious Cossacks. These turn out to be "friendly" Habsburg cavalry who proceed to rape them. The implication of this and many cultural statements about the Russian army was that Cossacks did not rape—a historical falsehood. In another Charskaya story, a Hungarian spy dresses as a Catholic nun—presumably an act of both cowardice and unmanliness.[22]

A crude and hastily made but exciting film called *Glory to Us, Death to the Foe* (1914) was directed by the talented Evgeny Bauer. News of war darkens the summer love of a young Russian manorhouse lady and her officer fiancé, played by the most popular actor of the age, Ivan Mozzhukhin. When he goes off to war, the heroine joins up as a nurse only to find him dying in a *lazaret* (field-hospital). She then crosses the lines disguised as an Austrian nurse and serves in the enemy field hospital in order to spy on them. When a young Austrian officer who has been flirting with her is given by his superiors a secret message to deliver, the nurse lures him to a rendezvous, stabs him, and flees with the document back to her own lines where she is rescued by Russians and decorated with military honors. This theme worked on a genuine social reality—Russian women on the medical front—but also elevated the female gender into heroic modes (on women see below, pp. 385, 388).[23]

The Turks came in third on the list of Russia's enemies. The anti-Ottoman theme drew on "orientalist" memories of the Eastern Question, the nine previous Russo-Turkish wars, and the Great Game involving Muslims further to the east. Since the sultan had declared a jihad or Holy War of Muslim peoples against their foes and slaughtered the Armenians, some films were devoted to

Turkish atrocities at the front. But usually the sultan was portrayed grotesquely in cartoons as a running dog and cowardly ally of the Kaiser: a cartoon in Kiev's *Dawn* of 1914 has the sultan urged on by the Kaiser with a sword at his backside. A facile producer of racy stories offered a salacious treatment of the German kaiser in *Wilhelm in the Sultan's Harem* (1914). Olga Bebutova's *Bloody Half-Moon* centered around the seduction and despoiling of "white women" by Turkish agents. Orientalism and the exotic dominated the Turkish theme and produced little of interest.[24]

It need hardly be said that the wartime abuses and atrocities of the Russian army and other authorities got no coverage in any cultural medium. The horrors of the scorched earth and the Great Retreat in Poland, the accompanying rape and murder and pillage of Jews and Poles, the treatment of all Jews as traitors, the death trains, the ugly Russification polices in Galicia, and the repression of the 1916 uprising in Central Asia—none of this was reflected in high or popular culture.

Victims and Friends

Loving the allies—the Entente powers, the little Serb Brother, and ravaged Belgium and Poland—offered outlets for the conflicting emotions of hate and love. News of the German occupation policies in Belgium—the false along with the true—came as a shock to Russians as to many others. The invaders looted, shot, raped, and pillaged as they tore through the tiny neutral country and pulverized ancient churches with their giant guns (Schaepdrijver, Jelavich, this volume). An early response in popular print medium was the first issue of library of the Great War—a cheap pamphlet series. *The Belgian Victim* (1914) offered vivid descriptions of early outrages by the Germans, the batteries at liege, shattered buildings and bodies, homes reduced to dust, Zeppelins bombing Antwerp hospitals, German soldiers singing "Watch on the Rhine," the patriotic song of the early nineteenth century, and "Deutschland, Deutschland, über Alles" to humiliate the Belgians. According to this account they also paraded a bear cub dressed as King Albert on the streets of Brussels. Another account showed a spike-helmeted firing squad executing citizens as women begged for mercy.[25]

Shaming of the Germans was supplemented by admiration of the victims. A Russian circus, in order to show the heroic resistance of the Belgians, performed a spectacle called "The Inundation of Belgium," dramatizing the opening of the dams to drown the German invaders. Andreev wrote a philosophical play on the same theme: *The King, the Law, and Freedom*. Seeing no contradiction to his famous anti-war story of the Russo-Japanese War of 1904-1905, *The Red Laugh* (1908), Andreev accepted World War I as a struggle of "world democracy against Caesarism and despotism." Publicly, he upheld a sacred union of tsar and people; privately he looked at the war as a prologue to a democratic Russia. Andreev did not think much of this play as a work of art; one critic called it "dramatized journalism." An admirer of Maurice Maeterlinck, Andreev modeled his main character on him. A civic-minded writer, this character joins forces with the philosopher king, Albert, in an act to save Belgium: the opening of the dams. Two of its premises were emblematic of pro-war writers: the power of word and thought; and the virtue of sacrificing people in order to save the Nation. Whatever its flaws, Andreev's play drew big audiences in Moscow and Petrograd.[26]

A more striking work of art was the extraordinary stop-motion film entitled *Lily of Belgium*, made by Czesław Starewicz for the Skobelev Committee. It presented Belgium as a forest idyll destroyed by marauding Germanic helmeted beetles, led by a Kaiser-beetle, who are repulsed by Russian pine cones, returning the land to a springtime of blooming lilies. In one regard—depicting Belgium as a ravished land—Symbolist efforts resembled Starewicz's treatment. Shocked by the horrors in this campaign, they produced a rash of sympathetic poems, stories, and plays. Sologub, in the poem, *The Belgian*, somewhat tactlessly made his hero an ivory trader from the Congo. Emile Verhaeren's *La Belgique sanglante* (1915) was translated into Russian, as was an anthology devoted to King Albert with pieces added by Alexander Kuprin and Merezhkovsky, who invoked a biblical commonplace by calling Belgium a Holy Land crucified. The great actress, Mariya Ermolova, joined literary figures in an evening on "The Spirit of Belgium" to honor Verbaeren, George Rodenbach, and Maeterlinck. Balletmaster Fokin used the same title in a dance number at the Marynsky.[27]

Some publicists and writers tried seriously to equate Poland with Belgium, thus projecting Germany as the evil villain of Polish destiny, erasing the Russian outrages then happening in Poland, and obscuring the troubled past of those two neighbors. In the film *Tears of a Ravished Poland* (with the Chopin funeral march played on the piano), patriotic producers mounted an image of German barbarism, Polish suffering, and Slavic solidarity. Certainly the Germans reduced Kalisz to rubble by bombardment and enacted cruel measures in their occupation. But Russian behavior was much worse, especially during the Great Retreat and scorched earth of 1915. The most active Polish patriot, Józef Piłsudski, formed legions to fight against Russia, while the noted cultural figures Henryk Sienkiewicz and Ignac Paderewski sought independence by lobbying abroad (Segel, this volume). And yet, the rightwing Russian Duma deputy, Vladimir Purishkevich, had the audacity to quote the great nineteenth-century Polish poet Adam Mickiewicz in parliament as some kind of proof of Russian-Polish historic solidarity.[28]

The Symbolists, while decrying the brutality of the Germans, were honest enough to air their own feelings of shame about historical repressions and the Russification of Poland and to hope for a glorious Russo-Polish partnership in the future. But they played down Russian cruelties and the renewed Russification efforts in Galicia. Valery Bryusov, with little tact, quoted in his "To Poland" the patronizing words of the Russian poet, Fёdor Tyutchev "On the Taking of Warsaw" (1831), suggesting that now the Polish Lazarus would be raised up by the Russian Jesus. This at a moment when, with half a million Poles fighting in the Russian army, no Catholic chaplains were serving at the front. In all fairness it must be said that Bryusov's well-meant literary atonement met with joy and acceptance among some Warsaw intellectuals. As a whole, the intelligentsia played the themes of brotherhood, forgiveness, and mutual healing, often echoing Mickiewicz's famous formulation of the "crucified Poland."[29]

Panslavism was also, in a sense, a matter of allies—present and future. Panslavism was an old Russian dream of a union of Slavonic peoples into a communion of nations under the Russian tsar. Poland had been excluded in most formulations. Now there arose among a wing of the intelligentsia the vision of a remarriage with Poland, a Galician annexation, a complete Balkan liberation, and the acquisition of Istanbul (Tsargrad in Russian), and parts of Anatolia by the Russian empire. It was no hard passage from the historiosophic smog of neo-Slavophilism (see below, p. 389) to Panslavism: "in the deep Russian sea, all the rivers of Slavia will merge" wrote Sologub. The dream of Tsargrad was nursed by Bryusov, Sologub, and Vyacheslav Ivanov—though not all Symbolists—and by various liberals and conservatives as well. Though they evoked no major works of culture, Panslavism and Tsargrad underlay the appeal of this war among many influential thinkers of the Russian intelligentsia and even made their way into a war song.[30]

The Russian Soul and National Bonding

Hovering around the theme of allies and friends and mutually reinforced in all genres was the oldest theme of all: Russia's destiny. Behind it lay a desperate vision and hope for national solidarity expressed in cultural and social unity. The forms it took were determined by a hundred years of Russian intellectual history: images of home and nation, concepts of Holy Russia and of Mother Russia, the Russian Soul, and neo-Slavophilism. In the cultural output of the war, these themes were wrapped around discussions of history, the folk, religion, cultural heritage, the tsar, and heroes of war.

The yearning for national unity was expressed in various ways—most of them rooted in ideas rather than realities. The monarch himself, Nicholas II, thought he saw it in the mystical bond he believed he possessed with the people, a bond made flesh in the dramatic show of patriotism on the square in front of the Winter Palace in August 1914. Duma leaders sought it in a Burgfrieden that they tried to build in the Progressive Bloc and in the vigorous voluntary associations that sprang up in the war: the Union of Zemstvos (local government) and Towns, the War Industries Committees, and the Red Cross. Feminists and other special interests called for a truce—to support the war effort in return for a new Great Reform era. Many writers hoped that a solidary show of patriotism would produce a permanent harmonious union of all classes and end Russia's enduring problem: the alienation of the elites from the masses.

Bryusov, as a war correspondent, at first saw national unity embodied in the brotherhood of the front, a front that in a few years would turn into a line of fraternization with the enemy.[31]

The most colorful cultural expressions of unity were the Patriotic Evening Concerts. Maria Dolina, a devoted monarchist and singer, gave hundreds of benefit concerts that offered folk songs, balalaika bands, martial ensembles, regimental choirs, songs set to the words of the famous anti-Semitic publicist Pavel Krushevan, and readings of official edicts and texts provided by the Russian right. Dolina presented *tableaux vivants* — actors dressed as Suvorov, Kutuzov, and other commanders of the past, frozen alongside common people for the visual contemplation of the audiences. The mixture of social orders promoted all-Russian solidarity and loyalty in a setting of solemn stasis. As Hubertus Jahn so aptly put it, "in this kind of entertainment, patriotism changed not at all; it remained static in the tight-fitting costume of convention and the stiff order of military bands." A remnant of authentic folk art was recruited in 1915 when the 72-year-old folk teller, Maria Krivopolenova, was brought from her native Archangel region to Petrograd. It was one of the last efforts in imperial Russian history to link the culture of the *narod* (peasantry or common people) to a state program. Some artists, giving concerts in military hospitals, avoided Dolina's chauvinism; but they did combine the high culture of the intelligentsia with military bands and folk songs. All of this was a natural attempt to suggest and promote the social-cultural unity of the Russian people in the face of a dangerous enemy — a unity that in 1917 was shown to be fictitious.[32]

The sincere quest for unity in the face of danger helps explain the bitter tone in the critique of domestic life that erupted in the press. Luxury and high life remained in place for the affluent. Although prohibition was proclaimed at the outset of war, complaints resounded in the press and in ministerial chambers about all-night restaurants and illegal consumption of alcohol. And, although motor cars were needed for war, fancy autos careened around the streets of the capitals carrying top-hatted dandies and furred ladies. To the ranks of high society spenders were added speculators and war-profiteers. As in all wars, draft-dodgers abounded and were much resented, whether they were the newly pious who entered monasteries to escape service, or public volunteers—the "Zem-Hussars"—who wore gaudy uniforms and saw no action except during their valiant nocturnal assaults on restaurants and cabarets. With heavy-handed humor, the satirical journal, *Scourge*, and other papers, flogged the draft-dodger in foppish monocle and morning coat, the homefront slacker, the profiteer, and other elements of society who were escaping the horrors of war—all of this highlighting the persistence of privilege in wartime when sacrifice and unity were supposed to be the order of the day.[33]

Bygone heroes were cast in the drama of national unity. The medieval prince Alexander Nevsky, Suvorov, and Kutuzov were regularly featured in cartoon and poster. One of the most interesting examples of historical cooptation was the double pamphlet *How the Russians Took Berlin in 1760*, whose title story presented a falsely optimistic picture of what would happen in the current war on the basis of what happened in 1760. The back-piece was a reprint of an 1882 speech by the nationalist and conservative hero of Balkan and Central Asian wars, General Skobelev. In this scandalous diatribe spoken before a Panslav group in Paris, Skobelev insulted the Germans as a people and foresaw an inevitable war between Teuton and Slav. Skobelev's name, redolent of so many past victories and synonymous with Russian jingoism, was constantly invoked and the state wartime committee on propaganda was named after him. The Russian army, however, produced no Skobelevs in the 1914-1918 war.[34]

Who then were the heroes? Since neither the tsar nor the commanders could qualify, heroic images were fashioned from the exploits of individual combatants: soldiers, Cossacks, flyers. The adventures of the first heroes—Kuzma Kryuchkov, the pilot P. N. Nesterov, and Vasily Ryabov—were put on film. The young Cossack lancer, Kryuchkov, allegedly killed eleven German soldiers in 1915. His face appeared everywhere—in the papers, on posters, on postcards, in the circus—and a rash of verse was poured out in his honor. One representation had him impaling the eleven men on his lance. Nesterov, a 36-year-old daredevil pilot, had made a dangerous loop over Kiev in August 1913; a year later to the day he was killed on the Austrian front by plunging into enemy bombers over Russian positions. As with other air aces of the time, a price had been put on his head by the enemy. Units and battles were also celebrated as in the circus spectacles of "Russian Heroes in the Carpathians" and "The Capture of Przemyśl," a major Russian victory that also inspired a motion picture. Real soldiers, judging from their letters to Gippius, seemed much more human and they wrote in a rather formulaic, coarse, boastful—even folkish—fashion about their wounds, their nurses, and the need for the public to buy war bonds. Although women fought in the war, they received little attention except in women's journals. Much more space was given to nurses, grand duchesses at their hospitals, the sanctity of women, war wives, and rape victims.[35]

War and Peace

The intellectuals who greeted the war that proved so utterly destructive could not in 1914-1915 see what was coming. Bryusov, idealizing the Russian occupation policies in Galicia, felt a "geographical patriotism" in the hope of Russian expansion and he saw this "Last War" as a prelude to a New World. Sologub rejoiced about Russian heroism from far away, gathering his information from newspapers. In a play Sologub coauthored with his wife—performed in Kharkov in November 1915—*A Stone Cast into the Water*, the outbreak of war unravels moral and sexual tangles that are enmeshing good people in a summer "nest of gentlefolk" during their "month in the country." Mechanics and agency are absent and the action is motivated by a transcendent force, a device wholly in keeping with Symbolist aesthetics. Other Symbolists, invoking the now exhausted cliché, likened the war to a "cleansing storm." Images of closure, finality, and apocalypse sprang off the pages of almost all the religio-philosophical writers of the time.[36]

The occultist movement, in particular the Russian Theosophical Society of Helen Blavatsky, saw war as a cosmic event of occult meaning another "cleansing fire" which could weld together a religious East and a scientific West. In the words of a recent historian, they spoke constantly of "crisis of conscience, dark forces, carrying the cross, Russian mission, Godbearing people (*narod-bogonosets*), sacrifice, crucifixions, spiritual renewal, new path, and bright future." Religious writers often utilized a rather watery Christology spiked with Romans and Pharisees, the cross, Golgotha, and resurrection; or they took off into stratospheric metaphysical climes. As a whole, the best thinkers of the time looked backward, upward, or inward rather than peering into the face of battle.[37]

The neo-Slavophiles identified the Germans with the traditional Slavophile images of Europeans as mechanized, narrow, smug, and affluent—in a word bourgeois. The old East-West dichotomy was reduced to Slav versus Teuton and soul versus machine. Sologub believed that a punitive victory over the Germans would enable the rebirth of Russia. (Interestingly, the new capital of his imagined renascent country was to lie deep in the interior at Yaroslavl on the Volga—considered a stereotypical Russian town.) Conversely, the old Crimean demons and "bourgeois" targets of abuse—England and France—were converted into suitable allies. Abhorring the concrete, the neo-Slavophiles and related thinkers defined reality as potential, essential, ontological—possessing no visible or provable attributes. "Holy Russia" was thus higher and therefore more real than the Russian state, despised by many Symbolists, Godseekers, and neo-Slavophiles. The Great War for them was a prelude to the spiritual regeneration of the Slavic soul, the Russian idea, *vsechelovechnost* (the all-human perspective), and the redeeming power of suffering.[38]

The Acmeist poet Nikolai Gumilëv, going well beyond the usual patriotic motives—hatred of the enemy and national ambitions—embraced war for the sake of war in the manner of Gabriele D' Annunzio and the characters of Ernst Jünger's novels. The sometime husband of Anna Akhmatova (a foe of the war), Gumilëv was later executed by the Bolsheviks for alleged monarchist plotting. His uniqueness stems not so much from heroic participation at the front as from his vision of the fighting as a personal adventure and a "grandiose spectacle" wherein he discovered the "mystery of the soul." Gumilëv's impulse was psychological and religious—not Panslav or Orthodox (though he was a devout believer), but rather a Nietzschean one of epiphany through danger, a masculine mysticism related to that of the love for the hunt (which Gumilëv possessed), the thrill of the kill, and the risk of being killed in the "cleansing fire" of battle. War for Gumilëv was not so much a sacred cause as a sacramental act. Recording his feelings in 1915 in *Note-book of a Cavalier*, Gumilëv exulted in the scorched earth, "burning everything that would burn." Disciple of the romantic cult of the horse and admirer of "The Turkestan Generals," Gumilëv aspired to be Superman and Conquistador; he saw man as beast among beasts and killing as a supreme work of art, a "festival of the spirit," a religious experience where man communes with God. Gumilëv stood virtually alone. Russia produced no group of well-known "trench poets" like those of other belligerents.[39]

How utterly different was the response of Konstantin Paustovsky, later a distinguished Soviet writer. "Symbolist poets," he recalled, "had completely lost all contact with reality [and] sang about pale ghosts of passion and the fires of otherworldly lusts." About an evening of Futurist poetry in 1914 in which Severyanin regaled a chic audience with sensual and witty verses, Paustovsky wrote: "it was savage to hear those words in days when thousands of Russian peasants were lying in rain-filled trenches, beating back the German armies with rifle fire." Paustovsky did not exult in the war, but he lived amidst the blood and the filth as a medical orderly on hospital trains and then in field medical units. Traveling from front to front through Poland, Galicia, and Russia, breathing in the smoke and stench of war, he began his life as a writer. "The 1914 war did not flood through our consciousness." He wrote years later about the home front in Moscow and elsewhere. "A life was going on in Russia which had nothing to do with the war."[40]

Another form of engagement was the wartime posture of the Orthodox Church. According to archival documents, the archbishop of Voronezh Province in 1916 affirmed the "duty of the clergy to use the symbols of the church to encourage and incite patriotic feelings for the war" through such means as communion masses for recruits, prayers for their safety, patriotic sermons, processions, and the distribution of crucifixes, icons, and religious and patriotic leaflets. Similar programs were preached and practiced all over Russia; and the front was well supplied with Orthodox chaplains who blessed and doused troops and weapons with holy water. Orthodox priests were also brought by train into conquered Uniate and Catholic Galicia.[41]

Not many people, apparently, thought the war funny enough to generate a lot of jokes. There can be little doubt that jokes abounded on the personal qualities of the enemy. One surviving example is about the German army breakfasting in Warsaw, lunching in St. Petersburg, dining in Moscow—and shitting it all out in Berlin. Another is plotted as the familiar dialogue between two Jews, now caught in the battle zone: one a German, the other a Russian, both "patriots." The former brags about the greatness of his Kaiser who rushes from front to front always at the head of the troops (a fiction, of course). The Russian Jew replies in scorn: "Your tsar has no dignity; he runs around like a chicken. Our tsar sits at Headquarters [in Mogilev] and the front comes to him!"[42]

The Impact of War

In trying to sum up the scope and meaning of Russian wartime culture, several points seem clear. First, the continuities between old and new expression. Those who addressed the war—whether in accents of high or popular culture—retained the forms and redressed the themes of their pre-war productions. That no great Russian war novel came out of this struggle is no surprise; most masterpieces about war are written out of memory and reflective contemplation. The gap between high and popular culture seems especially revealing. If we can believe that each possessed its own audience or "taste culture," then the division between the intelligentsia and the masses was very real. They saw it through different eyes and eventually divided over support of the war. For the intelligentsia, however removed they were from the war, it remained a burning issue and most of those who exalted a Russian victory maintained that position. For the common people—who suffered far more than the creative intelligentsia—the romance with war ended quickly, even though the common soldiers fought on. Culture as such had much less to do with this than the war's casualties and its economic effects.

In places where art branched off and moved into new directions—as with the avant-garde poets and painters—it had little or no connection to the war. Of all the cultural forms that flourished in the wartime period, none can compare with the glories of Russian visual art. It forms the middle period of a magnificent flowering from the turn of the century to about 1930 with the onset of Stalinism and the end of modernism and the avant-garde. The paintings, collages, studio events, and showings in Moscow and Petrograd in the 1910s have long been considered a peak moment in the history of twentieth-century European art.

The intelligentsia experienced the war largely as a philosophical exercise where moral values reigned supreme and the frontline world of troop trains and mountains of corpses remained in the less important kingdom of phenomenology. Readers of adventure and consumers of the popular arts wanted spectacle and entertainment—including sensationalist violence—that simplified the war as a Manichaean struggle between good and evil. At a deeper level, however, one may discern a striking difference between highbrow and lowbrow (or middlebrow) in their perceptions of the Russian people. The patriotic intelligentsia for the most part saw Russia's strength not in brute force, personal heroism, or material power— but rather in moral fortitude, thus in a sense making a virtue of physical deficiency. Popular culture, by contrast, offered heroes and heroines of physical brawn (for men), courage, and cunning. Cartoon soldiers and fictional female spies are tough and earthy. Their superior morality is assumed because they are Russian and on the "right side" and their inner character is never explored. One of the great political strengths of the Soviet socialist realist culture of the Stalin period was that it managed to weld these two elements into one whole—however fantastic that entity was.

Certain themes correlated well with certain arts or genres of art. Big philosophical dreams cannot be easily articulated in cartoons, songs, movies, cabaret, circus, or pulp fiction. The major thinkers avoided the realia of battle like the plague. Although their barbs at Germany were never expressed in comic low satire, they were full of spite and hatred. The anti-German theme suited the intelligentsia's positions as well as framing plots of adventure, suspense, action, and even love and violence. High and "low" art addressed the Belgium-as-martyr theme because it could be made both complex and simple. But no formula could deliver a satisfying presentation of ambivalence and latent guilt over Poland. The Jewish question got little space in popular culture probably because it would not sell to lower and lower-middle-class consumers.[43] As for the exaltation of the homeland, nothing was more amenable to any form of construction: philosophical, religious, or plain old patrioteering.

Very little research has been published on Russian "trench culture" in the Great War. Physical conditions are a partial explanation: the city-like labyrinths of the Western front had no counterpart in the East; trenches were dug and abandoned quickly until very late in the war. The war of movement in the East offered relatively few opportunities for leisurely creation. Another factor was the relative illiteracy in the Russian ranks. It is possible that many literate soldiers and officers wrote poetically—to themselves or to people at home—of love and death, suffering and despair, perhaps even of hope. But Soviet historiography on the war did not highlight or memorialize it and we have yet to see the literary remains of the Russian Bindings, Owens, and Sassoons. Books of composed songs appeared but they were remarkably similar to nineteenth-century ones. Collections from both eras displayed sentiments of monarchy, loyalty, patriotism, cheerfulness, and bravado. A 1915 songbook was merely updated with a few new items about allies and enemies and verses insulting to the Kaiser.[44]

The wartime use of the arts as propaganda or simply war-related morale building should not be exaggerated; both the producers and the public continued to rivet their attention on purely entertainment genres. Indeed the movie melodrama's popularity increased enormously during the war years. Russian jingoism took hold among all classes for a while—but it did not last long. In all the belligerent countries, culture—high, low, and middle—was enlisted by the state for patriotic purposes. Though hardly novel in 1914, this process was intensified by the technical means of communication. In Russia, one can find in the techniques of patriotic culture a preview of some of those used by the Provisional Government and the Bolshevik regime to legitimize their revolutions: the *tableau vivant*, the historical spectacle, the imaging of enemies in circus, graphics, and movies (which used not only plot, but casting, lighting, and costuming to satanize political and social foes).

Nothing like mass mobilization or nationalization of the arts took place in wartime Russia. A wave of patriotic enthusiasm did arise but did not last very long. To the extent that non-governmental cultural production reflects public opinion, its history shows starkly that enthusiasm for the war—though varying among the classes—sharply declined after the defeats of 1915. Private enterprise continued to churn out lurid graphics, mystical and satanic movies, detective tales, vulgar songs, straight comedy, and dance routines with no political or national content. This went on unhindered and indeed amplified after the fall of the monarchy in March 1917. It was only when the Bolsheviks came to power that state authorities began seriously to regulate the people's taste and then only in 1918 when Russia's war in Europe was ending. Russian wartime culture was wholly transformed after the February Revolution overthrew the tsar. Not that the war ceased being an issue. It was *the* central issue of 1917, but so tightly was it knotted to the revolutionary process that its history belongs to that epic struggle.[45]

Original publication: In *European Culture in the Great War: The Arts, Entertainment, and Propaganda, 1914-1918*, eds. Aviel Roshwald and Richard Stites (Cambridge, New York: Cambridge University Press, 1999), pp. 8-31.

In this essay, Stites refers to five other contributions to *European Culture in the Great War*:
p. 369, 384: Harold B. Segel, "Culture in Poland during World War I," 58-88.
p. 369: Aviel Roshwald, "Jewish Cultural Identity in Eastern and Central Europe during the Great War," 89-126.
p. 379: Roshwald and Stites, "Conclusion," 349-358.
p. 382: Peter Jelavich, "German Culture in the Great War," 32-57.
p. 382: Sophie de Schaepdrijver, "Occupation, Propaganda, and the Idea of Belgium," 267-294.

Notes

1   There is a very old pioneering Soviet work on literature: Orest Tsekhnovitser, *Russkaya literatura mirovoi voiny* (Moscow, 1937). But the best studies have been done by non-Russians: Hubertus Jahn, *Patriotic Culture in Russia During World War I* (Ithaca, 1995); Ben Hellman, *Poets of Hope and Despair: the Russian Symbolists in War and Revolution (1914-1918)* (Helsinki, 1995).
2   Mikhail Heller, "La littérature de la Première Guerre mondiale," in Efun Etkind *et al.*, eds., *Histoire de la littérature russe: le XX siècle - l'Age d'argent* (Paris, 1987), 641-648; Tsekhnovitser, *Russkaya literatura;*

Hellman, *Poets*, 80-84 (Gippius qu. 148); *Shchit: literaturnyi sbornik.* ed. M. Gorky, L. Andreev, and F . Sologub (Moscow, 1915), tr. as *Shield* (New York, 1917). Polish Jews were subjected by Russians to brutal deportation during the great retreat of 1915.

3   The best study is Hellman, *Poets of Hope and Despair.*

4   See Jeffrey Brooks, *When Russia Learned to Read* (Princeton, 1985) for the whole genre of popular reading and its audience; and Richard Stites, *Russian Popular Culture: Entertainment and Society Since 1900* (Cambridge, 1992), ch. 1. On war-scare fiction, see Stites, *Revolutionary Dreams* (New York, 1989), ch. 1.

5   Jean Benedetti, *Stanislavski* (London, 1988); Konstantin Rudnitsky, *Russian and Soviet Theater 1905-1932*, tr. R. Permar and L. Milne (New York, 1988), qu. 16, 17; Benedetti, *Meyerhold the Director,* tr. G. Petrov (Ann Arbor, 1981), 210; Eduard Brown, *Meyerhold: a Revolution in Theater* (Iowa City, 1995), 110-149. A light survey of *The Theatrical Gazette* (*Teatral'naia gazeta*) for the war years suggests that the war was wholly absent from high level comedy, avant-garde, and absurdist theater. Moscow and Petrograd were not unique: the Odessa *Theater and Movies* for December 1914, when war interest was still high, advertised classical opera, ballet, and drama; contemporary melodramas (only one of which sounds like it had a military theme [*On Manoeuvres*]); and Yiddish theater (*Teatr i kino*, 52 [24 December 1914]); *Epokha* in Kiev reveals a similar assortment, without the Yiddish component (2 [8 February 1915]).

6   For circus and other popular performances, Jahn, *Patriotic Culture*, is indispensable.

7   Arnold Haskell, *Diaghileff* (New York, 1935), 269-270; Jahn, *Patriotic Culture*, 14; Camilla Gray, *The Russian Experiment in Art, 1863-1922*, rev. ed. (London, 1986). Kandinsky, of course, was internally bruised by being forced to vacate his second "homeland," Germany, and by the loss in combat of two of his German friends: August Macke in 1914, Franz Marc in 1916: Peg Weiss, *Kandinski and Old Russia* (New Haven, 1995), *passim*. For a sampling of avant-garde utterances in 1915, see John Bowlt, ed., *Russian Art of the Avant Garde: Theory and Criticism*, rev. ed. (London, 1988), 112-135.

8   Postcard Collection in the Slavonic Library (Helsinki). The best treatment by far is in Jahn, *Patriotic Culture*, 11-85, with illustrations. I sampled fifty-six issues of *The War* (*Voina*) for the years 1914-1916.

9   Fritz Kreisler, *Four Weeks in the Trenches* (Boston, 1915), 64.

10   Arthur Lourié, *Sergei Koussevitzki and His Epoch* (New York, 1931), 140-148; Moses Smith, *Koussevitzki* (New York, 1947), 87-95. In Kiev, for example, Beethoven, Schubert, and Wagner were banned at the

outbreak of war: Michael Hamm, *Kiev: Portrait of a City, 1800-1917* (Princeton, 1993), 221-222. At least one critic tried for balance among allies and enemies: "the highest development of contemporary music," wrote Alexei Losev, "is that of Skryabin [Scriabin] and Wagner. Compared with it, [Verdi's] *Traviata* is vulgarity" (*Studenchestvo - zhertvam voiny* [Moscow, 1916], 120).

11 *Stravinsky: an Autobiography* (New York, 1936), 83 (the folk material was from the collection of the early nineteenth-century Slavophile, Pëtr Kireevsky, and later formed the basis of *Les Noces*); Faubion Bowers, *Scriabin*, 2 vols. (Tokyo, 1969), II, 265- 266.

12 Geoffrey Norris, *Rachmaninov* (London, 1976), 51; Barrie Martyn, *Rachmaninoff* (Aldershot, 1990), 253-287; Israel Nestiev, *Prokofiev*, tr. Florence Jonas (Stanford, 1960), 98, 111; Harlow Robinson, *Sergei Prokofiev* (New York, 1987), 101-120; Aleksei Ikonnikov, *Myaskowsky* (New York, 1946). The last of the Mighty Five, the aged Tsezar Kyui [César Cui], wrote some Panslav songs and a few war-related choral works: *Izbrannye pisma*, ed. I. L. Gusin (Leningrad, 1955), 692-693.

13 S. L. Grigoriev, *The Diaghilev Ballet 1909-1929*, tr. Vera Bower (London, 1953), 101-112; Romola Nijinsky, *Nijinsky* (New York, 1934), 276-298; Elizabeth Souritz [Surits], *Soviet Choreographers in the 1920s*, tr. L. Visson, ed. S. Bames (Durham, NC, 1990), 28-38; Tamara Karsavina, *Theater Street* (New York, 1931), 309-325. There are a few details of concert life in Maurice Paléologue, *An Ambassador's Memoirs*, 3 vols. (New York, 1923), *passim*. The Imperial Ballet did give a rare performance at the front in 1916. For other frontline entertainment, see Jahn, *Patriotic Culture*, 120-122 and Jahn, "Patrioticheski motivy v russkoi kulture perioda i mirovoi voiny," in *Patrioticheskie traditsii russkoi kultury* (St. Petersburg, 1992), 139.

14 Feodor Chaliapin, *Man and Mask: Forty Years in the Life of a Singer* (New York, 1932), 214- 219; Paléologue, *Memoirs*, II, 209-220.

15 Stites, *Russian Popular Culture*, ch. 1; Starr, *Red and Hot*, chs. 1-2. For one accordion photo of many, see *Solntse Rossii*, 299: 44 (November 1915), 6.

16 The best treatments: in English, Jahn, *Patriotic Culture*, ch. 3; in Russian, S. Ginzburg, *Kinomatografiia dorevolyutsionnoi Rossii* (Moscow, 1963), 155-385. See also Peter Kenez, *Cinema & Soviet Society, 1917-1953* (Cambridge, 1992), 18-27 and Jay Leyda, *Kino: A History of the Russian and Soviet Film* (1960; Princeton, 1983), 72-89. For the false analogy with 1812, see Bruce Lincoln, *Passage through Armageddon* (New York, 1994), 152 and, for the tsar's taste in film and light reading, 170-171.

17 *Raëk: Vilgelm Satana i nemetskaya voina* (Moscow, n.d.), in the Slavonic Library, Helsinki. See discussion in Jahn, *Patriotic Culture*, 31; he also

shows how vituperation against the Kaiser, a crowned head after all, was sometimes controlled by the censors (89). Virtually every other issue of *Voina* contained a withering depiction of the Kaiser by Lebedev. The airship poster, "Barbarism of the Germans" is reproduced in Frank Kämpfer, *Der rote Keil: das politische Plakat* (Berlin, 1985), 163.

18 Lidiya Charskaya, *Svoi, ne boites i drugie razskazy iz sovremennykh sobytii* (Petrograd, 1915).

19 J. N. Westwood, *Endurance and Endeavor*, 4th ed. (Oxford, 1993), 218-219and Lincoln, *Passage through Armageddon*, 138 for anti-German actions; Andrew Verner, "What's in a Name? Of Dog-Killers, Jews, and Rasputin," *Slavic Review*, 53:4 (Winter, 1994), 1046-1070; Gippius in Hellman, *Poets*, 150. A cartoon in *Voina*, 65 (November 1915) identified Russo-Germans with fat top-hatted, cigar-wielding bankers – precisely the image that Bolsheviks would use for capitalists in future.

20 Charskaya, *Svoi, ne boites*. See Stites, *Russian Popular Culture*, 34-36 with references; and Brooks, *When Russia Learned to Read*, 162, 314.

21 Hellman, *Poets*, 118-132.

22 Charskaya, *Svoi, ne boites*; for a sample of graphics on Austria, see Lebedev's back covers of *Voina*, 41 and 42 (January 1915). Russian soldiers mockingly called the multiethnic Austrian army "the Gypsy bazaar."

23 *Slava nam, smert vragam* (Director, Evgeny Bauer, 1914).

24 See Jahn, *Patriotic Culture*, fig. 32; Brooks, *When Russia Learned to Read*, 162, 314. *Voina* 14 (1914), contains a collection of crude ethnic jokes, fables, and anecdotes focusing on Turkish cunning, greed, and corruption. Bebutova, *Krovavyi polumesyats: strashnyi pauk* (Petrograd, 1915) is actually a sequel on the same theme begun in a pre-war novel subtitled *In the Land of the Odalisques* (1913).

25 *Belgiiskaya zhertva* (Moscow, 1914); *Voina Rossii s nemtsami: zverstva nemstsev* (Moscow, n.d.); *Voina*, 20 (1915).

26 Andreev, *Sorrows of Belgium* (*The King, the Law, and Freedom*), tr. H. Bernstein (New York, 1915); Ben Hellman, "Leonid Andreev v nachale pervoi mirovoi voiny: put to 'Krasnogo Smekha' k pese 'Korol, Zakon, i Svoboda'," *Studia russica helsingiensia et tartuensia*, II (Tartu, 1990), 81-101; Jahn, *Patriotic Culture*, 127-131.

27 *Liliya Belgii* (1915; rereleased in *Early Russian Cinema*, 10 vols., III, Milestone Video, 1992); Hellman, *Poets*, 63-7; S. N. Durylin, *Mariya Nikolaevna Ermolova, 1853-1928* (Moscow, 1953), 492; Souritz, *Soviet Choreographers*, 28-38.

28 B. S. Likhachëv, "Materialy k istorii kino v Rossii (1914-1916)," *Iz istorii kino*, 3 (1960), 45-57; Lincoln, *Passage through Annageddon*, 153-154. At the peak of the tragic events in Poland in 1915, a presumably serious dramatic treatment on the Vilna stage, *Polish Blood*, was a

failure, though I have not been able to locate it; on the same stage, Offenbach operettas, a favorite genre of pre-war audiences, did well. See *Teatral'naia gazeta*, 9:27 (5 July 1915). For the plight of the Jews, see Frank Schuster, *Der Krieg and der "inneren Front": Russlands Deutsche und Juden in Westrissischen Kriegsgebiet, 1914-1916* (Giessen, 1997).

29 Hellman, *Poets*, 67-80.

30 Ibid., 84-118 (qu. 99). The song "To the Slavs" is in *"Geroi Kryuchkov" i drugie pesni voiny* (Moscow, 1914), vii (the Slavic "Tsargrad" for Constantinople, seat of the Byzantine emperor, originated in the Middle Ages, well before Russia ever had its own "Tsar" - *ed.*).

31 For explorations of these lines, see Lewis Siegelbaum, *The Politics of Industrial Mobilization in Russia, 1914-17* (New York, 1983); Linda Edmondson, *Feminism in Russia 1900-17* (London, 1984), 158-176; and Stites, *The Women's Liberation Movement in Russia*, 2nd ed. (Princeton, 1991), 278- 289. Bryusov in Hellman, *Poets*, 102-111.

32 Jahn, *Patriotic Culture*, 116-118 and qu. 115; Heinz-Dietrich Löwe, *Antisemitismus und reaktionäre Utopie* (Hamburg, 1978), *passim* for Krushevan.

33 Press citations are numerous; for one example, see *Bich* (Scourge), 4 (14 September 1916), 5. Ministerial grumbling in: A. N. Yakhontov, *Prologue to Revolution: Notes on the Secret Meetings of the Council of Ministers*, 1915, ed. M. Cherniavsky (Englewood Cliffs, 1967), 83, 134-136; draftees into monks: Hamm, *Kiev*, 221-222; Zem-Hussars in Lincoln, *Passage through Armageddon*, 210. Apparently readers did not tire of reading about the high life: see Bebutova's society novel, *Zhizn'-kopeika* (Petrograd, 1916), describing a lavish ball.

34 *Kak russkie vzyali Berlin v 1760g.; Skobelev o nemtsakh* (Odessa, 1915). The war did, however, repeat his notorious massacres of Central Asians in 1916.

35 On Kryuchkov: *Geroicheskii podvig donskogo kazaka Kuzmy Firsovicha Kryuchkova* (Moscow, 1914) (trans. to appear in James von Geldern and Louise McReynolds, eds., *Russian Middlebrow Culture*) and *"Geroi Kryuchkov" i drugie pesni voiny. Shtabs-Kapitan P. N. Nesterov: geroi-aviator* (Moscow, 1914); Gippius, *Kak my voinam pisali* (1915) in *Poets*, 147-149; N. A. Vakhrusheva, "Soldatskie pisma i tsenzorskie otchety kak istoricheskii istochnik (1915-1917)," *Oktyabr' v Povolzhe i priurale* (Kazan, 1972),67-89; soldiers were in fact given canned letters which they could sign and send home: Jahn, *Patriotic Culture*, 48; Alfred Meyer, "The Impact of World War I on Russian Women's Lives," in Barbara Clements *et al.*, eds., *Russia's Women: Accommodation, Resistance, Transformation* (Berkeley, 1991), 208-224; see *Voina* 16 (1914) for exaltation of the Cossack style of combat and 24 (1915) for grotesque depictions of women at war.

36   Hellman, *Poets*, 33-34, 186- 190, and *passim*. One must consult this book as a whole for context and developing nuances among the Symbolists regarding the war. The theme of war as a simplifying and purifying force was taken up in popular fiction by Evdokiya Nagrodskaya in her *Evil Spirits*, in which the heroine's tangled love knot is cut in St. Isaac's Cathedral as the war breaks out: *Zlye dukhi*, 2nd ed. (Petrograd, 1916).

37   Maria Carlson, *No Religion Higher than Truth* (Princeton, 1993), 76-88.

38   Hellman, "Kogda vremya slavyanofilstvovalo: Russkie filosofy i per-vaya mirovaya voina," *Studia russica helsingiensia et tartuensia*. ed. Liisa Bückling and Pekka Pesonen, I (Helsinki, 1989), 211-239. France of course had been an ally since 1894 and Britain a semi-ally since 1907.

39   Hellman, "A Houri in Paradise: Nikolaj Gumilev and the War," *Studia slavicafinlandensia*, I (Helsinki, 1984), 22-37; Elaine Rusinko, "The Theme of War in the Works of Gumilëv," *Slavic and East European Journal*, 21:2 (1977), 204-213. A character in Mikhail Artsybashev's play *Voina* (Eng: *War* [New York, 1916], 43) muses over the "tragic beauty" of war, but he does so from a great distance and is ridiculed by other characters.

40   *The Story of a Life*, tr. J. Barnes (New York, 1964), 463, 274, 276 and *passim*.

41   Quotation in Chris Chulos, "Peasant Religion in Voronezh Province 1880-1917" (University of Chicago dissertation, 1993), 38l. Galicia: Lincoln, *Passage through Armageddon*, 89. Russians did not have enough time to set up in Galicia the kind of elaborate German cultural-occupation system found in Ober Ost (the Baltic, Lithuania, Belarus): see Vejas Liulevicius, *Warland: Peoples, Lands, and National Identity on the Eastern Front in World War I* (Ph.D. Dissertation, University of Pennsylvania, 1994).

42   Frank Golder, *War, Revolution, and Peace in Russia* ed. Terence Emmons and Ben Patenaude (Stanford, 1992). The two Jews: oral testimony.

43   For exceptions, see Jahn, *Patriotic Culture*, 113-14, 133. The Jews of Russia did raise their own voice, however. The Moscow journal *The War and the Jews* featured Jewish war heroes, including a cartoon of a ferocious Private Katz bayonetting Germans, and news about Jewish participation in the war and its effect upon the Jewish population in Poland. See *Voina i evrei*, 3 (1914). See also Segel and Roshwald, chapters 3 and 4, this volume.

44   Compare *Sbornik soldatskikh pesen* (Petrograd, 1915) with *Sbornik soldatskikh, kazatskikh, i matrosskikh pesen*, ed. N. K. Vessel, 2 ed. (St. Petersburg, 1886). In origin, these seem to be military equivalents of composed "folk songs." As with the Yanks in France, Russian soldiers probably adapted them to indecent lyrics. Nor could the occasional

forays to the front by popular entertainers (Jahn, *Patriotic Culture*, 98) be considered trench culture.

45 For an introduction to this rich history, see: Daniel Orlovsky, in Abbott Gleason *et al.*, eds., *Bolshevik Culture* (Bloomington, 1985); Christopher Read, "The Cultural Intelligentsia," in Roben Service, ed., *Society and Politics in the Russian Revolution* (London, 1992), 86-102; V. P. Lapshin, *Khudozhestvennaya zhizn' Moskvy i Petrograda v 1917 g.* (Moscow, 1983); and N. A. Nilsson, ed., *Art, Society, Revolution: Russia, 1917-1921* (Stockholm, 1979).

23

Soviet Russian Wartime Culture
Freedom and Control, Spontaneity and Consciousness

The mobilization of culture in the Great Patriotic War of 1941 must be seen in the context of the overall dynamic interaction of state policy and popular response. To make the point more clearly, one may compare the relation of state and culture in the Soviet experience to that in the Great War of 1914. Bluntly speaking, these two struggles had little in common except the fact that Germans and Russians fought each other. Two important books and some other recent studies are eloquent on the matter. The German scholar Hubertus Jahn's study of popular culture and entertainment in the visual and performing arts offers a picture of commercial opportunity combined with popular patriotism in the initial phases of war that resulted in a very large and interesting output of culture directly related to the war. As a rule this culture highlighted the bravery of Russian troops, the evil of the enemy, the nobility of the Allies (especially the "martyr nation," Belgium), and the reliability of the home front. This output began to fade after 1915 along with enthusiasm for the war among the population. The Imperial Russian regime, with a few exceptions, played a distinctly minor role in promoting anything like a vast propaganda machine.[1] The Finnish literary historian Ben Hellman's book on the symbolist poets during World War I goes well beyond its main topic and taps the very core of the cultural intelligentsia's response to the war. That response, though rhetorically patriotic, was couched in mystical formulations of the spiritual superiority of the Russian soul. It seldom touched on the realities of blood and battle. For the Russian intelligentsia, this war was fought in the realms of spirit, soul, and mind, an apocalyptic battle of ideas and national moralities.[2]

My own brief survey of high and popular culture in the War of 1914 emphatically confirms this view.[3] The wartime spy thrillers in print culture and cinema took the consumer to the front lines and into the machinations of the enemy behind the lines. Hero tales exalted the lancer, the machine gunner, the aviator, and the brave nurse; they vividly described the milieu—troop trains, mountains of corpses, field hospitals. Thoroughly mendacious in exaggerating German atrocities and denying or ignoring Russian brutalities during the Great Retreat of 1915, these works of pulp fiction and movie action melodrama nevertheless engaged the war itself—its material ambiance and its bodily exploits and suffering. After the disasters of 1915, even these genres turned back to the more traditional forms and themes of adventure, high society sexual melodrama, and even comedy. As a whole, the culture produced during the Great War metaphorically illustrates two great gaps: one between the state and the rest of society and one between elite and popular visions of the war.

One of the achievements of Stalinist culture—with all its distortions and banalities—was to close these gaps. The closure, or at least a major rapprochement, of the gap between state and society is well enough known: the monopolization and active guidance of literature and all the arts along the lines of "socialist realism." The machinery created in the 1930s ensured tight censorship, the silencing of dissonant voices, and the direct shaping of the arts, particularly the narrative arts—fiction, painting, opera, drama. The content and formulas of socialist realism closed, or attempted to close, the gap between intelligentsia and people, one might even say between mind and body. In fiction, the model for all the other arts, the intelligentsia was welded to the masses in every struggle—for production and against wreckers. The weld joined two elements of Soviet society. One was a mature mentor, often a learned and seasoned commissar, engineer, or scientist, cool and reserved, ready to shape the energies of the other. The other was the man or woman of the people—partisan, worker, collective farmer, aviator—hotheaded and locked in a battle against some obstruction, but too spontaneous to pull it off without the counsel of the mentor. However false the jointure, however unconvincing the obstacles and the solutions, this formula created the model for the culture of the Soviet war against the Axis powers between 1941 and 1945.

Soon after the initial shock of the 1941 invasion, social volcanoes began erupting on the Soviet home front. State policy, military operations, and mass reaction to the invasion took numerous forms. The government, party, and police mobilized the people, evacuated personnel and factories to the rear, moved whole segments of the population around on an immense scale, relocated government offices and cultural establishments, including film studios and theaters, and saw to the manufacture of weapons, the transport of troops, and the recruitment of ever fresh levees. As an example of massive direction of human energy, within six months over fifteen hundred large-scale enterprises, including over a hundred aircraft factories, were evacuated; about one-eighth of the nation's industrial assets were dismantled, relocated, and reassembled in the Urals, Central Asia, and Siberia. High school graduates of both sexes enlisted. Villagers melted into the forest and became partisans. Youngsters organized urban spy rings to wreak sabotage on the German garrisons. A million women served in the armed forces, not only in traditional wartime roles of nurses, doctors, and anti-aircraft gunners, but also as flyers, soldiers, tankers, and partisans.[4]

Nothing even faintly resembling this occurred during World War I. The regime possessed neither the will nor the power to make such things happen, nor would the population have responded in full array for war. This was partly due to the circumstances at the front. By 1915 the possibility of the Germans plunging into Great Russian territory was real, but at the outer limit of German expansion, they occupied only Poland and part of the Baltic provinces and then got stalled. Scattered atrocities occurred, of course, but nothing like the systematic bestiality that followed in the wake of Operation Barbarossa in 1941. In fact, during World War I, Russian outrages in Poland and Galicia were worse than anything the Central Powers perpetrated on the eastern front. Little of this filtered into Russian popular awareness, except for some publicity about the fate of the Jews who were cruelly used during the retreat of 1915.

In the Soviet war, state officials, propagandists of the Communist Party, and leaders of unions and mass organizations, carefully reading the psychology of the wartime masses, constructed new myths, legends, and cultural icons. Grafted onto the template of socialist realism, they were designed to draw upon the bottomless wells of national pride, to substitute visceral themes about the beloved homeland for the dry, bombastic official patriotism of the prewar period. For reasons both noble and ignoble, they reached out to find the heart of war in every Russian and to make it beat the rhythms of love, hate, anger, and ridicule—all directed toward smashing the "fascist" enemy and saving Mother Russia.

The level of hatred toward the German enemy differed greatly in the two wars. Except among a few circles of the pre-1914 Pan-Slavic intelligentsia, the teutonophobic rage was short-lived. Nothing like the Bolshevik buildup of the "fascist beast" had been present in pre-1914 Russia because, of course, fascism had not yet been born. In the Soviet 1920S the word "fascist" became a floating modifier for virtually any kind of enemy, including even Social Democrats who were seen as nothing more than servants of fascism disguised as socialists. In the 1930s, with Hitler in power in Nazi Germany, the term took on flesh, at least until the Nazi-Soviet Nonagression Pact of 1939. After two years of uneasy alliance it was not difficult to revive the old repulsive images. In order to retain some vestige of a Marxoid political category, the enemy was consistently labeled "fascist invader" by the official press. But eventually the more concrete "German" took over, especially in the hate poetry and journalism of eloquent writers such as Konstantin Simonov and Ilya Ehrenburg. When one sets the cardboard villains of Russian World War I spy thrillers, plays, and films beside the quintessential demons of World War II invaders, the former take on an almost comic hue.

In general accounts of the Soviet Union in World War II, the cultural dimension is still relatively neglected. Only religion and literature have been adequately treated. The expressive life of the wartime experience in communications, creativity, entertainment, the arts, hagiography and legend making, and the memorialization of the war has been addressed in a previous book, which focuses on the resurfacing into public life of emotional and even spiritual expression, recently suppressed or distorted in the media during the 1930s.[5]

Two major cultural-psychological currents were at large during this momentous struggle, coexisting and occasionally clashing.

The first was the official style of nationalism, authoritarianism, and hierarchy established in the 1930s—formal, impersonal, pompous, and unnervingly unemotional. It expressed itself in various terms: Stalinism, *partiinost* (high ideological consciousness and dedication to political business), socialist realism (the fantasy world of 1930s art that required folkloric structures and idealistic messages), heroicized traditional history, revolutionary glory, and proletarian robustness. Perhaps only the Russian adjectives *offitsioznyi* and *kazënnyi* can convey the terms of expression that in English suggest words like official, state, declamatory, inflated, bureaucratic, operatic, stylized, melodramatic, posed, monumental, utopian, and panegyric. The style was burdened with values of official boast and state talk as illustrated in the radio voices of Yurii Levitan and other announcers, government communiqués, *Pravda* headlines and editorials, and some films, songs, music, plays, graphics, and legends.

While such state-suffused cultural expression exists in all modern societies with mass communication, in the Soviet Union it was exceptionally amplified and hypertrophied, beyond even that of the Third Reich. The "public sphere" that usually lies between private discourse and official culture was unusually narrow because its basis—civil society—was almost eliminated by the nationalization of industry and all business, the collectivization of the countryside, the fear engendered by police, purge, and terror, and the swelling of the state. The small public sphere of expression—mass culture—was never wholly free of state content, even though much of it was very popular in terms of consumption. Needless to say, much that was private, unofficial, semiofficial, and countercultural remained outside the reach of the state, but its public utterance was severely restricted.

An acceptable aspect of unofficial and semiofficial cultural style rose to ascendance after the initial shock, however, and clearly expressed the feelings of a people at war. In vivid contrast to the official style, it was emotional, personal, relaxed, earthy, natural, spontaneous, autonomous, expressive, and honest about death, suffering, heroism, and hate. Wartime culture reflected the partial re-legitimation in Soviet public culture of personal life, intimate feelings, interior authenticity, and even quasi religiosity that had been muted during the "optimistic" thirties. Even the official party organ, *Pravda*, was, in the words of Jeffrey Brooks, "opened to new voices and new images of soldiers, partisans, civilians, and citizens."[6] Nina Tumarkin, interviewing veterans, tells of the sense of freedom that many participants felt on the outbreak of war. She quotes survivors saying that "those were our finest hours, the most brilliant time of our lives."[7] For those people the horrors, recalled with equal vividness, did not blot out the golden glow of that memory. Suffering and perhaps fear led to a passionate exaltation of Russian nature, its people, history, culture, and ancient religion. Art in every form could not fail to intersect with the changing mood.

Ironically enough, but not surprisingly, the popular culture of World War I had contained more bombast than emotional authenticity. Battlefield fiction and songs, including contrived hero stories, were suffused with "hurrah patriotism," particularly at the beginning of hostilities. Like the French, the Russians were planning to bivouac outside Berlin in no time at all. Heroic legends—not all of them false—were spun around individuals such as Kuzma Kryuchkov, who allegedly killed eleven German soldiers with his lance.[8] In World War II, the Red Army and the Soviet partisans had their share of individual exploits as well, but the "collective"—particular units, cities, and guerrilla bands—was much more prominent in the hagiography. Although some women went into combat during World War I, there were no partisan martyrs like Zoya Kosmodemyanskaya.

Many sources attest to the relative loosening of intellectual and creative controls in the years of the German occupation and the life-and-death struggle for national and state survival. Sad and terrible as it is to say, the war seemed to unleash creativity and create a kind of relieved joy. "When war flared up," wrote Boris Pasternak, "its real horrors and real dangers, the threat of a real death, were a blessing compared to the inhuman reign of fantasy, and they brought relief by limiting the magic force of the dead letter."[9] As the composer Dmitrii Shostakovich recalled, "the war helped. The war brought great sorrow and made life very hard. Much sorrow and many tears. But it had been even harder before the war, because then everyone was alone in his sorrow."[10] Those who did not collaborate with the enemy—the vast majority under occupation as well as those outside the occupied zones—formed a community of deep and shared sorrow as well as a nearly unanimous hatred of the enemy, which helped to reshape national consciousness to an extent that the old revolutionary élan could never again dislodge.

The notion of a "holy war" is almost oxymoronic, given war's essence and purpose. But almost all nations, particularly those who are attacked and invaded, try to sanctify the struggle. The USSR—with its Russian core—was no exception. The ideology of communism could not always evoke sacred feelings among the masses. Marxism, though not abandoned, was down played for most of the war: the Comintern was abolished, and patriotic slogans replaced international proletarian ones in an acceleration of the "nationalization" of Bolshevism that had first glimmered in the 1920s and then rose more rapidly in the 1930s. Significant is the fact that the official name of the war, the Great Patriotic (or Fatherland) War, did not contain the words "communist" or "Soviet." Wartime patriotism was couched in terms of reverence for the land, its history, and its treasure house of culture—all supporting the belief in the virtue of the Russian and Soviet peoples and the hideous bestiality of the German invader who sought their annihilation.

The Russian land as the matrix of home and family provided the central metaphor for wartime mood and culture. Germans lusted after Russian Earth, went the slogan; let them each have six feet of it. The land, with its familiar rivers, steppes, meadows, and endless birch forests, was a permanent backdrop to wartime culture. The motherland (*rodina*)—often represented in graphic art as a maternal figure—became an object of unabashed idolatry. Popular songs evoked simplicity and family happiness (real and imagined), with occasional visions of a rustic cabin or a hometown street. The memorable film song "Dark Is the Night" sings of bullets whistling across the steppe in fierce battle while far away the soldier's wife wipes away a tear beside the cradle of their child. Women were often represented as defenseless and menaced or victimized by a German. There was nothing tendentious about this: women and children were being slaughtered in cold blood by the thousands, a practice graphically exhibited in films of the period such as *She Defends the Fatherland* (1943), *Zoya* (1944), and *Rainbow* (1944). But women were also engaged in combat, a fact poorly reflected in official culture except for this trinity of thematically limited partisan women movies.

Heroes of the historical homeland were quickly reenlisted in the war effort. The 1938 film *Alexander Nevsky*, banned during the Nazi-Soviet Pact, was taken off the shelf and reissued after the invasion. Great military heroes of the medieval and tsarist past were refurbished: Nevsky in film, Kutuzov in drama, Suvorov on posters. Parallels with 1812 were heavily underlined. Dmitrii Moor's poster, "Then and Now, 1812-1941," foregrounded Hitler with a Napoleonic silhouette lurking behind him. The film short *Incident at the Telegraph Office* (1941) shows Napoleon sending Hitler a message: "I have tried it. I do not recommend it." All of this was as formal and contrived as the creation of hero cults at the time. Abstract populations, such as cities, were heroized for their endurance or resistance; Leningrad, Brest, Kiev, Odessa, Sevastopol, and Stalingrad were eventually named Hero Cities.[11] Mythic cults of human heroes and martyrs were woven around the Twenty-Eight Panfilov men, the Five Sailors of Sevastopol, the Young Guard of Krasnodon, and Captain Castello, who plunged his burning plane into an enemy armored column. Two stand out as the most famous: Alexander Matrosov, who allegedly threw his body across a German machine-gun nest, and Zoya Kosmodemyanskaya, who was tortured and hanged by the Germans early in the war. Both heroic images were stamped into the devotional life of wartime and postwar Russia through poetry, drama, radio, movies, photos, statues, and children's tales, and both are now subject to searching revision by historians.

Rosalinde Sartorti has examined the demythologizing of war heroes and their alleged exploits, asking the question, Which is more important, the "truth," or the truth that was believed? She argues that these heroes were in a sense created by the masses, whose aesthetic and moral demands help craft the deed and the person honored for doing it. Studies of the press also show that real people, "little" men and women, were being watched, interviewed, and chronicled without the mediation of the state. The radio and news correspondents who humanized and desolemnized their material—particularly Vasilii Grossman, Konstantin Simonov, and Ilya Ehrenburg—were the most popular with civilians and soldiers alike. It is interesting that many serious fiction writers served at the front alongside professional journalists—a thing that did not, to my knowledge, occur in Germany or the United States (where the most famous correspondent, Ernie Pyle, was a professional newsman, distant in psychology and style from a writer like Ernest Hemingway who had served in Spain). Jeffrey Brooks, in describing wartime *Pravda*, speaks of "new images of soldiers, partisans, civilians, and citizens," autonomous and sentient beings in contrast to the puppet-like figures interviewed on construction sites in the 1930s. State heroes were thus balanced by real ones—ordinary people caught up in the grimness of war. The space occupied by the cult of Stalin—now in temporary decline—was filled by popular heroism. And when heroism involved death, this was faced with honesty and dignity.[12]

The precious storehouse of Russian classics was linked with the national liberation. Novels and stories flooded the reading market. Tolstoy's *War and Peace*—now read for its promises—was issued in huge print runs and read by actors over the airwaves in a series of thirty radio shows. The same author's *Sevastopol Tales* was given a radio reading during the siege of that city. Many nineteenth-century novels, poems, and plays were read over the radio and thus perhaps became a part of mass culture for the first time. Soviet creative artists appeared on radio talk shows—as the composer Shostakovich, the writer Alexei Tolstoy, and the actor Nikolai Cherkasov (who had played the title role in the film *Alexander Nevsky*) did together—to appeal for a defense of Russian culture against the marauding enemy.[13]

Classical music was exalted as never before. In war-racked cities, the most mournful strains of Chaikovsky filled the concert halls and airwaves, and concerts were aired live from the Bolshoi theater. The journalist Alexander Werth recalled with astonishment "the extraordinary emotional atmosphere that summer, for instance at any routine Tchaikovsky concert-as though all Russian civilization were now in deadly danger. I remember the countless tears produced on one of the worst days in July 1942 by the famous love theme in Tchaikovsky's *Romeo and Juliet* Overture." Werth was puzzled by this. Yet any student of the sociology of music (or any sensitive listener for that matter) knows how easily music that conveys sorrow, even on a wholly unrelated theme, can release feelings and tears about one's own immediate grief. In a time of war or immense tragedy, personal grief can become part of a collective national lament. Soviet composers turned their talents to war-related subjects, Shostakovich's "Leningrad" Symphony being the most famous and most emotionally cathartic of these. Classical music lorded it on the airwaves, becoming in fact a popular art. This had been prepared for by the immediate efforts of cultural leaders to expose workers to "monographic" concerts of classical music right after the Revolution and by radio broadcasts of music education in the 1930s. Beethoven, Mozart, and Bach—though German—were not banished (as they were in some concert halls during World War 1); on the contrary they were used by artistic leaders to draw a line between "true and good Germans" and Nazis.[14]

The Germans also sacralized music, treating it as a popular as well as a national art. In the combat film drama *Stukas* (1940), two of the heroes play Chopin on the piano between raids against the French, even though, I have been told, public performance of Chopin's music was outlawed in German-occupied Poland, Chopin's homeland. The two aviators also play Wagner's *Rhine Journey*, arranged for two hands. When later in the film a young pilot becomes shell-shocked, he is cured by a performance of this music at Bayreuth where his nurse points out to him "the beauty of the German land." In another movie, *Wunschkonzert* (1942), a domestic scene shows the playing of Beethoven's *Pathétique* sonata (which has to be identified to the listeners on screen) as the camera cuts to the marching feet of booted soldiers on the street below. Art, nation, and heroism became a natural linking in popular imaging. But the "classics" in general were given much more widespread dissemination in the USSR than in other belligerent nations. This was because officially produced mass culture lacked sufficient emotional power, and the authorities preferred the "clean," respectable emotionalism of the classics, which induced reverent pride—but not a direct individual stake—in the homeland, to that of popular culture from below.

Wartime radio deepened the bond among Soviet citizens who listened to the open expressions of love, loneliness, despair, fear, and hope contained in letters to and from the front. Vladimir Yakhontov, a reader-actor, said, "living without listening to the radio was impossible. Radio informed, signaled and guided us, kept kin and loved ones linked together." Its programming helped to reshape national identity by fusing information, culture, and emotionalism into a picture of a just and martyred people beleaguered by an evil force.[15]

Frontline entertainment brigades of actors, singers, ballet dancers, folk musicians, and circus acts regaled the troops in mixed genre shows right behind the fighting lines. Some 45,000 men and women serving in 1,720 brigades performed over 400,000 concerts at the front. But these itinerant artists—like their counterparts in the American USO (United Services Organization)—had somewhat more freedom and could be more responsive to immediate needs of the soldiery than could those working in print media or on the air. Time and again, the state bodies that organized these companies tried to "direct" their repertoires and comportment, not always with success. Performers often hesitated to take their frothy wit or sassy song from the civilian stages of home to the roar and flame of the fighting lines. Yet they were always requested by frontline audiences to perform as they had on stage in the prewar days. The armed forces wanted songs of love, elegies of home, salty jokes, and anything that reminded them of home and normal life— certainly not politics and battle themes.[16] It is not at all paradoxical that Russian and other Soviet soldiers and sailors adored two kinds of music from the entertainment brigades above all: Russian folk songs and American jazz, either unmediated in the band of Edi Rozner or in the more adapted and sanitized versions of Leonid Utësov's band. Since the United States was an ally of the USSR in this war, the two wholly normal tastes of the ordinary eclectic consumer could be equally accommodated—an accommodation that would vanish in the postwar period.

The theme of hate was naturally prominent in the cultural offering. News about German atrocities introduced anger and loathing into high and popular culture. "With these hands of mine," wrote the poet Alexei Surkov about the Germans, "I want to strangle everyone of them." Konstantin Simonov's "Kill Him" was the culmination of a frenzied rage: "Kill a German, kill him soon / And every time you see one—kill him." Ehrenburg poured his racist abhorrence and contempt for the Germans into the pages of *Red Star*, the military paper that was devoured by the soldiers. Poster art depicted the Wehrmacht forces as rodents, insects, monkeys, pigs, and hyenas—beasts without feelings, sadistic brutes. The hate message was often conveyed through gross ridicule of Hitler, his minions, and his troops. They were portrayed in circus frontline shows and in graphic art as doomed descendants of Napoleon or "Winter Fritzes," blue-skinned and shivering, unaccustomed to the Russian frosts and addicted to stealing women's garments. Circus clowns had only to re-costume the old targets of the revolution: Kerensky, White officers, and fat capitalists.[17]

Three related phenomena reflect the deepening of the emotions in the stress of war and uncover dormant or suppressed layers of the human spirit: religion, populism, and folk culture. Stalin abolished the League of the Godless (founded in the 1920s) and arranged a temporary truce with the Orthodox Church; in return, the Metropolitan of Moscow publicly announced in 1942 that Stalin was "the divinely anointed leader of our armed and cultural forces leading us to victory over the barbarian invasion." Church reopenings were attended by multitudes of devout believers. The regime proudly communicated news about fund-raising efforts by churchmen and congregations to purchase tanks for the army; Ehrenburg openly described people praying; and Simonov wrote poetically and movingly of "the simple crosses on Russian graves." The earthy populism so endemic to the Russian manner was revived and displayed in the soldiers' mass response to the most popular epic poem of the period, Alexander Tvardovsky's *Vasily Terkin*, a tale about a coarse, witty, and humane soldier—the universal "little man" in the ranks who personified for the masses the notion that this was a war of the people. Folk singing and folk ensemble performance, though still bearing marks of its artificial styling, rose to the full amplitude of popularity in the patriotic war, erupted into a wave of festivals, and swelled majestically in the years to come, reflecting the depth of national feelings ignited by the struggle for existence.[18]

Propaganda and official pomposity never disappeared, of course. One finds it even in the genuinely popular and emotional films: in the final frames of *She Defends the Motherland*, the heroine stands on the gallows from which she has just been rescued and in her exalted speech mixes human feelings with clichés from the press as Soviet planes soar overhead. In *Zoya*, after the heroine is hanged, her smiling face is superimposed against Soviet flying aircraft and tanks rolling westward to victory. After Stalingrad, grandiloquent motifs of victory and military might suffused the media; and after the even greater battle of Kursk, resolemnization ensued on a vast scale. In response to these battlefield victories in 1943 and 1944, and in reaction to the sweeping spontaneity of popular emotion, the Soviets began reintroducing motifs of triumphalism and military might into the media on a vast scale: parades, the salute, epaulets and rows of medals for officers, and inflated communiqués. On the day of victory over the Germans the surgeons of official culture began to excise the great heart that had beat so spontaneously in the cauldron of battle. Wartime songs and films were, to be sure, repeated again and again for decades. But they were sanitized and passed through a filter of piety and self-congratulation that burnt out much of the original spirit of wartime culture. The multipurpose myth of war and victory extended down the years, but the heart of war had become a valentine for the state.

Neither this nor the stilted official cult of the war could stanch human memories of grief, fear, pride, heroism, and loss. This memory rang with the clarion sound of war for two generations. Understanding a nation's experience of war is often difficult for outsiders. War creates myth and memory embodied in great art and popular culture, and the persistent recollection of the moods it evoked in the minds of millions continued to configure attitudes. The human losses in this war were forty times greater than those of Britain and seventy times those of the United States—greater indeed than those of all the belligerents combined. Soviet people may not have known these comparative figures, but they knew through family memory as much as through public reminders that their collective suffering was colossal. The persistent recollection of the war in the minds of millions continued to configure cinema, songs, performance arts, and fiction long after 1945. For decades, Soviet people were constantly barraged by the regime with war images, but the solemnized memory sponsored by the government did not always converge with the actual recollections of the people.[19]

What did soldiers expect of the postwar period? Probably a return to the imagined joys of prewar peacetime life. A campaigner wrote to his wife in 1942 that every day would be like the movie *The*

Great Waltz.[20] It was not to be. A major backlash took place against satire, modernism, jazz, and "unpatriotic" or "rootless" elements (such as Jews). The purge of certain war novels (especially Fadeev's *Young Guard*) is well known. The entire postwar cultural pogrom—sometimes called the *zhdanovshchina* after its principal witch-hunter—was as much a reaction against wartime spontaneity, intimacy, emotionalism, and displays of eclectic desire for both native Russian and western entertainment forms as it was a reaction to the cold war. But the cold war and the perceived threat from the West certainly added a strong element of paranoid xenophobia. The replacement of the Holy War by the cold war brought a flourish of Russian chauvinism and anti-cosmopolitanism, a retightening of ideological orthodoxy and control, an austerity program that was covered over with a glistening cultural smile and the escalation of the Stalin cult to unprecedented heights. Consciousness reasserted itself over the spontaneity born of battle, hardship, heroism, and adventure. But once unleashed, the genie could not be thrust back into the bottle; when Stalin died, new waves of cultural "authenticity" in the high and popular arts resurfaced.

Original publication: In Robert Thurston, ed. *A People's War: Popular Responses to World War II in the Soviet Union*. Urbana-Champaign: University of Illinois Press, 2000, pp. 171-184. (Portions of this were originally published as "Introduction: Russia's Holy War." in *Culture and Entertainment in Wartime Russia,* Indiana University Press, 1966, pp. 1-8).

Notes

1   Hubertus Jahn, *Patriotic Culture in Russia during World War I* (Ithaca, N.Y., 1995).
2   Ben Hellman, *Poets of Hope and Despair: The Russian Symbolists in War and Revolution (1914-1918)* (Helsinki, 1995).
3   Richard Stites, "Days and Nights in Wartime Russia," in *European Culture in the Great War: The Arts, Propaganda, and Entertainment*, ed. Avid Roshwald and Richard Stites (Cambridge, 1999); also the preceding essay here.
4   John Barber and Mark Harrison, *The Soviet Home Front, 1941-1945: A Social and Economic History of the USSR in World War II* (London, 1991), 59-76, 127-32; Anne Griesse and Richard Stites, "Russia: War

and Revolution," in *Female Soldiers—Combatants or Noncombatants? Historical and Contemporary Perspectives*, ed. Nancy Goldman (Westport, Conn., 1982), 61-84; Reina Pennington, *Women, Wings, and War*, Ph.D. dissertation (University of South Carolina, 2000).

5   Richard Stites, ed., *Culture and Entertainment in Wartime Russia* (Bloomington, Ind., 1995).

6   Jeffrey Brooks, "*Pravda* Goes to War," in Stites, ed., *Culture and Entertainment*, 9.

7   Nina Tumarkin, "The War of Remembrance," in Stites, ed., *Culture and Entertainment*, 204.

8   On the cult of Kryuchkov see Jahn, *Patriotic Culture.*

9   Boris Pasternak, quoted in Geoffrey Hosking, *A History of the Soviet Union* (London, 1985), 276.

10   Solomon Volkov, ed., *Testimony: The Memoirs of Dmitri Shostakovich*, trans. Antonina Bouis (New York, 1979), 135.

11   For a case study of the sanctification of cities see Karl Qualls, "The Rebuilding of Sevastopol," Ph.D. dissertation (Georgetown University, 1999).

12   Rosalinde Sartorti, "On Heroes and Heroines," in Stites, ed., *Culture and Entertainment*, 176-93; Louise McReynolds, "Dateline Stalingrad: Frontline Correspondents," in Stites, ed., *Culture and Entertainment*, 28-43; Brooks, "*Pravda* Goes to War," 9-27.

13   James Von Geldern, "Radio Moscow: The Voice from the Center," in Stites, ed., *Culture and Entertainment*, 44-61.

14   Ibid.; Alexander Werth, *Russia at War, 1941-1945* (New York, 1964), 410; Robert Rothstein, "Homeland, Home Town, and Battlefield," in Stites, ed., *Culture and Entertainment*, describes how a female sound engineer could not record the famous film song, "Dark is the Night," because of her tears falling on the equipment, and of a chorus who could not get through "Dnieper Song" without weeping (87, 89). Those who lived in the United States during the war will recall perhaps how the music of Grieg, Dvorak, and Chopin, among others, was used to elicit sympathy for occupied peoples. And of course it worked.

15   Vladimir Yakhontov, quoted in Von Geldern, "Radio Moscow," 55.

16   For troop entertainment see Stites, "Frontline Brigades," in Stites, ed., *Culture and Entertainment*; I. N. Sakharova, ed., *Iskusstvo v boevom stroiu: Vospominaniia, dnevniki, ocherki* (Moscow, 1985).

17   Argyrios Pisiotis, "Images of Hate in the Art of War," in Stites, ed., *Culture and Entertainment*, 141- 56.

18   See Richard Stites, *Russian Popular Culture: Entertainment and Society since 1900* (Cambridge, 1992), 98-122.

19   Nina Tumarkin, *The Living and the Dead: The Rise and Fall of the Cult of World War II in Russia* (New York, 1994).

20 *The Great Waltz* was a prewar Hollywood musical based on the life of the nineteenth-century Austrian operetta and waltz composers, Johann Strauss, father and son. This and other American movies were captured by Soviet troops at various stages of the war.

24

Russian Representation of the Japanese Enemy

Iaponiia: The Intellectual Environment

One might say that negative and transferable orientalist images of the Japanese found a place among the Russians long before the conflict of 1904-5. Nothing is easier than to adapt clichés about one group of people to another. One need only recall, taking two examples, the nearly identical American popular depiction of Nazi spies in the early 1940s and Soviet agents in the late 1940s; or the similar application of the "gook" formula to the Japanese in World War II, the North Koreans and Chinese in the 1950s, and the Vietcong in the 1960s and 1970s.[1] British colonists in the days of the high empire freely wielded the term "wog" in reference to Arab, Persian, Turk, and any number of nationalities of the Indian subcontinent. Russians had been fighting against Asians for centuries prior to the clash with Japan: the steppe nomads of the Kievan period, followed by Mongols, Tatars, Ottoman Turks, Caucasian peoples, and Central Asians—to name only the most important. At the turn of the twentieth century, Russian forces in Beijing and Manchuria made little distinction between genuine Boxers and other Chinese who were liquidated as bandits. In 1904, many Russians saw the Japanese as just another "Asiatic" race to be properly disciplined and subdued by a superior European (Russian) force.

In spite of many episodic and fragmentary contacts with Japanese, to Russian society of the nineteenth century, Japan remained an exotic island kingdom shrouded in mystery. Writing about it first hand, the novelist Ivan Goncharov in the 1850s had depicted Japanese society as an "ant heap" in his book, *The Frigate Pallas*.[2]

Asian languages including Japanese were taught at the Vladivostok Eastern Institute but their graduates were not strategically deployed. For example, Japanese was not offered at the General Staff Academy until 1905, and the Russian army remained grossly under-informed about matters Japanese.[3]

The dynasty discovered Japan through the sly invocation by Kaiser Wilhelm of the alleged Yellow Peril and through the unfortunate 1891 voyage to Japan of the Tsarevich Nicholas, during which a would be assassin assaulted him. All this was heated up in the years of Russia's ill-considered expansion into Manchuria and Korea. When the Russo-Japanese war broke out in 1904, Nicholas II, now the commander-in-chief, "failed to perceive that Japan's army was more than a band of 'little brown monkeys' (macaques), as he called them"[4] in contrast to private expressions of admiration for certain aspects of Japanese life. Given the negative cue from on high, the official *Pravitel'stvennyi vestnik* (Government Messenger) was bound to follow suit and it painted an unambiguously negative picture of the enemy right up to war's end.[5]

The mass circulation press however did not always follow suit, and ignorance at the top failed to ascend to a level of massive self-mystification. Only a few of the bigger papers, such as A.S. Suvorin's *Novoe vremia* (New Times), kept up the beat of the war drums and anti-Japanese mockery all through 1904. The boulevard press also engaged in angry discourse about Russia's "historical mission" and the Japanese maniacs who resisted it. The nastier papers demonized the enemy in the crudest possible way, constantly speaking of *iaposhki* (Japs) instead of *iapontsy* (Japanese) even in news stories.

The content—as often happens in patriotic rhetoric—offered a predictable combination of sanctifying reverence for the Russian side and insulting abuse for the enemy in tones that were almost interchangeable from the output of 1812 and 1877 (and, beyond, of 1914 and 1941). But even here, messages were often mixed. Fiction contained more hysterical atrocity stories than the editorials; Japan-bashing was balanced by assaults on the ungrateful Europeans (i.e. Britain, Japan's ally) whom the Russians had allegedly saved from the Mongol devastation in the Middle Ages. Patriotic outrage sometimes alternated with more moderate views of the enemy. Since the thirst for news in rural Russian grew rapidly in this war, the stereotypes were distributed along with it as literate peasants on the home front read newspaper dispatches to other peasants.[6]

The star journalists of I. D. Sytin's *Russkoe slovo* (Russian Word), Vlas Doroshevich and V. I. Nemirovich-Danchenko (brother of the famous director), sent back dispatches from the front in which they denied the Yellow Peril thesis, spoke of the Japanese forces with respect, and openly criticized the government's ineptitude. Nemirovich-Danchenko called the struggle a "blind war." Sytin's paper tried to combine a position of patriotism with a critique of the autocracy and its war management (although his pamphlets voiced a far more chauvinistic view). His journalists assumed a posture familiar in our own time: unconditional support of "the boys at the front" and condemnation of the war itself.[7] A more radical and cohesive stance among intellectuals, socialism, clearly disassociated itself from a racist perspective on the Japanese during this war. The Socialist-Revolutionaries and both branches of the Marxist Social-Democratic Party (Bolsheviks and Mensheviks) preferred to distinguish between the workers-and-peasants-as-soldiers of both Japan and Russia on the one hand, and the warlords and capitalists of those countries on the other.[8]

Fiction, Stage, Graphic Arts

Russian literature, the vaunted conscience of the nation, often set the tone of cultural and moral discourse. In this war, the literary community divided roughly into moderate opposition, "transcendents," and patriots. The patriots or chauvinists who held no truck with philosophical or literary nuances ruled at the lower end of the mass press and the popular media. Opposition to the war took a number of different forms, most of them far removed from imagery of the Japanese. Leonid Andreev's famous anti-militarist novella *Red Laugh* (1905) focused on the "madness and horror" of combat. War itself, not Japan, was the real enemy. It not only crazed its participants, but turned decent men into Kurtz-like figures who reveled in the bloodbath. Leo Tolstoy's "Bethink Yourselves" (1904, published abroad) sympathized with the combatants on both sides. Tolstoy used his still burning literary flair to identify the foppery of tsarist military uniforms with false values and corrupt minds. And yet, when the news of Russia's disastrous defeat in the naval Battle of Tsushima arrived, Tolstoy displayed a particle of his sometimes submerged vestigial Russian patriotism by saying that non-Christian peoples won wars because their "highest ideal is patriotism and military heroism." Among the more humane of the anti-war literary accounts were those of Vikentii Veresaev, a physician and writer who actually served on the Manchurian Front. Aside from offering the usual critique of Russian military corruption, Veresaev berated the Russian troops for pillaging Chinese villages in Manchuria in actions unrelated to the war against Japan. Veresaev also rather touchingly reported (or invented?) how Russian soldiers could be converted instantly from ridiculing a Japanese prisoner by that prisoner's laughter.[9]

The Symbolists and related schools of literature whom I call "the transcendents" dominated Russian letters for the most part right up to 1917. Anticipating their response to World War I,[10] they tended to see the 1904-5 war as hardly more than a reflection of a larger reality, a dream world of apocalypse and/or regeneration. In the words of David Wells, they possessed and expressed an "idealized and aestheticized vision of the world" and thus of the war. Some poets attempted to voice their aloofness to the actual fighting by publishing Japanese art works in one of their journals, *Vesy* (The Scales), during the course of the hostilities. Others took sides. Valerii Briusov saw Russia's eastward thrust to the Pacific Ocean as a natural act of "manifest destiny," and both he and Viacheslav Ivanov sang a dirge over Russian losses at Tsushima. At the opposite pole stood Fedor Sologub who wondered why Russians would lament the loss of a useless place such as Port Arthur. Konstantin Balmont's opposition to the war was mainly a cry against the government. Zinaida Gippius, in line with some leftist writers, saw war as the murderer of sanity. Before his death in 1900, the philosopher Vladimir Solovev had floated the notion of Japan leading a "Pan-Mongolian" war against Western civilization. Although no direct allusions were made to this later influential trope, the Symbolists of the wartime era seemed to combine the specter of defeat with the idea of transcendent, purifying hope.[11] Generally speaking, as Yuliya Mikhailova has stressed, the intelligentsia tended to see the Japanese (and any Asian) foe within a philosophical (or historiosophical) context, often as something inevitable like a cleansing storm, rather than as satanic.[12]

One of the most popular modes of entertainment in late tsarist Russia was the so-called People's or Popular Theater, organized by religious, philanthropic, anti-alcohol, and business groups. These stages were host to spectacles as well as drama and musical shows. When their directors entered the realm of patriotism, they merely recycled themes and devices from previous wars, notably the Russo-Turkish War of the 1870s. Shortly after the outbreak of war with Japan in 1904, a Moscow Popular Theater run by temperance groups put on *Glory to All for the Faith, the Tsar, and the Fatherland*, a musical extravaganza set against a huge map of East Asia. At each evening performance, actors read out news telegrams from the front to the audience. In St. Petersburg, actors depicted a naval battle between Russia and Japan off the coast of Korea as *The Heroes of Chemulpo.* In spring and summer 1904, with victory fever still in the air, *Port Arthur* and Japan's *War with Russia*, were big hits. Such productions fell off in 1905 when the revolutionary turbulence of that year and Russian defeats in the war diluted the open display of patriotic fervor.[13]

On the visual front, the camera—first baptized in fire during the Crimean War in the 1850s—was very much in evidence in 1904-5. The poor reproductions of a dozen or so photographs from the period reproduced in I. I. Rostunov's well-known 1977 book on the war contain no pejorative imagery, either in framing, composition, or lighting; and they show no signs of major retouching. These are outdoor campaign pictures, probably made by war correspondents or their photographers, perhaps from both sides. Japanese infantrymen, gunners, and sailors are presented as well dressed and orderly, with no sense of pose. The candid angle of shot suggests a lack of rehearsal, and there are no parade lineups or eyewash. The Japanese infantry uniforms may jar or amuse the modern gaze because they might suggest bellhops with footwraps, but they were of their time. Smallness of stature in these pictures of Japanese foot soldiers is not an issue even when set beside their Russian opponents. This juxtaposition occurs once when Russian soldiers make a breach in a Japanese gallery resulting in hand-to-hand combat. The Japanese sappers wield rifle, spade, and pickaxe against the bearded intruders whose facial hair make them look older than their adversaries. In a river-crossing scene, the Japanese troops move smartly at an awkward right or left shoulder arms, instead of the safer and more logical position of port arms. The picture of a reconnaissance detail would, except for the uniforms, hardly differ from a hunting photo of the period. The ceasefire scene contains nothing like arrogance, morose submission, or mutual hatred in the visual surface of the photo.[14] Neither the Russian nor the Japanese fighters are heroized or demeaned. The presumably patriotic Russian cameramen had yet to learn or to employ the art of photographic falsification that would be so eagerly used by the British in World War I.

How utterly differently propaganda artists approached the foe. Liberated from the constraints of the lens and armed by prior commitment, they eagerly demonized the foe and lionized their own. Artistic representation obviously differed from the photographic in several ways. Photography was produced on the ground and had to be sent back to the capitals for distribution. The medium itself was inherently limited in its ability to distort. Popular graphic art was largely produced in Moscow and Petersburg, which allowed for rapid production and distribution. The imaginative element in the construction of imagery, in cartoon and print, was set free by its distance from the front. Furthermore, as Yuliya Mikhailova has stressed, the artist could repeat images over and over again and thus convert them into icons.[15]

Of all the graphic media, the *"lubok* cartoon" contained the most lurid scenes. *Lubok* or popular print (sometimes called "folk picture") was a centuries old art form, originally fashioned from woodblock, later by means of copper plate, and then lithography, including chromolithography. The raw colors and primitive lines of *lubok* underscored the sharpness of the mockery aimed at the enemy—whether of Prussian "cockroaches" in the eighteenth century, French dandies in 1812, sluggish Turks in the 1870s, or minuscule Japanese warriors in 1904.[16] Over 300 prints dealing with the Russo-Japanese war appeared in hundreds of thousands of copies, but only in the first six months of that war.

Historian Stephen Norris' extensive study of wartime *lubok* shows that in the Russo-Japanese War, stock figures of patriotism, such as the Cossack and the peasant, reemerged with a vengeance. The tsar rarely appeared, and the only high-ranking military leader featured as a hero (and martyr) was Admiral Stepan Makarov, who perished in the sinking of his warship. The images Norris offers reveal a national stereotyping far more vicious than those of previous wars.[17] The fantasy and exaggeration of some of these pictures—in contrast to the then current tendency for more realism in *lubok*— speaks of a desire to match visual shock to the trauma of war and, thus, to appeal to wartime consumer tastes.

A few samples from the Helsinki University Slavonic Library Collection of Graphic Materials from the Russo-Japanese War may give an inkling of their format and content. They consist of original pieces, each published by a different typography, three of medium size, one very large, all in rather florid colors. Enemy imagery in them ranges from a certain *Schadenfreude* at their injuries and suffering to extremely hostile contempt. *The Sinking of Four Japanese Ships* has the unlucky crews with European-looking faces and "slanted" eyes falling or floating amid the debris of shattered timbers and twisted metal of the merchant ships sunk by shore batteries and the Russian battleship, *Retvizan.*[18] A scene featuring the same victorious Russian warship transforms it into a minotaur with the body of a sturdy earringed and smiling Russian sailor protruding from the prow with a fist in the face of his counterpart, Togo Tashi, whose beastly apelike face is suffering a bloody nose and knocked-out teeth.[19] *A Japanese Crosses the Yalu* shows a rather natty and delighted Russian cavalry trooper, with a mustache like that of an Italian tenor of the era, dragging the enemy soldier across the river with a rope. The victim is grotesquely wrought, with almost vertical eyes and tongue bulging from a terrified face.[20] The cheerful visages of the Russian figures seem to suggest the happy optimism of good-natured warriors easily beating their inferiors, images designed to feed confidence about an easy Russian victory.

The only land battle treated in this sample of posters is that of Chong-zhou in March 1904. The Japanese troops, clearly outlined, are either dead, wounded, or in full retreat from the onrushing mounted soldiers of the tsar, sabers aloft—with various kinds of "Slavic" faces ranging from a bearded peasant to a figure resembling the Yalu dandy noted above. This bloody tableau contains well over a hundred figures and shows a good deal of gory detail.[21]

The depiction of Japanese in all these posters nevertheless pales in comparison with the sadistic violence shown in the once famous and popular collection of American war cards entitled "The Horrors of War" (1935-39), completed two years before Pearl Harbor. In this collection, interspersed with scenes from the Italo-Ethiopian War of 1935 and the Spanish Civil War of 1936-9, are cartoon representations of the Japanese fire bombing of the Chapai District of Shanghai, the Panay Incident, and the Rape of Nanking (Nanjing) in 1937. Needless to say, the American wartime images (1941-1945) surpassed even these in primitive and hateful imaging of the Japanese enemy.[22]

In the 1904-5 war, a much more sober and fair-minded approach to the enemy in graphic art than that of the posters can be found in *The Russo-Japanese War on Land and Sea* (1904), an eight-volume collection in album format with pictures and text.[23] Graphic art alternates with photography. Volume I opens with a triptych of pro-war demonstrations on St. Petersburg's Nevskii Prospekt, near the Winter Palace, and a few other places. This and all subsequent representations of the tsar and his commanders employ a standard pious dynasto-patriotic style, the colors varying to provide either jingoist or lachrymose effects.

The hard and soft combination of course was de rigueur in all European war imagery in order to promote both "the terror and the pity" of any tragedy: on the one hand, savage hatred or contempt for the enemy; on the other, the official devotion and love for tsar, faith, and fatherland as well as the more personal compassion for soldiers lost and families devastated. Oval-shaped tinted photo cameos of the leaders are presented in the manner of the "parade portrait" of the eighteenth and nineteenth centuries which was adapted from painting to photography at the very moment of its birth: full dress uniform replete with medals, erect posture, sober facial expression, and a classical frame of laurels or drapery.[24]

At the other end of the social-military scale, certain common soldier "types" are singled out for color sketches, such as the Siberian Taiga or the Buriat Mongol soldiers,[25] suggesting that these local figures — "Good Asians," so to speak — are well set for a war against fellow Asians because they know the terrain, are used to its rigors, and are genetically tough. In this sense, they are the Far Eastern equivalents of the Cossack who had always played the role of the most indomitable of Russian warriors. The artwork in these albums is generally poor but not garish, and there are no gory scenes or atrocities on either side. What distinguished their contents from the more lurid cartoon graphics of the time is the relative respect given visually to the enemy. Japanese troops, when being pushed back are shown in fear or in agony from wounds, but not as cowards. The portraits of General Ito and Admiral Togo are crude but objective, and that of General Kuroki displays stature and dignity.[26] Similarly, Japanese POWs are represented as clean-cut, glowering at their captors, but in no way cringing.

The religious element can be found all through the graphic collections, mostly of Orthodox clergy blessing the troops. One, from April 1904, stands out for its melodramatic energy. Father Stefan Shcherbakovskii commissioned this print of himself, standing atop a hill amid the forward lines of advancing Russian infantry. In a canonical triangular composition, the Orthodox cross held aloft in the priest's right hand provides the apex, and the sides are formed by his standing body, the soldiers, and the hill over which they are attacking with bayonets—indicating an imminent hand-to-hand engagement. Shcherbakovskii is looking back with turned head to see if the men are following him.[27] Missing from Russian propaganda was an attack upon the enemy's religion, in vivid contrast to the "paganizing" of Napoleon in 1812 or the mocking of Islamic symbols in the Russo-Turkish Wars.[28]

Dread: Rising Sun and Yellow Peril

Alexander Kuprin's novel *The Duel* (1905), conceived before this war, bitterly indicted the cruelty and perversion of the Russian military. His "Staff Captain Rybnikov" (1905) wrapped a critique of the army around a spy plot featuring a Japanese agent so skillful that he is able to pass as a Russian officer in St. Petersburg. The irony of Kuprin's perspective lies in the apparent blindness of his Russian characters to Japanese physical features at the very moment when graphic art was featuring Japanese monkey cartoons. The officer is unmasked by uttering the word "banzai!" in the arms of a Russian prostitute. Kuprin's has his Japanese spy Rybnikov described as "malicious, mocking, intelligent, even noble, but not human, animal instead, or more precisely of a face belonging to a being from a different planet." Kuprin also employs the words "yellow, monkey, machine, inhuman."[29] And the inclusion of "machine" in this catalogue of insults clearly exhibits the belief among many Russians that the Japanese were to be distinguished from the faceless "hordes" of old by their dangerous and "modern" skills. To paraphrase the Russian radical Alexander Herzen's mid-nineteenth century nightmarish metaphor of modern destructive power, Japan was Chinggis Khan with a fleet of destroyers.

The representation of "peril" in the poplar graphics came in two forms. One, the allegorical, featured in a 1904 print, *On the War of Russia and Japan.* It juxtaposes the familiar ultra-pious female figure of "Russia"—closely resembling Columbia, Britannia, Germania, and Marianne—to a ferocious but stylized Japanese dragon with the exaggerated "slanted" eyes and sharp teeth. In a print depicting a naval battle, the text compares the Japanese to the Mongol devastators of Russia in the Middle Ages.[30] Much more direct was an illustration, in the picture collection, *The History of the Russian Soldier from Peter the Great to Our Times*, of the peasant soldier, Vasilii Riabov, on his knees awaiting execution at the hands of the Japanese military.[31]

Contempt: Macaques in Uniform

But the theme of Japanese power and danger to Russia was rarely apparent in Russian views of Japan, especially in the early phases of the war. Bravura was the natural pendant to contempt. The enemy was seen to be physically small in stature and weak in state power. It possessed a military force that was, in the view of a non-Japanese-speaking Russian military attaché in Tokyo, "[although] no longer the rabble of an Asiatic horde…[sic] it is nevertheless no modern European army."[32] Such judgments, reinforced by the tsar's derisive view of the Japanese, and popularized in mass culture, seemed to bode well for the stalwart peasant host rattling its way to Manchuria.

Stephen Norris found in the Russian archives a cartoon titled "Regarding Russia's War with Japan: Napoleon Visits the Japanese."

It "depicts a ghostly French emperor standing in front of a table full of surprised Japanese officers. The text of the image has Napoleon warning the Japanese about the dangers of provoking the Russians into an attack."[33] This idea proved irresistible: virtually the same scenario featured in a propaganda short film of World War II, *Incident at a Telegraph Office*, which showed Napoleon sending Hitler a wire, warning him not to try it.[34] But the 1812 precedent had no analogue in 1904-5 any more than it did in 1915, when it was again invoked at the time of the "great retreat."

During the war, Alexander Pasternak (brother of the poet Boris) recalled that "the Japanese were uniformly portrayed as knock-kneed weaklings, slant-eyed, yellow-skinned, and, for some reason, shaggy-haired—a puny kind of monkey, invariably dubbed 'Japs' and 'macaques'." He described seeing a poster with terrified, spider-like Japanese soldiers trying desperately to crawl out from beneath an enormous imprisoning papakha (large Caucasian fur cap) with the caption "Catch them by the capful!"; and another of a huge hand crushing a bunch of Japanese-as monkeys.[35] A contemporary *lubok*, *A Cossack's Breakfast*, shows the huge Cossack devouring a tiny Japanese, a notion paralleled by a popular song containing the line "I'll tear your hide with my teeth."[36] Yet another features a Cossack lancer impaling Japanese soldiers as on a spit—a device elevated to a national icon in World War I.[37]

The relative stature of the two nations' people served as a contrastive theme as it had done in the past. In a popular tract issued during the Napoleonic invasion of Russia in 1812, the Moscow chauvinist Fedor Rostopchin had one of his fictional Russian men-of-the-people say of the French invaders: "Your soldiers are little dwarves and dandies."[38] While the insult "dandy" added specificity to Rostopchin's gallophobia, the "dwarf" designation both demeaned and discounted the enemy and physically magnified the Russian warrior. And so it did in 1904. A print of that year, *The Russian Hero-Knight [Bogatyr] in the East: the Knight and the Yellow Pygmies*, blended the mystique of size with the myth of history, as the Russian warrior on a white horse menaces with his lance a myriad of tiny Japanese troops, while modern warships in the background open fire.

Dragging old heroes onto modern battlefields is a familiar

device, used by the propagandists and morale builders of many nations, notably by the Soviet Union in World War II when on posters the shadow of Prince Alexander Nevskii was planted behind the Red Army fighter at the front. An image from the Russo-Japanese War, *The Enemy is Terrible but God is Merciful*, has an overconfident Russian Gulliver striding across the Sea of Japan with miniature Japanese sailors sticking out of his hand, his belt, and his boots. A bit more artful was *The Cossack Petrukha*, who is calmly dismembering and beheading doll-like enemy soldiers. Another print, while revealing one of Russia's devastating losses—the sinking of the warship *Variag*—has the tragedy being observed sympathetically by a group of other nationals. The caption warns that "there is no place for 'barbarian Asians' in the international club of civilized nations."[39]

After the first six months, this flood of imagery in prints began to ebb. Apparently, they were too conventional to counterbalance the evidence of defeat, not to mention the 1905 tremors of revolution (though the dry run started in October 1904). A similar thing happened in Russia in the first year or so of World War I—a period marked by both vigorous propaganda and a fairly widespread patriotism followed by a diminution of both.[40]

Worthy Adversary

The mask of illusion did not cover every face or remain intact through the war. Many publications of the military or by organizations close to the military addressed the Japanese foe as a "normal" enemy, one to be respected on the battlefield. And this image, after a year of warfare and hysterical Japanese-bashing, was conveyed to the new recruits in a little handbook published in 1905 by the Staff of the Moscow Military District, *Memo to Men in the Ranks on their Way to War with the Japanese*.[41] Aside from taking a new and kinder tone about the treatment of the local Chinese population in Manchuria, the handbook provided a realistic description of the Japanese opponent. "The Army of Japan is a good one; its soldiers are bold, brave, hardy, and cunning." The last word, in this context, does not resound with its usual negative overtones of calculating, cheating, or dishonest—but rather conveyed the image of savvy fighters, people to contend with, something close to a worthy adversary. The remaining instructions in the handbook catalogue in a business-like way the weaponry and practices of the Japanese army. Even more vivid is the testimony of a Russian held as prisoner of war who denounced the racist stereotyping of the Japanese. When converted to a different view by the kindness and humanity of his captors, he wrote that "the application of such a term [monkey] to a brave enemy was both undignified and shabby."[42]

In looking back at the variety of responses in print and in the arts, it becomes crystal clear that stereotyping propaganda had very little impact on the conduct or the outcome of the war. The years 1904-5 saw nothing like the anti-German hate propaganda of World War I that resulted in pogroms against and arrests of Russians with German (or Jewish, or Scandinavian) names. Neither the fanatical and malicious images of the enemy on the home-front nor the more respectful descriptions of them in the Russian army seem to have had the slightest effect on war fighting, victories, or defeats on the battlefield. Tactics, supply, leadership and a dozen other military factors completely overshadowed the cultural construction of that war.

Peace and Reconstruction

The images in the photos of well-run Japanese units were, to the Russian army at least, far more lasting in impact than those of satire. Russian military leaders were able to read from the organizational skills of the men in the field the deeper efficiency of the Japanese nation as a system. On the cultural front, a more complex picture emerged. On the one hand, we have a people who were pictured to be the modernizing and artful vanguard of a historiosophical Asian swarm. In the words of Barbara Heldt, "Japan stood both for the generalized Asiatic hordes and for a peculiarly cunning, intelligent, and disciplined form of evil against which good-natured old-fashioned Russian heroism was of little use."[43] On the other, we have admirers of Japanese poetry and the arts among the Russian figures of the Silver Age. Such cultural or symbolic ambivalences would not survive a major war to the death such as the two World Wars. Refined and nuanced evaluations of one nation by another in these wars quickly gave way to simplified and reductionist ones embedded in the effigies of hate.

And the reverse is true as well. Foes can quickly be converted into friends (cf. the Germany and Japan of 1945 and 1949, from the American point of view). Mikhailova, in a fine article on enemy imaging, writes that "enmification" tends to become permanent and difficult to erase, correctly citing the Soviet cartoon treatment of the Japanese during the frontier skirmishes of 1938 and 1939.[44] But one must not overlook the contrary example of World War I when Japan and Russia were allies. How easily nasty stereotypes could be erased is evident from the 1915 publication, *Our Allies in the Great War: Japan*.[45] The exoticism and orientalism are still there, but the demonization of 1904-5 has been replaced by a quaint romanticism in airbrushed photos of the emperor and other national leaders. This contrasts vividly with the demeaning wartime print of 1904, *Clever Wife*, which has the Mikado being henpecked by a vituperative empress.[46] In the 1915 presentation, benevolent pictures of the Japanese troops are framed by colorful and clichéd drawings of samurai, chrysanthemums, silk-screen designs, and praying Buddhists. Many of the figures are smiling and some of them are "de-Asianized." In fact those with the kepi and neck veil could hardly be differentiated from Russian forces in Central Asia or the French Foreign Legion in Morocco. The transformation cannot be surprising when we recall how this is done again and again from war to war by every nation engaged in building wartime images of friend and foe.

Original publication: In John W. Steinberg et al., eds., *The Russo-Japanese War in Global Perspective: World War Zero*. 2 vols. Boston, Leiden: Brill, 2005-2007, vol. 1, pp. 395-410.

Notes

1   Since 9 September 2001, the American media has largely avoided the "raghead" image that had often been applied indiscriminately to Palestinians, Iraqis, and Iranians. I wish to thank the many critical and helpful comments of my colleagues at the Washington, D.C., Seminar on Russian Studies (now the Russian History Seminar of Washington, D.C. - *ed*.) at Georgetown University, February 13, 2004.

2   Barbara Heldt, "'Japanese' in Russian Literature: Transforming Identities" in J. Thomas Rimer (ed.), *A Hidden Fire: Russian and Japanese Cultural Encounters, 1868-1926* (Stanford, 1995), 172. For the earlier encounters, see David Goldfrank, "Contrasting Contributions to the History of Russo-Japanese Relations," *Kritika*, 5, 2 (Spring 2004), 401-13.

3   David Wolff, "Winning a Thousand Daily Tsushimas: Russian Orientology in the Far East, 1899- 1917," ms.; David Schimmelpenninck van der Oye, "Russian Military Intelligence on the Manchurian Front, 1904-05," *Intelligence and National Security*, XI, no. 1 (1996), 26. For the background, see also Schimmelpenninck's *Toward the Rising Sun: Russian Ideologies of Empire and the Path to War with Japan* (DeKalb, 2001); and David Wolff, *To the Harbin Station: the Liberal Alternative in Russian Manchuria, 1898-1914* (Stanford, 1999).

4   Schimmelpenninck, "Russian Military Intelligence," 29.

5   Louise McReynolds, *The News Under Russia's Old Regime* (Princeton, 1991), 192.

6   McReynolds, *News*, 168-97; Jeffrey Brooks, *When Russia Learned to Read* (Princeton, 1985) 28-9; *Vestnik znaniia*, 11 (1904), 105-20.

7   McReynolds, *News*, 168-97 (qu. 187).

8   Kharuki Vada [Haruki Wada], "Solidarnost' iaponskikh i russkikh sotsialistov vo vremia russko-iaponskoi voiny," *Japanese Slavic and East-European Studies*, 2 (1981), 1-14, for their positions on victory and defeat.

9   David Wells, "The Russo-Japanese War in Russian Literature" in David Wells and Sandra Wilson (eds.), *The Russo-Japanese War in Cultural Perspective, 1904-1905* (Basingstoke, 1999) 118-24, 127-29 (qu. 119, 124).

10 Richard Stites, "Days and Nights in Wartime Russia" in Aviel Roshwald and Richard Stites (eds.), *European Culture in the Great War* (Cambridge, 1999), 9-11.

11 Wells, "Russo-Japanese War," 109-118 (qu. 109, 110).

12 Yuliya Mikhailova, "Images of Enemy and Self: Russian 'Popular Prints' of the Russo-Japanese War," *Acta slavica iaponica*, XVI (1988), 31, 45.

13 Anthony Swift, *Popular Theater and Society in Tsarist Russia* (Berkeley, 2002), 125, 163, 167 (and passim for other patriotic shows).

14 I. I. Rostunov (ed.), *Istoriia russko-iaponskoi voiny, 1904-1905 gg.* (Moscow, 1977), passim.

15 Mikhailova, "Images," 31.

16 Mikhailova, "Images," 33.

17 Stephen Norris, "Russian Images of War: the Lubok and Wartime Culture, 1812-1917" (University of Virginia Dissertation, 2002), 284-352.

18 *Russko-iaponskaia Voina: potoplenie 4-kh iaponskikh parakhodov* (M, 1904).

19 *K voine Rossii s Iaponiei: Russko-Iaponskaia Voina — Boi pri Chonchzhu 15 Marta 1904 g.* (Moscow, 1904).

20 *Iaponets lezet na Ialu* (Moscow, 1904).

21 *K voine Rossii s Iaponiei* (Moscow, 1904).

22 "Horrors of War": author's collection; John Dower, *War without Mercy: Race and Power in the Pacific War* (New York, 1986).

23 *Russo-iaponskaia voina na sushe i na more*, ed. Capt. M.N. von Krit, 8 vols. (SPB, 1904) I, I, II, pl. xx, and passim.

24 For the parade portrait style, see *Portret v russkoi zhivopisi XVIII- XIX vekov* (M, 1988).

25 *Russko-iaponskaia voina na sushe*, III, 44.

26 For example, ibid., V, 102-3. In another work, an unbound photo collection, the Russian captors are no taller than their Japanese prisoner: *Russko-iaponskaia voina, 1904-1905 g.g.* (N.p., n.d.), tab. 70.

27 *Russko-iaponskaia voina na sushe*, III, pl. xxii.

28 Norris, "Russian Images," passim. Japanese prints, in contrast, lacked the kind of hatred found in the Russian product. Personal communication from Jordan Sand, professor of Japanese and History, Georgetown University.

29 Heldt, "'Japanese' in Russian Literature," 175-5. See also the discussion in Wells, "Russo-Japanese War," 126-7.

30 Reproduced in Mikhailova, "Images," 35, 47.

31 Dmitrii Dubenskii, *Istoriia russkogo soldata ot Petra Velikago do nashikh dnei* (St. Petersburg, n.d.), pl. 12.

32 V. P. Vannovskii cited in Schimmelpenninck, "Russian Military Intelligence," 26.

33 Norris, "Russian Images." My thanks to the author for this material.

34 Stites, *Russian Popular Culture: Entertainment and Society Since 1900* (Cambridge, 1992) 112-13; Argyrios Pisiotis, "Images of Hate in the Art of War" in Stites (ed.), *Culture and Entertainment in Wartime Russia* (Bloomington, 1995), 141-56.

35 Pasternak's descriptions cited in Heldt, "'Japanese' in Russian Literature," 174.

36 Brooks, *When*, 314.

37 Hubertus Jahn, *Patriotic Culture in Russia During World War I* (Ithaca, 1995).

38 Quoted in Alexander Martin, *Romantics, Reformers, Reactionaries: Russian Conservative Thought and Politics in the Reign of Alexander I* (DeKalb, 1997), 127.

39 Mikhailova, "Images," 47, 49, 37.

40 Jahn, *Patriotic Culture.*

41 *Pamiatka nizhnim chinam otpravlaiushchimsia na voinu s iapontsami* (Moscow, 1905). I am indebted to Don Wright of Tulane University who found this in the Helsinki Military Library.

42 Cited in Norris, 332.

43 Heldt, "'Japanese' in Russian Literature," 174.

44 Mikhailova, "Images," 30, 45-6.

45 *Nashi soiuzniki v Velikoi voine: "Iaponiya"* (Moscow, 1915).

46 Mikhailova, "Images," 52.

IV

ELITE AND MASS ENTERTAINMENT UNDER SERFDOM

25

The *Veselukha* Tower
Social and Cultural Space in Old Smolensk

This brief essay is about the topography of social and cultural relations in a provincial Russian town—Smolensk—in the eighteenth century, particularly the interaction among classes and the interactive spaces where this occurred: market, tavern, restaurant, church, garrison, and Noble Club. It is built largely around a reading, supplemented with a few historical sources, of a popular novel published in 1845 and relating to the Smolensk of the 1780s: F. A. Ettinger, *Bashnya Veselukha ili Smolensk i zhiteli ego shest'desyat' let nazad* (*The Veselukha Tower, or Smolensk and its Residents Sixty Years Ago*). In genre it is an urban thriller resembling in style the historical novels of Zotov, Zagoskin, Lazhechnikov, and Walter Scott that were so popular at the time of writing. The author appears in the novel as a child character in a minor role. It is thus a kind of memoir wrapped in fiction. The plot revolves around politics, mystery, and love—but these rather conventional devices are held together and made vivid by historical, social, cultural, and topographical materials.

The Mystery of the Tower

The hero, a young Russian infantry captain, is an outsider to the town and is thus fed with exactly the kind of information that we other outsiders—historians—long for. In the words of the author of a modern introduction, the novel offers an accurate view of "the old way of life," of "provincial types in Catherinian Russia," and the "atmosphere, morals, and mores of a provincial town of the XVIII century" (p. 6). In this sense the novel resembles travel literature and ethnography. The plot can be summarized very briefly because its main axes run through the chief villain, Count Zmeyaysky (almost all the characters have the "speaking" names so widely used at the time). He is a truly serpentine figure of Polonized Belorussian origin who murders, kidnaps, makes counterfeit money, intrigues for his election as Marshal of the Nobility, and obscures his nefarious dealings by organizing devilish and ghostly apparitions on the walls of the Veselukha Tower, one of the great historical landmarks of Smolensk. For good measure, his corrupt nephew attempts to abduct and seduce an innocent maiden. Both villains' ambitions are foiled in the end and they are punished—and of course the young captain "gets the girl."

Around the three main plot elements—politics, mystery, and romance—are woven social commentary. Count Zmeyaysky, who has the audacity to establish his residence on the very site where Catherine II attended the opera on her 1780 visit, is the obverse of everything Russian: he wishes to embody and combine private lawlessness with the lawful and honorable function of marshal, to replace a loyal Russian family, the Khrapovitskys, and enrich himself and his entourage through appointments. To affect this he openly bribes (and also cheats) two weak and pitiful local potentates to gain their vote—their Russian names mean The Grabber and The Fatuous Pole. His partners in the purely criminal enterprise are a German, a Frenchman, and another Polonized Belorussian. Zmevaysky's bearing and dress are exceptionally foppish—even in an age know for foppery—thus reinforcing the feminization of the Poles and the Polonized that is found so widely in Russian culture. The author presents no real political issues in the election, of course, but uses it simply to bind together crime, political intrigue, and un-Russianness.

The mystery motif provides one of the puzzling and suspenseful elements of the story: nocturnal Walpurgis happenings featuring satanic creatures and minstrels with horns and tails atop the tower performing wild dances and playing bagpipes and balalaikas. On the final pages we learn that these "witches" are the hired help of the Count. But the conversations that run through the town about these events serve to divide the populace into two distinct cultural groups. All the lower class figures, servants, soldiers, the merchant families, and some of the gentry women—including a general's wife—are steeped in superstition and insist that the "evil force" is at work. It cannot be defeated, in the view of the wife of an old lieutenant, except by the intercession of the Virgin Mary. Against this are ranged the rationalists—the commandant (a Baltic German and in historical fact the author's father), the hero, his officer friends, and the two educated young ladies—who practice their "everyday Voltaireanism" at dinner parties by skeptically rejecting the magical interpretation of the events. In the end, they are of course vindicated. The discordance between upper and lower classes is never couched as a dispute but rather as deferential insistence by the latter on their beliefs. But when discord erupts among the upper ranks, it takes the form of good-natured disbelief by the rationalist as against an angry critique of enlightenment and "learned" people in general. The scenes at the homes of the commandant and the merchant characters suggest tiny islands of "Europeanized" modes of thought in a sea of urban superstition.

The love interest in this novel is pallid indeed, and very conventional. There are no great spurts of emotion—to say nothing of passion, lust, and sexual contact. Affection—between the captain and the heroine Nadya—is conveyed through inner thoughts, daydreaming, sighs, secret glances, and ineffable longing. In other words, love is clean, chaste, honest—without psychological complexity. The author can inject drama into it only by means of a *deus ex machina*: the classic villain of XVIII century domestic melodrama. Nadya is merely the object of a power intrigue by a lustful and parasitic young lord whose favorite preoccupations are gambling, drinking, sleeping, and seduction. His interest in the talented and beautiful Nadya is purely erotic, since he believes she is merely a merchant's daughter (a plot device). To add piquancy to the intrigue, the young rake makes use of a love potion given him by an alleged sorceress. For good measure, he kidnaps her at a masked ball. "In our enlightened age, why marry," he says to a friend. His plan is to give her away to some impoverished noble when he has finished with her. Enlightenment here is thus given another facet: the vulgarized freedom that comes from loosening traditional moral and religious bonds.

Social Classes

In this essentially upper class novel, only merchants and gentry
are shown in their own spaces. The lower classes come in and out
and interact with the masters, but rarely with each other. Thus the
tavern is talked about but never shown. The best one in town is
part of an inn run by a German in the town center and is said
to be clean, decent, and expensive. Other taverns are mentioned
as locales where coachmen, servants, and soldiers too often spend
their time and get tipsy. Everybody drinks in this story, but the
lower orders seem unable to hold their liquor—probably because it
is cheap, strong, and unaccompanied by food. Tolstoy, in *War and
Peace*, set thirty years later, names an inn and tavern, Ferapontov's,
in the suburbs where the servant of Bolkonsky stops. In the 1840s,
with roughly the same population, Smolensk had four taverns in
hotels or inns, and eight other "eating places." Decades later, the
geographer Przhevalsky complained of the proliferation of drinking places all over Smolensk province.

Servants, lower ranking soldiers, assorted townspeople, merchants, and women of all classes share certain things that set them
off from upper class men. All of them are infinitely more garrulous,
rhetorically colorful, humorous, and expressive. Their speeches are
long, rich in dialect, tumultuous in feeling. They also align themselves on the side of a "supernatural" interpretation of the events
in the Tower. And they are ruder to each other, especially those
who have servants. The educated male contingent is contained, reserved, ironic—often cool and dry in the face of the lexical blizzards they face from those around them. It might be observed
also that servants like to emulate their masters in taking on their
airs and postures and speech patterns and in giving orders to
those below; and that in the merchant home, one person must serve
as coachmen, butler, janitor, and valet.

The character and morals of the gentry characters vary greatly. At one end is the well-educated Captain Kaisanov, trained in
the Gentry Cadet Corps founded by Peter I for officers with a
broad literary culture and command of languages, who is keen on
fair play, social justice, and a vaguely Christian or Masonic morality. At the other end of the moral continuum, are characters

embodying various degrees of hypocrisy and greed, down to the arch-villain Zmeyaysky. The gentry regularly gather together at home and at public functions such as balls. The home entertainment format is not so different from that of merchants: drinks and appetizers, conversation, and then to table. Gentry food is more refined, more European. At one point, the villainous count, wishing to treat those he is about to bribe, orders "particularly Russian" dishes: fatty, sour, pungent, and salty. When the commandant entertains, he invites no merchants, but like the great English lords of his time, condescends to have in the doctor and the (Lutheran) pastor and their wives as well as fellow officers. Nearly everybody can speak German. The gathering goes well beyond the nine o'clock in the evening adjournment time for merchant dinners. The postmaster—an important position in town—claims to entertain dignitaries every night at his home where his wife plays the harpsichord and his son the violin while the guests engage in cards or conversation.

The local gentry possessed its own club of the nobility around which spun politics, entertainment, and social opportunity: where one could seek invitations, advantageous appointments, and available marriage partners, as well as plentiful food and dancing. Smaller affairs took place as often as twice a week. Two rather elaborate events are described in the novel. The first is a winter ball at election time financed by the gentry club and special contributions from the wealthy. The author ironically describes the flutter of preparation weeks in advance, the choosing of clothes, the primping, and the speculation about who will dance with whom. In one of his frequent introductions of real persons, the author introduces the prominent families who arrive in town from all over the province: Khrapovitskys, Meshcherskys, Vyazemskys, Rimsky-Korsakovs, Stankeviches, Von Lyarlyarskys, Anichkovs, Potëmkins, Milyutins, Yakushkins, Leslis, Engelgardts, and Glinkas. The dance, led off by the commandant, proceeds in strict order: two polonaises in column, a ring polonaise, a German quadrille, an *à la grècque*, an English promenade, an Allemande, and two Russian ballroom dances— the cakewalk and the duckwalk. At the ball hosted by Zmeyaysky, the guests arrive in Venetian masks and domino costumes, some of the men dressed as women.

The dance and the rituals of socialization that accompanied it was one of the markers of status that Peter introduced in his famous but relatively understudied social and cultural reforms. The Table of Ranks was supplemented by an entire code of conduct and dress as well as tightly ordered privileges: grooming, costume hairdo, speech style (and language) as well as rank, title, salary, list of duties and amenities—even down to the number of horses one's carriage could command at post stations. Eventually, the ball was ordered into a strict succession of dances, each of which mandated a certain kind of comportment and even style of talk. Such routinization was not yet locked in at the Smolensk affairs in the late eighteenth century. But the ball certainly served a social function. The young men and women danced; the older men played whist and macao after a few dances; older women talked. Younger men in clusters between dances discussed elections, cards, hunting, and women. In this public space between home life and official service, the ranks dissolved slightly and the women had a greater range of social intercourse available to them. Merchants and their wives, even had they been invited, could not have functioned at these events: aside from lack of common conversational bridges and foreign languages, their visible attire would have created an aesthetic anomaly—and the women, clad in dresses without a waist, could not have negotiated the intricate steps.

Home and ballroom gathering were modeled on life in the capitals. But few of the other amenities of high culture were available in Smolensk. The history of theater in this town is very fragmentary. Some claim from these fragments a continuous theatrical life there from the end of the eighteenth century. If so, this history begins in 1780 with the visit of Catherine II and Emperor Joseph II of Austria (see below). The governor, N.V. Repnin, in the spirit of potemkinesque panegyric shows, had a huge wooden theater hastily built and presented there Smolensk's first opera performance whose cast of presumably amateur gentry included his daughter. The house then went into disuse and later burned down. Characters in *Veselukha Tower* talk of comedy performances in the previous year (1782-3) when a field regiment was quartered in town. Two very old plays are mentioned: Sumarokov's *Narcissus* (1750) and Verevkin's *So It Must Be* (1773). There is also talk of circus acts and magicians. Theater life thereafter is problematic and the record is spotty: amateur plays at the Gentry Club, touring companies from time to time, and the first serf theaters that began appearing in Smolensk Province at about this time and which occasionally came to town. It was probably because of the serf theaters on rural estates that no permanent stage appeared until the 1850s.

A merchant family of the Second Gild plays a prominent role in the story. The Kubyshkins (money-box) are the adopted parents of the heroine who is actually of gentry birth and has been left to their care since infancy due to a turn in the plot, a familiar device of a secretly noble child raised in tender affection by those lower in the social scale. The Kubyshkins are prosperous, even though Smolensk was in a decline from earlier times; and its merchants were doing well since the town was a trade funnel from provincial estates to Riga and Poland. Judging from the conversations in their sitting rooms, merchants had no interest in politics but, if the editor of the novel is right certainly in civic affairs: he believes that Kubyshkin was modeled on prominent merchant of the time, V. G. Khlebnikov, who opened a home for orphans and abandoned or illegitimate children.

The social universe of the Kubyshkins is largely limited to their home (adorned with expensive silver-mounted icons in a redwood cabinet), the homes of other merchants, and church. The husband wears the full beard of pre-Petrine times; the more socially ambitious wife wears the ponderous expensive clothes traditional to her class but embellished with gentry items. Even in church, she is very much aware of her wealth. Kind to her "daughter," attentive to young officers, she displays sudden and peremptory coarseness in ordering carriage or a meal from her servants. Most of the females of all classes in the novel deploy more palpable power towards underlings than do the men. Thus the daily, if minor, wars of class and rank were also gendered. The Kubyshkins are not wholly cut off from the upper reaches of society. Their guests include junior officers and gentry acquaintances along with merchant friends. These guests divide into natural conversational groups: merchant met on prices and markets; older women on events in town; the young folks on each other. The relationship is cordial and cuts across classes but it is strictly one sided: the Kubyshkins are not invited "up" the social scale; the upper crust speak of them patronizingly as decent people with a daughter who exceeds them in education and manners.

Since Nadya has been educated in a gentry milieu but raised in a merchant family, the cultural contrast is interesting. Nadya reads the *Sobesednik liubitelei rossiiskogo slova* edited by the eminent Princess Dashkova, containing works by the empress, Kheraskov, Knyazhnin, Fonvizin, Derzhavin; and she reads other Russian and European literature including Rousseau's *New Heloise*. She also remembers the plays she attended a few years earlier during the visit of Catherine II. Her "mother" prefers religious reading material and dislikes society dancing. Her dancing is limited to family gatherings and weddings where the Russian *plyaska* or folk dancing is the thing, preferable she says, to the "German" *tanets* or European dances with their "twists, turns and figures," which seem both foreign and socially alien and perhaps slightly immoral since they are performed in public spaces rather than in the intimacy of the home. The differences between Nadya and her foster parents are clearly on display also of course in language forms and vocabulary—and by the fact that the young women converses freely in German and French and plays the clavichord.

The garrison, a battalion of guards, is a hub of continuous drill and military ritual of the clock, reveille and retreat matching the clock of the church with its matins and vespers. This little world also contains engineers, artillerists, veterans doing light guard detail, supernumeraries, cantonists, and soldiers' families. The attention paid by Smolensk "society" to Captain Kaisanov, "a dashing field officer" of the type rarely seen in Smolensk (at least until 1812) and his friend Lieutenant Blum suggests that the garrison troops and their commanders were looked on as a permanent part of the urban furniture, less than exciting, and not at all romantic. Since the visiting officers were there to gather recruits, there was bound to be some tension between serf-owners and military, both of whom wanted the strongest hands. This is not reflected in the story. The notion that the fighting man was somehow more manly and thus more erotically attractive to highborn young women lasted — though in attenuated form — right up to the winter of 1917. The most colorful character in the garrison community is the poorly educated wife of an aged junior officer. She is the most superstitious of the lot, the most ethnically conscious (the commander, she says, is a nice person but after all, "a German"), and the most folkish in her speech, pronouncing "general" as "eneral" and employing folk etymological constructions such as *kamindant* for *komendant*.

Meeting Places

In this small town of about 10,000 inhabitants (minus the garrison of about a thousand) stood thirty-five churches, including one Lutheran and only one Catholic (rather surprising, considering the long historical sojourn of Lithuanian-Polish power in Smolensk — 1395-1514, 1611-1654). The officers of German extraction frequent the Orthodox church. The German commandant, the lieutenant's wife complains, attends only on holy days and even then does not cross himself. On the eve of each of the numerous holy days, all-night services are held. Archbishop Parfenii Sopkovskii (served 1761-1795) officiated personally in the Uspensky Sobor, the town's most impressive church, then and now, towering over the Dnieper River and containing an astonishing iconostasis and various objects filled with religious and historical significance. Uspensky was the host church for imperial visits and is the preferred place of worship for the high and mighty, even though the believers of all ranks gather there. The very first romantic encounter between the heroes of the novel occurs during a three hour service in this cathedral.

There was one other space where all the population could gather: the great outdoors — castle walls, churchyard, streets, and squares. The most famous public square, then and now, was the Blone (still so called by the locals, though officially known as Glinka Park) right in the center of town. In the 1780s, after Catherine's visit and on her orders, the space was surrounded by official buildings. It was also ringed with birch trees. From then until 1830 when it was designated a city park. Blone was the *plats-parad,* a familiar feature of all Russian cities of the era, a kind of outdoor theater where daily units of the garrison battalion, bedecked in colorful uniforms, held parades, exercised highly choreographed changing of the guards, and drill.

Seasonally one could see church processions around the cathedral and around the city ramparts. By the 1840s, there were fourteen high holy processional days and several minor ones. One of the more amusing characters of *Veselukha Tower* belittles theater (*tiatr*) as frivolous compared to the outdoor festival (*gulyane*) of minstrels and gentry sleighs launched on Fat Tuesday by a previous commandant. And a merchant wife echoes the distaste for "theater" while praising the Russian Nativity puppet shows (*vertepy*) put on by seminarians and soldiers' children. In the 1840s, five festivals were held each year on designated holy days when the lower classes cavorted on swings, danced, and sang while the upper classes came to watch them, thus gaining vicarious fun. A rare account of lower class festivities at the end of the eighteenth century has them following dinner and church service with singing for the women, bowling for the men, and wall-to-wall fist-fighting on the ice in the middle of the Dnieper—the north side of town against the south—with merchants and even officials observing and wagering. At all these kinds of events, social mixing seems most recurrent.

The great outdoor event of the decade in Smolensk was the imperial visit of Catherine II and Joseph II in June 1780. Anxious to impress his sovereign, the governor had erected a triumphal arch and placed musicians around it to serenade the two monarchs. The monarchs then processed between two ranks of inhabitants: merchants and town dwellers on one side, two regiments on the other. Along the wide street descending to the Uspensky Sobor, an immense structure, they were greeted by women and girls in local costume. As they entered the cathedral, Catherine and Joseph were joined by the town's clergy and two differently dressed columns of male choirboys strewing flowers in front of them. The gentry of Smolensk were already assembled in the church. At night the governor presented the opera mentioned above. The entire town was illuminated and tables were laid outdoors for the commoners. On Catherine's second visit in 1787, the merchants and townsmen donated funds for the erection of a stone triumphal arch. Typically, when Emperor Paul visited in 1797, nothing happened: he spent the night and departed the next day. Imperial visits became important again under Alexander I and Nicholas I, as shown in the amplitude of the documents that fluttered around the chanceries in preparation for them.

The material in and around the novel about Smolensk shows that much of its life resembled that of comparable towns elsewhere—not only in Russia—and was at the same time a pale copy of the capital as, no doubt, were the provincial towns of central and western Europe at that time. Was there anything unique about it? The only statement on this by the author of *Veselukha Tower*—made with tongue in cheek—was that though the capitals dwarfed Smolensk in every respect, Smolensk drowned them both out in the volume of gossip and idle talk. Although the realia and the topography are interesting and specific to the place, it is the talk that makes the novel come alive. One is struck again by the well-known fact that the two dominant forces in Russian history—the State and the intelligentsia—were obsessed by the written word, the former constantly inscribing the actions and movements of its subjects (even down to today) and the latter inscribing what it took to be their spirit. But the common people were more prone to talk than write and the ear of the novelist captures for us what real conversations might have been like in Old Smolensk: the local dialects, the mispronunciations, the malapropisms of the pretentious, the coded communications of the French and German speakers—all familiar of course from Russian literature, but somehow made more vivid precisely by its concrete geographical and temporal setting. If we could multiply this crude picture of Smolensk life fifty times and capture some of the color of the other provincial towns, perhaps we could better put our fingers on a reality of the past that is not measured exclusively by its relation to a coming upheaval.

Original publication: In Natalia Baschmakoff, Arja Rosenholm, and Hannu Tommola, eds. *Aspekteja: A Festschrift for Professor Marja Lehnonen*. Tampere University, 1995 [Slavica tamperensia, V], pp. 295-304.

Sources

Avdusina, D. A. *Smolensk i Gnëzdovo: k istorii drevnerusskogo goroda*. Moscow, 1991.

Budaev, D. I., and N. M. Gorodskoi, *Iz istorii smolenskogo kraia* (Smolensk, 1958).

[Ettinger, F. A.] F. v. E., *Bashnya Veselukha ili Smolensk i zhiteli ego shest'desyat' let nazad*, intro. by V. Zakharov (St. Petersburg, 1845; Smolensk, 1992).

Istoricheskii ocherk Smolenska (St. Petersburg, 1894).

Ivanov, A., "Pervye spektakli," in *Rabochii put'* (Aug. 22. 1972), 3.

Koshelev, Yakov Romanovich, ed. *Smolenskii krai v istorii russkoi kul'tury* (St. Petersburg, 1973).

Lesli, I., "Zhizn' pomeshchikov tri chetverti veka nazad," *Smolenskaya Starina*, III/2 (1916) 1-98 (sep. pagination).

Lotman. Yu. M., *Roman A.S. Pushkina "Evgenii Onegin": kommentarii* (Leningrad, 1980).

Murzakevich, Nikifor, *Istoriya goroda Smolenska*. ed. I. I. Orlovskii (Smolensk, 1903).

___, *Istoriya gubernskago goroda Smolenska*, 2vols. in 1 (Smolensk, 1804).

Nikitin, Pavel, *Istoriya goroda Smolenska* (Moscow, 1848).

___, *Zapiski o Smolenske* (Moscow, 1845).

Ryabkov, G.T., "Novye yavleniya v ekonomike smolenskoi gubernoi kontsa XVIII-pervoi chetverti XIX stoletiya," *Sbornik nauchnykh rabot, posvyashchennyi 25-letniyu instituta (1930-1955 gg.)* (Smolensk, 1957).

26

The Creative Provinces in
Early Nineteenth Century Russia

Definitions of "antiquarianism" usually stress the difference between it and the serious study of history. The latter examines trends,
movement, ideas—big things—that try to explain events and patterns of behavior. The former is involved in a hobby-like way with
minuscule details—genealogy, furniture, battles, and other things
from the realm of factology. Numbing minutiae and irrelevance
characterize most of it. Antiquarianism has often plagued the study
of local history as well, with the "local" overshadowing the "history." But as we have seen so clearly from the papers at this conference and from the numerous professional monographs on local
history that have come down to us, local history and local studies
in general can be very serious. One is even tempted to paraphrase
a famous American dictum about politics and say that perhaps all
history is local. The point is to show how experience in a given limited locale is relevant not only for the people who lived and worked
and died there, but for the larger understanding of society as well.

That there are many approaches to local history is vividly illustrated by the existence of such alternate terms as "regional history"
and "microhistory" and the Russian word *kraevedenie*. The object
of investigation may be a rather large region such the Volga (researched by Orlando Figes), Bashkortostan (currently researched
by Jeremy Smith) or Karelia whose investigators are now very
numerous, especially in Finland. Or it may be a province such as
Tver' (recently studied by Mary Cavender), Voronezh the subject of
Chris Chulos' book, or Nizhnii Novgorod, now the focus of a book
by Catherine Evtuhov. Urban studies have long attracted attention
for all periods of Russian and Soviet history—the works of Ronald

Suny, Donald Raleigh, Lynne Viola, Anne Rassweiler, and Stephen Kotkin—to mention just a few—come immediately to mind. Even a single neighborhood within a city has come under examination: one of the precincts of Petrograd during the Russian Revolution and Civil War currently engaged by Alexander Rabinowitch.

My project differs somewhat from these approaches and in fact looks at the cultural relationship between centre and periphery— a rather patronizing term by the way. It is about art, music, and theatre in the capitals and the provinces of Russia during the last half-century or so of serfdom: 1800-1861. In doing this study I am attempting to avoid the constricting hierarchies that tend to dominate history in general and cultural history in particular: the hierarchy of capital over provinces, of high art over popular culture, of professional over amateur creativity, and of the works of art in and of themselves over the *experience* of the arts. In this spirit, I would like to present a brief summary of my research, now in progress, on the cultural life of Russians in the early nineteenth century.

Music: Listening around the Empire

Until the founding of the conservatories of St. Petersburg and Moscow in the 1860s, symphonic music in Russia possessed no central headquarters, so to speak: no training centre, no permanent concert hall, no public building of any sort that could be identified with the creation or performance of classical music. The St. Petersburg Philharmonia Society, founded in 1803, had no orchestra of its own. Its concerts migrated for a half a century from site to site, mostly to private homes or clubs. By mid-century the Philharmonia found a more or less regular home—though still on a rental basis until Soviet times—at the Gentry Club on what is now Square of the Arts. The Capella or Imperial Court Choir was virtually a branch of the tsar's household. It performed mostly sacred choral music for a very select audience at the site which bore (and still bears) its name. In the 1840s, a few other public concert opportunities arose, one of them at St. Petersburg university. Ironically the most popular place for listening to music in a public space was the Vauxhall in Pavlovsk, at the end of the line of Russia's first railway. From 1838 onwards, Petersburgers could reach this station in thirty-five minutes and settle down to an unending program of musical entertainment, featuring mostly opera overtures and "light" classics. (See Kratkii 1992; Stolpianskii 1989; Gozenpud 1992; Fradkina 1994 and Rozanov 1978.)

These offerings may seem meager indeed, if we think only in terms of classical music or of public performance space. Of course popular music could be heard almost everywhere: guitarists in their rooms, coachmen singing road songs, regimental bands, church choirs. And in private abodes, the homes and salons of rich music lovers, elite audiences could hear Louis Spohr, John Field, Liszt, Clara Schumann, and a dozen virtuosos—Russian and foreign. Some of the amateur salons mounted regular chamber recitals and even full-scale symphonic concerts in their homes with hired musicians. And of course, the palaces of the great magnates such as the Yusupovs and Sheremetevs resounded with the music performed by large serf orchestras.

Were the provinces "deaf and dumb" as the Russian word *glush* implies? Let us leave aside the ubiquitous peasant work songs, laments, and other forms of folk music and ask whether Evgeny Bazarov of Turgenev's novel *Fathers and Sons* (set in the late 1850s) had a right to be shocked when he said "Really, a man of forty-four, a *paterfamilias* in this out-of-the-way district, playing on the violoncello!" (Turgenev 1964, 237). Bazarov was referring to Nikolai Kirsanov who was probably playing Bach or perhaps a piece by the aristocrat and amateur cellist, Matvei Vielgorsky. In any case, hundreds of cellos and violins and flutes were playing classical music—Haydn, Mozart, Beethoven, Rossini, and dozens of now forgotten composers of that era. I estimate that there were approximately 300 serf orchestras at work in this period, mostly on provincial estates. One of them, that of Matvei's brother Mikhail Vielgorsky (an amateur composer) put on a great Beethoven marathon on his estate in the middle of Kursk Province in the Winter of 1822-1823. Thirty-three concerts were mounted during an intense cycle lasting four months. Among the performers—playing together—could be seen and heard hosts, neighboring gentry, hired German professionals, and serf musicians from the Chernyshev, Teplov, and Baryatinsky serf orchestras. This highly miscellaneous crew performed all of the then-current Beethoven symphonies as well as works by Mozart, Boccherini, Cherubini, Méhul, and Rossini (Shcherbakova 1990, 38).

Of course the audiences at estate concerts were also strictly limited to relatives and guests belonging to the gentry. But this is not the main point. Among the listeners were potential future performers and composers. One of these was Mikhail Glinka who drew his musical inspiration both from the peasant and coachmen's songs he heard around him and from actually playing music by Mozart and other composers in his uncle's serf orchestra as a small boy. Out of the forests of Smolensk Province thus sprang the commonly recognized first professional composer of genuine genius in nineteenth century Russia. Even more remote from the capital lay Nizhnii Novgorod where Mily Balakirev first heard orchestral music in the home of the ex-Decembrist amateur, A. D. Ulybyshev.[1]

There was also a primarily social dimension to the serf orchestras and choruses that adorned the manor houses of rich (and not so rich) gentry families: the role and fate of the serf musician. Some of these were trained to such a high degree of skill that playing among other serfs—often poorly trained—no longer satisfied their musical aspirations. The lucky ones of talent were freed by their masters and could go on to a career. But others were sold to unmusical masters in whose homes their talents withered; or sent back to the fields or stables from whence they had been recruited; or brutally punished by landowners for their "impertinence" and "pretension" at wanting to be freed or to study in the capitals. Although such stories also applied to serf actors and actresses and artists—as we shall see—those of serf musicians have rarely been told. Needless to say, artistic martyrdom was not the dominant theme among all serf musicians, most of whom apparently nurtured no "pretensions" and indeed were happy to escape the backbreaking labor of the fields. Yet they did not escape work itself, since they were usually made to alternate their musical duties with those of household serfs—serving meals and pouring wine for the guests before running to the pit to tune up. (See Kots 1926, further sources in Stites 1998.)

A much more common element of music in the provincial home than the serf orchestra was the piano and the song. A recent scholar has described the ideal view of the domestic sphere in Russia as "an oasis of purity, a source of civility, and a refuge from official society" (Wirtschafter 1997, 19). That oasis was a fertile site for social and cultural interplay. Private playing—as opposed to performance in concert—served as the lesser vehicle of musical expression analogous to the literary album. Albums formed a private genre of largely feminine expression and the pendant to the male universe of belles letters. Gitta Hammarberg has shown how the home album enlivened a flirtatious play with people and with literature and how the sentimentalized content of albums—private communications, poems, reflections written in personal books—was "feminized" and implied a female reader: "idylls, eclogues, elegies, songs," the intimate lyrical genres (Hammarberg 1996). Musical albums with romantic titles such as Erato, Jasmine and Rose, Gift, and Lyre of Grace offered tender love songs directed to the "fair sex" (Stolpianskii 1989, 141-146). In the musical parallel, the piano bench offered a fine base of flirtation not only with men but also with "serious music."[2]

Was the performance of all this music of high quality? Is the term "good provincial music" an oxymoron? These are the questions a musicologist would naturally ask. But the canonical approach—including the canons of performance art—does not take historians very far in exploring the relationship between music (or any art) and society, particularly the society that lay outside the bounds of the two capitals. The memoirs of the period bulge with references to listening experience as well as music making itself. Quite apart from the vexing social issues involved with creativity in an unfree society, we have on display all kinds of revelations about love, sensibility, ambition, inferiority complexes and a dozen other human feelings that were intimate ingredients of life and personality—even in the far flung bears' corners of the Russian Empire.

One further point. In addition to the music that was made in the provinces, provincials also heard performances brought to them from the Russian capitals and from the great music centres of Europe. It was in the tiny Ukrainian town of Elizavetgrad that Franz Liszt gave the very last concert of his career—one of many on his several tours through Russia. For most of the early nineteenth century, Russia was a great magnet for such touring virtuosos as the pianist Muzio Clementi, the violinists Ole Bull of Norway, Henri Vieuxtemps of Belgium, and Henryk Wieniawski of Poland, among others. However much contempt the metropolitans—and even some of the touring virtuosos—held for mere "provincials," the historian cannot ignore the moments of sheer bliss and astonishment of those audiences in the backlands, or the often comic and bizarre adventures of the hosts and guests during these musical events (See Walker 1983, 378; Piggott 1973; Herresthal 1987; Kufferath 1882; Ginzburg 1983; and Duleba 1974).

Theatre: The Provincial Circuit

Unlike music, theatre had a very firm institutional and physical base in the two capitals. The Imperial Theatre Directorate—like the Capella, a branch of the Court administration—ran three theatres in St. Petersburg (the Bolshoi, later replaced by the Mariinskii, the Malyi, and the Alexander); and two in Moscow (Bolshoi and Malyi). The Imperial Theatre School adjacent to the Alexander Theatre in St. Petersburg acted as the pedagogical feeder for this complex. These richly endowed, if often inefficient and corrupt, institutions made available to the public foreign and Russian drama, comedy, melodrama, vaudeville, opera, and ballet—sometimes at an extraordinarily high level of performance and staging. The season ran from autumn through spring, with an interlude during the Lenten Season—the time, incidentally, when orchestral concerts filled the gap. Seating, like society itself, was rigidly laminated—from the imperial box down to the standing room in the pit, with loges and stalls in between. The action backstage was easily as interesting as the works of Racine, Gogol, and Rossini on the stage itself. Scandals, fights, seductions, jealous fits, tyrannical outrages, and drunken binges were all a part of the unseen show and are well-documented in memoirs. By the early nineteenth century, theatre in the two capitals had become very much a part of the social existence of the Russian aristocracy and gentry, and, to a lesser extent, of wealthy merchants and middle officials.[3]

To turn again from the capitals to the provinces. Genuine cultural riches could be found in the outlying rustic regions—beautiful and luxurious estates with parks, formal gardens, stables, carriages, and hothouses. The stately homes were peopled with residents and guests who spoke foreign languages and with a legion of servitors dressed in livery. The richest of these were seats of literary culture, monuments of architectural and landscape wizardry, and centers of musical and theatrical creativity. Estate names copied from European royalty such as *Mon plaisir* and *Sans-souci* underlined the life of leisure that they wished to cultivate. Mobilized unpaid labor erected elegant mansions, Greek temples, lakes and canalettes, grottos, or Gothic pavilions. Trained serf artists, actors, singers, musicians, and architects were deployed to add to the grandeur. The great lords maintained serf theatres—about 175 of them have been counted—for their own and their guests' diversion.[4]

Musical theatre—opera and ballet—were the preferred genres on the estates, and the quality ranged from elaborate superlative performances of major spectacles with serf and professional casts to run-of-the-mill productions at a strictly amateur level. Serf actors were of course subjected to the same kind of exploitation and abuse as were musicians. But since a large number of stage performers were female, the issue of sexual exploitation came into play. On some "theatre estates," actresses were routinely passed around from owner to friends and guests. Stories and anecdotes abound about theatre harems and the mistreatment of uncooperative serf actresses. But most of these are based on a very few instances and we cannot know how common the practice was. As in the case of musicians, these incidents must be balanced with the experience of many servile performers who thrived on stage or—in a few well-known cases—managed to win their freedom through sheer talent. (See Kots 1926: Dynnik 1933; Senelick 1984; Medvedeva 1964.)

But the story of provincial performance does not end in estate theatre which was mostly rural. Towns—provincial and even district capitals—were also scenes of theatrical life. Some of the town theatres originated as estate serf theatres which the landowner moved into town in order to raise money. These were usually bought out by townsmen when the serf owner went broke or tired of its maintenance. The ownership and direction of town theatres was astounding in its variety: governors, land-owning magnates, merchants, foreigners, ordinary townsmen (*meshchane*), and even bonded serfs are found among them. A similar mix is apparent among the actors. From time to time one finds noblemen on stage in the provinces, a role that was prohibited to their class and unthinkable in the capitals. (The same thing was true in music: the talented violinist Count Alexei Lvov, composer of the tsarist national anthem, could not perform before the public in his own country.) And if theatre could accommodate a downward leap in class status in the eyes of one's peers, so could it be a springboard to freedom as it was for Mikhail Shchepkin, the most famous of the serf actors who managed to fight his way out of bondage after being "discovered" by a governor of the province where he was appearing (see Senelick 1984).

A virtual theatrical network grew up and enveloped an enormous stretch of European Russia—and a bit beyond. August von Kotzebue, while in temporary Siberian exile, found to his delight that his works were known and played in Kazan', Tobol'sk, and even remote Kurgan! (see Kotzebue 1965). Theatre venues were particularly thick in the central provinces of Orel, Kaluga, Tula, Kostroma, Voronezh, Riazan', Vladimir, and Iaroslavl'; further along the Volga from Nizhnii Novgorod down to Astrakhan'; and in the south: Kharkov, Kursk, Chernigov, and Poltava. The most notorious of the town theatres, because of the eccentricity and alleged cruelty of its owner, Count S. N. Kamensky, occupied a huge edifice in the centre of the city of Orel. His mistreatment of a serf actress formed the basis of Alexander Herzen's famous story, "The Thieving Magpie" (1848).[5] By general agreement, the best managed was that of Nizhnii Novgorod, founded as an estate theatre at the end of the eighteenth century, changing hands and subdividing over the decades, and offering a host of operas, ballets, and dramatic works in the town and at the fair. In the south of Russia and neighboring Ukraine, a whole interrelated chain of town and fair theatres arose that maintained permanent companies or hosted travelling ones. The endless Russian roads came alive with rattling carts and whizzing sleighs bearing the touring companies from one town to another. Villagers were astonished at the sight of a caravan of actors, sets, props, costumes bulging out of the sleighs. Memoirs have colorfully described their lives on the road with adventures including drunken stupor, fights with employees, expulsion from cities, and even arrest. The market for players became so active that a provincial actors' hiring hall was organized at Barsov's Tavern in Moscow (see Lavrov 1889; Nikulina-Kositskaia 1996; Gatsiskii 1867; Beliakov, Blinova and Bordiug 1980; Fitzpatrick 1990; Glagoleva 1993. On actors' labor exchange see Lavrov 1889, 168-171).

What did these players perform? The provincial repertoire was imitative of the capitals': chiefly translations, adaptations, or imitations of foreign tragedies, comedies, ballets, operas, and vaudevilles. The unaccustomed provincials who sat in the theatre reacted more or less the way such audiences did all over the Western world, often engaging with the plot which they temporarily saw as "real." On one occasion in 1844, during a performance in Astrakhan of Victor Ducange's *Theresa, or the Orphan of Geneva*, when the villain denied to the police the murder he had just committed on stage, an audience member cried out: "You lie, you son of a dog, bandit. You killed [her]. Look at these good folks [in the theatre]; they are witnesses. Am I right, friends?" The stalls and loges burst into laughter as the police took him away (Lavrov 1889, 50). Like audiences in the Western United States at the same time, local viewers had no trouble with works of "high culture," though they were admittedly adapted with immense freedom. Shakespeare, Molière and Schiller alternated with melodramas and rather coarse and bawdy vaudevilles.

When merchants and other classes joined the audience in greater numbers, one important fact soon became clear to the actors: the audiences outside the capitals where the class makeup was less exalted did not care much for the mountainous declamations by actors playing in the neo-classical drama of Corneille, Racine, or Voltaire. In drama, they wanted diction that was "natural" and—though happy with imported melodramas and operas—were particularly attracted to "Russian" situations, Russian speech patterns, and scenes from everyday life. They expected to see actors talk in terms they could comprehend. During the reign of Nicholas I in particular more Russian works appeared on stage. Thus, the "realism" in Russian theatre sometimes attributed solely to the work of Alexander Ostrovsky—to a great extent was shaped by the towns and the provinces—the birthplaces and training grounds of actors, playwrights, and critics; and by the everyday provincial life that was reflected in the emerging naturalist styles of acting and stage setting.

Although even by the 1850s fair-sized cities with dozens of churches still had no theatre, scores of towns and fairs were enjoying theatrical experience. Laurence Senelick (1984, 11) argued that serf theatre broadened and educated a theatre public among the lesser gentry, officials, military officers, merchants, and "even the common people." Adding to this the non-serf town and fair theatres and their audiences transforms the argument into unassailable fact. Provincial Russia was a major training ground for actors: I. I. Lavrov was "discovered" in a small town and brought to Moscow; Shchepkin dominated the Moscow stage for decades after he was drafted to the Moscow Maly Theatre; Liubov Nikulina-Kositskaia became the highest paid actress in that city and a major force in bringing to life the characters of Ostrovskii's plays. This was not simply a story of social mobility. It was also an element in the slow but massive Russianization of culture. For these actors carried with them to the Moscow stage the accents and inflections, the gestures and *emplois* of provincial performance, thus both "nationalizing" and, to a certain extent, democratizing Russian theatre.

Painting: Exploring the Interior

In the world of visual arts, we find an establishment similar to that of the theatre: the Imperial Academy of Fine Arts, founded in 1757 and chartered in 1764. This august establishment housed in a monumental structure on the Neva River was a training centre for painters, sculptors, architects, and those engaged in the decorative arts; a staging area for many of the great urban building projects undertaken in St. Petersburg during the reigns of Alexander I and Nicholas I; and—most important—the aesthetic arbiter of artistic taste and style. At the beginning of the century, its canonical approach—drawn from Europe—resembled that of drama and was termed neoclassicism. The Academy, like the rulers of the Imperial Theatres, ranked the Homeric cycle—as screened through the French masters—at the very pinnacle of art. Historical painting stood at the peak of the hierarchy and its professors were the most honored and highest paid. "History" was of course a very loose term which accommodated not only "real" historical events greatly distorted and embellished, but even more often scenes from the Bible and from Greek and Roman mythology. The nobility of heroic actions, sacred martyrdoms, and struggle with the gods was seen to reflect the elevated values and exalted sentiments of the nobility here on earth: the Russian gentry and aristocracy (see Imperator-skaia 1914; 1997; Savinov 1964).

At the Academy, portraiture for a long time was held in low esteem and it was a kind of insult to say "he is a portraitist" (Mikhailova 1982, 9). But this branch of painting had great appeal to state and private patrons and to the painters who made a living from it. The parade or ceremonial portrait, borrowing in part from the English "swagger portraits" of the eighteenth century, was much in demand. The sitter was posed and stage-managed by means of a lavish interior with classical props, lush drapes, and flattering light effects. With some brilliant exceptions, parade portraits tended to be flat and frozen, honorific, and suitable for hanging on the walls of the owner to give depth and legitimacy to his title or rank. Landscape stood even further down on the ladder of art, but again was popular among those who owned lavish estates and could deploy the talent of their serf painters or afford to hire professionals. Manorial representation employed the panoramic or prospect view, imputing to the owner and the viewer an elevated and enlightened vision of the world. Almost always working from one side of a pond or lake, the painter would plant the manor house on the far side and place the proud owner in the foreground, sometimes displaying his holdings to guests. Peasants and servants—if present at all—were mere extras, stick-like figures known as "staffage" in the lexicon of European art.[6]

Who were the artists? For the most part, they emerged from the lower and middle classes—sons of soldiers (a very small number of females passed through the Academy), artisans, townsmen, petty clerks, and *raznochintsy* of various kinds. These were admitted to the Academy's fixed curriculum which included further training in Rome for the most talented. Even serfs were admitted in the early years until they were excluded on the grounds as negative moral examples due to their alleged rowdy natures. For the gentry class, working with a saber or a gun was honorable; working with a brush was not. When the high ranking noble officer F. P. Tolstoy decided to enter the Academy of Fine Arts, he created enmity in his family and lost his fiancée, but eventually rose to become its vice-president and de facto director. Thus, the colossal edifice on the Neva, though functioning as an arm of the state and a conservative guardian of classical style, also served as an incubator of social mobility for hundreds of young men of talent, some of whom rose to eminence and even affluence in the first half of the nineteenth century. It was against this institution—particularly its curriculum and its canons—that the famous Revolt of the 14 occurred in 1863, followed soon after by the birth of the Peredvizhniki and the reign of "realism" in late nineteenth century painting.[7]

But long before that revolt, all kinds of changes began to erode the official system of representation and style promoted by the Academy of Fine Arts. And a good many of them arose in the provinces and small towns of Russia. First there was the explosion of graphic art—wood engraving, lithography, book illustration—that began in the capitals but made possible the spread of visual culture into the four comers of the empire. Simultaneous with this was the establishment of alternate art schools in the provinces: at Safonkovo in Tver' Province run by the Academy-trained painter Alexei Venetsianov; the school at Arzamas run by Alexander Stupin; those at Voronezh and Kozlov, and a few others—all of them with liberal admission policies. This not only broadened the social profile of the art community and put more art before the eyes of more people; it also affected the birth of new styles, usually characterized as "early realism."[8]

Venetsianov, a major teacher and stylistic innovator, worked out of his rural estate in Tver' Province and contributed to the expansion of artistic horizons in another way. He raised money to emancipate those of his pupils who were still enserfed. The most gifted of his pupils, however, Grigori Soroka, failed to gain freedom in spite of all his teacher's efforts. His owner, N. P. Miliukov, stubbornly insisted on his right to keep his "property." In this he was typical of those landlords who refused to manumit talented serfs in music, art, and theatre out of spite, fear of improper precedent setting, or simple pride of ownership. The records of the Academy, the Society for the Encouragement of Artists (founded 1821), and individual figures in their struggle to free artists constitute a relatively unstudied chapter in the discourse on anti-serfdom thought and action in the pre-reform period (see Sobko 1890; Stolpianskii 1928; Golubeva 1961).

Provincial artists helped open up new visual worlds by abandoning the gods, the warriors, and the saints of the Academic art world. One may say that they turned to the "exploration of the interior." Working and living in the provinces—the interior of Russia—they painted the real Russian out-of-the-way countryside as they saw it and captured peasants at work instead of picturing them as pastoral figures in an idealized landscape. When painting indoors, the realist artists did portraits and family scenes in the everyday *intérieur* and brought their gentry and merchant subjects down to earth. The more daring among them ventured into the under life. On their canvases, they caught Urals forgers sweating under the scorching heat of their workshops; drunks staggering outside a village tavern; coachmen battling their way through the spring mud; peasant women cleaning beets; and dozens of other genre scenes from the ordinary life of Russian people of all classes, far from the capitals, far from the ritualized round of the gentry world, far from the rules of Academic painting (see Alekseeva 1982; Mikhailova 1982).[9]

Some Thoughts

I have tried to evoke in this brief overview some of the mechanisms which were driving creative people to discover and represent their own country and how much of this drive was emanating from the provinces. I have done so by trying to accentuate the difference between the "cultural capital" of the cultural capitals and that of the rest of the country. Of course one should avoid exaggerating those differences and underestimating the contribution to this process of discovery made by urban creative figures, working on urban themes. After all, for most readers, it was the *feuilleton*, the physiological sketch, and the early stories of Dostoevsky, Grigorev, and others of the "naturalist" school of letters that introduced previously uncharted social terrain (see Oksman 1930). "Exploring the interior" was not the exclusive project of the provincials. The examination of "the inner city" was a key element in that quest. Urban painters in St. Petersburg and elsewhere, paralleling writers, found their subjects on street corners and squares—hawk and vendors of all sorts, laundresses, beggars, and "newly decorated" petty officials in their scrubby rooms, as in the paintings of Pavel

Fedotov.[10] Their subjects and styles of representation—including color, light, and composition—were eons apart from what was being taught and sustained in the Academy; and their works were appearing decades before the emergence of the much more celebrated Peredvizhniki.

I hope that this perspective, that of combining town and country, capital and provinces, high culture and everyday cultural experience will suggest ways of overcoming the sometimes rather exclusive and hierarchical approaches to history and to the history of culture in particular.

Original publication: In Natalia Baschmakoff and Paul Fryer, eds. *Modernization in the Russian Provinces*. Helsinki: Studia Slavica Finlandensia, XVII, March 2000, pp. 306-323.

Notes

1   For a brief introduction and documentation on Glinka, see Stites 1998. See also Garden 1967.
2   For domesticity and music elsewhere, see Loesser 1951; Weber 1975, 30-31; Leppert 1988; and Smith 1981.
3   I offer here only a few of the many general histories of Russian theatre and some specialised works: Istoriia 1977-1987; Istoriia 1982; Istoriia dorevolilitsionnnoi 1977-1978; Krasovskaia 1958; Grossman 1926; 19natov 1916; Karlinsky 1985; Rodina 1958.
4   See Roosevelt 1995 for the general ambience and for rich information of serf actors and artists; Sakhnovskii 1924; Stanyukovich 1927.
S   For the background and literature on this, see Stites 2000.
6   For a comparison, see Rosenthal, Payne, and Wilcox 1997.
7   On the "revolt" see Valkenier 1977. On the social origins of art students, see Perkins 1991.
8   For the graphics, see the discussion and notes in Bowlt 1983; Agin and Bernardskii 1892. For the new provincial schools, see note 9 below and Moleva and Beliutin 1963.
9   In addition to the many printed reproductions and the paintings hanging in the Tretiakov Gallery in Moscow and the Russian Museum in St. Petersburg, I have examined the un-hung pictures in the storage collection of the latter museum: Gosudarstvennyi russkii muzei, Fond zhivopisi XVIII-pervoi poloviny XIX veka. For comparison, see Barrell 1980; Brettell 1983.

10 Komelova 1960; *Vidy* 1960. There are literally scores of such works. Many of the originals are housed in the St. Petersburg Rossiiskaia Natsional'naia Biblioteka, Otdel Estampov. For one among dozens of studies of Fedotov, see Sarabianov 1985.

Bibliography

Agio, A. and Bernardskii, E. (1892): *Sto chetyre risunki k poeme N. V. Gogolia 'Mertvye dushi.'* Second ed. St. Petersburg.

Alekseeva, Tatiana (1982): *Khudozhniki shkoly Venetsianova.* Moscow.

Barrell, John (1983): *The Dark Side of the Landscape: the Rural Poor in English Painting, 1730-1840.* Cambridge University Press.

Beliakov, B. N., Blinova, V. G., and Bordiug, N. D. (1980): *Opernaia i kontsertnaia deiatel'nost' v Nizhnem-Novgorode — gorode Gorkom (1798-1980).* Gorkii.

Bowlt, John (1983): Nineteenth Century Russian Caricature. *Art and Culture in Nineteenth Century Russia.* Ed. Theofanis Stavrou. Bloomington: Indiana University Press, 221-236.

Brettell, Richard and Caroline (1983): *Painters and Peasants in the Nineteenth Century.* Geneva: Rizzoli.

Duleba, Wladyslaw (1974): *Wieniawski.* Kraków.

Dynnik, Tatiana (1933): *Krepostnoi teatr.* Leningrad.

Fitzpatrick, Anne (1990): *The Great Russian Fair: Nizhnii Novgorod, 1840-90.* New York: St. Martins.

Fradkina, Eleonora (1994): *Zal Dvorianskogo Sobraniia: zametki o kontsertnoi zhizni Sankt-Peterburga.* St. Petersburg.

Garden, Edward (1967): *Balakirev.* New York.

Gatsiskii, A. S. (1867): *Nizhegorodskii teatr (1798-1867).* Nizhnii Novgorod.

Ginzburg, L. S. (1983): *Anri V'etan.* Moscow.

Glagoleva, Olga (1993): *Russkaia provintsial'naia starina: ocherki kul'tury i byta Tul'skoi gubernii XVII-pervoi poloviny XIX vv.* Tula.

Golubeva, E. (1961): Iz istorii Obshchestva pooshchreniia khudozhnikov. *Iskusstvo,* No.10, 67-72.

Gozenpud, Abram (1992): *Dom Engel'gardta: iz istorii.* St. Petersburg.

Grossman, Leonid (1926): *Pushkin v teatral'nykh kreslakh: kartiny russkoi stseny, 1817-1820.* Leningrad.

Hammarberg, Gitta (1996): Flirting with Words: Domestic Albums, 1770-1840. *Russia, Women, Culture.* Ed. Helen Goscilo and Beth Holmgren. Bloomington, Indiana University Press, 297-320.

Herresthal, Harald (1987): *Norwegische Musik.* Oslo: Norsk Musikforlag.

Ignatov, N. N. (1916): *Teatr i zriteli. I: Pervaia polovina XIX st.* Moskva.

Imperatorskaia (1914): = *Imperatorskaia Sanktpeterburgskaia Akademiia khudozhestv: Kratkii istoricheskii ocherk.* Ed. S.K. Isakov i dr. St. Petersburg.

Imperatorskaia (1997): = *Imperatorskaia Akademiia khudozhestv: Vtoraia polovina XVIII, pervaia polovina XIX veka.* Moskva.

Istoriia (1977-1987): = *Istoriia russkogo dramaticheskogo teatra.* 7 tom. Moskva.

Istoriia (1982): = *Istoriia russkoi dramaturgii: XVII-pervaia polovina XIX veka.* Leningrad.

Istoriia dorevoliutsionnnoi (1977-1978) = *Istoriia dorevoliutsionnoi Rossii v dnevnikakh i vospominaniiakh.* I. Moskva.

Karlinsky, Simon (1985): *Russian Drama from its Beginnings to the Age of Pushkin.* Berkeley: University of California Press.

Komelova, G. (1960): *Russkaia graviura i litografiia XVIII-nachala XX vv.* Leningrad.

Kots, E.S. (1926): *Krepostnaia intelligentsiia.* Leningrad.

Kotzebue, August von (1965): *Das merkwürdigste Jahr meines Lebens.* München.

Krasovskaia, Vera (1958): *Russkii baletnyi teatr ot vozniknoveniia do serediny XIX veka.* Moskva.

Kratkii (1902): *Kratkii obzor deiatel'nosti S.-Peterburgskago Filarmonicheskago obshchestva.* St. Petersburg.

Kufferath, Maurice (1882): *Henri Vieuxtemps: sa vie et son oeuvre.* Bruxelles.

Lavrov, I. I. (1889): *Stsena i zhizn v provintsii i v stolitse.* Moskva.

Leppert, Richard (1988): *Music and Image: Domesticity, Ideology, and Socio-Cultural Formation in Eighteenth-Century England.* Cambridge University Press.

Loesser, Arthur (1951): *Men, Women, and Pianos.* New York: Simon and Shuster (1954; 2nd ed., Dover Publications, 1990 - *ed.*).

Medvedeva, Irina and Semenova, Ekaterina (1964): *Zhizn' i tvorchestvo tragicheskoi aktrisy.* Moskva.

Mikhailova, K.V. (1982): *Iz istorii realizma v russkoi zhivopisi.* Moskva.

Moleva, N. and Beliutin, E. (1963): *Russkaia khudozhestvennaia shkola pervoi poloviny XIX veka.* Moskva.

Nikulina-Kositskaia, Liubov (1996): Memoirs. *Russia Through Women's Eyes: Autobiographies from Tsarist Russia.* Ed. Toby Clyman and Judith Vowles. New Haven: Yale University Press, 108-157.

Oksman, Iu. G. (ed.) (1930): *Feletony sorokovykh godov.* Moskva.

Perkins, Etta (1991): Mobility in the Art Profession in Tsarist Russia. *Jahrbücher f. Geschichte Osteuropas,* N.F. 39/2, 225-233.

Piggott, Patrick (1973): *The Life and Music of John Field, 1782-1837: The Creator of the Nocturne.* London: Faber and Faber.

Rodina, T. M. (1958): La révolution du théâtre russe de 1800 à 1850. Special Issue of *Cahiers d'histoire mondiale,* 212-229.

Roosevelt, Priscilla (1995): *Life on the Russian Country Estate*. New Haven: Yale University Press.

Rosenthal, Michael, Payne, Christiana, and Wilcox, Scott (eds.) (1997): *Prospects for the Nation: Recent Essays in British Landscape, 1750-1880*. Studies in British Art, 4. New Haven: Yale University Press.

Rozanov, A. S. (1978): *Muzykal'nyi Pavlovsk*. Leningrad.

Sarabianov, Dmitrii (1985): *Pavel Andreevich Fedotov*. Leningrad.

Savinov, A. N. (1964): Akademicheskaia zhivopis'. *Istoriia russkoi iskusstva*. Ed. I. E. Grabar. tom. VIII/2, Moskva, 110-128.

Sakhnovskii, V. G. (1924): *Krepostnoi usadebnyi teatr*. Leningrad.

Senelick, Lawrence (1984): *Serf Actor: the Life and Art of Mikhail Shchepkin*. Westport: Greenwood Press.

Shcherbakova, T. (1990): *Mikhail i Matvei Vielgorskie: ispolniteli, prosvetiteli, metsenaty*. Moskva.

Smith, Bonnie (1981): *Ladies of Leisure. Princeton:* Princeton University Press.

Sobko, N. (1890): *Kratkii istoricheskii ocherk Imperatorskago Obshchestva pooshchreniia khudozhestv*. St. Petersburg.

Staniukovich, Vladimir (1927): *Domashnii krepostnoi teatr Sheremetevykh XVIII vek*. Leningrad.

Stites, Richard (1998): The Domestic Muse: Music at Home in the Twilight of Serfdom. *Intersections and Transpositions: Russian Music, Literature, and Society*. Ed. Andrew Wachtel. Evanston: Northwestern University Press, 187-205.

Stites, Richard (2000): The Misanthrope, the Orphan, and the Magpie: Melodrama and Sociodrama. *Melodrama in Russia*. Ed. Louise McReynolds and Joan Neuberger. Durham, NC: Duke University, forthcoming (2002, 25-54; also here, the next essay - *ed.*).

Stolpianskii, P. N. (1928): *Staryi Peterburg i Obshchestvo pooshchreniia khudozhestv*. Leningrad.

Stolpianskii, P. N. (1989): *Muzyka i muzitsirovanie v starom Peterburge*. Leningrad.

Turgenev, I. S. (1964): *Nakanune; Gamlet i Don-Kikhot; Ottsy i deti*. Moskva.

Valkenier, Elizabeth (1977): *Russian Realist Art, the State, and Society: Peredvizhniki and their Tradition*. Ann Arbor: University of Michigan Press.

Vidy (1960): = *Vidy S.-Peterburga i okrestnostei: litografirovannoe izdanie Obshchestvo pooshchreniia khudozhestv, (1821-1826)*. Kommentarii Komelovoi. Leningrad.

Walker, Alan (1987): *Franz Liszt: The Virtuoso Years, 1811-1847*. Volume l. Second ed. Ithaca, NY: Cornell University Press.

Weber, William (1975): *Music and the Middle Class: the Social Structure of Concert Life in London, Paris, and Vienna*. London: Croom Helm.

Wirtschafter, Elise (1997): *Social Identity in Imperial Russia*. DeKalb, IL: Northern Illinois University Press.

27

The Misanthrope, the Orphan, and the Magpie
Imported Melodrama in the Twilight of Serfdom

O, So Melodrama!

Traditional soviet readings of melodrama were not much different from the older, simple ones written in the western world. The *Theater Encyclopedia* of thirty years ago offered an elitist and politicized discussion of melodrama—barely admitting the genre's existence in Russia. Melodrama's cardinal sin was that its alleged concern for the poor and the weak was offset by an affirmation of the "bourgeois" order and a preachy message of class peace. The genre thus masked real, systemic social evils behind a war between abstractions of good and evil.[1] In actuality, the opposite may have been the case: Russian audiences who regularly saw legally permitted productions about the struggle of the poor and the weak against the rich and the strong in a secular setting may have become as attuned to social evils as did the far fewer readers of antiserfdom novels and essays. In any case, there is no denying melodrama's enormous popularity in the last half century of serfdom when it flourished on the Russian stage.

Today's viewers come equipped with a well-established anti-melodrama lexicon bulging with as many clichés as are found in the genre itself. In a world where horse opera has been with us for a century and soap opera for seventy years, it is not hard to be "sophisticated" about melodrama. Even some of its avid consumers utter the word as a sneer. Original melodrama as it emerged out of the French Revolution, the storm and stress of early romanticism, and "bourgeois sentimentalism" had its instant critics, but not a long history of dismissal. Melodrama was born on stage—a story in dialogue spoken by actors, visually decorated, and accompanied by music. The European public enthusiastically devoured vaudevilles and melodramas along with operas—many of which had melodramatic story lines. All evidence shows that audiences enjoyed the wonderfully outrageous plots. They identified with characters, wanted a certain plausibility, and accepted colorful exaggeration of that plausibility. When the genre was young, consumers of all classes were able to suspend disbelief. One did not have to be a gruff merchant or a poor clerk to immerse oneself in the toils of Pixérécourt or Kotzebue or Scribe.

In melodrama, certain character types and situations recur constantly.[2] A useful typology, although not rigorous or unfailing, suggests the melodramas of the grotesque, the adventure, and the family setting. The first drew on gothic novels of the eighteenth century, ruled in the "bloodbath theater" of London, and culminated at the turn of the twentieth century in the Paris Grand Guignole. The "cape and sword" adventure journeyed out to exotic places and back to historical times imagined. The family or domestic melodrama differed, and still does, from these two. In fact a more basic division lies between the melodrama of effect (or action) and that of affect (or emotion)—or, more bluntly, that of blood and that of tears. The gender appeal for the latter seems clear, and the playwrights of the age were fully aware of the growth of female audiences everywhere. Of the three works I will discuss, the Kotzebue domestic melodrama is of the second type and the two French pieces are of the first. Each partook of the other's modes; and all employed sensational devices. These devices were especially effective—because unexpected—in the family or domestic play, whose finale was often acted out in a wild place—from the mountains of Savoy in Pixérécourt's *Coelina* (1800) to the rushing ice floes of D. W. Griffith's film *Way Down East* (1920). The sensation could also be provided in the gritty urban version of domestic melodrama by a contrastive visit to back alleys and slums.

Melodrama is replete with much-scorned coincidences, with deus ex machina, and with the tricks of switched babies, mistaken identities, and the stirring moment of reconnaissance, or discovery of true identities. Such features are also found in classic drama, but in melodrama, justice—usually poetic—triumphs, wrongs are righted, and villains are punished. Tragic catharsis, the property of high art, never occurs. In the moral sphere, early European melodrama effected a transfer of revolutionary virtue and justice and populist values to the stage. Added pathos arose from inflicting evil on the already afflicted—the poor, the female, the weak, the child, the orphan, the blind, the deaf, the slave, the convict. The villains could come from outside the law—bandits and pirates; or they could emerge, slimy and unambiguously wicked, from respectable social milieux. A recurring conflict was that between a maiden ready to sacrifice her life to preserve her purity and the villain who falsely denounces her after his sexual advances are rebuffed. This surely resonates with Christian hagiography: Saints Agatha, Lucia, Margaret, and many others were martyrs not only to their faith but to the frustrated lust of men who brought about their deaths.

Scholars of great drama enjoy the advantage of being able to supplement textual study with live performance, however different the present versions are from the originals. It is now almost impossible to see melodramas of bygone days on stage. There is no market in the theater, and no interest in the academy. Historians must thus be doubly alert to what audiences might have seen and heard when melodramas were performed, including the setting, the seating, and the theater building itself. Stage effects in the more successful houses played for sensation: exotic locales and elaborate machinery imitating warships, fortresses, grottoes, alpine crevices, jungles. When the taste for historical, biblical, and mythological themes declined, more weight was given to urban contemporary settings, particularly in the 1840s in France under the influence of Eugene Sue's novel *Mystères de Paris*. Acting styles are hard to imagine even when we have script notes: the story was told by declamation, exaggerated gestures, coded movements, tirades, soliloquies, and asides—in which, for example, the villain would confide to the public his evil designs. A feel for the style may be gotten by watching the silent film melodramas of the 1910s.[3]

Music is often overlooked in theater history, and it is all but gone today on the drama stage where it was a vital component in the nineteenth century. Beethoven's incidental music to Goethe's *Egmont* and Mendelssohn's to Shakespeare's *Midsummer Night's Dream* was the fruit of a common practice even in high drama. Melodrama always used music, not only in the overture to get people seated but to signal entrances, exits, and dramatic moments; and as a means for emotional and character underlining—a plaintive flute for the innocent heroine, growling double basses to announce the villain, a lively tune for the comic. These devices were drawn straight from German musicological doctrine of the eighteenth century, a code known as *Affektenlehre* according to which minor slow meant elegiac; major slow, majestic; major fast, vigorous and triumphant; minor fast, menacing. This code guided composers of nineteenth-century melodrama music (and opera) and, later, of film scores.[4]

What follows is an attempt to delineate the experience that Russians had with European melodrama in the early nineteenth century, those last decades of serfdom when Russian theater was in fact a theater of war—a war of classic and romantic, state and private, elite and popular, capitals and provinces, declamatory and "natural" acting. The Russian experience of culture—what people saw and heard—is as important as Russian cultural production itself. This is particularly true for the melodrama of this era, which was largely imported. As in all other arts, when Russians came late to a genre they consumed what was available—in this case the French and German products. I offer in this essay a triptych of European melodramas that were popular everywhere in Europe and became an integral part of the Russian stage. Russian histories of theater usually dismiss them scornfully, yet without some understanding of these and similar works, what can we ever understand about the people in the theater itself—the cast, the writers, the translators and adapters, and those who outnumbered everyone else: the audience?

Mellow Drama: Kotzebue's First Hit

August von Kotzebue (1761-1819) is a name known—if at all—to students of European history as the German playwright in the service of Tsar Alexander I who was stabbed to death by a German nationalist student in 1819—a deed that launched Prince Metternich's infamous Carlsbad Decrees. But to hundreds of thousands of theatergoers in places ranging from the United States to Siberia, Kotzebue was a household name. Better known than Goethe and

Schiller in his day, Kotzebue wrote about 230 plays and boasted of being able to write one in a three-day period. All but forgotten now, his plays were translated into French, Russian, Danish, Swedish, Spanish, Romanian, Italian, Dutch, Greek, Bulgarian, Serbian, and English. In the German states, they made up one-fourth of the repertoire of plays performed in the years 1795 to 1825; in New York, fifty-two of the ninety-four theater performances in 1799 were of Kotzebue's plays. A student of his work has called Kotzebue "a phenomenon of literary and social history."[5] In Russia, Kotzebue effected a reorientation of theater taste as surely as did Beaumarchais in France a few decades earlier. His characters populated Russian stages in the capitals and in the provinces and helped launch the careers of well-known actors during the reign of Alexander I and Nicholas I.[6]

The great appeal of Kotzebue's works lay in their stageability, spectacle, immediacy of sentimental expression, and in their sense of empowerment and agency that was wholly absent in the neoclassical genre based on Greek models where the gods were in charge. Kotzebue wrote crisp dramatic material in plain language. His success—and his badge of shame to critical scholars—arose partly from his willingness to cater to a public weary of the tirade in rhymed verse of French neoclassical drama and comedy. The entertainment quotient of his work was provided by exotic settings in South America, the Near East, and on the ocean. Viewing his comedies, operas, one acts, farces , adaptations, and melodramas, audiences gaped at the animated impersonations of pirates, Gypsies, slaves, Peruvian Indians, uprooted Asians, rebels, impoverished nobles, and misused women—to say nothing of kings, sultans, and innumerable pseudohistorical figures attired in colorful costumes and backed by elaborate sets. Interwoven into the spectacle was the open expression of "naturalistic" feeling, with an occasional hint of sex and a down-to-earth sentimentalism. The socially expanding Russian audiences who were surfeited with—in Beaumarchais's scorching words—"the death of a Peloponesian tyrant or the sacrifice of a young princess of Aulis" could readily identify with his works.[7] People reared in the late eighteenth and early nineteenth century could relate more easily to everyday dramatic situations and to heroes who could triumph over evil than they could to exalted ancients locked in an uneven battle with the gods.

Kotzebue was a well-traveled bourgeois man of the world who claimed no depth of intellect. He skillfully played the strings of a sentimentalism that was already in literary vogue, and he spiced it with high adventure. Born into a family of Weimar petty officials in 1761, he moved in the environment of Schiller and Goethe, studied law, and became entranced by theater. He took up a minor post in St. Petersburg under Catherine II and began his dramatic career there with *Demetrius the Impostor,* one of many plays on this theme penned by European writers. Settling in Estland in a judicial post, Kotzebue immersed himself in amateur productions and founded the first theater in Reval (Tallin). For two decades from 1781 onward he lived on and off in the Baltic or in other parts of Russia before settling most of the time in Germany. Arrested under Tsar Paul in 1799, he was sent to Siberia on an unfounded suspicion of radicalism. Pardoned after a few months, Kotzebue returned, made his peace with Paul, and later became a favorite of Tsar Alexander I.[8]

An enlightened conservative, with a humanist outlook at least in his youth, Kotzebue in his works frequently criticized abuses of privilege and even of monarchical power. But in later years, like many of his contemporaries, he became an apologist of the Restoration and a keen foe of liberalism, democracy, constitutions, student rights, and a free press. Although not exactly a "spy" for Tsar Alexander I, he was certainly on his payroll as a nominal state councilor and supplied him with political intelligence, mostly in private correspondence. For all these reasons, Kotzebue was assassinated by Karl Sand in 1819. And this dramatic demise obscured Kotzebue's importance in history as a successful dramatist who dominated the stages of two continents for decades in all genres of melodrama.

Misanthropy and Repentance (1788), Kotzebue's first international sensation, premiered in Reval and then opened in Berlin where it was acclaimed by audiences composed of, in Oscar Mandel's words, "kings, lords and ladies, wealthy merchants, humble spectators — everyone except disgruntled intellectuals."[9] European readers and playgoers had been steeped in sentimentalism for decades before this play opened. As a "melodrama of affect" it was designed to appeal to popular sentiment, especially to female audiences. *Misanthropy and Repentance* was the ultimate gusher melodrama — both dialogue and stage directions are soaked in tears. It contains no villain and no violence, only the emotional turbulence in the finale when an errant wife repents to her husband in a lengthy dialogue and is forgiven. Baron Meinau, the male protagonist known as the Stranger, has spent three years of bitter hatred of self and of the human race as a result of the aberrant infidelity of his young wife, Eulalia. Repentant, she has gone into humble service to atone. The reunion is coincidental, their reconciliation organized by noble friends. The play presents an affecting dramatic treatment of the utter desolation of the two protagonists. Meinau, "an ice-cold man of clever mind" in the words of his servant, is an ancestor of those hard-faced, harsh-talking heroes with a soft heart who later inhabited westerns and crime melodramas on film. Eulalia, whose "heart bleeds and [whose] tears flow" at her fate, was an early model for heroines endowed with kindness, charity, and chaste modesty. In the very final moment of the play, after extended speechifying suspense, the afflicted couple are reunited in the presence of their children.[10]

The extraordinary impact of this play, and especially its heart-warming and eye-wetting finale, was conditioned not only by the sentimentalist literary movement of the time, but probably also by liberal life-affirming philanthropic currents among the bourgeoisie—the mainstay of Kotzebue's European and American audiences. This ideology encapsulated the antislavery crusade (Kotzebue wrote *Negro Slaves* [1796] on that theme) and other reformist movements. Eulalia was a perfect stand-in for the repentant convict so beloved of the penal reform movement of the time in many countries—especially in the Anglo-Saxon ones where Kotzebue flourished luxuriantly.[11] Having fallen afoul of the moral law, Eulalia has "paid the penalty" by years of separation from her loved ones, is now ready to "re-enter society" (family), and is given "a second chance." The emotional interplay of *Misanthropy* has direct analogies in prison literature. Meinau's friend and comrade-in-arms describes Eulalia in terms of her underlying virtue, her momentary lapse, her prolonged penance, and her worthiness of pardon. Eulalia, in the dialogue with Meinau, emphatically contrasts her own remorseful and atoning posture with that of "a hardened criminal," the unredeemable element in progressive penological discourse. [12]

Child of Love (1796), which dealt with illegitimacy, was the first

Kotzebue play performed in St. Petersburg. By the late 1790s, he was well known in the Russian provinces, and dozens of his plays had been translated into Russian, with *Misanthropy and Repentance* in the lead. Of the many versions of the play, a partial list includes two published in St. Petersburg (1792), two in Moscow (1796, 1801), one in Smolensk (1812), and two in Orël (1824, 1826). As early as 1800, during his brief sojourn in exile in Siberia, Kotzebue met people in Moscow, Kazan, and Tobolsk who knew his name and work. A friendly governor of Tobolsk province offered the playwright a chance to stage one of his new short comedies. On his way out of Tobolsk to his place of exile in remote Kurgan, Kotzebue was accosted by a Russian actress from an itinerant troupe asking him costume details about a play of his in which she was about to perform, *Virgin of the Sun*.[13]

On returning to St. Petersburg after his pardon, Kotzebue served at Tsar Paul's court theater. Kozebue's complaints about the stringent censorship are well known and often quoted. Less known was the reaction of the iron disciplinarian Tsar Paul—he was "deeply moved" to the staging in 1800 in French by French actors of *Misanthropy and Repentance* at the Hermitage Theater. Kotzebue's popularity thereafter grew apace: in the years 1800 to 1820 up to half of the plays in a season in Moscow and St. Petersburg were his. In 1806, a German correspondent in St. Petersburg reported that "the name of Kotzebue in the [theater] announcements is here always the surest magnet for a full house."[14] Within a decade Kotzebue was fully established in Russian provincial stages, serf theaters, and amateur productions. At Kazan University, his works inspired an amateur student theater in which Sergei Aksakov played the role of Meinau. Aksakov soon became known as a theater critic, long before his other reputation was made as the poetic memoirist of the Orenburg steppe or as the father of two Slavophiles.[15]

Audiences in Russia adored Kotzebue for what he delivered, whether in German, French, or Russian. Directors and theater entrepreneurs loved him for the full houses. And certain actors found in his work a natural vehicle for their talents. Kotzebue's plays required acting gifts untapped by the classical repertoire. Pavel Mochalov, Peter Plavilshchikov, Alexei Iakovlev, and "a whole series of major Russian actors" made their name in Kotzebue roles.

Mochalov, the icon of the "Moscow" emotional style (contrasted with the classical demeanor of the St. Petersburg players) found his first stage success in Kotzebue's plays. A memoirist recalls that when Mochalov played Meinau in *Misanthropy and Repentance*, "he would begin [his tale of woe] calmly, almost indifferently; but little by little his emotion rose to a pitch that seized the audience. Every added word expressing the accumulated bitterness of his soul moved their hearts more strongly, till finally they were unable to suppress their tears." Plavilshchikov's best role was Meinau, but Aksakov, while a student in the newly opened Kazan University, was thrilled by his performance in *Child of Love*. A. S. Iakovlev (1773-1817), the son of a Kostroma merchant, was a shop clerk when his talent was discovered. On stage, he privileged emotion over reason and when he played Meinau, not even "a heart of stone" could withstand his acting. Iakovlev turned on a "faucet of tears" in the audience and could bring tears to his own eyes at certain moments. A contemporary Russian critic, Stepan Zhikharev, comparing various well-known actors of the 1810s, observed that although they all played Meinau with merit, none could compare to Iakovlev who "made you cry."[16]

At the coronation of Tsar Paul in 1797, Alexandra Karatygina played Eulalia opposite Iakovlev as Meinau in *Misanthropy and Repentance*. She was noted for the "feeling and tenderness" of her style. It was, in the view of one scholar, the role of Eulalia that brought her talent to perfection. By contrast, the most famous actress of the age, Ekaterina Semenova, daughter of a serf, initially played the Kotzebue *emploi* but found her true line of business in classical and neoclassical plays. Her electrifying performance in *Medea* was as far from the Kotzebue genre as any could be. And it is Semenova who is canonized in theatrical history, although both her declamatory style of acting and her repertoire were on the verge of decline when she reached the peak of her career.[17]

A well-known soviet scholar of the 1920s called the Kotzebue oeuvre *meshchanskaia drama* (lower middle-class or philistine drama) and repeated the familiar Marxist cliché that melodrama, along with other popular forms, deflected popular passions away from the terrible reign of Nicholas I, just as it was doing in the France of Louis-Philippe. He also quoted contemporary classicists who called

Kotzebue's plays *kotsebiatina* (Kotzebue trash). Those writing from an aesthetic perspective fixed on the playwright's simplicity and lack of art. Kotzebue frankly admitted that he was a second-rate writer—but one who wished to give pleasure to the masses of theatergoers. Pleasing audiences, to certain critics then and now, can be considered pandering—a cheap and ultimately immoral act.[18] The Decembrist V. K. Küchelbecker (Kiukhelbekker), for example, detested the "sentimental-German" drama of Kotzebue "which gave the ladies of the Zamoskvorechie District [of merchant Moscow] much to rave about."[19] Here the resentment is leveled not only at the creator but at the very audience he serves, an audience that allegedly has been hoodwinked and is thus worthy of contempt.

But let us listen to a different voice, that of Rafael Zotov, novelist and dramatist, author of over one hundred plays, including melodramas and historical pastiches. He spoke for the seatless *parterre*, where stood teachers, journalists, youth, and officers who, he believed, came for the "theater" as opposed to the seated public who came for the "show." "The *parterre*," he wrote, "is a crucial element in the theater. Without it, the passion of the middle classes [*srednoe soslovie*] would not develop. The life that is imparted by the *parterre* encourages actors and makes them fear the stern and educational judgement that is located there." Elsewhere he wrote that "our audiences were raised on exclamations, shouts, and turgid phrases. But as soon as they were shown a domestic environment, the joys and sorrows of ordinary life, as soon as they saw verisimilitude and naturalness, as soon as they heard the voice of natural feelings—they joyfully jumped off the high horse of Sumarokov [the eighteenth-century classical dramatist] and with all their hearts attached themselves to the plays of Kotzebue."[20]

Kotzebue's numerous "cape and sword" plays, replete with nasty villains and exotic locales, also did well on the Russian stage, but none had the resonance in Russia of *Misanthropy and Repentance*. This is probably because the French imports in the "action" subgenre of melodrama were better and more timely (as will be discussed below) or because it was easier in Russia to translate them fast. *Misanthropy* appeared early and won patronage at court and in the German theater of St. Petersburg and elsewhere. It could be heard in three languages, sometimes in the same city. Although no detailed evidence of audience reaction is available, we do know that this melodrama gained instant popularity. It would be tempting to ascribe some peculiarly soulful element in the play that had special appeal for Russians. Were Russians especially sympathetic to the "agency" of a Eulalia or forgiving of her sin? Was there operating a moral equivalent of the European prison reform movement, a tendency to pity the wrongdoer? One thinks of the peasant habit of lining the road to Siberia and praying for convicts; and of the enduring tenderness in Russian literature to "fallen women."

The evidence allows no more than speculation. Like their European counterparts, Russian critics of the time differed over the pivotal moment in *Misanthropy and Repentance*: the moral propriety of forgiving an unfaithful wife on stage. But accounts of its public reception—in Russia and elsewhere—almost always focus on the favorable impression made by the final scene of reconciliation, clearly indicating that the key ingredient of the play was forgiveness and redemption, enduring features of New Testament Christian theology and ecclesiastical practice. In spite of the secularism launched by the French Revolution and the preceding Enlightenment, the deep wells of religion (and of Freemasonry) still offered sustenance to the public, perhaps all the more so when decked out in simple domestic fiction and acted on stage. Russian audiences who flocked to and wept through *Misanthropy* were cosmopolitan not so much in the sophisticated sense, but rather as sharers of that transnational collective surge of philanthropic emotionalism and charitableness that at this time was being exhibited—and constantly violated as well—all over the European continent.

An Orphan on the Provincial Circuit

Kotzebue has been compared to Guilbert de Pixérécourt (1773-1844), the "father of French melodrama."[21] The "melodrama of effect" in Pixérécourt's work and that of his Parisian rivals, Caigniez and Ducange, ruled the day. In the backdrop of melodrama hung the French Revolution with its own melodramas of violence, betrayal, pathos, rescue, and a world reversed. Pixérécourt fought on the side of both royalist émigrés and Jacobins, and he met real prototypes for the stock villain that he virtually invented for

Parisian audiences who frequented theaters located on what was called the Boulevard of Crime. Pixérécourt wrote about 120 plays, half of them melodramas, that were performed thousands of times in the first half of the nineteenth century. After the appearance of his first full-formula melodrama, *Coelina, or, The Child of Mystery* (1800), at the very moment of the transition between the inward turmoil of the Revolution and the outward spectacles of Napoleon, Pixérécourt was hailed as "the man who made all France weep."[22] Not far behind him came Victor Ducange, famous for breaking all the rules of drama by putting three generations of life on stage in *Thirty Years, or, The Life of a Gambler* (1827), a play about a compulsive gambler who kills a fellow train passenger for money to feed his gaming frenzy and subsequently discovers that the victim is his son. *Thirty Years* was very popular in Russia where the table and the deck could also be a lethal occupation (the well-known composer Alexander Aliabev was convicted of murder over a card game in the 1820s). But it was Ducange's *Theresa, or, The Orphan of Geneva* (1821) that achieved world acclaim.

The plot of *Theresa* is crucial in providing clues to audience reaction. Like *Misanthropy and Repentance*, it deals with high-born people. Kotzebue's cast resided in a castle; Ducange's characters live in the Swiss château of the widow de Sénange and her son Karl. The mysterious young woman who has been taken in by the châtelaine is Theresa, disguised as "Henriette," and she is about to be betrothed to Karl. The back story, slowly revealed, is her early life as an adopted (although in fact biological) daughter of a high noblewoman. When her mother dies, Theresa is revealed as the beneficiary of her vast fortune until the swindler Walther falsely accuses her of malfeasance and has her sent to jail. While she is out on bail, Walther concocts a plan—as he informs the audience in a long aside—to force her to marry him and thus get his hands on the fortune by revealing the truth about the will. But Theresa flees and finds shelter first with the kindly Pastor Egerthon and then with the de Sénanges. Walther appears at the engagement party and reveals Theresa's shameful arrest. At this point the plot accelerates into high, but still verbose, action. Theresa flees in shame to a hiding place arranged by Egerthon. Madame de Sénange and Walther learn of her whereabouts and both arrive when Theresa is absent. In the dark, Walther, now resolved to murder Theresa, mistakenly kills the older woman. When Theresa returns and discovers the body, she is suspected of murder. In court, however, Egerthon accuses Walther without telling him who the victim really is. The pastor confronts the killer with the live Theresa, and he is so frightened by what he takes to be a ghost that he breaks down and confesses. Theresa is absolved of all criminal activity.[23]

French melodrama flooded into Russia in the 1810s and 1820s. St. Petersburg and Moscow repertoires in the years 1813 to 1825 contained ten melodramas of Pixérécourt. (His works were so well-known that his *Pizarro, or, The Conquistador of Peru* was satirized by Dmitri Lenskii in Russia's most durable stage comedy, *Lev Gurych Sinichkin* [1839]). In those years, the capitals saw four plays of Caigniez and several of Ducange, including *Theresa*, which by then had already played around the world. Imperial Theater actors had to take the roles assigned to them and shift from serious tragedy to melodrama or vaudeville and even to opera and ballet. The classical star Semënova in St. Petersburg played de Sénange, with her sister Nimfodora Semënova as Theresa and Iakov Brianskii as Walther. Detailed sound effects and music are marked in the margins of a Moscow copy of the script. Many of the silent scenes demanded very expressive mimicry and clarity of movement in order to motivate the plot; as obvious as it sounds, we must remember that there are no closeups in theater. Stage movement was carefully taught by dancing masters, ballet being a mandatory part of the training of all dramatic actors in this era.[24]

I have no data on the reception of *Theresa* in the two capitals, but the experience of the provincials throws some light on the levels at which people saw melodrama. Frequent assertions to the contrary notwithstanding, theater flourished in the Russian provinces during the pre-emancipation era. The Imperial Theater system held a monopoly in its half-dozen houses in St. Petersburg and Moscow but was little concerned about what went on in the provinces. There, close to two hundred serf theaters operated at the apex of their development (ca. 1770s-1820), mostly on estates but also in provincial and district capitals. To these must be added commercial theaters owned by nobles, merchants, and other classes in the towns, and traveling troupes that crisscrossed the country in a permanent caravan of troikas and carriages, rattling with musical instruments, sets, machines, and costumes. At almost every one of the thousands of fairs one could find some kind of theatrical performance—not only puppet and folk entertainments but also *King Lear*, *Wilhelm Tell*, and Russian tragedies, comedies, vaudevilles, operas, and melodramas. Out of this circuit came some of the finest actors on the Moscow and St. Petersburg stages—including the most famous of all, Mikhail Shchepkin, a serf.

All three of the plays discussed here played this circuit. At the high end of the scale stood the once famous provincial theater of Nizhny-Novgorod, which flourished during the reign of Nicholas I. One of its standbys, borrowed from the capital stages, was *Theresa, or, The Orphan of Geneva*. For the highest-paid star of this theater, Anna Vysheslavtseva, Theresa was a bread-and-butter role. In her production, the murderer Walther used arson rather than the knife in order to enhance the spectacle.[25] At the lower end of the scale—fairground performance—we have the comments of the musician Iury Arnold from about 1835. While in Kharkov at the time of the Kreshchinskaia Fair, Arnold saw Theresa, disliked it, and conceded, rather sourly, that it was at the time a very popular melodrama.[26]

The comments of I. I. Lavrov, later an actor at the Maly and the lead singer at the Bolshoi in Moscow, offer a different perspective. Lavrov began life as the son of a petty merchant in Tambov province, worked as a peddler, a factory worker, and other menial occupations. In 1844 he began acting in a provincial repertoire that included Shakespeare, vaudevilles, operas, and melodramas. Lavrov's account of the provincial years—about sixty engagements in about thirty towns, villages, and fairs—is richly descriptive of theater life, including conditions of employment, audiences, managers, patrons, interfering officials, sudden dismissals, money matters, and backstage romances. It is also brutally frank about brushes with the police and about drunk and disorderly actors who were run out of town. How did Lavrov become an actor? During visits to the fairs along the Volga, while still a peddler, he became enchanted with carnival entertainment. The turning point of his life occurred in Astrakhan where in 1844 he saw his very first play, *Theresa, or, The Orphan of Geneva*. Lavrov was so captivated by the play and its performance that he was permanently hooked to life in the theater. In the pages of his memoirs, Lavrov pauses to give a plot summary of *Theresa* and to admit, after many years, that he wept for Theresa and felt a deep hatred for Walther.[27]

Lavrov recounts another incident at this performance. In the scene where Walther denies his guilt of the murder, a spectator cried out from the audience: "You lie, you son of a dog, bandit. You killed [her]. Look at these good folks [in the theater]; they are witnesses. Am I right, friends."[28] The public in the stalls and in the loges laughed and the police removed the spectator. This episode was fairly typical of audience behavior in the theater—and not only in Russia. According to an anecdote, at the premier of Rossini's opera *Otello* in Naples in 1816, when the singer playing Othello approached Desdemona in her bed, the audience shouted to the actress: "Watch out, he has a knife [*sic*]!"[29] Another example, related in Herzen's "Magpie," was the "old joke" about a good German viewer at a performance of *Don Giovanni* who shouted to those chasing Don Juan: "He fled down the alley to the right." If opera could induce this kind of belief, how much more could melodrama evoke such reactions, despite its artificial music and stylized gestures.[30]

The evidence on the reception of *Theresa* is thin and anecdotal, but certainly it can indicate its durability for at least three decades, and it can attest to its wide trajectory—from the imperial houses of the capital to commercial theaters at important Volga towns to the barns of the Kreshchinskaia Fair in Ukraine. What caused the classical composer and violinist Iury Arnold to curl his lip in scorn also drove a budding actor to tears (and to a career) and at least one spectator to near intervention. As in the other plays discussed here, the central figure *Theresa* is an agonized and finally redeemed or rescued woman. Theresa's status as an orphan doubtless had its own resonance; a Russian melodrama titled *The Lunatic Orphan Susanna* was playing the circuit during the same period. According to detailed topographical studies of Russian towns, virtually all of the towns possessed an orphanage and benefit performances for the support of orphans were common in provincial theaters.[31] Judging from what I have read of reactions to melodrama and related genres all over provincial Russia (and in the capitals as well), audiences delighted in both "pity and terror"—Aristotle's vaunted description of tragedy. But they also wanted agency, action, spectacle, and thrill. A murder plot twisted around the fate of a victimized young woman fit this formula to perfection.

The Flight of the Magpie

The origin of the story of the "thieving magpie," who unwittingly sent a young woman to her death, is obscure. One source on its genesis refers to a medieval legend, another to "a curious French legal case," and a third to a (probably the same) real event in which an innocent peasant girl was wrongly hanged for the theft of an article by a magpie.[32] This story was fashioned into a French melodrama in 1815 and adapted for Rossini's opera in 1817. Both won popularity in Russia. Alexander Herzen used the motif as the core of his famous story "Soroka-vorovka" (1848).

The melodrama, *The Thieving Magpie, or, the Maidservant of Palaiseau* is often attributed solely to L. C. Caigniez, author of

The Magpie or the Maid? A Melo Drame in Three Acts, Translated and Altered from the French by I. Pocock. London: 1815, Frontespiece.

The Judgement of Solomon, which is the first use in melodrama of a courtroom and of a biblical subject. In fact, the original author was J. M. T. Baudouin d'Aubigny, who submitted his play to a Parisian director. Unread, it was found by the director's child and given for rewrite to the already established melodramatist Caigniez. With music composed by Alexandre Piccinni, *Magpie* was staged in 1815 in the midst of Napoleon's Hundred Days, an event that had no effect on the box office. In fact, the director made such a huge profit from its many performances that he eventually retired on his earnings to a country place, aptly named the Hamlet of the Thieving Magpie.[33]

The action of *Magpie* turns around two linked problems, both involving the maidservant Annette. First, she is accused of having stolen her mistress's silver plate, which has actually been pilfered by a magpie attracted by its glitter. Second, she has, quite independently, sold one of her own cheap plates in order to help her old father who has deserted the army because of mistreatment and is fleeing his pursuers. The witnesses against Annette include an honest Jew who truthfully recounts his purchase from her of a plate, and, more important, a villainous magistrate who falsely accuses her because she has rebuffed his advances. Annette is found guilty and is sentenced to death. The audience knows the truth and the tension is generated, as in so many melodramas, by the fact that the innocent heroine cannot reveal the truth out of fear for her father's fate. The authors of the melodrama intervene to avoid the miscarriage of justice that apparently ended the original version, but the intervention is not immediate: after the tribunal renders its verdict, a march to the scaffold is staged, adding to the suspense. Annette, in a final act of sacrifice, sends a servant to deliver money to her father who is in hiding. As the comic servant counts the money, the magpie reappears and steals one of the bright coins. The man follows the bird to its nest and finds the stolen plate. Annette is cleared and her father pardoned.

Like *Misanthropy and Repentance* and *Theresa*, *Magpie* was an international success. It remained popular in France for a half century and was adapted in the United States and in Britain where one performance opened in London in 1815 at Covent Garden. The Russian version, *Soroka-vorovka*, premiered in Moscow in December

1816 as a benefit performance, which was followed by three more performances that month. In 1817 it played nine times—a record run for that era. For the 1816 St. Petersburg performance, Annette was played by M. I. Valberkhova, the daughter of the ballet master who also translated the play.[34]

The most enduring treatment of the magpie was the delightful opera *melodramma* of Gioacchino Rossini, *La gazza ladra*, which premiered at La Scala in Milan in 1817. The libretto by Giovanni Gherardini was adapted from the French original in 1816 for the then well-known Italian composer Giovanni Paisiello, who died that year. It was taken over by Rossini. His *Gazza* is an *opera semiseria*, a light melodrama with comic elements set against a continuous background of menace. Some names and character types were changed; for example, the villain in Gherardini's libretto is the mayor of the town. The cleverly wrought scene in which Ninetta (Annette) deliberately misreads to the mayor the description of the deserter in a letter of warrant for the hunted father was apparently copied for *Boris Godunov* by Alexander Pushkin, who saw the opera in Odessa during the 1823-1824 season. Rossini's music is charming— full of melodious arias yet occasionally darkened as in the prison scene, the trial, and the march to the scaffold, which introduced the novel (and to some objectionable) use of snare drums. *La gazza ladra* became a favorite vehicle for Giuditta Pasta, Maria Malabran, and Rossini's wife Isabella Colbran. It opened in St. Petersburg in February 1821 in Russian as *Soroka-vorovka*, with Nimfodora Semënova, who was also a singer, again in a melodrama lead, as Aneta (the Russian translation used the original names), and with Elizaveta Sandunova as the landowner's wife. Like its model, *Gazza* had a long stage life in Russia.[35]

Thus for about three decades, and perhaps longer, the thieving magpie flew around Russia as *La pie volleuse* in the French theater; as *Soroka-vorovka* in Russian theaters; and as an Italian opera. In both town and provincial estate theaters, the role of the wronged female was played by serf actresses, themselves subjected to all kinds of mistreatment and false accusations in their everyday lives. Although the irony is striking, it is difficult to say just what linkage audiences and performers made between the unjust system that undergirds all the magpie stories and their own social vulnerabilities. But the specific analogy was made by Alexander Herzen in his famous tale of serf abuse and sexual harassment, "Soroka-vorovka." To the theatrical inspiration of the story Herzen added historical material screened through a serf actress and a serf actor, and then he fictionalized it into an enduring critique of a particular aspect of serfdom that everyone knew of at the time but which is often down played in histories of that institution: house serfs as creative artists under the control of their owners. Herzen drew his tale from an episode in the life of a serf actress.

The villain of the true story was Count S. N. Kamenskii, a noble landowner and theatrical entrepreneur of Orël province. Orël was far from being a cultural backwater; on their estate, the Iurasovskii brothers in 1828 put on serf ballet, variety shows, and choral music. Another half-dozen landowners ran estate theaters, including the Turgenevs and the Taneevs, the latter offering opera, ballet, and drama performed by serfs and free provincial actors. A. A. Pleshcheev, a cellist and friend of Nikolai Karamzin, maintained a serf orchestra on his estate that was held to be the musical center of Kaluga, Orël, and Tula provinces.[36] Kamenskii possessed a serf theater on his estate and a commercial theater in the town of Orël, which lasted from 1815 to 1835 (the writer Nikolai Leskov recalled seeing it as a child). As one-story wooden structure occupying an entire block in Cathedral Square, Kamenskii's theater was as large, according to a contemporary, as Moscow's Apraxin Theater at the Arbat Gates. The interior consisted of stalls, *baignoire*, two upper circles, and a gallery—with tickets priced accordingly. Printed posters advertised productions, and one of the earliest provincial newspapers, *Drug rossian* (1816-1818) reviewed them.[37]

Kamenskii hired some actors, transferred serfs from his estate, and bought some from other serfowners. He purchased the Kravchenkos, an acting couple and their six-year-old tap-dancing daughter, for 250 male serfs. He also tried to acquire the then budding actor Mikhail Shchepkin, but without success. An officer serving in Orël in 1827-1828, M. D. Buturlin regarded the theater as a refuge from garrison life in what was otherwise a monotonous town. Kamenskii spared no expense on lavish sets and costumes, a German ballet master, and a large, well-trained serf orchestra.[38] But he was a rank amateur of theater and most of his actors were deficient in acting and singing. The eccentric owner, wearing his Turkish war decoration, the Order of St. George Second Class, would sit in the box office and sell tickets. Once a prankster officer friend of Buturlin bought his seat with a huge bag full of small coins in order to hold up the line. During performances, Kamenskii, armed with a stick and a script, sat in the first row, his family like royals, placed in a center box. The repertoire was the familiar one for provincial theaters: *comédies larmantes,* melodramas—including *Soroka-vorovka*—vaudevilles, ballet, and operas by Cherubini and Boiledieu. And even with all the unevenness of performance, the theater was rarely empty.

Kamenskii ran his home and his theater like a regiment. Lackeys and actors were uniformed in different colors and given court ranks, changing colors as they were promoted. The actresses were isolated and locked up at night in a harem-like complex in the courtyard. When two sisters in the company became the object of flirtation among local officers, one of them, caught in a correspondence, was flogged. Into this environment fell the victim of the real-life melodrama; she was one of Kamenskii's actresses who not only played Annette in *Soroka-vorovka* but acted out the role in real life as a woman falsely accused by a powerful man whose sexual overtures she rebuffed. The actress Kuzmina (or Kozmina; no other name is given in the sources) was originally a serf member of the landowner P. V. Esipov's estate theater about thirty miles from Kazan. When he opened a theater in the town of Kazan in 1803-1804 with a cast drawn from his estate theater, Kuzmina was brought along. Although Esipov apparently kept his actresses in a harem, Kuzmina's brief account of her life recalled him as a kindly master and made no reference to sexual relations. Esipov gave her an education, training, foreign travel, and exposure to a broad culture—but not her freedom. He promised to bequeath her emancipation at his death, but failed to do so. An improvident man, Esipov went broke in 1810 and died in debt in 1814. His troupe was dispersed and Kamenskii bought Kuzmina in 1814 or 1815. She first appeared on the Orël stage at its official opening. Her skills in roles such as Cordelia in *Lear* and "Edelmona" in *Othello,* as well as roles in the lighter genres, were much admired by the public and the press.

By 1822, the man who was to hear and tell Kuzmina's tale,

Mikhail Shchepkin, arrived in Orël. Shchepkin, a serf actor also enmeshed in a struggle for manumission, was already widely known on the provincial circuit and would soon be drafted by Moscow's Imperial Theater. Kamenskii hired him as a guest actor to play in Mikhail Zagoskin's popular *Gospodin Bogatonov, or, A Provincial in the Capital* (1817). While there, Shchepkin saw Kuzmina play Annette in Caigniez's *Soroka-vorovka*. Greatly affected by her performance, he was determined to talk to her and, after much pleading with Kamenskii, interviewed her for her story. Kuzmina had learned French, German, and English and had been happy in Esipov's service. Kamenskii, who she claimed had no understanding of theatrical art, had purchased the troupe for three hundred thousand rubles and paid her well. Then came the insinuations and flirtations. Puzzled when Kuzmina did not respond to his advances, Kamenskii made an open proposition. Kuzmina refused him and he retaliated by denying her good roles and costumes (a critical expense item for an actress all through the century). When the actress found money to buy her own dresses, Kamenskii insulted her, implying that she was selling her body to purchase clothing. She then told him that, although innocent of the charge, she would spite him by having a baby in a loveless match.

Kuzmina's account was in fact commonplace for actresses of the era and not only among serfs. She may have exaggerated the events of her story; and one must wonder why Kamenskii, who could have an actress flogged for a slight indiscretion, would limit his revenge to a mere insult. But what made her tale so famous in theatrical discourse is the dual treatment it received at the hands of Shchepkin and Herzen. As early as 1839 the actor began recounting the story of Kuzmina to his friends, and it allegedly brought tears to their eyes. He retold it many times before and after Herzen's story was written. The man who recorded Shchepkin's tale from dictation was the famed folklore collector Alexander Afanasev, who put it to paper in 1861. In the 1960s, his transcription was found in the archives by a soviet scholar, but Afanasev's version contains errors and shows signs that he had read Herzen's story before hearing it from Shchepkin.[39]

The most famous Russian radical of the age, Alexander Herzen, immortalized and fictionalized Kuzmina's experience in the short story "Soroka-vorovka" and also brought the ancient legend of the magpie full circle, ending his tale with the death of an innocent woman. Herzen took the main theme from the lips of Shchepkin himself in one of their many conversations. He wrote the story in 1846 and it was published in *Contemporary* in 1848 (with some of its language about serfdom and power toned down). The outer frame of Herzen's "Soroka-vorovka" is an ironic and amusing debate between a Slavophile and a westernizer, the former upholding the submission and silence of women and arguing that "Slavic" women—being modest creatures—were not suited to the stage where people disport themselves and rant their lines before the public. The westernizer refutes these and other arguments and then tells the tale; the teller is modeled on Shchepkin, and his account is also a frame within which the actress tells her own story.[40]

The villain of this prose melodrama, Skalinskii (Russian for crag), is modeled on Count Kamenskii (Russian for stone). He resembles in some ways the vindictive magistrate in Caigniez's *Magpie*—a powerful figure, rejected and vengeful. But the French villain is abstract, he could be almost any blackguard, whereas Herzen's figure, like the original, possesses concrete contours and colors. He is a landowner, a serfowner, whose power does not depend on his credibility in a court of law; he is deeply embedded in the social and political system of serfdom and seigniorial authority. Skalinskii, like Kamenskii, brooks no dallying among the actors; he imprisons one for sending a note to an actress. The fictional version of Kuzmina has ended up under Skalinskii's roof through an illegal trick added by Herzen to the Kuzmina tale: the suppression by relatives of her former benefactor's will granting her freedom. When Skalinskii's advances to the fictional version of Kuzmina fall flat, he voices his power over her with the ugly words: "You think you are an actress. You are *my* bonded property."

In Herzen's tale there are no upper-class sympathizers to help and rescue a blameless young woman, as in the plays of Ducange and Caigniez. The heroine-victim breeches the chaste rules of true melodrama by her own defiant act of sexual expression. But the reader is intended to find her deeper virtue in the courage and sense of fair play of that act. She is a powerless innocent devoted to her art who becomes her own "delivering hero" with the aid of a meaningless lover whom she takes as an act of vengeance on the count. There are no surprises or coincidences in Herzen's melodrama; it is a dark "society tale" rather than the melodrama of the original *Magpie*. And, to give his work more pathos and sharper social commentary, Herzen has the actress die from complications after childbirth.

Herzen's story and its layered sources offer an unusually complex study in intertextuality. A possibly real event from the European past had been clothed in legend, adorned, and then woven into a melodrama that was immediately plotted as an opera. A real-life Russian actress in servitude played on stage the role of the fictional servant wrongly accused. The serf actress was herself wrongly accused by her master of a different act—"stealing" her own body from him. Her version of the episode then emerged for a limited public as a sentimental morality tale recited in salons by a former victimized serf actor. Herzen fused the stage role of Annette with the real role of Kuzmina into an ideologically framed abolitionist tract. His magpie story is shorter and simpler in plot than the stage melodrama that partly inspired it, but its greater moral complexity lies in its three levels of villainy.

One level is outright testamentary fraud by the heirs of a master who had bequeathed manumission, an illegal act but hard to rectify in practice. To paraphrase Peter Brooks, this kind of act betrayed the "rules" of serfdom, which is itself a betrayal of the cosmic moral order.[41] The dominant villainy is the institution of the serf theater harem, a familiar although not endemic feature of the system. Law and custom were ambivalent on the practice and only rarely were abusive examples punished, usually at the local level. The third level of villainy was the wholly legal practice of promising, without delivering, freedom to serfs. This was a common custom among owners of serf painters, musicians, and actors. Some masters found it psychologically useful (although hardly necessary) to deflect offers of purchase of star artists by other landowners or by the Imperial Theater system. Others used the promise to keep their artists at least minimally happy and able to perform or create. Esipov, the benign first owner of Kuzmina, was a well-meaning villain by default. Because the victim is a woman, the emerging discourses on serfdom and on women's lot are melded. Herzen's melodrama adds a deus ex machina in the form of dishonest relatives, a device that actually vitiates the larger impersonal and systemic functioning of juridical unfreedom.

Abolitionist literature in the reign of Nicholas I—a subject not fully investigated by scholars—was sporadic and heavily constrained. Fictional references to the plight of bonded artists and the human degradation it could entail were episodic and couched in oblique language.[42] On the other hand, conversations and correspondence among nobles and between nobles and state artistic institutions abounded with entreaties, threats, negotiations, and contracts dealing with purchase, transfer, and manumission of serf artists. Societies composed of magnates and art patrons were formed precisely for these purposes.[43] Herzen's "Soroka-vorovka" was part of this discourse, a particularly clarifying tale that points up the issue of dependence, subordination, and abuse of power in the world of performing arts. To avoid the appearance of writing a tract, he employed the clever ruse of fiction and he invoked the plot from a popular genre that had great resonance. The tale was riveting, entertaining, full of pathos, and capped by the unhappy ending that punctuated the lives of so many real-life serf artists. The term for "villain" in French melodrama was either *tyrane* or *traître*. Herzen inserted both kinds of villains into "Soroka-vorovka"—the serfowner-tyrant and the falsifier-traitor—thus adding melodramatic effect to the social drama. After emigrating to western Europe in 1848, Herzen's pen was free to engage in the exposure of the arbitrary treatment of those serf artists who suffered the particular psychological agony of arrested development or the enchainment of talent.

Herzen's treatment of the victim theme suggests another process at work in the twilight of serfdom. Studies of late imperial reading tastes and popular fiction have described how news items sometimes fed into that genre, thus mediating the real event with the literary product.[44] No mass-circulation press was available to story-weavers of prereform Russia. But "media" sources from which they could draw certainly existed: the aforementioned epistolary discourse on abuse and liberation, salon or circle anecdotes such as Shchepkin's, and the villain-victim melodrama. Thus a distinctly entertainment genre could, as I suggested at the outset of this chapter, contribute not so much to popular consciousness of injustice as to the continuing formation of elite sensibilities about the evils of serfdom.

The Tale Is Told

The experience of imported cultural products cannot be divorced from native production or creation, because adaptation, translation, setting, and performance are themselves acts of creativity. The imported melodrama—not in spite of but because of its foreign themes, characters, and locales—found wide acceptance in Russia as entertainment. It might be tempting to say that these imported works were "Russianized" in their performance, but it would be more accurate to say that they were subjected to several local influences. Upper-class travelers from the capitals often found performances they had seen at home unrecognizable in the provinces. One ought not to postulate the unique popularity of melodrama. Everywhere in Russia until mid-century, when training began to bifurcate into drama and music roles, the same actors played in all genres, from tragedy to opera to vaudeville; and audiences consumed them all with apparently equal enthusiasm. Just as Shakespeare, performed with adaptations and adjustments, could thrill spectators of the Old West in early nineteenth-century America,[45] so could Schiller enchant dwellers in the outreaches of the Russian empire. Melodrama played a prominent but not exclusive role in entertaining the theater public. It is a well-established fact that, in previous times, certain works that are now canonized often lived vitally among the "low." The masters were loved by audiences of various classes; they were often adapted and performed in accordance with local audience expectations that bordered on entertainment. Even their best and truest translations commonly shared the stage with vaudevilles and comic interludes.

It is hard to speak about the moral or mental impact of melodrama on audiences, not the least because of the tremendous variation among audiences in terms of wealth, position, estate, geography, gender, and age. It is doubtful that many of those theatergoers who wept over the reconciliation of Meinau and Eulalia and who rejoiced over the deliverance of Annette and Theresa were ever aware of Herzen's adaptation of the form in his prose story, and it is doubtful also that those scenes on stage changed their lives. But theater events were certainly part of their lives, a part that is not often considered in recovering and reconstructing the sensibilities of the Russian people—and other peoples of the empire as well. This is especially true of provincial life, a subject still rather weakly developed in Russian historiography. The study of melodrama offers only a few peeks into it; broader exploration of all genres provides much more. But it is virtually certain that melodrama was the key viewing experience of most provincials. It was the genre they could best relate to, and probably the one that helped them "read" other more complex theatrical texts.

The biggest impact of melodrama on Russian theater was in stagecraft itself: costumes, sets, and especially acting. Acting did not become "realistic" overnight. Every generation, it seems, smiles at the "realism" of previous ones. This can only mean that every generation in turn had its own realism; that is to say that they experienced verisimilitude in the same way later ones did and do. But there did occur a clear divergence between the high-style declamatory method of neoclassical verse drama and the more earthy conversational delivery of melodrama. Melodrama sought illusion rather than stylized quasiballetic performance in order to drive the story and heighten suspense and sensation. Asides and soliloquies were reduced in number in favor of more "naturalistic" interaction of the players. The methods required to perform imported melodramas successfully were also those that made the plays accessible to audiences from increasingly broad social origins. Even actors on the capital stages found—or reinvented—themselves by acting melodrama. In the provinces, where stage rules and customs were relatively fluid, styles sprung from melodrama flourished more quickly. As Russian theater began to stage more works on contemporary Russian themes, the practice amplified of drafting provincial actors onto the imperial stages to play roles requiring special Russian inflections and sensibilities. And this practice laid the groundwork for the masterful performances of Russian theater in the second half of the nineteenth century.

Original publication: In Louise McReynolds and Joan Neuburger, eds. *Imitations of Life: Two Centuries of Melodrama in Russia*. Durham, London: Duke University Press, 2002, pp. 25-54.

Notes

1   *Teatral'naia entsiklopediia,* vol. 3 (Moscow, 1961-7), 787-88. For dates and performances, see A. I. Volf, *Khronika peterburgskikh teatrov s kontsa 1826 do nachala 1855 goda* (St. Petersburg, 1877).

2   See Vladimir Propp, *The Morphology of Folktales,* 3rd ed. (Austin: University of Texas Press, 1971); and Joseph Campbell, *The Hero with a Thousand Faces,* 2d ed. (Princeton: Princeton University Press, 1988.

3   Frank Rahill, *The World of Melodrama* (University Park: Pennsylvania State University Press, 1967), 83; Paul Ginisty, *La mélodrame* (Paris, n.d.) offers pictorial evidence of specific gestures and movements. For some modern perspectives on melodrama, see Jacky Branon, Jim Cook, and Christine Gledhill, eds., *Melodrama: Stage, Picture, Screen* (London: British Film Institute, 1994); Daniel Gerould, ed., *Melodrama* (New York: New York Literary Forum, 1980); Michael Hays and Anastasia Nikolopoulou, eds., *Melodrama: The Cultural Emergence of a Genre* (New York: St. Martin's Press, 1996); and Peter Brooks, *The Melodramatic Imagination: Balzac, Henry James, Melodrama, and the Mode of Excess* (New Haven: Yale University Press, 1976). Brooks's volume, although it applies dramatic and affective structures of melodrama to the later novel form, contains interesting insights on the plays as well.

4   On *Affektenlehre,* see Don Michael Randel, ed., *The New Harvard Dictionary of Music* (Cambridge, Mass.: Harvard University Press, 1969), 16.

5   Oscar Mandel, *August von Kotzebue: The Comedy, the Man* (University Park: Pennsylvania State University Press, 1990), 30.

6   Ibid.

7   Quoted in John Lough, *Paris Theater Audiences in the Seventeenth and Eighteenth Centuries* (Oxford: Oxford University Press, 1957), 237-78.

8   For discussion of the Russian years, see Gerhard Giesemann, *Kotzebue in Russland: Materialien zu einer Wirkungsgeschichte* (Frankfurt, 1968).

9   Mandel, *August von Kotzebue,* 35.

10 August von Kotzebue, *Menschenhass und Reue: Schauspiel in fünf Aufzogen* in *August von Kotzebue: Schauspiele,* ed. Jürg Nathes (Frankfurt/ Main, 1972), 46, 72. I thank Dr. Hubertus Jahn for securing this text for me. The earliest Russian translation I found is *Nenavist' k liudiam i raskaianie,* 4th ed. (Orël, 1826).

11 *Menschenhass und Reue* was staged as *The Stranger* in London every year from its debut until 1842 and many times after that.

12 Kotzebue, *Menschenhass und Reue*, 115, 122.

13 Ira Petrovskaia and V. Somina, *Teatralnyi Peterburg: Nachalo XVIII ve-ka-oktiabr 1917 goda* (St. Petersburg, 1994), 83; Giesemann. *Kotzebue in Russland*, 73-74: Avgust von Kotsebu, *Dostopamiatnyi god moei zhizni*, vol. 1 (n.p., 1879), 107, 128-31, 161-64; this is the Russian translation of *Das merkwürdigste Jahr meines Lebens* (1803; Munich, 1965), 136-37, 139-40, 170, 172.

14 Kotzebue, *Dostopamiatnyi god*, vol. 2, 74-76, 84-86, 99-100; *Das merk-würdigste Jahr*, 261- 62, 272.

15 Simon Karlinsky, *Russian Drama from Its Beginnings to the Age of Push-kin* (Berkeley: University of California Press, 1985) 191-1922; Giese-mann, *Kotzebue in Russland*, 175, 119.

16 Sergei Aksakov, *Sobranie sochinenii*, vol. 1 (Moscow, 1895-1900), 321; V. Vsevolodskii [Gerngross], *Istoriia russkogo teatra*, vol. 2 (Leningrad, 1929), 29, 58-59, 64-65; P. A. Karatygin, *Zapiski* (Leningrad, 1929), 91-92; Giesemann, *Kotzebue in Russland*, 104. On Iakovlev, see also Leonid Grossman, *Pushkin v tratral'nykh kreslakh: Kartiny russkoi stseny, 1817-1820* (Leningrad, 1926), 88. Boris Varneke, *History of the Russian The-ater*, trans. Boris Brassol (New York: Macmillan, 1951), 255.

17 Petrovskaia and Somina, *Teatral'nyi Peterburg*, 84; Irina Medvedeva, *Ekaterina Semënova: Zhizn' i tvorchestvo tragicheskoi aktrisa* (Moscow, 1964), 11, 16, 31, 37.

18 Giesemann, *Kotzebue in Russland*, 181; Vsevolodskii, *Istoriia*, vol. 2, 29, 33.

19 Küchelbecker is quoted in *Istoriia russkoi dramaturgii XVII - pervaia po-lovina XIX veka* (Leningrad, 1982), 258.

20 Zotov quotations from Grossman. *Pushkin*, 19; and Vsevolodskii, *Isto-riia*, vol. 2, 30.

21 This comparison is made by Hans Schumacher in August von Kot-zebue, *Die deutsche Kleinstädter* (1803), ed. Hans Schumacher (Berlin, 1964), 106.

22 Rahill, *The World of Melodrama*, 40, 44.

23 Viktor Diukanzh [Victor Ducange], *Tereza, ili zhenevskaia sirota, melo-drama* (Moscow, 1833), translation of *Thérèse, ou l'orphéline de Genève*. Lynn Hunt, discussing melodrama in *The Family Romance of the French Revolution* (Berkeley: University of California Press, 1992), makes much of mistaken identity in the genre, although in fact it is an ancient and continuous device in many genres of fiction and drama.

24 *Istoriia russkogo dramaticheskogo teatra* [hereafter *IRDT*], vol. 2 (Mos-cow, 1977-87), 140, 280, 286; Medvedeva, *Ekaterina Semënova*, 267.

25 On Vysheslavtseva and her roles, see A. S. Gatsiskii, *Nizhegorodskii teatr (1798-1867)* (Nizhny-Novgorod, 1867), 1-60.

26 Yury Arnold, *Vospominaniia*, vols. 1 and 2 (Moscow, 1892), vol. 2, 101. Arnold as a child had played in amateur theatricals in Kotzebue's *Misanthropy and Repentance* and *Child of Love* (vol. I, 26).

27 I. I. Lavrov, *Stsena i zhizn' v provintsii i v stolitse* (Moscow, 1889), 40-56.

28 Ibid., 50.

29 Charles Rosen, *The Romantic Generation* (Cambridge, Mass.: Harvard University Press, 1995), 602.

30 A. I. Gertsen [Herzen], *Sochineniia*, vol. 1 (Moscow, 1955), 337. Lawrence Levine cites similar instances in *Highbrow/Lowbrow: The Emergence of Cultural Hierarchy in America* (Cambridge, Mass.: Harvard University Press, 1988), 30.

31 S. P. Gagarin, *Vseobshchii geograficheskii slovar'* (Moscow, 1843).

32 The legend source is in Rahill, *The World of Melodrama*; the legal case in Herbert Weinstock, *Rossini: A Biography* (New York: Knopf, 1968); the real event in Richard Osbourne, *Rossini* (London, 1986).

33 L. C. Caigniez and J. M. T. Bandouin d'Aubigny, *La pie voleuse ou la servante de Palaiseau: Mélodrame historique* (Paris, 1815). The title page also indicates a ballet as well as the music by Piccinni. Commentary in Rahill, *The World of Melodrama*, 56-63; and Ginisty, *La mélodrame*, 121-38, 219.

34 The Russian translation by Valberkh is *Soroka-vorovka ili palezosskaia sluzhanka* (St. Petersburg, 1816). See also *IRDT*, vol. 2, 280, 288. The British adaptation "translated and altered from the French" by Isaac Pocock is *The Magpie, or, The Maid? a Melo Drame* (London, 1816). I thank Professor Abraham Ascher for securing a copy for me.

35 David Kimball, *Italian Opera* (Cambridge: Cambridge University Press, 1991), 358, 563; Osbourne, *Rossini*, 198-201; A. Gozenpud, *Opernyi slovar* (Moscow, 1965), 389-90; Weinstock, *Rossini*, 498, 77.

36 E. S. Kots, *Krepostnaia intelligentsiia* (Leningrad, 1926), 144-45, 148; Thomas Hodge, *Mutatis Mutandis: Poetry and the Musical Romance in Early Nineteenth Century Russia* (Ph.D. diss., Stanford University, 1992), 208.

37 My reconstruction is drawn from many accounts that largely overlap and conflict only on minor details. These accounts include Priscilla Roosevelt, *Life on the Russian Country Estate* (New Haven: Yale University Press, 1995), 139-41; N. Chernov, "Krepostnye aktrisy orlovskogo teatra," *Teatral'naia zhizn'* 4 (1961) : 28-29; M. D. Buturlin, "Teatr grafa Kamenskago v Orle v 1827 i 1828 godakh," *Russkii arkhiv* 7, no. 10 (1869): 1707-11; V. Putintsev, "Krepostnaia aktrisa Kuzmina," *Voprosy literatury* 9 (September 1963), 190-95; Lawrence Senelick, *Serf Actor: The Life and Art of Mikhail Shchepkin* (Westport, Conn.: Greenwood Press, 1984), 10, 48-49; T. S. Grits, "K istorii 'Soroki-vorovki,'" *Literaturnoe nasledstvo* 63 (1965): 655-60; and *IRDT*, vol. 2, 288, 423-26, 528.

Leskov's much later story about brutal treatment of serfs "The Toupee Artist" (1883) was inspired by the murder of Kamenskii's father; see Hugh McLean, *Nikolai Leskov: The Man and His Art* (Cambridge, Mass.: Harvard University Press, 1977), 438-41.

38 For information on serf orchestras, see Kots, *Krepostnaia intelligentsiia*; and Richard Stites, "The Domestic Muse: Music at Home in the Twilight of Serfdom," in *Interactions and Transpositions: Russian Music, Literature, and Society*, ed. Andrew Wachtel (Evanston, Ill.: Northwestern University Press, 1998), 187- 205.

39 For the Afanasev text, see Grits, "K istorii 'Soroki-vorovki.'"

40 Gertsen [Herzen], "Soroka-vorovka: Povest," in *Sochineniia*, vol. I, 327-50, 502-7.

41 Brooks, *The Melodramatic Imagination*.

42 One of the several streams of abolition thinking, the sporadic if never-dead reform discussion under Alexander I and Nicholas I, has been laboriously reconstructed from the record by a number of historians who all agree that very little came of government efforts. Most draw on the pioneering work of V. I. Semevskii, *Krest'ianskii vopros v Rossii v XVII i pervoi polovine XIX veka*, 2 vols. (St. Petersburg, 1888), see especially vol. 1, 316-17, 396-97. See also Peter Kolchin, *Unfree Labor: American Slavery and Russian Serfdom*, (Cambridge, Mass.: Harvard University Press, 1987); Jerome Blum, *Lord and Peasant in Russia from the Ninth to the Nineteenth Century* (Princeton: Princeton University Press, 1961). For the literary side, see William R. Dodge, *Abolitionist Sentiment in Russia, 1762-1855* (Ph.D. diss., University of Wisconsin, 1950).

43 P. N. Stolpianskii, *Staryi Peterburg i Obshchestvo pooshchreniia khudozhestv* (Leningrad, 1928); G. Lomelova, "Peterburgskoe Obshchestvo pooshchreniia khudozhestv i ego deiatelnost v 20-40-kh gg. XIX v," *Soobshcheniia Gosudarstvennogo Ermitazha* (1958): 34-36; E. Golubeva, "Iz istorii Obschshestva pooshchreniia khudozhnikov," *Iskusstvo* 10 (1961): 67-72.

44 For a superb introduction to this, see: Louise McReynolds, *The News under Russia's Old Regime: The Development of a Mass-Circulation Press* (Princeton: Princeton University Press, 1991) and Jeffrey Brooks, *When Russians Learned to Read: Literacy and Popular Literature, 1861-1917* (Princeton: Princeton University Press, 1985). For further enrichment, see Joan Neuberger, *Hooliganism: Crime, Culture, and Power in St. Petersburg, 1900-1914* (Berkeley: University of California Press, 1993) and Laura Engelstein, *The Keys to Happiness: Sex and the Search for Modernity in Fin-de-Siècle Russia* (Ithaca: Cornell University Press, 1992).

45 For comparison, see Levine's classic account, "William Shakespeare in America," in his *Highbrow/Lowbrow*, 11-81.

28

Cultural Capital and Cultural Heritage
St. Petersburg and the Arts of Imperial Russia

In the years after 1991, and a bit earlier under glasnost, the reconstructed memory of St. Petersburg's former cultural glories has often been mixed and sanitized in the elitist traditions not only of Soviet cultural conventions but of the Russian intelligentsia itself—especially its critical, curatorial, and historical establishments. The "bad" things—such as serfdom and imperialist wars—were sometimes omitted, and the "good" ones—such as aristocratic high culture—romanticized. St. Petersburg was trying to recover if not cultural hegemony at least equity with Moscow. Not many years ago, the historical and cultural "capital" that the former capital could claim was based upon three main identities: the home of the imperial style, the cradle of revolution, and the site of the Leningrad Blockade. The revolution is not only old news, but also bad news; the memory of the Blockade, long partly blockaded, is still being contested. And so only the grandeur of St. Petersburg imperial culture is left.[1]

What kind of culture was and is being revived or restored, and on what grounds: In other words, what drove and drives the selective memory of the cultural establishment? The study of memory, a major enterprise nowadays, sometimes threatens to overshadow the very objects of those memories.[2] Since events can never be recaptured, since all texts are unstable and all texts are unstable and all readings are potential misreadings, it may now seem less important to talk about "real" things that actually happened or about real persons who actually lived and died, created, organized, and consumed art and culture than to relate how we remember them. But such a metahistorical approach is simply substituting one epistemologically problematic task for another, since the evidence of memory is also created by the agency of real people creating real texts, rituals, and artifacts. Any discussion of recent choices being made about the presentation of the cultural heritage of St. Petersburg requires knowledge about what can be presented—in other words, about the canon and what lies outside it. I choose as my base point the late eighteenth and early nineteenth centuries, an era whose musical, theatrical, and artistic life is less studied than those of later periods and whose sociocultural underpinning was marked by high serfdom and a flourishing gentry culture, thus susceptible to all sorts of politicized nostalgia and screening. For the sake of making a few points, I will also mention some aspects of the later nineteenth century.[3]

St. Petersburg's exceptionally self-conscious possession of "cultural capital" in the Bourdieuian sense, invites a critical look at heritage practices and the deployment of cultural capital.[4] David Lowenthal's learned inquiry into "the heritage crusade" now raging throughout the world is particularly apt. "What heritage does not highlight," he writes, "it often hides."[5] Throughout the long monumental-memorial-historiographical reign of Soviet cultural managers—in Leningrad and in the nation at large—ideology and elitism rendered memory acutely selective. Of the cultural riches of the past, only what was "good" in elitist and aesthetic terms and "true" in ideological terms could be presented. Since the collapse of that system, the elitism remains in force, and Soviet ideology has been replaced by a new one, that of heritage: preserving, protecting, and exhibiting the culture that best seems to reflect the glories of the city's past. This process necessarily involves the selection and omission of certain works. The heritage mentality is not simply the pious aspiration to show one's best face. It is conditioned by what I elsewhere have called "market fossilism,"[6] the habit of presenting the old and familiar to patrons in order to fill museums and concert halls, an understandable posture given the economic rigors that beset the city and its cultural sites. The heritage approach combines these two impulses, which often conflict. Lowenthal has much to say about museums, though almost nothing about the performing arts. But it is clear that opera houses and concert halls operate like museums in two senses: the interiors are revered as hallowed sites of architecture; and the works are presented like the exhibited pieces in an art gallery.

A Night at the Opera

St. Petersburg is a window to the West through which its cultural leaders must constantly look for inspiration and for connection to the global system of high culture. But it also aspires to be a "window to Russia,"[7] a cultural gateway for foreign visitors. Russian dramatic theater suffers in terms of foreign audiences who have no command of the language. In Paris, the Comédie Française does well because so many visitors know enough French to follow; but far *fewer* Russian speakers visit St. Petersburg. Opera and ballet have always been more universal; listeners are used to hearing opera in other languages, and in any case visual splendors provide compensation, even when there are no subtitles. Therefore St. Petersburg draws its theatrical renown only from the Mariinsky Theater of Opera and Ballet. Luckily, it is headed by a very gifted and powerful cultural capitalist—in the Bourdieuian as well as the older sense of the word: Valery Gergiev. Gergiev and his orchestra also feature in Aleksandr Sokurov's surrealistic film *Russian Ark*, which, though exhibiting ambiguities about Russia's cultural past and its relation to the West, unfolds in the Winter Palace among tsars, courtiers, and heroes of high culture.[8]

One manifestation of Gergiev's leadership is the cooperative project of the Mariinsky and the Library of Congress to preserve that theater's priceless archive of music and librettos. The American side is headed by James Billington, who is not only the Librarian of Congress but a well-known historian of Russian culture, author of a pioneering book, *The Icon and the Axe* (1961). Preliminary examination of the archive has already uncovered some priceless old manuscript scores of Russian and European composers. The project itself is eminently valuable and a tribute to the concern of both sides in preserving a magnificent cultural heritage. It is also an impressive public relations feat that will call attention to donors, well-wishers, and audiences from all around the world who come to Russia precisely to sample its treasures.

The repertoire of the musical stage, long controlled by Soviet cultural managers, has expanded since the collapse of the USSR and, enjoying a free hand politically, continues admirably to seek new works, with modern music and dance vocabularies. Of nineteenth-century works (1836 to 1917), it has retained or restaged the canonical repertoire established late in that century and featuring the usual masterpieces of Glinka, Tchaikovsky, Borodin, Rimsky-Korsakov, Stravinsky, and a whole range of European works. When it comes to previously neglected operas of the eighteenth and early nineteenth centuries, however, selective memory comes into play. During my last extended visit to St. Petersburg, I witnessed the performance of a work that, to my knowledge, had not been performed in Soviet times.

An opera by Catherine the Great, *Under the Leadership of Oleg*, premiered in 1791 at the Hermitage Theater, with music by the Italians Giuseppe Sarti and Carlo Cannobio, and Polish-born Wasili Paszkiewicz (Vasily Pashkevich), with a libretto by the empress herself, assisted by Mikhail Lomonosov. Possessing a flair for showy effects, Sarti was wont to put on grandiose productions, embellished with hundreds of voices, the ringing of bells, and the roar of cannon to mark royal visits and military victories. Since he specialized in reworking themes of religion, mythology, and history (particularly Russia's past glory), the Soviet Musical Encyclopedia belittled his art as "academic, archaic classicism," a label that Sarti might have been proud of. A "historical representation" for reader, chorus, and orchestra, *Oleg* treats in a rather ponderous and didactic fashion the Kievan Prince Oleg's occupation of Constantinople in 907. This theme no doubt reflected Catherine's Greek Project, the lingering dream of taking Istanbul (Constantinople) from the Ottoman Turks and turning it into a Russian Tsargrad for her grandson Konstantin (so named with that ambition in mind). The music is up to Sarti's high standards, though jointly composed; the clever use of the folk melody "Kamarinskaya" in the peasant wedding scenes was later made famous in Glinka's arrangement. The enormous cast included 600 guardsmen of the Jaeger Regiment.[9]

The revival I saw on November 21, 1997, was astonishing in many ways. Its staging at the St. Petersburg Capella, among the most revered of the capital's musical venues, signified that the work was being honored as one of high prestige, catering to the city's elite. The composition of the audience in this elegant concert hall seemed to confirm as much: a reverent, well-dressed assembly of the intelligentsia. The 1997 public in no way resembled the courtiers and magnates who first saw the opera in the 1790s. Rather it was as if Alexander Benois, a well-known worshiper of eighteenth-century high culture, had brought an entire cénacle of elitists from the turn of a different century to relish the precious heritage of an aristocratic epoch (see Helena Goscilo, this volume). Given the size of the stage, the production was much less elaborate than the original, and it focused on performance art rather than on showy effects. The result was a success. Yet I could not help feeling that, by inducting the librettist, Empress Catherine II, into the charmed circle of Russian theatrical authorship worthy of public presentation, the organizers were bowing to the fashionable trend of reviving the reputation of long-gone monarchs and the opulence that surrounded them. Doing so is legitimate in the context of "heritage" culture. But for the historian of culture, the choice was more of a curiosity than one representing what many Russian opera audiences usually saw on stage in the decades after it was first produced.

A case in point, and one among many, is Aleksei Verstovskii — the most widely-performed opera composer in the reign of Nicholas I, but buried in oblivion during most of the twentieth century. Glinka's contemporary and a theater bureaucrat, Verstovskii maintained that "the dawn of Russian national opera music began in Moscow and not in St. Petersburg [with Glinka's *A Life for the Tsar*]."[10] By "Moscow" Verstovskii was referring to the performance there of his opera, *Askold's Grave* (1835), based on Mikhail Zagoskin's 1833 novel. It recreated a dark and gothic mood in tenth-century Kiev, with sinister doings by moonlight near the grave of Askold, a ruined church, kidnapping, and wizardry. These elements alternated with folkloric scenes of peasant revelry, Viking feasts, and references to the "broad and deep Dnieper River" and to "Kiev, mother of all Russian cities." The Moscow public was so delighted by its folkish and national themes, its choruses and melodies, that within days the tunes were heard on the streets. The opera also ran well in St. Petersburg and in the provinces. By 1859, the *Theatrical and Musical Gazette* could ask: "In what theater, in what corner of Russia didn't they sing this opera?"[11] It remained on stage throughout the next seventy-odd years, and by the early twentieth century, it had played 400 times in Moscow and 200 times in St. Petersburg.

In terms of stage life and the spread of its songs, for many years *Askold* did better than Glinka's *Life for the Tsar*; and the spinoff effect, according to the musicologist S. L. Ginzburg, lasted almost to the end of the Russian monarchy. For a time, at least, Verstovskii's large loyal following probably considered *Askold* the Russian national opera, until its eventual eclipse by Glinka's *Life for the Tsar*, which premiered a year after *Askold*. Both men were disappointed: Verstovskii because discerning critics preferred Glinka's opera, Glinka because of the continued popularity ofVerstovskii's music on stage and off. In recreating or "remembering" the operatic life of the mid-nineteenth century, the historian would have to give proper attention to Verstovskii. Though his music was on the lips of countless Russians, the mass of Russian listeners today and in the future might never know his name, let alone his earlier popularity. Verstovskii's work has been screened out partly because it is undeniably inferior to the work of Glinka, and partly perhaps because he was a director of the Imperial Theater system, Glinka's rival, and, for Petersburgers, a Muscovite to boot. The only performance of *Askold* during the Soviet era and thereafter that I know of, based on fragments of the music, was recorded in Kiev in 1959.[12] The new theater managements are certainly entitled to mount Glinka again and again, but I wonder if any of them will endeavor to stage other works that were extremely popular in the early part of the nineteenth century.

Evenings with the Orchestra

The history of high culture almost everywhere, in the past half-century, at least, has shown that excellence is not enough to promote or even preserve great monuments of cultural performance. Carnegie Hall in New York City was saved by a hair's breadth through the Herculean efforts of violinist Isaac Stern. The old Soviet subsidy system is largely gone, so that now culture has to stand on its own legs in what Lenin used to call "profit and loss accounting." The marketization of the arts has resulted in some terrible pain. The conservatory of music in St. Petersburg goes begging for support to maintain a magnificent collection of old recordings of music inaccessible anywhere in the world.[13] Sadder still is the sight of Petersburg conservatory musicians and students playing violins and xylophones for tips in the St. Petersburg underpasses and on the streets of Helsinki and other European cities. Changing the name of the conservatory and that of the one in Moscow, founded by the Rubinstein brothers, would not help in the least—though it would be an act of simple fairness. Those brothers pale in comparison to Rimsky and Tchaikovsky in terms of musical genius, but they were the main forces in founding the two conservatories in the 1860s. The plight of classical music in Russia is not unique: throughout Europe and the United States, such music has been relegated to the status of a poor relative and taken off the air by some public radio stations. Many labels finance classical recordings with the profits made by rock musicians.

Concert music in Russia and elsewhere does not possess the same draw as opera and ballet. The Great Hall of the St. Petersburg Philharmonia is among the most impressive concert sites in the world, with its extraordinary acoustics and classical decor. Few visitors realize that this accidental concert hall once and for a long time served as the ballroom of the St. Petersburg Noble Assembly. In tsarist times, the balcony—where Liszt, Shostakovich, and Stravinsky have stood—was used for a dance orchestra.[14] The cream of the capital's nobility first rented the ballroom of the Assembly to the Philharmonic Society in 1836, and from 1847 on a more or less permanent basis. But this venue—which in 1943 served as a virtual emblem of the city's wartime spiritual survival—was still very much a site of aristocratic leisure. The power of the capital's corporate gentry class in the mid-nineteenth century and the grandeur of its headquarters stand in contrast to the then relative insignificance of the Philharmonic Society, which subsequently gave the hall its name.

The St. Petersburg Philharmonia, for all its glorious past, cannot compete with the visual thrills that most visiting audiences seek in the musical theater at the Mariinsky: the edifice itself, with its red velvet plush, ornate carving, glittering chandeliers; and the spectacle presented on stage by bodies in motion, elaborate sets, and brilliant costumes (whether historically accurate or not). The names

Kirov and Mariinsky (like the Moscow Bolshoi) have had a magic ring for decades in a way that the Philharmonia has not, despite the eminence of those who have played or conducted there. The impoverished musical public of St. Petersburg may not be enough to sustain the expense required of such a major musical establishment.

A few years ago, in an effort to project the heritage image of the Philharmonia by connecting it to its hallowed past—and thus win audiences and possibly financial support—a live television broadcast from the Great Hall in 1997 commemorated its 150th anniversary as a concert hall in a recreation of an 1847 concert there: Haydn's Symphony No. 88; an aria from Mozart's *Clemenza di Tito;* Beethoven's *Fantasy for Piano, Orchestra, and Chorus*; a solo piano piece by Adolphe Henselt; and Mendelssohn's *Midsummer Night's Dream* music.[15] The program was superb, but it seems to me that the organizers deliberately chose a concert, rather atypical of that era, that included complete versions of canonical works. In the early nineteenth century, most Russian concerts were extremely eclectic and far from the balance and symmetry of modern programs; they offered excerpts and mixed genres, with longer works often divided between the first and second half of the concert. A much more typical program of a Philharmonia concert, given in March 1859, offered in the first half of the evening Beethoven's Fifth Symphony, an aria from Mendelssohn's *Elijah*, the first movement of the Beethoven violin concerto, the "Sanctus" from his *Missa Solemnis*, Wagner's *Tannhäuser* overture, and the finale of Glinka's *Life for the Tsar*; and in the second half the last two movements of the Beethoven concerto, an aria from Glinka's *Ruslan and Liudmila*, a solo piece for the ophicleide, an aria from Halevy's *La Juive*, and the finale of Mozart's *Jupiter Symphony*.[16] Russian audiences of that time were accustomed to this kind of sequence because it was the standard. The 1997 choice of program, which fits modern notions, was, I believe, more related to the compulsive tendency to show only the best moments of the past that is being recaptured than to celebrating a particular anniversary.

There are other ways of attracting attention to the great musical sites of Russian history that are still operating. Two examples: the Capella, which I have described above; and the Engelhardt House.

The latter was the original home of the St. Petersburg Philharmonia Society, founded in 1803, and the ancestor of the present Philharmonia. The founding occasion was a performance of Haydn's *Creation.* Although the Philharmonia's concerts had no permanent site, they were mainly performed on the second floor of the Engelhardt House near the corner of Nevsky Prospect and the Catherine (Griboedov) Canal—a building (with a Metro station beneath) that many readers of these pages have walked past a hundred times. Engelhardt House, the main site of Philharmonia concerts up to 1846, witnessed Petersburg audiences' raptures at performances by Franz Liszt, Clara Schumann, and Hector Berlioz—to name only the most famous of the visiting virtuosos and conductors who appeared there in the reign of Nicholas I. In the spirit of cultural versatility, the place also hosted testimonial dinners and masques for high society. Literary scholars best remember the Engelhardt House as the setting for Mikhail Lermontov's play *Masquerade.* Only in 1847, after this building was sold, did the House of Nobility become the regular home of the Philharmonia.[17]

Nowadays the musical offerings in the Capella and the Engelhardt continue, or in some cases revive, the best traditions of nineteenth-century music. But ticket-buying tourists largely neglect them, and only partly because of foreign audiences' preference for opera and ballet. The Engelhardt (now Glinka) concert hall is practically in the dead center of the city—and a block or so away from the Philharmonia itself, of which it is a filial. But its concerts are not well advertised or promoted. This neglect is chiefly the fault of tour guides, who know or care only about the big and famous tourist targets—the ones the tourists themselves are likely to know: the Mariinsky, the Circus, and, of course, the Hermitage. I have more than once heard Intourist guides apologize to their groups for not getting them into the Mariinsky, offering as poor compensation seats in the Engelhardt! The Capella, also in the center, has suffered the same fate, as has the Smolny Cathedral, which offers breathtaking performances of Russian sacred music.[18]

Pictures Not at an Exhibition

If, in the hierarchy of cultural establishments, the Mariinsky towers above the drama theater, as does the Philharmonia over its smaller sisters, then in even greater measure the Hermitage—set in the 1,100-room Winter Palace—far outshines the Russian Museum. In terms of tourist attraction, nothing in Russia except the Moscow Kremlin has greater resonance. The director of the Hermitage, Mikhail Piotrovsky, speaking to an influential group of women in Washington, D.C., in 1999, focused on two glories of his museum: the enormous and varied collection of European art, and the personal items that reflect the splendor of the Romanov dynasty—particularly the works of Carl Fabergé.[19] Piotrovsky's presentation was, in a sense, circular: He stressed those aspects of the Hermitage with which his audience would already be familiar, a perfectly understandable market strategy that is constantly reinforced by tour and museum guides.[20] The tone in all cases is prideful. The Soviets, of course, did the same thing, though with a different political subtext, one designed to underline the immense wealth that was amassed by the privileged few at the expense of the people.

In both eras, the Russian Museum has played second fiddle to the Hermitage. But managers of the recently renovated museum on the Square of the Arts have their own hierarchical agenda. On the walls of the Russian Museum, the public—Russians and foreign visitors—will find many of the great masterpieces of Russian art, from medieval icons to modern paintings. The curators have carefully selected them for exhibition. In the case of early nineteenth-century art, the sampling is extremely limited. But up in the dark recesses near the roof of the museum, and inaccessible to the public, is an attic storehouse that contains an unhung collection of thousands of pictures that are displayed only periodically or never at all.[21] Having spent several months working through this collection, I was amazed at its magnitude and richness. The numbered canvases are stored on racks. By means of an elaborate index file, one can find paintings on such themes as daily life in town and country, peasants at work, blacksmiths, metallurgical foundries, drunken tavern scenes, bourgeois interiors—the whole gamut of urban and provincial life in pictures, good and bad, that caused consternation among some authorities and critics when they were first painted. Tsar Nicholas I himself became outraged at scenes of drunken revelry and said so.[22]

In the attic of the Russian Museum, one can inspect both "minor" works of famous painters and the works of unknowns. These often deal with subjects unpalatable to art museum officials, who always want to exhibit the best to the art-viewing public. Of course, the works of the canonized early realists of the 1840s, and the "accusers" and Itinerants (*Peredvizhniki*) of the late nineteenth century are on public view, and some of these also show drunken priests, female suicides, and overworked children. Privileging works such as Karl Briullov's *The Last Day of Pompeii* and Aleksei Venetsianov's idealized peasant scenes, however, has sanitized the early part of the century. Viewing works like these without seeing the canvases in the attic, visitors witness a prettified and distorted tableau of what life was like and how art portrayed that life in the early nineteenth century. Curatorial strategies in the Russian Museum, which do not differ significantly from those elsewhere, presuppose that the quality of a painting should be the criterion for public showing because that is what the public actually wants to see. And yet in our postmodern age, there is certainly room for a more varied and more historically resonant approach, one that sets the masterpiece beside the inferior work of the same epoch in a way that permits a more nuanced visual understanding of the age. As long as pious and elitist selectivity prevails, such an educational juxtaposition is not likely to take place in the Russian Museum; and the exalted memory of the Age of Pushkin (another pious trope) will remain unsullied by the prose of reality.[23]

Whatever the arguments for curatorial elitism, less forgivable is the practice of falsifying by omission the record of Russian art in exported shows. Just a few years ago, I attended an exhibit of nineteenth century Russian art on loan from the Russian Museum to the White Hall on Senate Square in Helsinki. Vasilii Vereshchagin was one of the featured artists. Anyone who has been to the Russian Museum is not likely to forget the Vereshchagin room, with its striking canvases depicting the Russian campaigns in the steppes and deserts of Central Asia in the 1860s and 1870s. Amid the various scenes of "oriental" voluptuousness and brutality, one item stands out for its balanced view: a matched set of two canvases called Defeat and Victory. One shows two Kirghiz or Kazakh warriors admiring their trophy, the severed head of a Russian soldier. The other depicts corpses of the native warriors piled against the wall of a fort; standing over them and contentedly smoking a cigarette is a Russian soldier, decked out in the costume designed for desert warfare usually associated with the French Foreign Legion. The main message leaping out from this juxtaposition seems fairly clear: War generates violence and cruelty on both sides of the battlefield. A subsidiary theme may be that modern weaponry causes many more casualties than traditional ones. The exhibit in Helsinki, which hundreds of Finns and foreign tourists saw that summer, contained only the first painting of this set.

Let me conclude my remarks on the Russian Museum on a somewhat different note. This building was once the Mikhailovsky Palace, the midcentury residence of Grand Duchess Elena Pavlovna, where a kind of exalted political circle met in the 1850s to talk of coming reform and of the serfs' emancipation. Less well known, perhaps, is that in these same rooms, Elena Pavlovna hosted musical evenings and that her musician-in-chief was the celebrated founder of the St. Petersburg Conservatory, Anton Rubinstein. How this son of a Jewish merchant from the Pale came to move in such lofty Petersburg circles makes for one of the remarkable stories of pre-emancipation Russian history. During his sojourn at the Palace, Rubinstein not only composed what was once one of the most popular recital piano pieces in the world, the Melody in F, but also floated the idea to the Grand Duchess for a conservatory of music. A 1998 television special on the museum,[24] celebrating its upcoming centenary, made a big point about this aspect of the building's history, justly claiming that the St. Petersburg Conservatory was in a sense born at the Mikhailovsky Palace. Rubinstein was its inspiration, Elena Pavlovna its patron. The first rehearsals and classes of the Conservatory took place there. In the tastefully produced television program, the camera lovingly captured the exquisite White Salon, the site of the musical evenings. The entire effect was to broaden and enrich the setting and meaning of the edifice that would eventually house the Russian Museum (1898) and to take viewers back to a moment when the Mikhailovsky Square, as it was then called, was truly a square of the arts—framed by Elena Pavlovna's palace, the Mikhailovsky Theater, and the House of Nobility.

Truth, Beauty, History, Heritage

The period roughly from the 1790s to 1861—a period of high aristocratic culture, whose epicenter was St. Petersburg—also marked the twilight of serfdom, upon which that culture was built. The efforts to revive and make known to the public works of that period that were denied performance or exhibition in Soviet times are admirable. But the revivals—perhaps like all revivals—have been the result of selective memory. In the Soviet era, a tension existed among many cultural historians between their adulation for the art of the Tsarist era and their need to condemn the kind of society that produced it. The denunciatory literature assembled many stories, some true and some exaggerated, about the mistreatment of serf artists, musicians, and actors: overwork, physical punishment, sexual abuse, and the repression of serf talent. Against this emphasis on the dark side, the scholarly and curatorial approach to canonical figures such as Glinka, who also happened to own serfs, downplayed that aspect of their lives and even invested their art with some sort of proto-democratic sensibility.[25] That tension seems to have disappeared, at least judging from post-Soviet program notes and other commentary on the great masters of the early nineteenth century. But erasing the social context of creativity for aesthetic reasons has had the effect of romanticizing the imperial past, thus replacing the celebrated minus signs with pluses and sweetening memories that in fact should more closely resemble the sweet-and-sour taste of reality.

Though heritage practices and history writing differ in their aims, they need not annul each other. Honest historians strive to avoid falsification and to achieve an objectivity that they know can never be attained. Heritage managers are rarely concerned with these matters. Uplift, pride, and sometimes profit are inscribed on their banners. But, as Lowenthal persuasively argues at great length, despite these different approaches, each can inform the other.[26] Great culture, in St. Petersburg or anywhere else, can be enriched in presentation and reception by being acknowledged in a temporal and social context as well as in its accepted place in the narrative of excellence.

Original publication: In Helena Goscilo, Stephen M. Norris, eds. *Preserving Petersburg: History, Memory, Nostalgia*. Bloomington, Indianapolis: Indiana University Press, 2008, pp. 182-196.

In this essay, on p. 503, Stites refers to another contribution to *Preserving Petersburg*: Helena Goscilo, "Unsaintly St. Petersburg? Visions and Visuals," 57-87.

Notes

1   On forgetting, see Elena Hellberg-Hirn, "On the Art of Forgetting: the Siege Story," Conference on Selective Memory and Group Identity in Russia and Eastern Europe, Renvall Institute, Helsinki University, August 30, 2001. See also her *Imperial Imprints: Post-Soviet St. Petersburg* (Helsinki, 2003); on the Blockade, 102-115; on nostalgia for palaces and balls among the New Russians, 165-174.

2   Pierre Nora, *Realms of Memory: Rethinking the French Past*. 3 vols. (New York, 1996-1998), 3.

3   Direct observations about the city's cultural life are based on my residence in Russia in 1997-1998. I wish to thank the International Research Exchange Committee (IREX) for a grant that enabled my stay; Serafima Hager of the International Research Initiative of Georgetown University for additional support; and Elena Hellberg-Hirn of the Renvall Institute for inviting me to her project on St. Petersburg culture and memory. I wish to thank also the audience at the Baltic and East European Graduate School in Södertorn, Sweden, and at Cambridge University for provocative discussion of my ideas. Most of all, I am grateful to the staffs of the St. Petersburg theaters and concert halls I attended and to the art specialists in the Russian Museum.

4   Pierre Boudieu, *Distinction: A Social Critique of the Judgement of Taste* (Cambridge, MA, 1984).

5   David Lowenthal, *The Heritage Crusade and the Spoils of History* (New York, 1997).

6   Richard Stites, *Russian Popular Culture: Entertainment and Society since 1900* (Cambridge, UK, 1992) 165.

7   A difficult position to maintain, given the magnetism and easy travel access to Moscow. See the stimulating essays in Ewa Bérard, ed., *Saint-Pétersbourg: une fenétre sur la Russie, 1900-1935* (Paris, 2000).

8   For more on the film and its meanings, see the chapter by Norris in this volume ("Strolls through Postmodern Petersburg: Celebrating the City in 2003," in *Preserving Petersburg*, 197-218 - ed.).

9 *Nachal'noe upravlenie Olega* is often mistranslated as "The Early Reign of Oleg." See S.L. Ginzburg, ed., *Russkii muzykal'nyi teatr, 1700-1835 gg: khrestomatiia* (Leningrad, 1941) 150-156 for an excerpt. *Muzykal'naia entsiklopediia*, IV, 801; Vera Krasovskaia, *Russkii baletnyi teatr ot vozniknoveniia do serediny XIX veka* (Leningrad, 1958) 53-54; Tat'iana Dynnik, *Krepostnoi teatr* (Leningrad, 1933) 65, 203-205; Richard Wortman, *Scenarios of Power: Myth and Ceremony in Russian Monarchy*, 2 vols. (Princeton, 1994-2000) I. 138; Stephen Baehr, *The Paradise Myth in Eighteenth-Century Russia* (Stanford, 1991) 48-49, 212. In Simon Karlinsky's words, *Oleg* was "the most lavishly mounted stage presentation in the history of Russia": *Russian Drama from its Beginnings to the Age of Pushkin* (Berkeley, 1985), 88.

10 Quoted in O.E. Levasheva, "A.N. Verstovskii," *Sovetskaia muzyka* 6 (1949), 72.

11 *Teatral'naia i muzykal'naia gazeta* 8 (1859), 6 quoted in A.N. Verstovskii, *Askol'dova mogila: romnticheskaia opera*, Boris Dobrokhotov, ed. (Moscow, 1963), 5.

12 Mimoza [pseudonym], "Opera nashikh babushek," *Moskovskaia gazeta* (September 20, 1910), 4; S. L. Ginzburg, *Russkii muzykal'nyi teatr*, 286-300 (excerpt from the libretto). The aristocratic officer Mikhail Buturlin, a devotee of Italian opera, asserted that *Askol'd* produced an indescribable furor: *Russkii arkhiv* 5-8 (1897), 541. The full score has not survived: Boris Dobrokhotov, *A.N. Verstovskii* (Moscow, 1949), 40. But see Verstovskii, *Askol'dova mogila*, an arrangement for piano and voices from which a performance was mounted in 1959 by the Taras Shevchenko Academic Theater Orchestra and Opera Company of Kiev: Aleksei Verstovskii, *Askol'dova mogila*, recording in the fonoteka (recording room) of the Glinka State Central Museum of Musical Culture in Moscow. In 2005, the release of a CD containing selections by Verstovskii seems to augur a revival of interest in him.

13 Conversations with Neli and Vasily Kuznetsov, archivists of the Rimsky-Korsakov Conservatory recording collection, 1997-1998.

14 For historical pictures, see Eleanora Fradkina, *Zal Dvorianskogo Sobraniia: zametki o kontsertnoi zhizni Sankt-Peterburga* (St. Petersburg, 1994).

15 St. Petersburg TV, Nov. 25, 1997, a live concert accompanied by commentary and contemporary graphics.

16 Fradkina, *Zal Dvorianskogo sobraniia*, 55-56. Fradkina, reflecting both a twentieth-century elitism and a Russian purist version of it, is indignant over the patchiness of the 1859 program she describes. The ophicleide was a mechanical instrument popular at the time.

17 The current name is the Glinka Small Hall, Branch of the St. Petersburg Academic Shostakovich Philharmonia. Concert hall historical

placards and program notes for a concert hall historical placards and program notes for a concert, December, 1997; Malyi zal imeni M.I. Glinki (St. Petersburg, 1997); Evgenii Kuznetsov, *Iz istorii proshlogo russkoi estrady* (Moscow, 1958), 107n.

18 There is a big literature on the history of the Engelhardt and the Capella, once headed by Aleksei L'vov, composer of the tsarist national anthem (1833), who worked side by side with Glinka. For sources, see Richard Stites, *Serfdom, Society, and the Arts in Imperial Russia* (New Haven, 2005).

19 Mikhail Piotrovsky, speech at the Washington Museum for Women in the Arts, November, 1999.

20 A more spectacular example of the Hermitage's outreach is the recent Guggenheim Hermitage Museum in Las Vegas: *Aveniu: iskusstvo i kul'tura za rubezhom* 1 (2001), 16; *Financial Times* (Oct. 7, 2001), 9.

21 Stephen Norris visited the Russian Museum in May 2003 and noted that many pictures of the old capital had been taken from the storage attic and put on display for the exhibit "Sankt-Peterburg: Portret goroda i gorozhan." See his chapter in this volume and that of Helena Goscilo (for Norris, see note 8, and for Goscilo, see right above note 1 - *ed.*)

22 See Stites, *Serfdom*, chapter 8.

23 The architectural and art historian Grigory Kaganov has also noted that pictures showing the neighborhoods of St. Petersburg that resembled villages and provincial towns have been neglected in favor of art that focuses on the sectors of that city where the monumentalism of the Empire style prevails. Illustrated lecture at the Renvall Institute, Helsinki University, November 14, 2001.

24 "Russkii Muzei: Avtobiografiia," St. Petersburg TV Channel 2, January 22, 1998.

25 See Stites, *Serfdom*, passim, for references.

26 Lowenthal, *The Heritage Crusade*, passim.

29

Summertime
Petersburg Suburban Entertainment in the Era of Serfdom

In a recent film, *The White Countess*, featuring White Russian émigrés in Shanghai in the 1930s, the director's opening flashback poetically evokes the tsarist Old Regime with the standard image of an aristocratic ballroom scene. The countesses and princes and officers are clearly dancing indoors, and yet snowdrops are falling on them. Though using snow to suggest Russia is hardly a novel device, this scene takes winter as its signifier to new lyrical heights. In fact winter was the great season for upper class balls all over Europe—the *bal d'hiver*—with extensions back to autumn and into spring. They punctuated the hunt, local elections, Shrovetide, the pre-Lenten weeks, and numerous semi-official and family events. Summertime scattered the affluent noble families to country homes, spas, or foreign lands. So thinking about social and public entertainment in Old Russia as cold weather activities does not distort. But it does obscure the fact that dancing and musical diversions of all kinds took place in summer venues as well. Those catering to a broad range of social classes emerged in the late eighteenth and early nineteenth centuries.[1]

St. Petersburg, legendary capital of mystery-laden texts, of White Nights, and of stony and icy heartlessness, became encircled by several sites of summertime amusement, some open to a surprisingly broad ambit of the public. In addition to the private mansions and palaces of the high and mighty and the arenas of imperial display so brilliantly described in Richard Wortman's *Scenarios of Power*,[2] a number of public commercial entertainment centers sprang up to offer their diverse wares to the denizens of the city itself as well as to the suburban elite. The more famous and pretentious of them took the name Vauxhall. This word, taken from Falkes Hall, the estate of Sir Falkes de Breaute, a medieval Norman English knight, evolved into Vaux Hall and then Vauxhall, an eighteenth-century place for concerts and dancing in the Lambeth district of London. It became a generalized term for suburban summer gardens or amusement sites in Europe and in several Russian cities. For Petersburg in the reign of Nicholas I (1825-55), Ekaterinhof in the south of the city, the smaller northern islands, and the nearby town of Pavlovsk constituted its primary grounds for summer entertainment, stretching from May 1 to September.[3]

The first of these, created before the word Vauxhall came into usage, appeared under Peter I in the Ekaterinhof district of Petersburg where the Catherine Canal debouched into the gulf of Finland, and it functioned with many interruptions until the 1760s when its building burned down, the fate of many such buildings.[4] It continued as a site of the biggest funfair or seasonal festival of the Petersburg environs. A character in Ivan Goncharov's novel *Oblomov*, set in the 1850s, exclaims: "Not go to Ekaterinhof on the first of May! ...Why, everyone will be there!"[5] In that same decade summer concerts were being offered, thus making Ekaterinhof a combination of fair grounds and Vauxhall. The archipelago and adjacent lands north of the Neva and interspliced by it and its branches was largely stratified by class, roughly Stone and Elagin Islands for the gentry, Cross Island for middle and lower class elements, and Peter Island, mostly Germans.[6] These, together with the New Village and Black River districts offered a variety of summer delights such as the virtually all-class funfair, an ubiquitous event in villages, town, and cities throughout Russia that provided rides and games, peep shows, puppet theater, and huge arrays of food and beverages. From a boat landing on the Neva at the Summer Garden, a flotilla of private excursion barges and cheap ferries plied their way back and forth between the inner city and the islands.[7]

At the other pole, the extravaganzas of the very rich took place in more exclusive habitats. Residents of Stone Island in the 1840s could attend a French theater that played in a wooden house three times a week in summertime, though the audience remained thin.[8] A less respectable summer demimonde caroused till dawn. Sava Savvich Iakovlev, a millionaire wastrel and retired junior cavalry officer, became legendary for his hooliganism, decadence, and often salacious orgies. He brought in train an entourage, his so-called *mon-chers*, and a collection of "nymphs" of various backgrounds and languages.[9] Tivoli, the estate of Count G. A. Kushelov-Bezborodko in Poliustrovo on the Neva provided another variant of suburban entertainment. In the late 1840s he employed for his vast dances and entertainments the orchestra of Josef Hermann who specialized in light semi-classical and dance music performed in large tents. An 1851 program featured the waltzes of Lanner, Strauss, and Gungl; and operatic excerpts by Donizetti and Hérold.[10] Kushelov, owner of *The Russian Word*, patronized writers, journalists, gamblers, easy women, and foreign visitors of dubious merit and hosted such visiting celebrities as Alexandre Dumas.[11] The affluent bohème, a combination of great wealth, slumming, large scale entertainment, and a milieu of slightly sordid adventure—though not unique at the time—would become a growing phenomenon in the future. The Korolev family's Concordia dacha on the Vyborg Side, with maestro Henryk Gilman in charge of music, afforded yet one more example of the great social fluidity that popular music allowed and attracted.[12]

Between the strictly private gentry parties and hired entertainments on the one hand and the periodic public funfairs on the other, a site known as the Vauxhall of Artificial Mineral Waters—nicknamed Minerashi—became the central attraction of the islands. What divided it from the private dacha offerings was ticketing for the former and invitation for the latter. Located on the shore of the New Village district on land owned by Count Stroganov, it functioned in the morning as a spa which had been founded by Dr. Hermann Struve, brother of the noted astronomer.[13] I. I. Izler, an ex-pastry chef for Kushelov and the owner of the café-restaurant Dominique on the Nevsky, leased the grounds and buildings from noon onward late into the night. On Sunday August 22, 1837, he opened the Vauxhall, for an admission fee of five rubles, with a grand promenade through the brightly illuminated grounds to the sounds of an orchestra. Then followed a formal ball. Opened as a corporation, it contained a park, a ballroom, and the largest estrada theater and concert hall in St. Petersburg. Hundreds of employees served thousands of customers of various social classes. An imitator of Moscow's successful Petrovsky Park and a showman with a taste for extravaganza, Izler put on Bengal lights and fireworks operated by artillerymen and gave names to his evenings, such as the 1851 "One of the Thousand and One Arabian Nights," featuring 1500 lanterns. Petersburgers, a memorist related, called Izler "a genius and a magician."[14] The classical violinist Yury Arnold recalled in his memoirs its success and modishness, a place where, in the summertime, the cream of the capital's society gathered.[15]

By the 1850s, thousands of visitors—off-work commoners among them—arrived on Sundays by boat or diligence, paid a modest admission price, and availed themselves of refreshments in food tents, the music, and the shows. The concert hall opened with an eclectic program of the Horse Guards Regimental band, soloists, instrumentalists, and a Gypsy chorus. The estrada theater featured military songs and dances, acrobats, and the Schletzinger ballroom orchestra. By 1853, the repertoire at Izler was approaching that of a variety house—magic acts, acrobatics, ballet solo, Tyrolean singers, exotic acts from the "east." Skits were performed with music on topical themes about holidays on the islands. One bore the banal but appropriate name "A White Night on the Gulf of Finland." By the 1860s, French operetta with the can-can were appearing.[16]

The music played at these sites covered a wide range of styles and genres, local variants on the light music played in band shells and pavilions all over Europe at the time. Military wind bands that pumped out the oom-pah-pah alternated with waltz orchestras. One of the many "Viennese" waltz kings—until the Strauss family usurped the throne—Johann Gungl, was born in Hungary; Otto Dütsch, a Dane, came to Russia in 1848. The choir of I. E. Molchaninov sang folk songs; others preferred to deliver popular romances, "bandit songs," and ballads that soon became "folk" songs. Among the most popular ensembles were the then famous Gypsy choirs of Vasiliev, Sokolov, and the Brothers Malchugin.[17] In 1843, the inveterate musical snob, Vladimir Odoevsky, angrily argued that people who did not like or understand Mikhail Glinka's then new opera *Ruslan and Liudmila* were not Petersburg audiences but rather "the public which acquired its musical education at Sunday festivities in Ekaterinhof or on Krestovsky island from the sound of the Tyrolean guitar or the barrel-organ."[18] Odoevsky, like many music critics of that and any era, often exaggerated for effect and turned a deaf ear to the sound of popular music and failed to concede the legitimacy of popular taste.

By far the most renowned and elaborate of the summer entertainment suburbs—the Pavlovsk Musical Vauxhall—emerged as the offspring of Russia's first railroad line, the Tsarskoe Selo Railway. In September 1836, the first passenger car ran from Pavlovsk to Tsarskoe Selo in 15 minutes. The longer Petersburg-Tsarskoe Selo run, started in 1837, took on the average thirty-five minutes. Called "fabled steed" and "mechanical elephant," it made hardly slower speed than today's. The press reported that by a Sunday in June 1837, 1,833 passengers had ridden the line—more than half with 40 kopek tickets, the rest paying 80. By May 1838, almost 14,000 passengers had made the voyage. Both ends of the rail line became vibrant gathering centers, new public spaces in the empire's capital. The iron road to Tsarskoe Selo and Pavlovsk began at the station on Zagorodny Prospect in St. Petersburg—now the site of Vitebsk Station—a near contemporary of early stations in Europe and North America: Baltimore, Liverpool, London, Amsterdam, Leipzig, Potsdam, and Vienna.[19] Overnight, train cars and stations became topical themes in the entertainment world, such as P. S. Fedorov's vaudeville, *A Trip to Tsarskoe Selo by Rail*, and the merchant comedy, *Excursion to Tsarskoe Selo*. Sheet music followed suit and all copies of the popular "Steam Engine Mazurka" sold out at a music shop in the city.[20]

At the end of the line lay Pavlovsk which the new railway transformed into an entertainment site for almost a century. There is some irony in the fact that the busiest center of "popular" music in Russia during this era was founded right beside one of the great dynastic venues for classical music: the suburban palace of Tsar Paul and Empress Mariya Fedorovna. Pavlovsk, called Paul-Lust in 1780s, was the last of the great suburban palaces to be built—after Gatchina, Oranienbaum, Peterhof, and Tsarskoe Selo—and was given to Paul by Catherine the Great in 1777 on the birth of his son, Alexander. Paul preferred Gatchina which he ran like a military base, but his widow Maria Fedorovna (Sophia Dorothea of Würtemburg) turned Pavlovsk into a center of solo and chamber music played by professionals and amateur courtiers throughout

most of the reign of Alexander I. A keyboard pupil of Dmitry Bort-
nyansky, she held concerts in the elegant Grecian Hall of the palace
and patronized musical training for aristocratic girls. Tsar Nicholas
I's wife, Alexandra Fedorovna, had as court pianist the renowned
Adolphe Henselt. Amateur theatricals, serenades by boat-borne
musicians, and mock "village festivals" copied the styles then in
vogue at European courts. This and other lofty places were altogether closed to the general public. After Maria Fedorovna died in
1828, Tsar Nicholas's brother Mikhail replaced classical music with
the sounds of drums and martial music and the spectacle of drill.[21]

In the 1830s, the leafy town of Pavlovsk became a summer colony like Tsarskoe Selo, administered by a town council and a gathering point for Pushkin, Gogol, Zhukovsky, and other luminaries.
But since Pavlovsk boasted a population of only about 6,000, and
since the freight business remained weak, the railway authorities
needed something to induce a bustling passenger flow in order to
cover expenses. The director of the line, F. A. Gerstner, promoted
health concerns and argued that no capital in Europe required more
movement of its denizens to salutary climes in summer than did St.
Petersburg. He held a competition for the building of a Vauxhall
and hotel. It was awarded to the Petersburg architect, A. I. Stack-
enschneider and in July 1836 construction began. The new complex comprised a 40-room hotel, the huge Vauxhall with dining,
dancing, and concert facilities, a billiard room, a semicircular gallery, and adjacent buildings and pavilions—all set amid park-like
grounds adorned with fountains. The restaurant was run by Cou-
lon, the proprietor of the Hotel St. Peterbourg (later Hotel Europe,
completed 1834) and of the journal, *Northern Bee*. Live dining music
resounded from a gallery.[22]

The Pavlovsk Musical Vauxhall opened to the public in May
1838 almost two years after the inaugural excursion of the Peters-
burg-Pavlovsk train. The railway track was laid right through into
the grounds to the Circular Hall of the Vauxhall as the terminal of
the line, and a walkway linked the train to the hotel. The Pavlovsk
Vauxhall came to be associated with hoarding a train: thus the Russian word for it, *vokzal*, gradually became and remains the generic
word for railroad station in that language. The two wings of the
Circular Hall containing the hotel rooms were flanked by winter

gardens. Outdoors a band shell was erected for military band concerts in summer time. Indoors, a chorus or small ensemble in the
restaurant played music for dining and dancing. With a stage and
a ballroom modeled on those in gentry assemblies added, the Pavlovsk Vauxhall quickly became a fashionable gathering place for
the Petersburg *beau monde.* At various times, Karl Bryullov, Ivan
Turgenev, Fedor Dostoevsky, Ivan Goncharov, Avdotiya Panaeva,
Mikhail Glinka, Modest Musorgsky, and Cesar Cui resided nearby.
After an 1844 fire, insurance coverage allowed the owners to re-
build and remodel the Vauxhall within three months. Situated less
than an hour's ride from the city, Pavlovsk's free concerts brought
in bigger and more socially diverse audiences than did any other
concert hall in the country at that time.[23] Music became the great
attraction for passengers, particularly those who could not afford
the Philharmonia concerts or had no taste for its classical repertoire.

The peasantry of Russia had long been in the habit of riding
horses or carts to another village for a wedding; gentry shuttled
regularly by carriage and sleigh between estate, provincial ball, and
Moscow or Petersburg. And numerous other people hit the road
on pilgrimages, government business, commerce, or for just sheer
travel. For urban folks, however, the boat ride to the islands of St.
Petersburg in order to savor a day of rest and amusement linked a
mode of transportation to paid—for pleasure; so in a sense these
journeys constituted the beginnings of the excursion and domestic
tourism for large numbers of people. We can only speculate how
much the exotic chugging metallic monster belching smoke might
have enchanted day trippers off for evening of dinner and dance
along the straight steel roads. What did they see and hear on arrival?

Since the Pavlovsk entertainments began about nine months after the inauguration of the Izler establishment, it is no surprise that
the former drew from the latter—and its predecessors—in fashion-
ing its initial programs. Indeed performers often shuttled between
to the two sites. Estrada or variety acts alternated with instrumental
musical offerings. The former included dances, divertimentos, and
choral performance—often eclectically mixed in the manner of the
popular stage of that day. Among the vocal ensembles were V. G.
Zhukov's male factory choir and two groups who played at other

venues: the oft-mocked Tyrolean vocal quartet offering Alpine re-
frains, and the folk singing Malchugin brothers. The Malchugins'
success illustrated the growing mobility of performers from town
to town or—in the classic success narrative—from the provinces to
the capitals. They began as a local choir in Kazan and made it to St.
Petersburg in 1848. What they brought to the capital suburbs was
performance by a small team of tenor, soprano, three other voices, a
guitar, a piano, and the gestures and singing styles of lower townspeople.[24]

Most popular by far of those who offered non-classical vocal
music were the ubiquitous Gypsy choirs, sometimes comprising
real ethnic Roma or Gypsies, but often enough Russians or Ukrainians singing in the "Gypsy manner." Foremost among these, the already famed Moscow group of Ilya Sokolov arrived from Moscow
in the 1830s to play on both the Izler and the Pavlovsk stages. Sokolov pioneered in "russianizing" popular music by giving composed
folk tunes and the hugely popular urban romances of Alexander
Varlamov, Alexander Alyabev, and Alexei Verstovsky, a Gypsy spin
whose broad performance style suggested romantic abandon and
emotional freedom. This approach, which dramatized music by
means of body language and facial gestures associated with the
lower classes rather than stylized physical vocabulary of opera,
won the affection of people from every social strata right up to the
revolution of 1917 and—to the chagrin of Soviet elitists—beyond.[25]

The managers at Pavlovsk privileged orchestral dance music
by allowing visitors free entry to hear the singing but made them
pay five paper rubles to stay for the dance. Concert and dance music, originally offered by a military band, came under the purview
of a series of Germanic conductors and their orchestras. Within a
few years, the waltz had conquered Russian dancers, which led
Glinka to compose a fantasy waltz, a favorite of the audiences who
dubbed it the "Pavlovsk Waltz." The mostly Habsburg visiting
conductors—who called themselves Viennese wherever they came
from—brought with them a special Mitteleuropa style of "middlebrow" entertainment that had begun in beer gardens and spas and
eventually—as salon or palm court music—conquered restaurants,
cafes, hotel lobbies, and luxury steamships all over Europe and
beyond. At Pavlovsk and on the islands, the conductors, fiddle in

hand, offered a repertoire of light—meaning "feel good"—music, alternating band marches and waltzes, excerpts from currently popular operas, and topical tunes associated with the locale: a "Pavlovsk Polka" and a spate of "railroad" waltzes, marches, and gallops. Joseph Hermann of Vienna, arrived in 1838, and in time his waltz ballroom orchestra supplemented the salon music with an impressive array of Russian pieces, opera arias, and short classical pieces such as the Beethoven *Prometheus Overture.* He was spelled for a while by Joseph Labitski, a waltz prince and veteran of the Carlsbad spa who brought with him a fourteen-piece band. When the Hungarian-born Johann Gungl arrived from Berlin, the market for conductors produced a game of musical podia as the maestros moved from Pavlovsk to Izler to Korolev and back to Pavlovsk. In the 1850s, Johann and Josef Gungl—uncle and nephew—both had conducting posts in the St. Petersburg suburbs and for five years dominated the suburban musical scene: Johann at Izler and Josef at Pavlovsk.[26]

A media blitz over popular suburban music erupted when the most renowned among waltz royalty came to Pavlovsk: Johann Strauss Jr. In terms of celebrity and lasting fame, his reign every summer from 1856 to 1865 brought Pavlovsk to the pinnacle of its musical prestige. Classical virtuosos such as the cellist Adrien Servais and the violinist Henri Vieuxtemps had appeared—but only for one or two engagements. Strauss brought twelve men with him from Vienna and gathered the remaining musicians locally, eventually expanding to an orchestra of 42 players. Audiences loved his performance style: as he led the orchestra, he played the violin intermittently and danced around to the music, playing constantly to the audience in the Viennese gemütlich manner. The handsome and dashing twenty-nine year old also made a non-musical impression on female attendees who swooned over him. In the 1850s, a cartoon by N. Stepanov depicted outraged husbands infuriated by the conductor's popularity with their wives. In 1860, a crowd broke into pandemonium and destroyed music stands and instruments and dishes because Strauss had disappeared from the podium for a while—a habit of his. The cartoons, rumors, and gossip about Strauss attracted large crowds; commuters could buy autographed pictures of him for ten kopeks from the railroad company. On one of several such occasions, Strauss was honored on a Sunday in August 1857 by a benefit concert, a "Grand Musical Festival" with illumination and major fireworks that charged one silver ruble for entrance.[28]

Although Johann Strauss did fall in love while in the Russian capital, his primary concern was producing music and having the public listen to it. He abandoned the dining experience with music in favor of concertizing—both in the atmosphere and in the program. Strauss banned eating during his performance, allowing a military band to perform that service. His musicians began at seven in the evening and lasted until 11:00 when they played the national anthem, after which the guests boarded the last train for St. Petersburg. While Izler at the Mineral Waters was clinging to the recognized popular genres of the variety show and circus, Strauss' semi-symphonic ensemble played works by Beethoven, Bach, Mendelssohn, Schubert, Bellini, Verdi, and Wagner.[29] The *Theatrical and Musical Herald,* which catered to high culture, thanked Johann Strauss for not feeding the public overplayed Verdi tunes (though he did that too) and offering instead serious music.[30] And the arch-elitist critic Vladimir Stasov saw the Strauss concerts as a perfect training ground in the sounds of instrumental music for the Russian ear.[31]

From a broader perspective Johann Strauss and his fellow conductors echoed, on a different plane, developments in the larger world of music making in the Russia of this era. One was the effort of symphonic societies to educate audiences in non-programmatic classical instrumental music. Notable also was the hegemony of foreign, and especially "German," professional orchestral musicians and conductors in both realms. In the classical sphere, this led eventually to a successful campaign by the great Russian pianist, Anton Rubinstein, to create a conservatory in Russia for the training of serious musicians. Yet another parallel was the cult of the visiting virtuoso which had led to the lionizing of guests such as Berlioz, Liszt, and dozens of opera and ballet stars from European stages. Scholarship that explores the musical tastes of Russians in the era has largely focused on elite audience at classical concerts and the opera.[32] Yet, in the same early decades of the nineteenth century, a much broader social contingent was learning a good deal about the many varieties and styles that music could take, thanks to the eclectic mixes everywhere in the suburban sites and particularly due to the repertoire of Johann Strauss, who did not hesitate to insinuate a more serious program into the usual assortment of "light" music. And all of this may at least partly explain the enlargement of audiences for serious music after the emancipation of the serfs in 1861 and the opening of Russia's greatest outpouring of symphonic production.

In 1837, a newspaper reporting on the ball at Mineral Waters, commented that Izler had created "a melding of summer and winter"—since dance, according to polite custom, had been a strictly winter affair—with its gowns and rituals and lordly ambience.[33] Observations about audiences and reception must of course remain speculative. But perhaps this journalist was hinting that the Petersburg gentry had stretched the social code; or that the public at large could make their own social and amusement calendar; or even that urban society was emulating eternal habits of the peasantry who danced only in summer since they had no indoor gathering places to do it otherwise except in the narrow confines of the home. In any case at some of the balls and concerts, the audience was modestly clad.[34] This and other snippets of information reveal that summer audiences were socially variegated and that its lower ranks were able to mix, at least temporarily, with the more privileged classes. A broad public could, for a fee, enjoy some of the pleasures of the gentry manor house such as billiards and illuminated parks as well as those things provided to wealthy lords by their unfree serfs: dinner music, concerts, shows. While it would be unwise to claim that these few sites constituted elements of a burgeoning civil society, the spectacle of summer crowds, mingling in places of mass entertainment demonstrated that Russia contained growing alternative spaces to the manor house, gentry club, and village street.

Original publication: In Natalia Baschmakoff and Mari Ristolainen, eds. *The Dacha Kingdom: Summer Dwellers and Dwellings in the Baltic Area.* Helsinki: Aleksanteri Series, 3:2009, pp. 49-61.

Notes

1   See Kolesnikova, Anna (2005), *Bal v Rossii XVIII-nachalo XX veka.* Sankt-Peterburg: Azbuka-lassika; and Stites, Richard (1992), *Russian Popular Culture: Entertainment and Society Since 1900.* Cambridge: Cambridge University Press. For the hundreds of places fun fairs, folk festivals, village revels where peasants and townspeople made and consumed their entertainments as *narodnoe gulianie*, see Nekrylova, Anna (1988), *Russkie narodnye gorodskie prazdniki, uveseleniia, i zrelishcha: konets XVIII-nachalo XX veka.* Leningrad: Iskusstvo.

2   Wortman, Richard (1994-2000), *Scenarios of Power: Myth and Ceremony in Russian Monarchy,* 2 vols. Princeton: Princeton University Press.

3   Stolpianskii, P. (1989), *Muzyka i muzitsirovanie v starom Peterburge.* Sankt-Peterburg: Muzyka, 154; Stites, Richard (2005), *Serfdom, Society, and the Arts in Imperial Russia.* New Haven: Yale University Press, 40.

4   Kuznetsov, Evgenii (1958), *Iz proshlogo russkoi estrady: istoricheskii ocherk.* Moskva: Iskusstvo, 101.

5   Goncharov, Ivan (1963), *Oblomov* (tr. Ann Dunnigan). New York: Signet, 35.

6   Finland and Russia (1849), *Finland and Russia.* London. 510.

7   Bremner, Robert (1840), *Excursions in the Interior of Russia.* 2 vols. London. See vol. I, 143-4 and II passim; Stolpianskii 1989, 71-75.

8   *Finland and Russia,* 510.

9   Arnold, Iurii (1892-93), *Vospominaniia.* II, 3 vols. Moskva. 111.

10 Stolpianskii 1989, 77.

11 Panaeva, Avdotiia (1928), *Vospominaniia, 1829-1870.* 2 ed. K. Chukovskii (ed.). Leningrad: Academia, 312 and n. 1.

12 Rozanov, A. S. (1978), *Muzykal'nyi Pavlovsk.* Leningrad: Muzyka, 45; Stolpianskii 1989, 77.

13 Arnold 1892-93, 110-111.

14 Stolpianskii 1989, 75. Quote: Skal'kovskii, K. A. (1906), *Vospominaniia molodosti (po more zhiteiskomu) 1843-1869.* Sankt-Peterburg: Tipografia A. S. Suvorina, 98.

15 Arnold 1892-93, 110.

16 Kuznetsov 1958, 109-112; Iankovskii, M. O. (1937), *Operetta.* Leningrad: Iskusstvo, 212-15.

17 Stolpianskii 1989, 71-75; Kuznetsov 1958, 109-12.

18 Russians on Russian Music (1996), *Russians on Russian Music: 1830-1880: an Anthology.* Stuart Campbell (ed.). Cambridge: Cambridge University Press, 29.

19 Rozanov 1978, 24, 27, 30. See also Haywood, Richard (1969), *The Beginnings of Railway Development in Russia in the Reign of Nicholas I, 1835-42.*

Durham: Duke University Press; idem (1998), *Russia Enters the Railway Age, 1842-1855*. Boulder, East European Monographs. New York: Columbia University Press; Meeks, Carroll (1956), *The Railroad Station: an Architectural History*. New Haven: Yale University Press.

20 Rozanov 1978, 28, 30; A Century of Russian Ballet (1990), *A Century of Russian Ballet: Documents and Accounts, 1810-1910*. Roland John Wiley (ed.). Oxford: Clarendon Press, 112.

21 Timberlake, Charles (1982), "Pavlovsk Palace and Park." *Modern Encyclopedia of Russian and Soviet History*, XXVII. Gulf Breeze: Academic International Press, 101-3; Rozanov 1978, 1-23; Arnold 1982-93, 12-16, 138; Muzalevskii, V. I. (1961), *Russkoe fortepiannoe iskusstvo: XVIII-pervaia polovina XIX veka*. Leningrad: Iskusstvo, 130-2.

22 Rozanov 1978, 26-27.

23 Rozanov 1978, 24-30; Istoriia zheleznodorozhnogo transporta Rossii (1994), *Istoriia zheleznodorozhnogo transporta Rossii*. Tom. I: 1836-1917. Fadeev, G. M. & Kraskovskii E. Ia. (eds.). Sankt-Peterburg: Ivan Fedorov, 43-7, illustration, p. 46.

24 Kuznetsov 1958, 62-3, 102.

25 Kuznetsov 1958, 102; Rozanov 1978, 30-46; Stites 1992, passim.

26 Rozanov 1978, 30-46; Kuznetsov 1958, 102.

27 Findeizen, N. F. (2005), *Pavlovskii muzykal'nyi vokzal. Istoricheskii ocherk (1838-1912)*. Sankt-Peterburg, 57.

28 Rozanov 1978, 47-57; Massie, Suzanne (1990), *Pavlovsk: the Life of a Russian Palace*. London: Hodder and Stoughton, 119-23; *Teatral'nyi i muzykalnyi vestnik*, 55 (August 25, 1857), 445.

29 Rozanov 1978, 47-57; Stolpianskii 1989, 77.

30 *Teatralnyi i muzykalnyi vestnik*, 25 (June 29, 1858), 298.

31 Stasov, V. V. (1968), *Selected Essays on Music* (tr. Florence Jones). New York: Praeger, 16.

32 *Russians on Russian Music* 1995; Stites 2005, 88-125; Buckler, Julie (2000), *The Literary Lorgnette: Attending the Opera in Imperial Russia*. Stanford: Stanford University Press.

33 Stolpianskii 1989, 74.

34 Stolpianskii 1989, 77.

Richard Stites 1931-2010

Photo courtesy of Georgetown University.

A Meaningful Montage

by Anna Lawton

A controversial film director once said that it is only with death that human life achieves a meaningful montage.

To pay homage to the complex, contradictory and charismatic personality of the dear friend and colleague who recently completed the film of his life, I will assemble a few shots from a vast body of material, hoping that this selection, partial as it may be, will result in a meaningful montage of a most remarkable life.

Scene one

A large, comfortable office on the sixth floor of the Intercultural Center at Georgetown University; a solid desk, busy with books and papers but not cluttered—everything is neatly stacked; next to it, a brown leather chair for visitors. A window looking out on the atrium below takes an entire wall; tall bookshelves on the other three walls cover every inch of space from floor to ceiling. The books (how many?...several hundreds) are meticulously arranged—by theme, by author, chronologically, or by some other logical criterion—and perfectly aligned with the edge of the shelf, so that not a single volume would stick out and break the harmony of the display. A scribbled sign warns visitors: "Please do not touch or remove books from these shelves. —R. Stites."

Richard sits behind the desk, a cigarette between his fingers (only in the last few years, in our new sanitized, no-smoking society, he would refrain from lighting up his beloved Camel without filter in deference to a visitor). He is in his late seventies, a School of Foreign Service Board of Visitors Distinguished Professor in International Studies, the recipient of a mile-long list of awards and fellowships from the Russian Research Center at Harvard, the Kennan Institute, the Guggenheim Foundation, the Harriman Institute, the National Endowment for the Humanities, and others, including an honorary doctorate from the University of Helsinki. The list of his books, authored and edited, is just as long, without counting the dozens and dozens of articles and essays that could fill a few volumes. He is a legend in the Russian history field over two continents, and a dedicated and beloved teacher.

He's got his hair trimmed, not just because it was thinning, but because the longish cut had lost its provocative connotation (the 70s and 80s are well behind us). For the same reason, he removed the single ear stud, which looked so daring and exotic on him, when it became a common accessory of every pizza delivery man (democratic societies have a way of neutralizing the eccentric by absorbing the eccentricity into the mainstream). But he still wears the silver neck chain with an ornament that, supposedly, came from the tomb of a Scythian warrior. An open-collar sport shirt, his usual attire, keeps it in evidence.

Even at this mature age, Richard still cultivates his public image as the maverick scholar—exuberant, irreverent, mischievous, sporting a swashbuckling attitude full of self-irony. He lives aesthetically, like an actor on stage, fully savoring every minute of his performance. And yet, there is nothing unnatural or forced about him. His performance is genuine, no less genuine than his rigorous scholarship. Like an artist, he is able to project the truth through fiction.

I am closing up on his face now. I once heard Szabo telling the audience that actors must have a special face, good for close-ups—not just photogenic features that look pretty on screen, but a face that is captivating, engrossing, possessing an indefinable quality which keeps eluding the viewer. Asked to name a few, he said that he would be hardly pressed to find one in today's vapid, celebrity-filled gallery of stars, but that, in better times, Humphrey Bogart had it, Lawrence Olivier had it, Clark Gable had it, Marlon Brando had it…

Richard has it. No one is immune from his charm. His direct gaze and engaging grin conquer friends, colleagues, students, administrators, janitors, taxi cabbies and bar tenders alike—and, yes, women.

With the latter, the fascination is reciprocal: Richard has been in love with "woman" all his life. It is not by chance that his ground-breaking first book, *The Women's Liberation Movement in Russia*, was dedicated to the "woman question," a topic that in the late sixties was out of line in the history field even in the U.S., and that in Soviet Russia was treated with condescension and considered altogether bizarre.

Perhaps, the cause of his unrelenting pursuit of the feminine element is rooted in early childhood: in the image of a beautiful woman that too soon faded out of sight.

Scene two

The three-year-old sits on a highchair. The young woman cracks the shell of a boiled egg and gently feeds him, spoonful after spoonful. Afterwards, she wipes his face with a wet washcloth, warm and smelling of wild flowers. The woman smiles, the child's little heart fills up with happiness.

This is how Richard remembers his mother. He does not dwell on her reasons for leaving the family; his only feeling for her is a deep-seated nostalgia.

He grew up in the care of Aunt Florence (his father's sister) with two older brothers, in Fishtown, a working-class district of Philadelphia. Father was rarely around. He would visit with the kids from time to time, but the domestic setup was not congenial to him. He would soon get restless, would don a silk scarf and a smart fedora hat, and take off for another bout of adventure. He was a horse-race bookie.

In the neighborhood, a multi-ethnic enclave between the Delaware River docks and a large railroad yard, back-alley violence was a way of life. Richard, unlike his brothers, managed to keep out of trouble. How? He has an explanation: "There were Polish, Irish, Italian and Jewish gangs battling each other. But there was no Welsh gang. I could not afford violence, I had no backing. So, I turned to books."

Besides his ethnicity, he also credits Aunt Florence for this lucky outcome. The loving woman gave him books from a very early age and sent him to school. Year after year, his passion for books grew, together with an insatiable hunger for learning. This carried him successfully through the local schools and on to the University of Pennsylvania (B.A.), George Washington University (M.A.) and, finally, Harvard (Ph.D.). Before graduate school, he also took the time to serve in the army.

One of his closest friends and Georgetown colleagues, David Goldfrank, put it this way: "Richard rebelled against his childhood's environment by doing the right thing."

Scene three

A recurrent situation; some time in the past twenty years. A panel at a scholarly symposium, someone at the podium is reading a paper in a tedious, monotonous voice. In the audience many struggle not to fall asleep, thinking of the happy hours awaiting them in the hotel lounge. Mercifully, the presentation comes to an end. Next speaker. Richard takes the floor. He begins to speak—speak, not read...

The audience is suddenly electrified, wide awake. Richard's delivery style captivates the public. He has the talent of a brilliant performer who controls the audience with his stage presence. No doubt, he is an attraction. But there is also substance to his presentation: his argument is original, intriguing, related to his latest research. Richard is constantly cutting new paths through still uncharted areas.

After his pioneering study on the women's struggle, he turned his attention to culture. His second book, *Revolutionary Dreams*, dealt with the creative forms that emerged in the early Soviet period as a result of the intellectual fervor that permeated the building of the new society—festivals, parades, concerts, posters, art installations, movie shows.

Those spectacles were created for the masses, but still motivated by lofty ideals. In the next book, Richard abandoned the "revolutionary dreams" and immersed himself into the brewing cauldron of popular culture (*Russian Popular Culture*). Here he turned his attention to spontaneous, grass-root forms of entertainment: pulp fiction, movies, songs, vaudeville, rock music, the circus, jokes, those components of human experience that are very much part of history, and yet had been neglected by historians.

A few books already existed, each covering a specific aspect of popular culture, but Richard's contribution opened up a new field of studies. His classes at Georgetown were overflowed with students eager to get in, even though he was a demanding teacher and a strict grader. His classes were fun. For one particular course, the students were required to write a script on a given historical subject, and stage the skit instead of taking an exam. Richard has also been the dissertation advisor to a stream of doctoral candidates who, then, moved on to research and teaching in the new field.

Richard was able to bring culture and the arts—low-end as well as high-end—"into the mainstream of Russian history," as he put it. His fourth book, *Serfdom, Society and the Arts in Imperial Russia*, traces the history of the serfs' contribution to cultural development, especially as performers in the country home theaters of the nobility.

His last work, still unpublished, "The Four Horsemen," returns to the revolution theme that has fascinated him since his undergraduate years—he wrote his senior honor thesis on the French Revolution. This book explores the post-Napoleon revolutions of the 1820s in Spain, Naples, Greece and Russia, with a focus on the connections among the revolutionary subcultures.

Scene four

A serene cemetery behind the Orthodox Church of St. Elia in Helsinki. A thick coat of snow covers the grounds. In a corner, the white stillness is broken by a colorful display of flowers brought by the many friends who came to say goodbye.

Helsinki was Richard's second home. Initially, he went there because of the Slavonic Library, an alternative research source in the days when it was difficult to get access to archives and collections in the Soviet Union. But he found the place so congenial that it soon became his main residence abroad.

The Slavonic Library, with its superb collection of books and periodicals from Imperial Russia and a substantial amount of material from the Soviet era, was a hub of international scholars and a crossroads of ideas, projects, exchanges, discussions and discoveries. A place for learning and a place for partying—with hearty food and plenty of vodka and music (Richard was a fine connoisseur of classical music and a piano player of pop songs).

His research also brought him to Russia many times over the years, starting with a six-month stint at Leningrad University in 1967 that left on him a profound impression and changed the course of his life.

Richard was both a social person and a very private individual. He lived with gusto and valued the camaraderie of the group and the company of women. But he fiercely protected his private life. He was generous with his time, advising students, helping colleagues with their projects, editing other scholars' manuscripts, writing endorsements, serving on advisory committees and editorial boards (Richard was on New Academia Publishing's editorial board from the very beginning). But when he felt like retreating, he would raise an iron curtain around himself. Impenetrable. Until he decided to take it down again.

He was married three times and divorced three times. He had three sons and one daughter.

Andrei Stites, at a memorial service, remembered the recipe for a successful life that his father handed down to him: "Sing a song, tell a joke, and smile."

Obviously, it worked for Richard.

Original publication: Anna Lawton, "Instead of an Obituary," *Studies in Russian and Soviet Cinema*, 4. 2, (July 2010), pp. 129-134.

Books authored by Richard Stites:

The Women's Liberation Movement in Russia: Feminism, Nihilism, and Bolshevism, 1860-1930 (Princeton University Press, 1978; 2nd edn 1991)

Revolutionary Dreams: Utopian Vision and Social Experiment in the Russian Revolution (Oxford University Press, 1989; 2nd edn 1991; recipient of the 1989 Wayne S. Vucinich Prize of the American Association for the Advancement of Slavic Studies)

Russian Popular Culture: Entertainment and Society since 1900 (Cambridge University Press, 1992)

A History of Russia: Peoples, Legends, Events, Forces, co-authored with

Catherine Evtuhov, David Goldfrank, and Lindsey Hughes (Houghton-Mifflin, 2004)

Serfdom, Society, and the Arts in Imperial Russia: The Pleasure and the Power (Yale University Press, 2008)

*Passion and Perception: Essays on Russian Culture (*New Academia Publishing, 2010)

The Four Horsemen: Revolution and Counter-Revolution in Post-Napoleonic Europe (unpublished)

Books edited or co-edited :

The Russian Revolution by P. N. Miliukov, translated and edited by Richard Stites with Tatyana Stites, trs., 3 vols. (Gulf Breeze, FL: Academic International press, 1978)

Bolshevik Culture: Experiment and order in the Russian Revolution, Abbot Gleason, Peter Kenez and Richard Stites, eds. (Bloomington: Indiana University Press, 1985)

Russia in the Era of NEP: Explorations in Soviet Society and Culture, Sheila Fitzpatrick, Alexander Rabinowitz and Richard Stites, eds. (Bloomington: Indiana University Press, 1991)

Culture and Entertainment in Wartime Russia, Richard Stites, ed. (Bloomington: Indiana University Press, 1995)

Mass Culture in Soviet Russia: Tales, Poems, Songs, Movies, Plays, and Folklore, 1917-1953, James von Geldern and Richard Stites, eds. (Bloomington: Indiana University Press, 1995)

European Culture in the Great War: The Arts, Entertainment, and Propaganda, 1914-1918, Aviel Roshwald and Richard Stites, eds. (Cambridge: Cambridge University Press, 1999)